Sociology for AQA Volume 2

3rd edition

Ken Browne,
Jonathan Blundell & Pamela Law

SOCIOLOGY
FOR AQA VOLUME 2
2ND-YEAR A LEVEL

3RD
EDITION

First edition first published in 2009 by Polity Press
Second edition first published in 2014 by Polity Press
This third edition first published in 2016 by Polity Press

Polity Press
65 Bridge Street
Cambridge CB2 1UR, UK

Polity Press
350 Main Street
Malden, MA 02148, USA

ISBN-13: 978-0-7456-9694-2(pb)

A catalogue record for this book is available from the British Library.

Typeset in 9 on 12pt Utopia by
Servis Filmsetting Ltd, Stockport, Cheshire
Printed and bound in Italie by Rotolito S.p.A.

For further information on Polity, visit our website: politybooks.com

Contents

Acknowledgements

Ken Browne wrote chapters 1, 3, 5 and 6, and undertook general editing and compilation of the book; Jonathan Blundell wrote chapter 2 and Pam Law wrote chapter 4. We would all like to thank Penny Halliday, Heidi Fitzgerald, Charlotte Handy and Eirene Mitsos, and the various anonymous readers approached by Polity, who provided us with several ideas for activities and improvements, and some very constructively critical and supportive comments, many of which have been incorporated into the finished text. Peter Brierley was very kind in providing church attendance statistics, Greg Philo of the Glasgow Media Group provided very helpful comments on parts of the media chapter, and Steve Hall of Teeside University added very useful comments to the discussion of crime and moral panics. We would all like to thank the staff at Polity, particularly Jonathan Skerrett, who has once again proven to be a brilliant, supportive and understanding editor, who has shown resilience and good humour in his dealings with us. Clare Ansell and Breffni O'Connor did great jobs in producing and marketing the book, and Leigh Mueller once again demonstrated high levels of skill and knowledge in copy-editing the text.

We would like to thank all those who gave us permission to reproduce copyright material. The source of copyright material is acknowledged in the text. Should any copyright holder have been inadvertently overlooked, the authors and publishers will be glad to make suitable arrangements at the first possible opportunity.

Introduction to the 3rd edition

This third edition has been completely revised and updated to match the reformed AQA specification for the second year of A level, for first teaching in September 2016. The book is divided into chapters that provide coverage of every area in the new AQA specification. Each of these chapters is sub-divided into topics, which correspond directly to the bullet points in the AQA specification. This book is designed to accompany Ken Browne's *Sociology for AQA Volume 1: AS and 1st-Year A Level*, and together both books provide detailed coverage of all components for the new AQA Sociology A level.

The A level specification

The subject content of the first year of the AQA A level specification is identical to the AS level, and was covered in *Sociology for AQA Volume 1*.

The AQA A level specification involves the following subject content:

Compulsory Content

Education with
Theory and Methods:
Paper 1

Answer all parts of one stimulus response / structured question. The question is in six parts. On education, there are two short questions together worth 10 marks + two essay-style questions, one worth 10 marks, and one worth 30 marks. There is one 20-mark essay-style question, with stimulus, on research methods in the context of education. There is a further essay-style question on Theory and Methods worth 10 marks.
Total marks = 80, making up 33.3 per cent of the total A level marks. Exam is 2 hours.

Topics In Sociology: Paper 2

Section A: **One** of the following:

- Culture and Identity
- Families and Households
- Health
- Work, Poverty and Welfare

Section B: **One** of the following:

- Beliefs in Society
- Global Development
- The Media
- Stratification and Differentiation

Paper is divided into two sections. Section A covers the Topics in Sociology taught in the first year, and Section B covers Topics in Sociology taught in the second year. Choose one topic from Section A and one from Section B. Answer all questions on the chosen topics. Three essay-style questions, two with stimulus, on each topic, two worth 10 marks each and one worth 20 marks.
Total marks = 80, making up 33.3 per cent of the total A-level marks. Exam is 2 hours.

Compulsory Content

Crime and Deviance with
Theory and Methods: Paper 3

There are six questions, and you must answer all of them. There are four questions on Crime and Deviance: two short questions together worth 10 marks, and two stimulus response essay questions, one worth 10 marks and one worth 30 marks. There are two questions on Theory and Methods, one worth 10 marks, and one stimulus response question worth 20 marks.
Total marks = 80, making up 33.3 per cent of the total A level marks. Exam is 2 hours.

Assessment

At A level Sociology, students are assessed on three main objectives:

AO1 Knowledge and understanding

This involves demonstrating knowledge and understanding of sociological theories, concepts and evidence, and of the range of research methods and sources of information used by sociologists, and the practical, ethical and theoretical issues arising in sociological research.

Knowledge and understanding is tested in *questions* by the use of the following words:

Analyse	Explain
Define	Outline
Evaluate	Outline and explain

AO2 Application

This involves applying sociological theories, concepts, evidence and research methods to a range of issues.

The skill of *application* is tested in *questions* by the use of the following phrases, frequently used together with the *knowledge and understanding* words referred to above:

Applying material from item A...
Using one example...

To show that you are using the skill of *application* you might consider using the following words and phrases:

as shown by item A / recent events in ...	for example ...
this shows ...	as shown by Brainache's theory of / study of ...
such evidence may be misleading because ...	Brainache's study challenges/supports this view ...
this is a value-judgement because ...	Such statistics / other evidence show/s that ...

AO3 Analysis and evaluation

This involves things like being able to recognize and criticize sociologically significant information, to recognize the strengths and weaknesses of sociological theories, evidence and research methods, to present arguments, make judgements and reach conclusions based on the arguments and evidence presented.

The skills of *analysis* and *evaluation* are tested in *questions* by the use of the following words:

Analyse … (two changes/reasons/factors)
Evaluate … (the view / the usefulness / the contribution of / the problems of / the advantages or disadvantages of)

To show that you are using the skill of *analysis* you might consider using the following words and phrases:

the relevance of this is …	this indicates …
this is similar to / different from …	so …
therefore …	this means / does not mean …
hence …	a consequence of …
the implication of …	the contrast between …
put simply …	

For *evaluation skills*, you might use the following words and phrases:

a strength/weakness of this …	an argument for/against …
an advantage/disadvantage of …	the importance of …
this is important because …	this does not take account of …
however …	alternatively …
a criticism of this is …	others argue that …
a different interpretation is provided by …	on the other hand …
the problem with this is …	this does not explain why …
this argument/evidence suggests …	to conclude …

Two Core Themes

All students must develop an understanding of the significance of conflict and consensus, social structure and social action, and the role of values. In addition, there are two core themes or threads that run through the whole of the A level course:

- Socialization, culture and identity
- Social differentiation, power and stratification.

These are not expected to be taught as specific topics, but rather treated as themes that should be referred to throughout the course, and applied to particular Topics in Sociology. You will already have covered many aspects of these core themes during your first-year studies, and they are explored further in this book. For example, in the Beliefs in Society topic, you might consider the socialization of children into religious beliefs, inequalities of power and status between men and women in religious organizations, or religion as a source of identity in minority ethnic groups. In the Media topic, you might consider issues like the role of the media in socializing people into the dominant ideology, or the way the media support the interests of the powerful in society, or their role in socializing people into gender or other identities. Social differentiation, power and stratification are covered explicitly in chapter 4 on Stratification and Differentiation. Conflict and consensus approaches and the issues of social structure and social action are themes throughout this book, as seen in the differing approaches adopted by functionalist, Marxist and feminist sociologists, and by structural and action theorists, and they are also considered specifically, along with values and the study of society, in chapter 5 on Theory and Methods.

How to use this book

Each chapter of this book is designed to be more or less self-contained, and, together with the work in Volume 1, to cover the knowledge and skills required at A level Sociology.

Important terms are highlighted in colour when they first appear in the text, and in **bold type** in the page margins. These are normally explained in the text, and listed at the end of the chapter as key terms. They are also included in a comprehensive glossary at the end of the book. Unfamiliar terms should be checked in the glossary or index for further explanation or clarification. The contents pages or the index should be used to find particular themes or references. The bibliography consists of all research referred to in the book, in case you should wish to explore further any of the topics.

Chapter summaries and revision checklists outline the key points that should have been learnt after reading each chapter. These should be used as checklists for revision – if you cannot do what is asked, then refer back to the chapter to refresh your memory. There is a list of the key terms that you should know after studying each chapter. You should use this key terms list and the glossary as reference sources and a revision aid, as you can check the meaning of terms. At the end of each topic, some questions similar to those you could find in the examination are included to help you revise the topic, and at the end of every chapter, except for chapter 5, there is a typical practice question for that component. Students should attempt these under timed conditions, both as practice and to gauge how ready they are for the examination.

Websites

The internet is a valuable source of information for sociologists and for exploring the topics in this book. However, there is a lot of rubbish on some internet sites, and information should be treated with caution. One of the best search engines to search for topics generally is www.google.com. Try this for any research topic – putting 'UK' at the end usually helps, e.g. 'poverty uk'. There are some useful websites referred to throughout this book, but you can find more, and other resources, at **www.politybooks.com/browne**.

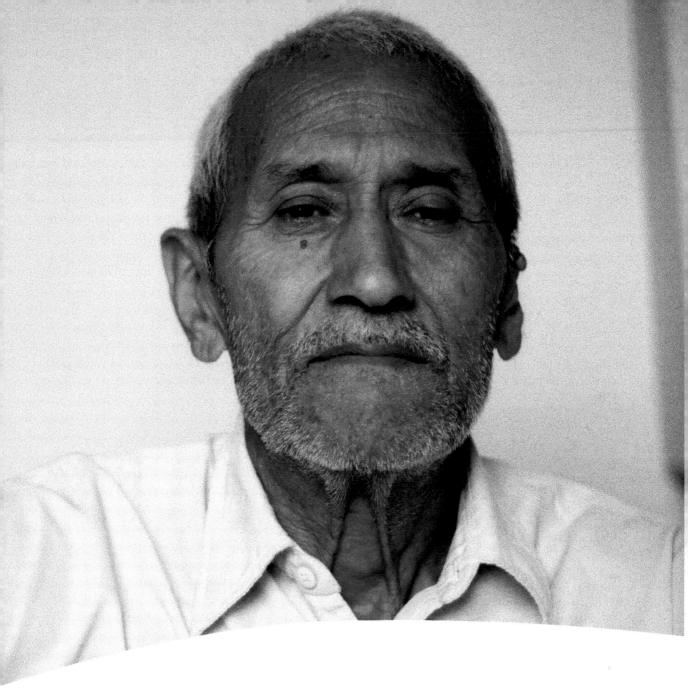

CHAPTER
1

Beliefs in
Society

KEN BROWNE

SPECIFICATION TOPICS

- **Topic 1:** Ideology, science and religion, including both Christian and non-Christian religious traditions
- **Topic 2:** The relationship between social change and social stability, and religious beliefs, practices and organisations
- **Topic 3:** Religious organisations, including cults, sects, denominations, churches and New Age movements, and their relationship to religious and spiritual belief and practice
- **Topic 4:** The relationship between different social groups and religious/spiritual organisations and movements, beliefs and practices
- **Topic 5:** The significance of religion and religiosity in the contemporary world, including the nature and extent of secularisation in a global context, and globalisation and the spread of religions

Contents

Beliefs in Society

Beliefs in society

Beliefs are ideas about things we hold to be true. There is a very wide range of beliefs in society, but this chapter will focus primarily on religious beliefs. These concern themselves mainly with beliefs in supernatural powers or forces of some kind, and deal with ideas about fundamental issues of human existence, like the meaning and purpose of life, the place of human beings in the cosmos, whether there is a soul, whether there is some kind of spirit or life force either within ourselves or watching over us, and what happens after we die. Religious beliefs include those found in the world's most common religions, such as Christianity, Hinduism, Islam, Judaism, Sikhism and Buddhism, but also a wide diversity of other beliefs and groups which concern themselves with similar issues, such as witchcraft (Wicca), paganism and Satanism. Religious beliefs are often also taken to include a range of activities that generally fall outside the framework of the world's established mainstream religions. These include beliefs in things like faith healing, astrology, horoscopes and fortune telling, superstitions of various kinds, magic, and a vast range of New Age beliefs, such as the spiritual or life-force dimensions of crystal healing, meditation, massage, aromatherapy and even beliefs in alien abduction and UFOs.

Before defining and exploring religion itself, it is first necessary to examine how religious beliefs differ from two concepts with which they have, at various times, been entangled: ideology and science.

Ideology

The term **ideology** is used in a wide variety of ways; it is most commonly regarded as a set of ideas and values shared by a social group that:

- Provides a particular vision or way of seeing and interpreting the world
- Presents only a partial, incomplete or false view of reality
- Expresses and justifies (legitimizes) the interests of particular social or political groups.

> **Beliefs** are ideas about things we hold to be true.

> **Ideology** refers to a set of ideas, values and beliefs that provides a means of interpreting the world, and represents the outlook, and justifies the interests, of a social group.

> **Pluralism** is a view that sees power in society spread among a wide range of interest groups and individuals, with no group or individual having a monopoly of power.

Different conceptions of ideology

There are many different types of ideology within this general definition, in part reflecting the wide range of ways in which the concept has been used. Four common forms of these are considered below.

Pluralist ideology

Pluralism is a view that sees the exercise of power in society as reflecting a broad range of social interests, with power spread among a wide variety of competing interest groups and individuals, with no single one having a monopoly on power.

Pluralist ideology is a view of the world which suggests that there are many different types of social group, each with its own ideologies, or sets of ideas and means of interpreting the world, which live alongside each other. None has any claim to be the only right way of seeing the world or has a privileged position of dominating or suppressing others, and there is no single dominant ideology that reflects the interests of a particular social group. However, pluralist ideology falls into the trap of itself claiming a form of superiority over other ideologies, as it aims to persuade people that the prevailing ideas in society reflect those of a broad range of social groups, with no single dominant ideology, and this is something to be approved of and welcomed. But in doing this, it is denying that there may be an unequal distribution of power in society, and that not all social groups are equally able to influence those with power or get their views accepted as part of the prevailing vision in society. In effect, the pluralist ideology tries to conceal the fact that there is an unequal distribution of power in society by trying to persuade us that this isn't the case.

Marxism: dominant ideology and hegemony

Marxists believe that the ideas that people hold are formed by their position in society, and ideology is therefore seen very clearly as the ideas of particular social groups reflecting their interests. The Marxist view is most associated with the view that there is a **dominant ideology** in society. This is a set of ideas and beliefs held by the most powerful groups and, in particular, of the ruling class in society. Mannheim (1985 [1936]) generally associated the dominant ideology with the deliberate obscuring of facts in order to conceal the inequalities of capitalist society and to preserve existing patterns of inequality and the privileged position of the dominant class, and to prevent any social change that might threaten their interests. Althusser (1971) suggested the dominant ideology was spread through a series of **ideological state apparatuses** – social institutions like the family, the education system, the media, the law and religion, which justified the power of the dominant social class.

Gramsci (1971) further developed the Marxist view of ideology with his development of the concept of **hegemony**. Hegemony refers to the process whereby the ruling class, through the dominant ideology, maintains its power by persuading other social classes, and particularly the working class, to adopt ruling-class ideology as part of their own beliefs and values, and therefore to consent to the rule of the dominant class rather than being forced to obey. An example of this – considered later in this chapter – is the way Marxists regard religion as part of the dominant ideology, establishing the hegemony and justifying the power of the ruling class.

Patriarchal ideology

Feminist writers have identified a **patriarchal ideology**, which is a set of ideas that supports and tries to justify the power of men in a patriarchal society, through beliefs like men being superior, more logical and less emotional than women, with women seen as more suited to childcare and family tasks rather than responsible positions requiring measured, unemotional and logical qualities. For example, some feminists regard many contemporary religions and religious organizations both to be patriarchal in structure and to reflect a patriarchal ideology. Many feminists would suggest that a wide range of other ideologies are also patriarchal, as they are much more concerned with promoting and protecting the interests of men than they are those of women.

Pluralist ideology is a set of ideas that reflect the pluralist view of the distribution of power, with no one particular ideology able to dominate others, and with the prevailing ideas in society reflecting the interests of a wide range of competing social groups and interests.

The **dominant ideology** is a set of ideas which justifies the social advantages of wealthy, powerful and influential groups in society, and justifies the disadvantages of those who lack wealth, power and influence

Ideological state apparatuses are agencies that spread the dominant ideology and justify the power of the dominant social class.

Hegemony refers to the dominance in society of the ruling class's set of ideas over others, and acceptance of and consent to them by the rest of society.

Patriarchal ideology is a set of ideas that supports and justifies the power of men.

Political ideologies

A political ideology is one that provides an analysis and interpretation of how society should work, and suggests how power should be used by governments to influence events and change society, through policy-making and political action. Political ideologies may be quite broad, such as nationalism, liberalism, fascism, communism or anarchism, which involve particular ways of seeing the world and how society should be run, or they might be very specific, like those held by political parties, like the Conservative, Labour, Green or Liberal Democrat parties in the UK, which suggest particular political policies they would favour implementing if given the opportunity.

Science as a belief system – scientism

For a very long time, science was so mixed up with religious beliefs, superstition and magic that it bore little relationship to the systematically collected research evidence, experimentation and rational argument we associate with science today. Even now, science and religion are often seen as competing ways of explaining the world, particularly when science takes the form of scientism, which directly challenges and dismisses all religious explanations.

Scientism is a belief system or ideology that suggests that the scientific method (see below and pages 404–5) provides the *only* means of gaining true knowledge about the world, with a strict commitment to only empirical evidence. It rejects any alleged truths and claims to knowledge that cannot be explained by the scientific method, such as those provided by religions. Scientism may be regarded as another form of ideology, protecting and justifying the interests of scientists.

Most scientists do not subscribe to scientism. They may hold science in high regard, and see the scientific method as a valuable tool in understanding the world, but many do not accept that science is the only means of understanding the world. For example, science cannot provide easy – or indeed any – explanations for human emotional dramas, such as why couples have fights, or why people have periods of non-clinical depression. It cannot explain many government policies or historical events, or social phenomena like racism and sexism. Many scientists themselves hold religious beliefs about the world and the meaning of life, representing the spiritual dimensions of their lives, alongside their attempts to use science to understand the world.

What is science?

Although there are differing views of science, it – as opposed to scientism – is generally seen as different from religion and ideology because its claims to be true rest on scientific methods producing explanations that are based on empirical evidence, collected under conditions of objectivity and value freedom.

Popper and the scientific method

Popper (2002 [1935]) suggests the scientific method involves:

1 *Hypothesis formation:* formulating ideas or informed guesses about possible explanations for some phenomena, which are capable of being tested against evidence derived from systematic observation and/or experimentation.
2 *Falsification:* the aim of testing hypotheses against the evidence is to try to prove them wrong, as just one exception can prove a hypothesis false.
3 *Prediction:* through establishing cause-and-effect relationships rooted in evidence, precise predictions of what will happen in the same circumstances in future can be established.
4 *Theory formation:* if the hypothesis is capable of being tested against evidence and cannot be shown to be false, and predictions appear sound, then there can be some confidence that the hypothesis is probably true. This may then become part of a scientific theory.

Scientism is a belief system or ideology that claims science and the scientific method alone can provide true knowledge and understanding of the world, and rejects any alleged truths that cannot be explained by the scientific method.

Empirical evidence is observable evidence collected in the physical or social world.

Objectivity means approaching topics with an open mind, avoiding bias, and being prepared to submit research evidence to scrutiny by other researchers.

Value freedom is the idea that the beliefs and prejudices of a researcher should not influence the way research is carried out and evidence interpreted.

5 *Scrutiny*: a scientific theory will be scrutinized by other scientists, and will stand only until some new evidence comes along to show the existing theory is false.

The application of the scientific method means that ideas and theories in science are not unquestionably accepted as an act of faith as they are in religion, but are open to constant challenge, change, correction and improvement as more and better evidence is collected.

Science as a social product: the social construction of scientific knowledge

Popper's principle of falsification suggests researchers should aim not to prove their hypotheses true, but to falsify them, or prove them wrong. This is because no hypothesis can ever finally be proven true, as there is always the possibility of some future exception. However, a hypothesis can easily be proven false, as just one observation to the contrary can disprove it. The more a hypothesis stands up to such attempts, the more likely it is to be a 'scientific truth'.

However, Kuhn (2012 [1962]) challenges whether scientists really do in practice set out to collect evidence with the specific aim of attempting to falsify their hypotheses. Kuhn argues that, on the contrary, scientists work within **paradigms** – sets of values, ideas, beliefs and assumptions about what they are investigating which are not called into question until the evidence against them is overwhelming.

> A **paradigm** is a framework of scientific laws, concepts, theories, methods and assumptions within which scientists operate, and which provide guidelines for the conduct of research and what counts as proper evidence. These are rarely called into question until the evidence against them is overwhelming.

Paradigms and scientific revolutions

A paradigm is like a pair of coloured lenses through which scientists look at the world. The paradigm colours their views of the nature of the problem or problems to be investigated, the approved methods which should be followed to tackle these problems, and what should count as proper and relevant scientific evidence.

Kuhn argues that, when scientists test their hypotheses through observations and experiments, they try to fit their findings into the existing paradigm, rather than attempt to falsify their hypotheses. The power of the paradigm may mean that scientists focus on what they are looking for, and overlook or fail to see evidence which doesn't fit the paradigm. When findings do not fit into the existing paradigm, they are likely to be dismissed as having resulted from experimental errors or freak conditions. This suggests that what passes for scientific truth may often be more an act of faith in scientific values than of scientific rigour. Only when there are so many anomalies, or things the existing paradigm can't explain, will the established paradigm change, as scientists begin to question their basic assumptions and produce a new paradigm which explains what the old paradigm could not. Kuhn therefore argues that science changes in dramatic leaps, resulting in 'scientific revolutions', as one scientific paradigm breaks down when a series of discoveries cannot be fitted into the dominant paradigm, and another comes along to take its place.

> **Activity**
>
> Try to think of times in your own science lessons at school when you got the 'wrong' result. Did you immediately question the validity of the theory or just assume that you had, for example, a dirty test-tube or did something wrong? Did you investigate the new finding – or stick with the paradigm, and keep trying until you got the 'right' result?

Social influences on the nature and direction of scientific research

There is a range of other factors suggesting that scientific research is not as objective as it claims to be. For example:

- The values and beliefs of researchers will influence whether or not they think issues are worth studying
- The career aspirations of scientists lead to an understandable desire to prove their own hypotheses right, for experiments to succeed, to publish scientific papers showing their successes, and to research what are seen as cool or lucrative research areas

- The search for funding may determine which research is carried out and how it is approached – for example, research for military or defence purposes, or to develop new drugs for pharmaceutical companies, will attract funding more readily than research into help for disabled people
- Objectivity may be limited by the institution or funding constraints within which the scientist is working – for example, in medical research on the effects of smoking funded by the tobacco industry, or research on genetically modified crops funded by the biotechnology industry.

The points above suggest that science may in some respects be itself a form of ideology, justifying the interests of the mainstream scientific community, and that it is not always as objective, value-free and independent of prejudices and social pressures as scientists might like to claim. Scientists do not always ruthlessly pursue evidence to attempt to falsify their theories, as Popper believes they should, but often protect favoured theories and fit their findings into the prevailing scientific ideology (or paradigm) of the time – an approach more akin to religion or ideology than the ruthless pursuit of truth associated with the scientific method.

Defining religion

Defining religion is quite important, as the definition adopted will decide what should be examined as a religious phenomenon and what should not, whether society is becoming more or less religious or whether religious belief is simply changing the forms it takes.

The sacred and the profane

Durkheim (2001 [1912]), writing from a functionalist perspective, defined religion as 'a unified set of beliefs and practices relative to sacred things, that is to say, things set apart and forbidden'. Durkheim contrasted this with the 'profane' – the everyday, mundane world. Durkheim's view of religion will be discussed shortly, but his notion of the 'sacred' has been questioned as a useful definition of religion, since many people hold as sacred and 'set apart and forbidden' a range of things that most would not really regard as religious in any conventional sense of the word. This very broad view of religion as 'all things held sacred' is part of what is known as the functional and inclusivist definition, which is generally contrasted with a narrower view called the substantive and exclusivist definition.

The functional and inclusivist definition of religion

This is a very broad definition of religion, which covers a wide range of beliefs to which people give a religious or sacred quality, but which does not necessarily include beliefs in a supra-human, supernatural being. This definition, seen in Durkheim's approach, focuses on the function of beliefs in society, and the way in which things that people regard as sacred can, for example, contribute to social integration by binding societies or groups together through shared values. As well as conventional religious beliefs, this wide definition might also include beliefs that many would not regard as religious. For example, interests in football, music, the lives of celebrities and royalty take on an almost sacred quality for some people, and play a similar role in their lives to conventional religions. For most sociologists, and for the purposes of this chapter, the main definition of religion that will be used is the substantive and exclusivist definition, which is discussed below.

The substantive and exclusivist definition of religion

This is a narrower definition, and focuses on what religion actually is (its substance or content), and involves supernatural beliefs of some kind, in something supra-human. It therefore excludes those views that suggest that anything that people regard as 'sacred' can be regarded as a religion. This definition fits with what most people would regard as religion, such as Islam, Christianity, Buddhism, Sikhism and Hinduism, though it also includes non-conventional supernatural beliefs like Wicca (witchcraft), paganism and Satanism.

This definition, with a supernatural dimension, is the one adopted by most sociologists. Bruce (1995), for example, defines religion as 'beliefs, actions and institutions which assume the existence of supernatural entities with powers of action, or impersonal powers or processes possessed of moral purpose'. Berger (1990) views religion as a 'sacred canopy' or shield providing supernatural protection against, and explanation of, random and apparently meaningless events (this is discussed later in the chapter).

Features of religion

In accordance with the substantive and exclusivist definition, religions are likely to include all or some of the following five features:

1 *Beliefs*: beliefs in the supernatural and/or incomprehensible powers (often some sort of belief in God or gods) or in symbols which are in some way regarded as sacred and representing these supernatural or incomprehensible powers, such as a cross, totem pole or holy water.
2 *Theology*: a set of teachings and beliefs, usually based on some holy book, such as the Bible or the Qur'an.
3 *Practice*: a series of rituals or ceremonies to express religious beliefs, either publicly or privately. For example, most religions contain religious ceremonies of worship, and rituals such as getting on your knees to pray, covering your head in places of worship, singing, fasting, ritual washing or lighting candles.
4 *Institutions*: some form of organization of the worshippers/believers, such as by priests or religious leaders, and buildings like churches, mosques and temples.
5 *Consequences*: a set of moral or ethical values that are meant to guide or influence the everyday behaviour of believers.

> ### Activity
> Refer to the five features of religion above.
> 1 If you wanted to carry out research into the strength and extent of religious belief in a society, outline two indicators for *each* feature you might use to measure this (excluding the following examples). For example, for the religious practice dimension, you might use the number of times a week a person visits their local mosque, church or temple; and for theology, you might devise questions about holy books, religious history or doctrines.
> 2 Outline reasons why the indicators you have identified may not provide a valid, or true, genuine and authentic, picture of the strength and extent of religious belief in a society.

There is a range of theories of religion, such as functionalist, Marxist/neo-Marxist, interpretivist, feminist and Weberian theories. These focus on the roles religion performs in society and for individuals, and whether it acts mainly as a force to maintain existing society in its present form, or whether it acts as an agent for social change. These theories of religion are discussed in the next topic.

Ideology and religion

Religion, like ideology, also offers a vision of and a means of understanding, interpreting and explaining the world. However, unlike ideology, religious beliefs are not necessarily tied to the interests of a particular social group, and, as Giddens (2006) put it, religion involves 'shared beliefs and rituals that provide a sense of ultimate meaning and purpose by creating an idea of reality that is sacred, all-encompassing and supernatural'. There are three main aspects to religion:

1 *Belief in the spiritual and supernatural* – a person, entity or other extra-worldly spiritual force or being of some kind, which ultimately provides a sense of meaning and a means of interpreting and explaining the world.

2 *Faith on the part of believers* – a strong sense of trust and conviction in a person or entity, which is not based on observable, testable or falsifiable evidence.

3 *A body of unchanging truth* – religions usually contain certain fundamental and unchangeable beliefs, like Christ being the son of God, or Mohammed being Allah's Prophet, and new discoveries are fitted into these existing frameworks.

Religion differs from ideology in that ideologies are not necessarily based on faith in supernatural beliefs, but on the interests of social groups. However, religion may become part of an ideology, as a social group may seek to use religion for its own ends, such as promoting and protecting its own interests. Marx, for example, regarded religion as part of the ideology of the dominant class in society (what he called the 'dominant ideology'), forming part of the worldview and helping to justify the interests of that class, and acting like the drug opium to dull the senses and pain of those that it exploited. This will be considered later in the chapter.

More recently, fundamentalist Christians in the United States, and increasingly in Europe, have transformed some religious beliefs into a campaigning ideology called 'intelligent design' (sometimes also called 'creative design'). This is a religious belief that the universe and living things, including the human race, are not products of the scientifically accepted process of natural evolution, but are, rather, created by an intelligent force (God). This religiously based ideology is aligned to conservative American politicians, who seek to have intelligent design either taught alongside or replace in schools the teaching of the scientific theory of evolution.

Activity

If you want to learn a bit more about intelligent design, and why it might be regarded more as an ideology or religious faith than a science, you can explore it on the following websites:

- www.intelligentdesignnetwork.org – Intelligent Design Network
- www.actionbioscience.org/evolution/nhmag.html – An article from the *Natural History* magazine debating intelligent design theories
- www.venganza.org – The site of the Church of the Flying Spaghetti Monster, which has developed the Pastafarian creation theory. This spoof site challenges intelligent design theories through absurdity, showing how its own made-up theories are no different – in the sense of being unscientific – from those of intelligent design.

As a result of your investigations, explain why intelligent design might be regarded more as a religious faith or an ideology than as what most would regard as a scientific explanation.

Science and religion

Open and closed belief systems

Although scientists operate within paradigms, and science is subject to the social influences discussed above, what makes science different from ideology or religion is that it *aspires* to be what Popper called an **open belief system**. This means that scientific research, even within the dominant paradigm, is open to scrutiny, questioning, criticism and testing by others, and scientific knowledge is always provisional as it is liable to change as a result of these processes. By contrast, ideology and religion are what are known as **closed belief systems**. This is because they assert an all-embracing and unchanging body of belief, and make claims that cannot be disproved or overturned, and any evidence that seems to challenge these beliefs is either dismissed by their believers or followers, or explained away by fitting them into the existing religious belief system or ideology.

Science and the displacement of religious explanations in modernity

There is still a great deal in the world that remains unexplained, and certainly science has not provided all the answers to questions that religion answers by appeals to faith. However, Bruce (2008)

An **open belief system** is one that is open to questioning, testing and falsifying by others, and may subsequently change as a result of these processes.

A **closed belief system** is one that cannot be disproved, because it relies on faith or beliefs rather than empirical evidence, and rejects or explains away any evidence that challenges that belief system.

argues that it is the scientific method rather than specific scientific discoveries that has provided the greatest challenge to religion as a belief system. This challenge to religion from the scientific method grew as society moved towards modernity, with a growing concern with evidence-based causes and effects of natural phenomena, rather than the search for the meaning of such phenomena.

Modernity refers to the period of society from the Enlightenment of the seventeenth century to the middle of the twentieth century. It includes a rational outlook on social issues and highlights the role of science and the scientific method as a basis for understanding the development and organization of human societies. It was the development of modernity that brought with it science as we know it today. Aldridge (2007) describes Comte's view of how the transition to modernity through three stages changed human understanding from a more religious to a more scientific explanation of the world:

1   *The theological stage*, in which phenomena are explained as arising from the actions of spirits, gods or other supernatural beings.
2   *The metaphysical stage*, in which the supernatural element of the previous stage is diminished, and phenomena are explained as arising from the action of more natural, though abstract, entities and forces, like the power of Nature.
3   *The positive or scientific stage*, in which theological and metaphysical explanations are displaced by rational scientific explanations based on evidence derived from observation and experimentation, logical thought and reasoning. It is at this stage that there is what Weber (1993 [1920]) called a growing 'disenchantment with the world'. By this, Weber meant that the magical and mystical elements of life – the province of religion – are displaced by science and scientific explanation. Deciding whether a particular understanding of the world was true or not would no longer be based on appeals to religion, faith, intuition, tradition and superstition, but on evidence and rational argument.

Bruce suggests that, in modernity, religious explanations and superstitions are gradually displaced by scientific explanations as many religious beliefs are shown to be false. For example, science proved that the Earth moved around the Sun and not vice versa as religion once taught, and the theory of evolution displaced the biblical account of the creation given in the Book of Genesis in the Christian Bible.

When phenomena occur that are hard to explain or understand – such as strange lights in the night sky, paranormal events like ESP (extra-sensory perception) or psychokinesis (moving objects with the mind), apparently 'miraculous' cures, an attack of disease or an accident – we are now more likely to look for scientific explanations than explanations based around supernatural beliefs, like the power of a god or gods, the devil, witches, spirits and so on. An example of this is the so-called 'miraculous' cure that put the Catholic Mother Teresa on the track towards sainthood in 2003. Dr Ranjan Mustaphi, one of the doctors treating the patient whose tumour was allegedly cured in 1998 after Mother Teresa's divine intervention, was astonished at the Vatican's belief that Mother Teresa ever performed a miracle. He described the claim that it was a miracle as a farce, and claimed that it was scientifically proven that the tumour was linked to tuberculosis and that the so-called 'miracle' was simply a patient responding to anti-tubercular drug treatment.

If we accept Popper's approach to the scientific method – that a hypothesis must be capable of being falsified by empirical research and observation or experimentation – then science might be expected gradually to displace religion, as there is no evidence that can prove or disprove the existence of God, or that Christianity, Islam, Buddhism, Hinduism, Sikhism, Judaism or any other religion is 'true'.

Modernity refers to the period of the application of rational principles and logic to the understanding, development and organization of human societies.

Disenchantment refers to the process whereby the magical and mystical elements of life are eroded, as understandings of the world based on religion, faith, intuition, tradition, magic and superstition are displaced by rational argument, science and scientific explanation.

Has science displaced religion?

The preceding sections suggest that the growth of a scientific understanding of the world in modernity might be expected to relegate religion to the position of a relic of a pre-modern, non-rational age. Nonetheless, this has not happened. Many millions of people identify themselves with the great religions of the world, such as Islam, Judaism, Christianity, Hinduism, Sikhism and Buddhism, and

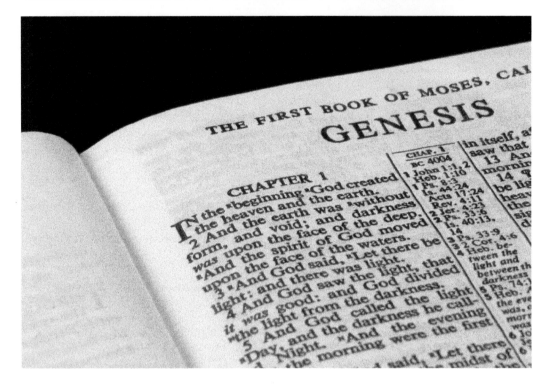

Scientific explanations have replaced many religious ones – for example, the theory of evolution displaced the biblical account of the creation given in the Book of Genesis in the Old Testament

all manner of religious and supernatural beliefs and superstitions continue to have extraordinary power over human behaviour. In 1978, for example, 913 members of the People's Temple religious sect, including more than 270 children, committed suicide, and in the first decade of the twenty-first century, hundreds of religiously motivated people killed themselves as suicide bombers, including those who killed 3,000 people in the attack on the World Trade Center in New York in 2001. Buddhist monks led an unsuccessful uprising against the military dictatorship in Burma in 2007, and in 2013 Britain and the USA were engaged in a long-running war in Afghanistan against an Islamic fundamentalist-inspired Taliban movement. Islamic **fundamentalism** is a significant force in the world, and Christian fundamentalists of the New Christian Right have substantial political influence in the United States.

> **Fundamentalism** means a return to the literal meaning of religious texts and associated behaviour.

Many individuals hold beliefs in some abstract, unseen, mysterious extra-human forces with the capacity to intervene in life for individual or social benefit, including those who may not see themselves as religious in any conventional sense. Many continue to cling to beliefs in magic, superstition, ghosts, demonic possession, extrasensory perception, the tarot, séances, spells, potions, chants, good luck charms, fortune telling, horoscopes and so on. Whichever way you look at it, religious and other supernatural beliefs of some kind remain significant features of life in many contemporary societies.

Postmodernist approaches to ideology, science and religion

Postmodernism, which is discussed in more depth in chapter 5, argues that society is now changing so rapidly that it is marked by chaos and uncertainty. No longer can the world be interpreted or understood through the application of what Lyotard (1984) called **metanarratives** – general theories or belief systems that try to provide comprehensive explanations and knowledge of the world.

> A **metanarrative** is a broad, all-embracing big theory or story providing an explanation for how the world and societies operate.

For postmodernists, religion, science and ideology are all metanarratives, claiming to provide comprehensive explanations of the world, and often also claiming a monopoly on truth. Postmodernists suggest such metanarratives are now just one 'story' among others that are all equally valid. In a sense, they are all just ideologies, expressing the different beliefs of a diversity of social groups.

THE SCIENTIFIC APPROACH
HERE IS THE EVIDENCE - WHAT CONCLUSION CAN WE DRAW FROM IT?
A+
B=
C

THE RELIGIOUS APPROACH
HERE'S OUR FAITH - WHAT EVIDENCE CAN WE FIND TO SUPPORT IT?
HOLY BOOK

THE IDEOLOGICAL APPROACH
HERE ARE OUR INTERESTS - HOW CAN WE USE THE EVIDENCE TO JUSTIFY THEM?
OUR INTERESTS

Ken Pyne

Explain how the cartoon suggests that science, ideology and religion differ from one another. What arguments might you give that the cartoon is oversimplifying these differences?

Activity

Drawing on the material in the previous sections, answer the following questions:

1 Outline and explain **two** ways in which science might differ from ideology.
2 Outline and explain **two** ways in which a scientific understanding of the world differs from a religious one.
3 Outline and explain **three** reasons why scientific knowledge might be regarded as socially constructed.
4 Outline and explain **two** ways in which the development of science might have displaced religious explanations of natural phenomena.
5 Outline and explain **two** reasons why religion might be seen as an ideology.
6 Outline **two** reasons why religious and other supernatural beliefs and superstitions continue to be held by many people in contemporary society.

Postmodernism and science

Postmodernists argue that science can no longer lay claim to the superiority of its scientific method, and its claims of enabling humans to control and improve the world have become discredited as it repeatedly fails to rise to the challenges it faces. Creutzfeldt-Jakob ('Mad Cow') disease, antibiotic-resistant superbugs such as MRSA, global warming and climate change, environmental pollution, nuclear power station meltdowns, and weapons of mass destruction are all products of science, and science has failed to provide cures for many of the killer degenerative diseases in Western societies, such as cancer and heart disease. Many scientists have shown themselves to be serving the interests of wealthy corporations and governments, rather than pursuing objective and value-free research. Such circumstances mean that science has lost its authority in society, and some claim that belief in the superiority of science is as much an act of faith as belief in a god or gods, or other supernatural forces, or any ideology.

Postmodernism and religion

In postmodern societies, many people have lost faith in religious metanarratives, and their capacity to explain and give a sense of meaning to the world. Postmodern society is characterized by growing individualism, choice and diversity, and people increasingly establish their identities through consumer culture – through the products they choose to buy (their consumption patterns) and the lifestyles they build; this includes the various beliefs they buy into.

Postmodernist approaches to religion are explored in different contexts throughout this chapter, and the following briefly outlines the contribution these approaches make to the study of religion.

You may wish to return to this section again later when you have a better grasp of the context and explanations in which the following issues are raised.

The decline of metanarratives, the fragmentation of belief, secularization and the growth of do-it-yourself spirituality

Postmodern societies are characterized by a fragmentation of belief and a wide range of different religious, spiritual and other beliefs. The decline of metanarratives is accompanied by people abandoning once taken-for-granted religious belief systems, and they are less willing to accept what religious authorities – in the form of organized religions and priests – say they should believe, what they should think about, and how they should interpret and explain the world. People now hold a wide diversity of beliefs, including the rejection of religious beliefs. The declining attachment to traditional religious explanations and organizations has contributed to growing **secularization** – the decline in the importance of religious thinking, practice and institutions in society.

Postmodernists regard the beliefs people hold as purely a matter of personal taste; people are choosing to pick 'n' mix beliefs as they go shopping in the spiritual supermarket, and buy into, or reject, beliefs in accordance with what most suits their personal lifestyle choices and the identity they wish to project, in much the same way as they select and change clothing as consumer tastes and fashions change.

> **Secularization** is the process whereby religious thinking, practice and institutions lose social significance.

Religion as a consumer product and lifestyle and identity choice

Postmodernists suggest that religion has declined as a source of collective identity based on traditions handed down by the socialization process. Religious beliefs – or lack of them – sit alongside other consumer choices people make as they establish their individual identities. The postmodern world is consumer-driven. Religion is just another consumer product, and people shop for beliefs in a global spiritual marketplace the same way they shop for any other consumer products. They are choosing to create their own do-it-yourself personalized cocktails of beliefs – which may not be religious or spiritual at all – centred on themselves and construction of their identities. The spiritual cocktail, where this is chosen, may be blended from a wide range of beliefs of all kinds, such as established religious faiths, religious sects and cults, and the diversity of beliefs which go under the label of New Age spirituality.

The global spiritual supermarket in a media-saturated society

Postmodern societies have become dominated by global media, including the internet, in what Baudrillard (1988, 2001) called a 'media-saturated' society. People now have access to a huge range of ideas, which enable them to pick 'n' mix beliefs from across the world adapted to their own personal lifestyle choices.

The 'vacuum of meaning' in postmodern society

Bauman (1992) suggests there is now a 'crisis of meaning' in postmodern society, as people reject traditional religious (and other) metanarratives they no longer regard as credible. Postmodernists suggest this has contributed to the rise of new religious movements (sects and cults) and the diversity of New Age ideas as individuals search for new sources of meaning, purpose and identity to fill the vacuum left by the lack of spirituality in contemporary societies.

The Disneyization of religion

In postmodern society, religion is forced to market and package itself in many different guises, in an attempt to appeal to a wide variety of consumer tastes and attract customers as it competes with a whole host of other consumer products and leisure activities. One way religion does this is by **Disneyization** – blending religion, consumerism and popular culture and placing an emphasis on fun and amusement, and merchandising (selling) itself like the fantasy-world of the Disneyland theme park to increase its appeal in the spiritual marketplace (see pages 77–8).

> **Disneyization**, or Disneyfication, is the process whereby something is transformed into a diluted or simplified, trivialized and sanitized version of its original form, to create an inoffensive neutral product resembling the Disneyland theme parks.

Evaluation of postmodernist approaches to religion is best considered in the context in which the points just outlined are discussed – for example, the usefulness of postmodernist contributions to issues like secularization or the growth of New Age spirituality can be weighed against other explanations for these issues. Once you have studied the rest of this chapter and chapter 5, you should also have plenty of ammunition to evaluate postmodernism generally, and to illustrate it with examples drawn from religion.

Practice questions

1 Outline and explain **two** ways in which religious interpretations of the world might differ from scientific ones. **(10 marks)**

2 Read **Item A** below and answer the question that follows.

Item A

Both religion and ideology are belief systems that provide a means for understanding, interpreting and explaining the world. Religion and ideology often differ, as religion usually involves faith in spiritual and supernatural forces of some kind to explain the world, while ideologies are more generally concerned with explanations that protect and promote the interests of social groups. Religion, though, can sometimes also act as an ideology.

Applying material from **Item A**, analyse **two** differences between religion and ideology as belief systems. **(10 marks)**

3 Read **Item B** below and answer the question that follows.

Item B

The greatest challenge to religious beliefs has come from scientific discoveries. The use of the scientific method and empirical evidence – observable evidence collected in the physical world – to establish the causes and effects of natural phenomena has shown many religious beliefs and explanations to be false, such as the origins and evolution of the world. Religious explanations and superstitions are therefore increasingly being displaced by scientific explanations.

Applying material from **Item B** and your knowledge, evaluate the view that science has replaced religion as the main influence on people's knowledge and beliefs in society today. **(20 marks)**

Topic 2

SPECIFICATION AREA

The relationship between social change and social stability, and religious beliefs, practices and organisations

Theories of religion

Sociological theories of religion are primarily concerned with religion's role for individuals and society. These theories can be broadly divided into two main debates:

1 *Religion acting as a conservative force.* Religion seen as a **conservative force** involves three aspects:
   - Building and maintaining **social solidarity** and social stability
   - Protecting traditional values and the existing state of affairs in society (but see the next point), *or*
   - Changing society to restore traditional values and ways of life that may be at risk of disappearing or have already disappeared.
2 *Religion acting as a force for social change.* This is concerned with how religious beliefs and organizations can change society and move it forward, rather than simply acting as a conservative force or moving society backwards to the way it was at some previous time.

Religion as a conservative force 1: the functionalist perspective

The functionalist perspective sees religion as mainly a conservative force, promoting social harmony, social integration and social solidarity through the reinforcement of a **value consensus** – a widespread agreement around the main values of a society which is the basis of social order. The functionalist perspective is essentially concerned with analysing the role of religion in meeting the **functional prerequisites** or basic needs that society has in order to survive. For example, society can only survive if people share at least some common beliefs about right and wrong behaviour. Religion is seen by functionalists as part of the culture or way of life of a society, and it helps to build a collective identity and maintain cultural traditions and establish the basic rules of social life. Bruce's (1996) ideas of **cultural defence** and **cultural transition** illustrate this. Cultural defence is where religion functions as a focal point for the defence of community identity, which is seen as under threat in some way from an external force. Cultural transition is where groups, like minority ethnic groups, move to a different country or culture, with religion providing a source of identity and support during the period of transition and adaptation to the new culture.

Durkheim

Durkheim (2001 [1912]) believed that social order and stability could only exist if people were integrated into society by a value consensus. He saw religion as an important element in achieving this, by providing a set of beliefs and practices which united people together.

Durkheim argued that all societies divide the world into the 'sacred' and the 'profane'. The 'sacred' refers to things that members of society regard as special, as 'set apart and forbidden', that are spiritual, religious or holy and that are in some ways extraordinary, inspiring awe, reverence,

---

A **conservative force** is one that maintains, or seeks to restore, traditional beliefs and customs and maintains the status quo (the way things are currently organized in society). This may sometimes involve supporting social change in order to return to traditional values and ways of life that are at risk of disappearing, or have already disappeared.

Social solidarity refers to the integration of people into society through shared values, a common culture, shared understandings and social ties that bind them together.

A **value consensus** is a widespread agreement around the main values of a society.

Functional prerequisites are the basic needs that must be met if society is to survive.

Cultural defence is where culture, such as religion, acts as a focal point for the defence of community identity which is seen as under threat in some way from an external force.

Cultural transition is where groups make the transition to a new culture, for example through migration, with their own culture, as shown through such facets as religion, providing a source of identity and support during the period of transition and adaptation to the new culture.

A **totem** is a sacred object representing and having symbolic significance and importance for a group.

The **collective conscience** refers to the shared beliefs and values which form moral ties binding communities together, which is necessary to maintain social order by regulating individual behaviour.

fear and so on. The 'profane' refers to the ordinary, everyday, non-sacred, non-spiritual, non-religious or unholy aspects of life. Religion relates to the sacred aspects of a society. Durkheim emphasizes that the sacred does not necessarily have to be a god, spirits or other supernatural phenomena, but can be anything that people regard as sacred – such as a stone, a tree, a place, a river, a book, a person or an animal.

Activity

1 In your own words, explain Durkheim's distinction between the 'sacred' and the 'profane', using examples from contemporary society.
2 Look at the photos on the next page, and explain how and why each of the items might be regarded as sacred according to Durkheim – use the internet to find out if you're not sure.
3 Suggest examples of things beyond conventional religion in contemporary Britain that might fit Durkheim's view of the sacred.

Durkheim studied the practice of totemism among the central Australian Arunta tribe of aborigines. He argued that totemism – the practice of worshipping a sacred object, known as a **totem** (usually named after a tribe or group) – represented religion in its most basic form.

Durkheim argued that the totem is created by society and is so sacred because it is a symbol of the group or society. When worshipping the totem, people are really worshipping society. Religious beliefs, such as totemism, and accompanying ceremonies and rituals, act as a kind of social glue, binding people together and building bonds between them. By sharing beliefs, giving them a sacred quality and worshipping together, people develop moral ties between themselves, and a sense of shared identity, commitment and belonging – what Durkheim called the **collective conscience**. This collective conscience exists outside of individuals, but controls individual behaviour and regulates how members of a community relate to one another, and is necessary to maintain social order.

For example, in minority ethnic communities in contemporary Britain, religious beliefs and customs are often a means for these groups to maintain their own cultural identity and traditions (the cultural defence referred to above), and provide guidelines on how individuals should conduct themselves in their daily lives. Sikh and Hindu temples and Muslim mosques often play an important role in integrating such communities, acting as focal points of community life as well as religious life.

Although Durkheim saw religion playing a key role in building the collective conscience, he believed that the supernatural dimensions of religion would eventually disappear, and that other 'civil religions' might take on this role in people's lives. Civil religion suggests that sacred qualities are attached to aspects of society itself, with non-religious rituals and ceremonies performing similar functions to religion, though not necessarily having any link with the supernatural. Examples of this idea of civil religion might include the devotion some people display towards royalty, the lives of celebrities, popular music or football in contemporary Britain. However, once we abandon the link between religion and some form of belief in supernatural forces, then it is questionable whether we are still really talking about religion at all, rather than just the various other non-religious ways that people are socialized and integrated into the societies to which they belong.

Malinowski

Like Durkheim, Malinowski (2004 [1926]) saw religion as reinforcing social norms and values and promoting social solidarity. However, Malinowski also saw religion as providing explanations for events that were hard to explain, as well as security in the face of uncertainty. Religion fulfils a need for emotional security and relieves situations of emotional stress which threaten social stability and solidarity. Events such as death, serious illness, suffering, accidents and disasters, as well as other life crises like divorce or unemployment, can produce anxiety and tensions which may threaten social solidarity as people experience bitterness, disillusionment, uncertainty or loss of meaning as they encounter events which they can't fully control, predict, explain or understand. Religion can provide a source of comfort, explanation and meaning for individuals when faced by such crises.

Images of the sacred. Durkheim said that anything can be held sacred. The photos above show, left to right: a sacred rock (Uluru or Ayer's Rock); a river (the Ganges); places (Mecca and Glastonbury); a book (the Qur'an); a person/symbol (crucified Christ on the cross); an animal (a painted cow in India); a building (a temple).

Funeral services, for example, act as a source of comfort for the bereaved – either through beliefs in life after death, or by the support gained in such moments of stress through the gathering of friends and relatives. Church attendances soar during wartime.

Parsons

Parsons emphasizes the role of religion in providing and underpinning the core values of any culture, and the social norms which regulate people's behaviour. The set of moral beliefs and values in religion may become so deeply ingrained through socialization that it may have an effect on the everyday behaviour of believers and non-believers alike. For example, if the social rules about killing, stealing and adultery are broken, most individuals will experience a guilty conscience about doing something wrong, and this is a powerful socializing and controlling influence over the individual. Like Malinowski, Parsons also sees religion giving meanings and explanations to, and thereby enabling people to make sense of, otherwise inexplicable and uncontrollable life crisis events which might threaten order and stability in society. He argues that religion provides what he called a 'mechanism of adjustment', providing a means of emotional adjustment in the face of the various crises that occur in life, and providing a means of returning to some sense of normality.

For the functionalists Durkheim, Malinowski and Parsons, religion reinforces social solidarity and restricts both deviance and social change, because the existing social and moral order is regarded as 'sacred'. It provides stabilizing and regulating influences for both individuals and society, as evidenced perhaps by the continuing significance of religion and religiosity in the contemporary world (see pages 84–5 in Topic 5). Religion is therefore acting as a conservative force – maintaining the status quo and keeping society as it is. Figure 1.1 provides a summary of the functionalist view of religion.

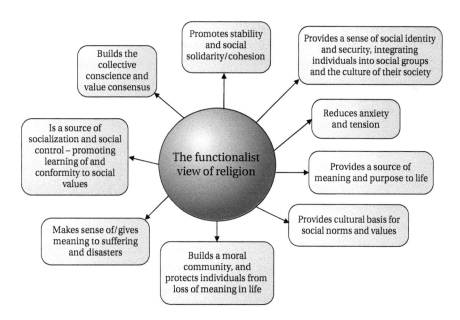

Figure 1.1 The functionalist view of religion

Activity

1 Outline ways in which religion might provide guidelines for everyday conduct.
2 Outline two ways, with examples, in which religion might act as a 'mechanism of adjustment' helping people to adjust to crises in life.
3 How do religious rituals help to control situations of stress and anxiety?
4 In what ways do these religious rituals strengthen social solidarity?
5 Give examples of any contemporary rituals which might strengthen social solidarity.

Criticisms of the functionalist view of religion

Downplaying social change

The functionalist perspective sees religion as a conservative force, promoting social harmony and protecting the status quo. However, this downplays the role that religion can sometimes play in social change, as discussed later.

Declining religiosity and secularization

Religion can only fulfil some of the functions that functionalists claim if people actually hold and practise religious beliefs. However, there is diminishing **religiosity** and growing secularization – a decline in religious thinking, practice and institutions – in many Western European countries.

Religious thinking, practice and institutions are becoming less important both in the lives of individuals and in society as a whole, and those involved are a dwindling group. This is shown, for example, by dramatic falls in attendance at services in all the main Christian Churches in the UK; less than half of the population now say they believe in God. This secularization issue is considered extensively in the final topic of this chapter.

> **Religiosity** refers to the extent of importance of religion, and religious beliefs and feelings in people's lives.

Religion can be a disruptive and socially divisive influence

While it is possible to see a common religion bringing people together, establishing a value consensus and integrating small-scale communities, it is hard to see how it can perform this role in contemporary societies, where there is a wide diversity of different beliefs and faiths. Indeed, religion can often do – and perhaps more often than not does – the opposite. Different religions and religious beliefs and values can tear people and communities apart, and pose threats to social order and stability.

Historically, religion seems to have played a far greater role in dividing people than in uniting them, as can be seen in countless religiously based wars or community conflicts. It is often the case that the stronger the religious belief, the stronger is the sense that other religious beliefs are wrong, heretical or evil and need to be defeated, as found among Christian and Islamic fundamentalists.

Examples of religion causing conflict and instability might include:

- *Conflicts within the same religion*, as between Protestant and Catholic Christians in Northern Ireland over hundreds of years, disputes in the Anglican Church over homosexuality and women bishops, and between Sunni and Shia Muslims in Iraq.

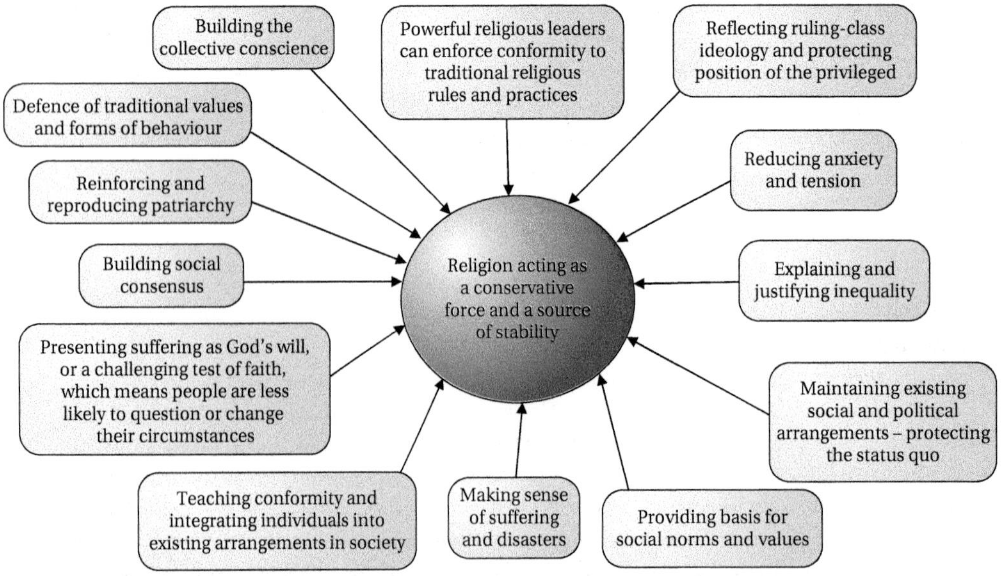

Figure 1.2 Religion as a conservative force

Building the collective conscience

Powerful religious leaders can enforce conformity to traditional religious rules and practices

Reflecting ruling-class ideology and protecting position of the privileged

Defence of traditional values and forms of behaviour

Reinforcing and reproducing patriarchy

Building social consensus

Presenting suffering as God's will, or a challenging test of faith, which means people are less likely to question or change their circumstances

Reducing anxiety and tension

Religion acting as a conservative force and a source of stability

Explaining and justifying inequality

Maintaining existing social and political arrangements – protecting the status quo

Teaching conformity and integrating individuals into existing arrangements in society

Making sense of suffering and disasters

Providing basis for social norms and values

- *Conflicts between religions*. Huntington (2002) suggests religion and religious identity are important aspects of different civilizations in the contemporary world, which can cause conflict and a 'clash of civilizations' as different lifestyles, beliefs and cultures clash with one another (this is discussed further in Topic 5 – see page 87). An example might be the clash between the predominantly Christian West and Islamic fundamentalism, often linked to terrorism, such as the attacks on the World Trade Center in New York in 2001. Other examples of religion as a source of conflict include those in the Indian subcontinent, where warfare between Muslims and Hindus was in part responsible for the division of a once-united India into two separate countries, India and Pakistan. In the 1980s and 1990s, these divisions were added to by conflicts between Hindus and Sikhs. In the 1990s, the former Yugoslavia disintegrated into warring factions of Serbs, Croats and Bosnians, often aligned on religious lines. Conflicts between Christians and Muslims flared up in Nigeria in the 2000s. In contemporary Britain, there are growing tensions between the majority white culturally Christian population and the Muslim community.

Religion as a conservative force 2: the traditional Marxist perspective

Marx saw religion as a part of the dominant ideology – the ideas or belief system of the ruling class which shapes people's view of the world and reproduces and reinforces the false class consciousness (or lack of understanding) among the working class of the fact that they are being exploited. Althusser (1971) saw religion as an ideological state apparatus, an institution which spread the dominant ideology and manufactured what Gramsci (1971) called hegemony – consent and acceptance by people that their positions were unchangeable and inevitable.

Marx thought religion did two main, interrelated things:

1 It acted as the 'opium of the people', cushioning the pain of oppression and exploitation in unequal societies.
2 It legitimized and maintained the power of the ruling class.

Religion as the 'opium of the people'

Marx regarded religion as 'the sigh of the oppressed creature, the heart of a heartless world, and the soul of soulless conditions' and, most famously, as 'the opium of the people'. He saw religion acting like a hallucinatory, pain-relieving drug creating illusions among the oppressed which helped them to accept their position and thereby maintained the power of the dominant class. Religion eased the pain produced by poverty, exploitation and oppression in unequal class societies, and helped to overcome the effects of the alienation (lack of control, fulfilment and satisfaction) of individuals in capitalist society by providing some control, purpose and meaning in their lives.

The Marxist approach suggests that religion eases the pain of oppression and exploitation in three main ways:

Alienation refers to the lack of power, control, fulfilment and satisfaction experienced by workers in a capitalist society, where the means of producing goods are privately owned and controlled.

1 Religion promises an eventual escape from suffering and oppression in this life with promises of an ecstatic future in life after death. Some religions make a virtue of suffering and poverty on this earth. If people believe that what happens to them is God's will, and possibly a test of their faith to be rewarded in the afterlife, they are more likely to accept, or even welcome, their fate and not try to change or improve their circumstances. For example, the Christian Bible promises that 'the meek shall inherit the earth'.
2 Religion sometimes offers hope of supernatural intervention to solve problems on earth. For example, the Jehovah's Witnesses believe that God will intervene to destroy the wicked and eliminate the present system of things on earth in the battle of Armageddon – the showdown between God and Satan. Survivors, along with millions of others who will be resurrected, will form a new paradise on earth where they will live forever ruled by a heavenly government. This

promise for the future, found in many of the world's religions, can encourage people to accept their position and not act to change society.

3   Religion provides a religious explanation and justification for inequality. For example, the Hindu religion provides a religious justification for the inequalities of the Indian caste system and an individual's position in the social hierarchy. In the caste system, there are strict rules about how people should behave, what they should wear and eat, the jobs they can do and who they can and can't marry. People have obeyed these rules because they believe in reincarnation, and if they don't obey the rules of their caste they will be reborn on a lower level. This has kept the caste system in place for over 1,000 years; it is still found in contemporary India, despite efforts to remove the system, because people still hold the religious beliefs that underpin it.

Religion and the power of the ruling class

Traditional Marxists see religion as an instrument of social control and oppression, used by the ruling class to legitimize (justify) their power and material wealth. Inequalities of wealth, income and power are presented as God-given and therefore legitimized and inevitable. The inequalities between rich and poor can't be challenged or changed without questioning the authority of religion or God itself. The Hindu caste system referred to in the previous section is one example of this, which protects the position of those in the highest castes. In the past, religion has justified the power of kings through a doctrine called the 'Divine Right of Kings', which suggested it was the will of God that gave monarchs the right to rule. Religion has even turned kings into gods – for example, the Pharaohs of ancient Egypt. Marxists have pointed out that many religious organizations, such as the Church of England and the Roman Catholic Church, are conservative organizations. They are often extremely wealthy and politically powerful, and have close links with the state, elite groups and the key power holders in society (see, for example, the discussion of the institutional power of churches on page 80). Their teachings, such as on marriage, divorce and abortion, accept, justify and promote the dominant norms and values of society and in general tend to support the status quo and the existing power structures in society. In such ways, religion acts as a barrier to social change.

Criticisms of the Marxist view of religion

Like any drug, religion can only act like opium, performing an hallucinating and pain-relieving role, if people actually take it. In other words, religion can only perform the role Marxists suggest if most people believe and if religion has some institutional power – neither of which is true in Britain or in most contemporary Western capitalist societies.

Neo-Marxist criticisms: religion as a force for change

Neo-Marxists (new Marxists) are later Marxists who have tried to develop and update Marx's ideas, found in traditional or classical Marxism, to overcome weaknesses in his theories and to apply them to more recent changes in society. Neo-Marxists disagree with classical Marxism that religion is simply a part of the dominant ideology and always serves the interests of the ruling class. They suggest religion can have some relative autonomy, or some independence from the interests of the ruling class.

Gramsci, for example, saw religion could sometimes be a focus for a counter-hegemony – a set of ideas providing a basis for challenges by the poor to the power of the ruling class and ruling-class ideology, and showing alternative ways of organizing societies. The way that religion can sometimes act as an outlet and focus for grievances against and resistance to the powerful, undermining their authority and promoting social change, rather than acting simply as a conservative force, is shown by the following examples:

1   Some early Christian sects became a focus for resistance and opposition to Roman rule, as Marx's collaborator, Engels, recognized.

Relative autonomy is the idea in neo-Marxist theory that social institutions, like religion, can have some independence from the interests of the dominant class.

Christ as a revolutionary, like Che Guevara, is the sort of image that liberation theology wanted to promote in the 1960s

MEEK. MILD. AS IF.
Discover the real Jesus. Church. April 4.

2   Liberation theology. The neo- (new) Marxist Maduro (1982) showed how Catholic priests in South America in the 1960s and 1970s played major roles in fighting against military dictatorships, poverty and exploitation. Through a doctrine mixing the teachings of Marx (communism) and Christ (through Catholicism) called 'liberation theology', Catholic priests supported and encouraged the poor to overthrow governments that oppressed and exploited them. Liberation theology sought to present an image of Christ portrayed more as a reforming revolutionary than the passive peacemaker presented in mainstream Catholicism.

3   The role of the Catholic Church in supporting the struggle for equal rights for Catholics in the Northern Ireland Civil Rights Movement in the 1960s, and in Poland in the 1990s, when it became a focus for the struggle for democracy and against Russian domination.

4   In the 1960s, some of the Christian Churches in the southern states of the United States played an important role in supporting the Black Civil Rights Movement, led by the Baptist minister Dr Martin Luther King.

5   Islam, particularly Islamic fundamentalism, is often a vehicle for resisting the global influence of Western cultural imperialism, fighting the Americanization of the world's culture, and resisting the dominance of Western corporations in the world economy.

6   In Iran, Islam produced revolutionary change, with a revolution led by Ayatollah Khomeini leading to the overthrow of a dictatorial monarchy (the Shahdom) and the establishment of an Islamic republic in 1978–9.

Cultural imperialism refers to the way in which Western, and especially American, cultural values are forced on non-Western cultures, with the consequent undermining of local cultures.

Functionalism and traditional Marxism compared

- Both explain the origins and functions of religion in terms of social factors.
- Both see religion as a human creation, with the supernatural having no reality.
- Both see religion as a conservative force, integrating society and maintaining the status quo.
- Functionalists see religion's role as necessary and justified, while Marx saw religion as repressive – an ideology legitimizing the power of the dominant class, misleading ordinary people into conforming to, rather than challenging, societies in which the majority are exploited by the minority.

Religion as a conservative force 3: the interpretivist perspective

Structuralist theories, like traditional Marxism and functionalism, tend to see religion as an external force, working on people to mould them into social conformity. Interpretivist approaches, by contrast, study the meanings and interpretations of people in order to understand their behaviour. They therefore look at the way religion is used by followers to create meanings and interpretations of the world, and to understand the meanings sacred symbols have for individuals – such as crosses, rivers, places, people, statues and items of clothing. The Shroud of Turin, for example, is an old piece of cloth, and in itself has no value, meaning or importance. However, some attach sacred meanings to it, as they believe it to be the burial shroud of Christ, with his face revealed on it.

Some believe that the Shroud of Turin is the cloth in which Jesus Christ was buried, and, because people give it this meaning, it is regarded as a sacred object. Can you think of other examples in which people place a high value on objects because of the meanings they give them?

A universe of meaning, theodicy and the sacred canopy

Berger (1990) argues that religion provides what he calls a 'universe of meaning'. This is a set of beliefs and values that helps people make sense of the world, and enables them to give life some focus, order and meaning.

The universe of meaning provided by religion gives individuals a sense of meaning and explanation in the face of a chaotic world. As part of this universe of meaning, religion provides a theodicy, a religious framework that enables people to make sense of seemingly inexplicable and fundamental questions about human existence, such as the meaning of life and death, and why poverty, injustice and inequality, accidents, disease, suffering, pain, evil and death exist in the world.

Berger sees religion as a kind of sacred canopy stretching over society, providing a shield that protects people from the uncertainties, meaninglessness and pointlessness of life, by helping them to interpret and make sense of the world and their position in it.

By suggesting that religion provides universes of meaning and theodicies to explain the darker sides of daily life, interpretivists are arguing that it is contributing to the maintenance of social stability. To that extent, therefore, they are allied with functionalists and traditional Marxists in that they all see religion acting as a conservative force in society.

A **universe of meaning** is a set of beliefs and values which enables people to give life some focus, order and meaning.

A **theodicy** is an explanation for the contradiction in the existence of a God who is assumed to be all-powerful and benevolent, while at the same time there is widespread suffering and evil in the world.

Does religion still provide a universe of meaning and a sacred canopy?

Berger argues that in modern (and postmodern) societies, religion is losing its role for most people as the provider of a universe of meaning. This is because, as discussed earlier, reason, logic and science have largely replaced faith and superstition in people's consciousness as the means of understanding and making sense of the world, and there is growing secularization and disenchantment with the world. In a media-saturated, globalized, postmodern society, there is increasing diversity and fragmentation of beliefs and lifestyles, and religion is losing its validity as a universe of meaning and as a theodicy for human suffering. Berger suggests that the sacred canopy of religion has therefore been lost, and that religion no longer provides a source of meanings and morality, or the sacred shield against life's insecurities and uncertainties.

Activity

1 Identify ways in which religion creates universes of meaning that enable people to give some focus to life, and order and meaning to inexplicable events like pain, accidents, suffering, death, disease and disasters. Try to draw on examples from a range of religions.
2 To what extent do you think this role of religion is still significant in contemporary society? Explain your answer.
3 What other sources of meaning are available to people, apart from religion?

Religion as a conservative force 4: religion as a compensator

Stark and Bainbridge's (1996) theory of religion echoes the concerns of Berger, as well as functionalists, as they examine the meaning and the functions of religion for individuals in society. Stark and Bainbridge see religion meeting the needs of individuals when their sense of social order is disrupted by economic hardship, loneliness, grief, accidents, death, disease and ill-health. They argue that belief in God, religion and religious organizations provides a means for individuals to make sense of and come to terms with such events, as well as answering universal fundamental questions – for example: Why are we here? Why is there suffering in the world? What is the purpose of life? Stark and Bainbridge see religion acting as a general compensator – a belief that if individuals act in a particular way, they will eventually be rewarded. Providing hope for life after death is an important compensator, with the promise of future rewards in an uncertain world. Stark and Bainbridge therefore suggest that religion in some form or another will never disappear, as it provides answers to universal questions – much like Berger's universes of meaning – and offers general compensators meeting universal human needs.

Stark and Bainbridge suggest that religion, by acting as a compensator, is contributing to the maintenance of stability in social life, and to that extent it is acting as a conservative force in society.

Religion as a conservative force 5: feminist views on religion and patriarchy

Many feminists see religion acting as a conservative force. This is because they regard many religious institutions as patriarchal – serving the interests of men – with religious beliefs reflecting a patriarchal ideology which justifies, reinforces and reproduces inequality based on male dominance and control of women by men. This is achieved by:

Marginalization refers to the process whereby some people are pushed to the margins or edges of society or organizations (marginality), often by poverty, lack of education, disability, discrimination and so on.

- The subordinate roles of women shown in religious scriptures/sacred texts, and the portrayal of women as morally polluting and corrupting
- The marginalization of women in organized religions, such as either their total exclusion from, or their restriction to lower levels of, the priesthood, their segregation in places of worship and their restriction to lower levels in religious organizations
- Patriarchal religious doctrines, allocating women to traditional roles as wives and mothers, particularly in Islamic and New Right Christian fundamentalism
- Religious laws and customs giving women fewer rights than men, such as in divorce and property rights.

Feminist views of religion and its role in society are discussed in depth in Topic 4 (see pages 49–54).

Religion, social change and conflict

Is religion always a conservative force?

While most sociologists agree that, in general, religion helps to maintain the status quo and that changes in society lead to changes in religion, there is an alternative view which argues that religion can also cause social change and conflict, and therefore doesn't always or necessarily act as a conservative force. Some of the criticisms in the previous sections have already shown how religion can act to challenge the powerful and change society.

Max Weber

Weber (1864–1920) was a social action theorist, who believed that, to understand human behaviour, it was necessary to examine the meanings people give to events and ideas. People's ideas and beliefs, which make up their worldview or image of the world, can have important consequences for the way they think and act. Religion is often an important component of this worldview, and Weber attempted to show that the evolution of new religious ideas can stimulate social and economic change as people act in terms of their beliefs.

Through cross-cultural analysis of the links between religion and social change in a number of societies, Weber sought to explain why capitalist industrialization developed first in Western Europe rather than in other parts of the world, even when they had similar levels of technological development. Weber's analysis was explored in *The Protestant Ethic and the Spirit of Capitalism* (2001), which was first published in 1904.

The Protestant Ethic and the Spirit of Capitalism

Weber studied the rise of Calvinism in Europe. Calvinism is a form of ascetic Protestantism (Puritanism) characterized by austerity and self-denial, with strong self-discipline to maintain these. Weber's study showed that Calvinist religious beliefs had an important influence on the development of an industrial capitalist economy and the emergence of a capitalist class.

Weber argued that, for capitalism to develop, both the normative conditions (the necessary values) and the material conditions (factories, technology, etc.) were needed. He saw Calvinism, which developed in seventeenth-century Western Europe, producing the normative conditions – the set of ideas, ethics and values making up the Protestant ethic – which provided the 'spirit of capitalism' that encouraged capitalist development.

Weber emphasized the following features of Calvinism and the Protestant ethic:

1 Calvinists believed in predestination – followers believed that their fate was already decided by God. However, a believer had no way of knowing whether he or she was one of the 'saved' or 'chosen ones'.

2 The solution to this problem of not knowing one's destiny was to become involved in 'intense worldly activity', since hard work and material success were seen as religious virtues and a likely sign of being one of God's chosen.

3 The Protestant ethic emphasized values and virtues like hard work, thrift, trade, profit, modesty and punctuality and the avoidance of idleness, time-wasting, excessive sleep and self-indulgence. Living life according to these values, with hard work leading to material success, became signs of God's grace and an indication that the individual was 'chosen'.

4 Weber argued that this Protestant ethic was a major reason why capitalist industrialization developed first in Western Europe rather than elsewhere. The Protestant ethic valued the pursuit of wealth and making money, which was something people had always done and still did in a wide range of societies with different religions. But the Protestant ethic also promoted as virtues the reinvestment of profits back into the business – rather than spending them on luxuries, conspicuous, self-indulgent consumption and high living – and working regularly with self-discipline rather than erratically and whenever you felt like it. Hard work, self-discipline

and self-denial, and making money to reinvest and expand a business, were therefore part not just of good capitalist business practice, but also of good religious morality.

5   Weber therefore came to the conclusion that Calvinism, alone of all the religions, provided the rationality and religious ideology and ethics which encouraged the development of capitalist industrialization first in the Protestant countries of Europe.

Weber's study of religion and the Protestant ethic led him to conclude that religion could be an important force in social change, including economic change, and this contrasts with those functionalist and Marxist theories that emphasize the conservative roles of religion.

Evidence that religion can act as a force for social change

There is abundant evidence that religion can act as a force for social change, rather than simply maintaining the status quo. A number of examples of this have been mentioned previously, such as the role of religion in civil rights movements in Northern Ireland and the United States, the Catholic Church in Poland, liberation theology in South America and the Iranian revolution in 1978–9. A good contemporary example is presented by the world growth in Islamic fundamentalism.

What is religious fundamentalism?

Religious fundamentalism means returning to the fundamentals of any religion, usually based on the literal interpretation of sacred texts. Religious fundamentalism may embrace different religions, and groups within religions, as is found in the New Christian Right in the USA, Jewish fundamentalism found in Israel, Islamic fundamentalism found in various Muslim countries and communities around the world, or Hindu fundamentalism in India.

Bruce (2008) suggests fundamentalism may involve some or all of the following:

- Beliefs based on a literal interpretation of sacred texts, like the Christian Bible or the Qur'an in Islam, which are seen as the complete word of God and as without error.
- A belief that a Messiah of some kind (such as Christ, or the Mahdi – the hidden Twelfth Iman – in Islam) will return and either put the world to rights or bring this world to a dramatic cataclysmic or apocalyptic end on a 'Day of Glory'.
- Certainty of the rightness of their beliefs, and therefore a hostile intolerance of other religions or religious beliefs.
- Strong opposition to secularization and modernization, and a robust defence of traditional beliefs and moral rules. Fundamentalists often wish to reverse social and religious changes that have already taken place, and hark back to some imagined past time when the excitement and commitment of the true religion existed, such as seventh-century Mecca and Medina for Islam.
- A strong desire to reshape the world in accordance with their beliefs, with public policy and laws promoting a distinctive way of life conforming to religious requirements, such as Sharia law in Islam.
- The use, sometimes, of violence, such as bombing abortion clinics (Christian fundamentalists in the USA) or Jihad (Holy war to defend Islam), to further these aims, and to hasten the desired Day of Glory.
- The use of modern technology, like the internet, satellite phones and mobiles, and cable television networks, as the establishments that the fundamentalists oppose control the major forms of communication.

Fundamentalism often emerges as a response to the threat to traditional religious beliefs and identity posed by modernization, the growth of science, the spread of secular culture through globalization, and the growing uncertainty and insecurity of postmodern societies.

Religious fundamentalism is a good example of religion acting as a conservative force – maintaining traditional values and resisting modernization – by supporting social change to return to traditional values that are at risk of disappearing or have already disappeared. It is also a good example of religion as a source of social conflict, for example between Islamic fundamentalism and Western cultural imperialism.

Globalization refers to the growing inter-connectedness of societies across the world, with the spread of the same culture, consumer goods and economic interests across the globe.

Islam became a major international force for social change in the late twentieth century, and the present spread of Islamic fundamentalism has attempted to forge social changes in much of the Islamic world, and beyond the Islamic world, based on literal interpretations of the Qur'an. The terrorist attacks on the Twin Towers of the World Trade Center in New York on 11 September 2001, the London bombings on 7 July 2005, the war in Afghanistan from 2001, and the terrorist campaigns of ISIS (Islamic State) in Iraq and Syria in 2014 onwards, have all been, at least in part, motivated by Islamic fundamentalism and its opposition to Western values, culture and global dominance.

> **Activity**
>
> To what extent do you think Islamic fundamentalism is an example of religion acting as a force for social change, or an example of religion acting as a conservative force, for example as it tries to maintain or restore traditional values and resist change?

Conclusion: is religion a conservative stabilizing force, a force for social change or a source of conflict?

There is a range of evidence discussed above that can be used to support the functionalist, Marxist, interpretivist and feminist views that religion acts as a conservative, stabilizing and integrating force, promoting social stability and protecting the patriarchal status quo in society.

Religion can also act *at the same time* as a conservative force and as an agent of social change by seeking to change society back by reversing what many might regard as progressive change. For example, in Afghanistan during the 1990s the Taliban regime set about reversing the modernization of Afghan society by establishing an extreme Islamic fundamentalist regime. Laws were based on a strict and narrow interpretation of the Qur'an, with very harsh punishments for those who did not conform, such as amputations of limbs for theft, public flogging for not wearing traditional dress, and death by stoning for adultery. The example cited earlier of the Iranian revolution of 1979–80, which deposed the Shah of Iran, led to the establishment of the present Islamic state, based on Sharia law defined by the Qur'an, which sought to reverse a perceived threat to traditional Islam posed by the modernization and westernization of Iran.

The rise of the extremist so-called 'Islamic State' in Syria and Iraq has led to the persecution of many minority groups in the region, including centuries-old Christian communities. The global response against ISIS (here showing Christian and Muslim leaders) shows how religion can act to both condemn and encourage such actions.

Many sociologists accept that religion is not necessarily or always a conservative force; it can also act as a destabilizing source of social division and conflict, and, as the Weberian approach and neo-Marxists like Gramsci and Maduro suggest, as a means for radical change. There is a danger of overstating the importance of religion, whether in the context of conservatism and social stability or in the context of social change or conflict, as there are often a number of other social, economic and political factors which also influence the nature and extent of religion's role in society.

McGuire (2001) and Robinson (2001) suggest that there are four major interrelated factors which influence whether religion acts as a conservative force or a force for social change:

1 *The nature and extent of religious beliefs.* If most people in a society hold religious beliefs and a religious view of the world, and these beliefs have strong moral codes which conflict with some features of existing society, then religion is more likely to lead to criticism of society, and attempts to change it.

2 *The significance of religion in a society's culture.* If religion is a central part of the culture and everyday life of a society, as with Catholicism in many South American countries, or in those where Islam is the main religion, religion is more likely to be used as a means of justifying behaviour and change. Examples might include the role of Catholicism in Ireland, where the Catholic religion is embedded in the culture, and where Catholicism has historically been aligned with Irish Republicanism in the fight against British rule in Ireland. In Islamic countries, reference to Islam is often very important in justifying social changes. By contrast, in the UK, religion is fairly marginal and irrelevant in most people's lives, and so plays little role in social change.

3 *The extent of the social involvement of religion.* In societies in which religious organizations, priests and other religious figures are close to and involved with the people and play important roles in the political and economic life of societies, then religion is more likely to influence social change. An example might be the role of Islam in contemporary Iran or Saudi Arabia, or the Catholic Church in the Middle Ages, when religion had a major influence on social and political decision-making. This aspect of the social involvement of religious organizations in affecting social change is likely to become of even greater importance in societies which lack democracy, where protest and change have to be fed through religion as other means are blocked by the political power of governments. This is what occurred with liberation theology in Latin America, in countries where Catholicism was very deeply embedded and where Roman Catholic priests attempted to lead protest and change against dictatorships when the dictators themselves claimed to hold Catholic beliefs. This social involvement of religion meant the church was able to exercise influence in a way that was almost impossible for ordinary people.

4 *The degree of central authority in religious organizations.* In societies where religious organizations have strong central authority, religion is in a much better position either to promote change or to prevent it. This is most apparent in Islamic countries like Saudi Arabia or Iran, where Islam has very strong centralized authority, and this authority is effectively used to influence the extent of changes in society.

Activity

1 Outline two examples illustrating ways in which religion has undermined stability and been a source of conflict in society.

2 Outline two examples illustrating ways in which religion has promoted social change.

3 On the basis of your work so far on religion, do you consider religion to be mainly a conservative force or a force for social change? List the arguments for your view, backing them up with examples drawn from contemporary societies, and preferably from a number of different religions.

Practice questions

1   Outline and explain **two** ways in which religion may act as an agency of social control.

(10 marks)

2   Read **Item A** below and answer the question that follows.

> **Item A**
>
> Religion once provided what Berger calls a 'universe of meaning', and religion acted as a 'sacred canopy' stretching over society. These helped people to interpret and make sense of the world and their position in it. Religion gave some focus, order and meaning to their lives, and protected them from the uncertainties of life. However, in many contemporary societies, religion is losing this role for a lot of people.

Applying material from **Item A**, analyse **two** reasons why for many people religion may no longer be acting as a 'universe of meaning' and as a 'sacred canopy' today.   **(10 marks)**

3   Read **Item B** below and answer the question that follows.

> **Item B**
>
> Some sociologists argue that religion acts as a conservative force that prevents social change. Through its teachings, religion reinforces dominant norms and values, and justifies existing inequalities in social and power structures. Religious organizations like the Church of England and the Roman Catholic Church are extremely wealthy and powerful, and have close links with the state, elite groups and the key power holders in society.

Applying material from **Item B** and your knowledge, evaluate the view that religious beliefs and organizations act as conservative forces in society.   **(20 marks)**

Topic 3

SPECIFICATION AREA

Religious organisations, including cults, sects, denominations, churches and New Age movements, and their relationship to religious and spiritual belief and practice

Religious organizations

There have been various attempts made to categorize the different types of organization through which people express and practise their religious beliefs, to provide a basis for comparing different kinds of group. This categorization, or **typology**, is based on factors like their organizational structure, their relationship with the state, their attitudes to the wider society around them and other religious beliefs, their size and type of membership, and the commitment required from members. There are four main categories: church, denomination, sect and cult.

The four categories are summarized in table 1.1, drawing on the work of Weber (1993 [1920]), Niebuhr (1957 [1929]), Troeltsch (1992 [1931]) and Wallis (1984). These typologies are really generalizations or **ideal types**, with features that apply in many, but not all, cases, and no religious group will conform exactly to the categories outlined. Any particular religious organization may combine aspects of each type, and may develop and change in character over time. Much of the work on these categories is based on Western Christian religions, and therefore they do not necessarily apply to other faiths like Islam or Hinduism.

Table 1.1 includes Wallis's categorizations of organizations as world-rejecting, world-accommodating or world-affirming. Although Wallis developed these in relation to the new religious movements which have developed since about 1945, discussed later, they can also be usefully applied to older traditional religious organizations.

> A **typology** is a generalization used to classify things into groups or types according to their characteristics, which do not necessarily apply in every real-world example.

> An **ideal type** is a model of a phenomenon, like a religious organization, built up by identifying the essential characteristics of many factual examples of it. The purpose of an ideal type is not to produce a perfect category, but to provide a measuring rod that enables the researcher to compare particular examples and identify the extent to which they are similar to or different from the ideal type.

World-rejecting, world-accommodating and world-affirming groups

Wallis (1984) suggested there were three main types of religious group, categorized by their relationship to the world around them:

- *World-rejecting* groups are in opposition to the world, and reject many of the dominant norms and values of society, and replace them with alternative beliefs and practices. Members are likely to live their lives in different ways from other members of society.
- *World-accommodating* groups generally accept the dominant norms and values of society, and members will live similar lifestyles to other members of society.
- *World-affirming* groups accept society as it is, and offer individuals the opportunity for self-improvement within it. Members are likely to live similar lives to other members of society, apart from their interest in what many regard as deviant, bizarre, esoteric or obscure matters.

Churches and denominations

Churches and denominations have relatively minor differences between them, other than their size, influence and relationship to the state. Churches and denominations both have a bureaucratic structure, which means they have a hierarchy of officials with different amounts of authority. For example, the Pope is the head of the Roman Catholic Church, presiding over a bureaucracy of cardinals, archbishops, bishops and so on, down to the local priest, with clearly spelt-out rules and regulations about the form that services and rituals should take, the dates of important events, appropriate forms of dress and literature and so on.

Table 1.1 Religious organizations: churches, denominations, sects and cults

	Churches	Denominations
Example	Church of England; Roman Catholic Church.	Methodists & religious organizations in countries where there is no established (official) church.
Organizational structure	Bureaucratic, hierarchical power structure with paid officials – often large, wealthy, with powerful leaders.	Hierarchy of paid officials & bureaucratic structure, but some division of authority roles and higher degree of democratic participation (more lay preaching).
Attitude to wider society and the state	WORLD-ACCOMMODATING Conservative – likely to accept dominant norms and values of society & in general tend to support status quo. Often close links with the state e.g. Britain's Queen is head of the Church of England.	WORLD-ACCOMMODATING Generally accept dominant norms & values, though perhaps some minor differences and restrictions on members e.g. alcohol and gambling by Methodists. More concerned with spiritual behaviour & everyday morality than 'other worldly'. Often no links with the state.
Commitment required – demands on members/ followers	Integrate with the social & economic structure of society. Few demands or restrictions on members, who play full part in social life and not expected to withdraw from society. Accept the social environment in which they exist.	Integrate with the world. Accept secular culture. No rejection of the wider society. Members often disillusioned members of established churches, other denominations or sects, but live conventional and conforming lives outside their religious activities.
Membership	Universalist and inclusive – embraces all members of society, and don't have to demonstrate faith to be a member. Often born into it, and all members of society assumed to be members unless opt out.	Members recruited by self-selection (conversion) or family tradition. Open membership.
Social base	Members drawn from all social classes, but higher-status groups tend to be over-represented in membership.	Hardly ever a social majority. Membership drawn from all levels of society but less closely identified with upper classes than a church, and lower working class least likely to be represented.
Attitude to other beliefs/religions	Tend to be intolerant of other groups and claim monopoly of religious truth.	Tolerant of other groups and religions, and don't claim monopoly of truth. See themselves as one denomination among many.

	Sects	Cults
Example	People's Temple; ISKCON (International Society for Krishna Consciousness – the Hare Krishnas); Unification Church (the Moonies); Jehovah's Witnesses.	Transcendental Meditation, Scientology.
Organizational structure	Often no hierarchy of paid officials or bureaucratic structure. More egalitarian power structure. Tightly knit community, often under control of single charismatic leader.	Loosely structured, tolerant and non-exclusive. Often lack some of features associated with a religion e.g. religious buildings, collective rituals of worship, developed theology, ethics.
Attitude to wider society and the state	WORLD-REJECTING Radical – in opposition to or in tension with the world. Many involve a radical rejection of the wider society and its institutions, including the state. Reject many dominant norms and values & replace them with alternative beliefs and practice. Some may face state disapproval and/ or persecution.	WORLD-AFFIRMING Accept world as it is, offering individuals special knowledge, personal insight, and access to either spiritual powers within themselves and/or supernatural powers, providing the opportunity to be more successful, secure and happy in existing society. No opposition to or links with the state, but some may face state disapproval and/or persecution e.g. Scientology.

Table 1.1 (continued)

	Sects	Cults
Commitment required – demands on members/ followers	Strict entry criteria, with members required to demonstrate strong involvement and commitment, change their lifestyles, and sometimes expected to withdraw from/make sharp break with conventional life outside sect (but some contact with outside world allowed for recruitment & fundraising). Tight social control of members, and risk of expulsion if fail to conform.	Often 'followers' rather than formal members, who carry on normal lives, with little social control over them by the cult.
Membership	Members recruited by self-selection or family tradition. Voluntary adherents. Small, elitist, exclusive, close-knit closed membership; initiation ceremonies. Hostile to non-members.	Cults are non-exclusive and open to all. Many are highly individualistic, selling services to individuals, with use of these services, 'salvation' or other rewards a purely personal matter.
Social base	Often a small, exclusive dispossessed or alienated minority, drawn from groups who experience relative deprivation, and/or are marginalized and/or drawn from poorer social groups.	Followers often have above-average incomes, who feel something is lacking in their otherwise successful lives. Less likely to have deprived members or followers since cult services are often for sale (at high prices) and purchased by supporters.
Attitude to other beliefs/religions	Claim a monopoly of the truth, and only members have access to the religious knowledge that offers the only true path to salvation, which is reserved for this 'saved' or chosen minority. Intolerant of other religious groups and those outside sect.	Tolerate existing religions, and coexist alongside them. Followers may belong to/ support and buy services from other religious organizations or cults.

Is the concept of the church now obsolete?

Bruce (1996) suggests that the concept of 'the church' is really outdated in most Christian countries now, and should only be applied in cases where a single religious organization really does dominate society and can reasonably claim to be administering to all members of society. Such examples might include Roman Catholicism in medieval Europe, when the Catholic Church was all-powerful and the only major religion, or where particular religions have state support and legal privileges, such as the Orthodox Church in contemporary Greece, the Roman Catholic Church in Ireland, Spain or Italy, or Islam in countries such as Iran, Saudi Arabia and Pakistan.

Should the term 'church' now only be applied in societies where a single religious organization dominates society and has legal privileges, as with the Greek Orthodox Church in contemporary Greece?

Many Western societies are now experiencing **religious pluralism**, with a wide diversity of minority-interest religions and religious organizations. This is accompanied by growing secularization (a decline in religious belief and practice), and many churches and denominations do not either expect or get a high degree of commitment. Bruce (1995) argues that the Church of England, for example, although it is still the established or 'official' church in England, now commands such little support among the population as a whole that it really only has the status of one denomination among others. Churches and denominations are becoming more alike, more tolerant of other groups and beliefs, and coexist quite happily alongside other churches and denominations. The idea of a church-type organization may therefore now be obsolete, with the term 'denomination' more accurately describing the major religious organizations in societies where there is religious pluralism.

Religious pluralism refers to a situation in which there are a variety of different religions, different groups within a religious faith, and a range of beliefs of all kinds, with no one religious belief or organization reasonably able to claim to hold a monopoly of truth or to have the support of most members of society.

Sects and cults

Whereas churches and denominations are generally seen as fairly respectable and mainstream organizations, sects and cults tend to be seen as more deviant – involving beliefs and behaviour that are seen as odd, weird or bizarre, or as a threat to existing society. Somewhat confusingly, the terms 'sect' and 'cult' are often used interchangeably, particularly in the media, with the same group sometimes classified as a sect and sometimes as a cult. For the sake of clarity, sects and cults are defined differently and kept clearly separate here (see table 1.1).

Barker (1989) has suggested that the terms 'sect' and 'cult' have such a stigmatized and pejorative (strongly negative) meaning attached to them that they should be abandoned altogether. This is because media treatment of sects and cults has meant they are associated in the popular imagination (often quite unfairly) with groups seen as evil, controlling, extremist and manipulative, as brainwashing their members into unthinking robots, and as harmful to both their own members and the wider society.

Sects

Wilson (1982) suggests that sects have the following main features:

- They exist in a state of tension or conflict with the wider society, frequently rejecting that society and its values.
- They impose tests of merit on would-be members, and members claim elite status as alone having access to what they regard as the only route to salvation.
- They exercise stern discipline, regulating the beliefs and lifestyles of members and using sanctions against those who deviate, including the possibility of expulsion.
- They demand ongoing and total commitment from members, overriding all other interests.
- They are often led by a charismatic leader – a person with a powerful, imposing and 'magnetic' personality that gives him/her power over other group members.

Cults

Wallis (1974) and Bruce (1995) see cults differing from sects in that, whereas sects are very tightly knit, closed groups, with strong demands on the commitment of members and strict internal discipline, cults are often very loosely knit groupings, open to all and highly individualistic. Giddens (2006) suggests that the focus on the individual, and individual expression and experience, are the main features distinguishing a cult from a sect. There is often little discipline or commitment demanded of cult followers. Cults generally don't claim any monopoly on the truth, and often lack the clearly defined and exclusive belief systems associated with sects. Aldridge (2007) suggests that cults see themselves offering just one route to self-realization or salvation out of a choice of others, with followers making individual choices and drifting in and out of cults depending on what works best for them at the time. Followers of cults are more appropriately regarded as clients or customers, rather than as members, as they often purchase services which cults sell to individuals.

Cults can embrace a wide range of beliefs, some of which may not appear as religious in any accepted sense. These include things like alternative medicine and therapies, belief in UFOs, occult beliefs and practices and, as Aldridge suggests, for most people, they are more like therapies than religions, used as relaxation and stress-busting techniques.

Audience cults, client cults and cult movements   Stark and Bainbridge (1985) identify three types of cult.

1   *Audience cults* provide little beyond information services of some kind for individuals, and there is little if any organization or involvement of followers. The service is often consumed individually and spread by the media, through the internet, books and magazines, for example. Such cults might include New Age ideas (discussed on pages 39–41) such as astrology, horoscopes, interest/belief in UFOs, and reincarnation.
2   *Client cults* have more organization, and offer services to followers (who are seen as customers), such as therapy and courses, which are often sold to clients by practitioners. Examples include spiritualism offering contact with the dead, or various forms of alternative medicine and treatments.
3   *Cult movements* are more organized, involving a wider range of activities, support and personal involvement and commitment. Scientology is an example of a cult movement, which is very highly organized and commercial, claiming to offer its followers a route to improved mental health.

From audience cult to cult movement – the example of Scientology

Scientology originated in 1950 as an *audience cult*, primarily focused on the marketing of founder Ron Hubbard's books on mental health, then developed into a *client cult*, as it began to form networks and provide counsellors to sell clients therapeutic services and courses based around Hubbard's concept of Dianetics (his 'science of mental health'). From the late 1950s it developed into a cult movement, as it grew to become the highly organized and wealthy global Church of Scientology it is today. For further information on Scientology, go to www.scientology.org/home. html.

Activity

1   Refer to table 1.1 and the sections on churches, denominations, sects and cults. Mark the following statements as true or false:
     (1)   Churches are world-rejecting institutions
     (2)   Cults are world-affirming movements
     (3)   Denominations have close links with the state
     (4)   Sects are large, world-accommodating organizations
     (5)   Sects are often controlled by people with powerful personalities
     (6)   Churches are intolerant of other religions and beliefs
     (7)   Cults often appeal to the more well-off sections of society
     (8)   Sects are often hostile to or suspicious of those not belonging to the sect
     (9)   Cult members can carry on with their existing religious beliefs if they want to
     (10) Denominations tend to be a bit more critical than churches of the present state of society
2   Explain, with an example of each, the difference between world-rejecting, world-accommodating and world-affirming religious organizations.

New religious movements (NRMs)

New religious movements (NRMs) are those that have emerged in the period since the end of the Second World War in 1945, and particularly since the 1960s. Many have little in common with established churches, denominations or religious sects, although, as Wallis pointed out, many of them draw upon traditional Christian or other religious faiths, like Hinduism and Buddhism. NRMs are mainly sects and cults, and as Aldridge (2007) notes, although they consist of a very diverse range of groups, they contain some of the most controversial social movements in the modern world, posing threats both to the lives of their own members and to the wider society. Some of these, like Heaven's Gate, the Branch Davidians and Scientology, are described shortly. The media frequently attack and stereotype NRMs for being bizarre, weird and sinister, and for brainwashing and mind-control, controlling, abusing and harming individuals, as in the People's Temple or Heaven's Gate. However, some NRMs, like Transcendental Meditation, have support from highly respectable people and business corporations.

The features of NRMs

Barker (1989) suggests that new religious movements have some or all of the following features:

1 They are religious in so far as they are often concerned with spirituality and/or the supernatural, and with similar questions shared with mainstream religions – for example: Why am I here? What is the meaning of life? Is there a God? Is there life after death?
2 They are most likely to find supporters among young adults, who are first-generation converts, rather than born into the sect or cult.
3 There is a high turnover of members, suggesting that the need fulfilled by new religious movements is temporary.
4 They are likely to be led by a charismatic leader – a person with a powerful, imposing and 'magnetic' personality that gives them power over other group members.
5 They are certain that they hold the only correct 'truth', and that they are the 'chosen' ones.
6 There is frequently a sharp divide between 'us' – the 'good and godly' group – and 'them' – the 'bad' and, perhaps, 'satanic' outsiders.
7 There is often suspicion or hostility from wider society, particularly the mass media.
8 Many are short-lived or transient, particularly world-rejecting sects, as the heavy commitment required is hard to maintain, and younger people grow older and look to more normal lives, or support dwindles when the leader dies.

There are many different new religious movements, with wide differences in beliefs, membership, organization and rituals. Wallis developed his threefold typology of world-accommodating, world-rejecting and world-affirming groups (see page 31) in relation to the NRMs, though he recognizes that no group will conform exactly to the categories he outlines. Wallis notes that the ideas and beliefs of most NRMs are hybrids, in that they combine ideas from different belief systems into a new hybrid belief system of their own.

World-rejecting NRMs

These are among the most controversial groups, and are often targeted by so-called 'de-programming groups' who attack them for brainwashing. World-rejecting NRMs are typically hostile to the wider society, and often receive hostility in return, from the media and sometimes from state authorities too. They have the characteristics of sects, and examples include the Unification Church (the Moonies), the International Society for Krishna Consciousness (ISKCON or Hare Krishna), the People's Temple and Heaven's Gate (see the box on pages 37–9). Some of these groups have very high levels of control and discipline over their members, who are expected to show uncritical obedience to leaders. Membership often entails a sharp break with conventional life and significant lifestyle changes, like diet, hairstyles and dress, and sometimes involves communal/group living.

World-rejecting NRMs are sometimes committed to **millenarianism**. This involves beliefs (millenarian beliefs) that some form of extra-worldly or supernatural intervention will change the world rapidly and suddenly, in what Aldridge calls 'an imminent apocalyptic collapse of the existing world order and its replacement by a perfect new dispensation' (2007: 31). Such groups are sometimes referred to as doomsday cults.

Millenarianism involves beliefs (millenarian beliefs) that existing society is evil, sinful or otherwise corrupt, and that supernatural or other extra-worldly forces will intervene to completely destroy existing society and create a new and perfect world order.

The Branch Davidians (see the box on page 39) were an example of a Christian-based millenarian NRM. They believed that the Second Coming of Christ to earth was imminent, and would be accompanied by the Apocalypse and the final battle of Armageddon mentioned in the Bible. Aldridge cites the example drawn from Islam of the millenarian belief in the reappearance of the Mahdi – the 'hidden imam' who will establish a world in accordance with the will of Allah.

Despite the threats to society that the mass media sometimes allege these NRMs pose, they generally have a tiny membership, and, as Barker (1984) found, they are very bad at holding on to members – there is very high turnover, due in part to the harshness of the regimes they are expected to follow.

World-accommodating NRMs

These are mainly denominations or offshoots of mainstream Christian churches and denominations. They are more concerned with rediscovering a spirituality thought to have been lost, and revitalizing the spiritual life of their members, than with everyday worldly affairs. Religion is seen as a personal matter, with members living conventional and conforming lives outside their religious activities. Examples include neo-Pentecostalism and the Charismatic Movement, which involve themselves in things like speaking in tongues, faith healing and exorcism.

World-affirming NRMs

Wallis sees these as mainly cults. They often lack many of the features associated with traditional religions or religious organizations, such as having religious buildings, religious services and rituals, and ethical and moral codes. Many are more like therapy groups than religious organizations, and they claim to be able to provide the techniques and knowledge that will enable individuals to access spiritual powers within themselves, to unlock their human potential, meet their personal needs and solve their problems. This helps people to remain or become successful in terms of existing society and its values. Examples include Scientology and Transcendental Meditation, both of which claim to provide access to the techniques and knowledge enabling personal growth and problem-solving.

Aldridge notes that most of the people who use the services of world-affirming movements do so as consumers, buying services that are for sale to anyone who can afford them, with commercial marketing of courses, conferences, books, therapies and so on. Followers of world-affirming NRMs live otherwise conventional lives, and the services they buy are meant to help them to do this more successfully than ever. Aldridge points out that although these groups are world-affirming and generally the most in tune with the contemporary world, the services they offer can come into conflict with established professional groups, such as the medical profession. Scientology, for example, is uncompromisingly hostile to modern psychiatry, and campaigns against the use of mood-altering psychoactive drugs like Prozac.

Seven new religious movements

The following organizations, and all other religious organizations mentioned in this chapter, can be explored further at www.religioustolerance.org.

Heaven's Gate (www.heavensgate.com)

A *world-rejecting sect* which believes that UFOs contain extra-terrestrial beings, and whose members believe that, by committing suicide together at the correct time, they will themselves be reborn as extra-terrestrials. In March 1997, when the Hale Bop comet, which members believed had a spaceship behind it to offer them rebirth, was at its nearest to earth, thirty-nine men and women voluntarily committed suicide.

The People's Temple

A *world-rejecting sect*, founded by Jim Jones in the United States, but based finally in Guyana. Jones developed a belief called *Translation*, according to which he and his followers would all die together in a mass suicide, and would move to another planet for a life of bliss. Following a shooting in 1978 carried out by the Temple's security guards, with 11 wounded and 5 killed, including a US Congressman on an inspection visit, Jones initiated a group suicide. In all, 638 adults and 276 children died, with most dying after drinking a grape drink laced with cyanide.

The International Society for Krishna Consciousness (ISKCON or the Hare Krishnas) (www.iskcon.com)

A *world-rejecting sect*, this has around 1million members worldwide, and follows, with some exceptions, much of conventional Hinduism. While some members live in temples and ashrams (monasteries) as monks and nuns, most ISKCON members practise Krishna consciousness in their own homes, and congregate in temples for worship. Hare Krishna monks are often seen in public places, and are highly visible when spreading their message – dressed in brightly coloured orange and saffron robes, chanting, playing drums, selling their literature and incense; the men's heads are distinctively shaven.

Church of Scientology (www.scientology.org/home.html)

A *world-affirming cult*, founded by science-fiction writer L. Ron Hubbard in the USA in the 1950s, this claims a membership of about 8 million worldwide. It has been widely persecuted, but has now become more accepted. It believes that individuals can improve their lives through the application of the philosophy of Dianetics, and the removal of 'engrams' which cause mental health problems through 'auditing' by a member of the clergy using an 'E-meter' (an electronic device used to measure electrical characteristics surrounding the body).

The Unification Church (the 'Moonies') (www.unification.org)

A *world-rejecting* (Christian-based) *sect*, this was founded in 1954 in Korea by the Revd Sun Myung Moon (hence the nickname the 'Moonies'). Membership estimates range from 1 to 3 million in more than 150 countries. Many of their beliefs are similar to those of other Christian groups, though

Founder of the Unification Church, the Revd Moon

the Moonies also believe that the Revd Moon has been asked by God to complete the work that Jesus Christ started, and to unite all Christians into a single body.

Transcendental Meditation (TM) (www.tm.org)

A *world-affirming cult* founded by Maharishi Mahesh Yogi in India and brought to the West in the 1950s. This merges a simplified form of Hinduism with science, and believes that meditation can develop human potential and intelligence, and provide better health and career success; it is believed that individuals are eventually able to develop paranormal powers, such as levitating or flying in mid-air (yogic flying). Well over a million people have taken basic TM courses, and there are estimated to be tens of thousands of members worldwide.

The Branch Davidians (www.rickross.com/groups/waco.html)

This *world-rejecting* (Christian) *sect* was led by David Koresh, and believed in the imminent Second Coming of Christ to Earth. This would only occur when at least a small group of Christians had been 'cleansed' by David Koresh, who was sent by God to do this. Koresh and seventy-five followers, including twenty-one children, died in a shoot-out with the FBI in 1993 in Waco, Texas, USA, believing that the beginning of the Apocalypse and the final battle of Armageddon mentioned in the Bible was beginning at their compound.

Activity

Refer to the box on 'Seven new religious movements', the features of new religious movements identified on page 36, the differences between world-accommodating, world-rejecting and world-affirming organizations outlined on pages 31 and 36–7 and audience cults, client cults and cult movements on page 35.

1 Explore two of the new religious movements, or two of your own choosing, using a Google search, www.religioustolerance.org or the websites mentioned in the box.
2 Identify those aspects of each group that fit the features of a new religious movement, and the reasons they may be classified as either sects or cults.
3 Classify them as world-accommodating, world-rejecting or world-affirming, and explain your reasons.
4 Explain in your own words, with an example of each (use the web), the differences between an audience cult, a client cult and a cult movement. Explain how your examples show the form of cult you identify.

New Age groups

The term 'New Age' is used to refer to a wide diversity of mind–body–spirit ideas, interests and therapies from across the globe that first began to become prominent in the 1980s. New Age ideas draw on and combine religious and occult traditions from the fairly conventional to the obscure, esoteric and bizarre. Many of the ideas have little to do with the supernatural dimension which is normally seen as a defining feature of a religion. Heelas (1996) sees the New Age consisting of two related features:

1 *Self-spirituality* – a range of beliefs in self-spirituality in which everyone becomes their own spiritual specialist, dipping into whatever beliefs and practices they fancy.
2 *Detraditionalization* – the rejection of traditional external religions and spiritual authority – such as established religions, priests and sacred texts – and their replacement by spirituality achieved by searching within oneself through personal experience.

What is New Age religion?

Bruce (2002a) suggests New Age religion consists of five main features:

1 *The emphasis is on the self,* and freeing the 'self within', which is seen as essentially good and divine.
2 *Everything is connected.* This involves a holistic approach, with the mind, body and spirit all connected, and individuals connected to the environment and the supernatural.
3 *The self is the final authority.* There is no authority higher than the individual, and no single truth: the truth is what the individual believes and what works for them. Personal experience is the only test that matters.
4 *The global cafeteria.* There is a vast range of beliefs, therapies and techniques drawn from across the globe, and people can mix these as they choose.
5 *Therapy.* New Age ideas are designed to be therapeutic: to make you more successful, healthier and happier.

The box 'What's included in the New Age?' lists a range of things that might reasonably be included in the broad category of the New Age. The New Age also has its own music associated with it. This is gentle, relaxing, other-worldly inspirational music, created with medieval instruments like the flute, harp and lute, with the human voice used for chanting and humming. It is used for relaxation therapy and to accompany meditation, healing and massage.

What's included in the New Age?

astrology	organic foods
clairvoyance	paganism
crop circles	psychotherapy
Eastern and Native American mysticism	reincarnation
Feng Shui	spirit guides
Gaia (Mother Earth) as a living entity	Tai Chi
green and environmental issues	the energizing and healing power of crystals
herbalism	the i-ching
hypnosis	the tarot
ley lines	traditional therapies
magic and spells	UFOs, extra-terrestrials (aliens) and alien abductions
massage	vegetarianism/veganism
meditation	Wicca (witchcraft)
natural healing and alternative remedies/ medicine	wizards and fairies
near-death experiences	

Stonehenge is a place that has significance for some New Age followers. Search the internet to find out why

Is there a New Age movement?

Sutcliffe (2003) suggests that the New Age refers to a diverse range of ideas and lacks features like premises, leaders and shared beliefs and rituals to such an extent that it can't be regarded as being a movement or movements. He suggests it is more a means for individuals to pursue their own self-development and explore their inner spirituality. The nearest it comes to an organizational form is perhaps the loose network of like-minded individuals, who might keep in touch through the internet and social networking sites, or the occasional meeting, workshop or conference.

New Age ideas are mainly spread through the media and through specialized New Age shops, such as those selling rock crystals and various Eastern and Native American artefacts and services, found in many towns and cities. The New Age requires very little commitment by those who are interested, and Heelas (1996) sees its supporters as subscribing to alternative spirituality through involvement in the commercialism of the mainstream marketplace, such as through buying products or magazines and books. The New Age is therefore best understood, to combine the concepts of Stark and Bainbridge and of Wallis, as either one or many world-affirming audience or client cults, rather than as a movement or movements.

Activity

1 To find out the range of ideas included under New Age spirituality, go into a local bookshop and browse the shelves on 'New Age' or books on the mind, body and spirit.
2 Visit the Kendal Project at www.kendalproject.org.uk. This explores religion in one town in Britain, and contains an array of findings about religion, including New Age spirituality, and discussion of methods for exploring it.
    (a) Find out and explain what is meant by the 'Holistic Milieu'.
    (b) Go to the Holistic Milieu questionnaire and identify five groups or therapies listed as part of this milieu.
3 Using ideas from the Kendal Project, devise and carry out a small survey among your fellow students to explore the following:
    (a) What, if anything, do people understand by 'New Age ideas'?
    (b) To what extent is there belief in or support for New Age ideas?
    (c) Are there any differences, in terms of age, gender, ethnicity or social class, in understanding of and support for New Age beliefs?
    (d) Analyse your findings and suggest explanations for them.

Reasons for the appeal and growth of sects and cults, new religious movements and new age spirituality: an explanatory toolkit

Why do people get involved in sects and cults, including new religious movements and New Age spirituality?

Churches and denominations are predominantly part of mainstream conformist life, and why people get involved with them does not require much explanation, since for many it is simply an aspect of the socialization process as they grow up, seeing going (or not going) to church/mosque/temple/synagogue, etc., as part of normal adult life. However, what does need explaining is why people join or support deviant religious sects and cults, and particularly the world-rejecting ones, like some of the new religious movements and the New Age audience and client cults. This can't simply be explained as a result of the stupidity or gullibility of individuals, as most people can be persuaded to support something only if it fulfils some need or offers them some reward. This section provides a range of reasons for the appeal and growth of sects, cults and New Age ideas. How these explanations apply will vary between more traditional religious sects and the NRMs, and whether they are world-accommodating, world-rejecting or world-affirming. These explanations should therefore be regarded as a kind of toolkit, with different combinations necessary to understand any particular religious group.

Practical or pragmatic reasons

1 *The key to success.* Heelas suggests that what he calls 'self-religions' – world-affirming NRMs and New Age ideas – appeal to more affluent, university-educated, socially integrated and generally successful middle-class groups, whose members nonetheless find something missing in their lives. They seek techniques to recapture their inner selves, and they also have the money to pay for the services on offer. Wallis suggests that world-affirming movements like Transcendental Meditation and Scientology are likely to appeal to such groups for various reasons: they claim to offer knowledge, techniques and therapies that enable people to unlock spiritual powers within themselves, helping them to reduce stress and anxiety at work, find career and financial success and a happier personal and spiritual life – making them better people in both work and personal terms.

2 *Escape.* Some groups may provide short-term practical solutions for those escaping from personal crises in their lives, such as some difficult family, personal or work circumstances. In her study of the world-rejecting Unification Church (the Moonies), Barker (1984) argued that the sect offered a type of substitute family, providing support and comfort.

Secularization

Weber saw the modern world as one in which there had been what he called a 'disenchantment with the world'. By this, he meant that the spiritual, magical and mystical aspects of life had diminished or disappeared, and the world had become more rational, or planned and predictable. Secularization (discussed later in this chapter) is part of this growing rationality and disenchantment, with developments in science and technology undermining religious beliefs.

Many traditional churches and denominations have watered down their beliefs to accommodate a more secular world, and have become more worldly, less spiritual and lacking in firm beliefs and commitment. Giddens (2006) suggests that 'people who feel that traditional religions have become ritualistic and devoid of spiritual meaning may find comfort and a greater sense of community in smaller, less impersonal new religious movements'. Bruce (1996) sees the growth of New Age ideas and cults as a consequence of growing individualism in modernity, and some people's loss of faith in and disillusionment with traditional religious leaders and beliefs. He suggests the attraction of world-affirming groups lies in the techniques they offer to bring into people's lives self-improvement and spiritual dimensions they may otherwise lack.

Traditional religious sects and new religious movements, and New Age ideas, may attract those turned off by mainstream religion, and provide a refuge for those seeking the spiritual and supernatural, and firm beliefs and commitment, in a secular society.

Filling the 'vacuum of meaning' in postmodern society

Linked to the secularization discussion above is the view of Lyotard (1984) that, in postmodern society, there has been a loss of faith in metanarratives – the all-embracing 'big' theories which try to explain everything, such as science and what Berger called the universes of meaning provided by traditional religious ideas. People have lost faith in traditional sources of authority, such as doctors, scientists and organized religions and priests. Bauman (1992) suggests there is now a 'crisis of meaning' in postmodern society. Heelas (1998) believes the rise of New Age ideas is part of a 'spiritual revolution' providing a means for individuals to fill the 'vacuum of meaning' left by the decline of traditional religions and the lack of spirituality in contemporary societies.

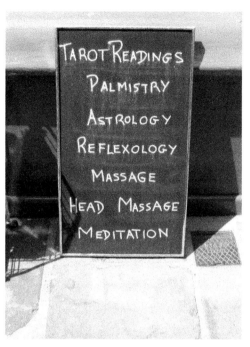

A New Age window display (left), and a typical menu of services available outside a New Age shop (right). Is the New Age just another part of mainstream consumer culture?

Joining sects or following cults may therefore provide new sources of meaning and purpose for individuals.

Identity formation and individual choice in postmodern society

Postmodernists suggest that traditional sources of identity, like social class, gender and ethnicity, have become more fragmented in contemporary societies. People increasingly form their own identities through consumer culture – through the products they buy (their consumption patterns) and the lifestyles they build – and this includes the various beliefs they buy into. Joining a sect or following a cult, as well as providing a sense of meaning and purpose for individuals, may therefore also meet their personal needs and individual choice in terms of identity formation and lifestyle choices.

Globalization and the media

Globalization, particularly in the media, including the internet, has meant that people now have access to a huge range of ideas from around the globe. We now live in what Baudrillard (1988, 2001) called a 'media-saturated society', and people are able to pick and choose, and mix and match, beliefs from across the world. The NRMs are able to communicate with larger numbers of people than ever before through the media, especially the internet, and this has raised the visibility and profile of these groups, particularly among younger people.

Social deprivation, marginality and theodicies of disprivilege

Weber (1993 [1920]) argued that sects are most likely to emerge among marginal groups in society. These are people who are pushed to the edges or margins of society, and are not integrated into mainstream society. Wilson (1970) suggests that a variety of factors may lead to marginalization, such as economic deprivation – including poverty, homelessness and unemployment – racism, or because people are in trouble, lonely, have personal or family problems or are disillusioned with or

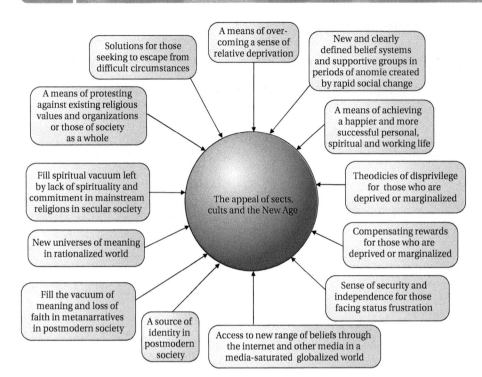

Figure 1.3 The appeal of sects, cults and the New Age

The following are contained in boxes surrounding the central sphere labelled "The appeal of sects, cults and the New Age":

- Solutions for those seeking to escape from difficult circumstances
- A means of overcoming a sense of relative deprivation
- New and clearly defined belief systems and supportive groups in periods of anomie created by rapid social change
- A means of protesting against existing religious values and organizations or those of society as a whole
- A means of achieving a happier and more successful personal, spiritual and working life
- Fill spiritual vacuum left by lack of spirituality and commitment in mainstream religions in secular society
- Theodicies of disprivilege for those who are deprived or marginalized
- New universes of meaning in rationalized world
- Compensating rewards for those who are deprived or marginalized
- Fill the vacuum of meaning and loss of faith in metanarratives in postmodern society
- Sense of security and independence for those facing status frustration
- A source of identity in postmodern society
- Access to new range of beliefs through the internet and other media in a media-saturated globalized world

alienated from wider society for some reason. Weber suggests that religious sects appeal to these groups by providing what he called a '**theodicy of disprivilege**'. This is a religious explanation and justification provided by sects for the social marginalization (or disprivilege) of their members.

As traditional Marxist theories of religion might suggest, sects also sometimes turn social deprivation and poverty into a virtuous test of faith, and offer compensation for suffering in this world. Stark and Bainbridge, for example, saw many of the world-rejecting NRMs acting as what they called 'compensators' to help deal with problems of marginality, particularly as the secularization of mainstream religions has meant they are less able to perform this role. Pentecostalist sects among African Caribbeans in the UK, or those like the Jehovah's Witnesses or the Branch Davidians, provide access to a close-knit group of members in a similar position, a sense of security, clear values and the reward of being one of the chosen few who will achieve salvation either in the afterlife or in a future new heaven on earth.

Wallis suggests that many well-educated middle-class young people were attracted to world-rejecting new religious movements in the 1960s and early 1970s because they felt marginalized and disillusioned following the failure of the radical student and hippie movements and their challenge to dominant norms and values. Also, such young people, as Barker found among those in the Moonies, can afford to 'drop out' for a while, with their backgrounds giving them reasonable prospects of re-entering conventional society after their temporary break.

A **theodicy of disprivilege** is a religious explanation and justification for social inequality and social deprivation, explaining the marginalization (or disprivilege) of believers, often used as a test of faith with the promises of compensating rewards in a future after death.

Status frustration

Status frustration means that people are frustrated at their lack of status in society. Marginality, discussed above, may cause status frustration, but it is particularly associated with young people going through the long period of transition from childhood to full independent adult status, brought about by longer periods in education and their lack of work and family commitments. Wallis (1984) suggests this may explain why new religious movements are most likely to appeal to young people, as membership can provide some support for an identity and status independent of school, college or family, and overcome the sense of status frustration. Barker suggests that the fact that young adults often lack the responsibilities of work, paying rent or a mortgage, or looking after children gives them the time and freedom to get involved should they so choose. Both Barker and Wallis argue that world-rejecting groups appeal to such unattached young people, as they join

Status frustration is a sense of frustration arising in individuals or groups because they are denied status in society.

them together in a supportive community of others facing similar experiences, bringing them both companionship and a sense of independence.

However, such periods of status frustration are generally short-lived, and Wallis concluded that 'the new religious movements involve only a very small proportion of the population … and even then often for only very brief periods during the transition to adulthood'.

Relative deprivation

Membership of sects and cults is not exclusively limited to the socially deprived, the marginalized or the status-frustrated young, and sometimes those from more advantaged, middle-class social groups join them. Stark and Bainbridge suggest that the concept of relative deprivation may help to explain this.

This refers to the subjective feeling of being deprived or lacking something compared to those in the social group with which individuals identify and compare themselves. This may be a sense of status or income, but could be a sense of spiritual or emotional inadequacy compared to others, even if there is no material deprivation. The ideas and support derived from sect membership or cult following may help to overcome this.

> **Relative deprivation** is the sense of lacking something compared to the group with which people identify and compare themselves.

Anomie and social change

Wilson (1982) argues that periods of sudden or rapid social change can provide fertile ground for the growth of sects. Such periods may create what Durkheim called anomie. This refers to a sense of normlessness, or uncertainty and insecurity over social guidelines for behaviour, as rapid change undermines or disrupts traditional norms and values and universes of meaning.

Sects and cults may provide solutions to such periods of uncertainty, by providing new and clearly defined belief systems and close-knit supportive social groups – a sense of certainty in an uncertain world. Wilson (1970) suggests that the rise of Methodism, which began as a sect in eighteenth- and nineteenth-century Britain, was a response to the rapid social change and insecurity of life in the new industrial towns. Similarly, the rise of NRMs might be seen as a response to the uncertainties generated by rapid social change since the 1960s.

> **Anomie** refers to a sense of normlessness, confusion and uncertainty over social norms, often found in periods of rapid social change and other disruptions of the routines and traditions of everyday social life.

Protest

Glock and Stark (1965) suggest that sects emerge as a form of religious or social protest of some kind, as many embody elements of protest against existing society. They may therefore appeal to those who find that their values, for a variety of reasons, are at loggerheads with those of the existing society around them, or of other religious groups, which they see as watered down or corrupted. Examples might be the Nation of Islam in the USA, which is a religious group for black people embodying protest against white society, or Pentecostalist sects. The growth of NRMs in the 1960s is sometimes seen as part of the protest movement among young people against existing society and their disillusionment with it, and the search for new alternative beliefs and lifestyles.

Activity

Refer to the toolkit of explanations above.
1 Outline reasons why individuals might join
   ● A world-rejecting group
   ● A world-accommodating group
   ● A world-affirming group
2 Outline reasons why new religious movements are more likely to be supported by young people, and why membership is often only for short periods.
3 Outline arguments and evidence for and against the view that the growth of new religious movements might be a response to the secularization of modern society.

The dynamics of sects

The dynamics of sects is concerned with how and why they may change over time. Niebuhr (1957 [1929]) suggested that sects tend to be short-lived, as they will, over time, either turn into denominations or disappear altogether. For example, both the Quakers, or Society of Friends, and the Methodists originally began as world-rejecting religious sects, with members living distinctive lifestyles in opposition to existing society. However, both abandoned a long time ago their world-rejecting features, and have evolved from sects into the highly respectable world-accommodating and tolerant denominations they are today. On the other hand, some sects, like the Jehovah's Witnesses, have retained their features as world-rejecting sects over a long period of time, while others, like the People's Temple, have completely disappeared. What influences whether a sect is short-lived or long-lived, whether it turns into a denomination or whether it disappears?

Why are sects thought to be only short-lived?

Many writers have argued that sects are short-lived and transient, and that there is little possibility of a sect surviving for long periods of time. There are a number of reasons given for this.

1   *The problem of maintaining commitment and fervour.* Barker (1989) suggested that, particularly in world-rejecting new religious movements, people may find it difficult to cope with the strict discipline and rules imposed on members, and the heavy commitment required is hard to maintain, leading people to eventually leave the sect.

    Niebuhr thought the enthusiastic fervour and commitment of sect members is hard to sustain after the first generation – the commitment and beliefs of parents who converted to the sect are hard to keep going in their children. Either the sect will then gradually wither away, or it will need to become less of a protest movement and modify its beliefs and practices to accommodate, and be more tolerant of, mainstream society and other beliefs. This would then allow its members to live more normal lives, and give it a better chance of retaining members, but this entails the sect becoming more settled and denomination-like. Becker (1950) identified this process, when he described a denomination as 'a sect that has cooled down', as it loses some of its initial fervour, and becomes more tolerant, world-accommodating and 'respectable'.

2   *The loss of charismatic leaders.* Sects that are founded and led by a single charismatic leader, whose inspirational personal magnetism and leadership attracted people into the sect, may lose support and disappear once the leader dies.

3   *The changing circumstances of members and appeal of sects.* The variety of personal reasons and social circumstances that were discussed earlier, and which originally attracted people to the sect, may, after a period of time, disappear and make sect membership redundant. For example, original reasons for joining, such as social deprivation, marginality, anomie and the search for meaning, or personal crises in their lives, may cease to be relevant. This is particularly likely in generations following the first generation of converts.

    Barker suggests that, in new religious movements, as younger people grow older, the reasons that drove them into the sect diminish, and they begin to look for more normal lives. This may mean that the sect disappears, or that it loses its world-rejecting features and becomes more like a denomination.

4   *Religious diversity in postmodern societies.* Postmodern societies are characterized by a fragmentation of belief and a wide diversity of religious, spiritual and other beliefs. Postmodernists tend to see the beliefs people hold as purely a personal matter, and they can experiment without long-term commitment and go spiritual and religious shopping, picking, choosing and changing beliefs as freely as they might chop and change washing liquids in their local supermarkets. There is greater tolerance of all beliefs today, and this may mean that religious sects have a short shelf-life as consumer tastes and fashions change.

Are all sects necessarily short-lived?

Are disappearance (death) or denomination the only options for sects? Aldridge (2007) argues that the suggestion that sects must over time either disappear or turn into denominations is false. He points out that:

- Many sects have existed a long time while still retaining their features as sects
- Not all sects depend on charismatic leadership
- Many sects have been successful in socializing their children into acceptance of the sect's beliefs and practices, while also converting adults
- Sects can maintain strict standards of conduct, including expelling those who fail to conform to these standards, over long periods of time.

Aldridge points to sects like the Jehovah's Witnesses and the Amish to illustrate this (see the box).

Jehovah's Witnesses are a worldwide world-rejecting Christian Adventist millenarian sect, and have managed to survive as such and maintain their religious fervour, despite not completely isolating their members from contact with wider society, or being led by charismatic leaders; they are also fairly wealthy and very bureaucratic. They try to protect their members, including children, from 'evil' – birthdays and Christmas are ignored. They encourage friendships to be formed only with other Witnesses, but their children attend the same state schools as other children. They are most famously known in Britain for refusing blood transfusions under any circumstances, and for going round in pairs knocking on doors and attempting to convert people.

The Amish are a Christian introversionist sect found predominantly in Pennsylvania in the USA. They have no interest in converting others to their way of life and have cut themselves off from the modern world, both physically and socially. They live in their own rural communities modelled on communities in the past, and reject features of modern life like TV, cars and modern technology, using their own horse-drawn carriages, as shown here. They live according to their own principles, based around spiritual experience, self-discipline and self-control, and have distinctive styles of dress and speech (see photo).

Wilson (1959) has also rejected the view that the disappearance of a sect or its becoming a denomination are the only alternatives, pointing to the Jehovah's Witnesses and the Seventh Day Adventists as examples of long-standing established sects that have retained their sect-like features and not become denominations. Wilson suggests that what will affect whether a sect can retain its status or will turn into a denomination will depend on what its members see as being required in order to be 'saved'.

Conversionist sects

Wilson suggested that what he called 'conversionist' sects were the most likely to develop into a denomination. These are sects which think that the best way to save the world is not to be hostile to and isolated from it, but to be engaged with it, and to try to change or convert individuals by spreading the religious message and 'saving souls'. Should they be successful, and win a lot of support, they may turn into a denomination, but this doesn't prevent them carrying on as they were when they were a small sect. The Salvation Army is an example of a small former conversionist sect that has turned into a conversionist denomination.

Introversionist and Adventist/revolutionary sects

There are two types of sect that Wilson saw as not being able to survive in denominational form – the introversionist and the Adventist or revolutionary sects.

1 *Introversionist sects* are those, like the Amish, which believe that the only route to salvation involves total withdrawal from the corrupting influences of the world and becoming inward-looking (introverted). Such sects can only succeed and last by keeping apart from the world. Trying to convert people by going outside the sect to preach is likely to be a polluting and corrupting experience, and would compromise and destroy the fundamental beliefs of the sect. Such sects therefore cannot survive in denominational form.

2 *Adventist or revolutionary sects* are those, like Jehovah's Witnesses, who hold millenarian or doomsday beliefs that suggest there is going to be some form of imminent, sudden, dramatic and catastrophic change in the world, brought about by the Second Coming (advent) of Christ, Judgement Day, Armageddon, or other revolutionary divine interventions. This will destroy the evil and ungodly world, and only the exclusive few selected members of the sect will be saved. Like Jehovah's Witnesses, they may try to spread their beliefs, but there can be no question of compromise with the world, watering down of beliefs, or tolerance of other beliefs, as otherwise they would be counted among the sinners and cast aside when Judgement Day arrives. Such sects cannot take on denominational form and compromise with other beliefs without abandoning the very beliefs and values and exclusivity on which their own sect is founded.

Practice questions

1 Outline and explain **two** ways in which the growth of new religious movements and New Age spirituality may be a response to conditions of rapid social change.   **(10 marks)**

2 Read **Item A** below and answer the question that follows.

> **Item A**
> Contemporary Western societies involve a wide diversity of religious, spiritual and other beliefs. Postmodernists see the beliefs that people hold as purely a personal matter. They can go spiritual and religious shopping, and pick and mix religious beliefs to suit their own lifestyles without long-term commitment to any religion or religious organization. This means that many religious cults and sects are short-lived, as consumer tastes and fashions change.

Applying material from **Item A**, analyse **two** influences on whether a religious sect or cult is short-lived or long-lived.   **(10 marks)**

3 Read **Item B** below and answer the question that follows.

> **Item B**
> Scientific and rational thinking has led to what Weber called growing 'disenchantment with the world' – a decline in the spiritual or religious aspects of people's lives. Postmodernists point to a loss of faith in metanarratives, such as the universes of meaning once provided by traditional religions. Some suggest that individuals turn to new religious movements and New Age ideas to fill the vacuum of meaning left by the decline of traditional religions.

Applying material from **Item B** and your knowledge, evaluate sociological explanations for the development of new religious movements and New Age spirituality.   **(20 marks)**

Topic 4

SPECIFICATION AREA

The relationship between different social groups and religious/spiritual organisations and movements, beliefs and practices

Gender and religion

Feminist approaches to religion

Most feminists focus on the way in which many existing religions are patriarchal, with writers like de Beauvoir (1953) and El Saadawi (1980) seeing religion and religious ideology playing a part in maintaining the male domination over women that is found in many aspects of contemporary social life. This is achieved by religious ideas that seek to control women's sexuality, and that emphasize their once-traditional roles as partners of men, mothers and carers in the family.

Feminists differ in their attitudes to religion, depending on their more general beliefs:

1 *Liberal feminists* are likely to aim for more equality for women within existing religions, by seeking to remove obstacles that prevent them from taking on positions of authority, such as those of priests, religious teachers and leaders.
2 *Radical feminists* tend to see most contemporary religions as existing for the benefit of men, and either present a fundamental challenge to religion altogether or seek to reshape it by recapturing the centrality of women in religion of early times.
3 *Marxist feminists* tend to emphasize the Marxist view that religion acts as 'the opium of the people', focusing on the way religion acts as a means of compensating women, particularly working-class women, for their double exploitation through their status as being both working-class and women.

Patriarchy and religion

Most, but not all, mainstream contemporary religions and religious organizations tend to be patriarchal, and women and men are rarely treated equally. Evidence for this is seen in a number of ways:

1 *Religious scriptures.* Women are either invisible or occupy subordinate positions to men in most religious scriptures/sacred texts. For example, in the Christian Bible, Eve is formed from a rib taken from a man, and it was Eve the evil temptress who led Adam astray and laid the basis for original sin in Christianity and Judaism. God is always seen as male and a father figure, Jesus is male, and Christ's twelve apostles were all men. In Islam, Mohammed is a man. Aldridge (2007) notes that, in the Qur'an, women are legally inferior to men, lacking the same rights as their husbands, to whom they must submit. De Beauvoir (1953) argues that most scriptures in most religions suggest that 'man is master by divine right'.
2 *Being barred from the priesthood.* Women are excluded from the priesthood (or equivalent) in Roman Catholic and Orthodox Christianity, in Islam and in Hinduism. In Buddhism, female nuns are always given less status than male monks. In Orthodox Judaism, only males are allowed to take a full part in ceremonies. Even in Sikhism, where all religious offices are theoretically equally open to men and women, only a small minority of women take on important positions. When women have been able to become priests, as in the Church of England since 1992, this has been accompanied by bitter controversy, and only after long and difficult campaigns to achieve it.

3   *The (stained) glass ceiling.* Within religious organizations, women are often found at the bottom of the career ladder, facing the same 'glass ceiling' that they face in many other organizations – an invisible barrier of prejudice and discrimination that stops them from rising higher up the hierarchy. For example, although the Church of England ordained its first woman priest in 1994, there were no female bishops in the Church of England until 2015, even though women make up around one-fifth of all full-time Anglican priests. There are deep divisions within the Church of England concerning women becoming bishops, and many regard the church as marred by institutional sexism, with women facing what has been called a 'stained glass ceiling'. The rejection of the introduction of women bishops by the Church of England in 2012 confirmed this, and the Archbishop of Canterbury suggested the decision meant the church had 'lost credibility' and could be seen as 'wilfully blind' to modern trends and priorities. This decision was subsequently reversed in 2014, and in January 2015, the Church of England consecrated its first female bishop, albeit as a suffragan (assistant) bishop.

4   *Patriarchal religious doctrines.* Feminist writers like Walby (1990) and de Beauvoir suggest that the doctrines (or teachings) of many of the world's religions contain an ideology emphasiz-ing women's traditional roles as wives and mothers in the family. For example, in Christianity, respect for the Virgin Mary as a submissive mother is widespread, particularly in Roman Catholicism. Similarly, Barrett (1977) and Pryce (1979) suggest that Rastafarianism, a religion that appeals mainly to African-Caribbean men, involves an assumption that women will take on the traditional roles of housewife and mother in the family, which Rasta men believe will protect women from racial and sexual harassment by white society. However, such an appar-ent defence of women in effect gives power to men, by discouraging women's more active engagement and participation in society. Writers like Holm and Bowker (1994) point out that many religious fundamentalist movements, such as 'Born Again' (New Right) Christianity and Islamic fundamentalism, reinforce patriarchy and seek to reverse women's growing independ-ence by returning women to their traditional roles in the family, as wives and mothers. In some Islamic countries, like Iran and Saudi Arabia, women may face very serious punishments for violating traditional gender roles, for example by wearing unapproved clothing, make-up and being out in public in the company of a man who is neither their husband nor a close relative.

5   *The veiling of women.* Aldridge notes the veiling of women (by head coverings like the hijab and niqab, or full body covering with chadors and burqas) in some Islamic cultures has been inter-preted as a powerful symbol of patriarchy, keeping women invisible and anonymous (but see page 51 for an alternative view of this).

6   *The portrayal of women as morally polluting and corrupting, and as sexual predators.* Aldridge notes that sexual pleasure, particularly for women, is disapproved of or condemned outright in many religions. Sexuality is often presented as something that should be linked only to reproduction, and non-reproductive sexual acts are strongly discouraged in Roman Catholicism, and are regarded by most Muslims and conservative Jews as forbidden. This explains, for example, Roman Catholic opposition to the use of artificial methods of contra-ception, and reinforces women's primary roles as mothers. Women are often, too, presented as sexual predators, with endless desires, who are out to seduce and snare men, divert-ing them from their proper religious duties. As Holm (1994) notes, women's menstruation is nearly always regarded as polluting, and Hindu and Muslim women, for example, are generally forbidden from entering sacred places (like a mosque) or touching sacred objects (like the Qur'an or a family shrine) during their monthly periods.

7   *Women have fewer rights than men in many religions.* Religious laws and customs often give women fewer rights than men, such as in their access to divorce, and how many marriage partners they may have. For example, a man having more than one wife at the same time (polygyny) is permitted in Islam under some conditions, but the opposite, a woman hav-ing more than one husband (polyandry) is forbidden. This is also found in fundamentalist Christian Mormon sects in the USA, such as the Fundamentalist Church of Jesus Christ of Latter-Day Saints, which practise plural marriage. Woodhead (2002) argues that the Catholic Church demonstrates its opposition to women's equality with men through its ban on

contraception, abortion and women's access to the priesthood, and its stress on the traditional caring and nurturing roles of women as wives and mothers in the conventional nuclear family unit.

Are all religions patriarchal?

Although women are subordinate within most religions, this has not always been the case, and it is not true of all religious denominations or faiths. In many ancient religions, like those of ancient Egypt or Greece, in Hinduism, and in modern New Age religions, like the pagan witchcraft-based Wicca, there are female goddesses, and women seem to dominate in New Age spirituality. Three examples are shown in the images below. While these goddesses have mainly been replaced by monotheistic (single-God) religions such as Judaism, Christianity and Islam, with patriarchal teachings, beliefs and practices, Aldridge suggests that gender equality can be found among contemporary groups like the Society of Friends (the Quakers), the Unitarians, the Baha'is and some spiritualist movements.

The Egyptian goddess Isis was the patron of women, mothers, children, magic, medicine and the Ritual of Life.

The Greek Aphrodite (Roman name Venus) was the goddess of love, beauty and fertility.

Kali is a Hindu goddess associated with death and destruction, here shown with her foot on the male god Shiva. Kali is now highly regarded as a benevolent mother-goddess in contemporary New Age spirituality.

Writers like Ahmed (1992), Watson (1994) and Woodhead argue that the veiling of women in some Muslim communities in Britain and some Islamic countries can be interpreted as a form of resisting patriarchy, by providing an independent female identity and freeing women from the male gaze and sexual harassment. The veil can also be seen as a symbol of female and ethnic identity, and as a sign of Muslim pride in resistance to a patriarchal Western culture which treats women as sex objects.

Do you think the wearing of the veil by Muslim women – either the headscarf (hijab), head and face veil (niqab) or full body covering with chadors or burqas – reveals patriarchy, or is a form of resistance to it? Is it a means of asserting an independent identity and freedom from male harassment? Does it make a difference whether the wearing of the veil is imposed on women, rather than them choosing to wear it?

Gender and religion: the facts

Given the patriarchal nature of many of the world's religions, it is perhaps surprising that women remain the biggest consumers of religion. Although in much of Europe, most men and women don't participate in organized religion, women are more likely than men to have religious beliefs and to practise their religion, and this appears to be true across nearly all faiths and religious organizations, including the new religious movements and New Age spirituality. The only exception to women's higher participation appears to be Islam, in which men seem to show greater commitment and involvement than women. In the UK, the trends in the loss of men from Christian churches is such that, at the current rate of loss, by 2028 men will have all but disappeared from the church.

Compared to men, women are more likely:

- To express a greater interest in religion and, as Voas (2015) found, to have firmer belief in God
- To have stronger personal faith and belief in life after death, and to have a stronger personal religious commitment
- To involve themselves in religious rituals and worship – e.g. they are more likely to attend religious services, do so more often and more regularly, and they participate more in religious life generally
- To see private prayer as important, and to practise it
- To join or involve themselves with new religious movements and New Age movements, as Bruce (1996) found.

Why are women more religious than men?

It is ironic that, despite the patriarchal nature of many of the world's religions, with women relegated to the margins or lower levels of many religious organizations and given minor or subordinate positions in many religious beliefs and texts, women do appear to be more religious than men. There have been a number of possible explanations proposed for women's greater religiosity and religious participation.

Socialization, motherhood and femininity

Men and women continue to be socialized into different roles. Miller and Hoffmann (1995) suggest that gender socialization means females are brought up to be more submissive, passive, obedient and nurturing than males, and more involved with feelings, cooperation and caring. These factors may explain women's greater involvement in religion in the following ways:

1 *Guardians of family life.* Women are often expected to be the guardians of family life, to be defenders of tradition in the family and to take on the major responsibilities for looking after

the home, family and children. Halman and Draulans (2006) note that these roles give women a greater focus on the family, and it is women, rather than men, who are more likely to feel it necessary to take charge of their children's moral development and to introduce them to approved social values, including religious beliefs.

2   *Visions of God.* Davie (1994) suggests that women associate God with love, comfort and forgiveness, which are linked with traditional femininity and family roles. In contrast, men associate God more commonly with power and control. The fact that women lean more to people-orientation than to concerns with power may explain their greater involvement in religion.

3   *Nurturing.* Bruce (1996) suggests that women's socialization into the nurturing aspects related to traditional femininity, together with their child-bearing and child-rearing experiences, make them less confrontational, less aggressive, less goal-oriented, less domineering, more cooperative and more caring. This would explain their greater involvement not just in the mainstream denominations, but also in religious sects, and the New Age ideas which were discussed earlier in this chapter. These include ideas such as Gaia (Mother Earth as a living entity), natural solutions and therapies associated with well-being – like herbalism, yoga and meditation, homeopathy, aromatherapy and massage, horoscopes, astrology, fortune-telling and tarot – which Glendinning and Bruce (2006) found appealed far more to women than men.

4   *Life, death and the changes in life.* Greeley (1995) suggests that caring tends to be associated with a more religious outlook, and Walter and Davie (1998) see women as more exposed than men to the ups and downs and changes of life. This is because of their biological involvement through childbirth, and through their greater participation in paid caring jobs, for example as teachers, nurses, social workers and care assistants, and as informal carers of children, the elderly, the disabled and the sick and the dying in the family. Davie (1994) suggests that these factors give women a closer association with birth and death than men have, and these are also central issues for many religions. They make women more aware of the vulnerability of human life, and more attuned to the spiritual dimensions of human existence.

Greater life expectancy

Women live longer than men, and this means they are more likely to be widowed and living on their own as they grow older. They may therefore turn to religion as a source of support and comfort, and as a means of building support networks in their communities.

Social deprivation, marginality and theodicies of disprivilege

Women are more likely than men to face social deprivation and marginality, and may experience more disillusionment and alienation from wider society. Women, compared to men:

- Are more likely to experience poverty
- Are likely to experience personal or family problems more acutely (for the reasons suggested above)
- Are often less self-confident, sometimes marginalized, and they are therefore more likely to seek self-improvement, perhaps through New Age cults and new religious movements
- Are more likely to be less powerful in a patriarchal society, particularly working-class women and women who are isolated in the home and not in paid employment.

These circumstances mean that women may seek and find some solace in religious groups, and particularly in religious sects and new religious movements which provide theodicies explaining their feelings, as well as solutions and support.

Status frustration

Status frustration may be experienced by some women, who lack personal fulfilment or status as a result of being confined to the home by the constraints of housework and childcare, or are in unsatisfying lower-middle-class jobs, which are mainly done by women. Religious participation, particularly in religious sects or New Age cults, may help to overcome or compensate for this.

The declining participation of women

Despite women's generally higher participation in nearly all forms of religious activity, women's levels of participation are declining. Since the late 1980s, women have been leaving the main Christian churches in the UK at a faster rate than men. Aune et al. (2008) suggest this could be because of a range of factors, including:

- *The women's movement and feminism*, which have led women to question the roles of women as wives and mothers with which the traditional Christian churches, and other religions, have been associated. This is accompanied by changing sexual attitudes, with a much more sexually permissive society, including gay and lesbian sexuality, and the church's attitudes to these seems increasingly old-fashioned and out-of-touch with changing times, driving younger women away.
- *The changing roles of women*, with most women now in paid employment, and more than ever following and succeeding in demanding career jobs. These demands have displaced religion as a focus of activity, as well as reducing the time available to pursue religious activities. Participation in paid employment also gives women, particularly younger women, alternative sources of identity beyond those of family and religion.
- *Changing families and relationships*. Contemporary societies have a growing diversity of family types and living arrangements, with high levels of divorce, remarriage, lone parenthood, step-families and cohabitation. Such arrangements have met with disapproval or discouragement from the traditional churches, further alienating the involvement of women.

Activity

1 With reference to the sections you have just read, outline reasons why:
   (a) Older women might be more likely to participate in religious activities than younger women;
   (b) Men are less likely to hold religious beliefs and participate in religious activities than women;
   (c) Women with children might be more likely to participate in religion than those without;
   (d) Women in full-time employment might be less likely to participate in religious activities and to hold religious beliefs than those who are not;
   (e) Women might be more likely than men to participate in new religious movements or New Age spirituality.
2 Devise a questionnaire to test the extent of people's religious beliefs, such as whether or not they believe in God, and the extent of their participation in religious activities – for example, whether they attend church, mosque, temple, etc., how often they attend and what religion means to them.
3 Use this questionnaire to carry out a small survey in your school, college or community, using equal numbers of males and females, to see whether there are any differences between men and women. Analyse and suggest explanations for your findings.

Ethnicity and religion

Ethnicity refers to the shared culture of a social group which gives its members a common identity in some ways different from that of other social groups. A minority ethnic group is a social group which shares a cultural identity that is different from that of the majority population of a society, such as African-Caribbean, Indian Asian and Chinese ethnic groups in Britain. An ethnic identity is one where individuals assert their identity primarily in terms of the ethnic group and culture to which they belong.

An important element of the identity of minority ethnic groups in the UK is their religious faith. As a result of immigration, mainly from Pakistan, India, Bangladesh and the Caribbean in the 1950s and 1960s, Britain is now characterized by religious pluralism, with a diversity of religious faiths, as shown in tables 1.2 and 1.3.

The 2011 census collected information about religious identity, asking the single question 'What is your religion?' This question assumed that everyone had a religion, and without making any distinction between practice, belief or religious background (see table 1.2). Table 1.3, based on research carried out in 2011–12, asked people whether they regarded themselves as belonging to any particular religion, without assuming everyone had a religion, which produced rather different results.

Table 1.2 England and Wales by religion, 2011 census*

Response	Thousands	Percentage
Christian	33,243	59.3
Muslim	2,706	4.8
Hindu	817	1.5
Sikh	423	0.8
Jewish	263	0.5
Buddhist	248	0.4
Any other religion	241	0.4
All religions	37,941	67.7
No religion	14,097	25.1
Not stated	4,038	7.2

*Respondents were asked 'What is your religion?', and tick-boxes were provided for six of the main world religions. A write-in box was provided for any non-specified religion and respondents could also tick that they had no religion.

Source: UK Census, ONS 2013

Table 1.3 Great Britain by religion, 2011–2012, British Social Attitudes Survey[1]

Response	Percentage
No religion	50
Church of England/Anglican	20
Other Christian (excluding Roman Catholic)	15
Roman Catholic	9
Non-Christian[2]	6

[1] Respondents were asked 'Do you regard yourself as belonging to any particular religion?' If yes, which?
[2] Includes Hindu, Jewish, Islam/Muslim, Sikh, Buddhist and other non-Christian religions.

Source: British Social Attitudes 28, National Centre for Social Research, 2012

Activity

Refer to tables 1.2 and 1.3
1 What percentage of the population of England and Wales reported having a religion in 2011?
2 After Christianity, which was the most common faith in England and Wales in 2011?
3 What percentage of the British population said they did not regard themselves as belonging to any particular religion in 2011–12?
4 In 2011, what percentage of the population of England and Wales said they had no religion?
5 Suggest reasons why in the British Social Attitudes Survey the percentage of people saying they had no religion was so much higher than in the 2011 census.

Minority ethnic group religions

African Caribbeans

The main religion among African Caribbeans is Christianity, and African Caribbeans made up about 17 per cent of all those attending Christian churches on an average Sunday in 2007. Many African Caribbeans were Christians before they originally came to Britain, but often encountered racism in the established Christian churches. Their Christianity had developed mainly in the Pentecostalist and charismatic tradition (see box), and they found the established British churches rather boring, with a preponderance of older women, an emphasis on doctrine and teachings, with very passive congregations – quite different from what they were used to. Consequently, they began to establish their own churches.

Pentecostalism (see box) is today the largest Christian group among British African Caribbeans. According to Christian Research, congregations in half the Pentecostal churches in England are predominantly black, and Pentecostalism is the fastest-growing group within Christianity, globally and in the UK, and is in third place behind Catholics and Anglicans in terms of attendance. Rastafarianism (see box) is another faith that is found in the African-Caribbean community, particularly among young men, and often gives them very distinctive group identities. African Caribbeans are generally well assimilated into mainstream British society. Modood et al. (1994) found that, unlike in Asian communities, religion amongst African Caribbeans, as in the white population, is much less important to their ethnic identity, and is mainly a matter of individual choice.

Pentecostalism (including the charismatic movement)

This is a Christian denomination that places an emphasis on experience rather than teaching doctrine and dogma. Religious services are very vibrant, family-centred and have high entertainment value. They involve elements like call-and-response interaction between the priest and the congregation, shouting and clapping, singing and dancing, fainting, trances, prophesying, speaking in tongues, impromptu healing and praying, and exorcism.

Rastafarianism

Rastafarianism emerged in Jamaica among the black working-class and peasants in the early 1930s. It regards Haile Selassie I, the former Emperor of Ethiopia, as a god figure, with the Jamaican black separatist Marcus Garvey seen as a prophet. It is associated with dreadlocks and the spiritual use of cannabis, and became widely known across the world through reggae music, particularly that of the Jamaican singer and songwriter Bob Marley, who has become an icon of Rastafarianism.

Asian religious groups

While those originally coming from the Caribbean were entering a country with which they shared the dominant Christian beliefs, those from Pakistan (and, later, Bangladesh) and India had non-Christian backgrounds and had to establish their own temples, mosques and other places of worship, as there were none already in existence. The main religions are Islam, Hinduism and Sikhism.

In contemporary Britain, young people from minority ethnic groups are being brought up in a society with equal opportunity laws, including equal rights for men and women and gay people, and laws against sex discrimination in work and education. This means some of the values associated with these religions are under pressure and difficult to sustain. For example, the caste system, which is rooted in Hindu religious beliefs, has religious rules about the kind of work that can be done, whom one can eat with and whom one can marry. Similarly, Islam sees it as desirable for men and women to be educated and raised separately, and treated differently. Arranged marriages, when couples are matched by parents in terms of social suitability rather than necessarily through a love match, are encountering resistance among some younger people. All these things can be difficult to sustain in a society where human rights and equality legislation exist.

Religious commitment in the minority ethnic groups

Research has repeatedly shown that the major minority ethnic groups in Britain (African Caribbeans, Bangladeshis, Indians and Pakistanis) are, in general, significantly more religious than the white ethnic majority, though they share some similarities in that younger people are less religious than older people, and women show more commitment than men (though the opposite is the case among Muslims). Religious practice, such as attendance at a place of worship, is highest in the minority ethnic religious groups, and lowest in the predominantly white Christian ethnic majority.

Evidence for the greater religious commitment among minority ethnic groups is shown by the following examples:

1   The Department of Communities and Local Government 2009/10 *Citizenship Survey* found those from ethnic minorities were far more likely than Christians to practise their religion – 79 per cent of Muslims, 74 per cent of Sikhs and 70 per cent of Hindus compared to 33 per cent of Christians.
2   While only around 6 per cent of the British population went to a Christian church on an average Sunday in 2007, around one in six of them were African Caribbeans – around five times their proportion in the population.
3   The 2011/12 British Social Attitudes Survey found that only 23 per cent of those who identified with a non-Christian religion never attended a religious service, compared to about half of those who identified themselves as Church of England/Anglican.
4   There is a growth of mosques and temples, while Christian churches are closing. In 1961 there were just 7 mosques, 3 Sikh temples and 1 Hindu temple in England and Wales, compared with nearly 55,000 Christian churches. By 2005 the number of churches had fallen to 47,600, with another 4,000 likely to disappear over the next 15 years, according to Christian Research. Between 1969 and 2005, 1,700 Church of England churches were closed – almost the same as the number of mosques there now are in Britain.

Since 1969, the number of mosques in Britain has grown to almost the same number as that of Anglican churches that have closed

5   There are growing demands for state-funded schools 'with a religious character' or faith schools for minority ethnic religions, as are already provided for Christian faiths. Demands are particularly strong for Muslim schools, where girls and boys can be educated separately according to Muslim religious principles. These are very controversial, as they are seen as discriminating on religious (and, in Muslim schools, gender) grounds and as a threat to social cohesion. Opinion polls regularly show a majority of the public oppose more faith schools, and a 2014 Opinium survey for the *Observer* suggested around 58 per cent of voters were against state funding for faith schools of any kind. In 2011, there were around 6,900 state-funded faith schools in England, making up 37 per cent of primary and 19 per cent of second-ary schools. The vast majority (99 per cent) are Christian, with 38 Jewish, 11 Muslim and 4 Sikh schools.

Activity

1 Consider the reasons why the establishment of new faith schools is very controversial, particularly the establishment of Muslim schools, when there are already many Church of England and Catholic schools.

2 In two columns, list all the arguments you can think of for and against faith schools, and discuss these in your group.

Why are minority ethnic groups more religious?

Many of the reasons for higher levels of religious commitment in minority ethnic groups have been considered throughout this chapter, in both the theories of religion and in the section on religious organizations, so they will only be briefly outlined here.

Community identity and cultural defence

Bruce (1996) suggests higher religiosity among minority ethnic groups may not necessarily be a sign of greater religious commitment but more an assertion of community solidarity and pride. Religion can act as a focal point for community identity and cohesion, and as a means of *cultural defence* of the culture, language and traditions of the community which may be under threat in some way – for example, at risk of disappearance through assimilation by the dominant culture, or through racism. Bruce also says religion can act as a source of identity, self-esteem and support during periods of *cultural transition*, as immigrant groups face a period of upheaval and adjustment and threats to their established identities when they move to a different country or culture. These views are similar to those of functionalist writers like Durkheim, who emphasized the role of religion in social integration, in building group solidarity, shared values and identity.

    Davie (1994), like Bruce, suggests that higher levels of religiosity in minority ethnic groups may be a means of maintaining tradition, group cohesion and community solidarity. She links this to other aspects of ethnic identity, such as art, marriage, cooking, diet, dress and language. Mosques and Sikh temples, for example, are community centres as well as places of worship, and provide a focus for social life as well as a means of protecting and promoting cultural values and traditions which may be seen as under threat by the dominant white culture. Modood et al. (1994) found that religion was important in the lives of minority ethnic communities as a source of socialization, and as a means of maintaining traditional morality, such as conceptions of mutual responsibility, trust, and right and wrong. It also helped to cope with the worries and pressures in life, perhaps arising from the hostility and discrimination caused by racism in the wider society which many from minority ethnic groups encounter.

Social deprivation, marginality and status frustration

Social deprivation and marginality, as well as the sense of dissatisfaction with a lack of status in society (status frustration), may account for higher levels of religiosity. People may turn to religion as a secure and solid source of identity, status and community, which they find lacking in mainstream society. Some older Asian women, particularly, may feel marginalized in mainstream society, as they may have a poor grasp of English.

Pakistani and Bangladeshi households are the poorest in Britain: around two-thirds of working-age adults from Bangladeshi and Pakistani ethnic backgrounds were living in low-income households in 2011–12. Many African Caribbeans face higher levels of unemployment, and racism affects all black and Asian minority ethnic groups. Marx's view of religion – as the 'opium of the people' providing comforting diversion from attacking the causes of their poverty and the racism they encounter – might explain higher levels of religiosity. Religion may also provide a 'theodicy of disprivilege', as Weber suggested, and the compensators that Stark and Bainbridge identified. This may explain the Pentecostalism found among African Caribbeans, and the Rastafarianism among alienated young black men.

Family pressures

Family structures are much more tightly knit in Asian communities, with strong extended families. This, combined with generally closer community life, may result in pressure to conform to religious values and behaviour.

Social identity

Religion in minority ethnic groups can provide individuals with many markers of identity, such as their customs, dress and food, and also rituals and festivals, such as Divali (Hindus and Sikhs), Ramadan and Al-Hijra (the Muslim new year). By asserting an identity drawn from religious elements of their cultures, members can resist the denial of status and the devaluing of their own culture by racism.

Johal (1998) suggests that many younger British Asians have forged a single new hybrid identity, which he calls 'Brasian', derived from blending both British and Asian cultures. This involves establishing an identity by adopting *selected* elements of the religion of their parents, with strong dimensions of personal choice. For example, the religious beliefs of Brasians might be important to them, but they might expect to marry whomsoever they wish, rather than have an arranged marriage or a partner from the same ethnic or religious group, and they may not necessarily follow traditional religious customs, such as constraints over diet, drinking alcohol or dress. Butler's (1995) interviews with 18- to 30-year-old Muslim women in Bradford and Coventry came up with similar findings. While these young women had some attachment to the religious values of their culture, and saw religion as important in shaping their identities, they also challenged some of the restrictions that traditional Asian Muslim culture imposed on them and wanted more choice and independence in their lives.

Jacobson (1998) explored the issues of religion and identity among young British-born Pakistanis in the East End of London. She found that a Muslim identity, rather than just an Asian or Pakistani identity, appealed to young people, as it provided them with stability, security and certainties when they faced much uncertainty in other aspects of their lives.

Islam and identity in the UK

The discussion above explains a number of possible reasons for the greater religiosity among the minority ethnic religions. However, the growing commitment and fervour and the public controversy that have surrounded Islam in the 2000s in Britain deserve further discussion.

Since the attacks on the World Trade Center in New York in 2001 and the London bombings of July 2005, both of which were carried out by Muslim extremists, the media reporting of the activities of a tiny minority of Muslims in Britain has formed the basis for the stereotyping of all Muslims in the popular imagination. The word 'Muslim' all too often conjures up images of terrorism and extremist preachers. As a result, Islam has become an important, and growing, marker of identity for many in the Muslim community in Britain – whether they want it to be or not. Media reporting has also meant that being identified as 'Muslim' has become almost a **stigmatized identity**,

A **stigmatized identity** is an identity that is in some way undesirable or demeaning, and stops an individual or group being fully accepted by society.

bringing with it harassment and fear for the vast majority of Muslims who have no sympathy with extremists or terrorism of any kind.

Growing numbers of young male and female Muslims in the UK, but especially young men, are choosing Islam as their prime marker of identity. Islam and its symbols and values have become central features in building a positive identity which they see as otherwise denied to them by a white, racist, Islamophobic British culture. About 70 per cent of British Muslims are under the age of 25, so this pattern is likely to signal long-term trends, as the young Muslims of today are the parents of tomorrow.

The rise of religiosity and a specific Muslim identity among young British Muslims was explored by Mirza et al. (2007) and Mirza (2008). Mirza found an increase in religiosity and identification with Islam among young second- and third-generation Muslims, shown by things like more younger Muslim women wearing the headscarf (hijab), greater identification with the worldwide Muslim community, and growing membership of Islamist political groups and youth associations. There were also growing demands among the young for education, financial and legal arrangements that complied with Islamic (Sharia) law. Although well over half of all British Muslims in all age groups say they'd rather live under British law than Sharia law, around 35 per cent of 16- to 24-year-olds expressed a preference for Sharia law, as shown in figure 1.4.

> **Islamophobia** is an irrational fear and/or hatred of or aversion to Islam, Muslims or Islamic culture.

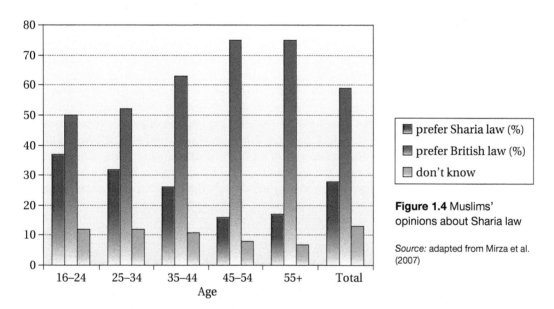

prefer Sharia law (%)
prefer British law (%)
don't know

Figure 1.4 Muslims' opinions about Sharia law

Source: adapted from Mirza et al. (2007)

Mirza suggests that the rise of a Muslim identity among the young might be related to three main factors:

1 *British foreign policy.* Many Muslims saw British foreign policies in the 2000s, such as the invasions of Iraq and Afghanistan, as anti-Islamic acts.
2 *The decline of other sources of identity,* like political parties, nationality, trade unions, or social class and ethnicity. This drives young Muslims, whose status is more insecure than that of older ones, to seek new sources of meaning, identity and belonging by asserting an Islamic identity.
3 *Multicultural policies.* These policies are found in many areas of life in British society, and have been a major feature of the British education system for many years. These policies are based on the idea that it is important to recognize, learn about and respect the cultural differences between ethnic groups. Such policies involve treating groups differently as a mark of respect for their cultures, and to make them feel included, rather than excluded and marginalized, in mainstream society. Mirza suggests that these policies have led to Muslims demanding things like more faith schools, laws against blasphemy (insulting references to God) and permission to wear traditional dress at work – for example, allowing Muslim

women police officers the option of wearing the hijab instead of the traditional uniform cap. Mirza suggests that multicultural policies, which are designed to include and protect Muslims, may have had the opposite effect. This is because they make Muslims feel different and excluded from mainstream society. At the same time, they generate hostility among the white ethnic majority, and possibly other minority ethnic religious groups, as Muslims are seen as being unreasonable in asking for special treatment, and unwilling to adapt to mainstream British society. This hostility then drives young Muslims further into embracing an Islamic identity, as they are constantly reminded of their difference, and increasingly lack other sources of identity.

Although Mirza is primarily concerned with explaining the growth of extremism among some young Muslims, much of what she says offers general explanations for the growing assertion of a Muslim identity among all young Muslims, the vast majority of whom are neither extremists nor terrorists. Mirza's work may also provide some general explanations for the importance of religion as a marker of identity among other minority ethnic groups.

Activity

1 Identify and explain three reasons why levels of religious commitment and participation are generally higher among minority ethnic groups.
2 Explain the meaning of the following concepts, and how they might explain greater levels of religious commitment among minority ethnic groups:
   ● Social cohesion
   ● Cultural defence
   ● Cultural transition
   ● Identity
   ● Status frustration
   ● Theodicy of disprivilege
   ● Marginalization
3 Suggest reasons why some of the rules and beliefs associated with minority ethnic group religions, like arranged marriages, might be under pressure and hard to sustain in contemporary Britain. Give examples of at least three rules or beliefs (use the internet if you want to explore the rules of different religions).
4 Explain why 'Muslim' has tended to become a stigmatized identity in contemporary Britain.
5 Design a small survey in your class to explore whether people claim to have a religion, their level of commitment to it, and what it means to them. If possible, try to get answers from a range of ethnic and religious groups, drawn from different ages and both sexes. Analyse your results, and identify and discuss any significant findings, such as any differences between men and women, ethnic groups and ages. Suggest explanations for your findings.

Age and religion

In general, people seem to develop a greater attachment to religion as they grow older. Belief in God is lowest among those under 34, and highest among those over age 55. With the exception of young Muslims, as discussed above, young people are not only less likely to participate in mainstream religious activity than older people; more than half of them say they don't regard themselves as religious at all, as shown in such studies as the British Social Attitudes Survey and the European Values study. This contrasts with only about 2 per cent of those over the age of 65 who make this claim. Bruce (2001) found that the age gap between churchgoers and non-churchgoers had widened in all Christian denominations over the past 25 years. Christian Research suggests that the age of churchgoers is high and increasing, and will continue to increase if current trends continue, as shown in table 1.4. Heelas et al. (2004) found that the majority of those involved in New Age ideas

Table 1.4 Proportions of Sunday churchgoers in each age group, Great Britain, 2000–2050

Age group	2000 %	2025* %	2050* %
Under 15	19	5	1
15 to 19	5	1	0
20 to 29	9	5	2
30 to 44	17	12	7
45 to 64	25	25	18
65 and over	25	52	72
Base (= 100%) All churchgoers	4.4 million	2.3 million	0.9 million
Average age of churchgoers	47	59	67
Average age of population	40	42	44

* Estimate.

Source: Christian Research

Activity

Refer to table 1.4:

1 Describe, giving figures, what the table shows about the relationship between church attendance and age groups in 2000.
2 Identify two trends that are shown in the table.
3 How many people are there estimated to be attending Christian churches in 2050?
4 What proportion of churchgoers are estimated to be under the age of 30 in 2050?
5 Suggest reasons for the pattern of churchgoing identified in the table.

and activities, which might be expected to appeal more to less traditionally minded young people, were middle-aged or older.

Older people and religion

The attachment of older people to religion is often explained by three main factors:

1 *Disengagement.* Disengagement means that, as people get older, they become detached from the integrating mechanisms of society, such as participation in workplaces through paid employment. Older people may face a growing privatization of their lives, with increasing social isolation as partners and friends die. Participation in religious organizations provides a form of social support in this situation, and a network of people to relate to.
2 *Religious socialization.* Older people are more likely to have had a greater emphasis placed on religion through the education system and socialization in the family when they were younger. This may have laid seeds that flower as they grow older, as they rediscover a religiosity they may previously have ignored.
3 *Ill-health and death.* Older people tend to be faced with declining health, and death looms on the horizon. These are the very things that religion concerns itself with. The ageing process and disengagement from society may therefore generate an engagement with religion for comfort, coping, meaning and support.

Religion deals with the fundamental questions of the meaning of life and death, and this may explain the greater religiosity of older people

Younger people and religion

Young people are undoubtedly less religious in terms of their expressed religious belief in surveys and their participation in the mainstream Christian religions. The 2011 census found that, since the 2001 census, there had been a significant drop in the number of Christians among 5–14- and 30–39-year-olds in England and Wales, despite an increasing population. Voas (2010) notes that in most developed countries young people, compared to older people, are less willing to identify with a religion, attend services or describe religion as important in their lives. Catto (2014) suggests young people are more likely to rely on their own consciences, rather than religious rules, to guide their behaviour; family, friends, social media and popular culture all have greater significance than religion in their lives, and a religious identity is now very much a minority, non-mainstream one among young people. This is not true among young Muslims, who are more likely than older people to identify themselves as Muslim. As discussed earlier, young people seem more attracted to New Age spirituality and new religious movements, but the vast majority do not participate in either, and the majority of New Age followers are middle-aged or older. This does not necessarily mean that young people are lacking all spirituality or religious feeling and belief. Explanations are suggested below for the apparent lower religiosity and religious practice of young people but it may be that these are simply being expressed in new, private ways which are difficult to record in statistical surveys.

Why do young people seem to be less religious than older people?

The declining attraction of religion
The mainstream religious organizations are very unattractive to most young people. In many cases, they find services to be boring, repetitive and old-fashioned, full of old people, and out-of-touch with the styles and attitudes of younger people. Controversies in religion over issues like abortion, contraception, the ordination of women priests and bishops, gay priests and gay rights in general, sex before marriage and so on seem bizarre to many young people, and alien to the values they hold. A former Archbishop of Canterbury, George Carey, said in 1991 that he saw the Church of England as like 'an elderly lady, who mutters away to herself in a corner, ignored most of the time'. If even the head of the Church of England saw it that way, then it is perhaps not surprising that many young people see mainstream Christianity as 'uncool', and stay away.

The expanded spiritual marketplace

Cusack (2011) suggests that in the early twenty-first century, while in Western countries the number of teenagers who are formally affiliated with a particular religious tradition or institution has declined significantly, their interest in religion and spirituality remains high. She suggests that, although young people are now less likely to be socialized into the religion of their parents, as they were in the early twentieth century – which typically meant a range of mainstream Christian denominations – they now exercise more choice in their construction of personal and group identities. They are now more likely to express their religious and spiritual identity through transnational religions, including Pentecostal Christianity, and to form their identities through a range of spiritualities and subcultural groups including paganism, Satanism, Goth culture and vampirism. Lynch (2008) suggests that young people may be turning away from conventional ideas of religion as there is now what Roof (2001) called an 'expanded spiritual marketplace'. This involves growing exposure and access to a wide diversity of religious and spiritual ideas from which young people can pick 'n' mix and consume, as with other products, to form their identities. This includes the religions that have become more significant as a result of immigration, such as Islam, Hinduism, Sikhism and Buddhism, but also the wide diversity of new religious movements and New Age spirituality, like Wicca and paganism, to which young people are more likely to be exposed as the greatest consumers of the media and the internet. These have opened up new avenues for exploring religion and spirituality. Lynch suggests that these have meant there are now more sources for young people to draw on to build religious and spiritual beliefs, identities and lifestyles, and these may be finding expression outside traditional religions and religious organizations.

The privatization of belief – believing not belonging

Young people may be choosing to treat their religion, of whatever faith or mix of beliefs, as a private matter. Even if they have some general spiritual or religious beliefs, they may not feel they belong to any particular religion, or are committed to any specific religious doctrine. They may prefer not to make any public display of whatever they believe through involvement in religious organizations, or admit to them in surveys. Davie (1994) expressed this in the words 'believing without belonging'.

Secular spirituality and the sacred

Lynch suggests that, although young people may be diverted from religion as it is normally conceived, they may be finding religious feelings inspired in them by aspects of what are generally regarded as non-religious or secular life. He develops an argument along the lines of Durkheim's conception of the 'sacred' and the inclusivist conception of religion discussed at the beginning of this chapter. He argues that when people become particularly attached to objects, experiences, other people or things – such as celebrities, clubbing, football or music stars, nature or the environment – these can take on the form of the 'sacred' in their lives. This may cause them to reflect on the meaning of their lives and the ways they live them. Lynch suggests, then, that young people may not have lost all religiosity, but that it is simply finding new forms, many of which are associated more with the secular and non-religious world than with religion as it is presently understood by most people.

Secularization and the decline of metanarratives

As discussed earlier, secularization is concerned with the general decline of religious thinking, practice and institutions, and growing disenchantment with the world. Postmodernists like Lyotard (1984) suggest that metanarratives like religion have lost their power to influence how people think about, interpret and explain the world. Young people may be becoming less religious simply because they no longer believe the old religious explanations, and they can pick, mix or reject any beliefs they choose.

Declining religious education

Bruce (2001) points out that the Church of England is increasingly unable to recruit young people by socializing them into religious thinking through such things as church Sunday schools or religious education. Sunday schools are in a state of terminal decline – Christian Research says that a century ago over half of all children attended a Sunday school, but by 2000 this had reduced to just

To what extent do you think that the fervour and commitment shown by some young people towards things like clubbing have replaced traditional ideas, and are new forms of expression of spirituality and religiosity?

one in twenty-five children. If the current rate of decline continues, there will be hardly any Sunday schools left by 2016. Although secondary schools are meant by law to hold assemblies of a broadly Christian character, most generally resort to a kind of secular moral or personal education, or ignore it altogether. This means that the majority of young people don't get any religious education at all, but it also reflects the fact that most of them don't want it.

Pragmatic reasons

There is also a range of possible more practical or pragmatic explanations for the decline of religious belief and commitment among the young. Leisure has become a much bigger part of life, and shops, clubs and pubs all open for very long hours, including on Sundays. Young people have more demands on their time, and they may simply have more interesting and enjoyable things to do. It is also seen as very 'uncool' to be religious in many young peer groups, which exerts social pressure not to be religious. Former prime minister Tony Blair, a committed Christian, admitted in 2007 that while he was in office he had to play down his religious beliefs for fear of being seen by the public as a 'nutter'. It is perhaps not surprising, then, if young people choose to do the same.

Activity

As a student, you are probably young, and you may or may not hold some kind of religious or spiritual beliefs. You should therefore have some insights and views on the issues above. Apply them to the following:

1 Study the various explanations offered here for the lower levels of religious belief, commitment and participation by young people. Put them in order from those you think are the most convincing to the least, and explain your reasons.
2 Identify and explain any other reasons you can think of why younger people might, in general, be less religious than older people.
3 We have suggested that 'Controversies in religion over issues like abortion, contraception, the ordination of women priests and bishops, gay priests and gay rights in general, sex before marriage and so on seem bizarre to many young people, and alien to the values they hold'. Do you agree or disagree? Explain your reasons, or discuss it in your group.
4 Lynch (2008) 'decided to explore the Hard House and techno dance scene to see if the people involved in it saw it as having any kind of religious or spiritual significance'. To what extent do you agree or disagree with Lynch's suggestion that young people may be finding spirituality or having mystical or religious experiences by giving a 'sacred' quality to secular activities like clubbing and football and to their engagement with the lives of celebrities? Explain your reasons, including how you think these activities relate to religion.

Social class and religion

There is not much reliable information available on the social class of those who participate in religious organizations, and even less on those who hold religious beliefs.

Traditional Marxist approaches suggest that religiosity and religious participation should be greatest among the most deprived social classes, for whom religion provides a means of coping with poverty and oppression, while at the same time the dominant class uses religion as a means of establishing hegemony and justifying its continuing power and control. Weber's idea of a theodicy of disprivilege would suggest religion might appeal most to disadvantaged and marginal groups. On the other hand, neo-Marxists like Maduro suggest that religion may also be used by the poorest social classes to fight their oppression, as in liberation theology in South America.

However, although the theories above might suggest the greatest appeal of religion would be to the most disadvantaged, in practice mainstream religions are inclusive, and recruit from a broad range of classes, with religion part of the experience of all social classes. It is hard to make overall statements about the links between social class and religious participation, but the following generalizations might be made.

Churches and denominations

The upper and upper-middle classes, especially women, tend to be over-represented in churches, though members of all social classes attend. A YouGov survey in 2015 found that more than 60 per cent of people who regularly attend church are middle class, and this drops to 38 per cent among working-class people. Established churches like the Church of England are middle-class-dominated, with its leaders tending to come from privileged backgrounds. Ashworth and Farthing (2007) found that churchgoing (in all Christian faiths) is largely a middle-class pursuit. Those in the higher social classes (classes A and B: professionals, senior and middle management) were the most likely to be regular churchgoers (at least once a month) and fringe and occasional churchgoers (less than monthly but at least once a year), while the manual working class had the lowest proportion of regular churchgoers. Those in the poorest social groups, which includes those entirely dependent on the state, for reasons like sickness, unemployment or old age, had the highest proportion who did not attend church. Many denominations seem to appeal mostly to the lower-middle and upper working class, and tend to have the highest proportions of working-class members.

Sects, cults and the New Age

Sects seem to gain their strongest support from the most deprived and marginal social groups, who perhaps use them as a means of coping with their disadvantage – through the Marxist idea of religion acting as the 'opium of the people', or the Weberian idea of a theodicy of disprivilege. Many new religious movements seem to appeal most to the young middle class.

Cults attract a cross section of society, including deprived and marginal groups. However, Bruce (1995) and Heelas (1996) suggest New Age client cults and world-affirming new religious movements have their greatest appeal for those who are fairly affluent members of the middle class, like young professionals. This is because followers are customers, who have to spend money to buy into the products associated with these cults. They may thereby access what they hope will be a means of filling a spiritual void in otherwise successful lives, of self-improvement, and of becoming more successful in their working and personal lives.

New Age ideas and spirituality, such as yoga and meditation, according to Heelas, appeal mainly to middle-class women, who can afford it, while astrology and fortune-telling appeal more to working-class women (though both appeal to only a tiny minority of people); similarly, all manner of New Age therapies – such as aroma-, sound, primal and colour therapies – and spiritual healing appeal mainly to the middle class, not least because of the costs involved in buying these services.

1   Outline and explain **two** reasons why people from some ethnic minority groups seem to participate more in religious activity than other social groups. **(10 marks)**

2   Read **Item A** below and answer the question that follows.

> **Item A**
>
> Compared to older people, young people are generally less religious in terms of their expressed beliefs in surveys and their participation in religious activities, although this is not true among young Muslims, who show greater religious participation and commitment. Young people seem more attracted to New Age spirituality and new religious movements, but the vast majority do not participate in either.

Applying material from **Item A**, analyse **two** differences between the religious belief and participation of young people compared with those of older people. **(10 marks)**

3   Read **Item B** below and answer the question that follows.

> **Item B**
>
> Feminists see many religions as patriarchal. For example, women are relegated to the margins or lower levels of many religious organizations, and given minor or subordinate positions in many religious beliefs and texts. Religious teachings often seek to control women's sexuality, and emphasize their roles as partners of men, mothers and carers in the family. Despite this, women are more likely than men to hold religious beliefs and to practise their religion.

Applying material from **Item B** and your knowledge, evaluate sociological contributions to the understanding of the relationship between gender and religious behaviour and beliefs.

(20 marks)

Topic 5

SPECIFICATION AREA

The significance of religion and religiosity in the contemporary world, including the nature and extent of secularisation in a global context, and globalisation and the spread of religions

The secularization thesis

A contested concept

The word 'secular' means 'non-religious'. The secularization thesis is the suggestion that religious beliefs are becoming less plausible (believable) and less appealing to those who might once have believed in them, and religion is therefore of declining importance both in society and for the individual. Secularization is an extremely contested concept, in the sense that there are deep and controversial theoretical and methodological debates over what it is, how to measure it, and whether or not it is occurring.

Defining secularization

The definition of secularization given by Wilson (1966) is one of the clearest: 'the process whereby religious thinking, practice, and institutions lose social significance'.

- *Religious thinking* refers to the influence of religion on people's beliefs and values, such as the importance of religion in their lives, whether they see themselves as a religious person, whether they believe in things like God, spirits, good and evil, and life after death.
- *Religious practice* refers to the things people *do* to carry out their religious commitment, such as the extent to which they actively participate in acts of religious worship and devotion, like attending church, mosque or temple.
- *Religious institutions* here refers to the extent to which religious institutions have maintained their social influence in wider society, and how far they are actively involved in and influence the day-to-day running of society.

Activity

Fox (2005: 354) describes the following exchange in a doctor's waiting room between a mother and her 12-year-old daughter, as they fill in a medical form and come to the religion question:

DAUGHTER: 'Religion? What religion am I? We're not any religion are we?'
MOTHER: 'No, we're not, just put C of E.'
DAUGHTER: 'What's C of E?'
MOTHER: 'Church of England.'
DAUGHTER: 'Is that a religion?'
MOTHER: 'Yes, sort of. Well, no, not really – it's just what you put.'

1 What does the mother–daughter conversation above tell you about the difficulties of measuring religious belief?
2 Take each of the three aspects of secularization – religious thinking, religious practice and religious institutions – and in each case outline two ways you might measure whether secularization is occurring.
3 Using the measures you have drawn up, suggest two ways in each case that the indicators may and may not provide reliable evidence of a decline of religion in society.

Inclusivist and exclusivist definitions of religion

There are theoretical problems in defining secularization. One key theoretical issue is how religion is defined in the first place, as the definition of religion will influence the methodological indicators used to measure it, and therefore the extent of secularization that is found. The following definitions were discussed at the beginning of this chapter (see pages 8–9), and you may wish to refer back for more detail.

1   The *exclusivist definition* is a narrow definition, which sees religion as involving beliefs in some supernatural, supra-human being(s) or forces of some kind.
2   The *inclusivist definition* is a wide definition, and does not necessarily require beliefs in a supra-human, supernatural being or force, but may include a wide range of beliefs and activities, including conventional religion, to which people give a 'sacred' quality. These might include beliefs and activities that many would not regard as religious, such as New Age therapies and inner-directed spirituality, as well as, for example, civil religions like football, clubbing or the lives of celebrities, which seem to have a sacred quality for some people. Such a wide definition means that religion is never likely to decline, as alternative activities which replace religion in people's lives simply become redefined as religious. As Aldridge (2007) suggests, such all-embracing evidence for the continued existence of religion is not telling us anything about the world, but is a 'mere trick of definition'. The following discussion of secularization will focus primarily on the exclusivist definition of religion.

Measuring secularization – methodological problems

Measurement and interpretation are major difficulties in the secularization debate, as they depend heavily on the researcher's definitions and judgements of what religion and religiosity are. Three important methodological issues include:

1   *Validity.* Do the findings of research on religion actually provide a true, genuine or authentic picture of what is being studied? Do they show what they claim to show?
2   *Reliability.* Do historical statistics on religion (against which any decline over time is measured) meet contemporary standards of accuracy in data collection? Would another researcher achieve the same results? Does the way statistics are gathered mean that different researchers can get different answers? Does the way questions are asked change the information obtained? Do different religious organizations use the same methods of counting membership?
3   *Representativeness.* Can the results obtained from surveys of religion be generalized or applied to the whole population?

Some examples of these methodological difficulties are considered below.

Measuring decline: was there ever a 'Golden Age of Faith'?

Secularization means that religion is declining in some ways compared to the past, so supporters of the secularization thesis need to show that society was once more religious than it is now. Often, this is based on assumptions about some past 'Golden Age of Faith', when nearly everyone believed in God and went regularly to their churches, most of which were generally packed out. However, there are problems with this reference to the past:

- Historical records about the strength of religion in the past are sparse
- Data collection methods weren't as reliable and didn't use the sophisticated survey methods used today
- There were no opinion polls or interviewers carrying out surveys to explore whether people believed in God, whether they attended church voluntarily or because it was expected, and what religion meant to them
- Most people even 150 years ago couldn't read or write, so the few records that do exist are based on the views of a small privileged section of the population, and probably tell us little about the religiosity of ordinary people.

Such records may therefore lack validity, reliability and representativeness, and the Golden Age of Faith from which a decline is said to have occurred may well be exaggerated. Even in the first Census of Religion carried out in 1851, in England and Wales only 40 per cent of the adult population attended church.

The meaning and interpretation of evidence

The evidence collected may not give a full picture of what is really happening, and deciding whether or not secularization is taking place will depend on how that evidence is interpreted, as the following examples suggest:

1 *High participation doesn't necessarily mean strong belief.* Even if church attendance remains high, it doesn't necessarily mean people still believe in religious ideas, but they may attend for non-religious reasons, like social support, being seen as socially respectable or, in some cases in contemporary Britain, because they want to get their children places in a faith school. Martin (1969) argues, for example, that in Victorian Britain church attendance was a socially necessary part of middle-class respectability. High levels of church attendance in the contemporary United States are, as Aldridge (2007) points out, part of the American way of life, based on the secular – not religious – values of fitting into the community. Church attendance requires only a superficial commitment, with few demands placed on those who go.

2 *Low participation doesn't necessarily mean lack of belief.* People might have strong religious beliefs but prefer to treat them as a private matter and never go near a religious institution, and so won't be recorded in attendance statistics, despite their religiosity.

3 *Quantitative versus qualitative data.* Quantitative data, like statistics on church attendance and other forms of participation in religious ceremonies and acts of worship, may suggest that religion is in decline, but qualitative data gained through in-depth interviews exploring people's religious beliefs and thinking may give a very different impression.

Asking questions about religion

Questions about religious belief involve quite personal and sensitive issues, and when questioned by opinion pollsters about their religious beliefs and activities, people may exaggerate or lie, perhaps because of a sense of guilt or because they feel they should give what they see as approved answers. What people say may therefore not be what they really believe, and may in any case have no influence over their behaviour.

Surveys are also very vulnerable to the wording of the questions being asked, which can affect the reliability and validity of the information obtained. For example, in response to the 2011 census question 'What is your religion?', 68 per cent of people described themselves as having a religion and 25 per cent said they had no religion (7 per cent didn't answer the question). A YouGov survey for the British Humanist Association in the same year asked the question, 'Are you religious?', and only 29 per cent said yes. The difference might, in part, be explained by the more open nature of the YouGov question, which allowed for the possibility that people might not be religious at all, while behind the census question was the assumption that people would have a religion, and so people, when so pushed, chose the one they felt closest to.

Membership, attendance and other statistics on religious practice

Statistics on religious practice are difficult to interpret.

1 What counts as 'practising' a religion may vary between individuals and religious groups. Some sects demand very high levels of commitment to be counted as a practising member, while some mainstream churches demand very little.

2 Information about smaller religious groups is often unavailable, and some sects and cults might wish to overestimate their membership to increase their sense of social importance and give the impression they are more established than they really are.

3 A lot of religious practice may not be recorded at all, so is not taken into account in official attendance statistics. Examples might include participation in the growing Christian house church movement, in which people meet to worship in private homes, or the Christian

'emerging church' – sometimes referred to as the 'emergent movement' – and other forms of expression of religious belief outside established religious institutions.

4 Different denominations use different criteria of membership, so apparently similar types of figures may be recording different things. For example, the Church of England and Catholic churches use criteria like the number of those who have been baptized and confirmed, whether they attend or not, while sects like the Jehovah's Witnesses include only those who show the high levels of commitment demanded.

The causes of secularization

The pages that follow contain a range of explanations for why secularization is thought to be occurring, and why traditional religious organizations may have lost support. These explanations include:

1 Traditional religious organizations are increasingly seen by many as conservative and old-fashioned, and out of touch with contemporary society.
2 Religious ministers, particularly in the Church of England, have lost status in society.
3 Many of the functions that used to be carried out by religious organizations, like education and welfare, have largely been taken over by the welfare state, which means religion has become sidelined in people's daily lives.
4 Traditional religious organizations have faced challenges to their traditional teachings and organizations from the growth of alternative spiritual organizations, like sects and cults and New Age spirituality.
5 Changing leisure patterns and more fragmented and individualized consumer-based lifestyles have meant that Sundays have become a time for leisure outings and shopping rather than religious observance.
6 The growth of science and what Comte and Weber saw as the rationalization of the modern world have displaced religious faith as a means of understanding the world.
7 The decline of metanarratives, including both religion and science, which, postmodernists assert, may have meant more people are abandoning once taken-for-granted belief systems, and picking 'n' mixing beliefs as they go shopping in the spiritual supermarket for whatever mix of beliefs suits their personal lifestyle choices.
8 In contemporary multi-faith societies, with religious pluralism, religion no longer commands the respect of the whole of society, with religion no longer able to perform the integrating function that functionalists like Durkheim and Parsons once saw as so important in maintaining social cohesion and stability.

These are the kind of factors, considered further below, which have led some to believe there is an inevitable and irreversible process of secularization taking place in many contemporary Western societies.

The evidence for secularization

1 The decline of religious thinking and belief

Declining religious belief and the desacralization of consciousness

Desacralization refers to the loss of the capacity to experience a sense of sacredness and mystery in life.

Bruce (2002b) suggests the growth of scientific explanations for why things happen, and the application of technology have undermined religious faith and beliefs. Weber thought growing disenchantment with the world would create a **desacralization** of consciousness – 'a loss of the capacity to experience a sense of sacredness and mystery in life'. Opinion polls seem to confirm this, as they have repeatedly shown a general decline in religious belief. For example, a Eurobarometer (2010) survey in 2010 found that only 37 per cent of people in the UK believed there was a God, compared

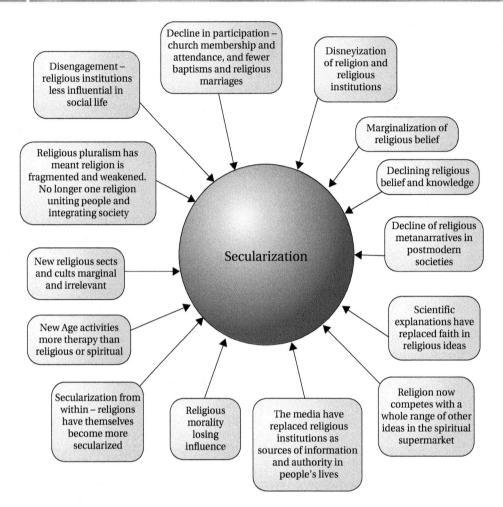

Figure 1.5 Indicators of secularization

to around 60–70 per cent in polls in the 1980s. The 2011 census found that one-quarter of the population of England and Wales said they had no religion at all.

The marginalization of religious belief

Following from the point above, Bruce (2008) suggests that religion and related beliefs have now been marginalized – they have been relegated to the sidelines of life. Religious beliefs are now, for most people, only a last resort, concerned with those areas of human life over which science and technology have no control, such as incurable illness. As Bruce puts it, 'when we have tried every cure for cancer, some of us pray'.

The declining influence of religious morality

Various churches' traditional disapproval of divorce, contraception, abortion, sex outside marriage, illegitimacy and homosexuality appears to have little impact on people's behaviour. The rising number of divorces, lone-parent families, children born outside marriage and couples living together without getting married; the growing acceptance of gays and lesbians, extra-marital sex and the widespread use of contraception among Catholics in direct opposition to Catholic teachings; and drug abuse, pornography and violent crime – these are all often used as evidence for the declining importance of the influence of religious beliefs on people's behaviour.

The fragmentation of belief

There is no longer one set of beliefs which most people share, but a wide diversity of religious faiths and organizations, fragments drawn from different faiths, and New Age ideas. Traditional religions now have to compete with tarot cards, paganism, Native American spirituality, self-help therapies, spiritual healing, New Age mysticism, palmistry and horoscopes, astrology, witchcraft, vampirism and beliefs in the paranormal (like extra-sensory perception).

The decline of metanarratives and the growth of do-it-yourself spirituality in postmodern societies

Postmodernists like Lyotard (1984) argue that, in postmodern societies, metanarratives like religion have lost their power to influence how people think about, interpret and explain the world; people are taking more control over their own lives and are less willing to be told by religious authorities what to believe. In contemporary consumer-driven societies, people are choosing to create their own pick 'n' mix, do-it-yourself cocktail of beliefs, centred on themselves and construction of their identities, after shopping around in the spiritual supermarket. Religion is now just one form of belief competing with many others.

The emphasis, particularly in New Age spirituality, is now on the quality of experience rather than the truth of the doctrine. Many of these New Age 'spiritual cocktails' have little religious meaning to those involved in them. Bruce (2002a) points out that most involvement is shallow and barely goes beyond reading a few books or listening to a few lectures. The most popular parts of the New Age are mainly secular therapies, like relaxation techniques, meditation, yoga and massage, and not alternatives to traditional religion, like the occult or Hindu philosophies. Bruce points out that 'much of the New Age is not an alternative to traditional religion; it is an extension of the doctor's surgery, the beauty parlour and the gym'.

The myth of belief in a 'spirit or life force' as an indicator of religiosity

Bruce (2002a) suggests that, although many people still claim to believe in a 'spirit or life force', this is an indicator of growing secularization, not of continuing religiosity. It simply represents a halfway house, in which people place themselves as they move away from religious belief, but can't yet bring themselves to admit that they are nonbelievers.

Declining religious knowledge

The evidence suggests that many people now know very little about religion. For example, even those who describe themselves as Christians, like the 59 per cent of the population in the 2011 census, don't know much about the life of Jesus, the Bible, or the religious meaning of important events like Easter and Christmas. For example, an Ipsos MORI poll for the Richard Dawkins Foundation for Reason and Science in 2011 found, of those who identified themselves as Christians, only around one-third were able to identify Matthew as the first book of the New Testament, when given only four answers to choose from; this is perhaps unsurprising as the majority (60 per cent) had not read any part of the Bible, independently and from choice, for at least a year, and a third hadn't done so in the last three years.

---

2 The decline of religious practice

Whether or not people claim to hold some religious beliefs and values, most do not have much attachment to religious institutions, and nearly every indicator of religious practice in the mainstream religions shows a decline. For example:

1 *There is declining membership* in all the major Christian denominations (see table 1.5 on page 75), and this decline is progressive: as many existing members grow older, and as they die off, they are not being replaced by younger recruits.
2 *There is declining attendance.* Compared to about 40 per cent in 1851, in 2007 only around 2 per cent of the population attended religious services on most Sundays, and these were mainly older people. Two-thirds of the population attended a religious service (excluding baptisms, weddings and funerals) no more than once a year or less, or never. The 2011–12 British Social Attitudes Survey found that, even among those who either identified themselves with a religion or were brought up in a particular religion, 56 per cent attended a religious service less than once a year or never (excluding baptisms, weddings and funerals). There are also declining

attendances at Christmas and Easter – the most important events in the Christian calendar. This trend is likely to get worse, as there is little evidence of religious participation by younger people to replace the present generation of older worshippers.

3   Only about a third of marriages now involve a religious ceremony; fewer than one-fifth of babies are now baptized, compared with about two-thirds in 1950.

4   A century ago, half of all children attended a Sunday school. If current trends continue, Sunday schools will be extinct by 2016.

The myth of belief without belonging

Bellah (1976), Bellah et al. (1996) and Davie (2002) claim that a decline in religious practice does not necessarily mean a decline in belief (see page 79). They suggest that people still believe and just no longer practise through, or belong to, religious organizations. Voas and Crockett (2005) say this view is mistaken, as they found that in Britain and many other European countries both belonging *and* believing are falling, and at a similar rate. A majority of those who don't belong (or are 'unchurched', in Davie's words) either do not consider themselves as religious or have no belief in God at all.

The myth of resacralization

While involvement in new religious movements, religious sects and cults, and New Age spirituality has been growing, it is difficult to see this as a process of **resacralization** (the renewal of religious belief and practice). Tiny numbers of people are involved, and any growth is insignificant compared to the membership loss of the major denominations. Bruce (2002b) argues the influence of such groups is marginal, and they can hardly be seen as taking the place of established churches and religions as significant or important religious and spiritual movements in contemporary society.

Resacralization refers to the renewal and continuing vitality of religious beliefs.

Wilson regards religious sects as the last outposts of religion in a secular society, showing that the only way religious belief can survive is by isolation from the secularizing influences of the wider society. New religious movements and New Age spirituality are of no significance in the lives of the vast majority of people, and almost irrelevant to society as a whole. Some of these activities are in many cases little more than a form of self-indulgent pseudo-religious titillation for society's drop-outs, except perhaps when they provide exciting and sensationalized stories in the media. Many of the most popular new movements and activities are, in any case, of the world-affirming type, driven by secular rather than religious concerns – such as self-improvement so individuals can be more successful and get on in their careers.

Glendinning and Bruce (2006) pointed out that the research collected in the Kendal Project (see the activity on page 41, and page 78), often cited as evidence of a growing reorientation of religiosity and of a 'spiritual revolution', showed that fewer than one in fifty people in the area around Kendal were engaged in New Age activities in a typical week, and fewer than half of them saw these as spiritual activities. They suggest that this is hardly evidence of resacralization or a 'spiritual revolution'.

3 The decline of religious institutions

Bruce points out that the church in the Middle Ages was the dominant social institution in Europe, with enormous wealth, power and influence, and dominated people's lives. Church leaders exercised real power in terms of the secular areas of law-making, education, politics and social welfare. Religion therefore affected many aspects of people's lives and was a major influence on the way people viewed the world.

Compared to this, religious institutions today have become increasingly marginalized, as they are no longer directly involved in every important area of social life. They therefore lose significance and influence, and most people can now live their lives completely untouched by religious institutions, and, by extension, the religious beliefs they seek to spread. This declining power and significance of religious institutions is demonstrated by the following types of evidence:

1   Church buildings are closing and crumbling today, while in the much poorer society of the past elaborate and ornate cathedrals and churches were built, expensively decorated, well maintained and repaired, and even the poor donated generously to church funds.

Table 1.5 Membership of churches and other religions: United Kingdom, 1995–2015

Church or religion	1995	2005	2010	2015[1]
Trinitarian[2] Christian churches: thousands				
Anglican	1,785	1,537	1,458	1,336
Catholic	1,921	1,667	1,473	1,326
Presbyterian	1,099	918	741	578
Methodist	403	295	238	181
Baptist	224	208	198	192
Pentecostal	209	342	435	530
Other Christian	663	877	972	1,042
Total Trinitarian Christian	6,304	5,844	5,515	5,185
% of population	13.6%	12.3%	11.2%	10.3%
Other religions: thousands				
Non-Trinitarian[2]	458	516	521	524
Muslims	632	894	1,082	1,245
Hindus	242	359	425	467
Others[3]	378	460	497	515
Total other religions	1,710	2,229	2,525	2,751
% of population	2.2%	3.7%	4.1%	4.3%
All religions: thousands	8,014	8,073	8,040	7,936
% of population	15.8%	16%	15.3%	14.6%

[1] Estimate.
[2] Trinitarian Christian churches are those who believe God consists of three persons: father, son and Holy Spirit. Non-Trinitarian religions do not believe this, and they may or may not be Christian, and include groups like the Mormons, Jehovah's Witnesses and some new religious movements.
[3] Includes Sikhs, Jews and Buddhists, and some new religious movements.

Source: adapted from: Christian Research, *Religious Trends 2003/2004 and Religious Trends No. 7*; Dr Peter Brierley, *UK Church Statistics 2005 to 2010*

Activity

Study table 1.5 and answer the following questions:
1 How many people belonged to Anglican churches in 1995?
2 By how many did the membership of the Catholic Church decline between 1995 and 2010?
3 What percentage of the population belonged to a Christian church in 2005?
4 Identify two trends shown in the membership of Christian churches.
5 Which three churches or religions are estimated to increase membership most between 1995 and 2015?
6 How might the evidence in the table be used to show that religion is not necessarily declining in the United Kingdom?
7 There has been a decline in the number of religious marriages in Britain, and more than two-thirds of all marriages today are civil (non-religious) ceremonies. Do you think this necessarily means there is a decline in religious belief? What other explanations might there be?
8 Suggest reasons why most surveys on attendance at religious services don't count baptisms, weddings and funerals.

2 The status of the clergy is steadily declining; they are poorly paid and hard to recruit.

3 In schools, religious education is more like personal development or social studies, and Sunday schools are on the verge of extinction. In September 2015, the Church of England reported that it was struggling to find enough Christian headteachers for its primary and secondary schools, and they were instead being forced to recruit from those with other faiths, or even from those with no faith at all.

4 Religious institutions are unable to command respect for even the major Christian festivals, like Christmas and Easter. These have little religious meaning to most people in British society and are for most people simply an excuse for a holiday, and/or an orgy of shopping, overeating and excessive drinking.

5 Religious institutions have, as Martin (1969) described it, 'disengaged' from society. This refers to the withdrawal of religious organizations from many areas of life in which they used to be involved. Parsons (1951) saw this as part of a process of **structural differentiation**, whereby new, more specialized social institutions emerge to take over functions that were once performed by a single institution, such as the church. For example, the welfare state and other agencies and experts now provide free state education, social services, the NHS, welfare benefits, care homes for older people and care and support for the sick, the poor, the unemployed and other disadvantaged groups that were once a near-monopoly of the church. This reduces the significance of religion in people's lives.

6 There are increasing numbers of alternative sources of knowledge. The development of the media – particularly global cable and satellite television and the internet – and free education have now effectively eliminated the monopoly of knowledge once enjoyed by religious institutions. The media and the internet have replaced religion as the main sources of authority and knowledge for many people, and these are likely to have far more influence on people's thinking than religion has. The erosion of the influence of traditional religious institutions is accelerated by globalization. This has meant that people are now exposed to a vast array of new doctrines, books, knowledge and ways of thinking by the ever-growing globalized mass media and the internet. This was confirmed by Halman and Draulans (2006), who found that the more globalized a society became – measured in terms of IT facilities (e.g. internet access) – the less religious the people in that country were.

7 The church is no longer closely associated with the state and the machinery of government, with the possible exception of the twenty-six bishops (the 'Lords Spiritual') in the House of Lords, and the fact that the Archbishop of Canterbury still crowns the monarch.

8 The church now has little influence over social policies. For example, gay men and lesbians can now marry on the same basis as heterosexual couples, but the Anglican Church still tears itself apart when it comes to issues like, for example, appointing a gay bishop.

9 Ceremonies marking the 'rites of passage', such as birth, marriage and death, which were once a church monopoly, can now be performed not only without a religious ceremony of any kind, but in almost any location, like a hotel or a pub.

10 The ecumenical movement is a movement among different Christian denominations to achieve greater unity between them. Ecumenicalism is sometimes seen as a sign of the weakness of religious organizations. Once-powerful independent institutions, tossed about aimlessly in a sea of apathy and indifference, are now forced to clutch at the straw of ecumenicalism and compromise with other denominations to try to save themselves from drowning.

11 Institutional religion has become fragmented into a vast and diverse range of competing religions, beliefs and religious organizations. As Bruce suggests, there is no longer one main church or body of shared religious belief around which people are united, but religious pluralism. This means that religion is no longer able (if it ever was) to provide a single universe of meaning or act as a social glue binding people together, integrating them into society and building social solidarity and social cohesion. As Aldridge (2007) notes: 'The very fact of religious diversity introduces doubt: why should one particular faith be the truth and command our allegiance when there are so many others, each with its own truths, vying for acceptance?' The fragmentation of beliefs and religious pluralism reduces the power of religious institutions, marginalizes their influence in society and, as a study by Halman and Draulans (2006) found, corrodes religious belief and practice among the population as a whole.

> **Structural differentiation** refers to the way new, more specialized social institutions emerge to take over functions that were once performed by a single institution.

Do you think the fact that religious institutions now promote themselves through popular 'Disneyized' advertising is a strength or a weakness of contemporary religion?

Secularization from within: the secularization of religious institutions

In order to survive in a secular society, religious institutions have been forced to move away from traditional doctrines and concern with the supernatural, and have compromised and watered down their beliefs and become less religious, and more like the secular society in which they're set. Herberg (1960) called this 'secularization from within'. Examples of this collapse of traditional doctrines and teachings include things like the acceptance of cohabitation as no longer 'living in sin', easier divorce laws, the abolition of Latin in Catholic services, the ordination of women priests and bishops, the growing – though still very controversial – acceptance of lesbians and gay men by the church, and the downplaying of doctrines concerning miracles and literal interpretations of heaven and hell.

Religious institutions are now so weak that they can no longer set trends, but have to follow them. This adaptation of religion to secularization has been the case for years in the USA, as Herberg found. There, membership and attendance of religious organizations is high, but mainly because traditional doctrines and the supernatural/spiritual aspects have been played down. Religious participation has become an almost secular part of the American way of life rather than involving any serious religious belief and commitment.

The Disneyization of religious institutions

Bryman (2004) uses the term 'Disneyization' (sometimes called *Disneyfication*) to describe the transformation of something into a diluted or simplified, trivialized and sanitized version of its original form, to create an inoffensive neutral product resembling the Disneyland theme parks.

Lyon (2000), from a postmodernist perspective, uses the example of the Harvest Day Crusade held at Disneyland in California to illustrate the way Disneyization diminishes religion through trivializing it, or making involvement with it appear less than fully serious. At this event, the organizers saw 'Disneyland as an opportunity to bring God's kingdom to the Magic Kingdom', which enabled religion to interact with the artificial, simulated, virtual, fantasy world of Disney, with Christian artists and performers replacing the regular attractions and rides. Lyon argues that, in postmodern societies, people want to establish their identities, including the beliefs they hold, by customizing their own personalized contemporary packages rather than those formed by social class, gender, ethnicity or beliefs handed down by traditional religious institutions. He argues religion has become like any other product to consume, and Disneyization blends religion with consumerism and popular culture to increase its appeal in the spiritual marketplace. In postmodern society, religion is forced to market and package itself in many different guises, in order to attract customers by appealing to a wide variety of consumer tastes, as it competes with a whole host of other consumer products and leisure activities. One way religion does this is by trivializing itself and placing an emphasis on fun and amusement, and merchandising (selling) itself like the fantasy-world of the Disneyland theme park. Lyon therefore suggests that religion has been 'Disneyfied', with participation seeming little more than a joke, and packaged as a commodity like washing powder or Mickey Mouse, for sale to consumers in a market in which rival belief manufacturers jostle desperately to sell variations of the same product in the face of declining demand.

The evidence against secularization

1 Religious thinking and belief

Many people still show signs of religiosity

Surveys show that, although around 70 per cent of the population think that religion is losing its influence, around 70 per cent still claim to believe that there is a soul, and almost as many believe in sin. Eurobarometer (2010) found that, while just 37 per cent of people in the UK believed in a God, a further 33 per cent believed in some sort of 'spirit or life force'. This suggests that up to 70 per cent of people still have some elements of religiosity in their thinking (though note Bruce's view earlier, on page 73, that the claim to believe in a spirit or life force is simply a halfway house, in which people place themselves as they move away from religious belief, but can't yet bring themselves to admit that they are nonbelievers).

Secularization and resacralization: the reorientation of religious belief

In an age of uncertainties and unpredictability, and with the decline of traditional religious meta-narratives, people are still searching for new meanings and commitment in, for example, New Age ideas, new religious movements and cults like Scientology, in order to re-establish religiosity in their lives and get clues to what their future holds. Heelas et al. (2004), using data gathered in Kendal (see www.kendalproject.org.uk), found there was a 'spiritual revolution' with growing involvement with what they called the 'holistic milieu' – New Age mind–body spirituality of some kind, such as yoga, Tai Chi and alternative therapies. They argued that while there may be secularization in relation to traditional religions, there is, at the same time, a process of resacralization – a renewal and continuing vitality of religious beliefs – as people shift from conventional religion and reorient themselves to a more individualistic spirituality centred on the self. Such research suggests that religious belief is not disappearing, but is simply being reoriented – taking a new form in which people pick 'n' mix their spirituality from the wide range of beliefs on offer, tailored to what they feel they need and what works for them (but note the earlier section on 'the myth of resacralization' on page 74).

> **Activity**
>
> Go to the site of the Kendal Project (www.kendalproject.org.uk) and answer the following questions:
> 1 Explain what is meant by the terms 'Congregational Domain' and the 'Holistic Milieu' and explain the differences between them.
> 2 How was the congregational attendance count carried out?
> 3 What was the purpose of the street survey, and what method was used? Identify three things it asked about.
> 4 Go to the Holistic Milieu questionnaire and identify three of the reasons offered in the questionnaire for people attending activities or therapies.
> 5 Identify any evidence found in the Kendal Project to support the claim of a 'spiritual revolution'.

Traditional religious beliefs remain strong

Various forms of Christian beliefs (and practice) in the UK remain strong. As discussed earlier, Pentecostalist denominations are growing, and Evangelical Christianity is the fastest-growing form of Christianity in Britain and in the rest of the world. Evangelicalism is a broad collection of

Christians sharing a fundamentalist belief in the Bible – accepting that the Bible is God's literal word and should be followed strictly. Many Evangelicals believe in the Second Coming of Christ, faith healing, speaking in tongues, miracles, casting out of demons and possession by evil. They campaign against witchcraft, Satanism, black magic, any form of occult activity, smoking, drinking, sexual promiscuity and homosexuality. The religious fundamentalism this involves cannot be regarded as 'watered-down' religion. Much the same may be said of the commitment required by many new religious movements. As seen in Topic 4, high levels of commitment are still shown in the minority ethnic religions in the UK, such as Hinduism, Sikhism and Islam.

The Eurobarometer (2010) survey cited earlier suggested that up to 70 per cent of people in the UK still have some elements of religiosity in their thinking, but the same survey found it is even higher in parts of Europe. Nearly four out of 5 (77 per cent) of European Union citizens had religious or spritual beliefs. Such evidence suggests that traditional religious belief is still very strong among many people.

The continuing vitality of religiously based moral values

Rates of crime, divorce, births outside marriage and so on have a wide range of causes, and cannot be explained as simply arising from declining religious beliefs. The rapid growth of Christian fundamentalism, particularly in the USA, and Islamic fundamentalism across the world is in part a reaction to modernization and secularization. The liberalization of religiously based moral values on issues like abortion, sex before and outside marriage, and homosexuality, found in postmodern pick 'n' mix societies, has created a reaction amongst those desiring to reassert traditional values. This shows that there is still some life left among those defenders of religiously based moral values.

---

2 Religious practice

Belonging without believing

Attending religious services does not necessarily mean believing in God. In the past, many people may have attended church regularly only because churchgoing was seen as necessary to achieve respectability in the community. The decline in church attendance today therefore may not necessarily mean that there has been a decline in belief, only a decline in the social pressure to attend church.

Believing without belonging: 'fuzzy fidelity' and the privatization of religious practice

Believing in God does not necessarily mean having to attend religious services. Bellah (1976) first suggested nearly forty years ago that declining church attendance in the USA did not mean a decline in religiosity, but a search for more immediate and personal religious experiences than traditional religious institutions were able to offer. Bellah et al. (1996) suggested there had been a reorientation from public participation in traditional religious institutions to more private worship. Davie (2002), looking across a number of European countries, has also argued that declining religious attendance has not been accompanied by declining religious belief. She suggests that people are simply becoming 'unchurched' – that is, they don't attend or belong to churches, even though they still claim to hold religious beliefs. Davie (1994) used the words 'belief without belonging' to describe this situation, in which people hold religious beliefs without participating in religious organizations. Voas (2009) refers to this casual loyalty to tradition among those who are neither regular churchgoers nor self-consciously non-religious as 'fuzzy fidelity'. The 'fuzzy faithful' are those who may hold religious beliefs without joining traditional religious organizations, and may simply be disillusioned with the traditional churches, or may be developing more individual spiritual beliefs. Although religion usually plays only a minor role in the lives of such people, they may be choosing to practise and express their beliefs in more private ways, such as in their own homes, in 'house groups' or through engagement with religious information provided by the mass media, such as that provided by the rising number of worldwide religious channels available on cable and satellite TV, internet websites and religious radio stations. However, note Voas and Crockett's earlier comments (see page 74) that this view is mistaken, as they found that in Britain and many other European countries both belonging *and* believing are falling, and at a similar rate.

Not all denominations and faiths are declining

Christian Research statistics (www.christian-research.org) in 2010, derived from a number of the major UK Christian denominations, suggest that the decline in the numbers of people attending worship during the later years of the last century has now become more stable. Christian Research therefore suggests the view that churchgoing numbers are in a nose-dive and the country is becoming either more secular or 'fuzzy faithful' is wrong.

As table 1.5 (page 75) shows, there has actually been an increase in membership of some Christian groupings, such as the Pentecostal and other Christian denominations, and of other religions, including Islam and Hinduism among the minority ethnic groups, and new religious movements. New religious sects and cults, and New Age ideas, are constantly emerging, and more people are getting involved. These may be responding to a deep-seated spirituality that people find lacking in existing religious institutions and faiths.

Despite an overall decline in church attendance, many people continue to make use of religious ceremonies for the 'rites of passage' such as baptism, marriage and death. This suggests they still believe it is important for religion to 'bless' the important stages in their lives. About 90 per cent of funerals involve a religious ceremony of some kind.

---

3 Religious institutions

The institutional power of churches remains

The Church of England (C of E) remains the established (or 'official') church in England, and the British monarch must be a member of the Church of England, is crowned by the Archbishop of Canterbury and, since the time of Henry VIII, has been head of the Church of England and 'Defender of the Faith'. Church of England bishops continue to have seats in the House of Lords (the 'Lords Spiritual'), despite extensive reform of the House of Lords in the early 2000s. The C of E is extremely wealthy, with investment funds of around £5.2 billion at the beginning of 2013, and it is one of the largest property owners in the country. The Roman Catholic Church is the world's largest Christian denomination, and retains extensive powers and influence over the state in several European countries (for example, Ireland, Spain, Italy and Poland) and in many South American countries.

Religious institutions remain very influential in education in Britain

Britain has very many C of E and Catholic faith schools, with a growing number being provided by other faiths. This power of religion in education is also shown by the legal requirement for schools to hold a daily religious act of worship, and religious education is a compulsory part of the National Curriculum.

The strengthening of religious institutions

The Church (the main Christian churches, at least) has disengaged from secular society in many ways, through the process Parsons described as *structural differentiation* (see page 76), in which new, more specialized social institutions emerge to take over functions that were once performed by the church. While this may weaken the influence of religion in many areas of social life, Parsons suggests this might also strengthen the place of religion in people's lives. This is because the church is now more focused on spiritual matters than at any time in the past, and avoids 'pollution' from involvement in non-religious affairs.

This suggestion that religious organizations are becoming stronger as they disengage from secular society, because they are purer and untouched by secular concerns and so can concentrate on religion, may or may not be true. What certainly is true is that if they are concentrating more on their religious message, there is very little evidence that they are getting through to enough people to offset their loss of influence and the decline in people's participation.

Religious institutions remain very important in the minority ethnic communities

Mosques, temples and synagogues are often a focus of social and cultural life as well as religious life, and are very important symbols of identity in minority ethnic communities. As Bruce suggests (see page 58) religion can act as a means of cultural transition and cultural defence in such communities, undermining the view that secularization is occurring. Minority ethnic group religious leaders are becoming increasingly influential, particularly in Muslim communities, and are often consulted by governments in relation to social policies relating to those communities.

Activity

1 Outline and explain three reasons why religious ideas may be of declining importance to many people.
2 Explain what is meant by 'religious pluralism', and outline two reasons why religious pluralism might weaken the influence of religion in society.
3 Outline and explain two reasons why New Age mind–body spirituality: (a) might be used as evidence against the secularization thesis; (b) might be used as evidence to support the secularization thesis.
4 Review this topic, and identify all the contributions postmodernists make towards our understanding of the process of secularization.
5 Make yourself a revision summary of the arguments, evidence for and against secularization and the explanations for them. List in one column one-sentence summaries of each of the arguments for secularization, and then in a second column, list one-sentence counter-arguments alongside each of the arguments given in the first column.

Secularization in a global context: the significance of religion and religiosity in the contemporary world

Most sociologists would agree, on the basis of the evidence presented above, that in the UK and much of Europe, *traditional* religious thinking and beliefs, practice and institutions are declining. However, as suggested at the beginning of this topic, secularization is a contested concept, and the question of the extent of this secularization, or whether religion is simply reorienting itself and appearing in new guises, has no simple answer. However, it would be misleading to think secularization is a universal, global process. In the United States and in many other countries of the world religious participation remains high (see below), and in some countries religion is actually growing in strength and commitment. Norris and Inglehart (2011), for example, point out that the world as a whole now has more people with traditional religious views than ever before, and they constitute a growing proportion of the world's population.

Religious market theory, also known as rational choice or market supply theory, suggests that religious organizations are like businesses that compete in the spiritual marketplace for customers. Diversity, choice and competition between religious organizations leads to a greater variety of religion and improved quality of religious products tailored to the needs of consumers, which leads to more religious participation.

Explaining the distribution and strength of religion in the world

There are two main theories – religious market theory and existential security theory – which have been used to explain why in some countries religious participation is in decline, while in others it remains strong and in some cases is growing.

Religious market theory

Religious market theory, sometimes called rational choice or market supply theory, is associated with the work of Stark and Bainbridge (1996) and Stark and Finke (2000). They argue that there is a basic and constant demand for religion, as people have an essential need for certain compensators and rewards (see page 25) that only religion can provide, such as knowing the meaning of life, the promise of a better life to come, and life after death. Stark and colleagues suggest religious organizations are like businesses, supplying religious products to meet the demands of consumers in the spiritual marketplace. Though demand for religion may be constant, whether people choose to participate in religious organizations will depend on the supply – the quantity, quality and attractiveness – of the religious products that are made available to them. Like businesses, religions and religious organizations that grow are those which supply and market attractive religious products that appeal to a wide range of spiritual tastes and beliefs, and constantly adapt their products to the demands of their potential customers as these customers go shopping for faith in the spiritual supermarket.

Stark and colleagues suggest people make rational choices when they 'buy' or consume religion; they make a cost/benefit analysis – weighing up the costs against the benefits or rewards – before choosing whether or not it is in their interests to participate in religious activities.

- *Costs* involve things like financial donations, time commitment, and any tensions with wider society arising from conformity with religious values.
- *Benefits* involve rewards or compensators, such as reduced stress and tension, spiritual fulfilment, a promise of future salvation, life after death, a useful social network of friends and contacts, and status in the community.

In this situation, religious organizations need to make themselves as attractive as possible to customers, by offering the greatest rewards at the lowest costs and the widest possible choice in the religious marketplace. Stark and Finke argue that religious pluralism, with a wide choice of religious products supplied by a diversity of competing religious organizations, is the key factor that underlies high levels of religious participation in any society. This is because in a competitive religious market, there is a greater likelihood that everyone will find a faith that fits his or her beliefs, which increases the take-up of religion. They suggest the United States, for example, has very high levels of religious participation because there is an exceptionally large number of religious options available in a highly competitive religious market, with no state religion and little religious regulation. This involves a huge diversity of churches, sects, temples, synagogues and mosques, all actively striving to attract members, supplying a vast range of religious products appealing to the needs of people from different social classes, regions, ethnic groups and so on. People therefore have a great deal of choice when they weigh up the costs and benefits of religious participation, and are almost certain to find something to satisfy their demand for religion.

Stark and Finke suggest that, despite low participation rates, secularization is not occurring in Europe, and that people still have religious beliefs. However, in contrast to the United States, in European societies one religion (normally traditional Christian churches) tends to be highly favoured by governments and protected through legislation or subsidies, and they are dominated by official state churches, such as the Church of England in the UK. This means there is limited availability of religious choices or competition between religious suppliers (religious organizations) to encourage them to offer their potential customers a selection of attractive religious products tailored to their needs and appealing to all consumer tastes. This lack of suppliers and choice means that only a fraction of people's beliefs are catered for, and this dampens down religious participation.

Criticisms of religious market theory

1 Sharot (2002) argues that the theory of Stark and colleagues:
   - Makes little reference to religions other than mainstream Christianity
   - Only applies to the USA, and is unable to account for levels and patterns of religiosity elsewhere, particularly in non-Western societies
   - Has little application to other forms of non-mainstream religiosity outside of established religious organizations, such as new religious movements and religious groups which allow followers to have a diversity of beliefs.
2 Stark and colleagues suggest it is the lack of supply of religion, rather than secularization, that is leading to declining religious participation in Europe. However, as Herberg pointed out, there is a process of 'secularization from within' going on in the United States (see pages 77–8), with competition and marketing 'dumbing down' religion, reducing the costs of religious participation to such an extent that it has become more a part of social life rather than an expression of any real religious belief or commitment. Lyon referred to this dumbing down as Disneyization (see pages 77–8), as religion in the USA develops into a less than serious activity.
3 As shown below, and as Norris and Inglehart (2011) point out, rational choice/religious market/market supply theory fails to explain variations in religiosity between different societies. It is

inaccurate as there is no evidence of any link between religious choice and religious participation: there continues to be high levels of religious participation even where there is a limited supply and little choice of religious organizations. This is the case in many Catholic countries in Europe, such as Ireland, Italy and Spain, and in the Orthodox Christian countries like Cyprus, Greece, Serbia and Romania. In some countries, like Iran, Saudi Arabia and Kuwait, Islam has a near-monopoly backed by the state, yet this does not appear to have led to any decline in participation. Bruce (1996) points out that, even in the United States, there are large areas, like the southern states, that do not have a wide diversity of religious groups, yet participation still remains high.

Existential security theory

Norris and Inglehart (2011) broadly accept the criticisms of religious market theory suggested above, particularly that it fails to explain variations in religious participation between different societies. They accept the secularization thesis, though they believe that secularization is occurring much more in Europe than in the United States, and that it is not occurring in all countries of the world.

They suggest that different levels of religious participation arise not because there is more or less religious choice, as the religious market theorists suggest, but because of different amounts of **existential security**, which they define as 'the feeling that survival is secure enough that it can be taken for granted'.

Norris and Inglehart argue that one major function of religion is to provide a sense of confidence and predictability in a threatening and uncertain world – where there are low levels of existential security. Based on studies of very many different countries of the world, they found that the demand for religion varies between social groups and societies according to the degree of existential security. They found that virtually all prosperous advanced industrial societies are more secular than poorer developing nations, with the poorest having the greatest demand for religion as they face the lowest levels of existential security.

> **Existential security** is the feeling that survival is sufficiently secure for it to be taken for granted. Religious participation is highest in societies or groups with low levels of existential security, and lowest in societies or groups with high levels of existential security.

Low levels of existential security

These are found in societies in which the majority of people face threats, vulnerability, insecurity, anxiety and personal risks in their lives. Their survival is uncertain due to factors like poverty, disease, threats from natural disasters like drought or flood, inadequate food, lack of safe drinking water, basic healthcare and schooling, and risks of war. In such societies, religions claiming to provide answers and reassurance about the future and the afterlife have widespread appeal. Norris and Inglehart (2010) showed that some of the poorest developing societies, like Chad, Rwanda and Mali, give the highest priority to religious values and have high levels of religious participation because of this lack of existential security. Norris and Inglehart suggest that it is high birth rates in the poorest countries (and low birth rates in the richer, more existentially secure, countries) that explain why there are now more people in the world with traditional religious views than ever before.

High levels of existential security

These are found in societies in which the majority of the population grow up with feelings of well-being. They are the more prosperous and secure advanced societies, with well-developed economies, and welfare states providing comprehensive healthcare, education and social services, offering some security during unemployment, periods of ill-health or disability, and in old age, and safety nets to reduce poverty and protect those at the bottom from insecurity. Norris and Inglehart suggest this explains why some of the most prosperous societies in the world, led by Sweden, Norway, Denmark and Britain, are the most secular, as in such societies, and many European countries, high levels of existential security diminish the importance of religion in people's lives.

The anomaly of the United States

Some suggest that existential security theory fails to explain the high levels of religious participation in the world's richest country – the churchgoing United States – where it might be expected people would have high levels of existential security. Norris and Inglehart (2010) suggest that this is no exception to the theory, but high participation arises because of the way resources in that society are unequally distributed. The sharp inequalities of US society, combined with inadequate social welfare and healthcare systems, create high levels of poverty and insecurity for the poorest groups, which helps to explain higher levels of religiosity. This insecurity may even apply to the non-poor, who may face, for example, the threat of huge crippling medical bills if they fall ill. Norris and Inglehart emphasize that even in affluent societies, there are groups who fall through the safety net of the welfare state and experience poverty, and their research shows that in most societies, including richer ones like the United States, religious participation is highest among the poorest social groups who face the greatest threats to their existential security, and lowest among the most affluent groups.

Activity

1 What do the religious market/rational choice/market supply theorists outline is the main reason for the high levels of religious participation in the United States, and the low levels of participation in Europe?
2 Outline three reasons why poor societies, or poorer social groups in rich societies, tend to have higher religious participation rates than more prosperous societies or groups.
3 Outline two reasons why many Western European countries appear to be more secular than the United States.
4 Outline and explain two reasons why secularization is more likely to be found in advanced developed countries than in poorer developing societies.
5 How does existential security theory explain the fact that the United States has much higher levels of religious participation than most European countries, despite being one of the world's richest countries?

The continuing significance of religion in the world

Religious belief and practice remain high in many countries of the world

1 *Religion remains strong among ethnic minorities in the UK*, as discussed in Topic 4 (see pages 57–9), though whether this is for reasons of cultural defence, cultural identity and community solidarity rather than religious belief is open to discussion.
2 *Religious belief and practice remain high in many countries, and is growing in others.* In Catholic countries such as Ireland, Spain, Italy, Portugal, Poland and many South American countries, and in the Christian Orthodox countries, for example Greece, Cyprus, Romania and Serbia, religious belief and practice remain high. In the USA, regular attendance at religious institutions is much higher than in the UK, with around 40 per cent attending regularly. Christianity is actually growing in South America, and radically changing as it mixes with native beliefs. Christianity is also growing in Africa and much of Asia, where it traditionally hasn't had much influence, and the estimated Christian population of China is around 50–150 million, where a century ago it was almost zero. Nanda (2008) suggests that, even in a rapidly modernizing and economically developing country like India, where religion might be expected to be losing influence, the level of religiosity has gone up among Hindus, with 30 per cent saying in 2007 they had become more religious. Nanda explains this as Hinduism being adapted and used by the modernizing and wealth-seeking class to give a 'divine stamp of approval' to their activities. At the same time, she says, Hindu values have become a focus for Indian culture and identity, and have become an explanatory factor for India's rapidly growing economic success.
3 *Religion still dominates in a number of societies across the world.* For example, in Iran, the Islamic Revolution of 1979 brought political power to religious leaders, which continues today. In Iran, Saudi Arabia and some other Muslim countries, the law is rooted in religious doctrine, and special religious police are used to enforce conformity to it, such as in dress and behaviour. In such societies where religion is so deeply embedded in the culture and the state, it is practically impossible to remain unaffected by religion in everyday life.

Religious fundamentalism

Religious fundamentalism (see pages 27–8) is a significant force in the world today. Bruce (2008) suggests that fundamentalism is a rational response of traditionally religious peoples to social, political and economic changes that threaten their religious values.

- *Christian fundamentalism*, particularly in the United States (as mentioned earlier in this chapter), is politically active in the New Christian Right, and often wields substantial political influence. It has been instrumental in getting the teaching of the theory of evolution banned in some schools, and actively campaigns very vigorously against, for example, abortion, sex before or outside marriage and homosexuality.
- *Islamic fundamentalism* is an important and growing force in the Muslim countries of the world, and among some members of Muslim minority ethnic groups in Western societies. Bruce suggests Islamic fundamentalism may be seen as a rational means of defending traditional Islamic beliefs and values threatened with elimination by the combined global influences of Western cultural imperialism, the Americanization of the world's culture and the dominance of Western corporations in the world economy. These bring with them Western values and culture and declining existential security, and Islamic fundamentalism emerges as a means of what Bruce (1996) called cultural defence against this cultural imperialism.

Globalization and the spread of religions

The impact of globalization on religion

Globalization refers to the process whereby there is growing interconnectedness of societies around the world, with the spread of the same culture, consumer goods and economic interests across the globe. The impact and some possible consequences of globalization in relation to religion are outlined below, and summarized in figure 1.6.

Globalization has meant that different cultures and religions have come into closer contact than ever before. This has been caused, particularly, by the globalized media, including the internet and social networking sites, and, combined with cheaper and faster travel, mass tourism and migration of huge numbers of people from one country to another, a wide range of different religious ideas and religious organizations have consequently spread across the globe.

Meyer et al. (2011) suggest that this has meant growing religious diversity, and that the world's religions are becoming less and less tied to particular geographical locations or countries, or linked to the histories and cultures of particular nations and ethnic groups. There has, in other words, been a process of cultural globalization and a **deterritorialization** of religion. This means that there has been a blurring or severance of the connections between a religion, a specific society and a territory, and religious beliefs and organizations have become part of global religious systems.

Deterritorialization is the blurring or severance of social, political or cultural practices, like religion, from their original places and populations.

The internet and social media sites have been particularly significant in making it easier to gain access to information regarding the teachings and activities of other religions, and enabling individuals to adopt elements of a variety of religions and belief systems which appeal to them, picking and mixing elements of different ones without being limited to those found in their own society or culture. The internet has also enabled individuals to access knowledge about religious beliefs and practices outside the power and control of existing religious organizations. This creates a more user-oriented religious market, and can at the same time undermine the authority and control, and monopoly of knowledge, of traditional religious organizations.

Singleton (2014) points out that globalization and deterritorialization have meant that Islam, for example, has been reconstituted as a transnational religion, which is no longer tied to specific geographical areas of the world, and has led to a growing emphasis on the idea that Muslims constitute an *ummah*. This is an Arabic word referring to a supra-national worldwide community of faith, with shared doctrines, beliefs and practices and a collective identity that transcends national borders, cultures and ethnicities. He illustrates this by the example of the publication in 2005 of cartoons of the Prophet Muhammad in a Danish newspaper. These were regarded as insulting to the Prophet, and led to worldwide protests – a global response reflecting a collective identity among the world's Muslims, who, despite their cultural diversity, were unified by the global *ummah*.

Many of the world's religions, like Islam and Christianity, are now transnational, with the spreading and interpenetration of religious organizations, beliefs and practices across national borders. No part of the world is now constituted exclusively of one set of religious ideas, and followers of every religion are found virtually everywhere. For example, the spread of Islam around the globe has meant around one-third of the world's Muslims now constitute minority groups in the countries in which they live, as millions of Muslims have settled voluntarily in Western countries which are predominantly culturally Christian. For example, there are large Muslim communities in the UK and in New York in the USA. Similarly, there are large Christian communities in China; followers of Tibetan Buddhism in Hollywood; a large Jewish presence in Argentina; there are now more Russian Orthodox parishes outside than inside Russia; and Celtic goddesses are very popular in the United States. Pentecostalism is a growing worldwide Christian denomination, which now makes up more than 10 per cent of all Christians, and is particularly strong in the developing world where it poses a serious challenge to other, more established, denominations. Similar examples of this spreading of religions through globalization are the Mormons (the Church of Jesus Christ of Latter-Day Saints), the Jehovah's Witnesses and new religious movements such as the Unification Church from South Korea (the 'Moonies'), which is found in around 150 countries.

This spreading of religions has meant that global transnational religions have become intertwined with local cultures and created greater cultural diversity. Increased immigration from Buddhist, Muslim and Hindu countries has transformed Western societies. For example, the spread of Islam, Hinduism and Sikhism into personal and public life in the UK has led to an increase in public religious observances, such as festivals like Diwali and Ramadan, and more signs of Islamic dress (such as the veiling of women) and a rise in banks offering Sharia-friendly current accounts and loans.

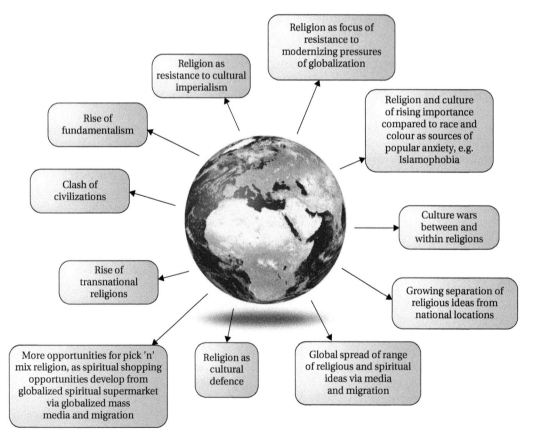

Figure 1.6 The impact and some possible consequences of globalization in relation to religion

The consequences of globalization for religion

The 'clash of civilizations' and culture wars

Huntington (2002) sees religion and religious identity as an important aspect of different civilizations in the contemporary world, which have differences between them in lifestyles, beliefs and cultures. He suggests there can be conflict – a clash of civilizations – as these come more into contact with one another through globalization. For example, the growth of Islam – particularly Islamic fundamentalism – increasingly comes into conflict with Christian-based Western civilization. Such clashes are like those found between Western governments and the fundamentalist Taliban in the war in Afghanistan, and the 9/11 attacks on the World Trade Center in New York in 2001, or the London bombings on 7 July 2005. Huntington, however, does not consider the possibility of clashes within civilizations, such as between Protestants and Catholics in Northern Ireland, or between Hindus, Muslims and Sikhs in India.

Kurtz (2012) says globalization has spurred a revitalization of religious traditions. He suggests the growing encounter of different religions as globalization continues fuels 'culture wars' between religions, and sometimes between modernizing and traditional groups within the same religion, such as between Muslim communities in the West and those in the Middle East. Kurtz suggests conflicts between people, ethnic groups, classes and nations are often now framed in religious terms, as the struggle of good against evil. In some ways, globalization has meant that religion and culture may have displaced race and colour as the main sources of popular anxiety, as people encounter and learn more about other religions. For example, Islamophobia (see pages 59–61) – a fear and hatred of the culture and religion of Muslims – may be a more significant issue in some communities in the UK today than racism. However, religious prejudice and racism are not easy to disentangle if the religion concerned is mainly held by a particular ethnic group: Islamophobia in the UK may in fact be concealing anti-Pakistani or anti-Bangladeshi racism.

Ben-Nun Bloom et al. (2014) suggest that globalization has contributed to declining levels of religious freedom across the world. More countries are interfering with worship or other religious practices, and regulating religious symbols, literature or broadcasting. They suggest this arises from the desire of religious or cultural groups to protect themselves from the perceived threat to existing traditions, values and identities they feel when they are exposed to different religious beliefs and customs, and interact with members of other religions. This leads to more restrictions on the religious activities of minority groups, such as the 'burqa ban' in several European countries.

The rise of fundamentalism, cultural defence and identity

The spread of Western culture, particularly American culture, through globalization, and the modernizing processes which accompany this, may threaten traditional ways of life, including religious beliefs and values. Both Christian and, particularly, Islamic fundamentalism may emerge as a means of what Bruce called cultural defence – protecting and attempting to restore traditional culture and religious values – and as an attempt to provide some security in a rapidly changing world marked by growing uncertainty and change.

Religion more generally may become a focus for what are seen as threats to traditional values posed by cultural imperialism, and the modernizing and the perceived corrupting influences of globalization. The Western world's threat to traditional social norms, such as the treatment of sexuality, including homosexuality, the use of women as sex objects, attitudes to divorce and gender roles, and the breakdown of family life has led to a re-emergence and strengthening of traditional religious and fundamentalist ideas as a focus of resistance to what is seen as growing Western dominance and dilution of traditional norms and ways of life.

Singleton (2014) suggests the dramatic rise of Islamic fundamentalism can be seen as a response to globalization. This has brought about the end of the Muslim world as a distinct geographical entity, and given rise to resistance to Western influence penetrating Islam. Fundamentalism is a device to look for purity beyond nationality, ethnicity, language and culture, thus transforming Islam into a set of transnational doctrines.

Religion may also become simply an expression and assertion of national identity in the face of globalization, as Nanda suggested in relation to Hinduism in contemporary India, where the religion has become a source of national pride and identity, and is credited with India's growing success in the world economy.

The global spiritual supermarket

As suggested throughout this chapter, postmodernists believe that in contemporary societies people increasingly form their identities through consumer culture – through the products they buy (their consumption patterns) and the lifestyles they build – and this includes the various religious or spiritual beliefs they may or may not buy into. Postmodernists tend to see the beliefs people hold as purely a personal matter, and they can experiment without long-term commitment. In contemporary consumer-driven societies, people are choosing to create their own pick 'n' mix, do-it-yourself cocktail of beliefs, centred on themselves and construction of their identities, after shopping around. In the contemporary globalized, media-saturated world, the spiritual supermarket is now more than ever a *global* supermarket, with beliefs to choose from every part of the world, including many that, before the advent of the internet, the globalized media and mass migration, would have hardly been heard of except in the geographical area or community in which they originally existed.

Activity

1 Identify and explain two reasons why the extent of secularization varies between societies.
2 Explain what is meant by 'globalization', and outline two reasons why globalization might threaten traditional religious beliefs.
3 Outline three ways that globalization might undermine the view that the contemporary world is becoming more secular.

Practice questions

1 Outline and explain **two** ways in which a decline in participation in religious institutions may not mean that society is becoming more secular. **(10 marks)**

2 Read **Item A** below and answer the question that follows.

Item A

Sociologists disagree about the extent of secularization in the modern world. For example, some suggest that the development of science and technology has displaced religious faith as a means of interpreting the world. Postmodernists point to the decline of metanarratives, which mean people are abandoning once taken-for-granted belief systems, like religion. Other sociologists suggest religion is not declining, but simply changing and appearing in new forms.

Applying material from **Item A**, analyse **two** ways in which religion, rather than declining, is changing and appearing in new forms. **(10 marks)**

3   Read **Item B** below and answer the question that follows.

Item B

Globalization has meant that many of the world's religions are now transnational, and no longer tied to particular geographical locations, countries or cultures. A wide range of different religions has spread across the globe, creating more religious diversity. Despite suggestions that participation in traditional religions has declined in most European countries, there continues to be a great deal of religious activity in the world today.

Applying material from **Item B** and your knowledge, evaluate the view that globalization has led to major changes in religious beliefs and practices in the world today.   **(20 marks)**

CHAPTER SUMMARY AND REVISION CHECKLIST

After studying this chapter you should be able to:

- Explain what is meant by religion, ideology and science, and the differences between them

- Outline pluralist, Marxist and feminist accounts of ideology

- Explain different views of science and the scientific method, including the concepts of falsification and paradigms, and the various factors influencing the social construction of scientific knowledge

- Explain the concept of modernity, and examine the extent to which science has displaced religious belief

- Explain the difference between the inclusivist and exclusivist definitions of religion

- Explain and criticize different theoretical approaches to the role of religion in society, including the functionalist, Marxist, interpretivist, feminist, Weberian and postmodernist approaches

- Explain, with evidence, the various ways religion can act as a conservative force and as a force for social change

- Identify and explain the factors that influence how and whether or not religion will influence social change

- Explain, with examples, what is meant by the concepts of church, denomination, sect and cult, and the differences between them

- Explain the meanings of world-accommodating, world-affirming and world-rejecting groups, and the differences between them

- Explain the meanings of, and differences between, audience and client cults and cult movements

- Explain, with examples, what new religious movements and New Age groups are, who might support them and why

- Explain and criticize the view that sects are necessarily short-lived organizations

- Examine the evidence and explanations for why, in general, women are more religious than men

- Discuss the view that religious organizations are mainly patriarchal institutions

- Examine the links between minority ethnic groups and religion, and why religiosity appears to be higher in minority ethnic groups

- Examine the extent to which younger people are less religious than older people, and reasons for this

- Explain what is meant by secularization, why it may be occurring, and the theoretical and methodological difficulties involved in defining and measuring it, and examine a range of arguments and evidence both for and against the view that it is occurring, both in the UK and globally

- Explain how postmodernists see religion in contemporary societies, and what is meant by 'pick 'n' mix' spirituality, the 'spiritual supermarket' and Disneyization

- Describe religious market and existential security theories, and how these might explain why some countries might be experiencing secularization, while others are not

- Explain how globalization affects religion, including the view that contemporary societies are becoming more secular.

KEY TERMS

Definitions can be found in the glossary at the end of this book, as well as these terms being defined in the margin where they first appear in the chapter.

alienation	empirical evidence	millenarianism	scientism
anomie	ethnic identity	minority ethnic group	secularization
beliefs	ethnicity	modernity	social solidarity
closed belief system	existential security	objectivity	status frustration
collective conscience	functional prerequisites	open belief system	structural differentiation
conservative force	fundamentalism	paradigm	stigmatized identity
cultural defence	globalization	patriarchal ideology	theodicy
cultural imperialism	hegemony	pluralism	theodicy of disprivilege
cultural transition	ideal type	pluralist ideology	totem
desacralization	ideological state apparatus	relative deprivation	typology
deterritorialization	ideology	religiosity	universe of meaning
disenchantment	Islamophobia	religious market theory	value consensus
Disneyization	marginalization	religious pluralism	value freedom
dominant ideology	metanarrative	resacralization	

There are a variety of free tests and other activities that can be used to assess your learning at

www.politybooks.com/browne
You can also find new contemporary resources by following @BrowneKen on Twitter.

See also the revision guide to accompany this book:
Sociology for AQA Revision Guide 2: 2nd-Year A level

Please note that the above resources have not been endorsed by AQA.

PRACTICE QUESTION

Topic B1 Beliefs in Society

Answer **all** the questions on this topic   **Time allowed: 1 hour**

| 1 | 3 | Outline and explain **two** ways in which the emergence of religious fundamentalism may be a consequence of globalization.   **[10 marks]**

| 1 | 4 | Read **Item A** below and answer the question that follows.

Item A

Churches and denominations are generally seen as fairly respectable and mainstream organizations, whereas sects and cults tend to be seen as more deviant. Media treatment of sects and cults has meant they are associated in the popular imagination (often quite unfairly) with groups seen as evil, controlling, extremist and manipulative, as brainwashing their members, and as harmful to both their own members and the wider society.

Applying material from **Item A**, analyse **two** ways in which churches and denominations may differ from sects and cults.   **[10 marks]**

| 1 | 5 | Read **Item B** below and answer the question that follows.

Item B

Metanarratives are general theories or belief systems that claim to provide comprehensive explanations and knowledge of the world. Postmodernists see secularization arising in part from the general collapse of metanarratives. Secularization has relegated traditional religious beliefs and organizations to the margins of contemporary society. Personalized beliefs have replaced the metanarrative of religion, and people pick 'n' mix whatever beliefs they choose from a global spiritual supermarket.

Applying material from **Item B** and your knowledge, evaluate the view that religion is of declining significance in people's lives in the world today.   **[20 marks]**

CHAPTER

2

Global Development

JONATHAN BLUNDELL

SPECIFICATION TOPICS

- **Topic 1**: Development, underdevelopment and global inequality
- **Topic 2**: Globalisation and its influence on the cultural, political and economic relationships between societies
- **Topic 3**: The role of transnational corporations, non-governmental organisations and international agencies in local and global strategies for development
- **Topic 4**: Development in relation to aid and trade, industrialisation, urbanisation, the environment, war and conflict
- **Topic 5**: Employment, education, health, demographic change and gender as aspects of development

Contents

CHAPTER
2

Global Development

Topic 1

SPECIFICATION AREA

Development, underdevelopment and global inequality

Introduction

The topic of global **development** is about global divisions between the rich and privileged on the one hand and the poor and underprivileged on the other, and about the attempts to eliminate those divisions. The world today is more unequal than ever before.

Development: the process by which societies change; a controversial term, with different writers having different conceptions of what processes are involved and what the outcome should be.

> **Activity**
>
> Here are some resources that will help you gain an understanding of development issues, and that you can return to as your studies progress.
> 1 Visit www.gapminder.org. This website, run by Hans Rosling, provides a lot of data on development and allows users to map development against a wide range of criteria. You will also find several talks by Rosling on the TED web site.
> 2 Visit www.worldmapper.org
>   Hundreds of maps of the world, covering many issues and providing you with new ways of seeing the world.
> 3 There are a number of films and television programmes that can help your understanding of this topic area:
>   The film *Black Gold* (2006) uses a case study of coffee in Ethiopia to explore issues about trade, aid and the role of transnational corporations.
>   Eight films for television called 'Why Poverty?' are available free online at www.whypoverty.net, and there are supporting resources provided by the Open University.
> 4 The *New Internationalist* is a monthly magazine devoted to development issues. Its website is www.newint.org.
> 5 For current events and analysis of them, follow the *Guardian* newspaper's Development section www.theguardian.com/global-development. The *Guardian* website has many useful articles, including audio and video.

Defining and measuring development

What is meant by development?

Development is the most important concept in this area of sociology. The term is used in several different but related ways, which can be summed up as 'good change'. It is the first and third senses – as given in figure 2.1 below – of development as an ideal state to be achieved by human effort, which are the most common meanings adopted in this book (Thomas 2000).

What is meant by 'good change'?

Economic growth: the growth of national income, usually measured by Gross National Income.

First, economic development – or economic growth – means that an economy gets bigger, producing more goods or goods of higher value. Economic development involves a change from an economy based on subsistence agriculture and small workshops to factory-based mass production of goods, mass consumption and service industries such as finance and banking. Economic growth means a rise in living standards and less poverty, but not everyone will benefit equally, and some may lose out. Economic growth also affects the environment.

Second, social development covers a range of aspects of social life, including:

Sustainability means that something can continue at the same level indefinitely; for example, using trees from a forest for fuel is sustainable only if the wood is taken at the rate that the trees grow, so that the number of trees in the forest remains constant.

- Education
- Health
- Democracy
- Human rights
- Gender equality
- Happiness and well-being
- Sustainability.

Finally, combining both economic and social aspects is the idea of development as the reduction or eradication of poverty.

Measuring development: how do we know when countries are developing?

Economic well-being

Gross National Income (GNI) is the total value of goods and services produced by a country in a particular year.

The economic well-being of a society is usually measured by Gross National Income (GNI). This measures the total value of goods and services produced in an economy in a year. GNI is usually given as a 'per capita' (per person in the population) figure to allow for differences in size of populations between countries, and is given in US dollars. GNI figures reveal the dramatic scale of inequality between the developed and developing worlds.

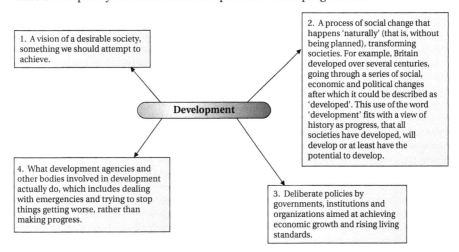

1. A vision of a desirable society, something we should attempt to achieve.

2. A process of social change that happens 'naturally' (that is, without being planned), transforming societies. For example, Britain developed over several centuries, going through a series of social, economic and political changes after which it could be described as 'developed'. This use of the word 'development' fits with a view of history as progress, that all societies have developed, will develop or at least have the potential to develop.

Development

4. What development agencies and other bodies involved in development actually do, which includes dealing with emergencies and trying to stop things getting worse, rather than making progress.

3. Deliberate policies by governments, institutions and organizations aimed at achieving economic growth and rising living standards.

Figure 2.1 The meaning of development

Changes in GNI from year to year give a measure of economic growth. At the moment, some economies in the developing world, such as China and India, are experiencing rapid growth, faster than developed countries both now and in the past. At the same time, some economies, notably in Africa, have suffered a fall in GNI, from already low levels, over recent years. Sociologists use GNI with caution, and in combination with other measures, for a number of reasons:

1   Economic growth does not cover all the aspects of social development which sociologists are interested in; a rise in GNI per capita does not necessarily mean that education, health and so on are improving.
2   GNI per capita is an average for the whole population, and so conceals inequalities. A high GNI does not necessarily mean a high standard of living for all members of the population. This applies even to developed countries, where a high GNI per capita can conceal significant minorities living in poverty.
3   GNI only counts what happens in the 'official' economy; some important activities are outside the market and are not counted, such as growing food for one's own consumption. These are likely to be more important in developing countries than in developed countries; moreover, they are often activities carried out by women, so that GNI can be seen as a gender-biased measure (Storey 2003: 30).
4   Continuous economic growth is very unlikely to mean **sustainable development**. A rise in GNI can also be accompanied by problems such as rising crime rates and the loss of community as well as environmental degradation.
5   It is difficult to calculate GNI accurately. In 2008, the size of Ghana's economy was recalculated, and estimated to be 60 per cent higher than previously thought. About $23 billion of economic activity had been missed out; Ghana moved from being a low- to a lower-middle-income country (Jerven 2012).

Social development

Some commonly used measures include:

1   Education: the percentage of school-age children attending school; and literacy (the proportion of the population who can read and write).
2   Health: child and infant mortality rates; mortality rates in general; maternal mortality rates; the number of doctors and hospitals in relation to population.
3   Democracy: whether there are free and fair elections, in which everyone can vote; whether opposition parties are allowed to organize.
4   Gender equality: differences between males and females in education, health, politics and other measures.

Several measures of development combine different indicators of development to create a score for each country. Countries can then be put in rank order, and changes over time can be measured.

The Human Development Index

The most important of these measures is the **Human Development Index** (HDI), produced by the United Nations Development Programme (UNDP). Each country is given an HDI score which is calculated by considering what the UNDP takes to be the three most important aspects of development, covering both economic and social aspects:

1   Material standard of living (measured by Gross National Income per capita).
2   Education (measured by the mean years of schooling that those aged 25 had and the expected years of schooling of children of school entering age).
3   Health (measured by life expectancy).

Each country's score is between 0 and 1, with 1 being the highest. Countries can then be ranked in order of HDI score. The 2014 *Human Development Report* showed Norway, Australia and Switzerland at the top. The lowest-ranking countries were Niger, the Democratic Republic of

Sustainable development is development that sustains the natural environment, thereby ensuring that **future generations** can have the same level of development.

The term '**future generations**' means that the concept of sustainable development requires consideration of the future of today's children, and also of people not yet born, even though there is no established way of representing their interests.

The **Human Development Index** is a composite measure of social and economic indicators, giving a statistical value to the level of development.

Congo and the Central African Republic. The HDI also classifies countries as having very high, high, medium or low human development. There were 102 countries classified as having very high or high human development and 43 as having low human development. Of the thirty countries with the lowest human development, twenty-seven were in Africa.

In many developing countries, there are doubts about the accuracy of some of the statistics used because of the difficulties in collecting data; figures are not always available for all countries. It can also be argued that not all important aspects of development can be measured quantitatively. The three measures of development seem rather arbitrary (there are other ways of measuring health and education) and they are equally weighted. Nevertheless, HDI is useful in giving a broad impression of development and of the links between the economy and social well-being. In addition, the reports in which the HDIs are published have broadened the scope of development by covering, for example, human rights and political freedoms and sustainability.

It is instructive to compare the GNI and HDI of nations. Countries that are much higher in the HDI table than they are in the GNI table are those where the wealth created is being used for social development. Examples include Cuba, New Zealand, Uruguay and Sri Lanka. On the other hand, where countries are lower in the HDI table than in the GNI table, this suggests that the wealth is not being used for social development. Examples include Equatorial Guinea, Gabon, Saudi Arabia and the United Arab Emirates.

Table 2.1 Highest- and lowest-ranking countries, by HDI and by GNI per capita, 2013

Highest-ranking countries by HDI, 2013		Highest-ranking countries by GNI per capita, 2013	
1	Norway	1	Qatar $119,029
2	Australia	2	Liechtenstein $87,085
3	Switzerland	3	Kuwait $85,820
4	Netherlands	4	Singapore $72,371
5	United States	5	Brunei Darussalam $70,883
6	Germany	6	Norway $63,909
7	New Zealand	7	Luxembourg $58,695
8	Canada	8	United Arab Emirates $58,068
9	Singapore	9	Switzerland $53,762
10	Denmark	10	United States $52,308
...		...	
14	United Kingdom	28	United Kingdom ($35,002)
Lowest-ranking countries by HDI, 2013		**Lowest-ranking countries by GNI per capita, 2013**	
178	Mozambique	178	Eritrea $1,147
179	Guinea	179	Guinea $1,142
180	Burundi	180	Togo $1,129
181	Burkina Faso	181	Guinea-Bissau $1,090
182	Eritrea	182	Niger $873
183	Sierra Leone	183	Liberia $752
184	Chad	184	Burundi $749
185	Central African Republic	185	Malawi $715
186	Democratic Republic of The Congo	186	Central African Republic $588
186	Niger	187	Democratic Republic of The Congo $444

Source: data from *Human Development Report* 2014 (http://hdr.undp.org/en)

Activity

Use the data above and the *Human Development Report* website (http://hdr.undp.org/en) to investigate:
- Which countries score highly on both GNI and human development;
- For which countries are there major differences between their rankings for these two measures? What might account for these differences?

The *Human Development Report* includes three other indices of development:

1 *The Multidimensional Poverty Index (MPI)*: this is a new measure which has replaced the Human Poverty Index. It sees poverty as multidimensional, looking at measures of health, education and living standards.
2 *The Gender Inequality Index (GII)*: this measures the disadvantages faced by girls and women in reproductive health, empowerment (measured by educational attainment and parliamentary representation) and participation in the labour market.
3 *The Inequality-adjusted Human Development Index (IHDI)*: if a country's people are all equal, its IHDI is the same as its HDI; if not, the IHDI goes down. The difference can be given as a percentage.

Alternative indicators

These represent attempts to broaden what is meant by development to include factors seen to be important but which are difficult to quantify.

Gross National Happiness

In 1972 the King of Bhutan, in response to criticisms of his country's slow economic growth, proposed a plan for development that rejected the pursuit of economic growth as a good in itself and reflected Bhutan's Buddhist values. Gross National Happiness also takes into account spiritual and psychological aspects of development. www.grossnationalhappiness.com

Happy Planet Index

This measure, created by the New Economics Foundation, gives a higher score to countries with smaller ecological footprints. It also includes experienced well-being and life expectancy. Costa Rica was at the top of this index in 2014. www.happyplanetindex.org.

Good Country Index

This new measure tries to quantify the contribution each country makes to what it calls 'the common good of humanity' rather than their own leaders, businesses and citizens. www.goodcountry.org.

Measuring poverty

The poverty of whole countries can be measured by GNI, but for individuals and households a different measure is needed, because GNI can only give an average. As a criterion for measuring success in achieving the **Millennium Development Goal** (MDG) of halving the proportion of people living in extreme poverty by 2015, the World Bank uses income of less than US$1.25 a day, adjusted for purchasing power. On this definition, about 1.2 billion people live in poverty.

Having less than US$1.25 dollars a day to live on is a measure of *absolute* poverty; another way of conceptualizing poverty is by defining it in relation to others – this is called *relative* poverty. For example, poverty might be defined as living on half the mean income in society, or being excluded from full participation in society. The poverty line is set at a higher level for developed countries

Millennium Development Goals were a set of eight development goals adopted by the United Nations in 2000, to be achieved by 2015.

Having less than US$1.25 a day to live on has very different consequences in different parts of the world, e.g. an industrial city in the UK compared to a slum in South Africa. What sorts of issues need to be considered when measuring poverty?

because it is necessary to have a minimum level of consumer items to take part in what is accepted as normal everyday life.

The Indian economist Amartya Sen argues that development is about overcoming poverty because this allows people to develop their potential – it increases human freedom. Improving health and education and gaining greater political freedom are both ways of achieving development and its goals. His work focuses on measuring poverty as a means towards greater development (Sen 1999).

The Millennium Development Goals (MDGs)

Development was also measured by progress towards the Millennium Development Goals. These were set by the United Nations as targets for the world to achieve by the end of 2015; they can be seen as representing agreement by the world's nations on how development can be defined in specific terms. The goals are shown in Table 2.2

Table 2.2 Millennium Development Goals

Goal	Target		Assessment
1		Eradicate extreme poverty and hunger	
	1A	Halve, between 1990 and 2015, the proportion of people whose income is less than $1.25 a day	Achieved by 2010 but this still leaves more than 1 billion people below this income
	1B	Achieve full and productive employment and decent work for all, including women and young people	Fewer workers are below the poverty line but there is still a gender gap
	1C	Halve, between 1990 and 2015, the proportion of people who suffer from hunger	Expected to be almost met but this still leaves 842 million undernourished people
2		Achieve universal primary education	
	2A	Ensure that, by 2015, children everywhere, boys and girls alike, will be able to complete a full course of primary schooling	Primary school enrolment is up to 90 per cent but 58 million children still do not go to school and there are concerns about the quality of education offered
3		Promote gender equality and empower women	

Table 2.2 (continued)

Goal	Target		Assessment
	3A	Eliminate gender disparity in primary and secondary education, preferably by 2005, and in all levels of education no later than 2015	Equality has been achieved in primary education but women still experience inequality at other levels
4		To reduce child mortality	
	4A	Reduce by two-thirds, between 1990 and 2015, the under-five mortality rate	17,000 fewer children die each day than in 1990 but each year more than 6 million children still die before their fifth birthday
5		To improve maternal health	
	5A	Reduce by three-quarters, between 1990 and 2015, the maternal mortality ratio	Maternal mortality has fallen by 45 per cent
	5B	Achieve, by 2015, universal access to reproductive health	Only half of women in developing countries receive the recommended healthcare during pregnancy
6		To combat HIV/AIDS, malaria and other diseases	
	6A	Have halted by 2015 and begun to reverse the spread of HIV/AIDS	New HIV infections of adults fell by 44 per cent from 2001 to 2012
	6B	Achieve, by 2010, universal access to treatment for HIV/AIDS for all those who need it	9.5 million people in developing countries receive retroviral treatments
	6C	Have halted by 2015 and begun to reverse the incidence of malaria and other major diseases	42 per cent fall in malaria mortality between 2000 and 2012 but malaria still killed an estimated 627,000 people in 2012
7		To ensure environmental sustainability	
	7A	Integrate the principles of sustainable development into country policies and programmes and reverse the loss of environmental resources	Global emissions of CO_2 are increasing and we are losing forests at an alarming rate
	7B	Reduce biodiversity loss, achieving, by 2010, a significant reduction in the rate of loss	14 per cent of land and coastal marine ecosystem areas are now protected
	7C	Halve, by 2015, the proportion of the population without sustainable access to safe drinking water and basic sanitation	Met five years ahead of schedule but 2.5 billion people still lack basic sanitation such as toilets or latrines
	7D	Achieve, by 2020, a significant improvement in the lives of at least 100 million slum dwellers	Already met but 863 million people live in slums
8		To develop a global partnership for development	
	8A	Develop further an open, rule-based, predictable, non-discriminatory trading and financial system	Official aid is higher than ever

Table 2.2 (continued)

Goal	Target		Assessment
	8B	Address the special needs of least developed countries	Aid has shifted away from the poorest countries
	8C	Address the special needs of landlocked developing countries and small island developing states	These states now receive more aid
	8D	Deal comprehensively with the debt problems of developing countries	The debt burden has been reduced
	8E	In cooperation with pharmaceutical companies, provide access to affordable essential drugs in developing countries	Little improvement
	8F	In cooperation with the private sector, make available benefits of new technologies, especially information and communications	Big increase in numbers online but still less than half the world's people

Source: www.un.org/millenniumgoals/global.shtml

> **International governmental organizations** (IGOs) are organizations established by states, such as the IMF, the World Bank and the World Trade Organization (WTO).

By early 2015, some goals had been met but it was clear that others would not be met. Some targets were unrealistically ambitious for some countries, and the commitment by richer countries to help achieve them was sometimes lacking. But the MDGs do seem to have been useful in focusing the world's states, international governmental organizations (IGOs) and non-governmental organizations (NGOs) on outcomes, and they probably were responsible for increases in aid, which doubled between 2000 and 2005. In September 2015 a new set of goals, the Sustainable Development Goals (SDGs), was adopted by the United Nations. There are 17 goals, and 169 targets. Some goals reflect how ideas have changed since 2000; for example, there is now a much greater emphasis on environmental issues and sustainability. Other goals are a response to criticisms of the MDGs. For example, achieving the MDG of halving the number of people living on less than US$1.25 still left a billion people in poverty, so the new SDG is to eliminate extreme poverty completely. The SDG on education focuses on the quality of education now that most children do receive primary education.

> **Non-governmental organizations** (NGOs) are non-profit groups which are independent of the state; they are largely funded by private contributions and are mostly involved in humanitarian activities.

Activity

The post-2015 development agenda: the Sustainable Development Goals (SDGs)

Visit this website to find out about the 17 SDGs. Each of the icons leads to a page explaining the goal and why it matters in development. For each goal, work out whether it is new or whether it builds on the Millennium Development Goals. If the goal does build on the MDGs, what has changed and why? www.undp.org/content/undp/en/home/mdgoverview.

Terminology

There is no agreement about the right terms to use to describe the ways in which the world is divided. Always choose the terms you use carefully for your purpose, and note that the terms used by different writers may indicate assumptions and judgements. In this chapter we have used a variety of terms depending on the context.

Three Worlds

Dating back to the period of the Cold War (1948–89), one of the conventional ways of describing differences between groups of countries has been to divide the world into three:

1 *First World*: the industrialized capitalist world – USA, Western Europe, Japan, Australia, New Zealand.
2 *Second World*: the industrialized communist world – the Soviet Union and its Eastern European satellites (Poland, Bulgaria, Czechoslovakia, Hungary, etc.).
3 *Third World*: the rest of the world – Central and South America and the Caribbean, Africa, Asia and the Middle East.

The terms 'First' and 'Second World' were (and still are) much less used than 'Third World'. The Third World covered a vast range of countries in different circumstances and at different stages of development. The idea of a distinct group made sense because many countries saw themselves as having a shared interest against the superpowers, and joined together in a non-aligned movement (that is, not aligned to either the USA or the Soviet Union). Many of these countries actively sought a 'third way' between capitalism and communism. In addition, almost all shared the experience of having recently been colonies of European powers.

After the collapse of the Soviet Union in the late 1980s there was no Second World, and the term Third World became used less. Around the same time, it became obvious that some Third World countries were developing and others were not; differences within the Third World became more distinct, and it no longer seemed sensible to treat it as a single group. The non-aligned movement also became less important; the Third World acted even less as a unified group.

North and South (and West)

The developed, industrialized countries are mainly in the northern hemisphere and the poorer, undeveloped countries in the tropics or further south. From the 1970s on, the former became referred to as the North and the latter as the South. The distinction was used by the Brandt Commission, which recommended strategies to reduce world poverty in 1980 (Brandt 1980).

This is a geographical way of distinguishing between countries that involves two groupings rather than three. The term 'West' is also often used as a shorthand way of meaning the most industrialized and wealthiest countries. The main problem with this approach is that not all countries fit neatly into the geographical pattern. For example, Australia and New Zealand are geographically in the south but in terms of development, they belong in the category of North.

Majority and minority worlds

These two terms are a more recent attempt to describe more accurately the state of the world, but their use has not become widespread. 'Majority' refers to the Third World and to the fact that two-thirds or more of the world's population live there; 'minority' refers to the rich world, drawing attention to the fact that the living standards of the rich world are available only to a privileged minority of the world's population.

Developed and undeveloped countries

The difference between 'undeveloped' and 'underdeveloped' is one of perspective. 'Undeveloped' suggests that the poor world is simply further behind and can catch up; it has not yet experienced progress. 'Underdeveloped' suggests that the poor world has been made poor through exploitation by what has become the rich world. The significance of these terms will be explained in the later section on modernization and dependency theories.

The Sustainable Development Goals (SDGs) are a set of 17 development goals adopted by the United Nations in 2015, to be achieved by 2030 and replacing the earlier Millennium Development Goals (MDGs).

Industrialized countries are those whose economies are based on industry rather than on agriculture or extraction.

The **Third World** is a term used to describe the world's poorer countries, distinct from the First World (developed capitalist) and Second World (developed communist, or, today, ex-communist).

Capitalism is an economic system in which investment in and ownership of the means of production, distribution and exchange of wealth is made and maintained chiefly by private individuals or corporations, whose primary aim is to make profits.

North refers to the world's richer countries – developed nations; sometimes known as the 'Global North' or the 'first world'.

MEDCs, LEDCs, LLEDCs

More economically developed countries (MEDCs), less economically developed countries (LEDCs) and least economically developed countries (LLEDCs) are terms used to refer to economic development, with social development being assumed to go with this. Although these terms demonstrate the hierarchical nature of the world today, they inevitably put into the same category countries that are actually very different.

South refers to the world's poorer countries, those that are developing; sometimes, the 'Global South'.

The bottom billion

The **bottom billion** is Collier's term for the poorest billion of the world's population – also described as 'Africa plus'.

The economist Paul Collier (2007) has used the term the 'bottom billion' as a way of acknowledging that many parts of what were once described as the Third World have achieved some degree of development. The remaining problem, Collier argues, is the lack of development in most of Africa and in a fairly small number of other countries (including Haiti, Bolivia, the central Asian countries, Laos, Cambodia, Yemen, Burma and North Korea), which are affected by war and other factors. Collier refers to these 58 countries together as 'Africa plus'. They account for about a sixth of the world's people, though most of the countries are small and, even combined, they have fewer people than either China or India. Collier argues that in India, China and other countries that are achieving some level of development, economic growth will eventually bring progress on social indicators, so the world needs to concentrate its efforts on the countries of the bottom billion, where economic growth is non-existent or too small to make a difference. The Millennium Development Goals, in Collier's view, were misguided, because the focus needs to be on the bottom billion only.

All the terms discussed above are about differences between countries. However, most countries are in some ways both developed and underdeveloped. There are extremes of rich and poor within as well as between countries. There are people in poor countries who are incredibly wealthy by any standards, while most rich countries have substantial numbers living in poverty. Within all countries, there are also structured inequalities of gender and ethnicity.

Theories of development

Modernization theory

The dominant theory of development over the past fifty years has been modernization theory; it is related to and overlaps with the broader sociological perspective, functionalism.

Modernization **theory** was the dominant development theory of the 1960s, based on factors internal to Third World countries inhibiting their development.

Modernization theory arose in the early 1960s, during the Cold War period. It assumed that development means capitalist development and offered the newly independent nations of the Third World a route out of poverty provided they adopted Western, capitalist ways. After the Second World War, in 1947, the USA launched the Marshall Plan to rebuild the shattered economies of Western European countries, including the UK, France, West Germany and Italy, at a cost of US$17 billion. The success of the Marshall Plan, which also ensured that the European economies provided markets for the USA's growing manufacturing industries, was seen as a precedent for the Third World. The generosity of the USA and its allies, providing technological and other assistance, would lift the rest of the world out of poverty.

Modernization theory is closely associated with American policies, and its best-known exponent, W. W. Rostow, worked in the US State Department. The theory sets out to explain how, following the example of Western nations, poorer countries could achieve development through economic growth, and also how communism could not be the way to achieve development. The theory needs to be seen in the context of the Cold War, with the USA offering reasons to newly independent countries to encourage them to ally themselves with the West and not with the Soviet Union. Rostow subtitled his most popular work 'an anti-communist manifesto' and described communism as 'a kind of disease which can befall a transitional society if it fails to organize effectively those elements within it which are prepared to get on with the job of modernization' (1960: 164).

Modernization theory is essentially an ethnocentric approach; it argues that the only route to development is to follow the example of the USA, and success is measured by whether the economy is based on mass consumption, as in the USA. The USA and other developed countries are seen as having reached the destination of being modern; the rest of the world is behind, needing to follow the same road in order eventually to catch up – following in the footsteps of the West.

From traditional to modern

For modernization theorists, the process of development meant 'total change': poorer countries had to move from being traditional to being modern. The changes needed included:

1 Technological – from simple and traditional technology to applying scientific knowledge and using more advanced technology.
2 Agricultural – from subsistence farming to commercial production.
3 Industrial – from using human/animal power to machines.
4 Geographical – from farm and village to town and city – urbanization.
5 Political – from hereditary chiefs and kings to liberal democracy.
6 Social and cultural – from extended kin groups to nuclear families; from traditional to modern values and attitudes – such as from instant to deferred gratification – and becoming entrepreneurial.

The dichotomy between traditional and modern can also be found in the work of the structural functionalist sociologist Talcott Parsons. For Parsons, the most significant differences between traditional and modern societies were that the former were collective and based on ascribed status, whereas modern societies were individualized and based on achieved status. Parsons argued that societies passed through evolutionary stages, marked by 'evolutionary universals' such as the decline of traditional kinship patterns like the extended family and the emergence

Many developing countries model themselves on developed nations with the aim of 'modernization' – such as Shanghai in China following the precedent of New York's skyscrapers

of a system of stratification. The dichotomy between traditional and modern is questionable, because some of the supposed characteristics of traditional societies survive even in the most developed societies, and some supposed characteristics of modern societies can be found in less developed societies.

What prevents development?

According to modernization theorists, obstacles to development are internal to the poorer countries, and include:

- Having traditional values and attitudes
- A lack of necessary modern values and attitudes. Modern values that are needed include deferred gratification and what McClelland referred to as the 'need for achievement', so that, for example, people would be willing to work for longer than necessary and willing to move to where there were jobs
- High birth rates and rapid population growth – because of traditional values, people want to have too many children
- A shortage of people with entrepreneurial skills and a desire to compete and succeed in business
- A lack of the necessary institutions and organizations for economic growth, such as banks, and lacking capital
- A lack of the necessary technology.

Need for achievement refers, in modernization theory, to the desire to be entrepreneurial and to make money, essential for modernization.

Differences within modernization theory

Emphasis on economic modernization

Rostow (1960) argued that societies need to pass through five **stages of economic growth** (see table 2.3). He suggests that there is a period of about sixty years from take-off to maturity. It was therefore possible to foresee the whole world having achieved American standards by the mid twenty-first century.

Rostow saw the role of the USA as providing assistance to poorer countries, supplying them with some of what they needed in order to modernize – capital, expertise and technology such as tractors – and putting them on a 'fast track' to modernization. Generating economic growth would mean people being paid higher wages and the income generated would eventually 'trickle down' to the whole population. Most importantly, the goodwill towards the USA that this would create would ensure that the countries helped in this way would become American allies in the Cold War.

Stages of economic growth refers, in Rostow's version of modernization, to the five stages through which societies pass as they move from being traditional to fully developed.

Emphasis on social obstacles

Functionalists such as Hoselitz (1952) applied the functionalist model of change to the Third World and argued that developing countries needed to modernize socially and culturally as well as economically. Obstacles to modernization included social systems that impeded social mobility and getting people to accept new patterns of work. They saw the main assets of modern society as being educational opportunity, individual freedom and the rule of law. Other methods suggested for achieving the transition to modern values and attitudes included:

- Cities could act as centres of Western values and spread them to rural areas
- Education – not only Western-style schools in the Third World, but also bringing the future rulers of developing countries to schools and universities in the USA and Western Europe so that they would absorb Western values
- Mass media – radio in particular could be used to spread Western ideas.

Modernization theory today

Like functionalism in sociology more generally, modernization theory tends to be dismissed as no longer being of great relevance. Yet, like functionalism, it has laid foundations that prove durable, for example:

1 Communism proved not to be a way to achieve development; China's economic growth under a communist government has been achieved through capitalism. Western standards

Table 2.3 Rostow's five stages of economic growth

Stage 1	Traditional societies based on **subsistence farming**. There is limited wealth, and traditional values hold back social change.
Stage 2	Preconditions for **take-off**. Western values and practices begin to take hold, establishing the conditions that are necessary for development. There may be new technologies to modernize agriculture, improvements in infrastructure such as roads and bridges, more education, and money to invest in business. These provide the fuel for 'take-off' in stage 3.
Stage 3	Take-off. The society's economy grows as modern values and practices pay off; the changes become self-reinforcing. A new class emerges which is willing to take risks in investing in business – a sign of traditional values being eroded. The society begins to produce on a large scale, including for export, and the newly created wealth begins to reach the mass of the population.
Stage 4	Drive to maturity. The economic benefits produced in stage 3 continue and investment in education, health services and mass media lead to rising living standards. The society is now becoming modern.
Stage 5	Age of high mass consumption. The society achieves the kind of levels the USA had reached by the 1960s: high mass consumption; high standards of living for most with access to education and health; most people living in cities; and so on.

Subsistence farming is a system whereby crops and livestock are produced for consumption by the family rather than for sale in the market.

Take-off, in Rostow's five stages of economic growth, is the third stage, at which societies achieve a momentum that ensures development.

of economic growth and of consumption remain the aspiration of many in developing countries.

2 The rich countries continue to use development aid to try to help poorer countries develop.

3 Rostow saw India and China as being at the stage of take-off in the late 1950s; his estimate of sixty years to maturity seems prescient given recent growth rates in those countries.

Dependency theory

Dependency theory developed in the 1970s as a response to modernization theory. In many respects, it is the opposite of modernization theory, although they agree on the importance of economic growth and of state-led industrialization. Like modernization theory, dependency theory originated in the Cold War period. Alternative and revolutionary movements were strong in many parts of the Third World as well as in the West. Dependency theory developed at a time when Marxist and radical theories were strong, and at a time when protest movements, such as that against the war in Vietnam and those for greater rights for women and for minorities, were widespread.

Where modernization theory comes clearly from the developed world, dependency theory takes the perspective of developing countries; it can be seen as 'a view from the South'. Much of it is based on analysis of Latin American economies, such as the work of the best-known dependency theorist, André Gunder Frank (1969). For Frank, development and **underdevelopment** are two sides of the same coin; the underdevelopment of the Third World made possible the development of the West. Similar conclusions were reached by writers studying other parts of the world – for example, Samir Amin's study of Côte d'Ivoire in West Africa (1976). The title of Walter Rodney's book *How Europe Underdeveloped Africa* (1972) sums up the dependency approach.

Dependency theory is an alternative Marxist-influenced theory to modernization, focused on external factors which impede development, including relationships with developed countries.

Underdevelopment is a term used by dependency theorists to describe the process of exploitation by which the North became and stayed rich at the expense of the South.

What prevents development?

Unlike modernization theory, dependency theory sees the obstacles to development as imposed from outside rather than being internal. Third World countries have been forced into a position of

Colonialism is a system in which European powers had direct political control over most of today's developing countries.

Neo-colonialism refers to the continuation of past economic domination by former colonial powers over ex-colonies.

Metropolis refers, in dependency theory, to the centre of economic activity, profiting from an exploitative relationship with satellites.

Satellite refers, in dependency theory, to the deformed and dependent economies of the underdeveloped countries.

dependency on the developed world. The end of colonialism did not end exploitation, only bringing in neo- (new) colonialism, whereby the exploitation continues but is less direct and obvious. Political independence is not enough to allow poor countries to escape from their dependency. The problem is the world capitalist system, and, in order to develop, Third World countries need to break away from this system. Relationships with richer countries are the problem, not the solution; where modernization theorists see a helping hand being offered to the less fortunate, dependency theorists see neo-colonialism and exploitation.

The nature of dependency theory

1   It rejects modernization theory – the problems are not internal to Third World countries, but imposed upon them from outside.
2   It is anti-capitalist – capitalism has spread all over the world, but is a system based on exploitation.
3   The situation today is seen as a direct result of the history of capitalism, world trade and colonialism. This contrasts with modernization theory, which tends to assume that the historical experience of Third World countries is unimportant.
4   The developed capitalist countries benefit by cheap access to raw materials and markets for manufactured goods.
5   Dependency theory led to an emphasis in Third World countries on nationalism, national unity and self-reliance, rather than a reliance on aid.

How is underdevelopment seen by dependency theorists?

The developed countries have made the poorer countries poor, and it is in their interests to keep them poor – by, in Ha Joon Chang's metaphor, 'kicking the ladder away' (Chang 2003). This happens through a chain of relationships between the metropolis or core nations in the rich world and the satellite or periphery countries of the Third World. This is called the 'chain of dependency'. The development of the metropolis causes the underdevelopment of the satellite. The metropolis 'buys off' the elites of poorer countries by allowing them a small share of the profits. This ensures that most poor countries are ruled by groups, sometimes called the comprador bourgeoisie, that are involved in exploiting their own people and whose interests involve preventing changes which would benefit the majority of the people. These groups are exactly those that modernization theorists would expect to lead their country's development.

How did we reach this situation?

Dependency theorists see history as essential to understanding the situation we are in today. They point out that the rich countries were never underdeveloped in the sense of being dominated and exploited; they are better described as having been undeveloped (Frank 1966). The historical experiences of developing countries mean that they are in a very different situation, and cannot follow in the footsteps of the West as suggested by modernization theorists. Moreover, the spread of capitalism will lead to greater underdevelopment, not development.

According to dependency theorists, non-Western societies were often wealthy and economically complex when they first came into contact with the West. They cite, for example, the civilizations of the Aztec and the Inca in the Americas before the arrival of Europeans, and the complexity of Chinese and Indian civilizations. It would have seemed unlikely 600 years ago that the European powers would come to dominate the world. The world's leading civilizations were probably Ming Dynasty China, the Inca in Peru and the Ottomans. Europe was relatively poor, ravaged by wars, and had lost a lot of its population in the Black Death. What has happened since can be traced through three broad historical periods, which can be seen as stages of dependency and underdevelopment.

Stage 1: Mercantile capitalism
In the fifteenth and sixteenth centuries, merchants in Europe travelled to many parts of the world in search of goods which would command high prices in Europe, such as spices, cloths and jewels.

Production in Europe of goods that could be traded increased as well. The merchants were often able to impose favourable terms of trade, threatening or using force, and sometimes what happened was plunder and looting rather than trade. This period also saw the beginning of the slave trade and the **triangular trade** involving West Africa, the Americas and Europe, shown in figure 2.2 on the next page. Stable and complex societies that were as economically and socially advanced as the Europeans were damaged and sometimes destroyed by contact with the Europeans. Many suffered huge declines in population through war and disease. Small numbers of Spanish explorers looted vast quantities of gold and silver in the Americas, destroying civilizations such as the Aztec and Inca. They brought with them Christianity and horses, and diseases that wiped out native peoples such as the Arawak, who had little resistance.

> **Triangular** trade refers to the slave trade linking West Africa, Europe and the Americas.

Stage 2: Colonialism

During this period, which occurred at different times in different parts of the world, the European powers, and particularly Britain and France, took direct political control of lands around the world rather than simply trading with them. The colonies were exploited for cheap food, resources and labour; industries such as cotton in India were destroyed to ensure they could not compete, social divisions were encouraged, and borders that bore no relation to where people lived were imposed. The cash economy was introduced, and people were forced into paid work by the need to pay taxes in cash. Subsistence farming and the cultivation of crops for sale locally were replaced by **cash crops** for export to the colonial power. British people, for example, benefited from tea from India and sugar from the West Indies. These changes led to a lasting legacy of inequality and of economic changes that benefited the colonial powers.

> **Cash crops** are crops grown for sale in the market, and especially for export; colonialism imposed cash crop cultivation as the main form of agriculture in many colonies.

Stage 3: Neo-colonialism

The period of colonialism came to an end for most colonies in the mid twentieth century, when the European powers had been weakened by the world wars. People in the colonies had been influenced by Western ideas about freedom, democracy and independence and demanded the right to rule themselves. In some cases, long and bloody wars were fought, as in Malaysia and Algeria, and the colonial powers gradually relinquished their rule. However, according to dependency theorists, although they gave up direct political control, they did not give up their economic control and the economic dependency of the ex-colonies continued. The newly independent colonies struggled for stability and growth; they had no tradition of self-rule or democracy, and few entrepreneurs. They had to overcome the colonial ideology which had tried to persuade them that the colonial power was benevolent, and that they were unable to rule themselves. The ex-colonies came to rely on aid, continued to be underdeveloped and remained in a state of dependency.

Neo-colonialism and the legacy of colonialism

Dependency theorists argue that the history of developing countries puts them in a fundamentally different situation from that of developed countries before their development. They are locked into one-sided relationships with developed countries, for example, exporting cash crops. They have inherited from colonialism inappropriate political, educational and healthcare systems and institutions. Even the borders between countries, especially in Africa, were fixed by colonial powers and do not correspond to where different groups of people live. Ways in which neocolonialism works today at preventing development, according to dependency theory, include:

- Tied aid, and aid with conditions attached
- Political alliances through which developed countries dominate developing countries
- Transnational corporations
- Terms of trade
- Global finance and debt.

How can underdeveloped countries develop?

For dependency theorists, underdevelopment appears permanent; the only way out of dependency is for an underdeveloped nation to escape from the capitalist system and the 'master–servant'

Figure 2.2 The triangular trade

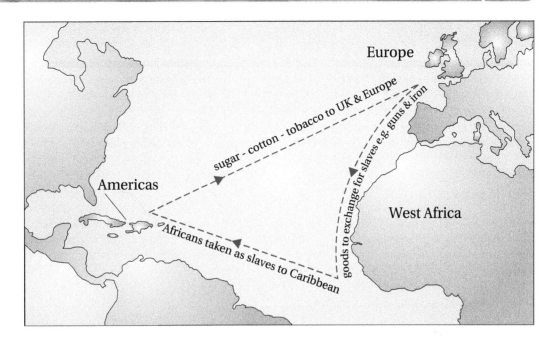

relationship, taking action itself rather than relying on outside help, though it might be able to work with others in the same situation. Action taken would involve:

1 *Development needing to be led by the state itself,* because the national or comprador bourgeoisie are tied to the interests of the First World, and it would involve keeping out foreign capital.
2 *Isolation, which involves an attempt to be self-reliant and to have little contact with the rest of the world* – e.g. China until the 1980s, North Korea even today, and Cambodia under the Khmer Rouge from 1975 to 1979. This is very difficult, because countries attempting this are poor to start with, their only source of money for capital being their own population's savings. These attempts have sometimes been disastrous – for example, China's Great Leap Forward, attempting to transform the country through rapid industrialization, led to famine and millions of deaths.
3 *Breaking away at a time when the metropolitan power is weak,* such as during war or recession. South American countries were able to do this when the European colonial powers such as Spain were weakened by war in the early nineteenth century.
4 *'Associate development' or 'dependent development'.* Some later dependency theorists suggested that limited development is possible even when remaining locked in the capitalist system. For example, industries developed in Brazil and Argentina. This development remains limited, however.

Dependency theory today

Dependency theory never provided much direct guidance to Third World countries on how to develop, having a pessimistic message that any development would be limited. Even communist countries today, such as China, Cuba and North Korea, see a role for the market and are not attempting a completely non-capitalist route to development. In South America, however, a group of nations with left-leaning governments have tried, led by Venezuela under the late Hugo Chavez, to reduce their reliance on the USA and develop an alternative route to development. Dependency theory can be seen more as an analysis of some of the obstacles to development than as a guide to action.

Traditional Marxism

While dependency theory can be described as a neo-Marxist approach, it is clearly different from a traditional Marxist approach to development. Marx himself saw capitalism as a dynamic system with an unmatchable potential for economic growth. Capitalism was the best way to achieve growth; the problem involved the inequalities that were produced at the same time. The traditional Marxist view is that developing countries need capitalism in order to develop. Economic growth under capitalism is progress, and the wealth created can later be distributed equally under socialism. In many ways, traditional Marxism is similar to modernization theory, except that it expects sudden revolutionary change rather than gradual evolutionary change, and that it foresees a further stage, socialism, beyond fully developed capitalism.

This Marxist view, which is far more optimistic about development than dependency theory is, was revived by Bill Warren (1980). Warren claimed to find evidence of industrial growth in Third World economies, indicating that independent development was possible. Colonialism had introduced capitalism to the Third World, where it had taken root. Economic relations with the First World were strengthening independent capitalism, and the absence of growth, or its slow pace in some countries, was more the result of internal factors such as the mistaken policies of Third World governments influenced by dependency theory.

World systems theory

This is associated with the work of Immanuel Wallerstein from the early 1970s onwards and developed from dependency theory, sharing with it a basis in Marxism. Where dependency theorists tended to focus on the experiences and prospects of individual countries, world systems theory describes the world as consisting of a single unified capitalist system: the modern world system (MWS). This comprises a hierarchy of countries from the core (developed), through the semi-periphery (countries such as Brazil and South Africa, with some advanced urban sectors), to the periphery (the least developed). The MWS came into existence as European trade expanded in the late fifteenth and early sixteenth centuries, and, because of its global scale, was a new kind of social

> The **modern world system** (MWS) refers, in world systems theory, to the global capitalist system.

Canary Wharf in London is currently the centre of a large part of the world's financial affairs. However, this is only because UK law has made it an attractive base for large companies, which could easily move to another country in the search for more profit – taking their capital with them

system the world had not experienced before. The processes by which underdeveloped countries are exploited are the same as in dependency theory, with an emphasis on economic issues and on external rather than internal factors. However, the MWS is a dynamic system and countries can move up and down the hierarchy. This is because capitalism does not respect national borders; capital will move to wherever money is to be made, so the MWS continually changes as capitalism searches for profit (Wallerstein 2004).

The theory impasse

By the 1980s, both modernization and dependency theories were clearly unable to explain adequately how the world was changing. The certainties that both sides had held were challenged. In 1985 David Booth wrote of a 'theory impasse', and within a few years the end of the Cold War and recognition of globalization added to the feeling that the old theories could not hold.

Reasons for the impasse

1 *The failure of development.* In the 1960s and 1970s most developing countries made some progress towards economic growth as well as progress on indicators of social development such as life expectancy and literacy. The following decade, however, saw a slowing down or even reversal; the 1980s are now referred to as 'the lost decade' for development. On rates at the time, it would take developing countries many generations to approach Western standards. Modernization theory could not explain the failure to take off, while dependency theory could not explain the significant differences in the situations of developing countries that were becoming evident, notably the rapid growth of the 'Asian tigers'. The end of communism in Europe also undermined the legitimacy of Marxist and neo-Marxist theories.

2 *Postmodernism.* Postmodernist ideas in the social sciences began to undermine the 'meta-narratives', not only Marxism (which underpinned dependency theory), but also the very idea of development. Postmodernists argued that development and the development theories carried assumptions about social evolution and progress, and were based on Western values. This questioning of the metanarrative of development led some writers to talk of 'post-development' (see page 112).

3 Social scientists began to discuss *globalization*; not all accepted it as a real phenomenon, but the concept opened up new debates that increasingly overlapped with debates about development. These are discussed in the next section (and see Schuurman 2002).

4 *Environmentalism.* There was growing concern that development meant industrialization, which would cause environmental damage and would not be sustainable.

People-centred development and environmentalism

These related new approaches began to affect development practice from the late 1980s. They were reactions against the way most development had been attempted until then – that is, involving large-scale projects run by governments or by large organizations. These did not seem to be lifting people out of poverty. They argued that development should be based on:

- Sustainability; for example, using locally sourced renewable resources and local knowledge and skills
- Participation: communities have to be able to set their own development goals and take decisions about their own lives
- Justice: including, for example, democratic decision-making and the involvement of all groups – especially women, who had previously often been excluded
- Meeting people's basic needs.

People-centred development is sometimes described as 'grassroots development', or as a 'bottom up' approach rather than a 'top down' one.

People-centred development projects are usually run by non-governmental organizations (NGOs) (see later section pages 128–30). Projects tend to be small scale, because they are decided on by local communities, which tend to be traditionally organized and fairly small. The number of NGOs grew considerably when people-centred development became a favoured approach, with some money that had previously gone to governments being channelled to NGOs.

People-centred development involves a lesser role for governments, and so it fits with neoliberalism (see below) which advocates reduced government spending and a more limited role for governments. Where successful, it can greatly improve the lives of poorer people, but is unlikely to lift a country out of poverty. It can also be seen as a means for governments to evade the responsibility of promoting development.

The relationship between the environment and development is explored later in this chapter (see pages 149–52). Environmentalist approaches to development focus on sustainability. Although the term 'sustainable development' is now widely accepted, some environmentalists argue that economic growth is by definition not sustainable and that what is needed is 'degrowth' – a reduction in production and consumption which they say would be compatible with increased happiness and well-being.

Post-development

The study of development was from the 1990s onwards affected by the growing influence in sociology of postmodernist and post-structuralist approaches. The whole idea of development was criticized as being based on Western, and therefore ethnocentric, assumptions about progress and poverty, with Western nations being seen as superior. These ideas were forced on the developing world. Dependency theory, from this point of view, makes the same error as modernization theory in the discourse that it uses and the way that development is set up as something to be achieved by changing social life. Post-development writers such as Arturo Escobar accept that changes are needed, but argue that there can be no universal model of development and that people need to be fully involved in the changes. Some of them would question whether the term 'development' is useful at all, because assumptions about Western superiority are so much a part of it.

Neoliberalism

Neoliberal economic theory replaced modernization theory as the guiding 'official' approach to development in the 1980s. Like modernization theory, it takes the obstacles to development to be internal, but focuses on economic policies and institutions which are seen as holding back development because they limit the free market. Neoliberalism insists that developing countries remove obstacles to free market capitalism and allow capitalism to generate development. The argument is that, if allowed to work freely, capitalism will generate wealth, initially for a minority who are successful, for example as entrepreneurs, but eventually for all, as the wealth 'trickles down'. The policies proposed are those that were tried first in Chile in the 1970s, then in Britain under Thatcher's Conservative governments (1979–90), and elsewhere. They involve a much reduced role for that state, because state interference is seen as distorting the balance between supply and demand. Neoliberal policies include:

- Privatization: selling to private companies and investors industries that had been owned and run by the state – in many countries power, water, telecommunications and broadcasting, etc.
- Cutting subsidies by which governments kept the prices of essentials such as food and fuel low; in some countries the resulting price increases led to riots
- Getting rid of 'parastatal' institutions, often with names such as 'marketing boards', through which governments regulated production, distribution and pricing of particular goods
- Cutting state spending, especially on welfare, so that the state would be less important in the economy
- Cutting taxes: leaving people free to spend their money rather than the government taking a large share and spending it

Neoliberal economic theory was dominant in influencing development policies in the 1980s and 1990s, based on a minimal role for states and liberalization of trade to allow the free market (capitalism) to work without restrictions.

Parastatals are state-run organizations such as marketing boards, which played a leading role in the development policies of many states before neoliberal policies were enforced.

- Free trade: removing tariffs and restrictions on both imports and exports
- Integration into the global economy.

Some countries willingly adopted these policies, believing they would work; in other countries, they were imposed as part of **structural adjustment programmes** (SAPs) created by the **International Monetary Fund** (IMF) and other international government organizations (IGOs). The agreement by the **World Bank** and IMF on these policies as a development strategy, together with liberal democratic political systems, is referred to as the **Washington Consensus**.

Although they try to get developing countries to adopt these policies, the MEDCs do not always practise what they preach. The EU and the USA have tariffs and trade barriers to protect their own agriculture and industries.

Advocates of neoliberalism argue that it has worked in some countries and that opening to the free market is the explanation for the recent economic growth of, for example, China and India, and that, where it seems not to have worked, this is because the policies have not been fully implemented. Its opponents, however, point out that after thirty years or so of neoliberal policies, development has proceeded at only a slow pace in most countries. There is also, arguably, a contradiction in that imposing free markets requires a strong state that has to undermine its own role.

Assessing the impact of neoliberal policies

A report from the Center for Economic and Policy Research (CEPR) compared the period from 1960 to 1980, when most countries had more restrictive, inward-looking economies, to the period 1980 to 2000, the period of neoliberal policies in trade and imposition of policies by the IMF and World Bank. It considered indicators such as income per person; life expectancy; mortality among infants, children and adults; literacy and education. The report found that progress was greater before 1980, and that there has been a decline since. For example, in poor countries child mortality fell faster and school enrolment increased faster before 1980 than after. The report's authors do not claim that liberalization of trade and capital flows has caused the decline in progress, but they do say that supporters of neoliberal policies have not yet produced proof for their claims that the Washington Consensus is the best route to development (Weisbrot et al. 2001).

Practice questions

1 Outline and explain **two** factors that, according to modernization theorists, impede development.
(10 marks)

2 Read **Item A** below and answer the question that follows.

> **Item A**
> Changes from year to year in a country's Gross National Income give a measure of economic growth. Some countries such as China are experiencing high economic growth, while the economies of other countries, notably in sub-Saharan Africa, are showing little growth. However, some sociologists are critical of measuring development in this way and suggest that other factors should be considered as well.

Applying material from **Item A**, analyse **two** reasons why some sociologists would challenge the view that development can be measured solely by economic growth. **(10 marks)**

Sidebar definitions:

Structural adjustment programmes (SAPs) refer to a set of policies imposing neoliberal policies on governments, used by IGOs, especially the IMF.

The International Monetary Fund (IMF) is a key IGO, which gives loans to members and has spread neoliberal economic globalization.

The World Bank is a key IGO, which gives aid and loans to members to fight poverty; it is often accused of spreading neoliberal economic globalization.

The Washington Consensus is a set of neoliberal policies which were argued to be essential for reforming economies and promoting development.

3   Read **Item B** below and answer the question that follows.

Item B

Some sociologists argue that, in order to develop, Third World countries need help from the West in the form of aid, expertise and trading relationships. This, they argue, will help these countries climb the ladder of development and become like the West. However, this view is rejected by others who argue that development is not possible as long as Third World countries are relying on the West.

Applying material from **Item B** and your knowledge, evaluate the view that in order to achieve development, developing countries today must break away from dependency on the more developed countries.   **(20 marks)**

Topic 2

SPECIFICATION AREA

Globalisation and its influence on the cultural, political and economic relationships between societies

Globalization

Globalization is a relatively new term, which quickly became a 'buzz word' – widely used without its meaning and implications always being fully examined. Even within sociology, it is always worth asking what a particular writer means by globalization.

The context for globalization is the end of the Cold War and the collapse of the Soviet Union in 1989. Together with rapid changes in communications technology, this made possible the spread of free market capitalism, which has been imposed on many developing countries through structural adjustment programmes and the pressure to get debt relief.

There is a series of debates about globalization, which include questions such as:

- Is it happening or not? (Does the term refer to a new phenomenon, different from earlier social changes?)
- When did it begin?
- Is it irreversible?
- Who benefits from it?
- Is it, overall, a positive or negative force?

What is meant by globalization?

'Globalization' refers to several connected changes that have made the lives of people around the world more global. These include faster and more frequent communications, more travel, more trade and the development of global organizations and of a global infrastructure supporting them.

Sometimes, however, 'globalization' is used to mean the globalization of capitalism or the free market, accompanied by democratic freedoms and greater consumerism. In this sense globalization is supported strongly by neoliberals but opposed by dependency theorists and radicals. It can be seen as creating greater inequalities within and between nations, as well as greater wealth.

If this second sense of globalization is accepted, then accompanying it is what can be called 'alternative globalization'. This includes global movements and developments such as Fair Trade, gender equality and human rights, based on ideas that have globalized. The spread of demands for greater political freedoms, for example in the Arab Spring of 2011, could also be seen as part of this.

Globalization can be seen as having cultural, political and economic dimensions. The following section discusses some of the arguments and evidence that have been put forward for globalization; we then consider the different interpretations of the evidence and arguments which have led to different theoretical positions on globalization.

Evidence for economic globalization

The **new international division of labour** (NIDL) refers to the new global economic order said to be produced by factory production moving from the developed world to some developing countries.

The case for economic globalization, as presented below, is that there is now a single fully integrated global economy based on the new international division of labour (Frobel et al., 1980), with growing trade and economic connections between different parts of the world. This has replaced the 'traditional' division of labour which had been established in the colonial period and under which the colonies provided raw materials for the industries of the colonizing powers. Industries in the colonies themselves were discouraged; in India, for example, the cotton clothing industry was destroyed so that it could not compete with Britain's cotton mills.

From the 1970s onwards, manufacturing production moved away from developed countries and increasingly to developing countries. The spread of TNCs and improvements in global travel and communication changed the earlier pattern. The new international division of labour (NIDL) is a result of economic globalization and refers to the situation whereby manufacturing takes place in the developing world, with goods exported to and consumed mainly in the North. This idea is a useful one because it draws attention to the increasing use of cheap labour in poor countries to produce goods for rich countries. However, the term can be seen as misleading. Many poor countries still rely heavily on exporting food and raw materials, while rich countries still have some manufacturing industries, so the old (traditional) division of labour survives alongside the new. Other evidence for economic globalization includes:

1 *The spread of capitalism (the 'free market') around the world.* Even nominally communist countries, such as China and Vietnam, have moved away from state control of the economy and allow capitalist businesses. The adoption by many countries of neoliberal policies, sometimes under pressure to follow structural adjustment programmes, has extended the market even further, into areas that once were under the control of the state (for example, supplying energy and water).

2 *The growth and strength of* **transnational corporations** *(TNCs).* The supply of resources, production and consumption have all been globalized. These giant companies (or their subsidiaries or franchises) make the same products (with local variations) in many countries, using supplies imported from a wide range of different countries, which they then sell all across the world. The products of companies such as Unilever, Nestlé and Sony are household names which are recognized globally. Other TNCs, such as those involved in primary extraction of resources – for example the mining TNC Glencore – are less widely recognized names.

Transnational corporations (TNCs) are large business enterprises which produce and sell globally and have global supply chains.

Austerity cuts in public spending over recent years, such as on education, have been passionately protested against. The initial impetus for the cuts can be traced back to the 2008 financial crises, which ultimately began due to problems with home owners in the US being unable to keep up with their mortgage repayments. In an economically globalized world, the ripples from the US crisis have far-reaching – and long-lasting – effects.

McDonaldization is Ritzer's term for the ways in which the organizing principles of a fast-food restaurant chain are coming to dominate and standardize many aspects of economic and cultural life globally.

3   *The ways in which TNCs tend to operate* has led to social changes which George Ritzer refers to as **McDonaldization** (see the box below).

4   *Finance and money markets have also been globalized.* Financial events on the other side of the world can quickly affect us. Banks and stockbrokers are often transnational operations, and money can be moved very quickly around the world. This became evident with, for example, the 'credit crunch' and recession in 2008, which spread very quickly from one economy to another across the globe, showing how closely the economies of different countries were interconnected.

These changes to the world's economy have been facilitated by the falling costs of transport and of sending data around the world.

McDonaldization

Since George Ritzer wrote *The McDonaldization of Society* in the 1990s, the word has caught on and been used in a wide variety of contexts. Many people find it a useful shorthand term for a range of ways in which we can see social life changing, and others have adapted it, talking of 'McJobs', 'McUniversities' and so on. McDonaldization is a global process and an aspect of globalization. Here are Ritzer's dimensions of McDonaldization (Ritzer 2000):

1   *Efficiency*. McDonald's is all about getting customers from hungry to full as quickly as possible. Staff are trained to prepare food and serve customers in a precise series of steps that delivers efficiency.

2   *Calculability*. Quantity replaces quality; a Big Mac's selling point is its size, not its taste.

3   *Predictability*. The restaurants will look the same inside and out, the menus will be the same, the food will taste the same and the staff will say the same things to customers.

4   *Control*. The experience of eating at McDonald's is carefully controlled to ensure that people eat quickly and leave as soon as they have finished. Wherever possible, McDonaldization replaces people with machines.

Evidence for political globalization

Some writers assume that, as capitalism spreads, so will the political system of liberal democracy (based on political parties, regular elections, freedom to speak and vote).

Around the world, the number of liberal democracies has grown considerably since the early 1990s and there are far fewer dictatorships. Not all political systems and elections are 'free and fair', with the opposition allowed to organize freely, but elections are almost always now observed by international monitors and there are procedures to try to reduce bribery, vote rigging and so on. Having free and fair elections is now often a condition of receiving aid.

A second aspect of political globalization is that nation-states become less important compared to TNCs and global or supranational political entities such as the European Union, and, at the same time, local political structures. National governments increasingly face problems that are too big for them to deal with on their own, for example climate change, pollution, terrorism, the drugs trade, the power of TNCs, AIDS and refugees. The big political questions now require global decision-making. This has made governments willing to concede some powers to international organizations like the United Nations and the European Union, and willing to negotiate agreements with other countries. In the long term, the logical outcome would be a world government.

Global decision-making refers to states acting together and taking decisions at a global level through IGOs to resolve issues that states acting alone are unable to do.

Nation-states have also given up some political power to smaller and more local political structures; for example, in the UK there are now devolved assemblies in Scotland, Wales and Northern Ireland. New social movements often operate across several countries or even globally; national boundaries no longer restrict political activity. Important global political 'actors' include Greenpeace, the Red Cross, Amnesty International and many non-governmental organizations, as well as movements working on environmental and political issues.

The major problems of today, such as pollution and climate change, drug-trafficking and nuclear threats, are too large for single nation-states to regulate, and require global cooperation

Evidence for cultural globalization

Cultural globalization is very closely linked to economic globalization, and includes:

- The existence of worldwide information and communication systems
- global patterns of consumerism
- Cosmopolitan lifestyles
- World sport
- World tourism.

Most of the attention is focused on the spread of highly visible aspects of American consumer culture – McDonald's, Coca-Cola, fast-food chains, baseball caps, jeans, hip hop and rap music and so on – but other aspects include the growth of Christianity, Islam and other religions, the dominance globally of the English language and the spread of Western values regarding families, relationships and lifestyles. Ideas such as gender equality and human rights have spread globally.

Activity

For an account of globalization that sees it as having deep historical roots, and that has useful examples including how a virus has globalized, view Nayan Chanda's powerpoints at http://yaleglobal.yale.edu/about/history.jsp. This site has a lot of other useful material about globalization; the flash presentation on the globalization of television supply chains illustrates economic globalization, and there are interviews with experts such as Paul Collier.

Theoretical perspectives on globalization

Globalists are those in the globalization debates who argue that globalization is a positive and irreversible force from which all will eventually benefit. They are associated with neoliberalism.

According to McGrew (2000), it is possible to distinguish three theoretical accounts of globalization.

(1) The neoliberals

Neoliberals (also referred to as positive globalists or optimists) see globalization as the worldwide extension of capitalism, or, as they would prefer to call it, the free market. They see this as good because a global free market will lead to economic growth, the eradication of poverty and the spread of democracy all around the world. A new world order is being created which will ensure peace and prosperity. Neoliberals would say that countries that are embracing the global free market are the ones where development is happening now (for example, India and China), while the continuing problems in Africa are because that continent remains largely outside the global free market. Globalization spreads the benefits of capitalism around the world. Allowing people to use their entrepreneurial skills by liberalizing markets will, they argue, produce wealth that will eventually 'trickle down' to the whole population. Liberal democracy tends to be seen as the inevitable accompaniment to the spread of the free market. In the long run, there will be no losers, only winners, from globalization. Cultural globalization involves the spread of Western values, which are essential in a globalized world.

Radicals are those in the globalization debates who argue that globalization is a powerful negative force; associated with dependency theory and neo-Marxists.

(2) The radicals

Radicals agree with the neoliberals in seeing globalization as essentially the global spread of capitalism, but they see this as negative. This position is often associated with Marxism and with Wallerstein's world systems theory. Economic globalization is seen as spreading globally an economic system which impoverishes many and, because it is based on high consumption, is environmentally not sustainable. Globalization widens the gap between rich and poor – even if some countries benefit, the rich world, or at least the majority there, benefits even more, and the poor are excluded. Globalization creates a global system based on *structural violence*. This is a term used by Galtung (1969) to describe the way in which, even in an apparently peaceful society, a group (usually distinct because of, for example, its gender, ethnicity, religion or caste) can be exploited by the systematic denial of their rights. This condemns parts of the South to poverty and stagnation. Radicals see cultural globalization as cultural imperialism – that is, globalization is seen as leading, through a process of cultural homogenization, to a single global culture based on American or Western culture. The mass advertising of Western cultural icons (Coca-Cola, McDonald's, etc.) through the media is present everywhere, suggesting to people (especially children) that they should try to adopt a Western consumer lifestyle – which radicals fear will undermine or even destroy unique local cultures. Some writers call this Americanization or 'coca-colonization'.

Cultural imperialism, associated with neo-Marxism, refers to the imposition of Western, and especially American, cultural values on non-Western cultures, and the consequent undermining of local cultures and cultural independence.

Cultural homogenization refers to the removal of cultural differences, so that all cultures are increasingly similar.

For the radicals, what is happening now is a deepening or intensification of long-standing trends. Capitalism began its global expansion centuries ago, but is only now completely dominant. What is new is that transnational corporations (TNCs), supported by the IGOs, have replaced the developed nations as the driving force of these changes. The new world order which is emerging seems more like disorder: the North cannot be safe and secure as long as its wealth is based on intensifying the poverty of the South.

Transformationalists are those in the globalization debate who see globalization as a force whose outcomes are uncertain, but which can be controlled and used to promote development.

(3) The transformationalists

The transformationalists, such as Cohen and Kennedy (2012), see globalization as a very important development, but disagree with both the neoliberals and the radicals on several grounds:

- Globalization may not be unstoppable – it may even slow or go into reverse
- It may be possible for people and countries to reject some negative aspects of globalization while embracing the more positive aspects
- Far from creating a homogeneous global culture, the meeting of different cultures creates

new hybrids (**hybridization**, or creolization) – of peoples, of music, of religions, of languages and so on – which is seen as creating greater diversity, and more vibrant, exciting cultures. For example, although McDonald's seems to be iconic of everything American, in many countries the food the company offers has been adapted to local tastes and incorporates local food traditions. The media too have been adapted for different cultural traditions, so that, for example, the Bollywood film industry in India draws on classical Hindu themes and mythology. The adaptation of a global idea, product or service to local conditions is called **glocalization**.

- Reverse cultural flows mean that the developing world influences the culture of the West
- The world is still unequal, but globalization is transforming the old hierarchies of North/South and First World/Third World.

> **Hybridization**
> refers to the creation of a new third hybrid culture when aspects of two different cultures combine.

> **Glocalization**
> refers to the processes leading to the permanent intertwining of the global with the local, and the way, for example, global products might be adapted to fit local cultural needs.

Ankie Hoogvelt: a radical view of the globalized world

Hoogvelt (2005) has argued that globalization has transformed the world social order so that geographical boundaries are no longer relevant. Rich and poor live alongside each other in the world's great cities, not in different countries. She sees the world order as a three-tiered structure of circles: the affluent and elites (the 'bankable'); the insecure; and the excluded. In the rich countries, she says, the proportions are 40:30:30; in poor countries, 20:30:50; in Africa, more like 10:10:80.

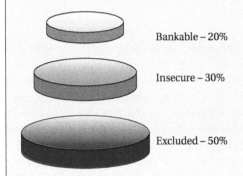

Bankable – 20%

Insecure – 30%

Excluded – 50%

Figure 2.3 The three-tiered structure of the world

How far has economic globalization gone?

It is far from complete. There are still many national companies, and even the largest corporations have clear national bases and so are more properly MNCs than TNCs. Even if national governments have less control over their economies than in the past, regional groups of governments (like the European Union) can provide some protection for workers and insist on basic rights (such as the Social Chapter), placing limits on the power of TNCs.

Hirst and Thompson (1999) argue that economic globalization is a myth. Outlining ideal types of the international economy and the global economy, they argue that we are still much closer to the former. Nation-states remain important actors, with the ability to control the direction taken by the world economy. Although there is greater global economic activity, Hirst and Thompson see no evidence of a fully developed global economic system. The global economic downturn since 2008 may have slowed economic globalization further.

How far has political globalization gone?

Governments still have considerable scope to influence developments and it is national governments that are entering into the agreements that create the international organizations. National governments still wage wars and raise taxes. More countries have adopted the trappings of liberal democracy. Dictators such as Robert Mugabe in Zimbabwe can hold and win elections and claim to be democratically elected even though little has changed there. The USA and its allies still tolerate undemocratic regimes as long as they are on their side (e.g. Saudi Arabia). On the other hand, there has been progress, with a decline in the number of dictatorships or authoritarian regimes and a rise in the number of democracies (see figure 2.4).

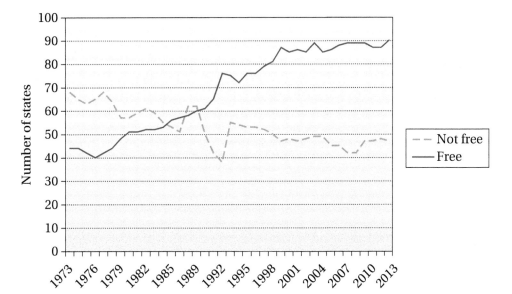

Figure 2.4 Political freedom around the world

The terminology 'Free' and 'Not Free' is used by Freedom House and is based on political rights and civil liberties

Source: compiled with data from Freedomhouse.org

Where people have attempted to resist globalization, this has sometimes led to asserting strong national, ethnic and religious identities. For example, it can be argued that Islamic fundamentalism and jihadism are reactions to Westernization but ones that themselves make use of some aspects of globalization – for instance, using the internet for propaganda and recruitment.

The transformationalist case has been put forward by McGrew (2004), arguing that although nation-states are not in terminal decline, there is plenty of evidence of a transformation of politics, with the development of global decision-making structures and also a diffusion of power. The ways in which people become active in politics have also changed, with more global and international movements and organizations, at the same time as traditional political activities such as party membership and voting are declining in the North. The problems that people face increasingly require both global and local change, and politics is changing to reflect this.

If economic globalization does mean a much reduced role for nation-states, as neoliberals claim, then the idea that this also means greater democracy is questionable. While the citizens of more countries may be able to join parties and vote as the number of liberal democracies grows, the politicians they vote for are no longer able to take really important decisions. Those are taken by transnational corporations, whose leaders are not elected and which are accountable only to shareholders.

> **Activity**
>
> **TTIP**
>
> Find out about the Transnational Trade and Investment Partnership (TTIP). As this book went to press in 2016, negotiations, mainly in secret, between the EU and USA were being held to reduce the powers that national governments can use to control the activities of big businesses. If these negotiations result in an agreement, there will be a shift in power away from governments towards corporations.

How far has cultural globalization gone?

Evidence of Western or American culture is hard to avoid anywhere in the world now. The giant media and communications corporations are all based in the North. But not everything American spreads globally: baseball and American football have limited appeal outside the USA (the baseball 'World Series' is always between two North American teams).

The cultural flow is not always one-way from North to South. Bollywood and the Japanese and Hong Kong film industries challenge the supremacy of Hollywood in global cinema. Migration of people means that Southern cultures have significant presences within developed countries (for example, Islam in Britain). The cultural products of the developing world are often highly valued (world music, 'ethnic' fashions and jewellery, Eastern religions, 'ethnic' foods and so on). Reverse cultural flows have brought Asian martial arts and traditional medicines to the West, and have made brands such as Pokemon and Hello Kitty a part of Western childhood.

Some welcome American culture, but others actively resist it. Western culture can be seen as degrading or even as destroying local cultures, and also as creating a generation gap as young people embrace it while the older generation reject it. Some countries vigorously oppose Western cultural values, turning to religious fundamentalism (Iran), or isolationism (North Korea). This in itself can be seen as proof of globalization: globalization so unsettles people that they retreat to old familiar values simply as a way of making sense of a world that seems out of control. However, the meeting of cultures seems often to lead not to the disappearance of the non-Western, but to new hybrids in which the non-Western can survive in a new form. Encounters between cultures create 'third cultures', in which aspects of different cultures are combined. Traditions may also be kept alive, or resurrected, for tourists, many of whom highly value what they take to be an authentic cultural experience. While tourists may only be presented with a simplified version of an aspect of culture, or one removed from its original context, this can still promote a sense of the value of one's own culture and the cultures of others.

Cultural globalization seems to involve an unprecedented level of difference and variety, with the variety extended by hybridization and reverse cultural flows; this can be seen, for example, in the range of foods or types of music available. At the same time, on the other hand, there is an unprecedented level of cultural homogenization.

The expansion of the internet and global telecommunications have greatly increased the access of many of the world's people to information and ideas. By 2014 Facebook had 1.23 billion monthly active users (prnewswire.com) and mobile telephone ownership in Africa grew to an estimated 56 per cent of the continent's population (*BBC News*).

In some countries, however, governments restrict access to the internet and social media or use them for surveillance of dissidents. The traditional mass media remain largely controlled by a very small number of huge global conglomerates such as Walt Disney, News Corporation and Time Warner.

Cultural globalization is not a one-way phenomenon. Bollywood-inspired cinema is attracting larger audiences in the West, with an associated interest in Indian dancing. World music, such as reggae, has been embraced by popular culture, and martial arts from East Asia are commonly practised by children and adults in the West

Global tourism can help to keep local traditional cultures alive, albeit in a sometimes artificial way. For example, travellers to Thailand are often keen to see the cultures of local tribes, such as the Akha pictured here

Who benefits and who loses from globalization?

The **transnational capitalist class** is a global power elite or ruling class made up of the owners and controllers of transnational corporations and the globalized media, top officials, professionals and politicians who operate globally, and top business people who trade in global markets.

The neoliberal case is that, in the long run, everyone can benefit. Globalization will bring economic growth to the whole world. Initially, this is likely to create inequalities, but eventually living standards will be higher.

The case against globalization from the radical perspective is that its negative effects seem to outweigh any advantages. It has failed to deliver peace and prosperity or economic stability. Progress towards development has been slow; some countries in Africa have even slipped backwards on some development measures. It is poorer people in poorer countries – Collier's 'bottom billion' – who seem not to be helped by globalization. The growth of consumerism that is part of globalization is leading to growing environmental problems (see pages 149–52). The winners, from this point of view, are what Sklair (1995: 8–9) has called the 'transnational capitalist class': a global ruling class no longer tied to national boundaries. It has been questioned, however, whether these people have enough in common to act together as a class. For Naomi Klein (2000), the winners are TNCs; she argues that globalization is a project by TNCs to further their own interests and profits. The neoliberals respond that the poor are only missing out because they are not yet sufficiently integrated into the global economy. Cohen and Kennedy (2012) argue that globalization has created both 'global winners' who have increased their power and privileges, and 'global losers' who have missed out.

Globalization then, whatever its benefits, seems to create two problems:

The **anti-globalization movement** is a loose network of groups and organizations globally opposing neoliberal economic globalization (but using globalized communications).

- A growing gap between rich and poor, or the secure and the excluded
- Growing environmental problems because of the spread of consumerism.

There has been an anti-globalization movement since at least 1995, a loosely organized coalition of many groups from around the world. They attracted global media attention with demonstrations at the WTO meeting in Seattle in 1999 and then in Genoa in 2001. Because of its disparate nature, the movement lacks a coherent programme, but is broadly in favour of decisions being taken locally rather than imposed by 'experts', and is mainly non-violent. Although opposed to neoliberal globalization, the groups involved take full advantage of the possibilities of cooperating globally using the internet and other global telecommunications.

Globalization today

The terrorist attacks of 11 September 2001 were a setback to optimistic views of globalization. One of the darker aspects of globalization, the ability of terrorist networks to organize and operate globally, had become unavoidable. It became clear also that there was considerable hostility to the USA and the rich world more generally. Islamic and other cultures showed no signs of being about to disappear under Western cultural imperialism. The USA then acted without UN support and against strong public opinion in the developed world in invading Iraq in 2003, suggesting a return to international politics dominated by nation-states.

Kunstler (2005) argues that there is nothing inevitable about globalization, and that it is coming to an end. He sees globalization as a product of two factors: the relative peace of the post-Cold War period and the simultaneous availability of cheap energy sources, especially oil. These two factors are fading: US troops (and others) became involved in wars in Iraq and Afghanistan and the West is also under continuing threat from Islamic terrorism; oil reserves are limited and much of the remaining oil is under the control of states that resent or are hostile to the West. Even without considering global warming, the West's oil-led lifestyle has a very limited future. Kunstler therefore expects an imminent end to globalization.

Saul (2004) sees globalization as having reached its high point in the mid-1990s, with the creation of the World Trade Organization (WTO), but then being challenged by a reclaiming of power by some nation-states from the supposedly all-powerful global economic forces. Malaysia broke all the neoliberal rules to successfully escape the 1997 Asian crisis; Argentina ignored IMF advice after its economic collapse in 2001, and recovered; India shrugged off WTO pressure to allow genetically modified (GM) seeds; and countries across South America and elsewhere have elected governments opposed to globalization. In the developed world, the response to the economic crisis and the imposition of austerity led to radical movements challenging neoliberalism, including the election of the Syriza-led governments in Greece in 2015. But Saul sees positive signs of more benign aspects of globalization emerging as neoliberalism retreats, in non-economic international treaties and the setting-up of the International Criminal Court.

The global recession of 2009 is a recession of globalization, with effects everywhere, even slowing growth in China. Wealthier nations became preoccupied with their own economies, and global trade fell. Some aspects of globalization, though, seem likely to continue: global communications, the internet and social media have made possible global actions and seem unlikely to be reversed. Transformationalists see these as opening up possibilities for ensuring that the 'global losers' can also benefit.

Practice questions

1 Outline and explain **two** ways in which local peoples and cultures may respond to global influences. **(10 marks)**

2 Read **Item A** below and answer the question that follows.

> **Item A**
> In the past, although there was trading between different regions and countries, most economic activity was local: many goods were made from local resources and produced and consumed locally. The economies of different parts of the world were very different from each other. Some sociologists argue that globalization has now led to the creation of an integrated global economic system.

Applying material from **Item A**, analyse **two** reasons why some sociologists argue that there is now a global economic system. **(10 marks)**

3 Read **Item B** below and answer the question that follows.

> **Item B**
> According to its advocates, globalization will bring higher living standards and greater freedom to the world's citizens as they adopt Western values and business practices. However, others are concerned that the economic and political strength of the USA and of corporations based in the West mean that Western culture and values will be forced on people elsewhere, who risk losing their own values and traditions.

Applying material from **Item B** and your knowledge, evaluate the view that globalization usually means the spread of Western culture and values. **(20 marks)**

Topic 3

SPECIFICATION AREA

The role of transnational corporations, non-governmental organisations and international agencies in local and global strategies for development

Agencies of development

Agencies of development are those organizations and institutions that play a part in development. The specification says that you need to know about transnational corporations (TNCs), non-governmental organizations (NGOs) and international agencies; to give a fuller picture, this section starts by looking at the role of states in development.

States

States are not the same as governments. Governments are in temporary control of some or most aspects of the state, but, for example, the civil service, the military, the police and the judicial and legal systems, which are also part of the state, have greater continuity. Many developing states, especially in Africa, have borders imposed by colonial powers in the past. Often the population does not share a common identity and there are ethnic and religious tensions. This makes it harder to achieve a sense of national identity that could help development; the civil service and machinery of government will be inherited from the colonial power and may not be appropriate because they were set up to control a 'native' population rather than improve living standards and develop.

Neoliberals favour the state being as small as possible; their view of globalization is that states should have a fading role, while transnational actors, such as TNCs, should have a growing role. Neoliberals argue that states in the developing world have been too big, with over-sized bureaucracies and too much interference in the market. However, even neoliberals accept that states have the responsibility to create and maintain a stable and secure social situation in which the free market can operate. Countries in which states cease to be able to do this, such as Somalia, are referred to as 'failed states'.

Marxists and dependency theorists are opposed to capitalism and favour development being led by the state – provided it represents the people. In most countries, however, the state is controlled by the ruling class or bourgeoisie, and it therefore acts against the interests of the majority of the population and in favour of the elites of the North. A transformation of the state via revolution is needed.

A **development state** is one that sees its main purpose as development and leads the country's development programme.

The state can itself lead development, setting development as a goal it actively pursues. Many newly independent countries in the 1950s and 1960s attempted this. States ran industries, organized agriculture and bought products for marketing; they were large and employed many people. The state played an essential role in the few examples of successful industrialization and economic growth – for example, the rise of Japan and, later, the Asian 'tigers'. Adrian Leftwich (1995) argues that the common factor in the development success of the past fifty years (Japan and the Asian tigers) has been the presence of what he calls the 'development state', in which the state focuses on development goals and works closely with the private sector. These states tended to be authoritarian, with weak or absent opposition. In the twenty-first century, this is less acceptable, with aid and debt relief often dependent on being democratic, but China today is following this approach.

A **predatory state** is one that preys upon its own people, through appropriation and corruption, preventing development.

Alternatively, the state may prevent development. The state may be corrupt, with politicians and civil servants enriching themselves from aid or from the country's resources; these are known as 'predatory states'. An example is Zaire (now the Democratic Republic of Congo) under Mobutu, where the president and a small group around him became immensely wealthy by preying on the population, with support from rich nations and from the World Bank (Evans 1989: 571). Because of Mobutu's arbitrary power, it was impossible for either a civil service implementing agreed rules or a capitalist class investing in business to exist. Mobutu stayed in power for so long because of external support, especially from France and Belgium. He embezzled millions of dollars while Zaire defaulted on its debts.

Governments of developing countries face problems that make it difficult to achieve development. They have little money to spend because money raised from taxes is low. It has been estimated that Africa loses more than $50 billion each year through illicit financial flows such as fraud, mispricing and tax avoidance by transnational corporations (Anderson 2015).

Transnational corporations

The term 'transnational corporation' (TNC) refers to corporations that have globalized their operations; they produce and sell around the world, use global supply chains and employ people in many different countries. As a result of globalization and the new international division of labour (see pages 115–16), there are more, and larger, TNCs than ever before. Some writers have argued that, as economic globalization progresses, TNCs are at least as important as nation-states. The majority of the world's countries have economies smaller than the largest TNCs. Well-known names such as Nestlé, HSBC, Toyota, Shell, Unilever and Sony, as well as Japanese trading houses and corporations many people will not have heard of, have huge economic power; the question is how that power is used.

A distinction can be made between TNCs and multinational corporations (MNCs). The latter operate in different countries but retain a clear base in a particular country. MNCs have not yet become truly global in the way TNCs are. From the point of view of developing countries, the distinction is less important; both TNCs and MNCs are very powerful outside organizations that can affect development for better or for worse.

TNCs exist to make profits for their shareholders; it is not their purpose or aim to help a country develop, although all now accept the idea of corporate responsibility. The question is whether in doing this they can also contribute to development. Most countries actively seek investment by TNCs, setting up special areas where TNCs can operate without the usual restrictions (for example, they may be exempt from tax, planning laws or minimum standards for workers). Such areas are called Export Processing Zones (EPZs), but also are known by different names around the world. Countries that set up EPZs assume that the presence of TNCs will eventually have benefits, even if initially the situation seems more like exploitation.

> A **multinational corporation** (MNC) is one that has some global aspects, but is still clearly based in one nation, though the term is sometimes used interchangeably with 'TNC'.

> **Export Processing Zones:** areas in developing countries where the normal workplace regulations etc are relaxed to encourage TNCs to invest.

Corporate responsibility

Many companies now have corporate responsibility policies, or try in some way to show that they have social responsibilities, beyond complying with the law, which they take seriously. Some British supermarkets, for example, support community initiatives in developing countries. While sometimes the main aim may be to attract customers who approve of such practices, there can also be practical developmental and environmental gains. Corporate social responsibility (CSR) is voluntary, and can be seen as a way of heading off criticism and preventing regulations controlling what TNCs can do. Despite the popularity of CSR today, TNCs are frequently accused of abuses. This website reports on alleged wrongdoings of TNCs:

www.corporatewatch.org

Be aware when visiting this site that it is campaigning against TNC activities; for balance, visit the websites of some TNCs and look for information on their corporate or social responsibility policies and practices.

Applying the theories to TNCs

Modernization theory and neoliberal approaches see TNCs as essential, able to introduce modern values and to kick-start an economy. Any accompanying abuses are comparable to those that

Britain and other now developed countries went through during industrialization – painful but necessary.

Dependency theorists concentrate on the abuses, some of which are listed in table 2.4 under 'Costs'. The presence of TNCs is seen as intensifying dependency, preventing local industry from growing and ensuring that the country stays poor. The overall effect of the growth of the power of TNCs is to weaken workers and strengthen capitalism; for example, if the workforce in a factory proves troublesome by demanding higher wages or better conditions, the company can close its operation and relocate elsewhere, even in another country. Trade unions around the world recognize that, faced with transnational employers, they need to cooperate so as to provide a transnational voice for workers.

Table 2.4 Costs and benefits of TNCs

Costs	Benefits
Exploitation of workers: conditions and pay may be low; some TNCs have been implicated in employing children, not allowing trade unions, making overtime compulsory and other abuses. Developing countries compete with each other to attract TNCs, providing ever lower standards. TNC investment goes to those who will accept the lowest wages, least benefits and worst conditions. Charles Kerngahan described this, in his book about Bangladesh, as a 'race to the bottom' (cited in Jones 2006).	TNCs bring in investment in terms of money, resources, technology and expertise and creating jobs, often where local companies are unable to do this.
Exploitation of the environment: using up renewable resources, damaging ecosystems and creating pollution, with negative consequences for local people.	TNCs need trained workers and this should raise the aspirations of local people and encourage improvements in education.
Exploitation of markets: mis-selling of goods (e.g. baby food), dumping of out-of-date goods (e.g. medicines) and selling harmful goods regardless of consequences (e.g. faced with a shrinking market in the North, tobacco companies have turned to developing countries with marketing that plays down the health consequences of smoking).	The jobs and training often provide opportunities for women, who may not have had them before, promoting gender equality.
Jobs created, especially the better-paid ones, may go to expatriates from the developed world rather than to local people.	TNCs bring modern values, which may help development; for example, ideas about gender equality.
Profits are unlikely to stay in the developing country, and the TNC may avoid paying tax, so that the host country does not benefit financially.	TNCs need and will pay for infrastructure such as roads and power lines, from which local people may also benefit.
Products are for export to Western markets, so local people are unable to buy them.	TNCs encourage international trade and open up new markets.
TNCs have little loyalty to particular countries; when supplies of raw materials have dried up, or when labour is cheaper elsewhere, they will move on.	
Bio-piracy: TNCs are able to patent traditional medicines and sources of food, making money from resources that ought to belong to developing countries and also eliminating domestic firms that sold these products.	

Bio-piracy refers to the appropriation, generally by means of patents, of legal rights over indigenous knowledge – particularly biomedical knowledge – developed by indigenous groups, without permission from and without compensation to the indigenous groups themselves.

Why are TNCs able to act in unethical ways?

Global economic influence

The largest TNCs are more powerful than some developing countries, so they are able to put pressure on individual countries, and also on IGOs such as the World Trade Organization. For example, world trade rules now allow TNCs to patent medicines and foods that have been used for many years in developing countries and should really belong to their people.

Parent–subsidiary relationship

TNCs often operate through smaller, subsidiary companies. When there is a court case, the subsidiary is prosecuted and the parent TNC is protected, both financially and in terms of publicity and image. For example, chains of clothes shops such as Nike and Gap can claim to be unaware of use of child labour or other unacceptable practices in the factories in which the clothes are produced if they do not own the factories.

Regional economic influence

TNCs hold power within particular countries and regions; they can force or blackmail governments into overlooking what they do.

Whose legal system?

Where can a TNC be prosecuted? TNCs might break a law in their country of origin but there may not be a law in the developing country (e.g. some countries don't have laws against child labour).

How and whom to punish?

Where TNCs or their subsidiaries are prosecuted for breaking regulations and laws, fines are tiny as proportions of profits, and in any case the cost can be passed on to consumers. And who, at what level in a TNC, is responsible? If a chief executive resigns (prison sentences are unusual for corporate crimes), he or she will be replaced by someone with the same outlook following similar practices.

Activity

Research allegations made against the practices of TNCs in developing countries in one or more of the following:

- Shell's exploitation of oil in the Ogoni area in Nigeria
- Nestlé's selling of powdered baby food in developing countries
- The use of sweatshop labour for branded clothes, such as those of Primark, Nike and Gap, and by Apple in factories making iPhones in China
- The Bhopal disaster of 1984, involving a factory owned by Union Carbide
- Allegations against Coca-Cola of polluting water supplies in India and of being indirectly responsible for murders of trade unionists in South America
- Allegations that, in Zambia, mining corporation Glencore avoids paying tax and pollutes the air and water.

When you are studying Crime and Deviance, note that some of these are examples of corporate crimes or green crimes in the context of globalization.

Non-governmental organizations

There is a very wide range of non-governmental organizations (NGOs). These organizations are part of 'civil society', not part of government or businesses that exist to make a profit. They are essentially organizations of concerned citizens who want to act together for humanitarian and philanthropic ends, though many have grown beyond such small-scale origins and now employ many people and have huge budgets. Many NGOs work on local and domestic issues; this section is concerned only with those that work on global issues, development and the environment, referred to as **international non-governmental organizations (INGOs)**. Some focus on campaigning, others on charitable work via fundraising. Some work locally at grassroots level, others at the national or international level. Some of the best-known INGOs are associated with the people-centred approach to development and work on issues wherever there is a need; for example, Oxfam has helped people in poverty in the UK as well as in developing countries.

The amount of aid that INGOs can provide is small compared to aid from governments and multilateral aid provided by IGOs. INGOs have for many years had a vital role in emergencies, raising funds from the public for disaster relief. Some of the UK's largest INGOs work together in the Disasters Emergency Committee (DEC) to coordinate fundraising. Although this is the most visible aspect of their work, most also work on development aid. The health NGO Médecins Sans Frontières (MSF) played a central role in dealing with the outbreak of the Ebola virus in parts of West Africa in 2014, responding more quickly than the World Health Organization or governments of aid-giving countries. NGOs are growing in importance; because of the many criticisms of other forms of aid, more Official Development Assistance (see page 135) is being channelled through INGOs, allowing donors to claim that the money is benefiting the poor more directly.

Some INGOs have grown into large organizations which keep expanding and, arguably, lose sight of their original idealism. Not all practise as organizations what they are trying to achieve in their development work; ideals about social justice, equality and democracy do not always translate into decent wages for staff or involvement in decision-making. For the public of Northern countries, on whom INGOs rely for most of their income, another concern has been the amount of money absorbed by administration rather than helping people in developing countries directly. Edwards and Hulme (2013) studied a range of development NGOs and argued that they were losing touch with their roots and becoming closer to governments and other sources of funding than to the people they were trying to help.

Overall, INGO aid is worthy and often highly successful at a local level, but there is not enough of it to transform the global situation.

Medical intervention in crisis situations – such as the recent outbreak of Ebola in West Africa – is one of the most visible aspects of INGOs' aid work. This photo shows a medical worker with Médecins Sans Frontières (MSF) in Liberia

Strengths of INGOs

- Smaller and more effective than large state bureaucracies
- Continuity (unlike government aid, which can be affected by elections)
- Not driven by profit (unlike TNCs)
- Able and willing to take risks
- Able to undertake small-scale projects working as partners with local people
- Responsive to donors, on whom they rely for funding.

Criticisms of INGOs

Most of these criticisms apply particularly to the larger INGOs; smaller NGOs are more able to avoid the pitfalls.

- Working too closely with governments or relying on government funds
- Having links with TNCs
- Unclear accountability
- Inappropriate spending of funds – for example, flying in experts rather than using the knowledge and experience of local people
- Some NGOs have portrayed people in developing countries as helpless victims and objects of pity
- Some faith-based NGOs have been accused of prioritising converting people to their religion
- Being too concerned with good publicity and building a successful brand.

The 2004 tsunami

Mari Marcel Thekaekara, who co-founded the South Indian NGO Accord, was at first impressed by the response of INGOs to the tsunami in India. Thanks to the unprecedented generosity of people around the world, the INGOs were able to play vital roles, especially in the first few days, delivering money to people that the government failed to reach, providing support to orphaned children and so on. But as time went on, some of the worst aspects of INGOs became evident. Some thought they knew better than local people – for example, building unsuitable temporary houses rather than the traditional coconut palm structures local people would have preferred. They acted as 'disaster tourists', more interested in getting their brand name publicized than in the victims (Thekaekara 2005).

Global civil society

Global civil society (GCS) comprises a loose collection of INGOs, activist groups and others, overlapping with the anti-globalization movement. There is a debate as to whether there is a coherent GCS or whether the organizations are too different and lack any common focus.

The term 'civil society' refers to the networks of groups and organizations that exist in any society, between individuals and families on the one hand and the state on the other. It includes municipalities, business, political groups and voluntary organizations of all kinds. The size and vitality of civil society is often seen as a sign of the health of a society in general. Globalization has meant that a worldwide civil society is emerging, made up of all the groups and organizations whose interests and activities are no longer confined to one state. GCS includes INGOs, both those with permanent staff and large networks of volunteers, and much smaller ones without paid staff.

Many of the activist INGOs and groups focus on working on particular areas of concern – for example, for equality for women or for cancellation of debts – and can be seen as forming clusters working within, or constituting, a global social movement (GSM). These movements have grown in numbers and size as people around the world become disenchanted with traditional politics and the issues it tends to focus on, and seek new ways of expressing themselves and demanding change.

The growth of global civil society and of global social movements has led to the emergence of an anti-globalization (in the sense of opposition to *neoliberal* globalization) movement, also referred to as the global justice movement, or as globalization from below. Global activists have come together to protest at G8, IMF and WTO meetings, and also at the annual World Social Forum (WSF) usually held at Davos in Switzerland. This is a gathering of tens of thousands of people representing many GSMs and other groups. It acts as a voice for a very wide range of reformist, radical groups, creating a broad coordinating body for those who oppose neoliberal globalization. It meets annually at the same time as the World Economic Forum, a rather secretive meeting of many of the world's political and business leaders. The WSF, with its inclusive slogan 'another world is possible', seeks to provide a progressive alternative and to demonstrate the strength of feeling globally against neoliberal globalization.

> The **World Social Forum** is an annual gathering of the anti-globalization movement.

> The **World Economic Forum** is an annual gathering of the world's business and political leaders.

Activity

Here is a list of some well-known large INGOs, and also some smaller ones: Oxfam; Action Aid; Save The Children; Global Rescue Mission Sierra Leone; Tree Aid; Sponsor a Gambian Child. Research one or more of these by visiting their websites or requesting their publicity material. Ask yourself these questions:

1 What are the main aims of this INGO?
2 In the UK, do they work mostly on fundraising or on raising awareness of issues?
3 In which developing countries do they work, and on what sorts of projects?
4 How effective are they in promoting development?

International governmental organizations

States cannot solve problems alone, and so they cooperate to set up a growing number of suprastate organizations, referred to as international governmental organizations (IGOs). The largest and best-known of these is the United Nations (UN), founded in 1947. There are also organizations that cover specific regions, such as the African Union and the African Development Bank.

The United Nations (UN)

The UN was set up partly to promote development, but initially its activities in this area were limited by a lack of commitment from developed countries. By the 1960s, many colonies had become independent and had a vote in the UN General Assembly, so voices from the Third World began to be more influential. However, the General Assembly is mainly a debating forum and its votes are not binding. Real power in the UN is with the Security Council, which has fifteen members, five of whom are permanent members with a veto (China, Russia, France, the UK and the USA). The ten non-permanent members always include some developing countries. The UN also takes on a peacekeeping role in conflict situations.

The UN system comprises a wide variety of programmes and agencies. Many of these take a more radical and pro-South line than the IMF, the WTO and the World Bank, because of the numerical strength of the developing countries when voting is based on one-country-one-vote rather than on economic strength or financial contributions. So, for example, the *Human Development Report* produced by the UN Development Programme has a more radical interpretation of development than the World Bank's *World Development Report*.

UN programmes and agencies involved in development include the following:

- United Nations Development Programme (UNDP): provides grants for sustainable development and produces the *Human Development Report*
- World Health Organization (WHO)
- World Food Programme (WFP): provides food aid in disaster and emergency situations; the WFP buys food to distribute, but also accepts donations; some Northern countries have used this to dispose of food surpluses, which has sometimes resulted in culturally or nutritionally inappropriate food being distributed
- Food and Agriculture Organization (FAO): helps improve food production and food security

- Office of the United Nations High Commissioner for Refugees (UNHCR): provides protection and assistance for refugees, including, increasingly, internally displaced people.

The European Union (EU)

The EU brings together twenty-eight nation-states in Europe; the total amount spent on aid by EU states bilaterally and through EU institutions multilaterally is over $50 billion and makes the EU and its members the world's largest aid donor. The 2013 Eurobarometer survey found that most Europeans thought aid was important and that more should be given, but many did not know how EU aid was spent (https://europa.eu/eyd2015/en/content/about-2015). The discussion of aid in Topic 4, pages 135–8, can be applied to the EU's aid programmes.

The International Monetary Fund (IMF), World Bank and World Trade Organization (WTO)

The three major supranational organizations which run the world economy are the International Monetary Fund (IMF), the World Bank and the World Trade Organization (WTO). They are formally part of the UN system, but are, in practice, separate. A common criticism of them is that they seem to have taken on lives of their own. The first two were established at a meeting of forty-three countries in 1944 at **Bretton Woods**. In both cases, voting is based on financial contributions ('dollar-a-vote'), meaning that they are, in effect, under the control of developed countries, especially the USA. The president of the World Bank has always been from the USA and the managing director of the IMF has always been a West European. Neither organization can be held accountable by other parts of the UN system, and the developed countries have rejected attempts to reform the allocation of votes. Both are large bureaucratic organizations in which admirable goals such as poverty alleviation can be lost in the internal demands of the organization.

> **Bretton Woods** is the place in the United States where an agreement in 1944 set up the IMF, the World Bank and what became the WTO.

The International Monetary Fund (IMF)

The IMF's role was initially to control the system of fixed exchange rates based on gold. This system ended in the early 1970s and the IMF lacked a clear role until the debt crisis began in the 1980s. The IMF then became a sort of financial police for the countries in debt, giving loans provided that the countries adopted an IMF economic programme. By the mid-1990s, many developing countries had such structural adjustment programmes.

CRITICISMS OF THE IMF'S ROLE IN DEVELOPMENT

A number of general criticisms are levelled at the role played by the IMF in development.

- It adheres strictly to neoliberal policies, despite lack of evidence of their effectiveness.
- It is unconcerned with the human effects of SAPs.
- It imposes the same conditions on all, regardless of how far the country has developed or what resources it has – 'one size fits all'.
- It deals mainly with short-term economic problems, and is less interested in longer-term development.
- It has failed to foresee economic crises.

The verdict on IMF structural adjustment programmes, as presented by a former chief economist at the World Bank, is as follows:

> IMF structural adjustment policies – the policies designed to help a country adjust to crises as well as to more persistent imbalances – led to hunger and riots in many countries; and even when the results were not so dire, even when they managed to eke out some growth for a while, often the benefits went disproportionately to the better-off, with those at the bottom sometimes facing even greater poverty. (Stiglitz 2002: xiv)

The World Bank

The World Bank has always had a clearer development role than the IMF. The Bank raises money from finance markets at a much lower rate of interest than governments would be able to, and then passes this rate on to its members. This enables governments of developing countries to borrow at much lower rates of interest than they could get commercially. The Bank also provides International Development Association (IDA) loans to the poorest countries, at zero interest. It has recently focused much more on poverty eradication and the setting of the Millennium Development Goals strengthened this.

CRITICISMS OF THE WORLD BANK'S ROLE IN DEVELOPMENT

- In the past, it has been restricted to lending for specific projects, such as dams, which were often inappropriate.
- It works closely with the IMF, so is still associated with SAPs.

The World Trade Organization (WTO)

The WTO was set up largely at the instigation of the USA. Its mission is essentially to push for neoliberal reforms in the area of trade. Although in theory all its member nations have an equal say, no votes are taken and decisions are reached by consensus. This means that decision-making is often difficult, and WTO talks have recently usually ended without agreement.

CRITICISMS OF THE WORLD TRADE ORGANIZATION (WTO)

- Its decision-making is undemocratic, with poorer countries in theory having a vote but in practice excluded from important discussions.
- It is so far ineffective in making rich nations reduce subsidies and tariffs when they are determined not to.
- It gives free trade priority over all other considerations, including sustainable development.

The main forum at which developed countries meet is the Group of Twenty, or G20, where representatives of the governments and central banks of member countries discuss global economic issues. There are also IGOs which bring together groups of developing countries. These include the Group of 77 developing nations (which now has 132 members); the BRICS (Brazil, Russia, India, China, South Africa) group, linked by their large, fast-growing economies and regional influence; and the D-8 or Developing 8 group of developing countries with large Muslim populations.

Activity

Visit the websites of the big three IGOs:
- www.imf.org
- www.worldbank.org
- www.wto.org
and of the G20:
- www.g20.org

To what extent do these websites acknowledge the criticisms made of the IGOs? How successfully do they put across their case?
For criticism of the IGOs, see:
- www.brettonwoodsproject.org.

Activity

Which six three-letter acronyms are relevant to global development? What words do they stand for? Give a one-sentence explanation of each of them.

NGO	WHO	SAS
GCE	IMF	TNC
SAP	KFC	MBE
DHL	ITV	HDI

What are the six non-global-development acronyms? Tie break: can you find any way to link these to global development?

Practice questions

1   Outline and explain **two** ways in which transnational corporations might help the development process.   **(10 marks)**

2   Read **Item A** below and answer the question that follows.

> **Item A**
>
> The largest International Governmental Organizations (IGOs) play an important part in development. The International Monetary Fund (IMF) and World Bank effectively run the world's economy, giving loans to countries in debt and helping to finance large-scale development projects, and trying to improve the structure of economies by insisting that in return they adopt neoliberal policies that the IMF and World Bank see as essential for development.

Applying material from **Item A**, analyse **two** reasons why the role of IGOs such as the International Monetary Fund and World Bank in development is controversial.   **(10 marks)**

3   Read **Item B** below and answer the question that follows.

> **Item B**
>
> There is now a very wide range of non-governmental organizations (NGOs), many of which are well known, such as Oxfam and Christian Aid. These organizations vary enormously in size and in the areas they focus on. Because of criticisms of other forms of aid, more aid is now being channelled through NGOs as it is believed that this will benefit poor people and countries more directly.

Applying material from **Item B** and your knowledge, evaluate the view that NGOs are more successful than other organizations in supporting development.   **(20 marks)**

Topic 4

SPECIFICATION AREA

Development in relation to aid and trade, industrialisation, urbanisation, the environment, war and conflict

Aid

Aid refers to economic, military, technical and financial assistance given (or loaned) to developing countries.

Aid can be classified according to where it comes from:

1 Aid provided by voluntary agencies and non-governmental organizations (NGOs) such as Oxfam, Christian Aid, World Vision and Voluntary Service Overseas. This form of aid is considered in the section on NGOs.
2 Official Development Assistance (ODA): the Organization for Economic Co-operation and Development (OECD) comprises twenty-five developed countries. Its members have aid budgets – they allocate a part of their resources to ODA. ODA takes the form of grants and 'soft' loans to promote economic development and the welfare of developing countries. ODA can be given directly to a developing country (**bilateral aid**), or to multilateral organizations, such as the United Nations (UN), World Bank and European Union aid programmes (**multilateral aid**). Some other countries that are not OECD members also give aid.

Bilateral aid involves only the donor and the recipient, usually government to government.

Multilateral aid is that which donors contribute to a shared fund, from which aid is then given to recipients.

Conditionality is the setting of conditions on aid, so that it will be withheld if those conditions are not met.

In 1970, OECD members agreed to aim to allocate 0.7 per cent of their GNI to ODA. Most do not meet this target; in 2014, the only countries to do so were Sweden, Luxembourg, Norway, Denmark and the UK (www.theguardian.com/global-development/2015/jun/01/european-union-aid-target-deadline-2020).

The word 'aid' covers grants and loans (which have to be repaid), and also the writing-off of debt (so that the recipient country is not receiving aid at all in the expected sense). Aid is often tied – that is, it must be used for a particular purpose specified by the donor. The donor country may also specify that the money be paid to one of its own companies to carry out a particular project, such as building a road or dam or supplying technical equipment. Aid may also be subject to **conditionality** – that is, it will only be given if the recipient country abides by certain conditions. For example, aid may be cancelled if the recipient country fails to hold elections, or to reform its economy.

A recent development is the giving of aid by countries outside the OECD group of rich nations. Cuba, which for a relatively poor country has a successful healthcare system, has sent doctors and other medical aid to African and other developing countries for many years. In 2007, Cuba provided more medical personnel to the developing world than all the G8 countries combined: 'Cuba has 42,000 workers in international collaborations in 103 different countries, of whom more than 30,000 are health personnel, including no fewer than 19,000 physicians' (Huish and Kirk 2007: 78). Venezuela under Hugo Chavez used some of its oil wealth to give aid to South American governments, and is using this to push an alternative to the Washington Consensus, based on breaking all ties with the IGOs. Bolivia has ended its agreement with the IMF and long-standing structural adjustment, compensating for this with loans and aid from Venezuela which come with fewer conditions and can be used for projects involving the state (Forero and Goodman 2007). Neumayer (2003) points out that Arab countries such as Saudi Arabia, Kuwait and the United Arab Emirates are also important donors of aid, usually to poorer Arab countries and to Islamic countries. Compared to OECD aid, aid given by Arab countries is more generous and usually not tied to specific projects.

With the global economic downturn in 2008, OECD governments came under pressure to cut their ODA spending. In the UK, the Conservative and Liberal Democrat Coalition government (2010–15) did not cut aid spending, although public support for aid dropped (Glennie et al. 2012).

Under a law passed in 2013, UK governments now have to spend at least 0.7% of GNI each year on aid. British aid was redirected towards greater support for private business and towards countries whose security was seen as important in preventing Islamic terrorism spreading. At the time of writing, these policies have continued under the majority Conservative government elected in 2015.

The case against aid

The very word 'aid' suggests something positive, yet the arguments against aid, or at least against the way it has usually been given, are strong and come from both sides of the political spectrum – from neoliberals and neo-Marxists. Emergency aid is usually, though not always, seen as above these criticisms, though it too can create dependency and worsen conditions.

The neoliberal view: aid creates dependency

The use of the word 'dependency' here points to considerable shared ground between right and left on the subject of aid. Neoliberals make similar criticisms of aid to those they make of the welfare states providing social security in the North: aid is seen as teaching people to be dependent on handouts, taking away their initiative and their ability to help themselves. Countries are seen as poor because of their own failings, such as laziness, corruption or inefficiency, and giving aid does not help overcome these failings and may even encourage them. Third World countries then demand aid as a right just as, from this view, social security 'scroungers' do, and become trapped in a culture of dependency. If a project is viable, it should be able to attract investment so that aid is unnecessary. If it can't attract private-sector funding, it can't be worth doing.

A strong and controversial statement of these views was made by Peter Bauer (1995), an economist who popularized these views and became known as Lord Anti-aid in the British media (he was made a baron in 1983 by Margaret Thatcher). The main argument for aid is that it supplies what developing countries do not have, but Bauer argued that aid could not be necessary for development, because Northern countries did not receive aid when they were developing. He suggested that aid implied that the Third World was incapable of achieving what the West had achieved. The term 'aid' is misleading, he said, because it implies something positive; a more neutral term would be 'government to government subsidy'. The term 'aid' allows governments to seem to be doing the right thing; it is hard to avoid calling them 'donors', which is another term loaded with positive connotations. Bauer said that the reality was that aid went to Third World governments, not to people. The aid industry has developed a logic and momentum of its own because it suits some groups in both the North and South.

Aid has also been criticized by writers from developing countries. The Zambian Dambisa Moyo (2010) argues that aid has been harmful to Africa because it has created dependency, fostered corruption and encouraged poor governance, and has not led to development. Aid, she says, should be phased out, to be replaced by encouragement of entrepreneurship and the market.

The neo-Marxist view: aid as imperialism

A good example is the work of Teresa Hayter, whose 1971 book is entitled *Aid as Imperialism*. She stresses how aid is conditional – it nearly always comes with strings attached. It is one way in which rich countries exercise power over poorer ones, and, as such, it is a form of **imperialism**. Hayter regards the claim made by Western governments that aid helps the South as hypocritical: most aid doesn't alleviate poverty, because it isn't meant to; its real purpose is to strengthen a system which damages the interests of the poor. Most aid doesn't go to the people or countries who need it, but to those who are of strategic or other importance to the donor country and who arguably don't need it. Aid creates jobs and export markets for the donors. Aid can also be used to win political support: the recipient country gets aid if it agrees to support the donor, perhaps by votes at international conferences, or by allowing its land and air space to be used for military purposes.

Imperialism: the process of empire-building associated with the colonial system.

The middle ground: a social democratic view

Aid can work, but it is often inappropriate or inefficient. This is not an objection to all aid, but a recognition that much aid is misdirected and abused, and a desire to see it used well. There have been many examples of aid which has not contributed to development:

- Aid that supports corrupt or undemocratic governments, or where the money is wasted through inefficiency
- Aid that is used to strengthen the armed forces
- Projects that are inappropriate and do more harm than good
- Projects that cause damage to the environment
- Projects that employ highly paid foreign experts who have little knowledge of local conditions and ignore the views of local people
- Projects based on ignorance or lack of thought – e.g. sending food to refugees in a war zone: the food is likely to be seized by combatants and will prolong the war and the suffering of the people it was intended to help.

The Sierra Leonian film maker Sorious Samura summed these criticisms up in his documentary 'Addicted to Aid' (BBC's *Panorama*, 24 November 2008) by describing aid as 'a leaking bucket' – more and more money is poured in, but the bucket never fills. The overriding criticism is that aid doesn't seem to work; fifty years of aid have not led to development. There are two possible conclusions to be drawn from this: either aid does not help development, or the aid given so far has not been enough and more needs to be given.

> **A case study of inappropriate Aid**
>
> The Pergau Dam in Malaysia was the most expensive UK government single aid project ever. £415 million was spent on a scheme to provide electricity for the capital, Kuala Lumpur. The project caused considerable environmental damage, including deforestation, and Malaysia could have produced electricity more cheaply from other sources. This was tied aid: the Malaysian government bought around £1 billion of military equipment from the UK. In 1994, a British court ruled that the allocation of aid money to this project was illegal because it was not of economic or humanitarian benefit to the Malaysian people (Lankester 2012).

The case for aid

The justification for aid comes originally from modernization theory: the rich world could provide aid in the form of capital, expertise or technology as a helping hand to those who were behind on the road to prosperity and mass consumption. It is still clearly the case that the North has much that can be shared with the South. A similar case to that of modernization theory has recently been put forward by Jeffrey Sachs (2005) who argues for a big push of large-scale, focused and integrated aid to lift developing countries out of poverty.

Aid has not solved the problems of world poverty, but it may have made things better than they would otherwise have been. Collier (2007) estimates that, over the past thirty years, aid has added one percentage point to the annual growth rate of the countries of the 'bottom billion'. This does not seem much, but it is significant; these countries would have been poorer without this aid. Aid may not have led to development, but it has stopped the situation being even worse.

Bauer's view of aid has been challenged on ethical grounds. He argues that Third World countries are responsible for their own poverty, but it is chance that leads to an individual being born in the Third World rather than the North. A person born in poverty in Africa does not have the same life chances as someone born in the North, and this is through no fault of their own. It can be argued on grounds of natural justice that giving aid is a moral imperative; not even to try to help is inexcusable. If aid helps improve life chances, it is worth it. This argument has gathered strength with the discourses of globalization and of the environment, which emphasize how we all share one small and fragile planet.

Does aid do more harm than good?

A lot depends on the type of aid that is offered. The right kind of aid – small-scale, aware of local needs, controlled at a local level, usually given by an NGO – can be very positive, but is not on its own going to transform a country. Aid in a disaster or emergency can be vital, although some aid of this kind has been misdirected and has often been restricted to relief rather than establishing foundations for a more secure future. Overall, however, the net flow of capital is *from*, not *to*, the South – for example, African countries send more money to the West in payment of interest on loans than they receive in aid. Aid needs to be seen in a bigger context, which includes debt and trade. The following sections explore these issues.

The debt crisis

The 'debt crisis' has its origins in the 1970s when banks in the rich world lent money to Third World governments. At this time, modernization theory led many people to believe that, if they were helped, poorer countries would quickly develop and begin to catch up with the rich world. The loans were seen both as good business for the banks and a contribution towards modernization. Interest was to be charged on the loans, but Third World countries took the money, believing that economic growth would mean they could pay the interest and eventually repay the loan.

Some of the money lent went into the pockets of dictators, and a lot was spent on arms, but there was briefly some real development. However, recession in the 1980s in richer countries reduced the export markets of Third World countries – but they still had to repay the interest on their loans. Many countries went deeper and deeper into debt, borrowing even more money to pay off the interest due on earlier loans. When governments were obliged to curtail their spending, they often found it easier to cut health and education budgets than, for example, to reduce spending on arms and the military (which risks a military coup by unhappy soldiers).

> The **debt crisis** refers to the inability (and sometimes refusal) of indebted countries to pay interest on loans or to repay the original loan; debt repayments hold back development by diverting money and resources.

The six boomerangs

People in developing countries are forced by debt to exploit their natural resources in the most profitable and least sustainable way; for example cutting down rainforest for timber to export. This leads to climate change, exhaustion of resources and depletion of biodiversity.

If the indebted countries were better off, they would be able and willing to buy from developed countries, so jobs have been lost for lack of markets.

For some countries in debt, the huge demand in developed countries for illegal drugs such as cocaine and heroin provides a tempting market, but with huge social and economic costs in the developed countries.

Many flee poverty by moving to the North or to other richer countries nearby. Economic migrants are not recognized as refugees.

People in developed countries pay taxes to give banks concessions so they can write off bad debts.

War

Debt creates social unrest, and can lead to war. Iraq's invasion of Kuwait, which led to the first Gulf War, happened partly because Iraq was under pressure to repay a $12 billion loan.

By the end of the century, debt had clearly become a huge obstacle to development, though it is impossible in practice to separate the effects of debt from those of globalization, trade and neo-liberal policies.

George (1991) introduced the term 'debt boomerang', arguing that debt was also creating problems for the North, and that action on debt was in the interests of the North as well as being ethically desirable. George's argument is important, because it suggests that debt cancellation is actually in the interests of those to whom the money is owed – it is not charity or compassion, but social and economic sense.

After pressure by the Jubilee Debt Campaign (http://jubileedebt.org.uk) and other organizations, the debt burden was reduced for many countries by the **Highly Indebted Poor Countries Initiative** (HIPC). This allowed debts to be written off provided the countries adopted IMF- and World Bank-approved economic policies.

The main argument for not cancelling the debts completely is 'moral hazard', a term used in the insurance industry referring to when people are not held responsible for what goes wrong as a result of decisions they have made. In this case, cancelling debts rewards those countries that did not use the money well (for example, spending it on a new presidential palace or private jet). Another argument is that banks would probably not loan money to the countries concerned in future. Much of the money is owed to the World Bank and the IMF; debt cancellation would leave them with limited funds to promote development. On the other hand, should people today be expected to repay loans if they didn't benefit from them? Is it their fault if a dictator wasted money twenty years ago, and should not the banks have realized that the money would be wasted?

The writing-off of debts has been hampered by so-called 'vulture funds', which buy the debts owed by poor countries at cheap rates and then sue those governments in order to make a profit. In 2007 the IMF found that eleven of the twenty-four countries in the HIPC Initiative had been sued by vulture funds, with a total of £1 billion being awarded to the vultures; in one case, a company called Donegal International bought an old debt owed by Zambia for £3 million, sued for £55 million and was awarded £15.5 million in a British court (Seagar and Lewis 2007).

In 2014, the Jubilee Debt Campaign reported that an increase in loans to developing countries was likely to lead to a new debt crisis. 'There is a real risk that today's lending boom is sowing the seeds of a new debt crisis in the developing world, threatening to reverse recent gains in the fight

Debt boomerang is George's term to describe the ways in which the debt crisis has negative effects in the developed world.

The (HIPC) **Highly Indebted Poor Countries Initiative** refers to a system by which heavily indebted countries can apply to have debt written off provided they keep to conditions.

One of George's boomerangs refers to the environment. Developing countries that are home to the world's last great rainforest – for example in South-East Asia and South America – are often forced to destroy huge swathes of rainforest to plant crops for fuel or food. This has serious consequences for climate change, which is of concern to the developed world as well as the developing world

against poverty and inequality', said Sarah-Jayne Clifton, director of the Jubilee Debt Campaign. 'The shocking thing is that public bodies like the World Bank are leading the lending boom, not just reckless private lenders hunting for returns' (Allen 2014).

> **Ghana's debt problems**
>
> In 2014, Ghana's external debt was $12.6 billion, having risen from $2.3 billion in 2006. Of this, 43 per cent is owed to multilateral institutions such as the World Bank, 31 per cent to private-sector organizations and 27 per cent to foreign governments. Ghana will need to borrow from the IMF to meet debt payments, and the IMF is likely to require cuts to the civil service and the removal of fuel subsidies.
>
> *Source*: http://jubileedebt.org.uk/blog/ghana-talks-imf-debt-problems-deepen

Trade

The extent and terms of trade between Northern and Southern countries are issues increasingly recognized as essential to an understanding of development. Trade was once seen as a rather dry concern of economists, but has now become the subject of popular debate and protest. In the last few years, Northern consumers have become aware of some of the issues through the growth of the **Fair Trade** movement and the availability of fairly traded goods – and the claim implicit in the term itself that normal free trade is not fair. Increased trade is an aspect of globalization; the ratio of exports to GNI, a measure of the extent of trade, has risen significantly for the whole world over the past fifty years, and for most developing countries (Coyle 2001).

Fair Trade is a movement to try to alter the terms of trade so that producers in developing countries receive a higher proportion of the profit.

The least developed countries are much less involved in world trade than the developed ones. Often, smaller countries rely almost entirely on one crop or material, and sometimes on exporting it to a limited number of countries (such as their former colonial power). For example, coffee accounts for 70 per cent of Burundi's exports (African Economic Outlook 2012). This leaves such countries, and the farmers or producers within them, in a very vulnerable situation. They receive only a tiny proportion of the final price of the crop or product, with the main profits being taken by the businesses which ship, process, package and sell – the middle-men. Even this small proportion is at risk, for several reasons:

This t-shirt is part of the social economy.

(ask me what that means)

A Fair Trade product, displaying the philosophy behind the scheme

Figure 2.5 Some of the principles of Fair Trade (Look for the FAIRTRADE mark on products. www. fairtrade.org.uk)

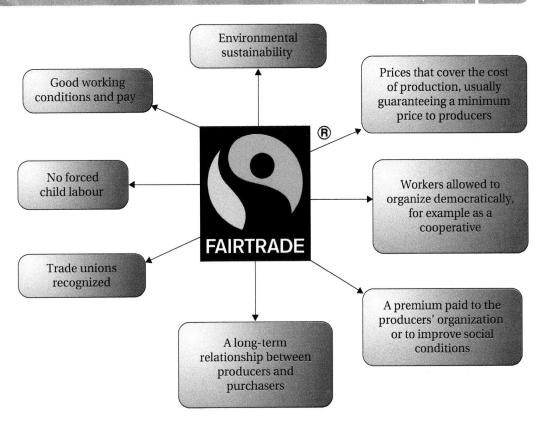

- Prices fluctuate according to supply and demand – if supply rises because more countries are producing a particular crop or material, the price is likely to fall
- Changing tastes and fashions in the North can affect demand
- Crops are vulnerable to severe weather conditions and disease – relying on one or a limited number of crops provides no insurance.

However, because terms of trade and prices of commodities change, developments which are positive for Southern countries can happen in an unplanned way. China's rapid industrialization means that it needs raw materials such as minerals, and some African countries have been able to supply these, with the demand pushing prices up. In return, Chinese goods are increasingly available in African markets and consumer goods such as mobile phones have become cheaper and more affordable (Dowden 2006).

Cocoa farming in Ghana

Ghana once produced a third of the world's cocoa (which is used to make chocolate). But in the late 1970s the world cocoa price fell, and many Ghanaian farmers switched to crops to feed themselves and to sell locally because they could not earn enough from cocoa. The Ghanaian government had relied on tax revenues from cocoa export and found itself in economic difficulty. It accepted a structural adjustment programme from the IMF and World Bank to 'rescue' the economy. This included removing subsidies to cocoa farmers, thereby increasing their difficulties. At the same time, chocolate producers in the West were cutting the cocoa content of chocolate, reducing demand and, as a result, pushing down the prices that Ghanaian farmers could get. Ghanaian chocolate has a reputation for its high quality and is now nearly all fairly traded, and Ghana's hope is that Western consumers will be willing to pay more for a high-quality and ethically sound product (Swift 1998).

Modernization theorists argue that developing countries need to become much more involved in international trade. This was one of the ways Western countries developed in the past, so the theory is that it should work for the rest of the world too. For dependency theorists and radicals, however, trade is one of the ways in which the North ensures the neo-colonial exploitation of the South. Under colonialism, the economies of the colonies were used for the benefit of the colonial power, by providing primary products (raw materials and cash crops). Despite political independence, developing countries remain heavily dependent on the export of these. However, the rich world uses its dominance in the world trade system to ensure that the prices that developing-world producers can get are low. The profits from such exports will never be sufficient to fund development, or even to keep many people out of poverty.

For neoliberals, free trade is fundamental. They favour trade liberalization – that is, the opening of national markets to international competition. This will, in theory, ensure that those who can produce goods for which there is a market, and at a price that customers are willing to pay, will do well. Trade liberalization includes the removal of protectionist policies in the developed world, where there are often tariffs on goods imported from the developing world and other barriers such as quotas, technical regulations and health and safety standards. Developed countries also subsidize agriculture and some industries, giving them an advantage in the global market. In practice, developed countries are very reluctant to reduce subsidies or to allow in cheap foreign goods that would undermine their own producers. In other words, they do not practise what the neoliberals preach. Developing countries, on the other hand, being in a weaker bargaining position, often have no alternative but to accept liberalization.

> **Trade liberalization** refers to the removal of barriers to free trade, such as tariffs and subsidies.

Mali and the cotton trade

The West African country of Mali grows high-quality cotton, but farmers there cannot sell it at a price that brings them a reasonable income. This is because the price of cotton on the world market is brought down by subsidies that the US government gives to its cotton farmers. American cotton farmers are able to sell cotton at a lower price than Malian farmers. Mali cannot afford to subsidize its farmers. Increasingly, Malian cotton is hard to find even in Mali, and across Africa people wear imported clothing rather than clothes locally made with local cloth. The World Trade Organization ruled in 2004 that the USA must reform its cotton subsidies, but by 2012 this had still not happened. West African cotton farmers lose about $250 million a year because of these subsidies (Bunting 2010).

Fair Trade

Products bearing a Fairtrade label have become more popular in the North, although they still only cover a limited number of types of product and have only a small share of the market. Fair Trade is an attempt to alter the terms of trade to give a fairer deal to producers in developing countries.

Neoliberals are opposed to fair trade because it interferes with the operation of the market. They argue that it is free trade, not fair trade, which will reduce poverty and improve living standards. They say that fair trade is in fact unfair, because it gives privileges to the relatively small number of producers who meet the criteria to take part in fair trade schemes – it is an intervention in the market that creates unfair advantages and disadvantages (Sidwell 2008).

Activity

Match the writers with their ideas:

Frank	One big push to solve world poverty
Bauer	The rich nations have kicked the ladder away
Hayter	Five stages to modernization
Collier	Aid as government-to-government subsidy

Rostow	World systems theory
Wallerstein	Focus on the bottom billion
Sachs	The debt boomerang affects the rich too
George	Dependency and underdevelopment
Chang	McDonaldization
Ritzer	Aid as imperialism

Industrialization

As we have found in our study of modernization and dependency theories, development is usually seen in terms of becoming more like the developed countries, and this involves becoming industrialized. Industrialization refers to the transition whereby the methods of production change, with accompanying social and cultural change.

The industrialization of the West

Britain was the first country to industrialize, with the Industrial Revolution usually dated roughly to the period from 1750 to 1850. Other countries, such as France and the USA, soon followed. Industrialization involved a 'total change', involving all aspects of society, which Polanyi called 'the Great Transformation'.

Achieving industrialization

Import substitution industrialization: an industrialization strategy based on domestic production of consumer goods to replace imported ones.

In the 1950s and 1960s, many Third World countries tried import substitution industrialization (ISI); already aware of the difficulties of breaking into the markets of the developed world, they produced goods for their own domestic market, in competition with imports from the developed world. This usually involved the state setting up industries, and protecting them by putting high tariffs or even complete bans on imported goods. Countries which attempted ISI on a large scale included Mexico, Argentina, Brazil and India. For example, India had its own car industry, producing the Ambassador car for sale in India rather than for export, and protected from foreign competition. Many expected economic growth to be fast and modernization to be achieved, but while ISI led to some development, especially in Latin America, it was not widely successful. A major problem was that the savings from domestic production of goods were balanced by the costs of importing the necessary raw materials (Hewitt 2000: 294). Neoliberals argue that the protection of 'infant industries' through tariffs on imports leads to inefficiency and lack of innovation, and therefore ISI could not be successful in the long term. Ha Joon Chang (2003), however, argues that today's developed nations practised protectionism while they were industrializing.

Export-oriented industrialization: an industrialization strategy based on production for export.

In the 1970s, there was a shift towards export-oriented industrialization (EOI). This had already been achieved by Japan, which produced goods cheaply and succeeded in marketing them in the developed world. A group of other countries followed Japan – notably South Korea, Taiwan, Singapore and Hong Kong, which became known as newly industrializing countries (NICs) and also as the 'Asian tigers'. The NICs protected their industries in the early stages and development states provided considerable support to companies. However, the success of Japan and each subsequent country seems to make it harder for other countries to succeed, because the world market is already under the control of developed countries. There are few opportunities left to exploit. The influence of neoliberal economics also means that countries are under pressure to allow free trade rather than protect their infant industries.

Newly industrializing countries: those that seemed to make rapid progress in the late twentieth century, notably the 'Asian tigers'.

An example of adjacent countries following different strategies is found in North and South Korea. Korea was divided after the Second World War with both parts of the country at roughly the same level of development – both were poor. The North followed ISI, the South EOI. Today South Korea is many times wealthier than the North, and scores much more highly on measures such as life expectancy.

Japan, China and Taiwan have all succeeded in export-oriented industrialization, mass-producing items for global distribution

Agriculture as industry

The strength of most developing countries is in agriculture, not industry, with especially those in tropical zones having good conditions for growing crops for export to the West. Growing crops has also been the main way of life for many, and the export of cash crops was established during the colonial period. So some countries have concentrated not on industry, but on agriculture, though sometimes treating it very much as an industry in order to increase production and to meet the standards required by Western consumers and supermarkets. Production and export is often controlled by TNCs, such as Del Monte and United Fruit. The **Green Revolution**, which started in the 1960s, was based on new high-yield varieties and enabled production to increase substantially – but it required ever greater use of environmentally damaging fertilizers and pesticides. Demand for Fair Trade and exotic produce such as 'superfoods' and for health products provides new opportunities for developing countries to grow for export.

Green Revolution: scientific and technological developments that improved agricultural yields, enabling more food to be produced in developing countries but creating some environmental problems because of heavy use of pesticides and insecticides.

New opportunities for industry

Globalization has opened up some new opportunities for developing industries, notably global tourism and using global communications technology to process data or develop software for customers in rich countries, as India has done in recent years.

Recently, many developing countries have been taking up new technologies. For example, mobile phone use in Africa has grown quickly. When a new technology is used without the previous version of the technology having been deployed, this is called **technological leapfrogging**. Often the older version of the new technology was less efficient and more polluting, and the newer version more sustainable. The best examples are the adoption of mobile phones without previous widespread use of land-line telephones, and of solar-powered tablet or laptop computers without previous use of desktop PCs. Leapfrogging only works for some technologies, and those that don't need an infrastructure or grid.

Technological leapfrogging refers to the use of a new technology when the previous version of that technology has not been used.

Tourism

International tourism is a huge industry, often regarded as the third-largest industry in the world after oil and vehicle production (Cohen and Kennedy 2012: 270, citing Sinclair and Tsegaye). Until recently, the main destinations for international tourists were a small number of developed countries, but non-Western destinations have grown in popularity.

For example, the small West African nation of The Gambia now relies heavily on tourism. To European visitors, it can offer winter sunshine, English-speaking staff and guides, and the chance to experience Africa, even though The Gambia lacks the charismatic wildlife species of East Africa (see table 2.5).

There is therefore a range of different strategies for developing industries that can be adopted. There are, however, some problems with the whole idea of a country having a development strategy.

- It can involve adopting the latest fashion, whether or not it is appropriate and likely to work.
- It is usually adopted by an elite and its main purpose may even be to line their own pockets.
- Any strategy will have different outcomes for different groups, but those involved are not usually consulted – for example, industrialization needs factory workers who will have to be persuaded to leave their agricultural livelihood, and move to a city.

The social historian Barrington Moore (1967) pointed out that there is no evidence to show that any population anywhere ever wanted industrialization, and plenty to show that many did not want it. Industrialization was favoured by members of the emerging middle classes, who saw opportunities for enrichment and to take power from the rulers of pre-industrial society. For the masses, there were fewer benefits. In Britain, industrialization was strongly opposed (by the Luddites and in the Swing riots of the 1830s for example) because it would end traditional livelihoods and would uproot people from their homes and destroy communities. Polanyi described the Great Transformation as a struggle between those who wanted to establish the market as the organizing principle of society and those who wanted to protect themselves, their land and their livelihoods against the new market forces (in Thomas 2000: 39–40). Industrialization requires one generation to pay a heavy social and environmental price in order that their descendants can (perhaps) benefit.

The **Informal sector** of employment is characterized by lack of regular work and wages, including petty trading, self-employment, casual work and so on; the dominant sector in cities in developing countries.

Table 2.5 Advantages and disadvantages of tourism to The Gambia

Advantages	Disadvantages
Formal-sector employment for Gambians, for example as hotel staff.	Environmental damage, especially to the coast, through hotel building and providing beaches.
Informal-sector employment for Gambians, for example selling fruit to tourists on the beaches.	The presence of wealthy tourists encourages begging, prostitution and theft.
Local farmers benefit from selling their crops to hotels.	Tourists sometimes act in culturally insensitive ways.
Tourists bring and spend money, most of which goes into the local economy (though not if spent in a foreign-owned hotel).	Growing inequality between coastal areas benefiting from tourist income and inland areas which do not.
	Tourism is seasonal, leaving people unemployed or underemployed for parts of the year.
	Relying on one industry is risky; a recession, rising costs or attractions of an alternative destination could destroy many people's livelihoods. Tourism in The Gambia was badly affected by the Ebola outbreak in other parts of West Africa in 2014, because tourists decided to stay away.
	Hotels often import much of the food they serve and the materials they use.
	Profits often do not remain in The Gambia, especially with package and all-inclusive holidays.

For more information about the problems of tourism in developing countries: www.tourismconcern.org.uk.

Urbanization

In 2007, for the first time, more than half the world's population were living in cities, a dramatic rise from 13 per cent in 1900. This is the result of urbanization. The urban population is expected to keep growing at nearly twice the rate of growth of the population as a whole. The growth of cities in developing countries will be much faster than that in developed countries. Rural populations are expected to remain stable overall, though with some variation between regions of the world.

Urbanization refers to the process by which the proportion of a country's population living in cities increases and also to the related economic, social and political changes. A city is usually defined as having more than 100,000 inhabitants; mega-cities have more than 10 million inhabitants. Urbanization occurs as a result of migration but also of smaller settlements growing so that they are reclassified as cities.

Historically, many cities were in what is now described as the developing world. For example, in the Middle Ages, China had several cities with populations of more than 1 million people. The phenomenon of most of a country's population living in cities is, however, relatively modern – it dates from industrialization and was first seen in England (in 1800, 20 per cent of the population lived in towns and cities; by 1900 that figure was 74 per cent).

In 1950, there were only two mega-cities: New York and Tokyo; by 2014, there were twenty-eight, most of which were in developing countries (see table 2.6).

Modernization theorists, looking back to the model of Western development, see the growth of cities as an essential part of economic growth. Cities provide a labour force concentrated in one place for factories and businesses. They are also important in promoting cultural change, because they remove people from the countryside, where traditional ways are strongest, and expose them to Western values. Modernization theorists would therefore expect that urbanization would be an essential part of the process of cultural and economic change leading to development.

However, there are several ways in which urbanization in developing countries today is different from the process that the now developed world experienced in the past.

1 Third World cities tend to be bigger and fewer. There is often a primate city, much larger than any other cities in the country, where there will be an international airport and other facilities.
2 Urbanization has not been accompanied by industrialization; city-dwellers often make a living from informal-sector work rather than being formally employed.

> **Urbanization**: the process by which a growing proportion of people live in towns and cities, and the social and other changes which accompany this process.

Table 2.6 The world's largest cities

	Population, millions
Tokyo, Japan	37.83
Delhi, India	24.95
Shanghai, China	22.99
Ciudad de México (Mexico City)	20.84
São Paulo, Brazil	20.83
Mumbai (Bombay), India	20.74
Kinki MMA (Osaka), Japan	20.12
Beijing, China	19.52
New York-Newark, USA	18.59
Al-Qahirah (Cairo), Egypt	18.42

Source: United Nations (2014)

3   The poor in the growing Western cities of the nineteenth century formed a proletariat, working in factories and workshops and often organized in trade unions, Marx saw this industrial working class as the group that would rise in revolution to overthrow capitalism. While traditional Marxists dismissed the urban poor as having no revolutionary potential, Franz Fanon (1963) in *The Wretched of the Earth*, turned this derogatory view around and said that their very marginality made them potentially revolutionary – they had nothing to lose.

Fanon's view is not widely shared when the poor in the cities of the developing world are considered today, because few strong political movements have arisen. Nancy Scheper-Hughes wrote of the people she studied over several years in South America:

> It is too much to expect the people of the Alto to organize collectively when chronic scarcity makes individually negotiated relations of dependency on myriad political and personal bosses in town a necessary survival tactic.... Staying alive in the shanty town demands a certain 'selfishness' that pits individuals against each other and that rewards those who take advantage of those even weaker. (Quoted in Beall 2000: 441)

Dependency theorists point out that colonialism has made it impossible for developing countries to follow in the footsteps of the developed world. Urbanization in developing countries today is fundamentally different because it is not a response to industrialization. Many cities in developing countries were established or grew dramatically under colonial rule, because they were used as administrative centres and as staging posts in exports of raw materials and cash crops. A two-tiered social system grew up, with the colonial administrators and some of their higher-ranking native allies enjoying a much higher standard of living and access to goods than the mass of the population. Dependency theorists argue that these characteristics have not changed under neo-colonialism, as TNCs have replaced the colonial powers. Cities play a key role in keeping countries underdeveloped by soaking up resources in unproductive ways.

Urban housing in developing countries

In developing countries, the number of people in cities far exceeds the number of jobs available, leaving many unemployed or underemployed. The poor usually have no access to regular

A shanty town in South Africa

housing, so they build their own. The areas they live in exist everywhere under different names: shanty towns, barrios, favelas, bidonvilles, bustees. They are often on illegally occupied land, and governments generally see them as problems, so that the residents live under constant threat of their homes being demolished. The housing is, at least initially, temporary and of low quality, but over time some more permanent features are created, with residents acting together to arrange resources and amenities. For the people who live there, they are often a viable solution to their problems, providing accommodation they can afford close to sources of income. Spontaneous settlements (a more neutral term than 'shanty towns') also offer new arrivals in the city a foothold and can encourage self-help and collective action; they can be, in Lloyd's (1979) term, 'slums of hope'. Not surprisingly, though, access to water, sanitation, education, health and other resources is limited. Residents are often unable to vote, because they do not have a legal address, and are vulnerable to exploitation by landlords, politicians, police and criminals (Slatterthwaite 2007).

Migration

Much urban growth is the result of natural population increase, but migration also plays a large part. Migration is often explained using the 'push–pull' theory, which focuses on rational decisions to move made by individuals. Migrants tend to be unmarried male adults who move for a variety of **push** and **pull factors** (see figure 2.6). The influx of large numbers of people without steady incomes contributes to urban squalor. Step migration is common – that is, people move from a rural area to a town to a city, and perhaps on to the developed world. Migration is often seasonal; migrants retain close links with rural family members and may return home to help with the harvest, for example, or they may send money home.

However, people often move in groups, or to settle with members of the same group. Extended family and ethnic ties are important, and this can be explained by the social networks theory of migration. Migration can also be seen in a wider historical and political context, in which people move because of social forces such as poverty and inequality (Raghuram 2009: 196).

Push factors refer to the disadvantages of rural life which push people into moving to cities.

Pull factors refer to the advantages of city life which attract people to move there from rural areas.

Differences between urban and rural poverty in developing countries

People in cities are usually closer to facilities and services than those living in rural areas – but that doesn't mean they have access to them. In the cities of developing countries, the living conditions of the poor are often worse than for those who live in rural areas. Such conditions include overcrowding, contaminated water, poor or absent sanitation, threat of floods/landslides and indoor pollution. In the case of water, supplies are now privatized in most countries as a result of free market policies and SAPs. In cities, piped water and sewerage is usually only provided for a minority in affluent areas (where the company supplying the service can expect to make a profit). Companies pursuing profit have no interest in providing services to people who cannot pay for them. So the poor buy their water from vendors – they pay more than their wealthier fellow citizens do and the water they buy is of a poorer quality (Beall 2000: 439). In rural areas, people are more likely to have access to natural water supplies, which are generally not privately owned and so are free to all. People in rural areas also benefit from having family members in cities who send home some of their earnings.

Cities and the environment

Cities are often seen as the main source of pollution and greenhouse gas emissions. However, having large numbers of people and industries in one place makes it easier to bring in new environmental regulations and lowers the cost of delivering water, sanitation and healthcare (Slatterthwaite 2007). Cities also provide opportunities to change the way people live more quickly, for example by designs which favour public transport, cycling and walking rather than cars.

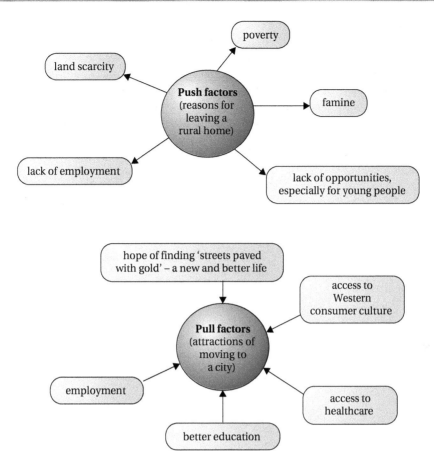

Figure 2.6 Push and pull factors involved in migration

The environment

Throughout history human activity has changed the environment. Most of what appears to be natural landscape has in fact been shaped by people. For most of history this was not seen as a problem, but as inevitable and even necessary; to survive and to prosper, people had to use what was around them (Woodhouse 2000: 141).

Concern about human effects on the environment can be seen in the Romantic movement in the early nineteenth century, which celebrated nature and deplored the new industrial landscape of factories and cities. By the second half of the twentieth century, it was recognized that pollution of air and water was a serious threat to health. The environment became an important political issue, and one intimately linked to economic growth and development. Within society and sociology, it became clear that human society was part of nature, not separate from and above it. In the field of development, the report of the Brundtland Commission, set up by the United Nations, highlighted the relationship between development and the environment (World Commission on Environment and Development 1987). The report coined the term 'sustainable development', which it defined as development that met the needs of the present without compromising the ability of future generations to meet their own needs. The use of the term 'sustainable' for the Sustainable Development Goals adopted in 2015 shows how sustainability and protection of the environment have come to be seen as very important.

Economic growth and industrialization, which developing countries are trying to achieve, will cause further environmental degradation if practised in the same way as by the West. China, for example, has large reserves of coal and will use them to meet its citizens' energy needs, despite the contribution to global warming that will accompany this. Green thinking in developed countries can involve, in effect, telling people in developing countries that they should not aspire to the life-style that people in the West have enjoyed.

Many environmental issues are now seen as being global, but both the causes and the effects are unequally distributed between regions of the world. The consumerist lifestyle of the developed world and its greater energy and fuel use mean that it creates and worsens many of the problems. People in the developed world have much larger ecological footprints than those in developing countries – that is, on average, they consume more resources and have a greater impact on the environment.

Although poorer people are the least responsible for environmental problems, they are affected by them more than wealthier people. They lack the resources to move or to change their situation. For example, it is the poor who live on land that is liable to flooding, or close to sources of pollution, because they cannot afford to move anywhere else.

Some current environmental issues

- Global warming and climate change, attributed mainly to carbon emissions (from factories, power plants, cars, aeroplanes, etc.)
- Deforestation, particularly loss of tropical rainforest
- Desertification, involving the loss of farm land
- Loss of biodiversity: extinction of species, depletion of the gene pool of other species and loss of variety of ecosystems to support biodiversity
- Over-use of non-renewable resources, such as coal and gas, and over-reliance on exhaustible resources which can be destroyed if overused, such as fish stocks
- Land, air and water pollution, damaging shared resources, including the dumping of waste, especially toxic waste in developing countries by TNCs or Western governments. For example, many of the West's discarded PCs end up in Agbobloshie in Ghana, where local people break them up for recyclable parts, exposing themselves to dangerous chemicals and other risks (*BBC News*)
- Ozone depletion: the only issue on which the world has so far been able to work together and make significant progress, by banning the use of CFCs (chlorofluorocarbons).

Environmental problems in developing countries

Environmental problems are not seen in the same way in the North as they are in the South. For the North, at least for those concerned with the environment, the focus is on issues such as global warming, deforestation and conserving habitats, often using the discourse of sharing a small planet. In the South, there is more concern about the effects of TNCs, uneven trade and Western consumerism in making it difficult for developing countries to avoid problems (Cudworth 2003: 148). The pressure to attract investment from TNCs leads some developing countries to weaken environmental controls – for example, having less stringent controls on pollution. The use of the best agricultural land by TNCs for cash crop production, employing few workers, pushes small farmers onto marginal land, for example on the edge of forests, and into unsustainable use of the forest and its resources.

Some Southern environmentalists have accused the North of using environmental concerns as a cover for its own interests, with international agreements that appear fair often seeming in practice to allow TNCs to carry on with unsustainable practices. The USA, in particular, seems unwilling to act if there is likely to be any impact on its corporate interests – for example, it refused to join 160 countries in signing the Kyoto Protocol on the reduction of carbon emissions.

The current emphasis in developed countries on recycling can have a negative impact in developing countries as well. Poorer countries are often dependent on the use of natural resources (timber, mining, etc.). Recycling of scrap materials and the substitution of synthetic materials reduces demand for these. Waste from the developed world often ends up in poorer countries, being recycled but also often bringing pollution and health problems.

The people-centred approach to development advocates sustainable development practices such as appropriate technology. This involves use of renewable local resources with minimal environmental impact. For example, wind-up PCs and radios remove the need for electricity gen-

---

An **ecological footprint** is a measure of the environmental impact of an individual's or country's lifestyle, taking into account what resources are consumed.

Global warming refers to the rise in global temperatures now acknowledged to be caused mainly by human activity, likely to lead to severe consequences such as rising sea levels and increased desertification.

Deforestation refers to the fall in the amount of land covered by forest as a result of human activity.

Desertification is the spread of deserts, as land on the edges of deserts loses its vegetation and top soil.

Biodiversity refers to the number and variety of species in ecosystems, threatened by human activity.

Non-renewable resources are natural resources which are finite, and cannot be replenished, such as coal and oil. They can be distinguished from renewable resources such as wind, solar power and (if used sustainably) timber.

Exhaustible resources are those that can be renewed, but that can also be exhausted and destroyed if overused – for example, fish stocks and forests.

Shared resources are those resources that are not privately owned and whose use is freely shared – for example air, water (unless you choose to buy bottled water) and parts of the countryside. They are also sometimes referred to as 'public goods'.

Appropriate technology is that which is people-centred, small-scale, energy-efficient and environmentally sound, and uses local resources.

Neo-Malthusians: modern followers of Malthus's main argument, that population growth will overtake food supply.

eration; and food in Africa can be stored and kept fresh in pot-in-pot refrigerators which need no power. The NGO Practical Action focuses on appropriate technology: www.practicalaction.org.

Clash of interests

Actions to try to protect the environment are political and run the risk of affecting some people adversely. The well-meaning attempts of outsiders may be met with hostility and may create social problems even as they try to solve environmental ones. George Monbiot gives this example:

> The Bambuti Ba'twa tribe of Pygmies who used to live in the low equatorial forests on the border of Rwanda and what is now the Democratic Republic of Congo had their lands designated a national park to protect gorillas. The Pygmies were evicted in the name of conservation and are now found in small groups living in squalor on the edge of the park.
> 'Life was healthy and good, but we have become beggars, thieves and prowlers', said one chief. 'This disaster has been imposed on us by the creation of the national park.' (Monbiot 2008)

Applying the theories

Neoliberals

Neoliberals see the solution of environmental problems in the extension of the free market. Capitalism may have contributed to environmental problems, but its nature as an unprecedented 'growth machine' (Saunders 1999: 269) means that it will generate solutions to the problems. So current problems such as the use of high-polluting non-renewable fuels for cars and other transport will be solved as costs rise, creating incentives to develop more environmentally acceptable alternatives. Such solutions are referred to as 'technological fixes', and both environmentalists and sociologists tend to be very sceptical about them. Environmental problems have their roots in complex social and economic contexts, so a 'fix' seems too easy. Moreover, the fix has to come from pursuit of greater wealth by individuals or corporations when most environmentalists would prefer a collaborative effort. Neoliberals also advocate privatization or commodification of public goods, extending the market into areas it has not reached before. The owners, they claim, would act as custodians and would promote sustainable use because this would make economic sense. Those who disagree say that this will just exclude the poor who, for example, may not be able to get water because they cannot afford the market price.

Neo-Malthusians and modernization theory

The **neo-Malthusian** view is put forward by those influenced by the writings of Thomas Malthus (explained in more detail below, on pages 167–8). They are concerned by the implications for the environment of population growth, especially in developing countries. For neo-Malthusians, those whose damage to their environment most needs curbing are poor people in developing countries, especially in rural areas. Their poverty leads them to degrade the environment. Even if they are aware of the long-term problems being created, short-term needs mean they use the available resources. Population growth contributes to this. Growing numbers of people mean that marginal land has to be farmed, with loss of soil and eventual desertification. This view has been adopted by writers following modernization theory approaches. It sees the problems as being internal to developing countries, rather than seeing them, as dependency theorists would want, in the context of an unequal global system.

Anti-Malthusians and dependency theory

For anti-Malthusians, who are often environmentalists, the people whose damage to the environment most needs curbing are the wealthiest people on the planet, because they consume a far greater share of resources and generate far more waste than poor people do. They would point to the fact that exploitation of the developing world's resources is for the benefit of consumers in the North. A poor family may take firewood from a forest, but it takes a timber company with an export market to devastate large areas of rainforest.

It is not population that is the basic problem, but consumption – not how many people there are, but how much they consume. The unequal global distribution of resources is the real underlying issue. This view fits in with dependency theory in its emphasis on seeing the problems in the context of an unequal global system. The world can sustain far more people if they have a lifestyle based on low use of resources than it can if they have a lifestyle like that in the West today. Anti-Malthusians argue that developed world consumers must reduce their consumption levels, and their ecological footprints. Environmentalists argue that this would allow some economic growth in the South, which would be necessary to achieve acceptable living standards, but disagree on how much growth is possible or desirable.

Activity

Ten of the words below are concepts used in the study of global development; the rest are not. Find the global development terms and then write one-sentence explanations of each of them:

Panthusian	Modernization	Mint imperialism	Sustainability
Satellites of love	Commodious	Underdevelopment	Malthusian
Cultural imperialism	Desertification	Urbane metropolitans	Malapropism
Dependability	Agribusiness	Herbivorous	Neo-anti-postmodernism
Neoliberalism	Metropolis	Structural violence	Structural isomerism

---

War and conflict

Conflict in the sense of struggles between groups or individuals is an inevitable feature of any complex society. Many sociologists emphasize conflict within societies, as opposed to consensus. If conflict is taken in this wider sense, rather than meaning violence, it can also be seen as necessary and positive, providing the impetus for change and progress. All societies develop ways of managing conflicts – for example, the democratic political process manages changes of government without coups or revolutions. But conflicts can develop into wars.

Rwanda as a structurally violent society

In analysing the roots of the Rwandan genocide in which more than half a million people died, Uvin (1998) has argued that Rwanda before the genocide was a structurally violent society. Its economy was growing, and many aid agencies were working there. But only a small group, the 'state class', was benefiting, and there was growing inequality, with education and health poor following a structural adjustment programme. An apparently peaceful society concealed mounting anger which was channelled into scapegoating of the Tutsi group in the genocide.

The nature of wars today

War can be defined differently depending on the answers to questions such as:

- How many deaths are there and over what period?
- What are the causes of death (only battle-related, or including disease which has spread because of the war)?
- Are regular armed forces involved?
- Is the purpose to control all or part of a state?

By most counts, there have been around thirty-five to fifty wars going on at any one time in recent years. Since the end of the Cold War, and with the exceptions of the US-led invasions of Iraq and Afghanistan, most wars have not been the conventional wars of history between two or more states for possession of territory. States have lost the monopoly on military violence. Most of today's wars are civil wars, and occur in some of the poorest developing countries. Kaldor (1999) calls them 'new

Structural violence: the term used by Galtung (1969) to describe the way in which even in an apparently peaceful society, a group (usually distinct because of, for example, its gender, ethnicity, religion or caste) can be exploited by the systematic denial of their rights.

Table 2.7 Old wars and new wars compared

Old wars	New wars
Total wars – mobilization of men and resources on a large scale	Often these are civil wars, sometimes based on ethnic differences
Fighting was on battlefields between armies, though since World War Two civilians have been targets more often	Battles are avoided; mainly guerrilla warfare. Civilians targeted and terrorized, leading to increase in number of refugees
Wars were justified by appeals to patriotism or democracy	There is now a globalized war economy. Armed groups may raise money by control of oil, diamonds or other resources, or by ransoming hostages
Mass production of weapons, ships, aircraft and later production of nuclear weapons	Leaders often influenced by globalized culture, e.g. wearing Rayban sunglasses and Rolex watches

wars', arguing that although they appear localized, they involve global 'shadow' economies and global networks such as the arms trade, diamonds and drugs. They are a result of globalization, and to some extent a reaction against it (see table 2.7).

Why are there so many civil wars in the poorest countries?

Neo-Malthusians would see uncontrolled population growth and environmental scarcity as the main factors. Countries such as Sierra Leone are those where the struggle to survive is most intense. This is the New Barbarism thesis, which is explained below on page 167.

Mohammed Ayoob (2001) argues that civil wars are part of the process of creating modern states. Medieval and early modern Europe experienced similar wars, with many warlords controlling often small areas and constantly shifting borders and alliances. In this view, related to modernization theory, civil wars will become less common as countries begin to modernize. Peace will come as a result of free trade and democracy.

Contrasted with these views are those, related to dependency theory, which see civil wars in the global context and look at external factors. For example, Duffield (2001) sees new wars in the context of globalization, which has increased inequalities and excluded many in developing countries from its benefits. At the same time, traditional ways of life and earning a livelihood have been disrupted and states have less control. Amongst the factors contributing to civil wars are:

- Relative poverty worsening: some groups in these countries are not benefiting from globalization and development, or are affected by SAPs
- Weak state institutions: the state ceases to be able to provide social goods such as security, health and education, and is less able to resist challenges such as rebellions (Hanlon 2006: 123)
- The presence of unemployed young men who see no future for themselves (for example, being unable to find a wife or support a family)
- Changes in terms of trade adversely affecting people; for example, the ending of the International Coffee Agreement by the USA in 1989, which drastically reduced the incomes of Rwandan coffee farmers – the resulting poverty contributed to the 1994 genocide
- The arms trade: large amounts of weapons and military equipment were produced during the Cold War period, and so arms have since 1990 been cheaply and easily available. Many weapons were originally sold legally to nation–states but today there is a substantial trade in arms controlled by transnational criminal networks
- Aid can help create the conditions for war if most of the benefits go to one group and so strengthen inequalities

- The presence of valuable resources such as oil or diamonds, which can be goals in themselves or can be used to buy arms and military equipment
- Ethnic or other divisions which can be exploited by politicians and others seeking power
- Interference by other countries.

Underlying and uniting all of these, it can be argued, is structural violence on a global scale – 'the deliberate maintenance of a global system based on fundamental and self-reinforcing inequality' (Richard Cornwell, quoted in Hanlon 2006: 124).

Civil wars

Civil wars tend to be marked by shocking brutality. A good example is the practice of Sierra Leonean rebels of cutting off the hands or feet of their victims, most of whom were civilians. This is partly because rules of war such as the Geneva Convention, to which most states subscribe, do not apply.

Most of the casualties in civil wars are civilians, who die because of reduced access to food and healthcare rather than in battle. It is therefore very difficult to calculate how many people have died, especially as civilian casualties may not be counted. People flee from their home areas because of fear, and so wars create refugees. Some will join an armed group as the best survival option.

Women and children are often the main victims of war, but both are also increasingly involved in the fighting too. War destroys families and leaves widows, widowers and orphaned children. It is often easier for a widower to find a new partner, because there are likely to be fewer men than women. A widow without family support may find it difficult to make a living, and to find a new partner, especially if she has been raped or become pregnant. Child soldiers (both boys and girls) have been a visible new feature of some recent wars, such as those in Sierra Leone and Uganda.

Intervention in civil wars

Wars often lead to intervention. This may be by a neighbouring country, but is more likely to be a multilateral intervention, by the United Nations or a regional grouping such as the African Union. Intervention can succeed in imposing a ceasefire, but this may just give the combatants time to regroup and re-arm. The end of fighting is not the end of the problem; unless the underlying causes of the war are removed, fighting is likely to resume. More than half of all civil wars restart within ten years.

A child soldier in South-East Asia. What consequences might there be for a society in which young children are required to fight in wars and conflicts?

The purpose of intervention is to stop the killing. This is, however, not always the most desirable outcome. A quick end to a war may bring a bloody dictator to power, with greater loss of life and probably little progress to follow. It may be better for there to be a long war to defend a popular elected government than to allow the government to be overthrown quickly in a coup. Luttwak (1999) has argued provocatively that it can be better to let wars run their course, because they will eventually end with a resolution of political conflict and with peace. Intervention prevents the two ways of wars 'naturally' coming to an end: by a decisive victory for one side or through exhaustion of both sides.

The effects of war on development

Many countries in the lower half of the Human Development Index have experienced an armed conflict in recent years; relatively few of those in the top half have done so. This suggests a strong link between low development and conflict.

Although poverty can lead to war, so too does war create poverty, for a number of reasons.

1 War is expensive, absorbing money that could be used for development.
2 War destroys the infrastructure that makes development possible: schools, hospitals and health centres and the roads and bridges that trade relies on.
3 The human costs of war can be enormous – for example, communities, families, homes and businesses are often destroyed, and people are left wounded and disabled as well as homeless.
4 Unexploded munitions and landmines cause deaths and impede agriculture for many years after a war.
5 Environmental costs can be very high, including damage by bombs and other arms that destroy or cause harm to, for example, forests, wildlife and agricultural land, from which it may take many years to recover. Such effects might be the direct result of explosions as well as due to the release of poisons into air, water and land.
6 Refugees are forced to use whatever is available to survive, resulting in further environmental damage – for example, they need to use any available wood for fires to keep warm, cook and boil water.
7 Civil wars in one country can also contribute to poverty in neighbouring countries: conflict can easily spread across borders, trade is reduced and there will be refugees.

War kills after the fighting has stopped

The Second Congo War, also known as the Great War of Africa, officially ended in 2003. Yet findings from the International Rescue Committee, based on a nationwide survey, found that the crude mortality rate in Congo from January 2006 to April 2007 was 57 per cent higher than the average for sub-Saharan Africa. The committee estimates that, from 1998 to 2007, there were 5.4 million excess deaths because of the war, and that more than 2 million of these were after the peace agreement. Less than 0.5 per cent of recent deaths were from violence; after the war, people were dying from infectious diseases, malnutrition, and pregnancy- and childbirth-related causes. The social and economic disruption caused by the war, with people displaced, infrastructure destroyed and health services and food supplies weaker, led to higher rates of disease and death. Children accounted for 47 per cent of deaths, but make up only 19 per cent of the total population (Coghlan et al. 2008).

Terrorism: in war and conflict, the use of tactics intended to persuade the opponents, or civilians, not to resist.

Ending and preventing war and conflict are therefore important for development. Collier (2007) argues that security and accountability are essential for both social and economic development.

Terrorism

Terrorism is now an inescapable part of war. In traditional wars, it is used sometimes as a supplementary measure, but in civil wars it has become more important than armed action. Groups that cannot sustain traditional armed action terrorize civilians. The word 'terrorism' was first used for state actions, and many states have used terror tactics against parts of their own population or others, or have sponsored terrorism. Although the distinctions between state-directed terror, state-sponsored terror and non-state terror are often blurred, in popular use the term now usually refers to non-state terror.

The US State Department defines terror as 'politically motivated violence perpetrated against non-combatant targets by subnational groups or clandestine agents, usually intended to influence an audience' (Cohen and Kennedy 2012: 203). According to this definition, incidents of terrorism fell from a peak of around 660 in 1987 to around 200 in the early 2000s. The Islamic jihadist attacks on the USA on 11 September 2001 came in a context of declining non-state terrorism. The Islamic jihadists are a globalized form of terrorism, present in small groups around the world and attacking globally dispersed targets. They also differ from earlier terrorists in not always claiming responsibility for attacks, in having few or no specific demands and in being more indiscriminate. These characteristics may indicate a change in the nature of terrorism; Giddens refers to 'new-style terrorism' (2006: 886).

Practice questions

1 Outline and explain **two** ways in which development can lead to environmental problems.
(10 marks)

2 Read **Item A** below and answer the question that follows.

> **Item A**
> The justification for giving aid to poorer countries is that it will improve the lives of poor people and help countries to develop. Although large amounts of aid have been lent or given to developing countries over the past fifty years, it is clear that aid has not achieved these aims consistently and some have argued that aid may not help in the ways that it has been assumed to help.

Applying material from **Item A**, analyse **two** reasons why aid from developed nations might not help developing nations.
(10 marks)

3 Read **Item B** below and answer the question that follows.

> **Item B**
> The expansion of free trade is often seen as essential to development. Poorer countries, it is argued, need to become more involved in international trade because this will increase the flow of capital and will stimulate economic growth. However, the terms of trade are often unfavourable to producers in poorer countries, and this has led to a movement arguing for Fair Trade rather than what it sees as unfair trade.

Applying material from **Item B** and your knowledge, evaluate the view that unfair trade is preventing development.
(20 marks)

Topic 5

SPECIFICATION AREA

Employment, education, health, demographic change and gender as aspects of development

Employment

There are many more people in developing countries than in developed countries who are not in full-time regular paid work, but few households where there is no income at all. The issues are different from those in the North, where some households have no paid work at all. Unemployment statistics would not give an accurate picture of work and non-work in the South.

Many people in the South, especially in cities, rely for their income on work in the informal sector. This includes self-employment, micro-enterprises, petty trading, casual and irregular work and personal services. Work in the informal sector is often labour-intensive and unregulated, and may be illegal. Informal-sector businesses are usually not officially registered and may not pay tax. People working in this sector make a living (just about) in an astonishing variety of ways, which reveal the extent of human ingenuity. But such work is precarious, often temporary, and the problems are especially acute for women, minority ethnic groups and disabled people. In the informal sector people tend to work very hard but productivity is low and they do not get paid well.

In addition, many people in developing countries support themselves and their families through growing food for their own consumption (subsistence agricultural production), or by hunting, fishing and gathering.

Work in the formal sector tends to involve large businesses with fairly stable employment, higher wages and regulated conditions (for example, paid holidays and sick pay), and workers may even be able to organize themselves as trade unions. The formal sector includes those working in the public sector, for example as teachers or in health services, and for TNCs, or for local businesses supplying TNCs. Where these can be described as sweat shops, there are normally regulations on pay and conditions, even if these are not being applied fully. Formal-sector work is in short supply (TNCs only account for about 5–6 per cent of the world's jobs, and many of those are in the developed world) (McGiffen 2002, p. 80) and is highly sought-after in most countries. Despite offering good pay and conditions by local standards, TNCs are still the target of criticism

A roadside fruit and vegetable stall in Guam in the Western Pacific, an example of the informal sector. What other examples of economic production might official figures not take account of?

from campaigners because workers receive only a very small proportion of profits in the form of wages and benefits, with most of the wealth created being taken out of the country.

The economy of developing countries therefore consists not only of the formal, recorded economy, but also of the 'informal' economy which is unrecorded and activities like production for own consumption, which replace money and market activities. Taken together, these are the 'real economy' (Wield and Chataway 2000: 108). A similar situation exists in developed countries, but there the formal sector is much larger and the other two sectors are smaller. These differences mean that it is very difficult to establish reliable statistics on employment or unemployment.

Where the informal sector is the main way of making money, some groups are in particularly difficult situations, for example:

1 *Children.* Even where schooling is free, time spent in school is time that could be spent earning money, so children may work rather than go to school.
2 *Older people.* The idea of retirement belongs to the formal sector, and there are unlikely to be state pensions.
3 *People with disabilities.* In the absence of state support, disabled people rely on family and community, or may generate income by begging. In Sierra Leone's civil war, the rebels often cut off the hands or feet of victims; a priority for both government and NGOs has been to train victims in skills that will help them find work.
4 *Women.* In some cultures it is unacceptable for women to work outside the home. Women are often reliant on husbands and fathers to earn money; for women alone, such as widows, making money may be very difficult. Even in the formal sector, women are often taken advantage of, working for lower wages than men and in poor conditions. Elson and Pearson (1981) showed how globalization led to many young women working in factories producing goods for export. This provided some financial independence but kept women subordinate with their supposedly limited skills ('nimble fingers') justifying low wages.

Although more jobs have been created as countries experience economic growth, globally the number of unemployed people has grown and will continue to grow because the number of people of working age will grow. The bigger problem concealed by the figures is the number of people who are underemployed, unable to work to their full potential and unable to work themselves out of poverty.

Globalization and the availability of cheaper international travel have enabled increasing numbers of people from developing countries to work in the North. Some are well trained and qualified, for example as doctors; others are unqualified. Some work legally, others not; some are abroad only for a short period and others stay for many years. In all cases, the big pull of the North is the availability of higher wages. Although to some extent these are absorbed by the higher costs of living, being able to send money home in the form of remittances to support families in the country of origin is an increasingly important aspect of many economies; Harris has described it as 'one of the most successful mechanisms for redistributing the world's income in favour of poorer countries' (Harris 1995). In 2014, according to the World Bank, remittances to developing countries totalled $436 billion. Remittances are important to families, but also help development by the flow of capital into a national economy (World Bank 2015).

> **Remittances** refers to the transfer of money by a migrant worker back to family and friends in their country of origin.

Helping people make a living

One way in which agencies have sought to support the informal sector is through micro-credit loans. Poor people are unlikely to be able to borrow money from a bank to start a small-scale enterprise; micro-credit fills this need with small loans, often supported by training – for example in how to track stock and keep accounts. The best-known scheme is the Grameen Bank, launched in Bangladesh by Mohammed Younus, but such schemes are now widespread across the South and have also been used in developed countries. Micro-credit schemes are not without problems, however. Many loans have been to women, for the best of motives, but not always with awareness of gender relations in the community and wider society, potential conflicts with men, and the potential difficulties of repaying the debt (Pearson 2000: 396–7).

> **Micro-credit:** schemes to allow poor people to borrow small sums of money.

Child labour

Many children around the world work; for example, those aged 14 and over in Britain can do some kinds of part-time work. Such work can be valuable preparation for work later in life, but the law limits the amount and type of work so that the child's education does not suffer.

In developing countries, families have often relied on children to work – for example, helping on the family farm or selling the produce at a market. This has been cited as one reason for families having several children: children who work are an economic asset to the family. The International Labour Office (ILO) makes a distinction between working children and child labour. The ILO works to abolish child labour, but recognizes that some work by children, depending on age and local conditions such as the availability of schooling, is acceptable and even essential.

Child labour normally refers to children under the age of 15 who work for more than fourteen hours a week (and who are usually not attending school). The ILO estimates that in 2012 there were 168 million child labourers, down from 246 million in 2000. Many were engaged in hazardous work directly endangering their health, safety and moral development. The great majority were in developing countries, and there were many more boys than girls. Both the number and percentage of child labourers have fallen in recent years as a result of international campaigns to reduce child labour, and the ILO believes that total abolition is possible, arguing that the cost of eliminating child labour is much lower than the benefits gained in health and education (ILO 2013).

Education

Education – schools in particular – is widely accepted as an essential aspect of development. On achieving independence, countries committed to development often spent highly on education. For example, the Indian economist Amartya Sen (1999) has argued that education is essential both to increase human capability to make choices for ourselves and because development is not possible without it. Between 2000 and 2015, following the Dakar Education Forum and the setting of Millennium Development Goals for education, there was significant progress in improving education in developing countries. By 2015, however, according to the UNESCO *Education for All Global Monitoring Report,* although the number of children not in school had fallen by a half, there were still 58 million children not in school and around 100 million who do not finish primary education. There is still some gender disparity, with girls less likely than boys to go to school, despite an

Education is recognized as important for development. Left: a community in Zambia. Right: Mansa-Colley Bojang School, Brikama, The Gambia

Table 2.8 Primary education globally, 2012

	Total primary enrolment		Primary education enrolment (adjusted net ratio)		Out-of-school children			Survival rate to last grade of primary education	
	2012 (000s)	Change since 1999 (%)	1999 (%)	2012 (%)	2012 (000s)	Change since 1999 (%)	Female (%)	1999 (%)	2011 (%)
World	**705,103**	**8**	**84**	**94**	**57,788**	**-45**	**53**	**75**	**75**
Sub-Saharan Africa	144,075	75	59	79	29,639	-30	56	58	58
Arab States	42,761	22	80	89	4,467	-43	58	82	83
Central Asia	5,479	-20	95	95	295	-22	52	97	98
East Asia and the Pacific	184,382	-18	95	96	6,923	-42	47	85	92
South and West Asia	192,650	24	78	94	9,814	-73	48	64	64
Latin America and the Caribbean	64,696	-8	93	94	3,763	-6	47	77	77
North America and Western Europe	51,349	-3	98	96	2,060	108	47	92	94
Central and Eastern Europe	19,712	-21	93	96	827	-53	48	96	95

Source: Education for All Global Monitoring Report, UNESCO 2015

1a In which regions did the net enrolment ratio (representing the proportion of children of the relevant age group enrolled in school) increase by most between 1999 and 2012?

1b In which part of the world did this fall? Can you think of a reason for this?

2a How many children of this age group were not in school in 2012?

2b What percentage of the total number of children of this age group globally is this?

2c Approximately what proportion of these were in sub-Saharan Africa?

2d What percentage improvement has there been between 1999 and 2012 in terms of the total number of children in school?

2e What percentage of those not in school were girls?

3 What proportion of children completed their primary education in 2011? How does this compare to 1999?

emphasis on education for girls because this is seen as effective not only in getting women into the workforce but also in raising general education and health standards. The gap between rich and poor has increased in education, with children from poorer families being far less likely to go to school than those from wealthier ones. As a consequence of inadequate education in the past, there are about 781 million illiterate adults; this is an improvement from 18% of the adult population in 2000 to 14% now.

Amongst the problems faced by schools and pupils in developing countries are:

1 Many countries cannot afford universal primary, let alone universal secondary, education.

2 Teachers are not well paid, so teaching is not an attractive career. It is not unusual for teachers to take on other jobs at the same time in order to supplement their pay. The country may also struggle to train teachers well, or may have to take on as teachers people whose qualifications are not really good enough.

3 Schools are under-resourced – they have access to few textbooks, and little science or other practical equipment.

4 Many schools are housed in inadequate buildings with few facilities.

5 Schools may charge fees that parents cannot afford. Parents may decide to keep children out of school so that they can earn a wage or help a family business.

6 Even where there are no fees, parents will be expected to pay for uniform and books. Children whose parents cannot afford this will be unable to go to school unless scholarships or other help are available.

7 The education system and the curriculum are often shaped by the experience of colonialism – for example, English literature is studied rather than the country's own literature.

8 Many African schools, in order to maximize use of buildings and resources, often operate on double shifts: one group of children is educated in the morning, a different group in the afternoon. This is a good use of resources but it means that children do not get a full day of schooling, and teachers who work both shifts will be overworked.

9 War disrupts education.

10 Pupils may have a lot of time off school because of illness, such as bouts of malaria. In Liberia and Sierra Leone, schools closed for many months during the 2014 Ebola outbreak, holding up the education of all school children in those countries.

11 Even for pupils who do well at primary level, there are often not enough secondary places available. Walking a long distance to school may be necessary.

12 To try to meet the Millennium Development Goals, countries were getting more children enrolled, but the facilities were not always there to ensure a good quality of education. Progress towards the MDG might have been achieved, but only with overcrowded classes, poor facilities and untrained teachers.

13 In Nigeria, schools have been attacked and teachers and pupils kidnapped or killed by the terrorist movement Boko Haram, whose name means 'Western education is sinful.' There have also been attacks on schools in Afghanistan and Pakistan by the Taliban.

Modernization theory

Human capital: the theory that a country's people are a potential source of wealth; by educating its people, a country can increase its human capital.

Modernization theorists argue that education is essential to development. They favour a Western-style education system and curriculum, able to spread modern values. Higher education is essential to train future political and business leaders. The level of education required is linked to the country's stage of economic growth: a fully modernized society will need a well-educated general population. The theory of **human capital** argues that investment in education, provided it is tied into developing the skills necessary for industry, can be a basis for modernization, and that human capital can to some extent make up for shortage of money capital. Education is a way to spread modern values, to encourage entrepreneurial skills and break with traditional values that act as a brake on modernization.

Dependency theory

Dependency theorists see education as it is normally practised as a form of cultural imperialism, imposing Western values. Dependency theorists argue that education was one of the main ways colonial powers exercised control over their colonies – existing education systems were replaced by new systems which trained a small elite in the colonial powers' values and rewarded them with jobs. The elite had a stake in the system and would support it. On independence, developing countries inherited inappropriate education systems geared to the needs of a minority. Copying Western-style education systems is today not appropriate, when the situation of developing countries is so different.

Beacon of excellence or a wasteful parody?

Kamuzu Academy in Malawi, Southern Africa, is modelled on Eton. Pupils wear boater hats with a green and gold uniform and have to study Latin and Greek to GCSE level. They have piano lessons and a golf course.

Dr Hastings Banda, President of Malawi from 1961 to 1994, founded the school to ensure that Malawi's brightest children could fulfil their potential, and in so doing to train the country's future leaders. When first set up, it took most of Malawi's education budget, so most other children received no education at all. When Banda died in 1997, the school went through a difficult period but is now doing well, with very good results at GCSE. A small number of poorer children who pass an entrance exam receive bursaries, but most pupils have their fees paid by wealthy parents – so wealthy that if Kamuzu did not exist, they would probably be sent to a boarding school in the UK or elsewhere (Carroll 2002).

Universal primary education

The second Millennium Development Goal made universal primary education one of the priorities for all countries. For governments of developing countries, though, this is not always accepted as the best use of resources.

Arguments for universal education as a priority

- Universal education in the North was associated with economic growth, rising living standards and improvements in health.
- Education is the best way of ensuring that there are people with the skills and qualifications needed for the country's development.
- Education, especially for literacy and numeracy, is a human right – it gives people some control over their own lives, and makes it more difficult for them to be exploited.
- Universal education of girls has positive outcomes in improving the health and nutrition of families and chances of employment, and limiting the number of children women have.

Arguments against universal education as a priority

- Where a country has limited resources, it may be better to educate a minority for leadership and management posts if the majority do not need an education for their work.
- A country may decide to achieve economic growth first, seeing education as something that cannot yet be afforded.
- Education may simply make people more discontented and rebellious if they cannot use their education to improve their lives (through a new career, for example); among the leaders of the rebels in Sierra Leone's civil war were well-educated young men who had come into contact with radical ideas in their education, but could see no future for themselves in Sierra Leone as it was (Richards 1996, pp. 25–7).

Health

There is a broad correlation between a country's per capita income and its levels of health, as measured by life expectancy, infant mortality, overall death rates and incidence of particular diseases. All over the world there has been considerable progress over the past thirty years, notably in increased life expectancy, but in some countries there has recently been a slip backwards.

Causes of death are strongly related to development. In sub-Saharan Africa, about 65 per cent of deaths are the result of infectious diseases and causes related to birth and maternity (see table 2.9 for statistics on maternal mortality), but in developed countries only 5 per cent of deaths have these causes. The great majority of deaths in developed countries are from non-infectious medical conditions such as cancers and heart disease (Sutcliffe 2001), both of which are associated with lifestyle factors such as rich and fatty diets, smoking and stress. These diseases are also more likely to occur the longer a person lives. In developing countries, although these 'diseases of affluence' are present, the main health problems are communicable diseases, which are often still big killers: diarrhoea, bacterial and viral diseases such as polio, cholera, hepatitis and typhoid, and also airborne diseases such as tuberculosis, pneumonia, meningitis, whooping cough, diphtheria and influenza. All of these are still found in developed countries, but there they can be treated effectively and are rarely fatal. Malaria is also a huge problem, with 207 million cases of malaria and 627,000 deaths in 2012; 90 per cent of these were in Africa, and many victims were children under 5 (World Health Organization 2015). Funding for prevention and control of malaria, through effective medicines and insecticide-treated bed nets, has increased considerably but is not sufficient.

Disease in the South tends particularly to affect children, who are often weakened by malnutrition, and also women, and is more rife amongst rural populations where there is less access to healthcare, clean water and sanitation.

Many of the diseases now commonly seen in developing countries were found in Europe in the recent past (and some, such as malaria, are threatening to return). Three factors led to the control of these diseases:

- Improvements in nutrition and diet
- Improvements in hygiene – piped water supplies, sewage disposal
- Changes in reproductive behaviour – the falling birth rate.

All three factors were helped by improvements in education and literacy. These factors were more important than advances in curative medicine or even vaccination and immunization.

Despite the progress in reducing deaths from infectious diseases, there remains a threat that they will return. Changes to lifestyles and the environment can lead to new disease threats, such as HIV, SARS and Ebola, and the re-emergence of others such as polio and tuberculosis.

About 1.4 billion people are affected by infectious diseases that are confined to, or are only significant problems in, developing countries. In 2012, an important new initiative was launched to try to eradicate or control these Neglected Tropical Diseases (NTDs) by 2020. These diseases affect mainly those without clean water, basic sanitation or healthcare, rarely killing, but leaving people weak or disabled, and they make it even harder for these people to improve their lives. The diseases targeted for elimination are guinea worm, leprosy, lymphatic filariasis, trachoma and sleeping sickness; those targeted for control are schistosomiasis, river blindness (onchocerciasis), soil-transmitted helminthes, chagas disease and leishmaniasis (www.unitingtocombatntds.org).

Another major health problem and cause of death is trauma – that is, accidents and injuries. Victims of trauma in developing countries are more likely to die or to suffer long-term consequences, because they are less likely to be treated effectively. The number of road accidents is increasing as car ownership grows, but in developing countries accident victims often do not get prompt and effective treatment.

With colonialism, developing countries inherited healthcare based on costly Western-style hospitals with unreliable modern technology in cities. Doctors are trained for this system and often run lucrative practices for urban elites; there is no financial incentive to work in poor rural areas – or indeed in developing countries at all, hence the 'brain drain' of doctors, nurses and other health professionals to the North. Many developing countries have shortages of doctors, nurses and other medical staff; there are fewer hospitals, treatment centres and ambulances than in the developed world; and there are likely to be shortages of medicines and medical equipment. Adopting a Western-style system based on highly trained staff, technology and hospitals in cities can leave the poor and those in rural areas with little access to healthcare.

Table 2.9 Maternal mortality: deaths of women in childbirth and pregnancy, 2008 estimates

UNICEF regions	Maternal mortality ratio (maternal deaths per 100,000 live births)	Number of maternal deaths	Lifetime risk of maternal death – 1 in:
Africa	590	207,000	36
Sub-Saharan Africa	640	204,000	31
Eastern and Southern Africa	550	79,000	38
West and Central Africa	720	115,000	26
Middle East and North Africa	170	17,000	190
Asia	200	135,000	210
South Asia	290	109,000	110
East Asia and Pacific	88	27,000	600
Latin America and Caribbean	85	9,200	480
CEE/CIS*	34	1,900	1700
Industrialized countries	14	1,600	4300
Developing countries	290	356,000	120
Least-developed countries	590	166,000	37
World	**260**	**358,000**	**140**

*Central and Eastern Europe and the Commonwealth of Independent States

Source: UNICEF Childinfo Statistics

1a How many women worldwide are estimated to have died in childbirth and pregnancy in 2008?

1b How many of these deaths were in developing countries? What percentage of these deaths were in developing countries?

2 In which region of the world is the maternal mortality rate: (i) highest; and (ii) lowest?

3 Approximately how many times greater is the risk of maternal death in West and Central Africa compared to industrialized countries? What factors might account for this difference?

Shortage of health workers

One of the reasons that the Ebola virus outbreak in West Africa in 2014 cost so many lives was the shortage of skilled health workers.

Liberia with a 4.2m population: 51 doctors (0.1 per 10,000 people); 978 nurses and midwives; 269 pharmacists.

Sierra Leone with a 6m population: 136 doctors (0.2 per 10,000 people); 1,017 nurses and midwives; 114 pharmacists.

In both countries some doctors died of Ebola contracted while treating patients. Nigeria, with a more developed healthcare system, was able to contain the virus.

Source: Afri-Dev.Info citing BBC News article by Farouk Chothia, published 24 September 2014

Developing countries can attempt to improve health by:

Selective biomedical intervention: in healthcare, interventions such as immunization campaigns to try to prevent the spread of disease.

1 *Selective biomedical intervention* such as mass vaccination programmes, distributing vitamin supplements or insecticide-impregnated bed nets. This can lead to rapid reductions in child mortality, but these cannot always be sustained – reducing one disease may only mean that children die later from another disease.
2 *Comprehensive, community-based primary healthcare* with an emphasis on health education and prevention of disease – e.g. draining ponds so that mosquitoes can't breed, disposing of rubbish safely.

Modernization theory

Epidemiologic transition: in health, the change from the main problem in a society being infectious diseases to it being 'diseases of affluence' such as cancer and heart disease.

Modernization theorists would expect health patterns of developing countries to follow those of the developed world in the past. Developing countries are still at the stage developed countries were at centuries ago, but are now entering the **epidemiologic transition**. Before the transition, infectious diseases are widespread and the major cause of death; life expectancy is low and infant and child mortality high. Improvements in nutrition, hygiene and sanitation lead to falling death rates from infectious diseases. After the transition, deaths from infectious diseases are negligible, infant and child mortality low and life expectancy much higher. Developing countries should draw on aid and expertise from the developed world, drop traditional medical practices and concentrate on centralized primary healthcare based on doctors and hospitals and on mass immunization against disease.

Dependency theory

Dependency theorists argue that there is no reason to assume that today's developing countries can simply follow the path of the rich world. Colonialism changed health in the colonies, and neo-colonialism continues. MacDonald (2005) argues that the gap in health between the developed and developing worlds is due to the relationships between them; health issues in LEDCs are made worse by the effects of, for example, debt, aid, trade and the activities of TNCs and IGOs. Health in developing countries is affected by a number of factors, as shown in Figure 2.7.

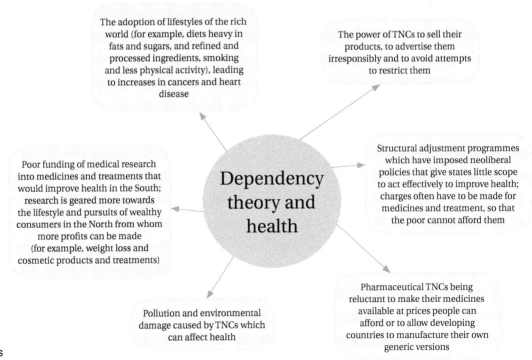

Figure 2.7 Factors affecting health in developing countries

Demographic change

Demographers study population. The study of demographic change, both in world population and in the populations of individual countries, is directly relevant to development. Amongst the terms demographers use are the following:

- *Mortality rate*: the number of deaths per 1,000 in the population in one year
- *Infant mortality rate*: the number of deaths of infants under the age of 1 per 1,000 of the infant population in one year
- *Child mortality rate*: the number of children who die by the age of 5 per 1,000 live births per year
- *Birth rate*: number of live births per 1,000 members of the population in one year
- *Fertility rate*: the number of live births per woman over her lifetime.

World population growth

Throughout most of recorded history there has been a slow rise in world population. The rise has accelerated over the past few centuries, with most of the increase in the past 100 years, from 2 billion people in 1925 to more than 7 billion today. Most of this increase has been in the developing world; the population of the developed world is now stable. The world's population in 2050 is projected by the UN to be 9.6 billion, 90 per cent of whom will live in today's developing countries.

Today's developed countries went through a demographic transition during the period of industrialization and urbanization.

The shape of populations also changes. Today's developed countries before industrialization, and developing countries today, had large numbers of children and young people and few elderly people; this is conventionally represented as a pyramid. After the demographic transition, the pyramid is inverted, with growing numbers of elderly people and proportionately fewer young people.

The experience of the developed countries is important because many developing countries seem to be passing through the demographic transition; the death rate is falling, but the birth rate is still high, and so many developing countries still have high population growth.

> **Demographic transition**: in demography, the change from high birth and death rates to low birth and death rates.

During the transition

High birth rate, high death rate
It made sense to have several children because children in pre-industrial societies were an economic asset – they would work from an early age, for example helping on the family farm. An extra mouth to feed became an extra pair of hands by about the age of 7. Also, without pensions or welfare, older people relied on their adult children to support them. Having more children meant a greater chance that at least one would survive to support you in your old age.

High birth rate still, death rate falling
Populations grew because the death rate fell. Fewer children died, and people began to live longer than had been the case. Life expectancy increased. This was partly due to improved systems of sewage and provision of clean piped water, which helped in the prevention of disease, and to advances in medicine, which reduced the numbers dying from disease.

Low birth rate, low death rate
Children are more of an economic burden in an industrial society. They have to be supported through formal education; they do not work, and their schooling can be expensive. Because infant and child mortality are low, children are much more likely to survive into adulthood – but with pensions and welfare adults are no longer dependent on them anyway. People therefore choose to have fewer children. The population of industrialized nations tends to stabilize, and may even begin to decline.

Figure 2.8
Demographic transition

Figure 2.9 Factors involved in population in developing countries today

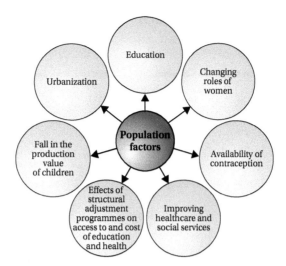

Modernization theorists would expect there to be a transition, because the developing countries are expected to go through the same process of modernization as developed countries did. However, just because countries in the past went through the transition, we should not assume that it is inevitable. Dependency theorists would argue that the situation today, as a result of colonialism and neo-colonialism, is fundamentally different. Demographic transition is a theory; it is not inevitable that it will happen, and some countries may get stuck in the transition phase – the 'demographic trap' (Hewitt and Smyth 2000: 128).

Population growth and consumption

The Malthusian view and modernization theory

At the end of the eighteenth century, an English clergyman, Thomas Malthus, put forward an influential argument about population growth. The population would inevitably grow faster than the food supply, because food supply would grow arithmetically (1, 2, 3, 4, etc.) whereas population would grow geometrically (1, 2, 4, 8, etc.). This, said Malthus, would bring about disaster: famines, and wars over food, which might end civilization. Malthus argued that it was essential to curb population growth. Today, followers of Malthus's basic idea – that the world cannot support a continually growing population – are referred to as neo-Malthusians.

For neo-Malthusians, population growth in developing countries is the main cause of their poverty, and also leads to economic stagnation, uncontrollable urbanization and environmental damage. Ultimately, it will also lead to disaster, in wars over resources such as food and water, because there will not be enough to go round. Controlling population growth is therefore the main objective of aid, because this is necessary for development to happen. This can be done by persuading people to have fewer children, by having family planning programmes and making contraception available. However, governments do not always see population control as a priority; they may even want to increase the population if they believe the country is under-populated.

The neo-Malthusian approach has been taken up by modernization theorists who see high birth rates and population growth as obstacles to Western-style development, keeping people in poverty.

Robert Kaplan (1994) drew on Malthus's ideas for his influential article 'The Coming Anarchy'. Based on his travels in West Africa and elsewhere, Kaplan argued that parts of the poor world were collapsing into anarchy because of population growth, urbanization, resource depletion and tribalism. These factors undermined already weak states and led to instability that, he thought, could eventually threaten the developed world too. This argument is referred to as the **New Barbarism** thesis; Richards (1996: xiv) describes it as 'Malthus-with-guns'. Richards's counter-argument is that what appears to be random and anarchic is in fact rational and can only be understood in the context of globalized modernity.

The doom foretold by Malthus and his successors has not yet occurred, despite the fact that the world population has grown to a level many in the past would have thought impossible. This is because their predictions were based on projecting existing trends; in practice, other factors have

New Barbarism: Kaplan's theory, a variant of Malthusian theory, that overpopulation and exhaustion of resources were leading to civil wars in developing countries.

intervened, such as improvements in food production. Improvements in agriculture have averted a food crisis, and deaths from war and disease have also restrained population growth, but neo-Malthusians would argue that these have simply postponed the inevitable.

How can population be controlled?

1 *Contraception*: birth control pills need to be taken regularly, which is not always practical in the developing world. Women may find it hard to persuade men to use condoms, although they are fairly easily available in most places. Some religions (e.g. Roman Catholicism) disapprove of contraception. Attempts to increase the use of contraceptives have sometimes tended to assume that, if they are available, they will be used, but people who want children will of course not use them – and poor people often want more children because of the economic benefit they bring.

2 *Abortion*: this is not practical on a large scale because it requires trained medical staff and is therefore expensive. It is also very controversial in the USA, and so American NGOs and government aid bodies do not support it.

3 *Sterilization*: people tend to only want to be sterilized after having several children. Compulsory sterilization is an abuse of human rights, but in India in the late 1970s poorer people were bribed with goods or money to accept sterilization.

4 *Financial incentives to limit family size*: this is what China practised with its one child per family policy between 1979 and 2015. An unintended consequence of this was female infanticide and a growing gender imbalance in the Chinese population, with many young men unable to find Chinese wives.

The anti-Malthusian view and dependency theory

This approach turns Malthus's view upside-down. Rather than seeing poverty and lack of development as the consequences of high population growth, it sees them as the causes. Adamson (1980) argues that where children still have an economic value, because they can work and earn and relieve the parents of some work, it makes sense to have several children. Where infant and child mortality rates are high, the more children a couple have the more chance that at least one will survive to support them in old age; children may be not just the best, but the only available, insurance policy. Where traditional values are strong, having many children may also give the parents status. People have many children because they are poor, rather than being poor because they have many children.

From this point of view, aid that focuses directly on controlling population is misguided. The way forward is to focus on alleviating poverty, bringing infant and child mortality down and improving the situation of women. The parts of the developing world where fertility has declined, such as Sri Lanka, Thailand, Cuba and the Indian state of Kerala, are those where women have good access to resources such as health and education (Hewitt and Smyth 2000: 135).

There is now a widespread acceptance that women's status and fertility are closely linked. The education of girls is seen as very important for several reasons:

- Educated women do not need to have children for status, because their education brings status
- They are more likely to be able to work to support their children, rather than relying on their children for work and income
- They are better able to look after the health of their children, reducing mortality
- They are likely to have better access to and willingness to use contraception
- They are more likely to take decisions about their own fertility, or negotiate with their husband, rather than accepting his authority.

Malthus's starting point was the relationship between population and food supply. Anti-Malthusians point out that a lot of land is used to grow fodder for animals to be consumed as meat in the developed world, by people and by pets. If this land was used to grow food for direct human consumption, the planet could support an even larger population. This suggests that it is the unequal distribution of the world's resources and excessive consumption in MEDCs that are the bigger problem, rather than overpopulation (see earlier section on the environment, pages 149–52).

Famine and undernourishment

The media tend to treat famines as freak natural disasters, and often suggest that a major cause is that there are too many people. They also tend only to report the final stages of a famine, when normal survival strategies have been exhausted and people have abandoned their homes and moved in search of food. If relief camps are established, infectious diseases often become a major cause of death. However, relief camps provide very good publicity and fundraising situations for INGOs. Famines can be precipitated by climate, for example a drought, but people in areas prone to drought will have survival strategies. Other factors will also be involved, and often these include war. Famine can even be used as a weapon of war; Keen (in Crow 2000: 62) argues that, in Sudan, famines can be seen as a deepening of the exploitation of poor groups that already exists in 'normal' times.

Rather than famine, it is undernourishment that is a continual fact of everyday life for large numbers of people. About 868 million people were chronically undernourished in 2010–12, according to the Food and Agriculture Organization of the United Nations (FAO), nearly all of them in developing countries. Long-term chronic hunger does not often attract media attention, but in the long run it costs more lives than spectacular famines. The problem is one of ownership and distribution, and poverty. Food is usually available but people cannot afford to buy it. Those most at risk are children, the elderly and women.

Gender

Women used to be invisible in the study of development. With the growth of feminism, this changed. It is now not only feminists but also the UN, IGOs, NGOs and global social movements which take gender issues very seriously. For example, the *Human Development Report* includes a Gender Inequality Index. The Millennium Development Goals, and the Sustainable Development Goals of 2015 which replaced them, include the promotion of gender equality, the empowerment of women and improvement in maternal health. However, women are still a long way from parity with men. Other sections of this chapter have referred to women's disadvantages in education, employment and health. Underlying these is women's usually subordinate position within households and communities, owning far less land and property and having less control over their lives than men.

Issues that particularly affect women and can be used to gauge the extent of gender freedom are shown in Figure 2.10.

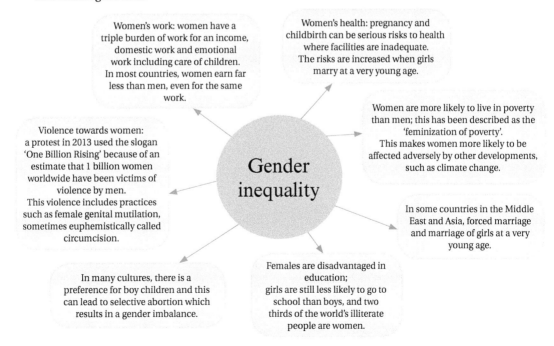

Figure 2.10
Issues affecting gender inequality

The continuing extent of gender inequality was vividly demonstrated in the 2004 Indian Ocean tsunami. 'Four times as many women died in tsunami': it was under this headline that the *Guardian* reported on 26 March 2005 the far greater loss of life among women than men. Among the reasons put forward were:

- Women were less likely to be able to swim
- Women were often trying to save their children as well as themselves
- Men were more likely to be away from home, for example working in cities, and were also more able to run and to cling to debris.

Oxfam reported that, because of the shortage of women, young women would be more likely to have to marry earlier (abandoning their education) and to try to take on the roles of the missing women.

The problem of child brides and forced marriages

In the rural villages of countries such as Egypt, Afghanistan, Bangladesh, Ethiopia, Pakistan, India and countries in the Middle East, many young girls are rarely allowed out of their homes unless it is to work in the fields or to get married. These uneducated girls are often married off at the young age of 11. Some families allow girls who are only 7 years old to marry. It is very unusual for a girl to reach the age of 16 and not be married. In Afghanistan, it is believed that between 60 and 80 per cent of marriages are forced marriages. Even though the legal age to get married in Egypt is 16, and in India and Ethiopia the age is 18, these laws are quite often ignored.

Poor health, early death and lack of educational opportunities lead the list of problems attributed to child marriage.

- Child brides have double the pregnancy death rate of women in their twenties.
- In developing countries, the leading cause of death for young girls between the ages of 15 and 19 is early pregnancy.
- Additionally, from having babies too young, child brides face an extremely high risk of fistulas (vaginal and anal ruptures).
- The babies of child brides are sicker and weaker and many do not survive childhood.
- Child brides have a higher risk of being infected with sexually transmitted diseases.
- Child brides are at increased risk of chronic anaemia and obesity.
- Child brides have poor access to contraception.
- Child brides have a lack of educational opportunities.
- Being forced into an early marriage creates a lifetime of poverty.
- Statistically, child brides have a higher risk of becoming a victim of domestic violence, sexual abuse and murder.

Source: www.globalissues.org/article/166/womens-rights

There has been considerable progress towards greater rights for women. For example, education of girls is now seen as normal and expected. Nikki van der Gaag (2008), however, suggests that this progress is being threatened. Economic globalization has led to an increase in trafficking of women and the growth of industries in which women workers are exploited. Globalization has also produced a backlash in which supposedly traditional values and practices are reasserted. Women's rights can be seen as associated with Western values. Thus, for example, the education of girls has been seen as threatening by Islamic fundamentalists and this has led to events such as the assassination attempt on Malala Yousafzai, who advocated the education of girls in Pakistan, and the kidnapping of schoolgirls in Nigeria by Boko Haram. There has also been an increase in violence against women in South Africa, which is seen as being caused by a perception that women have too many rights; this has been described as 'neo-patriarchy' – an attempt to reassert male superiority through a culture of sexual violence.

Applying the theories

Both modernization theory and dependency theory, arising before the impact of second-wave feminism in the 1960s and 1970s on theory and research, had little to say about gender issues. Both can be seen as part of the 'malestream' of sociology and of academic sociology more widely at the time.

Modernization theory was closely associated with the sociological perspective of functionalism, and took from it the idea of the nuclear family as the family type suitable for modern society, with husbands and wives having complementary roles. The role of the man was to work outside the home for money, the role of the woman to work within the household. This was seen as fair and equal. As countries modernized, then, women would be restricted to work within the home. As Leonard (2003) comments, this was a very masculine view of what it is like to be modern. In dependency theory, the focus is on relationships between countries rather than social groups, and both here and in world systems theory there is little discussion of women.

One of the reasons that women were overlooked in these theories is that the work women tended to do, within the household and subsistence agriculture, including essential survival tasks such as grinding grain and preparing food, was overlooked in measures such as GNI and official statistics. In 1970, Boserup (in Leonard 2003: 79), working from modernization theory and adding a liberal feminist view, argued that such measures needed to be extended to include women, especially by bringing them into paid work, so that they also could benefit from modernization.

In the following fifteen years, socialist feminist thinking began to have an influence. It was pointed out that Boserup was assuming that the modernization process was benign, and that attention needed to be paid to the ways in which women were exploited within the global capitalist system. Part of the problem was clearly male power, so discussion shifted from women to gender relations. Socialist feminism, looking at underdevelopment and neo-colonial exploitation, seemed more relevant to developing countries than radical feminism, which sees women's subordination to men as the most important issue. In the South, most women see a need to work with men with whom they share an unequal position compared to the developed world. Women in the developing world are united by their gender, but also divided by ethnicity, religion, class and culture. Recent work on gender and development acknowledges that gender relations vary around the world.

Socialist feminists and others draw attention in particular to a new form of exploitation, which they argue shows how the global spread of capitalism requires the exploitation of women. It is mainly young women who are employed in sweatshop factories in South-East Asia and elsewhere by TNCs. Companies pay little and treat female workers poorly, partly on the (false) grounds that the work is unskilled. This work can sometimes help young women achieve financial independence, but often the money goes straight to a man. The boss at work is invariably a man, and training and job security are rarely provided.

Gender issues today

One effect of globalization has been on the nature of services traditionally offered by women. Ehrenreich and Hochschild (2002) describe how millions of women leave developing countries each year to work as nannies, maids and sex workers in the rich world. They suggest that the move into work for many women in developed countries has created a 'care deficit' because they are unable to spend the time that previous generations of women did on family and home. The use of cheap labour from developing countries eases this situation, but, at the same time, creates a 'care deficit' in developing countries because the women are working abroad. The sex industry employs many women from developing countries, both in the North and in sex tourist destinations. Bales (2002) estimates that in Thailand, with a total population of about 60 million, there are between half a million and a million sex workers and that about 1 in 20 of these is enslaved.

Ecofeminists have argued that there is a special relationship between women and the environment, based either on innate nature or on social relationships which put women in a position of working with and understanding natural resources. Men are seen as responsible for most environmental damage, still treating the environment as something to be dominated and used rather than to be looked after. Women are therefore seen as vital to attempts to protect the environment.

Malestream is a word coined by feminists to describe the type of sociology that concentrates on men, is mostly carried out by men and then assumes that the findings can be applied to women as well.

Ecofeminism: feminist theory based on the idea that women have a different relationship with nature and the environment from men.

Activity

Ecofeminism

Two well-known women who have been described as ecofeminists are Vandana Shiva (1952– ; from India) and Wangari Maathai (1940–2011; from Kenya). Research their life and work and show in what ways they are both feminists and environmentalists.

Aid is not gender-neutral. It comes with Western values attached, and that usually means male-dominated values. For example, agricultural training programmes are offered more to men than to women, because it is assumed that men are more suited to technical and scientific training – but it is women who play a greater role in growing food. Aid often helps men rather than women with their work, again because women's work is still generally unrecognized or undervalued.

Practice questions

1   Outline and explain **two** ways in which healthcare problems in developing countries are different from those in developed countries. **(10 marks)**

2   Read **Item A** below and answer the question that follows.

> ### Item A
> The world's population has grown from 2 billion people in 1925 to well over 7 billion today. Most of that increase has been in the developing world, which has had both higher birth rates and higher mortality rates than the developed world. The rate of population growth is now slowing and world population is expected to stabilize later this century and then slowly decline.

Applying material from **Item A**, analyse **two** factors that influence rates of population growth. **(10 marks)**

3   Read **Item B** below and answer the question that follows.

> **Item B**
>
> Feminism began to have an influence on the sociology of global development from the 1970s onwards. Feminists argued that, in order to understand the development process, and to improve the lives of poorer people, it was essential to study and understand the problems that women in developing countries faced. However, there were some differences among feminists as to what they took to be the most important problems.

Applying material from **Item B** and your knowledge, evaluate the view that both the theory and practice of development have tended to ignore the experience of women.   **(20 marks)**

CHAPTER SUMMARY AND REVISION CHECKLIST

After studying this chapter, you should be able to:

- Explain the different ways in which development can be defined and measured
- Explain and evaluate theoretical explanations of development and underdevelopment: modernization theory, dependency theory, neo-liberalism, traditional Marxism and world systems theory
- Apply the main theoretical explanations to topics within this chapter, such as aid, education and health
- Describe aspects of cultural, economic and political globalization, and explain and evaluate theoretical explanations of globalization
- Evaluate the role of aid, trade and debt in development
- Describe and evaluate the role of states, transnational corporations, non-government organizations and international governmental organizations in development
- Describe and evaluate the strategies for industrialization and development open to developing countries
- Describe and explain the process of urbanization
- Describe and evaluate the relationship between development and the environment

- Explain and evaluate the relationship between development and war and conflict
- Describe the main patterns of employment in developing countries
- Describe education in developing countries and evaluate the importance of education in development
- Describe health issues in developing countries and evaluate the importance of health in development
- Describe the main patterns of demographic change, and evaluate Malthusian and anti-Malthusian explanations of the relationship between population growth, food supply and the environment
- Discuss the significance of gender for development and for topics such as education, health and aid
- Know about the Millennium Development Goals and Sustainable Development Goals and account for progress or lack of progress towards achieving them

KEY TERMS

Definitions can be found in the glossary at the end of this book, as well as these terms being defined in the margin where they first appear in the chapter.

aid
anti-globalization
  movement
appropriate technology
bilateral aid
biodiversity
bio-piracy
bottom billion
Bretton Woods
capitalism
cash crops
colonialism
conditionality
cultural homogenization
cultural imperialism
debt boomerang
debt crisis
deforestation
demographic transition
dependency theory
desertification
development
development state
ecofeminism
ecological footprint
economic growth
epidemiologic transition
exhaustible resources
Export Processing Zones
  (EPZs)
export-oriented
  industrialization
Fair Trade

future generations
global decision-making
global warming
globalists
glocalization
green revolution
Gross National Income
  (GNI)
Highly Indebted Poor
  Countries (HIPC) Initiative
human capital
Human Development
  Index
hybridization
imperialism
import substitution
  industrialization
industrialized
informal sector
international govern-
  mental organizations
  (IGOs)
International Monetary
  Fund (IMF)
malestream
McDonaldization
metropolis
micro-credit
Millennium Development
  Goals (MDGs)
modern world system
  (MWS)
modernization theory

multilateral aid
multinational corporations
  (MNCs)
need for achievement
neo-colonialism
neoliberal economic
  theory
neo-Malthusian
New Barbarism
new international division
  of labour (NIDL)
newly industrializing
  countries (NICs)
non-governmental
  organizations (NGOs)
non-renewable resources
North
parastatals
predatory state
pull factors
push factors
radicals
remittances
satellite
selective biomedical
  intervention
shared resources
South
stages of economic growth
structural adjustment
  programmes (SAPs)
structural violence
subsistence farming

sustainability
sustainable development
Sustainable Development
  Goals (SDGs)
take-off
technological leapfrogging
terrorism
Third World
trade liberalization
transformationalists
transnational capitalist
  class
transnational corporations
  (TNCs)
triangular trade
underdevelopment
urbanization
Washington Consensus
World Bank
World Economic
  Forum
World Social Forum

There are a variety of free tests and other activities that can be used to assess your learning at

www.politybooks.com/browne
You can also find new contemporary resources by following @BrowneKen on Twitter.

See also the revision guide to accompany this book:
Sociology for AQA Revision Guide 2: 2nd-Year A level

Please note that the above resources have not been endorsed by AQA.

PRACTICE QUESTION

Topic B2 Global Development

Answer **all** the questions on this topic   **Time allowed: 1 hour**

1 6 Outline and explain **two** ways in which education can contribute to the development process.

[**10 marks**]

1 7 Read **Item A** below and answer the question that follows.

Item A

Wars greatly hold back development in affected countries. Developing countries that have had civil or 'new' wars in recent years, such as Sierra Leone and the Democratic Republic of Congo, tend to be at the lower end of the Human Development Index. There are a number of factors that lead to poorer countries being more likely to have civil wars than other countries.

Applying material from **Item A**, analyse **two** factors that can lead to wars in developing countries.   [**10 marks**]

1 8 Read **Item B** below and answer the question that follows.

Item B

More than half the world's population now lives in cities and it is cities in the developing world that are growing fastest. The industrialization of what is now the developed world was accompanied by urbanization, with many people moving to cities to work in new industries. Some sociologists argue that urbanization in the developing world today is different because often industrialization is not happening at the same time.

Applying material from **Item B** and your knowledge, evaluate the view that urbanization is an essential aspect of development.   [**20 marks**]

Contents

CHAPTER
3
The Media

Topic 1

SPECIFICATION AREA

The relationship between ownership and control of the media

What are the media?

'The media' may refer to a number of different but related things:

1   The technology involved in communicating with large mass audiences without any personal contact, such as televisions, computers, DVD players/recorders, mp3 players, smartphones, games consoles and satellites
2   The institutions and organizations concerned with mass communication in which people work, such as the press, cinema, broadcasting, advertising, publishing and web-related industries
3   The products of those institutions, such as the news, movies, television soaps, newspapers, magazines, websites, books, films, CDs and DVDs and computer games.

The main media include terrestrial (earth-based), cable and satellite television, radio, newspapers and magazines, books, films, DVDs, advertising, CDs, computer games, the internet and smartphones.

Traditional and new media

The media are now often divided into the 'traditional' and the 'new' media.

The 'traditional media' refers to those mass media that communicated uniform messages in a one-way, non-interactive process to very large mass audiences, which were assumed to be homogeneous (all possessing much the same characteristics and interests). This is the type of communication associated with traditional broadcasting, like the terrestrial television channels (BBC 1 and 2, ITV 1, and Channels 4 and 5) and BBC Radios 1 and 2, and mass-circulation national and Sunday newspapers. There is little consumer choice, beyond a few TV channels, radio stations or newspapers.

The 'new media' refers to the interactive screen-based, digital (computer) technology involving the integration of images, text and sound, and to the technology used for the distribution and consumption of the new digitized media content which has emerged in the late twentieth and early twenty-first centuries. These include computers and the internet; electronic e-books; digital cable and satellite TV, digiboxes and DVD recorders enabling customized, individualized television viewing with a choice of hundreds of television channels; digital media like CDs, DVDs and mp3; internet downloads of films, videos and music onto smartphones and mp3 players; user-generated media content via Twitter and websites like Facebook and YouTube; and interactive video/computer games using PlayStations and Xboxes.

Social media

One of the most significant and popular forms of the new media is social media.

The term 'social media' refers to a group of online and internet-based applications that are used for social interaction among large groups of people. Through applications and websites like Twitter, Facebook, Google+, YouTube, Instagram, Tumblr and Blogger, people build social networks of friends and contacts with whom they share (and re-share) and exchange pictures and videos, news and other information, which they have either created themselves or which has been created by others. It is through social media that stories and images go 'viral' – reaching millions of people in a very short time – as they are shared and re-shared through social networks. Many people spend more time on social media sites than any other online or internet-related activity, and social media have become an extremely significant form of the media in the twenty-first century, sometimes rivaling more traditional mass media in their ability to get their views across to large media audiences.

Much of this chapter focuses on the nature, output and effects of the dominant large-scale mass media industry. This includes both traditional and new media, though the distinction between these is becoming blurred as mass media companies are increasingly adopting and using new media, including social media. There are references to new media, including social media, throughout this chapter, but there is a full discussion of the new media and their significance in contemporary society in Topic 6.

Social media include websites and other online means of communication that are used for social interaction among large groups of people, whereby they create, share and exchange information and develop social networks.

The power of the media: key questions

In the UK in 2014, according to Ofcom, around 96% of homes had digital TV, and viewers watched an average of about four hours of television every day. Around 77% of UK households had internet broadband connections, and 8% of adults had mobile broadband; 93% of adults owned/used a mobile phone (with 61% owning a smartphone), and 57% used them to access the internet. Digital broadcasting is leading to the creation of literally hundreds of terrestrial, cable and satellite television channels. Around 7.5 million national newspapers are sold every day.

The media have become a gigantic international business, with instant news from every part of the globe. International marketing of TV programmes and films to international audiences is backed by huge investments. The internet has millions more people going online every year, providing instant access to colossal amounts of information and entertainment from the entire globe. Bauman (2007) cites research that suggests 'during the last thirty years more information has been produced in the world than during the previous 5,000 years, while a single copy of the Sunday edition of the *New York Times* contains more information than a cultivated person in the eighteenth century would consume during a lifetime'.

Society has become media-saturated, with the media becoming important sources of information, entertainment and leisure activity for large numbers of people. They have become key agencies of secondary socialization, and often have an important formative influence on the individual's sense of identity and consumer spending choices. Most of our taken-for-granted knowledge and our opinions and attitudes are based, not on personal experience, but on evidence and knowledge provided by the media. Indeed, if the media didn't report an event, or distorted it, or totally made it up, the only people likely to know about it would be those who were actually involved. For most of us, the media are our only source of evidence, and they colour, shape and even construct our view of the world.

If most of our opinions are based on knowledge obtained second-hand through the media, then this raises important issues about the power of the media to mould and shape our lives and identities. Most people think and act in particular ways because of the opinions they hold and the knowledge they have. However, do the media inform us about everything, or do they 'filter' information, obscuring the truth and giving false, distorted or exaggerated impressions of what is happening in the world? Do they favour some points of view over others, spreading a dominant ideology that favours the more affluent over the poor, for example? Do they misrepresent or stereotype some social groups, like women, minority ethnic groups or the disabled? The main media are privately owned and controlled, and run to make a profit as are the technology and websites underlying social

Bias means
that a subject is
presented in a
one-sided way,
favouring one
point of view over
others, or ignoring,
distorting or
misrepresenting
some issues,
points of view or
groups compared
to others.

media. What effects does this pattern of ownership have on the content of the media? Does it create bias in them, with subjects presented in one-sided, distorted or misleading ways? Do the media actually have any influence on people? These are the sorts of questions which have interested sociologists and which will be explored in this and other topics in this chapter.

Formal controls on the media

Although the media in Britain are formally free to report whatever they like, and the government has no power in normal times to stop the spreading of any opinions by using censorship, there are some formal limits to this freedom.

The law

The law restricts the media's freedom to report anything they choose in any way they like. The principal legal limits to the media's freedom are shown in the box.

Legal limits to the media's freedom

- *The laws of libel* forbid the publication of an untrue statement about a person which might bring him or her into contempt, ridicule, dislike, or hostility in society.
- *The Official Secrets Acts* make it a criminal offence to report without authorization any official government activity which the government defines as an 'official secret'.
- *Defence and Security Media Advisory Notices or DSMA-Notices* are issued by the government as requests to journalists not to report defence and counter-terrorist information which the government believes might be damaging to national security.
- *The Racial and Religious Hatred Act* (2006) and the *Equality Act* (2010) forbid the expression of opinions which will encourage hatred or discrimination against people because of their ethnic group or religious beliefs.
- *The Obscene Publications Act* (1959) forbids the publication of anything that a court considers to be obscene and indecent, and likely to 'deprave and corrupt' persons who are likely to read, see or hear it.
- *Contempt of Court* provision forbids the reporting, expression of opinions or publication of material about cases which are in the process of being dealt with in a court of law and which is likely to jeopardize or prejudice a fair trial.

Ofcom

In 2003, Ofcom (the Office of Communications) was established as a powerful media regulator, with responsibilities across television, radio, telecommunications and wireless communication services. This has responsibility for:

- Furthering the interests of consumers
- Securing the best use of the radio spectrum
- Ensuring that a wide range of television, radio, electronic media and communications networks are available in the UK, with high-quality services having a broad appeal
- Protecting the public from any offensive or potentially harmful effects of broadcast media, and safeguarding people from being unfairly treated in television and radio programmes.

Activity

Go to www.ofcom.org.uk, and identify and briefly describe four issues that Ofcom is currently dealing with.

The BBC

The BBC is established by a Royal Charter and is a largely state-funded body, which is governed by the BBC Trust, whose members are appointed by the Queen on advice from government ministers. The Trust sets the strategic direction of the BBC and has a clear duty to represent the interests of licence fee-payers and to ensure the BBC remains independent, and resists pressure and influence from any source. The BBC is partly regulated by Ofcom, and partly by the Trust. The BBC is financed by the state through the television licence fee, plus income from a series of private spin-off companies, which top up the licence fee income with substantial profits. The state can therefore have some control over the BBC by refusing to raise the licence fee. Although the BBC is not a private business run solely to make a profit, like the independent commercial broadcasting services (independent TV and radio), and is not dependent on advertising for its income, it still has to compete with commercial broadcasting by attracting audiences large enough to justify the licence fee. In October 2015, the government had just completed a major consultation on the constitutional basis of the BBC – the Royal Charter – which expires at the end of 2016. The results of this consultation and the policies flowing from it were not known at the time of writing this book. This means that in the near future the current arrangements on the funding and control of the BBC, as described above, and the role of the BBC, may change.

Independent broadcasting

Independent broadcasting includes all the non-BBC television and radio stations. These are regulated by Ofcom, which licenses the companies which can operate in the private sector, and is responsible for the amount and quality of advertising and programmes on independent television and radio, and for dealing with any complaints.

The Independent Press Standards Organisation (IPSO)

The Independent Press Standards Organisation (IPSO) is an independent regulator for the newspaper and magazine industry in the UK. This was established in September 2014 by the newspaper industry itself. IPSO replaced the former Press Complaints Commission (PCC) which was discredited following its inadequate response to journalists hacking into people's mobile phones, which led to the Leveson Inquiry into the culture, practice and ethics of the press in 2011–12. IPSO seeks to monitor and maintain the standards of journalism set out in what is known as the Editors' Code of Practice, which deals with issues such as accuracy, invasion of privacy, intrusion into grief or shock, and harassment. IPSO considers and investigates complaints about the content of newspapers that breach acceptable standards, and the behaviour of journalists. In 2015, many saw IPSO as little different from the former PCC, and not as independent but as a puppet of the big newspaper corporations that would be more concerned with protecting their interests than those of the public. As a fairly new body at the time of writing (2015), it remains to be seen how effective it will be, and whether it has any real power or willingness to enforce effective sanctions in response to any breaches of acceptable standards or arising from complaints it receives.

How governments influence and control media output

Apart from the various formal legal and regulatory controls outlined above, governments try to influence the output of the media in a number of other ways.

1 By official government press conferences and briefings of journalists, which present the official government position on contemporary issues and thereby hope to get their line presented in the media.

2 Leaks and off-the-record briefings: these are more informal briefings of journalists through which governments try to manage what is reported in the news. These are non-attributable –

Julian Assange and his WikiLeaks website, which releases secret and confidential information from anonymous sources, have both caused controversy, particularly in a case in which the website leaked classified US government cables. Assange and WikiLeaks supporters have protested against the silencing and punishment of such sources in the name of free speech

that is, they don't quote any named source – and will often be reported in the form of 'sources close to the government said …' Journalists giving favourable exposure to the government as a result of such briefings are likely to be given preferential treatment in the future, such as privileged access to government sources.

3   The use of government spin doctors, who try to manipulate the media by providing a favourable slant to a potentially unpopular or controversial news item. Alternatively, they attempt to bury bad news by releasing information that shows the government in a bad light at the same time as the nation's media are distracted by a more sensational story, or releasing it during a holiday period, which means items of bad news hardly receive any attention as journalists and media audiences are on holiday.

4   Refusal to issue broadcasting licences to those whom it deems are unfit and unsuitable.

5   Refusal to allow the use of some forms of computer software, and the use of filtering and surveillance software to block access to some internet sites ('Sorry: the page you requested does not exist'). Google, for example, withdrew from China in 2010 because that government was hacking into Google to track human rights activists, and other Google services in China such as Gmail are plagued with frequent service disruptions, and some internet sites cannot be accessed because of the government's web-filtering system. Facebook has been blocked from time to time in several countries. The United States government ferociously attacked the WikiLeaks site (www.wikileaks.org) following its release in 2011 of secret emails allegedly posing a threat to the United States, resulting in the website being cut off from 95 per cent of its funds as major financial institutions refused to process WikiLeaks donations.

6   Electronic surveillance of emails, monitoring of websites and intercepts of mobile calls. In 2014, a new law was passed in the UK allowing police and security services to scrutinize the public's email, and social media communications through sites like Facebook and Twitter. Such measures could have the effect of restricting people's willingness to communicate freely, or even make tongue-in-cheek comments, for fear of repercussions. This is particularly likely to happen in autocratic regimes without democracy, where such state surveillance is used to crush all opposition to the government.

Ownership of the media

The ownership of the main mass media in modern Britain is concentrated in the hands of a few large companies, which are interested in making profits. Some aspects of this concentration of ownership are shown in table 3.1. Of the total circulation of national daily and Sunday newspapers, around 86 per cent is controlled by just four companies, and over half by just two companies (News UK and the Daily Mail and General Trust). One individual, Rupert Murdoch, is the major force behind News UK, which owns the *Sun* and *The Times*, newspapers which make up about 32 per cent of all national daily newspaper sales in the United Kingdom. Murdoch alone accounted

Table 3.1 Who owns what: national newspaper group ownership and some of their interests in publishing, television and digital media, United Kingdom, 2015

Company	Share of UK national daily (excluding Sunday) newspaper circulation % (May 2015)	National newspapers (all of which have related websites)	Also owns
News UK and News Corporation	32	*Sun, The Times, The Sun on Sunday, Sunday Times, Times Literary Supplement*	39% of Sky television, broadband and telephony; HarperCollins book publishers; wide range of websites
Daily Mail and General Trust	24	*Daily Mail, Mail on Sunday*	Second-largest regional newspaper owners, with over 100 papers, including the most widely read free daily paper, *Metro*; 20% of ITN; various radio stations and large range of websites
Trinity Mirror	15	*Daily Mirror, Sunday Mirror, Daily Record, People, Sunday Mail*	Over 130 local and regional newspapers; over 300 websites
Northern & Shell	12	*Daily Express, Sunday Express, Daily Star, Daily Star Sunday*	*OK!* magazine; various websites
Telegraph Media Group (part of Press Holdings Limited)	7	*Daily Telegraph, Sunday Telegraph*	*Spectator*
Pearson	3	*Financial Times*	Longman, Pearson and Penguin book publishers; FT.com; 50% of The Economist Group; *Rough Guides*
Guardian Media Group/Scott Trust	3	*Guardian, Observer*	*Guardian Weekly; Auto Trader*; Guardian Unlimited network of websites; shares in various consumer magazines, including *Sainsbury's* magazine
Seven companies	96		

Source: Data compiled from Audit Bureau of Circulation and various corporate websites

for about 35 per cent of the total daily and Sunday newspaper sales in 2015. As table 3.1 shows, this concentration of ownership extends also to other areas of the media, such as TV and book and magazine publishing. The same few companies control a wide range of different media, and therefore a large proportion of what we see and hear in the media. The details of who owns what are continually changing, as concentration of ownership is an ongoing process with take-overs and mergers occurring, providing a stronger financial base for competition in the international market. Who owns what can be researched at www.mediauk.com.

Features of media ownership: Lords of the Global Village

Bagdikian (1989) pointed out around twenty-five years ago that even then the concentration of media ownership meant that a handful of global media companies and moguls – what he called 'Lords of the Global Village' – dominated the world's mass media, and controlled every step in the information process, from creation of the product to all the various means by which modern technology delivers media messages to the public. These features of media ownership include the following.

1 *Concentration of ownership:* most of the media of all kinds are concentrated in the hands of a few very large companies.

2 *Vertical integration:* there is concentration of ownership within a single medium, such as one company owning several newspapers, and owning all stages in the production and distribution of a media product, like a film company that also owns the cinema chains showing the films. For example, a company like News Corporation owns film and TV studios and a large chunk of BSkyB (Sky), so they own both the programme- and film-making facilities, and the means of transmitting them to consumers who use Sky TV.

3 *Horizontal integration* or cross-media ownership: media owners have interests in a range of media, such as newspapers, magazines, book publishing, cable and satellite television, the film industry, music, websites and as internet service providers (ISPs).

4 *Global ownership:* media ownership is international – the owners have global media empires, with interests in many different countries of the world.

5 *Conglomeration and diversification:* media companies are often part of huge conglomerates – companies that have a diversity of interests in a wide variety of products besides the media. Virgin, for example, has an airline, a train company, a bank and other financial products, and mobile phones, on top of its widespread media interests.

6 *Global conglomeration:* the two points above converge, as not only is media ownership international, with media companies operating in global markets producing many different media products – such as films, newspapers and websites – in many countries, but the conglomerates they are part of are often also global conglomerates.

7 *Synergy.* **synergy** is what happens when media companies produce, promote and sell a product in a variety of forms, through all the various subsidiaries of a media conglomerate or in collaboration with other companies, thereby promoting and enhancing sales of that product and related spin-offs. For example, a film shown in cinemas might be promoted by advertising in newspapers and magazines, the film might then appear as a book, or be used to promote sales of the book on which the film is based, then sold as a DVD, with music released as a CD or download, turned into a computer game, and further promoted by merchandizing of toys, sweets, bed linen and so on. All or some of these products may be produced by the same media company. Each of these promotes the other products, enabling far more sales and greater profits than would be possible through one form of the product alone. Examples of this might be the Harry Potter and Star Wars franchises, which spanned a vast range of media and entertainment products licensed to a range of companies, and which turned Harry Potter and Star Wars into household names and money-spinning global phenomena.

8. *Technological convergence*: media companies try to maximize sales of their products by promoting and making them available in a variety of formats which can be accessed on a single device. For example, companies may collaborate and combine different media technologies so a single device like a smartphone or a tablet computer can be used to advertise a film, to watch the film, to download and listen to the music, to play the related computer game or to read the book.

Synergy is where a product is produced in different forms which are promoted together, either through different arms of the same company or through collaboration by different companies, to enable greater sales than would be possible through the sale of a single form of that product or by the efforts of one company.

Technological convergence is where several media technologies, once contained in separate devices, are combined in a single device.

The concentration of ownership is clearly illustrated by the media in the United States. Bagdikian (2004), confirmed by the 2011 *Fortune* 500 list, says that five global-dimension firms (Walt Disney, News Corporation, Time Warner, CBS and Viacom) own most of the newspapers, magazines, book publishers, motion picture studios, and radio and television stations in the United States. These firms have major holdings in all the media, from newspapers to movie studios. Each medium covers the entire country, and the owners prefer stories that can be used anywhere and everywhere. Bagdikian suggests this concentration of ownership 'gives each of the five corporations and their leaders more communications power than was exercised by any despot or dictatorship in history'. Whether the rise of the new media has undermined this power of the media moguls will be considered in Topic 6, but the concerns over media ownership raised by those like Bagdikian have given rise to three main and related questions:

- Are the media simply spreading a limited number of dominant ideas (the dominant ideology), thereby protecting the interests of the dominant class in society?
- Do the owners of the media control the content of the media?
- What effects do the media have on the audiences they aim at?

Activity

1 Outline reasons why the concentration of ownership of the media might be of some concern in a democracy.
2 Do you think there should be restrictions on the number of media that any one person or company should be allowed to own? Give reasons for your answer.

The media and ideology

Ideology refers to a set of ideas, values and beliefs that represents the outlook, and justifies the interests, of a social group. The ideological role of the media is concerned with the extent to which the media socialize audiences into a particular view of the world and the society in which they live, often manufacturing a consensus around some central set of values. This is often thought to be achieved by the media producing messages that they expect audiences to respond to in a particular way. This is what Morley (1999 [1980]) called the preferred (or dominant) reading – the interpretation of messages that those producing media content (newspaper stories, TV programmes, etc.) would prefer their audiences to believe.

Marxists see societies as having a dominant ideology, which is that of the dominant class in society. This dominant ideology is one which justifies the social advantages of wealthy, powerful and influential groups in society, and justifies the disadvantages of those who lack wealth, power and influence. It is spread through the rest of the population by what the Marxist Althusser called ideological state apparatuses. These are agencies like the media and the education system which seek to induce in the mass of people a false consciousness of their exploitation and their real interests. They do this by persuading them to accept that everyone benefits from the way society is presently organized and that it is fair and just, because persuading them and trying to obtain their consent is a far more effective means of controlling the population than using force.

Marxists like Miliband (1973) and the Glasgow Media Group (GMG) argue that the media play an important role in spreading this dominant ideology. They argue that the media control access to the knowledge which people have about what is happening in society, and encourage them to accept the unequal society in which they live. The media promote preferred readings which try to create a general consensus or agreement about what constitutes 'reasonable' and 'unreasonable' ways of thinking and behaving, which makes those who challenge the way things are presently organized seem unreasonable or extreme. This is because the media have the means to provide incomplete or distorted views of the world, and to ignore, attack, dismiss or present as unreasonable any groups, events or ideas which challenge or threaten the dominant ideology. The media thereby create a climate of conformity among the mass of the population which justifies the rule of the rich and powerful. This ideological role of the media is explored further in Topic 3. The following section examines whether the media are simply the tools of the dominant class.

Control of the media and media content

How ownership and control affect specifically the selection and presentation of the news are considered further in Topic 3 of this chapter. Within sociology, there are three main approaches to the issue of ownership and control of the media and how this affects the content of the media. These are known as the manipulative or instrumentalist approach, the dominant ideology or hegemonic approach, and the pluralist approach.

Ideology refers to a set of ideas, values and beliefs that represents the outlook, and justifies the interests, of a social group.

Preferred (or dominant) readings are the interpretations of the messages that those producing media content would prefer their audiences to believe.

The **dominant ideology** is one which justifies the social advantages of wealthy, powerful and influential groups in society, and justifies the disadvantages of those who lack wealth, power and influence.

Ideological state apparatuses are agencies that spread the dominant ideology and justify the power of the dominant social class.

False consciousness is a lack of awareness among people about what their real interests are, and the false belief that everyone benefits from the present organization of society which is presented as fair and just.

The manipulative or instrumentalist approach

This is a traditional Marxist approach, adopted by writers like Miliband. This suggests that the owners (the media moguls) directly control media content, and manipulate that content and media audiences to protect their profits, and spread the dominant ideology. Media editors, managers and journalists have little choice other than to run the media within the boundaries set down by the owners as they depend on them for their jobs; journalists will consequently self-censor their work, and produce biased, one-sided reports which attack, ridicule or ignore ideas or groups which threaten or criticize the interests of the dominant class and the status quo (the existing arrangements in society).

Curran and Seaton (2010) found evidence which suggested media owners did interfere and manipulate newspaper content, at the expense of the independence of journalists and editors, to protect their own interests, and supported or withheld criticisms of governments which defended those interests. For example, in February 2003, Rupert Murdoch of News Corporation was arguing strongly in interviews for a war with Iraq. It is unlikely to be coincidence that all his 175 newspapers around the world backed him. Murdoch admitted to the House of Lords Communication Committee in 2007 that he was 'hands on both economically and editorially' and exercised editorial control on major issues in the *Sun* and the now-defunct *News of the World*, like which party to back in a general election or policy on Europe. Even though the law ostensibly prevented him from instructing the editors of Murdoch papers *The Times* and the *Sunday Times*, former *Times* editor Harold Evans (2011, 2012) suggested Murdoch continued to undermine editorial independence and pressed editorial staff to adopt his right-wing, conservative views. The Leveson Inquiry (www.levesoninquiry.org.uk) in 2012, into the culture, practice and ethics of the press, uncovered a range of links between media owners and governments, with media support given to political parties in return for government policies favourable to the interests of media owners.

The manipulative/instrumentalist approach assumes the media audience is passive – a mass of easily manipulated, unthinking and uncritical robots, who unquestioningly swallow the preferred readings or interpretation of the limited range of opinions and biased reports found in media content. It is fed on a dumbed-down mass diet of undemanding, trivial and uncritical content, which stops them focusing on serious issues, or encourages them to interpret serious issues in ways favourable to the dominant class.

Neophiliacs are people who dislike and get bored with tradition and routine, and welcome, rapidly embrace and adapt to new technology and other changes.

Citizen journalism is where members of the public, rather than professional journalists and media companies, collect, report and spread news stories and information.

Criticisms of the manipulative or instrumentalist approach

1 Pluralists (see pages 189–90) would argue there is a wide range of opinion in the media, and the media's owners and managers are primarily concerned with making profits. This means attracting large audiences to gain advertisers and the only means of doing this is to provide what the audiences – not the owners – want.

2 The state regulates media ownership so no one person or company has too much influence. By law, TV and radio in the UK have to report news impartially, and can't therefore simply churn out biased, one-sided reports.

3 Audiences are not as gullible and easily manipulated as the manipulative approach suggests – people can accept, reject or re-interpret the preferred (dominant) readings of media messages, depending on their existing ideas and experiences. This is discussed in Topic 5.

4 Pluralists and neophiliacs (optimists who rapidly adopt and use new media) suggest the rise of the new digital media and the internet, and the growth of citizen journalism, has undermined the traditional influence of media owners, and has given more power to ordinary people to give their interpretations of events that happen in the world. This is discussed more in Topic 6.

The dominant ideology or hegemonic approach

This is a more recent, neo-Marxist approach, and is particularly associated with the work of the Glasgow Media Group (GMG) (www.glasgowmediagroup.org). This approach also suggests the mass media spread a dominant ideology justifying or legitimizing the power of the ruling class. It recognizes the power of owners, but, unlike the manipulative approach, it suggests that owners –

although they have influence – rarely have direct day-to-day control of the content of the media, which is left in the hands of managers and journalists.

This approach emphasizes the concept of **hegemony**. This is a term first developed by the neo-Marxist Gramsci, and refers to the idea that, through the spreading of the dominant ruling-class ideology, other social classes are persuaded to accept that the values and beliefs in that ideology are reasonable and normal, and form a consensus that becomes part of everyday common sense. This enables the ruling class to rule with the consent of those they rule over.

The hegemonic approach suggests that media managers and journalists have some professional independence; they still generally support the dominant ideology, but by choice – not because they are manipulated or ordered by owners to do so. The GMG points out that most journalists tend to be white, middle-class and male, and their socialization means they share a similar view of the world to that of the dominant class. They have a set of professional values which suggests that the most reasonable and sensible explanations of events and the way they should be reported are those in keeping with the taken-for-granted, common-sense assumptions of the dominant ideology. These assumptions mean the audience is exposed to only a limited range of opinions, in which groups, events or ideas threatening the status quo are presented as outside of the established consensus view of the world, and as unreasonable, extremist, ridiculous, funny or trivial, to be ignored, attacked, mocked or not taken seriously.

Media managers and journalists, while inevitably influenced by the desire not to upset the owners and to protect their careers, also need to attract audiences and advertisers, particularly if they are to produce profits for the owners. Journalists' **news values** (discussed later) mean that sometimes journalists do not always trot out the dominant ideology, but sometimes develop critical, anti-establishment views which strike a chord with their audiences – such as campaigns against government corruption, excessive bonuses for bankers, or wrongdoing by large companies. This means that there can be a range of media content, including some occasional content critical of the dominant ideology, which serves the purposes of attracting audiences, making money for the owners, and maintaining the pretence that routine media content is generally objective and unbiased.

The GMG suggests the consensus discussed above means, more often than not, some items are deliberately and routinely excluded from reporting in the media, and audiences are encouraged to think about some events rather than others – such as the appalling damage caused by rioters in British cities in 2011, rather than why people were rioting in the first place. This is known as **agenda-setting** and **gatekeeping** (discussed later in this chapter), and means audiences have little real choice of media content, as newspapers and TV programmes are produced within a framework of the dominant ideology. Philo (2012) illustrates this in a study of media coverage of the global banking crisis of 2008 onwards. He found the media focused attention predominantly on the views and solutions offered by the three main political parties, and the bankers themselves. This meant the people the media asked about solutions were those most supportive of the system which created the problems in the first place, and there was very little media discussion of solutions outside the existing system of financial arrangements.

By the processes described above, audiences are unconsciously persuaded to see the dominant ideology as a consensus – a wide agreement about what is worthy, good and right for all, and the only reasonable and sensible way of viewing the world. Over time, this reinforces and encourages continued acceptance and maintenance of ruling-class ideology and hegemony in society.

Criticisms of the dominant ideology or hegemonic approach

1   The approach underrates the power and influence of the owners. Owners do appoint and dismiss managers and editors who step too far out of line, and journalists' careers are dependent on gaining approval of their stories from editors. For example, former *Sun* editor David Yelland said that all Murdoch's editors 'go on a journey where they end up agreeing with everything Murdoch says … "What would Rupert think about this?" is like a mantra inside your head' (cited in the *Guardian*, 27 April 2012).

2   Agenda-setting and gatekeeping mean audiences have little real choice of media content, as newspapers and TV programmes are produced within a framework of the dominant ideology. This suggests a direct manipulation of audiences more in keeping with the manipulative or instrumentalist approach.

Hegemony means the dominance in society of the ruling class's set of ideas over others, and acceptance of and consent to them by the rest of society.

News values are the values and assumptions held by editors and journalists which guide them in choosing what is 'newsworthy' – what to report and what to leave out, and how what they choose to report should be presented.

Agenda-setting involves the power to manage which issues are to be presented for public discussion and debate and which issues are to be kept in the background.

Gatekeeping is the power of some people, groups or organizations to limit access to something valuable or useful. For example, the mass media have the power to refuse to cover some issues and therefore not allow the public access to some information.

3   As in the criticism of the manipulative/instrumentalist approach, pluralists (see below) suggest the rise of the new globalized digital media and the internet has undermined the traditional influence of media owners, and put more control of media content into the hands of media users. This is discussed more in Topic 6.

The pluralist approach

Pluralism is a view held by pluralists – sees the exercise of power in society as reflecting a broad range of social interests, with power spread among a wide variety of competing interest groups and individuals, with no single one having a monopoly of power.

> **Pluralism** is a view that sees power in society spread among a wide variety of interest groups and individuals, with no single one having a monopoly of power.

The manipulative and hegemonic approaches argue that those who own, control and work in the media shape their content, spreading the dominant ideology among media audiences and protecting the interests of powerful groups in society. The pluralist approach takes a very different view. They argue that media content is driven not by a dominant ideology or the political interests of owners, but by the fight for profits through high circulation and audience figures. There is a wide range of competing newspapers, magazines, television channels, websites and other platforms for the delivery of media products, reflecting a huge range of audience interests and ideas, including those which challenge the dominant ideology. The only control over media content is consumer choice, and the media have to be responsive to audience tastes and wishes otherwise they'll go out of business. This competition for audience prevents any one owner or company from dominating the media, and media regulators, like Ofcom, also act to prevent this happening.

Pluralists argue that the media are generally free of any government or direct owner control and can present whatever point of view they want. The same goes for journalists, who are not simply the pawns of their employers, pumping out the dominant ideology and biased stories to manipulate audiences; they have some professional and editorial honesty and independence, and have to produce stories that offer a wide selection of views, using news values (discussed later) which reflect the wishes and interests which are most relevant to their audiences, if they are to satisfy and maintain their audiences.

Audiences, too, are free to choose in a pick 'n' mix approach to whatever interpretation suits them, thanks to the wide range of media from which they can select; they have the freedom to accept, reject, reinterpret or ignore media content in accordance with their tastes and beliefs. The new globalized digital media and social media and the internet, particularly, enable all sorts of views to be represented through citizen journalism. More people, not just media moguls and large media corporations, have the opportunity to communicate with vast numbers of other people. For example, ordinary people can now publish their thoughts on Twitter (www.twitter.com), attack those in power on Blogger (www.blogger.com) and report on events excluded from other mainstream media by sending their own news stories and photos to citizen journalism sites like Demotix (www.demotix.com) or YouTube, or posting them on Facebook. This undermines Marxist views of control of media content by media owners.

Criticisms of the pluralist approach

1   Media owners appoint editors – and have on numerous occasions sacked uncooperative editors – and strongly influence who is appointed at senior levels. Owners, top managers and editors often share a similar outlook on the world.
2   While managers, journalists and television producers have some independence, they work within constraints placed on them by the owners. News is collected from a few news companies and agencies, often paid for by the media owners themselves.
3   Not all groups in society have equal influence on editors and journalists to get their views across. The main sources of information for journalists tend to be from those groups that consist of the most powerful and influential members of society, and it is they who are most likely to be interviewed on TV, to appear on chat shows, to be quoted in newspapers, and their views are given greater weight than those of less powerful groups.
4   Only very rich groups will have the resources required to launch major media companies to get their views across independently, and both governments and rich individuals have brought

political or legal pressure to bear to stop programmes, newspaper stories and books which threaten their interests.

5   The pressure to attract audiences doesn't increase media choice but limits it – the media decline in quality, and news and information get squeezed out or sensationalized, and turned into 'infotainment' (information wrapped up to entertain), as the media aim to attract large mass audiences with unthreatening, unchallenging and bland content. Barnett and Seymour (1999), in a study of TV schedules in 1978, 1988 and 1998, and Curran et al. (2009), in a content analysis of media in Denmark, Finland, the UK and the United States, showed how the media were becoming more market-oriented and entertainment-centred, leading to less serious kinds of journalism that limited citizens' knowledge of public affairs. Multi-channel television, less regulation, the challenge of the internet and the push to have large audiences led to a dumbing down and a marked increase in tabloidization (see glossary box) of media content. This means that different and competing media organizations have not led, as the pluralists contend, to more choice and a more open and honest media, portraying a range of opinions, but to a lack of choice as market pressures lead to lower journalistic standards, infotainment, endless repeats and US imports replacing original drama.

6   Hegemonic theorists argue that people have been socialized by the media into the belief that they are being provided with what they want. The media themselves may have created their tastes, so that what audiences want is really what the media owners want.

Table 3.2 summarizes approaches to ownership of the media and media content, and how ownership and control affect specifically the selection and presentation of the news are considered further in Topic 3 of this chapter.

Tabloidization refers to the process whereby there is a decline of serious news reporting, coverage of current affairs and documentaries, and their replacement by a more dumbed-down, entertaining, sensationalized or gossipy style of journalism – focusing on human interest stories, celebrity culture and scandal – and entertainment, crime drama, soap opera and reality TV shows.

Table 3.2 Ownership of the media and media content: a summary

	Manipulative or instrumentalist approach	Dominant ideology or hegemonic approach	Pluralist approach
Role of owners	Direct control and manipulation	Influence and persuasion	No direct control, and wide range of competing interests
Media content	Dominant ideology	Dominant ideology, but sometimes critical of it to attract audiences	Need for circulation and audience figures, and profits, means content is what audiences – not owners – want
Role of media managers and journalists	Told what to do by owners, or within framework set by them	Some independence from owners, but share dominant ideology, and so present most stories in that framework, but need to attract audiences and advertisers	Have high level of independence, so long as they attract audiences and therefore profits
View of audience	Passive – audiences manipulated by owners, and unquestioningly make only the preferred (dominant) readings of media content	Passive – audiences persuaded to accept dominant ideology, and unquestioningly make only the preferred (dominant) readings of media content	Active – audiences make choices between media and can accept, reject, reinterpret or ignore media content – they do not always accept the preferred (dominant) readings

Activity

Go through each of the following statements, identifying them as corresponding most closely to the manipulative or instrumentalist approach, or the dominant ideology or hegemonic approach, or the pluralist approach.

a) 'I'm in the business of making money, and I'll use the media I own to provide whatever the audience wants.'

b) Generally the media support the interests of the dominant groups in society, but a bit of criticism every now and then encourages people to believe the media are telling us the truth about society.

c) The concentration of media ownership means that the views expressed in the media reflect little more than the interests of the owners.

d) There is such a wide variety of media to choose from that everyone's views are represented somewhere.

e) The media are controlled and run mainly by white, middle-class males, so they mainly spread the existing dominant ideas in society.

f) Media audiences are exposed to only a limited range of opinions, and so over time people are persuaded to accept only a limited view of the world, mainly that of the most powerful groups in society.

g) Journalists are just the tools of the owners, and they can't criticize the interests of the powerful without losing their jobs.

h) If audiences aren't attracted, advertisers won't advertise and media companies will go out of business. Survival in the competitive world of the modern media means audiences are the ones who really decide what appears in the media.

i) The media cons people in subtle ways over a period of time so that the only reasonable view of the world is seen as that of the most powerful groups in society.

Practice questions

1 Outline and explain **two** ways in which media owners might influence the content of the media.
(10 marks)

2 Read **Item A** below and answer the question that follows.

Item A
Traditional Marxists suggest media owners control media content, and manipulate that content and media audiences to spread a dominant ideology which favours the most powerful groups in society. In contrast to this, pluralists argue competition between different media means the only control over media content is consumer choice. Media owners have to be responsive to audience tastes and wishes in order to stay in business.

Applying material from **Item A**, analyse **two** differences between Marxist and pluralist views on how ownership of the media affects media content. **(10 marks)**

3 Read **Item B** below and answer the question that follows.

Item B
The ideological role of the media is concerned with the media's role in socializing audiences into a particular view of the world and the society in which they live. Marxists see the media as spreading a dominant ideology that justifies both the social advantages of wealthy, powerful and influential groups in society, and the disadvantages of those who lack wealth, power and influence.

Applying material from **Item B** and your knowledge, evaluate the view that the output of the media mainly reflects the interests of wealthy, powerful and influential groups in society.
(20 marks)

Topic 2

SPECIFICATION AREA

The media, globalisation and popular culture

Globalization and popular culture

The speed of technological change is now so great that the world is rapidly becoming what McLuhan (1962) referred to as a global village. This term is used by McLuhan to describe how the electronic media, such as satellite technology and the internet, collapse space and time barriers in human communication; people from around the world can now interact with one another instantaneously on a global scale, and in a sense this 'shrinks' the world, which has become more like one village or community.

Many people are now exposed to the same information and messages through media which cut across all national frontiers. The internet and satellite, cable and Freeview TV, for example, have opened up access to TV programmes, entertainment and information from all cultures and countries of the world.

This is part of what is known as globalization, which refers to the way societies across the globe have become increasingly interconnected, and are exposed to the same cultural products across the world. This has led to a growing globalization of popular culture.

Popular culture

Popular culture is culture liked and enjoyed by ordinary people, such as TV soaps, and is sometimes called mass culture, and sometimes low culture. Mass culture, which is the popular culture enjoyed by the majority, is highly commercialized, involving mass-produced, standardized and short-lived products, sometimes of trivial content and seen by many as of no lasting artistic value. These cultural products are designed to be sold on the global mass market to make profits for the large 'culture industry' corporations that produce them, especially the mass media. The term 'low culture' is a derogatory term (critical and insulting) to describe popular culture. Its usage suggests popular or mass culture is of inferior quality to the high culture of the elite discussed below. The term 'popular culture' is often used as an alternative to low or mass culture, suggesting it is culture liked and enjoyed by ordinary people, worthy of study, and avoiding and rejecting the suggestion that it is somehow of an inferior quality or of lower value than high culture.

Popular culture is everyday culture – simple, undemanding, easy-to-understand entertainment, rather than something 'set apart' and 'special'. Such products aimed at popular tastes are typically the products of mass culture, such as mass-circulation magazines, red-top tabloid newspapers like the *Sun* or the *Mirror*, television soaps and reality TV shows, TV films, dramas and thrillers, popular music, feature films for the mass market, thrillers bought for reading on the beach and popular websites like Facebook.

Popular culture is largely linked to passive and unchallenging entertainment, designed to be sold to the largest number of people possible. Such products are dumbed-down – they demand little critical thought, analysis or discussion, and rarely provide any challenge to the existing social structure or dominant cultural ideas (see, for example, the discussion of dumbing-down in media content by Barnett and Seymour, and Curran, on page 190 in Topic 1). The mass media are now spreading a common mass culture across the globe, which is becoming the popular culture of millions as it appeals to people across local communities, different cultures and national divisions, and makes vast sums of money for huge media conglomerates.

A **global village** refers to the way that the media and electronic communications now operate on a global scale and so shrink barriers of space and time that the world has become like one village or community.

Globalization refers to growing interconnectedness of societies across the world, with the spread of the same culture, consumer goods and economic interests across the globe.

Popular culture refers to the cultural products liked and enjoyed by the mass of ordinary people. Often associated with mass culture.

High culture

Mass culture generally refers to commercially produced culture, involving cultural products produced as entertainment for sale to the mass of ordinary people. These involve mass-produced, standardized, short-lived products, which many see as of little lasting value and which demand little critical thought, analysis or discussion. Often linked with popular culture.

Popular culture is generally contrasted with high culture. High culture is seen as something set apart from everyday life, something 'special' to be treated with respect and reverence, involving things of lasting value and part of a heritage which is worth preserving – for example, ballet, opera and fine art. High culture products are often found in special places such as art galleries, museums, concert halls and theatres, and they are aimed at mainly upper-class and professional middle-class audiences with what might be viewed as 'good taste'. Such products might include 'serious' news programmes and documentaries, and quality newspapers, involving comprehensive detail, social and political analysis and discussion. Other products include classical music like that of Mozart or Beethoven, opera, ballet, jazz, foreign-language or specialist 'art' films, and what has become established literature, such as the work of Shakespeare, Dickens, the Brontës, Jane Austen or Virginia Woolf, and visual art like that of Monet, Gauguin, Van Gogh, Picasso or Kahlo.

The changing distinction between high culture and popular culture

Low culture is a derogatory (critical and insulting) term used to suggest popular or mass culture is of inferior quality compared to the high culture of the elite.

Postmodernists, particularly, argue that the distinction between high culture and popular culture is weakening. The global reach of contemporary media, the mass production of goods on a world scale, and easier international transportation make a huge range of media and cultural products available to everyone. This has been combined with a huge expansion of the media-based creative and cultural industries, like advertising, television, film, music, and book, magazine and web publishing, which makes the distinction between high and popular culture meaningless.

Such changes enable original music and art and other cultural products to be consumed by the mass of people in their own homes without visiting specialized institutions like theatres or art galleries. High culture is no longer the preserve of cultural elites, and people now have a wide diversity of cultural choices and products available to them and can pick 'n' mix from either popular or high culture.

Strinati (1995) argues that elements of high culture have now become a part of popular culture, and elements of popular culture have been incorporated into high culture, so there is no longer any real distinction between high culture and popular culture. Giddings (2010) points out that forms of high culture are now often used to produce products for the mass popular culture market. Video games, for example – which are considered to be part of popular culture – often bring together art, architecture, classical music, actors and writers which separately might be classified as 'high culture'.

High culture refers to cultural products seen to be of lasting artistic or literary value, which are particularly admired and approved of by intellectual elites and, predominantly, the upper and middle classes.

Technology has made it possible for mass audiences to see and study high-culture products, such as paintings by artists like Van Gogh, on the internet or TV, and have their own framed print hanging on their sitting-room wall. Internet websites, like those of museums and galleries and Google (see www.googleartproject.com) mean people can build their own private high-culture virtual museums and art galleries. The originals may still only be on show in art galleries and museums, but copies are available to everyone. High-culture images, like the *Mona Lisa* or Van Gogh's *Sunflowers*, are now reproduced on everything from socks and T-shirts to chocolates and can lids, mugs, mouse mats, tablemats, jigsaws and posters. Classical music is used as a marketing tune by advertisers, and literature is turned into TV series and major mass movies, such as Jane Austen's *Pride and Prejudice*, and Charlotte Brontë's *Jane Eyre*.

Evaluation of popular/mass culture

An **elite** is a small group holding great power and privilege in society.

Popular culture, in the form of mass culture, is often attacked for diverting people away from more useful activities, for driving down cultural standards (like those established in high-culture art and literature, or high journalistic standards) and for having harmful effects on mass audiences.

Marxists and critical theorists of the Frankfurt School see mass culture as simply mass-produced manufactured products imposed on the masses by global media businesses for financial profit. Popular mass culture is a form of social control, giving an illusion of choice between a range

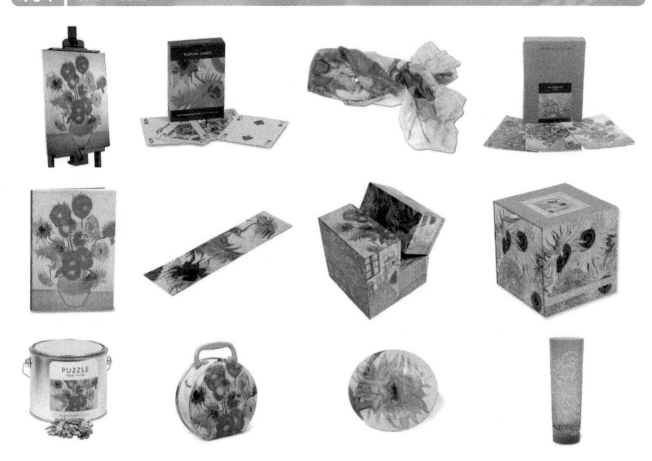

of similar dumbed-down, standardized, trivial and uncritical media infotainment and escapist fantasy, which maintains the ideological hegemony and power of the dominant social class in society. This is because consumers are lulled into an uncritical, undemanding passivity and mindless social conformity, making them less likely to challenge the dominant ideas, groups and interests in society. Marcuse (2002 [1964]), for example, suggested consumption of media-generated mass culture, with its emphasis on relaxation, fun, entertainment and consumption through advertising, undermined people's ability to think critically about the world. He saw this as a form of social repression – a means of locking people into the present system, promoting conformity and a passive acceptance of the way things are, and undermining the potential for revolutionary action to change society.

Strinati (1995) rejects these views, and doesn't accept the suggestion that there is a single mass culture and mass audience, which people passively and uncritically consume, and points to a wide diversity and choice within popular culture, which people select from and critically respond to. Livingstone (1988) found that the writers and producers of TV soap operas, a form of popular culture watched by millions, saw them as educating and informing the public about important or controversial social issues, presenting a range of political opinions, generating public controversies and discussion, and giving insights into the sometimes tough and grim lives of others. Rather than killing off public debate and lulling mass audiences into uncritical passivity, contemporary soap operas like *Hollyoaks*, *EastEnders* and *Coronation Street* have generated widespread critical discussion about issues that might otherwise rarely get aired in public, or only in crude media stereotypes. For example, in recent years the public has been encouraged through soap stories to discuss issues like child rape, incest, homelessness, false imprisonment, lesbianism, child abuse, domestic violence, eating disorders, homophobia, racism, bisexuality, religious cults, paedophilia, drug addiction and relationship breakdown. The controversies surrounding these soap stories have frequently dominated the headlines of the red-top tabloid press, promoting public discussions that might never otherwise have happened.

Mass marketing has broken down the distinction between 'high culture' and 'popular culture'. As seen here, Van Gogh's *Sunflowers* painting, an example of a high-culture art form, is now available as popular culture, as a canvas reproduction, on playing cards, a scarf, greetings cards, a notebook, a book mark, a puzzle cube, jigsaw puzzles, a lunch box, a plate and a vase

A global popular culture

Flew (2002) suggests that the evolution of new media technologies, such as satellite TV and the internet, has played an important role in the development of a global popular culture. Kellner (1995) argues that the media has the power to globally produce images of lifestyles that increasingly become part of everyday life and through which people form their identities and views of the world. This global culture is primarily American in origin.

Globalization has undermined national and local cultures, as the same cultural and consumer products are now sold across the world, inspired and promoted by global media content and advertising. These products become part of the ways of life of many different countries, spreading a popular culture which makes what were once different cultures more and more alike.

This process of a powerful media making the cultures of different countries become more alike, and merged into one uniform culture, is known as cultural homogenization, and it may now be more appropriate to speak of a homogenized global culture than national or local cultures.

Advances in multi-media technology, like satellite TV and the internet, and the digitization of cultural products like music and visual art, mean that today's media conglomerates operate in a global marketplace. As well as breaking down the distinction between high culture and popular culture, this new digital world also breaks down the cultural distance between countries, and popular culture is spread beyond the boundaries of particular nation-states, with the same cultural products sold across the globe.

Sklair (2012) suggests the media, largely American-based, spread news, information, ideas, entertainment and popular culture to a global market. The media blur the differences between information, entertainment and promotion of products, and sell across the world ideas, values and products associated with what is presented as an idealized, happy and satisfying consumerist American/Western lifestyle. This encourages acceptance of the dominant ideology of Western capitalist societies, which Sklair calls the 'culture-ideology of consumerism'. It is Western companies such as Microsoft and Google that have dominated the growth of the internet, which increasingly spreads this same Western culture-ideology of consumerism.

Inspired by the media-generated culture industry and global advertising and marketing, consumers around the world increasingly have a shared popular culture, with people watching the same Western/American TV programmes and films, listening to the same music, eating the same foods, following the same sporting events, wearing the same designer clothes and labels and sharing the same fashions, playing the same computer games, carrying the same smartphones and sharing many aspects of their lifestyles, beliefs and identities.

As Ritzer (2008) shows, companies and brands now operate on a global scale, promoting a global culture along with the consumer lifestyles associated with them, and also weakening local cultures. Companies like Apple, Google, Microsoft, Samsung, HSBC, McDonald's, Coca-Cola, Vodafone, Starbucks, Nescafé, Sony and Nike use the transnational media to promote their products on a global stage, and their logos are now global brands that can be recognized across the world.

Television and production companies – predominantly from the USA and the UK – sell their programmes and programme formats globally. For example, by 2012, *Who Wants to be a Millionaire?* had been distributed to 120 countries; *The Weakest Link* had been seen in 60 countries; *Strictly Come Dancing* (badged as *Dancing with the Stars*) had been bought by more than 30 countries; *Pop Idol* appears in 50 versions in 110 countries; and *Big Brother* in 64 countries. 160 million viewers in China were watching subtitled episodes of *Downton Abbey* in 2014, and localized versions of *Britain's Got Talent*, *Big Brother* and *The X Factor* have been huge successes, with hundreds of millions of viewers. Computer/video games are a global phenomenon – for example, *Grand Theft Auto V*, produced by the American firm Take-Two Interactive Software, in 2013 became the fastest-earning entertainment product of all time, hitting $1 billion in global sales in just three days.

It is the media that have made some US and British film, music and sports stars known across the world, enabling huge success in marketing their merchandise in global markets; and it is the media that have contributed substantially to English becoming the internationally dominant and preferred second language of most of the world.

Cultural and media imperialism

Fenton (1999) points out that the term 'global' rarely means 'universal', and normally disguises the domination of Western culture over other cultures. Most media conglomerates are now based in the United States, and US transnational media and communications corporations, like Microsoft, Google, Yahoo and AOL/CNN/Time-Warner, dominate global communications. This has been described as a process of cocacolonization (a derivative of the American soft drink 'Coca-Cola' and 'colonization') which involves cultural imperialism or media imperialism. This is the suggestion that the media-led global culture-ideology of consumerism described above has led to Western, and especially American, media products and cultural values being forced on non-Western cultures, and overwhelming a good part of the world with the consequent undermining of local cultures and cultural independence.

This global Western dominance is illustrated by the fact that nearly all the 500 top-grossing international films of all time, outside of the United States, are primarily American films, with the top 10 shown in table 3.3. You can explore the latest and a fuller version of the list at www.imdb.com/boxoffice/alltimegross?region=non-us.

The pluralist view of the media and the globalization of popular culture

Pluralists argue that there is no such thing as popular or mass culture. The internet, cable, satellite and digital television, and the global reach of modern media technology all offer a huge range of media products. This gives consumers across the world a wide diversity of cultural choices. Compaine (2005) argues that global competition is expanding sources of information and entertainment, rather than restricting them or dumbing them down. Tomlinson (1999) argues that globalization does not involve direct cultural imposition from the Western world, but that there is a hybridization or mixing of cultures. People pick 'n' mix and draw on both Western/global cultures and their own local cultures. Increased choice promotes different cultural styles around the world in which a range of local and westernized global cultural influences are combined into new hybrid cultures. For example, though there may be globalized TV formats, many TV programmes, such as *Who Wants to be a Millionaire?*, are 'glocalized' – merging the global and the local – as they are adapted to suit the tastes of local cultures, as was shown in the film *Slumdog Millionaire*. This means there is more, not less, cultural diversity in the world.

New media technology, like smartphones and the internet through websites like YouTube, Facebook and Blogger, enables consumers to create and distribute their own media products, and enables people to generate their own popular culture, rather than being the passive victims of Western media conglomerates.

Globalization means that the same product brands are now found in many countries of the world

Cultural imperialism refers to the imposition of Western, and especially American, cultural values on non-Western cultures, and the consequent undermining of local cultures and cultural independence.

Media imperialism is the suggestion that the media, particularly the internet, satellite television and global advertising, have led to the imposition of Western, and especially American, cultural values on non-Western cultures. Often linked to cultural imperialism.

Table 3.3 Top-10 grossing films of all time at the international (non-USA) box office August 2015

Rank	Film	Year	Country of origin	Total gross revenue (millions of US dollars) excluding USA
1	Avatar	2009	USA	$2,021
2	Titanic	1997	USA	$1,527
3	Furious Seven	2015	USA	$1,130
4	Harry Potter and the Deathly Hallows: Part 2	2011	UK/USA	$947
5	The Avengers: Age of Ultron	2015	USA	$942
6	Jurassic World	2015	USA	$928
7	The Avengers	2012	USA	$892
8	Frozen	2013	USA	$858
9	Transformers: Age of Extinction	2014	USA	$846
10	Iron Man 3	2013	USA	$806

Source: Internet Movie Database (www.imdb.com/boxoffice/alltimegross?region=non-us)

Hybridization is the process of creation of a new, hybrid culture when aspects of two or more different cultures combine.

A **hybrid culture** is a new culture formed from a mix of two or more other cultures.

As will be seen later in Topic 5, there are a variety of possible effects of the media, and media messages can be interpreted in a range of ways. Even if media conglomerates are spreading Western ideas, values and culture, this does not mean that all cultures will react in the same way or necessarily adopt the Western culture and consumer lifestyles the global media promote.

Rather than being doped into passivity, with people simply and uncritically swallowing what they see or hear, as some Marxists argue, consumers and audiences now have more choices and knowledge available to them than ever before in history. This, pluralists claim, makes it ever more difficult for any one set of ideas or culture to dominate in the world, leading to a promotion of democracy, growing cultural diversity through hybridization, and the blossoming of ideas that were never before possible.

A critical view of the media and the globalization of popular culture

The globalization of popular culture is of great advantage to the media owners, who gain colossal profits from exporting and advertising their products across the globe, along with promoting the identities and lifestyles that encourage people to consume them. Thussu (2007) argues that the globalization of television and competition between media conglomerates for audiences and advertising has led to TV news across the world becoming tabloidized or more like entertainment – what he calls 'global infotainment', designed both to entertain and to inform – with an emphasis on celebrities, crime, corruption and violence at the expense of reporting of public affairs. This US-style infotainment is accompanied by the promotion of a false global 'feelgood factor' based on Western, and particularly US, consumerist lifestyles. He argues this diverts people's attention away from more serious issues, like wars, the destruction of native cultures by global media conglomerates, the growing cultural hegemony of the West, and global inequality. This provides evidence for the Marxist view considered earlier (see pages 193–4), in that global mass culture lulls consumers into an uncritical, undemanding passivity, making them less likely to challenge the dominant ideas, groups and interests in society.

Critics suggest the global media have led not to more choice, but less, with output controlled by a few media 'lords of the global village', who preside over dumbed-down, standardized mass entertainment, creating a cultural sameness, with many repeats, similar programme content, American sitcoms and celebrity gossip dominating all forms of the media, and infotainment and docudramas (programmes that adopt a documentary-style to reconstruct events using actors) replacing serious and critical news reporting and documentaries. Local media and programme makers are increasingly unable to compete with the power and influence of global media conglomerates, and either get absorbed by the conglomerates or go out of business.

In light of all the material above, it might well be argued that media imperialism has moved the world's cultures towards a global cultural homogenization, and that the media-saturated global village is largely a North American and Western one, in which global audiences primarily consume the same American music, fashion, consumer goods and media images found everywhere.

Activity

1 Explain, with examples, what is meant by popular culture.
2 Explain carefully what you understand by globalization, and the role of the media in creating a global popular culture.
3 Identify a series of consumer products that are available all over the world, and explain how they illustrate the idea of a global culture.
4 In what ways do you think the media might be responsible for imposing Western or American values and lifestyles on countries across the world? What effects do you think this might have on local cultures?
5 To what extent do you think that the media might be creating a global popular culture of undemanding and uncritical consumers? Explain the reasons for your answer.

The postmodernist view of the media

Postmodernists view media globalization in ways that are more similar to the pluralist than the Marxist view. They regard the diversity of the globalized media as offering the world's population more choices in terms of their consumption patterns and lifestyles, opening up a greater global awareness and access to a diversity of cultures, bringing them more opportunities to form their identities unconstrained by the limited horizons of local cultures.

Baudrillard (1988, 2001) argues that we now live in a media-saturated society, in which media images dominate and distort the way we see the world. For example, media images replace reality to such an extent that laser technology and video reportage have eliminated the blood, the suffering and the corpses from war. The TV news presents a sanitized version of war, with wars as media-constructed spectacles to gaze at, which have such an air of unreality about them that it is hard to distinguish between image and reality, as they appear like Hollywood movies or computer games. Baudrillard calls this distorted view of the world hyperreality, in which appearances are everything, with the media presenting what he calls simulacra – artificial make-believe images or reproductions/copies of real events which bear little or no relationship to the real world and which are viewed simultaneously across the globe.

Postmodernists argue that the media no longer reflect reality but actively create it. Garrod (2004) suggests that reality TV shows like *I'm a Celebrity … Get Me Out of Here*, *Wifeswap*, *Fear Factor* and *Big Brother*, and social networking and video-sharing sites like Facebook and YouTube, are blurring the distinction between 'reality' and 'hyperreality', leaving audiences confused about what is real and what is media-created.

Strinati (1995) emphasizes the importance and power of the media in shaping consumer choices. Popular culture, such as the culture of celebrity, and media images and messages bombard us daily, through books, magazines, newspapers, TV, radio, advertising, smartphones, tablet computers and the internet, and form our sense of reality and increasingly dominate the way we define ourselves. In this media-saturated society, the media create desires and pressures to consume, and many of us actually define our identities – how we see and define ourselves and how we want others to see us – in terms of media imagery. Colour, form and media-induced trends become more important than the content or usefulness of products: it is not the quality of the clothes, drink or mobile phones

Hyperreality is a view of the world which is created and defined by the media, with the image of an event more real than the event it is meant to be depicting.

Simulacra are media images or reproductions and copies which appear to reflect things in the real world but have no basis in reality.

Postmodernists suggest we are now living in a media-saturated society, in which our view of reality is formed through media imagery and interpretations, and we increasingly live media-led virtual lives rather than real ones. What arguments might you give to support or oppose this view?

we buy that matters, but whether they conform to media-induced images, styles, brand names and trends. The media-promoted designer labels of popular culture become more important than the quality of the products. In films, it is not the story that matters so much as how good the special visual and sound effects are; not the script or the writing, more the icon and the big-name stars. There are any number of people who are famous for no reason at all except for being made into celebrities by the media.

In this media-saturated postmodern world, Baudrillard suggests we identify more with media images than we do with our own daily experiences, and we increasingly live media-led virtual lives rather than real ones. We are more likely to get excited about who is the best act in the *X Factor*, or engage with people we hardly know on Facebook or Twitter, or to identify with the lives and communities of television soap characters or reality TV characters, than we are to get involved with our next-door neighbours and the communities we actually live in. An example of this hyperreality was found in TV soap *Coronation Street* in 1998, when the character Deirdre Barlow was sent to prison *in the show* for a crime she did not commit. The British public started a big grassroots campaign, pleading with Granada Television to 'free the Weatherfield One'. Even more bizarrely, the real-world home secretary involved the then prime minister, Tony Blair, who, with only a touch of irony, attempted to intervene in this unreal world on Deirdre's behalf.

Criticisms of postmodernist views of the media

Postmodernist views assume that people approach the media without any prior experiences of their own, and that they do not discuss, interpret, ignore or reject media imagery and messages. Media images and representations of gender, age, ethnicity, disability and so on (see Topic 4) do not open up new choices of identity and lifestyle, but simply present and reinforce stereotypes. Many people, particularly in the poorest social groups and the poorest countries of the world, simply do not have access to new media, and cannot afford to make free choices between media-promoted lifestyles and identities, and buy the consumer goods associated with them, no matter how much they might like to. Marxists emphasize that the choice alleged by postmodernists is a myth, as transnational media conglomerates control the major media and forms of communication and influence.

The media are only one element – albeit an important one – in shaping our lives. For many of us, our gender, ethnicity, sexuality, age, social class, whether we are able-bodied or disabled, our experiences of school, college, work, friends and family, our political or religious beliefs all are likely to influence how we select, interpret and respond to the media. These issues will be considered further as we go through this chapter, and particularly in Topic 5.

Activity

1 Identify all the changes you can imagine might occur in the media over the next century. How do you think the relationship between the media and audiences might change?
2 How do you think the changes you imagine might affect our daily lives?
3 List all the ways you think the media influence you in your life, such as your knowledge about current affairs, opinions, tastes in music and fashion, and your views of different social groups, such as women and men, minority ethnic groups, the disabled and the elderly.
4 Do you think the media have a significant effect on your beliefs and values, your sense of identity and your consumer choices? What other influences on your beliefs and values might also be important?

Practice questions

1 Outline and explain **two** ways in which the media may contribute to the creation of a single global popular culture. **(10 marks)**

2 Read **Item A** below and answer the question that follows.

Item A

For postmodernists, the globalized media provide access to a greater diversity of cultures than ever before, and the world's population consequently has more choices of identities, consumption patterns and lifestyles. Marxists by contrast suggest that media imperialism imposes a Western-based uniform global popular culture. This destroys local cultures, and promotes lifestyles that most people in the world cannot afford.

Applying material from **Item A**, analyse two differences between postmodernist and Marxist approaches to the relationship between the media, globalization and popular culture. **(10 marks)**

3 Read **Item B** below and answer the question that follows.

Item B

Media or cultural imperialism refers to the way Western media conglomerates promote through advertising and sell the same media content, consumer and cultural products across the world. These products spread a globalized popular culture, which undermines national and local cultures, and consequently what were once different cultures become more and more alike.

Applying material from **Item B** and your knowledge, evaluate the view that media or cultural imperialism is a threat to the cultural identities of many countries. **(20 marks)**

Topic 3

The social construction of the news

The media obviously cannot report all events and issues happening every day in the world. This means that, rather than simply being out there waiting to be collected, what counts as 'the news' is necessarily selected and processed, or *constructed* by a range of social influences. The Glasgow Media Group (GMG) (www.glasgowmediagroup.org) has shown in a series of studies over many years that the selection and presentation of media news stories is not a neutral process, but that the news is a sequence of socially manufactured messages produced within the context of the dominant ideology of society.

Of all the happenings that occur, how is the content of the news selected? Who decides which of these events or interests is worthy of media coverage? Who decides who gets on TV and what questions they are asked? The content of the media, like any other product for sale, is manufactured. What factors affect the production and 'packaging' of this product? Is media content, and particularly the news, biased or does it present a balanced and truthful view? This topic will examine the process of news production in our society, and the way in which what counts as 'news' is socially constructed through selection, interpretation, editing and processing on a continuous basis.

The influence of the owners

Although the manipulative view discussed in Topic 1, with the owners controlling media content, is rather oversimplified, sometimes the private owners of the media will impose their own views on their editors, directly or indirectly. The political leanings of the owners and editors are overwhelmingly conservative. The influence of the owners on news content, including the issues discussed in Topic 1, can be summarized as follows.

- Owners occasionally give direct instructions to news editors.
- The owners, via editors, influence the resources made available to cover news stories, such as whether to allocate resources for reporters to pursue a story, or whether to have reporters or TV camera crews in different countries.
- Journalists, and particularly editors, depend for their careers on not upsetting the owners. This can lead to editors and journalists adopting a form of self-censorship, whereby they will avoid reporting some events, or reporting them in a way that risks offending the owners or directly challenging their political preferences.
- The owners are concerned with making profits, and this search for profit and the desire to attract large audiences in an increasingly competitive global media environment means that news and information get squeezed out or turned into unthreatening, unchallenging, inoffensive and bland 'infotainment' (see page 190). This encourages the development of a media culture in which unethical journalistic practices can thrive. These include things like illegal hacking into mobile phones, the invasion of individuals' privacy, bribery (cheque-book journalism) to encourage people to tell all, and the use of intrusive paparazzi to gain photos of celebrities and other famous people. It was such methods which led to the establishment of the Leveson Inquiry in 2011–12 into the culture, practices and ethics of the British press, following claims of illegal phone hacking at the then best-selling Sunday newspaper *News of the World*, and allegations of illegal payments to police by the press.

Making a profit

The mainstream media are predominantly run by large business corporations with the aim of making money, and the source of much of this profit is advertising, particularly in newspapers and commercial television and in social media and websites. It is this dependence on advertising which explains why so much concern is expressed about 'ratings' for television programmes, the circulation figures of newspapers and the social class of their readers, and the number of 'hits' on websites. Advertisers will usually advertise only if they know that there is a large audience for their advertisements, or, if the audience is small, that it is well-off and likely to buy their products or services.

Bagdikian (2004) suggests that the importance of advertising means news reports will be presented in such a way as to avoid offending advertisers, with some stories repressed or killed off altogether, and this was confirmed by Barnett and Seymour (1999) and Curran et al. (2009) (see page 190 in Topic 1). In order to attract the widest possible audience or readership, it becomes important to appeal to everyone and offend no one (unless offending a few helps to generate a larger audience). This leads to conservatism in the media, which tries to avoid too much criticism of the way society is organized in case it offends media audiences. This often means that minority or unpopular points of view go unrepresented in the media, and this helps to maintain the hegemony of the dominant ideas in society. This pressure to attract audiences in an increasingly competitive media market to, in turn, attract advertisers also can lead to a 'dumbing down' or tabloidization of news content, with serious hard news journalism – such as in-depth analytical coverage of politics, economics, foreign affairs and social issues – being replaced by human interest and celebrity stories, sports, sensationalism, gossip and scandal – 'infotainment' – and entertainment, like crime drama, soap operas and reality TV shows. Barnett and Gaber (2001) suggested that such pressures lead to a more conformist, less informed and less critical approach to reporting politics. Thussu (2007) found this move to tabloidization or 'infotainment' was found in TV news across the world.

Globalization, new technology and citizen journalism

The news market is now very competitive, and globalization means there are a mass of news providers from across the globe to choose from. New technology like satellite phones and cameras, email, Twitter, and news on digital TV, smartphones and internet websites means news is instantly available from practically anywhere in the world twenty-four hours per day. The mainstream news media can no longer rely on the attention of audiences, as they might once have done with the major evening news bulletins or the daily newspapers, as people are now tweeting, texting and surfing the web for news that interests them.

In the global market, news providers need to compete to survive. It is therefore crucial for media companies to be right up-to-date, and to tailor their media offering and the way news is presented to their market, if audiences and readers are to be attracted and retained – for example, short, simple, snappy, news reports, using the latest gadgetry, for more youthful audiences, or celebrity gossip-type human-interest news stories for mass consumption.

New media technology has at the same time transformed the news business by creating greater opportunities for citizen journalism. New media, like videos shot on mobile phones and uploaded to YouTube, Twitter tweets or Facebook posts, mean ordinary folk, rather than professional journalists and media companies, are more involved in directly collecting, reporting and spreading news stories and information, with minimal costs.

Such grassroots alternative sources of news and information can help to overcome or bypass suppression of stories, or biased or inadequate news reports, in established media. For example, Philo and Berry (2011) of the GMG found many British television reports on the Palestinians were over-reliant on official Israeli perspectives, with Israeli provocations and assassinations being routinely ignored by the media, while counterstrikes by Palestinian militants were widely reported. Ashuri (2012) showed how citizen journalism can overcome such bias. In a study of Machsom ('Checkpoint', in Hebrew) Watch – a women's organization whose members monitor the human rights of Palestinians at checkpoints set up by the Israel Defence Forces (IDF) – Ashuri showed how members of the group were able to offer an alternative view to the official one of some events

Electronic and digital media technologies and networks mean that news reporting is now almost instantaneous. It also means that news reporting is in the hands of anyone with a mobile phone. For example, students protesting against cuts to education spending are able to film their actions and police responses to them rather than relying on TV news channels to report their demonstrations. How do you think this might affect the presentation of the news, and the type of stories that get reported?

at checkpoints by posting their own reports, videos and photos on their website (www.machsom watch.org/en).

Bivens (2008) suggests citizen journalism through mobile phone picture and video recording at the scene of news events, publishing original news reports and commentary via publicly accessible blogs, and online criticism of mainstream news output are transforming traditional journalism. She points out these have increasingly been used to expose offensive, illegal or corrupt activities by politicians, celebrities, the police and armed forces, and public and private institutions which are worthy of public condemnation, but which may not have been otherwise covered by the traditional media. Citizen journalism has therefore made their activities far more accountable to the public.

When news-related videos are uploaded to websites like YouTube or individual blogs, very large global audiences can be attracted. By posting and sharing, news stories can go viral – be seen by millions in a very short time – and this can make it increasingly difficult for mainstream media organizations not to cover news stories they might once have chosen to ignore. Increasingly, the reports, blogs, videos and photographs of citizen journalists are being included in mainstream media, as seen in the reports of the uprisings in the Arab world and the reports of the riots in the UK in 2011. New technology therefore gives citizen journalists greater opportunities to shape mainstream news agendas. Citizen journalism also suits the mainstream media organizations' own needs, as they can obtain news items and supporting video at little cost to themselves, compared to sending out their own reporters and news cameras.

Organizational constraints

People's habits in the way they keep up with the news have changed, with less use of newspapers (where sales are falling) and TV, and growing use of social media to access and spread news. People now expect to be able to access up-to-date news at all times and wherever they happen to be, through their mobile phones, tablets and laptops, or computers at home or work.

Social networking sites like Facebook, Twitter and YouTube are now increasingly used to release and spread news stories on a global scale, and also to shape the reaction of others to them through commentaries. Twitter, for example, has around 316 million monthly active users and sees around 500 million tweets per day (in June 2015), with each tweet using a maximum of just 140 characters to break news, yet a single tweet can result in reports in mainstream news bulletins in a very short time. The intensity of news has changed, with news reporting becoming rolling 'breaking news', with digital news programmes and websites running constantly changing bulletins all day long – like *BBC News 24* or the BBC (www.bbc.co.uk/news/uk), *Guardian* (www.theguardian.com) or *Daily Mail* (www.dailymail.co.uk) websites.

These changes place growing organizational pressures on news media, and media organizations have little alternative but to respond to this changed situation, and journalists now often produce material first for the web, rather than for newspapers or TV. Competition means news organizations have to work within very tight time schedules to meet ever-shortening deadlines, which means that shortcuts to news gathering may need to be taken. There may be a greater emphasis on getting a news story first rather than getting it right, with inadequate evidence collected to justify any conclusions drawn. Stories aren't checked as carefully as they should be, to verify facts and to ensure it is real information rather than speculation (see also 'churnalism' below).

Agenda-setting

People can only discuss and form opinions about things they think they know about, and in most cases it is the media which provide this information. This gives those who own, control and work in the media a great deal of power in society, for what they choose to include or leave out of their newspapers, television programmes or websites will influence the main topics that people discuss or are concerned about. This may mean that the public never discuss some subjects because they are not informed about them.

The media's influence in laying down the list of subjects, or agenda, for public discussion is known as agenda-setting, and is particularly associated with the work of the Glasgow Media Group. The agenda-setting process was summed up by Cohen's (1963) comment that, while the news media may not necessarily be successful in telling people *what* to think, they are stunningly successful in telling audiences what to think *about*. McCombs (2004) suggests that the news media now increasingly not only tell us what to think about, but also *how* to think about certain subjects – for example, the images of politicians, or the perception of rioters or welfare benefit claimants.

The GMG, as shown earlier (see pages 187–8 in Topic 1), suggests the main media organizations, and the journalists within them, work within a framework of the dominant ideology which helps to form the list of subjects that the public are encouraged to think about, and so audiences have little real choice of the news they receive. Philo (2012) of the GMG noted that, during the global banking crisis of 2008 onwards, the media were very effective in channelling public anger towards the greed of bankers – 'scumbag millionaires', as the *Sun* put it – but focused public attention on solutions within the existing system (which had caused the problems in the first place). The media actively discouraged the public from thinking about solutions that challenged the existing financial system, by simply avoiding discussion of such alternatives. As Philo points out, the role of the mainstream media was largely to act as a forum for public grumbles and discontent, but not to explore serious alternatives. The media even went so far as to shift public attention away from the 'scumbag millionaires' by suggesting 'workshy welfare scroungers' were the reason for the crisis rather than the actions of the bankers.

The various economic and organizational pressures discussed above, including the desire to make money, to attract large audiences and hence advertising, and the organizational pressures generated by rolling news in the framework of global competition, mean that some news items are more likely to be ignored or treated less favourably than others, for fear of offending owners, audiences and advertisers. Through setting the agenda, and giving more prominence to some issues than others, the media are socially constructing the news, and encouraging audiences to think about what the most important issues are and what they should, and should not, be interested in or concerned about.

Gatekeeping

The media's power to refuse to cover some issues and to let others through is called gatekeeping. The GMG (1976, 1980, 1982), in a series of *Bad News* studies conducted between 1976 and 1982, suggested owners, editors and journalists construct the news by acting as gatekeepers, influencing what knowledge the public gains access to. As Philo's analysis of the media and the banking crisis above showed, the issues that are not aired – such as alternatives to the existing banking and financial system – are frequently those most damaging to the values and interests of the dominant social class. Sometimes the media do not cover issues either because journalists and editors think they lack interest to readers and viewers, or because they regard them as too offensive, controversial or threatening to existing society. For example, strikes are widely reported (nearly always unfavourably), while industrial injuries and diseases, which lead to a much greater loss of working hours (and life), hardly ever get reported. This means that there is more public concern with stopping strikes than there is with improving health and safety laws. Similarly, welfare benefit fraud by the poor is widely reported, but not tax evasion by the rich, with the result that there are calls for tightening up benefit claims procedures, rather than strengthening those agencies concerned with chasing tax evaders.

Norm-setting

Norm-setting
describes the
way the media
emphasize
and reinforce
conformity to social
norms, and seek to
isolate those who
do not conform
by making them
the victims of
unfavourable media
reports.

Norm-setting describes the way the media emphasize and reinforce conformity to social norms, and seek to isolate those who do not conform by making them the victims of unfavourable media reports.

Norm-setting is achieved in two main ways:

1 *Encouraging conformist behaviour*, such as not going on strike, obeying the law, being brave, helping people and so on. Advertising, for example, often reinforces the gender role stereotypes of men and women.
2 *Discouraging non-conformist behaviour.* The media often give extensive and sensational treatment to stories about murder and other crimes of violence, riots, benefit fraud, football hooliganism, illegal immigrants, and so on. Such stories, by emphasizing the serious consequences which follow for those who break social norms, are giving 'lessons' in how people are expected *not* to behave.

This norm-setting is also achieved through media representations, which are discussed in Topic 4.

The processes of agenda-setting, gatekeeping and norm-setting act as forms of social control as they mean some events are simply not reported and brought to public attention, and some of those that are reported may be singled out for particularly unfavourable treatment. In these ways, the media can define what the important issues are, what 'news' is, what the public should and should not be thinking about, and what should or should not be regarded as 'normal' behaviour in society.

Activity

Content analysis

1 Study the main newspaper headlines or major television, radio or internet news stories for a week. Draw up a list of the key stories, perhaps under the headings of 'popular newspapers' (like the *Sun* and the *Mirror*), 'quality newspapers' (like the *Guardian*, the *Daily Telegraph* and *The Times*), 'ITN news', 'BBC TV news' and 'radio news' (this is easiest to do if a group of people divide up the work). You might also research these on the web, using the following sites:
   - www.bbc.co.uk/news
   - http://news.sky.com/uk
   - www.itn.co.uk
   - www.telegraph.co.uk
   - www.theguardian.com
   - www.mailonline.co.uk
   - www.thesun.co.uk
   - www.mirror.co.uk
2 Compare your lists, and see if there is any evidence of agreement on the 'agenda' of news items for that week. If there are differences between the lists, outline reasons for them.
3 Try to find examples of norm-setting in the headlines and stories you have identified. Explain in each case what types of behaviour are being encouraged or discouraged.

The presentation of news

The way news items are presented may be important in influencing how people are encouraged to view stories. For example the physical position of a news story on a website or in a newspaper (front page or small inside column), the order of importance given to stories in TV news bulletins, the choice of headlines, and whether there is accompanying film or photographs, the camera angles used and so on, will all influence the attention given to particular issues.

Some issues may not be covered at all if journalists or camera crews are not available, especially in international news reporting, and the space available in a newspaper or TV programme will influence whether an event is reported or not. A story may be treated sensationally, and it may even be considered of such major importance as to justify a TV or radio 'newsflash'. Where film is used, the pictures shown are always selected from the total footage shot, and may not accurately reflect the event. The actual images used in news films may themselves have a hidden bias. For example, the GMG has shown how, in the reporting of industrial disputes, employers are often filmed in the peace and quiet of their offices, while workers are seen shouting on the picket lines or trying to be interviewed against a background of traffic noise. This gives the impression that employers are more calm and reasonable people and have a better case than the workers.

The media can also create false or biased impressions by the sort of language used in news reporting. Emotive language – which stirs up emotions – may be used to liven up a story, placing a dramatic angle on events and thereby grabbing the audience's attention and interest, and to encourage audiences to make a particular interpretation of events. For example, words like 'pointless', 'troublemakers', 'thugs', 'rioters', 'scroungers', 'scum', 'terrorist', 'atrocity' or 'brutal' encourage people to have a negative view of the people or events reported.

Inaccurate and false reporting and the creation of moral panics

Other sources of bias in news reporting lie in inaccurate reporting, because important details of a story may be incorrect. This partly arises because of the organizational pressures discussed on pages 203–4. Politicians, for example, often complain that they have been inaccurately quoted in the press.

False reporting, through either completely making up stories or inventing a few details, and the media's tendency to exaggerate and dramatize events out of all proportion to their actual significance in society, typical of much reporting of the royal family, are devices used to make a story more interesting and attract audiences. This is particularly common in the mass-circulation 'red-top' tabloid press, and their related websites. Such false, inaccurate or exaggerated and sensationalized reporting in the media can sometimes generate a moral panic. This is a wave of public concern about some exaggerated or imaginary threat to society.

> A **moral panic** is a wave of public concern about some exaggerated or imaginary threat to society, stirred up by overblown and sensationalized reporting in the media.

Moral panics are generated around activities or social groups which are defined as threatening to society or dominant social values. The classic study of the media and moral panics was Cohen's (2002 [1972]) study of the Mods and Rockers youth subcultures in the 1960s. This study, and a fuller discussion of moral panics and the role of the media in the social construction of crime and deviance, can be found on pages 515–23 in chapter 6, and *you should refer to this now.*

Moral panics show the media's power to define what is normal and what is deviant, unacceptable behaviour, and to reinforce a consensus around the core values of the dominant ideology, while at the same time making money through attracting audiences.

Moral panics usually begin when the media starts expressing concern over certain activities and the behaviour of certain groups, and exaggerating out of all proportion their real significance and the harm caused to society. This exaggeration, often coupled with false reporting and dubious hearsay anecdotal evidence, can create public anxiety and hostility towards that group or activity, and encourage agencies like schools, social services, the police and the courts to stamp down hard and take harsh measures against the alleged troublemakers. Such action, particularly by the police, can, in turn, generate more deviant behaviour, as people become alerted via the media to things they previously hadn't been aware of, or as the groups concerned play up their behaviour to gain media attention, or react with hostility to those who are attempting to stop their activities. This can

Deviancy amplification is the way the media may actually make worse or create the very deviance they condemn by their exaggerated, sensationalized and distorted reporting of events and their presence at them.

often make what was a minor issue much worse – for example, arresting people can cause a reaction like resistance and hostility to the police, riots and more arrests – and amplify (or make worse) the original alleged deviance. This is known as deviancy amplification.

In recent years, moral panics have arisen around groups like asylum seekers, radicalized Muslims and internet paedophiles, and issues like anti-social behaviour and gun and knife culture among young people.

Media-generated moral panics often arise from many of the pressures discussed so far in this chapter, such as the ever-growing need in the competitive world of the media to attract audiences through sensationalized, interesting and exciting dumbed-down news stories (even if there aren't any) and infotainment, and thereby make money from advertisers. Such methods mean the media can be accused of socially constructing the news and manufacturing unwarranted anxiety in their audiences.

Is the concept of moral panics still relevant in the new media age?

McRobbie and Thornton (1995) suggest that media-generated moral panics are now becoming less common. This is because new media technology and constant 24/7 rolling news reporting, and intense competition both between media organizations and between different types of media – such as web-based news, blogs, social networking through Twitter, YouTube and Facebook, and cable, print, broadcast and satellite news – have changed the reporting of, and reaction by audiences to, events that might once have caused a moral panic. Pluralists and postmodernists argue there is now such a huge diversity of media reports and interpretations of events, and of opinions and reactions to these events by the public through citizen journalism, that people are now much more sceptical of mainstream media interpretations and less likely to believe them. Most events that might once have generated a moral panic now have such short shelf-lives in sustaining audience interest that they are unlikely to be newsworthy for long enough to become a moral panic.

News values and newsworthiness

Events that are eventually reported in the news have been through some kind of gatekeeping or filtering process, with journalists, and particularly news editors, deciding what is newsworthy and what is not. Research has shown that journalists operate with values and assumptions – called news values – which guide them in deciding what events are newsworthy and therefore what to report and what to leave out, and how what they choose to report should be presented. So news doesn't just happen, but is *made* by journalists. In this sense, it is socially constructed. Galtung and Ruge (1970) suggested newsworthy items included some of the news values included in table 3.4. The idea of news values means that journalists tend to include and play up those elements of a story which make it more newsworthy, and the stories that are most likely to be reported are those which include many newsworthy aspects. The importance of news values is also underpinned by the economic pressures of needing to make a profit, by constantly striving to attract readers and viewers through news flashes, scoops and exclusives of all kinds.

News values and immediacy

Stories are also more likely to be reported if the media, particularly TV and the new media, can combine news values with the impression of *immediacy* – of being present at events as they unfold. The new media have enabled news organizations to give a perception to audiences of immediacy, as they are now able to provide instantaneous, live coverage of events as they happen. This is aided by the growing volume of material recorded on mobile phones through citizen journalism. This was particularly evident during the Japanese earthquake and tsunami of 2011, during the popular uprisings in the Arab world in the Arab Spring in 2010–11, and the Israeli military operation in Gaza in 2014, when the mainstream media organizations included much video footage shot on mobile phones when they had no reporters of their own present, or were unable to access some locations.

Table 3.4 News values

News Value	Features
Composition	Events that fit the style of a paper or TV channel, the balance of items (human interest stories, political news, domestic and foreign news, crime stories, etc.), its political slant and the values of the journalists.
Continuity	Events that are likely to have a continuing impact – the running story, which is also convenient as the news reporters and cameras will already be there.
Elite nations or people	Stories or pictures which involve what journalists and media customers perceive as important – powerful nations, people or organizations, are seen as more newsworthy than lesser ones. West European and American political leaders, celebrities and countries, for example, are seen as more newsworthy than ordinary people or more distant countries and cultures, like Benin or Chile.
Frequency	Events that fit into the routine schedules of a newspaper's or news programme's or website's reporting and broadcasting or publishing cycles are more likely to be covered. Events that occur quickly or unexpectedly, and are of short duration, such as disasters and murders, are more likely to make it into the news as they fit the schedules better.
Meaningfulness	Events which, it is assumed, will have meaning and be of interest to the readership or audience. This essentially involves giving the readers and viewers what journalists and producers think they want; this is of great importance if the audience or readership is to continue to be attracted and viewing figures kept up, papers sold or websites referred to.
Negativity	Bad news is nearly always rated above positive stories. A good news story is often bad news, as bad news, such as death, violence, urban riots, disasters, floods and hurricanes, involves many newsworthy aspects that encourage journalists to report the event.
Personalization	Events that can be personalized and linked to individuals in some way, and given a human interest angle, with some human drama attached to them, such as disputes between two political leaders or scandal involving the activities of famous personalities or celebrities.
Proximity	This generally involves items which will have some cultural meaning or proximity to news audiences. For example, what happens to British citizens is seen as more newsworthy than what happens to foreigners from remote cultures. Events in Britain are generally considered more meaningful than those happening in the rest of the world, and national events are generally considered more important than local ones.
Threshold	Events that are considered large and significant enough to be in the news, and to have an impact – a single rape might make it into a local paper, but a serial rapist might become a national story.
Unambiguity/ clarity	Events that are clear, easily understood and not too complicated, without the need for lots of background explanation and detail.
Unexpectedness	Events that are in some way unexpected or out of the ordinary. Events that involve drama, conflict, excitement and action, such as natural disasters or terrorist attacks, are more likely to be reported than predictable everyday events.

Activity

1 Refer to the three news stories here, or any major news stories which are currently receiving wide coverage in the media. List the features of these stories which you think make them 'newsworthy'. To find more details on any story, try a Google search on the internet.

2 Imagine you wanted to run a campaign to prevent a waste incinerator being built in your neighbourhood (or choose any topic of interest to you). In the light of the issues identified in this chapter relating to the social construction of news, suggest ways you might get the attention of journalists so as to achieve media coverage of your campaign. Explain why you think the activities you identify might be considered newsworthy.

The 'Twin Towers' of New York's World Trade Center before their destruction

The terrorist attack on the 'Twin Towers' of the World Trade Center in New York on 11 September 2001 was a massive international news story. Two passenger aircraft were hijacked, and deliberately crashed into the Twin Towers, causing both towers to collapse, and killing around 3,000 people. This dominated world news for weeks and months afterwards, and provoked a range of conspiracy theories on the internet.

Three-year-old Madeleine McCann vanished from her holiday apartment in Praia da Luz, Portugal, on 3 May 2007. Thanks to a high-profile campaign run by the McCann family (the image here shows her parents at a press conference in Berlin, Germany), Madeleine's face was rarely out of the public consciousness. At the time of writing, it was still not known what happened to Madeleine. The mystery of Madeleine's disappearance led to a feeding frenzy in the red-top tabloid press, with a mass of unsubstantiated theories and wild speculation about her disappearance. In 2015, Madeleine McCann stories were still hitting the headlines, and a full one-hour reconstruction on the BBC's *Crimewatch* in 2013 achieved the programme's highest-ever ratings, six years after her disappearance.

The town of Ofunato in Japan after the devastating 2011 tsunami

On Friday 11 March 2011, one of the most powerful undersea earthquakes ever recorded since modern record-keeping began took place off the coast of Japan. This triggered tidal waves, or a tsunami, which travelled up to 6 miles inland, and caused extensive and severe damage. More than 20,000 were killed, missing or unaccounted for, with many more injured. It also caused a number of nuclear accidents, with meltdowns at three nuclear reactors, causing the evacuation of hundreds of thousands of residents.

The assumptions and activities of journalists and the rise of 'churnalism'

The GMG, which generally supports a neo-Marxist-dominant ideology/hegemonic approach to the media, emphasizes the importance of the assumptions of journalists in forming media content and suggesting interpretations of issues to media audiences. The group emphasizes a number of features that affect the content of the news.

1   Journalists operate within what Becker (1967) called a hierarchy of credibility. This means they attach the greatest importance to the views of powerful and influential individuals and groups, such as senior politicians, senior police officers, civil servants or business leaders and bankers, rather than ordinary people. Hall et al. (1978) suggest such people are primary definers who regularly feature in the media as 'experts' and are in a position to set the news agenda and influence what journalists define as the news and how they present it. For example, the media are likely to consult the police and Home Office for comments on crime policy, or politicians, city analysts and bankers for comment on economic policy. The views of primary definers appear more 'reasonable' to journalists than those of the least powerful or 'extremists' who present the greatest challenges to existing society. Manning (1999) suggests journalists are under increasing pressure from market competition to use primary definers as a cheap and readily available source of news, as governments and large businesses are forever trying to manipulate the media and manage the news through their press and public relations departments.

2   Journalists tend to be somewhere in the moderate centre ground of politics, and so ignore or treat unfavourably what they regard as 'extremist' or 'radical' views.

3   The GMG has pointed out that journalists tend to be mainly white, male and middle-class, and they broadly share the interests and values of the dominant ideology. This influences whose opinions they seek for comment, what issues they see as important, and how they think issues should be presented and explained to audiences (this is also linked to the news values discussed on pages 207–8). The GMG has shown how the explanations given in the media often favour the views of dominant and powerful groups in society, such as managers over workers, or police over protesters.

4   Journalists are doing a job, and they like to keep their work as simple as possible. To reduce time and costs, they often produce articles based on information provided by news agencies, government press releases, spin doctors, public relations consultants and so on, without checking facts

A **hierarchy of credibility** means that greatest importance is attached by journalists to the views and opinions of those in positions of power, like government ministers, political leaders, senior police officers or wealthy and influential individuals.

Primary definers are powerful individuals or groups whose positions of power give them greater access to the media than others, and therefore puts them in a more privileged position to influence what and how journalists define the news.

or digging out the news themselves. This has been described as 'churnalism', which is discussed below. News reports are then often based on what others claim about events rather than what reporters have discovered for themselves. This means that primary definers drawn from powerful and influential groups such as businesses, the government and political parties, and powerful and wealthy individuals, are more likely to be able to influence journalists.

Churnalism is a form of journalism in which journalists produce news articles based on pre-packaged material in press releases provided by sources such as government spin doctors, public relations consultants and news agencies, without doing further research or checking facts.

The rise of churnalism

The term 'churnalism' was originally devised by BBC journalist Waseem Zakir, to describe the trend whereby journalists were uncritically churning out articles based on second-hand news agency reports, and pre-packaged material from press releases and other sources, rather than digging out the news for themselves, doing further research or checking whether the 'facts' were true or false.

Davies (2008) found that 80 per cent of stories in *The Times*, the *Guardian, Independent, Daily Telegraph* and *Daily Mail* were wholly, mainly or partially constructed from second-hand material, provided by news agencies and by the public relations industry. Only 12 per cent of stories were generated by reporters. He found that this routine recycling of second-hand material mainly originated from wire agencies like the Press Association and public relations activity which was promoting some commercial or political interest. Jewell (2014) showed how 'advertorials' – branded content paid for by advertisers and promoting their products but masquerading as journalists' news articles – were increasingly appearing on the online news sites of mainstream media brands like the *Guardian* (theguardian.com) and the *Daily Mail* (dailymail.co.uk). Such branded content appears with headlines like 'Watch it here first! M&S unveil magical Christmas ad.' The result of this process is a blurring of advertising, information, news and entertainment and a reduction of quality and accuracy, as what is presented as news is wide open to manipulation and distortion.

The rise of churnalism is linked to many of the issues discussed so far in this topic: the desire of media owners to cut costs, and attract audiences and advertisers in a hugely competitive global media market, coupled with the time pressures arising from the intensity of 24/7 rolling news in the context of ever-expanding new media.

Activity

Go to one or more of the following websites, and try to find three contemporary examples of churnalism in news reports.

- www.spinwatch.org – an independent non-profit-making organization which monitors the role of public relations and spin in contemporary society
- www.churnalism.com – a search engine to distinguish journalism from churnalism, run in association with the Media Standards Trust
- www.medialens.org – which aims to show how news and commentary are 'filtered' by the media's profit-orientation, by its dependence on advertisers, parent companies, wealthy owners and official news sources

---

Conclusion: A propaganda model of the media?

The features covered in this topic suggest that the media generally present, at best, only a partial and biased view of the world, with some subjects posing a threat to powerful interests either distorted or ignored by the media. What counts as 'the news' is a manufactured product that reflects the interest of powerful groups, and is produced within a framework of the dominant ideology in society. The range of influences on the news discussed in this topic, which are summarized in figure 3.1, lead Marxist-influenced writers to be highly critical of what counts as 'the news' in contemporary society.

Herman and Chomsky (2002) adopt a propaganda model of the media. They suggest that mainstream media news and commentary are shaped by and propagandize on behalf of the powerful social interests that control them. Structural factors – such as ownership and control, market forces, the media's profit orientation, and dependence on advertisers – create a network of shared interests and

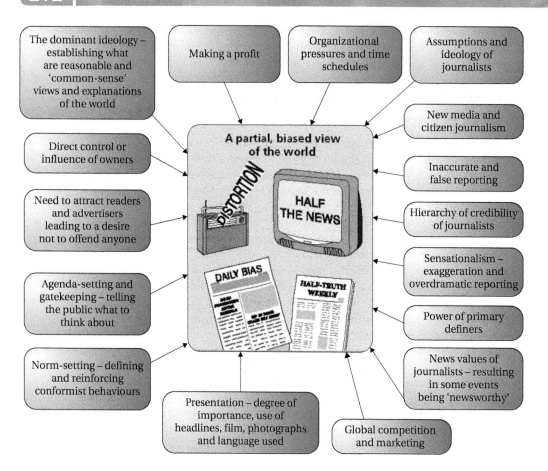

Figure 3.1 Factors contributing to the social construction of the news

relationships between the media, those who make the news and those who have the power to define it and explain what it means. These factors influence what journalists do, what they see as newsworthy and the ideas they take for granted as they do their work. Herman and Chomsky therefore see the mainstream media essentially as a propaganda system for the elite interests that dominate in contemporary society. In a similar vein, Edwards and Cromwell (2009) argue that many leading journalists and editors are servile to those who hold power in society, and are little more than cheerleaders for government, business and war, and that they are engaged in the 'dark art' of smearing dissidents of all kinds who pose any challenge or threat to the dominant ideology and existing social structure of society.

However, pluralists point out that media competition and the need to attract audiences also mean that journalists do occasionally expose injustice, or corruption in government and business, and therefore are not always or simply in the pockets of the powerful. The rise of the new media has also begun to undermine the power of the mainstream media organizations, as citizen journalism opens up the possibility of alternative views to those of the media establishment being made available to millions of people across the globe.

Activity

1 Outline **three** reasons why journalists might be reluctant to write articles critical of the most powerful groups in society.
2 With reference to figure 3.1, identify and explain **six** reasons why both the selection and presentation of the news might be regarded as ideologically controlled.

Practice questions

1 Outline and explain **two** ways in which the news values held by journalists might influence the selection and presentation of the news. **(10 marks)**

2 Read **Item A** below and answer the question that follows.

> ### Item A
> Agenda-setting refers to the media's ability to select subjects for public discussion. This gives the main news media a great deal of power in telling people what to think about. The media also tell us how we should think about some subjects, such as the way we perceive politicians or welfare benefit claimants.

Applying material from **Item A**, analyse **two** ways in which the news media may influence the subjects people think about and how they perceive those subjects. **(10 marks)**

3 Read **Item B** below and answer the question that follows.

> ### Item B
> Media news is often regarded as an objective and neutral reporting of the most important events that have happened in the world. Many sociologists disagree with this. They argue that what counts as 'the news' is socially constructed through complex processes of selection and presentation. Media news represents a biased and partial view of the world, which is mainly concerned with protecting the interests of the most powerful groups in society.

Applying material from **Item B** and your knowledge, evaluate the view that 'the news' is a socially constructed, manufactured product mainly concerned with protecting the interests of the most powerful groups in society. **(20 marks)**

Topic 4

SPECIFICATION AREA

Media representations of age, social class, ethnicity, gender, sexuality and disability

Media representations and stereotyping

One of the issues that has interested media sociologists has been the categories and images that are used to portray social groups to media audiences, such as images of minority ethnic groups, men and women, the disabled, gays and lesbians, and different social classes and age groups. These portrayals are known as media representations.

Media representations very often conform to and create stereotypes – generalized, oversimplified views of the features of a social group, allowing for few individual differences between members of the group. Media stereotypes act like codes that give audiences quick and easy-to-understand images of groups, while at the same time they construct meanings and interpretations, and such stereotypes may form the basis for treating members of some groups differently from others.

The media gaze

The term 'gaze' was first used in a media context by Mulvey (2009 [1975]) to describe the way men look at women as sexual objects (the 'male gaze'), but it can equally well be used to describe a 'media gaze' of the media establishment on society. This 'gaze' of the media establishment means that media content does not reflect the social diversity that characterizes our society, but the perspective of the predominantly male, able-bodied white upper and middle class who own and control the media, and produce media content.

Symbolic annihilation

One of the recurring themes in media representations is the way that some groups, often based on factors like their ethnicity, age, sex, sexual orientation, or social class, are omitted, condemned or trivialized in the media, under-represented (not appearing as much as they should given their proportion in the population) or only appear in a limited number of roles. Gerbner and Gross (1976) and Tuchman et al. (1978) referred to this process as symbolic annihilation and suggested that this could give a distorted impression of some social groups, or erase them from public consciousness altogether.

The following sections examine some of these representations in the media. As you read, it is important to remember that media representations and stereotypes do not necessarily mean that people will behave in accordance with these representations. The various theories of media effects discussed later in Topic 5 (the hypodermic syringe, two-step flow, cultural effects, selective filtering/decoding and uses and gratifications theories), suggest that media audiences do not necessarily react to or interpret the same media content in the same way. Gauntlett (2008) cautions that there is a diversity of media, a diversity of representations and a diversity of audiences, and it therefore can't be assumed media representations will either be consistent or have the same effects on audiences. For example, media representations of ethnic minorities or of disabled people may not have the same meaning to those who are from a minority ethnic group or who live in multicultural communities, or to those who are disabled or know disabled people, as to those who lack such experiences. People may therefore ignore, accept or reject media representations, or even, in the postmodern age, pick 'n' mix media representations in a creative way to forge their own identities.

Media representations are the categories and images that are used to present groups and activities to media audiences, which may influence the way we think about these activities and groups.

The **male gaze** is the way men look (gaze) at women as sexual objects.

The **media gaze** is the way the media view society and represent it in media content.

Symbolic annihilation refers to the lack of visibility, under-representation and limited roles of certain groups in media representations, as they are omitted, condemned or trivialized in many roles.

Nonetheless, such media representations, whether true or distorted, can become realities for many people, particularly when they have no experiences of their own by which to judge media imagery. In a media-saturated society, Baudrillard (2001) suggests media representations can become a form of hyperreality, which become more real than reality itself. In this sense, the media don't reflect reality, but actively create it.

The Glasgow Media Group (GMG) point out that media representations and stereotypes are formed within the context of the dominant ideology of society. This means they generally reinforce the cultural hegemony of the dominant social class in society, and justify existing patterns of inequality in wealth, power and social status.

Activity

1 Outline, with examples, two ways in each case that the media might provide for individuals a source of: (a) identity; (b) role models.
2 Go to www.mediasmarts.ca and/or www.mediaknowall.com. Outline **four** contemporary media representations, and explain in each case:
   (a) The ways they are stereotypical – for example, Muslims represented only as terrorists or associated only with brutal punishments; disabled people defined only by their disability;
   (b) Why they may be harmful to the groups concerned.

Representations of age

Different age groups tend to be represented in different ways in the media. The media gaze is filtered through the eyes of young to middle-aged male adults, and this influences the representation of children, young people (youth) and older people. Overall, older people are under-represented in the media, and youth are over-represented.

Representations of children

Children (up to the age of about 14) are generally represented in a positive way, and often figure as consumers of toys and games in advertising, or as comedy sources in sitcoms.

Children's Express, now *Headliners* (www.headliners.org), a journalism site run by young people, monitored national newspaper output for one week in 1998. The researchers found 'seven deadly stereotypes' of children. In order of frequency, and described in some of the young people's own words, these were:

1 *Kids as victims* – children portrayed as good children led astray by bad influences, or as victims of crimes committed against them by others.
2 *Cute kids* – providing the feel-good factor in advertising and other stories.
3 *Little devils* – stories of evil children and young hooligans, often in comedies and drama.
4 *Kids are brilliant* – exceptional children who excel in some way, like getting into Oxford or Cambridge universities at age 10, or donating their pocket money to the Third World, or 'who ride down Everest on a unicycle while simultaneously discovering a cure for cancer', (as a young journalist put it).
5 *Kids as accessories* – where children are used to somehow enhance their parents' image, like those of celebrities.
6 *Kids these days!* – stories which show adults' nostalgia for the past, with young people knowing so much more than their parents used to at their age, which includes stories of children being corrupted by computers and 'pretty pupils getting off with a choir master with adults commenting that it didn't used to happen in their day'.
7 *Little angels* – children who can do no wrong; children who endure terrible illnesses or disability with a smile, or risk their lives by hauling a toddler back from a cliff edge.

Such stereotypes are often generated by the gaze of the adult middle-class media establishment, and media stories based around these stereotypes often do not take into account the views of the children they write about.

Representations of youth

Youth (from around age 15 to the early 20s) are often the subject of negative media stereotyping. They are frequently portrayed as a rebellious and selfish problem group in society: as troublemakers, layabouts and vandals, fuelled by drugs and alcohol, and depicted in the context of crime, gang, knife and gun culture, anti-social behaviour and binge drinking. Such images are particularly associated with young working-class males.

A 2005 analysis of the local and national press conducted by MORI for *Young People Now* magazine showed that the majority of stories about young people were negative (57 per cent), with just 12 per cent positive, with 40 per cent of articles about young people focused on crime, vandalism and anti-social behaviour. A survey commissioned by Women in Journalism in 2009 found that teenage boys most frequently appeared in the media in stories about crime, and were most commonly described using terms like 'yobs', 'thugs', 'sick', 'feral' (wild), 'hoodie', 'lout', 'heartless', 'evil', 'frightening' and 'scum'. White et al. (2012), in a report on a survey of viewers and industry experts, found broadcasters negatively stereotyped young people, and more than 40 per cent of young people were dissatisfied with the way they were portrayed on television as 'disrespectful' and living 'unproductive and vacuous lives'.

These representations are driven by media news values, as exciting stories and sensational headlines which exaggerate the occasional deviant behaviour of a few young people out of all proportion to its real significance in society help to sell newspapers and attract TV viewers. For many people, the media provide the only source of information about events, and therefore distort people's attitudes and give a misleading impression of young people as a whole. Older people, who tend to be more home-based, are particularly vulnerable to believing such stereotypes, as their impressions are likely to be formed strongly by the media.

Cohen (2002) argues that young people are relatively powerless, and an easily identifiable group to blame for all of society's ills. Consequently, young people – particularly young African-Caribbean males – have often been used as scapegoats by the media to create a sense of unity in society, by whipping up a moral panic among the public against the **folk devils** who allegedly pose a threat to society, and uniting the public against a common 'enemy' and encouraging them to support tough action against them. As a result of these media-generated moral panics, all young people may then get labelled and stereotyped as potentially troublesome or as an anti-social problem group.

Folk devils are individuals or groups posing an imagined or exaggerated threat to society.

It should be remembered that it is these same young people who are the major users of the new media. This means that media stereotyping can be combated by young people themselves through texting, tweeting, YouTube and the other devices of citizen journalism. This growing preponderance of youthful new media users means that mainstream media organizations may over time be forced to change their traditional media stereotypes of young people.

Representations of older people

Older people, say in their late 50s onwards, are often either largely invisible in the media, or presented in quite negative ways. Cuddy and Fiske (2004) showed that, in the United States, TV portrayed just 1.5 per cent of its characters as elderly, with most of them in minor roles, and that older adults were more likely than any other age group to appear in television and film as figures of fun and comic relief, usually based on impaired mental, physical or sexual capacities. Biggs (1993) found UK TV sitcoms presented older people in similarly negative ways, such as being forgetful and difficult.

Elderly people suffer from negative stereotyping in the media perhaps more than any other identifiable social group apart from youth. Old age is generally represented as an undesirable state. Being poor, in ill-health, a burden, forgetful, anti-social, interfering, incapable of work, not interested in sex, and personally difficult, stubborn and grumpy are typical stereotypes.

The Dove Pro·Age campaign sought to market a range of beauty products avoiding traditional media stereotypes of gender and age. Study the four images, and suggest ways they may, or may not, challenge media stereotypes of gender and/or age

There are sometimes different stereotypes for men and women. It is not uncommon to see older men presented in a positive light, for example as sexual partners of younger women in Hollywood movies, or as distinguished, experienced and informed 'wise old men', such as political and religious leaders, successful businesspeople, experts of various kinds, and as established and authoritative media journalists and commentators. By contrast, there are few positive images of older women, who are often rendered invisible – symbolically annihilated – because women are, in media imagery, expected to be forever young and youthful, and there are not many positive roles for them as they grow older.

White et al. (2012) found that older viewers thought they tended to be stereotyped on television, and that there was a lack of representation of middle-aged and older women on TV. Viewers accused the media of being 'insulting' and 'out of step' with the ageing society, with negative stereotypes of older people focusing on their incapacity, their reluctance to move with the times and their tendency to moan.

In a study of the views of advertising executives in nineteen London agencies about the types of products and services which they considered appropriate for representation by older people, Szmigin and Carrigan (2000) found they were wary of using models in their advertisements that they considered might alienate younger audiences. However, the growing numbers of older people in the population with money to spend – the 'grey pound' – mean we might expect more positive images of ageing to emerge, and more positive roles for older women, as media conglomerates pursue the growing older people's market, as shown in the Dove Pro·Age campaign marketing beauty products to older people.

Representations of social class

General features of representations of social class

1   The mainstream media gaze means representations of social class are filtered through the eyes of the rich and powerful upper-class media owners and the middle-class media professionals who produce media content. This results in:

- More favourable stereotypes of the upper and middle classes than the working class or the poor
- An over-representation of the upper and middle classes and an under-representation of the working class
- The portrayal of the working class in a more restricted range of roles than the middle class. These may colour people's conceptions of social class, wealth and poverty.

2 Jones (2011) suggests the media gives the impression 'we're all middle class now', with the values and lifestyles of the middle class as the norm, to which everyone should aspire. By celebrating the lifestyles of the upper and middle classes, the media create the impression that the interests and worries of the well-off are, or should be, important to everyone. The working class and the poor/underclass are presented as in some ways abnormal/deviant and/or as figures of fun.

3 Class is generally represented as a lifestyle choice rather than as an economic category. Lawler (2005) suggests 'taste' is used as a symbol of class identity. People's lives are seen as shaped by their individual choices and tastes in the consumer goods they buy to form their lifestyle. The focus is on the individual, rather than on their social class and the patterns of structural inequality in the distribution of wealth, income and life chances.

4 Media news values means news about the rich and famous, such as crimes by or against them, are more likely to be reported than similar stories about working-class people. McKendrick et al. (2008), in a content analysis of UK media output in 2007, found poverty was a marginal issue, comprising only a small proportion of media output. Journalists who were interested in poverty acknowledged that they were only likely to secure coverage if they were able to find angles to make it newsworthy, such as examples of extreme cases which highlighted the individual failings of undeserving people, rather than the wider social causes and consequences of poverty.

5 The media give different representations of different social classes, and Weltman (2008) notes that across a range of media entertainment formats, including sitcoms, soaps, drama and reality TV, working-class people are devalued relative to the middle class. Marxists and neo-Marxists like the Glasgow Media Group emphasize that media representations reflect the interests of the powerful. There is little media content that explicitly discusses class privilege, class inequality and power differences, and the tensions and conflicts between classes are concealed or seen as irrelevant.

Representations of the working class

The working class and the poor are generally under-represented in the media, but when they are represented they are typically stereotyped in negative ways, with their failings seen as arising from their lack of conformity to middle-class values, norms and lifestyles.

Curran and Seaton (2010) argue that the content of newspapers aimed at working-class audiences, such as the mass-circulation red-top *Daily Star, Sun* and *Daily Mirror* – though the same applies across the whole range of media aimed at working-class audiences – suggests that the working class has little interest in public affairs, except for the personalities of politicians, and is predominantly interested in over-dramatized, exaggerated or made-up human interest stories, celebrity lifestyles, entertainment, sex, sport, TV and women's issues, such as fashion and diet which are themselves often linked to stories about celebrities.

There are four main media representations of the working class, which often overlap:

1 *As dumb and stupid buffoons.* Butsch (2003), in a study of US TV programmes, argues TV creates a persistent image of the working class as buffoons or figures of fun – well-intentioned but flawed individuals, who are immature, irresponsible, inarticulate, incompetent, lacking in common sense, and who are coping only ineptly with life. The sitcom the *Royle Family* illustrates this, with a family of couch potatoes watching TV all the time and holding totally absurd non-conversations. Butsch argues this reinforces the ideological hegemony of the dominant values in popular culture. It also justifies existing patterns of inequality, as the higher status and power of the middle classes is justified by their need to supervise the amusing but incompetent working-class buffoons, and to provide role models of how they might live successful lives.

2 *As a source of trouble and conflict.* Working-class people are often presented, like working-class youth, in the context of trouble, with the working class presented as undesirable welfare scroungers, as lone parents, and as inadequates who are unable to cope with their uncontrollable delinquent children and other difficulties. Neo-Marxists like the GMG see such negative representations as the media acting against groups which challenge the dominant ideology.

3 *As living in idealized/romanticized working-class communities.* The working class is often presented most positively in the stereotypical context of traditional working-class communities, where people are seen as respectable and hard-working, and as working-class heroes who struggle to overcome adversity in their lives.

These are the stereotypes portrayed in programmes like *EastEnders* and *Call the Midwife*. Here, life rotates around pubs, shops and close and supportive networks of family and friends. This traditional working-class imagery is also linked to macho behaviour, masculinity and physically hard work, and this is often the representation found in advertising, for products such as jeans and beer. The values in these communities are often praised, but they have little relation to reality, as such working-class communities have largely disappeared with the decline of traditional industries like coal-mining, shipbuilding, the steel industry and docking.

Jones suggests these images of working-class communities are somewhat romanticized, and are filtered through the middle-class media gaze. For example, the former *EastEnders* script writer David Yallop said *EastEnders* was 'created by middle-class people with a middle-class view of the working class which is patronizing, idealistic and untruthful' (cited in Jones (2011: 132)).

With the decline of these communities, Jones points out that, in the 2000s, there has been a change in the representation of the working class from being patronized to being despised, with the emergence of the fourth stereotype discussed below – of the working class as an underclass of white trash and scum – chavs.

4 *As white trash and scum: 'chavs' and the demonization of the working class.* With a media ideology suggesting most people are now middle class, this media stereotype is of an underclass, in which the working class and the poor are merged. Various terms like 'white trash', 'social scum' and 'chavs' have been used to describe this group, but the most common, and the most offensive, is now 'chav', and sometimes 'chavettes' for female chavs. This is the most demeaning and hostile stereotype of the working class, emerging first in the late 1990s / early 2000s, and is now probably the most dominant one in the media, which seems to have replaced media notions of the hard-working and respectable traditional working class.

Lawler (2005) said this stereotype represents the working class as 'worthless, disgusting, contemptible, frightening and threatening chavs, with bad clothes, bad food, bad behaviour and bad taste'. The box below summarizes the key features of 'chavdom'. Weltman (2008) suggests the chav stereotype is one of the media techniques used to devalue working-class taste and

---

What is the chav stereotype?

The chav underclass stereotype has a huge range of 'failings': ignorance, immorality, vulgarity, bad taste (bling jewellery, fake designer gear), lack of education, drug abuse, alcoholism, crime, sexual promiscuity, lone parenthood, waste, obesity and a tendency for violence. Chavs are thugs who own dangerous dogs, irresponsible parents with out-of-control children, aggressive men and excessively fertile women, who are workshy, welfare dependents, committing benefit fraud, who subsist on junk food and live in filthy council houses on run-down estates, with unwashed dishes and clothes everywhere, and where dogs crap on threadbare and filthy carpets.

A still from the Channel 4 documentary *Benefits Street*, criticized for perpetuating a negative chav stereotype attached to those in deprived areas

culture, and Tyler (2008) suggests the word 'chav' has now become a common form of middle-class abuse of the poor white working class. Lawler suggests it is one way the middle class helps to secure and maintain its identity, through a sense of its own superiority over white working-class culture.

The chav stereotype appears in a wide range of media, and regularly appears in some form in most newspapers. On TV, in the 1990s, Jones reports early chavs in the form of filthy, foul-mouthed, chain-smoking, benefit-dependent Wayne and Waynetta Slob, characters invented by comedian Harry Enfield. In the 2000s, the characters Lauren Cooper (catchphrase 'Am I bovered?') and her friends (in *The Catherine Tate Show*), Vicky Pollard (in *Little Britain*) and Kelly Bailey (in *Misfits*) all possessed chav characteristics. The confrontational ITV daytime chat show *The Jeremy Kyle Show* frequently features for the entertainment of viewers chav-like dysfunctional working-class people whose lives are in turmoil. A 2014 Channel 4 documentary series, *Benefits Street*, filmed in Birmingham, was highly controversial because of the way it fuelled the chav stereotype of those living in deprived communities.

Shildrick et al. (2007) point out that the media explain these features as arising from the character deficiencies, moral failings, depravity and weakness of individuals, rather than from the structural inequalities of wealth and consequent social deprivation. This reinforces the popular impression that the poor are poor because of their own failings – the 'undeserving poor' – and neutralizes any public sympathy for their plight. Such media stereotypes encourage audiences to laugh at rather than understand the lives of those living in deprived communities, reinforcing the cultural hegemony of the dominant class and a perception of the normality of middle-class life.

Representations of the middle class

The middle class is over–represented in media content – there is more exposure of middle-class lifestyles than is justified by their proportion in the population as a whole. In contrast to the representation of the working class, the middle class is generally presented in a positive light – as mature, sensible, educated and successful, and coping with problems. Middle-class families are represented as well-functioning units, and the consumption and taste making up the middle-class lifestyle are presented in drama, sitcoms, advertising, magazines and newspapers as the norm to which everyone should aspire.

Such positive representations, combined with negative portrayals of the working class, are the product of the media gaze of a middle-class-dominated media establishment. These representations confirm and promote the dominant and hegemonic ideology of the normality of middle-class life, and help to legitimize or justify the existing class structure and class inequalities. They do this by suggesting that people who are higher up the class structure are more competent, successful, and able to cope, and therefore more worthy of respect than those below them.

Representations of the upper class

The most obvious and extensive media representation of the upper class – rich and powerful aristocrats, businesspeople and celebrities – is through coverage of the monarchy, such as gossip about royalty, the antics of royal princes and princesses, and royal visits, weddings and jubilees.

The upper class is generally presented as being 'well bred', cultured and superior, with posh accents, country estates and a taste for shooting and hunting. Sometimes the upper class is portrayed as a bit eccentric or odd, but fundamentally decent and respectable. It is often portrayed in a romanticized, nostalgic way in the context of costume/period dramas like *Upstairs Downstairs* or *Downton Abbey*, which suggest that somehow life was once better, even for the poor who worked for the upper class.

The lavish lifestyles of the upper class, particularly in the form of luxury homes, cars, exotic holiday locations and expensive fashion accessories, often provide media content for mass audiences, in TV, the mass-circulation tabloid press and magazines, especially in celebrity magazines like *OK*, *Hello* or *Now* and their related websites. Pluralists see such coverage as simply providing what media audiences want, but neo-Marxists see this as a celebration of hierarchy and wealth which encourages admiration and envy by other social classes who aspire to it. This promotes – as in the representations of all social classes – the dominant ideology, and seeks to legitimize the existing social hierarchy as natural, normal and desirable, and to undermine opposition to patterns of inequality.

Activity

1 Based on your own media use, try to identify a contemporary example of each of the stereotypes of the different social classes described above. If you're in a group, collect your answers and explain how each of the examples demonstrates a stereotype, and discuss whether the various examples you've found provide an accurate or fair view of the social classes concerned.
2 Outline and explain **three** reasons why media stereotypes of the working class might be regarded as newsworthy by most of the media.
3 Go to www.urbandictionary.com and look up 'chavs' to get a flavour of both the nature of chav culture and hostility to it.
4 Try to read (at least) the first chapter ('The Case of Shannon Matthews') of Owen Jones's *Chavs: the Demonization of the Working Class* (2011). Identify **four** reasons why the stereotyping of communities like those in which Shannon Matthews lived gives a misleading impression of life in such communities.

Representations of ethnicity

General features of representations of ethnicity

1 Ethnic minorities are under-represented in senior management of the media companies and in producing programmes. Neo-Marxists like the GMG point to the way representations of minority ethnic groups are therefore filtered through the gaze of a predominantly white middle-class-dominated media establishment, or, as Hall (2003) put it, 'the white eye through which they are seen'.
2 Cumberbatch et al. (2014), in a content analysis of the most popular TV programmes across three genres and four channels in 2013–14, found just over one in seven roles was filled by a person from an ethnic minority group, slightly greater than their share in the population as a whole, though Black African Caribbeans were over-represented and South Asians were under-represented. Ethnic minorities were also clustered in certain types of programmes, particularly entertainment. They were under-represented in lead roles in fictional programmes, and very rarely appeared as presenters.
3 Ethnic minority interests and representations are *ghettoized* in the mainstream media. This means they are marginalized and featured mostly in specialized programmes on minority group issues, like programmes dealing with issues of stereotyping, discrimination or prejudice, or religion.
4 Malik (2002) found that African Caribbeans were more likely to be found in programmes dealing with social issues, music, sport, light entertainment and comedy, rather than in heavy-weight roles, such as those of political commentators or experts, or in subjects of a serious nature, such as politics; and were less often found in major roles in big-budget British films. Beattie et al. (1999) of the GMG, in their study of TV presenters and hosts, showed black and Asian people were more likely to appear in supporting roles and as temporary guests than as hosts. Although they found there was a growing representation of black people and Asians as hosts and presenters, this was more in the margins of TV output, like children's TV, rather than in prime-time television and in political, current affairs programmes, except for the news.
5 In advertising, Beattie et al. found that black people were less likely than whites to be shown in professional roles, and more likely to appear as musicians, sports persons and in exotic dress. White actors were more likely to be given speaking parts. Data from Clearcast showed that in 2010, actors from black, Asian or other ethnic minorities appeared in just 5.3 per cent of UK TV adverts screened in 2010 – less than half the proportion of those from ethnic minorities in the population as a whole.

6   Gill (2007) points to the narrow range of representations of black women in the media, and Beattie et al. cite black supermodel Naomi Campbell's complaint about the under-representation of black women models in the advertising industry: 'You've got to understand this business is about selling and blond and blue-eyed girls are what sells.'

7   Minority ethnic viewers, especially Asian viewers, rarely see the reality of their lives or the issues that concern them reflected on TV channels. Hargrave (2002) found ethnic minorities were themselves concerned about the content of such portrayals. Asians thought they were stereotyped as all the same, with the cultural and religious differences between, for example, Pakistani, Bangladeshi and Indian Asian groups not being recognized in the media. In particular, they complained about negative stereotyping, unrealistic and simplistic portrayals of their community, negative or non-existent images of their countries or areas of origin, and tokenism (including Asian or black actors only because programme makers thought they should do to avoid accusations of prejudice and discrimination).

The points above suggest that there does appear to be a form of *symbolic annihilation* of the main minority ethnic groups, let alone those from other ethnic groups, like the Chinese, Greeks or Poles. Media representations of ethnic minorities are also characterized by stereotyping, with these stereotypes combining with the news values of the predominantly white media establishment to produce stories which attract media audiences, advertisers and profits for media owners.

Media stereotypes of ethnicity

Black and Asian people are frequently negatively stereotyped and used as scapegoats in the media. Hall (2003), for example, suggests they are represented as cheating, cunning and capable of turning nasty, and as the source of social problems and of conflict that otherwise would not exist. As revealed by a range of research over time, such as Hall et al. (1978), Alvarado et al. (1987), van Dijk (1991) and Cottle (2000), black and Asian minority ethnic groups are often represented in a limited range of degrading, negative and unsympathetic stereotypes, and as scapegoats on which to blame a range of social problems.

1   *As deviants and law-breakers.* Minority ethnic groups are frequently represented in the context of drug-dealing, terrorism, welfare fraud, 'mugging' (street robbery with the actual or threatened use of violence) and gang, knife and gun culture. Hargrave (2002) found that black people were more than twice as likely as white people to be portrayed on terrestrial television as criminals. REACH (2007) reported that black boys and young black men are often portrayed as a dangerous and threatening group, with their lives focused around criminality, such as drugs, guns and gangs. Black people committing crime is far more likely to be reported than black people who are the victims of crime, such as attacks and intimidation by white racists. These images generally fit the news values of the white media establishment.

Hall et al.'s (1978) neo-Marxist analysis of media reporting of mugging (street robbery) during the 1970s showed how the media exaggerated the extent of black crime, and suggested that black people were more prone to criminality than whites. This led to a media-fuelled moral panic over the problem of the 'black mugger', who came to be seen as a folk devil. Hall et al. suggested the black mugger became a symbol which functioned to reassert the hegemony of ruling-class ideology by distracting the public's attention away from a wider economic and political crisis at that time.

Similar media representations of young black people as folk devils continue to be presented in the media in contemporary Britain, with reports of things like gang, drug, knife and gun culture symbolized in gangsta rap music.

2   *As posing a threat.* This stereotype presents ethnic minorities as possessing a culture which is seen as 'alien' and a threat to British culture – a kind of 'enemy within'. Immigration, for example, is presented as a threat to the British way of life and the jobs of white British workers. Media reports of rare events like forced marriages (in which one or both of the parties is forced

into marriage against his or her will), and honour killings (the murder of a family member, usually of women, by other members, due to a belief that the victim has brought dishonour on the family), give a misleading impression of all minority ethnic groups. Muslims and Muslim culture are frequently presented as a threat to British values (see page 224). Such stories are very newsworthy, as they conform to the news values of journalists.

3 *As causing social problems, conflict and trouble.* These include representations linked to racial problems, ethnicity-related riots, disruption caused by underachieving black students in schools, illegal immigrants, welfare scroungers, lone parents and so on. These are often presented in the context of people with individual inadequacies or 'badness', rather than as people with social problems generated by things like poverty, racial discrimination, poor housing, and racist intimidation and attacks by white people. Asylum seekers are often represented as bogus, as really economic migrants seeking to work illegally, rather than as people escaping from persecution, including possible torture or death, in the countries from which they have fled. Periodically the media generate moral panics over such issues, with stories which might seem almost amusing and absurd if it weren't for the consequent prejudice against wholly innocent people arising from media reporting. For example, in 2003, the *Sun* dedicated the front page to a story entitled 'Swan Bake', with a similar story in 2011, maintaining asylum seekers were killing and eating swans from ponds and lakes in London, and in the same year the *Daily Star* had a similar story about Somalian refugees, with its front page headline 'Asylum seekers eat our donkeys'.

4 *As having limited talents and skills.* This stereotype portrays minority ethnic groups as people who have either few skills and talents, or only a narrow range of them. They are often shown in low-paid work, in jobs like cleaning, or as educational failures, or as people who do well in sport and music, but are rarely portrayed as academic or professional successes.

5 *As having problems internationally.* Developing countries are often portrayed as countries that are run chaotically, that suffer from AIDS epidemics (in Africa) they are unable to get under control, that use children as soldiers and labourers, that live in famine conditions (images of starving babies), that are always having tribal conflicts, civil wars, military coups and so on, and that need the white Western populations to help solve their problems for them (through aid agencies, for example). The Glasgow Media Group (2000), in a study of British television coverage of developing countries, and audience reactions to it, found disasters and terrorism were the main categories of news story, but there was little explanation or context given in most news accounts. Audience studies found the developing world was perceived very negatively, with the respondents describing the developing world with words like 'poverty', 'famine', 'drought', 'wars' and 'disasters', and this was accompanied by audience impressions of corrupt governments. Audiences were left with a view of the developing world as not much more than a series of catastrophes.

The stereotypes considered above have in recent years also been applied to white people from Eastern Europe and countries close to Russia, like the Ukrainians, Poles, Latvians, Bulgarians, Romanians, Lithuanians and Slovakians. These groups have been blamed for virtually every problem that has beset Britain, and frequently blamed for things that either aren't true or are not their fault. For example, as Dowling (2007) showed, in the 2000s, immigrants from Eastern Europe were being attacked and blamed in the media for being benefit scroungers and lone parents, stealing unwanted clothes, causing a shortage of £50 notes, taking British jobs, having road signs put up in foreign languages, drunken driving, car crashes, driving down wages, groping women, cheaper heroin, counterfeit money, cheap guns, selling babies, overcrowding in churches, bad service in restaurants, and causing anglers to stop fishing as immigrants were stealing and devouring fish stocks, as well as killing and eating swans, ducks and deer. These media stories were all either completely absurd, untrue or massively exaggerated, but they may well have had a negative influence on audiences, creating, confirming and reinforcing the public's racial prejudices, by blaming minority ethnic groups for problems that are not created by them at all.

Activity

1 Outline **three** reasons why media stereotypes of minority ethnic groups might be regarded as newsworthy by most of the media.
2 Based on your own media use, go through each of the stereotypes listed above, and suggest examples of particular contemporary TV programmes, newspaper stories, advertisements and other media content that show these stereotypes. Consider whether these stereotypes are applied mainly to particular minority ethnic groups, or whether they are applied to all of them.
3 Suggest criticisms of the media stereotypes you have identified, and the ways they may or may not give a misleading impression of the relevant ethnic groups.

Islamophobia and the media: 'Muslim' as a stigmatized identity

Media coverage of the worldwide terrorist network of Al-Qaeda, which was behind the bombing of the Twin Towers in New York in 2001 and the London bombings in July 2005, suicide bombings by Islamic fundamentalists across the world, and in 2014–15 the participation by some British youth in the terrorist activities of ISIS (Islamic State) in Iraq and Syria, has meant the activities of a tiny minority of Muslims in Britain has led to the stereotyping in the popular imagination of all Muslims as a threat to social values and public safety. A 2007 report commissioned by the Mayor of London showed that, following research into one week's news coverage, 91 per cent of articles in national newspapers about Muslims were negative. Muslims have been demonized in the mass media, and stereotyped as fundamentalists who threaten British values, for example by oppressing women, such as by forcing them into wearing the hijab (headscarf) or burqas (a full body cloak) or into marriages they don't want, and seeking to establish Sharia law (Islamic law) to replace British law in some communities.

Media reporting and representations of Muslims in the 2000s generated a moral panic, with the very word 'Muslim' practically becoming what Goffman (1990b [1963]) called a stigmatized identity – an identity that is in some way seen as abnormal, undesirable or demeaning, and which excludes people from full acceptance in society. This has contributed to creating Islamophobia (an irrational fear or hatred of Muslims) in the white majority population, leading to what Baroness Warsi, who was then co-Chair of the Conservative Party and the first-ever female Muslim cabinet minister, in 2011 called 'fashionable Islamophobia'. She suggested that anti-Muslim prejudice and hatred in Britain were now seen as so normal that they had passed what she called 'the dinner-table test', which meant it had become acceptable to talk about Muslims at middle-class dinner parties in a prejudiced, bigoted way without attracting the social stigma attached to prejudice against other religious and ethnic groups. As Phillips (2007) pointed out, the balance of media reporting of Muslims in the 2000s was such 'that the very word "Muslim" is conjuring up images of terrorism and extremist preachers, rather than Mrs Ahmed down the road, who might be the mother of your son's best friend'.

As Hargrave found, Muslims are very concerned about such negative media portrayals, and the way only certain aspects of the Islamic faith, such as the views of fundamentalists, are depicted. Such media representations and moral panics bring with them harassment and fear for many British Muslims, who have little sympathy with Islamic fundamentalism, much less terrorism of any kind, and whom surveys repeatedly show are moderates who accept the norms of British life and Western democracy.

A **stigmatized identity** is an identity that is in some way undesirable or demeaning, and excludes people from full acceptance in society.

Islamophobia is an irrational fear and/or hatred of or aversion to Islam, Muslims or Islamic culture.

Explanations for stereotyping of ethnicity

Pluralists see media representations of ethnic minorities as simply reflecting the news values of journalists, and providing material that media audiences want.

Cottle (2000) suggests that media representations of ethnicity encourage media audiences to construct a sense of their identity by defining who 'we' are in relation to who 'we' are not, in terms of 'us' and 'them'. This means that majority white audiences may be encouraged by representations of the cultural differences of ethnic minorities to secure their white identity by defining themselves as different from and superior to 'them'.

The two stories depicted above both appeared in British newspapers in one week in November 2007. One concerned a British woman, Gillian Gibbons, who was teaching in the Sudan. Because she allowed a teddy bear in her classroom to be named by the children as Mohammad, she was jailed for fifteen days, and there were angry protests in the Sudan against the alleged insult to the prophet Mohammad. In the same week, a teenager in Saudi Arabia was sentenced by the courts to 200 lashes after being gang-raped by seven men. Look at the reporting, pictures and wording of the stories above. What kind of impression of Muslims do you think they give? Do you think such reporting might give a distorted impression of Islam, and increase anti-Muslim feeling in Britain?

Neo-Marxists like the GMG point to the way negative media representations are created through the white eyes of the media establishment and the ideology and news values of journalists. These representations may be creating, maintaining and reinforcing racist stereotypes. These can make ethnic minorities vulnerable to discrimination, while at the same time reinforcing the cultural hegemony of the dominant white ideology and the alleged supremacy of white culture. Racist stereotypes and the scapegoating of ethnic minorities for the social and economic problems experienced by white workers, when these aren't their fault, divide black and white workers by fuelling racism. This diverts attention away from the structure of inequality in society, and in particular the inequalities and deprivation faced by many people from all ethnic groups. This protects the interests of the dominant social class. Media-generated moral panics, like that shown in Hall et al.'s study of mugging discussed earlier, or over the alleged threat posed by Muslims, are therefore seen by neo-Marxists as a way of reasserting and reaffirming ruling-class hegemony in society generally.

Changing stereotypes of ethnicity?

Media stereotypes of black and other minority ethnic groups do appear to be changing. Appreciation of black culture has grown, and there are more major black and Asian figures appearing in music, arts and the media generally. There have been greater policy commitments in television to recruit more people from ethnic minorities as presenters, and Beattie et al. showed this was most obvious in the areas of children's television, education and the news.

There are more programmes, TV channels, websites, radio stations, DVDs and magazines being targeted at black and Asian audiences, and digital technology and satellite and cable TV enable black and Asian people to extend the range of programmes they can receive, and they are adopting the new media faster than the white ethnic majority – particularly younger people, who make up the fastest-growing section of these minority ethnic groups. These changes are ones terrestrial TV networks need to take account of if they are to retain viewers and therefore justify the licence fee (in the case of the BBC) or retain advertisers (in the case of commercial channels).

The new media, of which young people from minority ethnic groups are greater users than the average in the UK, means they have greater access to things like YouTube, Twitter, Facebook and the internet to put across their own views and counter negative ethnic stereotypes and reports in mainstream media.

We are seeing black and Asian actors moving into more popular dramas and soaps. Abercrombie (1996) shows these changes are most apparent in soaps like *EastEnders* and *Coronation Street*, where black and Asian actors are now appearing more as ordinary, routine characters, who share the same interests, worries, concerns and lifestyles as white people, rather than in roles focused only on their ethnic identity. *EastEnders* has a long history of featuring black and Asian characters, and is the third most popular series among ethnic minorities, watched on average by 43 per cent of the non-white TV viewing audience. This suggests there is a growing acceptance in the media of ethnic minorities as a normal, mainstream part of British society.

Representations of gender

General features of representations of gender

1 *The under-representation of women in the media industry.* Women are under-represented in positions of power and influence in the management of the media industry, and among editors, journalists and TV producers. The IWMF (International Women's Media Foundation; 2010) found that in UK news companies women were marginalized in newsrooms and decision-making hierarchies, and that women faced a glass ceiling – an invisible barrier to progress in their careers – that was fixed at the junior professional level. These jobs are important in the gathering of news but not normally in defining what news should be reported or in shaping policy or company decisions. Those are the senior professional roles, 60 per cent of which were filled by men, with women making up around a third of those in media management. According to Women in Journalism, in 2011, 74 per cent of news journalists on national newspapers were men, and there were twice as many male editors as women. The *Guardian* newspaper (5 December 2011) found, in a study of TV and radio programmes and newspaper reports, that in a typical month an average of 77 per cent of reports were by male journalists with just 23 per cent by women. A 2012 study by Women in Journalism of nine national daily newspapers found that, over a period of four weeks, 78 per cent of all front-page articles were written by male journalists.

2 *The male gaze.* Neo-Marxists like the GMG and Marxist feminist and radical feminist writers point to the way representations of gender are filtered through the media gaze of the predominantly male-dominated media establishment. This means, particularly, that women are portrayed through what Mulvey (2009 [1975]) called the male gaze, whereby men look (gaze) at women as sexual objects, with images of women focusing on their physical appearance and sexuality, using camera angles that focus on women's sex appeal, their breasts, suggestions of or actual nudity, often in a way to provide erotic pleasure for men. This is at its most blatant in pornography, but female sexuality is a constant theme in advertising, and appears very often in the mass-circulation tabloid press and many men's magazines. The Leveson Inquiry report (Leveson 2012) into the culture, practices and ethics of the press commented that the tabloid press often failed to show 'consistent respect for the dignity and equality of women', and that there is a 'tendency to sexualise and demean' women.

3 *The under-representation and stereotyping of women in media content.* Women in Journalism in the 2012 study previously referred to found that men accounted for 84 per cent of those mentioned or quoted in lead articles. Globally, women are the subject of news stories far less than men. The Global Media Monitoring Project (2010) in a study of media across the world found about 76 per cent of the people heard or read about in print, radio and television news and on news websites were male, compared to only 24 per cent female. When women were interviewed or heard in the news, they appeared mainly as 'ordinary' people, whereas

The **glass ceiling** is an invisible barrier of discrimination which makes it difficult for women to reach the same top levels in their chosen careers as similarly qualified men.

men were presented more often as 'experts'. Women were also four times more likely to be identified by their family status than men ('Mrs so and so, a mother of two ...'). Nearly half of news stories reinforced gender stereotypes – almost eight times higher than stories that challenged such stereotypes. The report concluded that the world depicted in the news remains predominantly male. Cumberbatch et al. (2014), in a content analysis of the most popular TV programmes, showed that women also appear on TV in the most popular shows less often than men, especially as prominent presenters and in supporting roles. This is particularly the case for older women, who are under-represented compared to their proportion in the real world, while older men are over-represented. Martinson (2014) noted that, out of all the over-50s appearing on BBC TV, 82 per cent are men, and across all major broadcasters women over 50 make up just 5 per cent of on-screen presenters of all ages and both sexes. As Cumberbatch et al. note, women are less likely than men to grow older on television. Women also tend to appear in a narrower range of roles than men across the media, often conforming to the gender stereotypes which are discussed in the next sections.

4   *Patriarchal ideology and the symbolic annihilation of women.* Feminist writers suggest features like those identified above mean that the media tend to be patriarchal (controlled mainly by men) and spread a patriarchal ideology – presenting a male view of women and femininity in the interests of men. The way women are either invisible, under-represented or represented in a limited range of stereotyped roles and identities was described by Tuchman et al. (1978) as the *symbolic annihilation* of women, involving the three aspects of trivialization, omission and condemnation of women in the media.

The media and the social construction of gender differences

The media are generally considered as an important influence on the social construction of gender differences between men and women. Connell (2005) considers that gender identities are in part constructed by the media reproducing hegemonic or culturally dominant stereotypes of the roles and relations between men and women. The gender stereotype of men involves what Connell called a 'hegemonic masculinity', but we could also consider there to be a 'hegemonic femininity'. Some possible features of these are summarized in table 3.5.

The media create and reinforce these hegemonic gender stereotypes in a number of ways. For example, the media, and particularly advertising, often promote what Wolf (1991) calls the 'beauty myth'. This is the idea that women are assessed primarily in terms of their appearance, and expected to conform to male conceptions of female beauty. Tebbel (2000) suggested that at no other time in history have women been so preoccupied with the shape they are in, with newspapers, magazines, the advertising industry, TV and films all promoting the prevailing 'ideal' body shape for women as more like a Barbie doll than a real woman. The bodies of real women have, in effect, been rendered invisible and symbolically annihilated in the media, and replaced by an idealized, youth-obsessed beauty cult, with airbrushed images of female beauty, like size zero models, that are unrealistic and unattainable for all but a very small number of women. The cosmetics, fashion, diet and cosmetic surgery industries all promote this imagery because they profit from it. The beauty myth is found right across the media spectrum, and women are often expected to be young and attractive, whether as actors, presenters or other media personnel, no matter how successful or powerful they might be.

There are often very different types of story and magazine aimed at males and females. Romantic fiction is almost exclusively aimed at a female readership. A glance at the magazine shelves of any large newsagents will reveal 'Women's interests' and 'Men's interests' sections, reflecting the different hegemonic masculine and feminine identities which men and women are encouraged to adopt. A 2012 survey of girls between the ages of 7 and 21 by Girlguiding UK, *Girls' Attitudes Explored ...Role Models*, found many used a limited range of role models drawn from reality TV and celebrities.

Children Now (2001) found that female characters were severely under-represented in video games, accounting for only 16 per cent of all characters, and the majority of female characters

Table 3.5 Hegemonic masculine and feminine characteristics

Hegemonic masculine characteristics	Hegemonic feminine characteristics

Heterosexuality	Heterosexuality
Sexual dominance	Sexual passivity (or a 'slapper' if sexually active)
Repression of emotions/emotional distance (except in sport, when males tend to get very emotional indeed)	Expression of emotions/emotional warmth, caring and sensitive
Physically strong/muscular/tall	Physically weak/fragile/small
Aggression	Gentleness and non-aggression
Independence and self-reliance	Dependence (on men)
Competitiveness and ambition	Lack of competitiveness
Lack of domesticity (housework and childcare) – only occasional practical DIY round home	Concerned with and responsible for housework and practical and emotional aspects of childcare, personal relations and family life
Rational and practical	Emotional and unpredictable
Risk taking	Avoidance of risk
Task-oriented – focus on 'doing things' like work success, playing sports, making things, DIY in the home or activities to escape from work	People-oriented – focus on forming and maintaining friendships, family, children, and 'customer care' (keeping customers happy).
Lack of concern with or interest in personal appearance, taste in dress or personal health and diet	Major concern with physical appearance (being slim and pretty), health, diet, dress sense and attractiveness to men

Activity

1 Discuss the suggested features of the hegemonic stereotypes of masculinity and femininity shown in table 3.5. To what extent do you think these stereotypes are shown in the media in Britain? Back up your view with evidence drawn from the media, such as magazines, advertising, TV programmes, films, music videos or YouTube and other websites. Refer to examples of both child and adult behaviour.
2 Outline ways, with examples, that these media stereotypes might be changing.

were scantily clad and highly sexualized. Male and female character roles and behaviours were frequently stereotyped, with males more likely to engage in physical aggression and females more likely to scream, wear revealing clothing and be nurturing. Some popular video games, such as the *Grand Theft Auto* series, even portray, and some say glorify, violence against women.

As the images above show, Lads' mags continue to present women almost exclusively as sex objects, and the images from the *Sun* and *Daily Star*, which between them sell just over 3 million copies every day, are typical of the representation of women in much of the mass-circulation 'red-top' tabloid press

Female representations and stereotypes

As Wolf and Tebbel each suggested, women in the media have traditionally been shown as young, pretty and sexually attractive. Whatever the role, television, film and popular magazines are full of images of women and girls who are typically white, extremely thin and heavily made-up, even when playing in action roles. Women are more commonly shown indoors than outdoors – in the private sphere of the home rather than in the public world of the workplace and the street. They are frequently presented as emotional and unpredictable, and in their relationships to men, whether they be brothers, husbands, bosses, fathers or lovers, and in a limited number of stereotyped roles. These stereotypes include:

1 *The WAG* – the wives and girlfriends of men, or the *femme fatales*, who are concerned with beauty, love, romance, being pretty and sexually attractive, being a good partner and getting and keeping their men.
2 *The Sex Object* – the slim, sexually seductive, scantily clad figure typically found in the red-top daily press, such as the *Sun* and *Daily Star* newspapers, and their related websites like page3. com, in advertising, or as objects of male fantasy in pornography.
3 *The Supermum* – the happy home-maker or part-time worker, who is primarily concerned with childrearing, housework, cooking and family relationships. She keeps the family together and is both source and manager of family emotions.
4 *The Angel* – who is 'good', displays little sexuality, and is sensitive and domesticated; she supports her man.
5 *The Ball Breaker* – who is sexually active, strong, selfish, independent, ambitious and career-minded, and not dependent on men.
6 *The Victim* – as in many horror and crime films and TV dramas, with men as both the cause of their problems and – sometimes – their saviours.

The 'cult of femininity'

Ferguson (1983) argued that teenage girls' magazines traditionally prepared girls for feminized adult roles, and generated a 'cult of femininity'. This cult of femininity included themes like getting and keeping a partner, being a good wife/partner, keeping a family happy, what to wear, how to be a good cook and so on. These themes socialized young girls into the stereotyped values and roles of femininity as established in our society, and are often reflected in adult women's magazines, with their concerns with personal and emotional relationships, family, beauty, health and fashion.

Male representations and stereotypes

In contrast to women, men appear in a much wider range of roles, most often in the public sphere outside the home. They are generally portrayed both in a wider range of occupations and in those carrying higher status, for example as the boss or manager rather than the secretary or PA, which has long been identified as a female and subordinate role. Male voices are more likely to be used in 'voice-overs' in TV and radio programmes and advertising, presenting and reinforcing the idea of men as authority figures, opinion formers or experts. The dominant role of men is also shown in media representations in which older men are shown as sexual partners of younger women, with the opposite rarely being depicted. The stereotyped hegemonic masculine identity of the tough, assertive, dominant and rational male – what Gilmore (1991) described as 'the provider, the protector and the impregnator' – often appears, but not as exclusively as the stereotypes of women. Men are presented as having interests that are seen as part of the hegemonic masculine identity. A look at men's magazines reveals these to be things like sport, photography, computers and gadgetry, DIY and all manner of transport: cars, motor-bikes, aircraft, trains and boats. The 'top-shelf' soft-porn magazines are aimed exclusively at men.

Various media analysts and researchers argue that media portrayals of male characters fall within a range of stereotypes. Three related American reports (see Children Now 1999), identified six media stereotypes of male characters which reinforce 'masks of masculinity'. These stereotypes are:

1 *The Joker* – who uses laughter to avoid displaying seriousness or emotion.
2 *The Jock* – who avoids being soft, and who shows aggression to demonstrate his power and strength to win the approval of other men and the admiration of women.
3 *The Strong Silent Type* – who is in control, acts decisively, avoids talking about his feelings or showing emotion as this is a sign of weakness, and is successful with women.
4 *The Big Shot* – who is economically and socially successful and has high social status with possessions to match.
5 *The Action Hero* – who is strong but not necessarily silent, and who shows extreme aggression and often violence.
6 *The Buffoon* – who is well-intentioned and light-hearted, but is the bungling or inept figure found in TV ads and sitcoms, who is completely hopeless when it comes to parenting or domestic matters (confirming that men shouldn't be doing these things).

Activity

1 Refer to the stereotypes of females and males referred to in the previous sections. While using your favourite media, make a note of examples of each of these stereotypes, explaining how they illustrate them in each case.
2 Outline **three** reasons in each case why media stereotypes of gender might be: (a) newsworthy; (b) of appeal to advertisers.

As will be considered in Topic 5, it is a matter of debate whether media stereotypes will have any effects on the roles of men and women. Some or many women and men may reject such representations, dismissing them as simple media manipulation serving the interest of advertisers. Media stereotyping may, though, have a long-term influence (as the cultural effects model discussed in Topic 5 suggests) in socializing men and women in such a way that what they allegedly want is what the media have persuaded them to want. The end result of this process may influence the perceptions of men and women about their respective positions in society. At present, these stereotypes are clearly to the benefit of men, with women presented as no threat to male dominance.

Theoretical explanations for gender stereotyping

- *Pluralists* suggest that stereotyping occurs because that is what media audiences want. Media organizations, including advertising, are driven by the need to attract audiences to make money. Stereotypes provide a simple and effective way of satisfying the wishes of both audiences and media organizations.

- *Liberal feminists* see media representations as a product of the under-representation of women, as chief executives, senior managers, editors and journalists in male-dominated media organizations, which encourages a male view of the world. This will change as women gain more power and equal opportunities in media organizations, enabling them to break through the glass ceiling.

- *Marxists and Marxist feminists* see media imagery of gender as rooted in the need to make profits. Media owners and the producers of media content need to attract advertisers, and the advertisers need stereotypes (primarily of women, but increasingly also of men) to promote sales of all manner of cosmetics, fashions, diet and anti-ageing products. If audiences weren't persuaded to be concerned about these things, there would be no market and no profit. This demand for stereotypes by advertisers and their power over media owners, managers and journalists were shown by the experiences of Cyndi Tebbel. Tebbel was in 1997 the editor of the Australian *New Woman* magazine. She decided to feature a size-16 model on the magazine cover. This was well received by readers, who welcomed the representation of real women for a change, but a major advertiser – a cosmetics company – subsequently withdrew its advertising. Tebbel, who later resigned, was forced to discontinue promoting what the advertisers saw as 'unhealthy' (for sales of their products) imagery.

  Marxist feminists share with radical feminists the view that gender representations are driven by patriarchal ideology, but they particularly emphasize that this ideology is linked to social class inequality. Media-generated patriarchal imagery projects a lifestyle in which working-class women can least afford to participate. This confirms their own sense of inadequacy and reasserts the hegemony of the normality of male-dominated middle-class and upper-class lifestyles.

- *Radical feminists* see media representations as arising from the necessity to promote and reproduce patriarchy and patriarchal ideology. The media world, like the world in general, is a man's world, which seeks to keep women in a narrow range of stereotyped roles, where they continue to be subordinate to men, where they conform to the beauty myth and look good to satisfy the male gaze. Media-generated stereotypes of femininity discourage women from making the most of the opportunities available to them, and undermine any threat to male dominance in society.

The explanations above combine to explain why the news values of journalists, discussed in Topic 3, are often influenced by patriarchal ideology, with women facing symbolic annihilation as their interests are either ignored, given trivial treatment or removed or ghettoized by moving them into special women's TV or radio shows, or the women's pages of newspapers. Women's interests are simply not seen in the media as being as important or as newsworthy as those of men.

Are media stereotypes of gender changing?

McRobbie (1994) suggests that, in postmodern society, there is much more fluidity and flexibility in the representations of men and women in the media, in keeping with the changes in wider society. Gauntlett (2008) suggests there is growing social expectation that women and men should be treated equally, and this is increasingly reflected in the media, in which representations of gender are changing all the time. He sees the media as presenting a wider range of gender identities beyond traditional gender stereotypes, which are opening up new choices for both men and women, as they reassemble different media representations to construct gender identities of their own.

Changing representations of females

There is more emphasis now on independence and sexual freedom for women, and there is a growing diversity of imagery: women's position in society is changing rapidly, they are becoming more successful than men in education, and they are doing better than ever before in the job market. As the pluralist model predicts, new magazines now cater for working women, reflecting a world in which advertising revenue and profits are driving forces of the media, and these forces may well lead to reduced gender stereotyping, as women demand more from the media than increasingly outdated and patriarchal stereotypes.

McRobbie (1999) argues that a new form of popular feminism has emerged, shown in young (pre-teen and teenage) women's magazines, like *Mizz*, *More* and *Sugar* (now defunct, but replaced by www.sugarscape.com). These promote female assertiveness, being in control and enjoying sex as entitlements, and encourage their readers to be more self-aware, self-confident, ambitious and independent. McRobbie argues this new form of assertive femininity is embedded in contemporary 'girly culture', with 'girl power' now part of a popular culture in which girls are no longer presented as 'sweet' and innocent, and women are no longer 'ladylike'.

Inness (1999), in a study of female roles in TV dramas and films, showed women are being presented more as powerful 'tough girls', such as detectives, confronting danger and taking on roles that were once the preserve of men. Female roles are becoming stronger, more assertive, more resourceful and complex characters. Examples of these include Katniss Everdeen in *The Hunger Games* books and films, Hanna Heller in the film *Hanna*, and Lara Croft in the *Tomb Raider* film and computer games. There are stronger female leads in soaps, and in TV dramas such as *Scott and Bailey*, which stars a pair of female cops, overseen by a powerful female boss, as opposed to the traditional way women were often portrayed in such dramas – as the wife, sidekick or subordinate of men.

Activity

The contemporary media move and change so fast that examples of TV dramas, films and other media in textbooks like this can rapidly become outdated (though the ones mentioned above can all be researched on the internet). Based on your own media use, identify contemporary examples of 'tough girls' – female action heroes, women warriors and wonder women – and any other assertive female characters portrayed in the media, and suggest ways they might defy traditional gender stereotypes.

Knight (2010) points out that although the portrayals described above show women who can take care of themselves in ways that have historically been seen as typically male, this apparent reversal of women's traditional roles is accompanied by an underlying conventional femininity. These are nearly always *attractive* and *glamorous* women, like Angelina Jolie, Sarah Michelle Gellar, Milla Jovovich and Lucy Liu. They are not becoming masculinized or unfeminine, and remain traditionally attractive, thereby conforming to the male gaze and the beauty myth, and posing no threat to a patriarchal society. Nonetheless, Knight suggests that female action heroes and other new gender representations have at least opened up choices for girls which enable them to explore and construct new identities outside the norms of traditional femininity.

Changing representations of males

Gauntlett (2008) suggests that media portrayals of men are also changing, with a wider range of representations of masculinity, opening up new choices for men to construct identities different from traditional hegemonic masculinity. Men's lifestyle magazines are offering some new ways of thinking about what it is to be a man, and, as Gauntlett says, while 'sometimes going overboard with macho excess, [they] encourage men to understand women, and face up to modern realities'. New male identities that have made appearances in the media in recent years include the Emo Boy, the Metrosexual and the New Man, who are more caring, sharing and emotional, and more in touch with their feminine sides. (You can find out more about these new identities by a Google search.) A further change in male representation is the transformation of male bodies into sex objects in advertising to sell things, in much the same way that women's bodies have always been used.

These changing masculine identities are reflected in the growing concerns of men with such issues as their appearance and sexual attractiveness, their body size and shape, their diet, health and dress sense, and the growing use by men of cosmetics and cosmetic surgery. Combined with the increase in eating disorders among men, these all suggest that the factors that have traditionally affected women are now also beginning to have effects on men.

Explaining changing representations

Behind these changing representations of both men and women lie the traditional explanations: the power of advertisers, and the need to attract media audiences. Advertisers have found new ways of tapping into a lucrative men's market for consumer cosmetics and the like. Women are becoming more successful and have growing power in society, and traditional stereotypes have ever less appeal or relevance to their lives, and media representations need to reflect this if they are to maintain female audiences. In addition, if traditional mainstream media don't change, women will increasingly opt out of the traditional media, and discuss their concerns and issues through Facebook, Twitter and blogs like The Vagenda (www. vagendamag.blogspot.co.uk), where they may transcend and challenge media stereotypes.

Despite the growth in the presence and influence of women in media management and production, and the changes considered above, gender stereotypes continue to thrive in the media we consume every day, particularly in the mass-circulation red-top tabloid press, advertising, video games and music videos. New media technology, while it offers both men and women opportunities to challenge the way they are represented in media stories, has led to the exploitation of women as sex objects and as victims of sexual violence more extensively than ever. For example, the growth of the internet has led to a huge expansion of porn sites, which overwhelmingly feature the commercial and sexual exploitation of women's, rather than men's, bodies.

Activity

1. Outline and explain **two** ways in each case that (a) men and (b) women might use gender representations in the media as a source of personal identity and meaning.
2. Outline and explain **three** examples of how men are being represented more as sex objects in the contemporary media, including advertising.
3. Outline and explain **three** ways that the new media might be used to counteract and challenge mass media stereotypes.
4. Drawing on your own experiences of the media, discuss examples of the ways new masculine and feminine identities might be emerging in contemporary society.

Sexuality refers to people's sexual characteristics and their sexual behaviour.

Heterosexuality involves a sexual orientation towards people of the opposite sex.

Sexual orientation refers to the type of people that individuals are either physically or romantically attracted to, such as those of the same or the opposite sex.

Representations of sexuality

Representations of heterosexuality

In contemporary Britain, the dominant view of 'normal sexuality' is that of heterosexuality, which is where people have a sexual orientation, or a physical or romantic attraction, towards people of the opposite sex. This has always been a central aspect of both the hegemonic masculine and feminine stereotypes discussed in the previous section.

Sexuality – people's sexual characteristics and behaviour – has always been a central part of the hegemonic feminine stereotype, as, in Britain and other Western countries, women have been defined largely by their physical attractiveness and sexual appeal to men. They have traditionally been regarded as sex objects, subjected to what Mulvey called the 'male gaze', particularly in the mass media, such as advertising and through media pictures and stories of the exploits of female celebrities.

Increasingly, changing social attitudes have meant men are also becoming represented as sexualized objects. This is reflected in the growing coverage in men's magazines of men's appearance and sexual attractiveness, their diet, health and dress sense, and their growing use of cosmetics and cosmetic surgery. Men's bodies have also become much more sexualized in advertising: naked men's bodies appear in the media and advertising on a greater scale than ever before, and there is a growing importance attached to men's physical body image.

McRobbie (1994) has argued that men are beginning to face the same sort of physical scrutiny, by both women and other men, as women have always had to put up with, and, as she put puts it: 'The beauty stakes have gone up for men, and women have taken up the position of active viewers.'

A new male stereotype has emerged in the media – the 'metrosexual'. These are heterosexual men who embrace their feminine side, are in touch with their feelings, use moisturizer and designer cosmetic products, have refined tastes in clothing, and may adopt elements of the gay lifestyle.

Nonetheless, women are still much more likely to be seen as sex objects than men are, particularly in pornography, with even young boys and girls widely exposed to sexualized images of females. Porn now seems quite deeply embedded, through the internet and mobile phone technology, in the culture of young men.

Representations of homosexuality

The media are controlled by middle-class white predominantly heterosexual men, so the media view of homosexuality is formed through a heterosexual media gaze. The fear of loss of profits if investors, advertisers or media audiences are offended has meant that male **homosexuality** (gays) and female homosexuality (lesbians) have been traditionally treated by the media as deviant and perverse. Women were stereotyped as butch lesbians, and gay men as effeminate and camp, or sometimes as macho camp – super-macho men with large, bodybuilder-type muscular bodies. Gays and lesbians have been portrayed as marginal to society, as odd and colourful 'camp' characters and as figures of fun, or as dangerous and violent psychopaths. Such portrayals often corresponded to a range of media news values, and provided titillation for heterosexual audiences by giving them insights into what they regarded as abnormal or perverse sex. This treatment of gays and lesbians meant the media tended to present distorted views of homosexuality, portraying it as a social threat, and occasionally generated moral panics over what they saw as abnormal sexuality. This was particularly true during the early stages of the AIDS epidemic in the 1980s, when the disease was treated as the 'gay plague'.

Homosexuality involves a sexual orientation towards people of the same sex as oneself

The symbolic annihilation of gay and lesbian sexuality

Gross (1991) argues the media have often symbolically annihilated gays and lesbians by excluding them altogether, or trivialized, condemned or made fun of them. Gauntlett (2008) argues that, although things are changing, gays and lesbians are still under-represented and/or portrayed negatively in mainstream media.

Gay and lesbian sexuality may traditionally have been treated unfavourably by the mainstream media, but there are thriving traditional and new media catering for the gay market, such as *Gay Times* (*GT*) and *Attitude*. There are also a host of websites such as www.thegayuk.com and www.stonewall.org.uk

Stonewall (2010), the lesbian, gay and bisexual charity, in a study of TV programmes most popular with young people, found lesbian, gay and bisexual people were portrayed in less than 5 per cent of the total programming studied, with three-quarters of this in just four programmes – *Hollyoaks*, *I'm a Celebrity ... Get Me Out of Here*, *How to Look Good Naked* and *Emmerdale*. Half of all portrayals were of gay/lesbian stereotypes, and 36 per cent of portrayals were negative, in which gay people were depicted as figures of fun, predatory or promiscuous.

Cowan (2007) found that almost a fifth of people think TV is responsible for anti-gay prejudice, and Cowan and Valentine (2005), in a study of representations on the BBC, found that gay people were five times more likely to be portrayed negatively than positively. Gay life was most likely to appear in entertainment programmes, and was rarely featured in factual programmes, like documentaries and the news.

When gay and lesbian characters have appeared in the media, they are usually cast and defined in terms of their sexual orientation, rather than being other characters who also just happen to be gay or lesbian – this happens even in more recent sympathetic treatment of homosexuality, like the 2006 film *Brokeback Mountain*, or in soaps like *Hollyoaks* or *EastEnders*.

Growing tolerance, changing stereotypes and the 'pink pound'

Although the media still tend to under-represent and distort the lives and experiences of gays and lesbians, this is changing and there is a growing acceptance and tolerance of a diversity of sexual orientations. There is evidence of some change in traditional representations of masculine and feminine and gay sexuality, and the camp gays/butch lesbians stereotypes have largely disappeared. Soap operas and reality TV shows give us insights into lesbian and gay relationships, and other images of sexual identities with which we may not be very familiar. The popularity of gay media celebrities like Matt Lucas, Alan Carr and Gok Wan would seem to confirm that media representations and audience reactions are beginning to change.

Media companies have woken up to the fact that the gay and lesbian consumer market – the 'pink pound' – is large and affluent. As the pluralist approach would suggest, they are now slowly beginning to respond to what the gay and lesbian audience wants, by actively courting it through advertising campaigns and the provision of media products, particularly in the new digital media and the plethora of gay and lesbian websites.

The sanitization of gay sexuality

Gill (2007) suggests that, to avoid the risk of offending heterosexual audiences or of putting off advertisers, mainstream media represent gay sexuality only in a 'sanitized' way. She points out that gay men are rarely portrayed in a sexualized way, like kissing, touching or having sex. They appear mainly as stylish and attractive figures with beautiful bodies in adverts or other media content designed to appeal to women, not to other gay men. Gill suggests the opposite applies for lesbians, who rarely appear in advertising and other media in anything other than a highly sexualized manner, which appeals to one of the oldest heterosexual male sexual fantasies – that of watching women engage in intimate sexual conduct. Such representations have the triple effect of:

- Appealing to the gay and lesbian market
- Not offending heterosexual media audiences and advertisers
- Not challenging heterosexual ideology, but actively securing its continued hegemony as the norm.

The media thirst for newsworthy, headline-grabbing stories around sexuality is now more likely to be quenched by stories about paedophilia (adult sexual interest in young children) and the 'grooming' of children by paedophiles using internet chatrooms, or the growing sexualization of childhood, whereby young children are exposed to sexual influences and adopting sexual behaviours typically associated with adult sexuality (such as sexual acts, body language, dress styles and internet pornography). Both paedophilia and the sexualization of childhood are fairly regularly the stuff of newspaper headlines and moral panics.

Representations of disability

The social construction of disability

Disability refers to a physical or mental impairment which has a substantial and long-term adverse effect on a person's ability to carry out normal day-to-day activities. An impairment is some loss, limitation or difference of functioning of the body or mind, either that one is born with or arising from injury or disease. An impairment is not the same as disability. Disability is not caused by an impairment, but is created by interaction between people with impairments and their social environment, in which social and environmental barriers limit the opportunities for people with impairments to take part in society on an equal level with others. Shakespeare (1998) suggests that disability should be seen as a social construction – a problem created by the attitudes of society and not by the state of our bodies.

Shakespeare argues that disability is created by societies that don't take into account the needs of those who do not meet with that society's ideas of what is 'normal'. The stereotype in any society of a 'normal' or acceptable body may generate a disabled identity among those with bodies that do not conform to this stereotype, particularly those with a physical impairment, even when the impairment does not cause mobility or other physical difficulties for that person. An example of this might be people of very small stature (those with dwarfism), or with facial disfigurements causing an adverse reaction among others.

Whether someone is disabled or not is then a social product – it is social attitudes which turn an impairment into a disability, as society discriminates against those with impairments.

Most of us learn about disability as part of the socialization process, rather than as a result of personal experience. Popular views of those with impairments, for those without direct experience, are often formed through media stereotyping. Those who control the media industry are predominantly white, middle-class and able-bodied men, so the media gaze which forms representations of disability is that of the able-bodied. This media gaze nearly always represents disability as a problem for the individuals themselves who have impairments, rather than as something that is created by society.

> **Disability** is a physical or mental impairment which has a substantial and long-term adverse effect on a person's ability to carry out normal day-to-day activities.

> An **impairment** is some loss, limitation or difference of functioning of the body or mind, either that one is born with or arising from injury or disease.

The symbolic annihilation of disability in the media

Around a quarter of all adults (over age 16), one child (under 16) in twenty, and about 8 million people of working age (20 per cent of the working age population) in the UK were covered by the Disability Discrimination Act (DDA) definition of disability in 2011. Yet these disabled people are so seriously under-represented among those who work in the media industry and in the whole range of media content, and are so often portrayed in negative ways, that they effectively face symbolic annihilation.

Cumberbatch et al. (2014), in a content analysis of the most popular TV programmes in 2013–14, found that people portrayed as disabled represented just 2.5 per cent of the television population, compared to more than one in five in the real world. In two-thirds of cases, the impairment played a part in the participant's on-screen portrayal: that is, they appeared either as or playing disabled people, rather than as people or characters who happened to have an impairment, but which had no relation to their role in the programme. Ofcom (2005) found more than four in ten appearances (42 per cent) of disabled people were in the context of programmes highlighting issues of prejudice, stereotyping and discrimination.

The Broadcasting Standards Commission (2003), Ofcom and Cumberbatch et al. each found over three-quarters (80 per cent) of the impairments portrayed were related to mobility, sensory impairments, disfigurement and physical or mental illnesses/impairments. Sancho (2003) noted the wheelchair is often used as an 'icon' or index of disability by those wishing to represent disability in the media. Cumberbatch et al. found over one-third of participants with impairments in the programmes they reviewed were seen using disability aids, with wheelchairs (including wheel trollies and motorized shopping buggies) seen most often, followed by sticks and crutches.

Negative representations of disability

Briant et al. (2011) of the Glasgow Media Group (GMG) found, in a study comparing media coverage of disability in five newspapers in 2010–11 with a similar period in 2004–5, that there had been a reduction in the proportion of articles describing disabled people in sympathetic and deserving terms, particularly those with mental health-related disabilities. The proportion of articles linking disability to benefit fraud had more than doubled in five years, and nearly one in five articles discussed disability using terms like 'scrounger', 'cheat' and 'skiver', including the idea that life on benefits had become a 'lifestyle choice' for some disabled people, suggesting such people were 'undeserving'.

Philo et al. (2010) of the GMG found such negative stereotypes were also applied to people with disabling mental health conditions. In a study of TV drama and entertainment, they found nearly half of peak-time programmes with mental illness storylines portrayed people with mental health problems as posing a threat to others; 63 per cent of references to mental health were negative, in the sense of being critical, flippant or unsympathetic, with mental illness used as an easy source of violent tragedy, or as something to poke fun at. In the latest follow-up to this research, the GMG and Time to Change (2014) found, from a content analysis carried out in the first three months of 2014, encouraging signs that TV soaps, dramas and sitcoms were beginning to move away from the 'mad and bad' stereotypes of mental illness that Philo et al. found in 2010. There were more positive, authentic and sympathetic portrayals, and fewer overly simplistic stereotypes which stigmatized mental illness. However, the mad/bad/violent 'psycho' stereotypes were still quite common.

Media stereotypes of disability

Only rarely do the media treat disability as a perfectly normal and incidental part of everyday life, and there are few programmes that deal with disability without grotesque fascination, like media freak shows, or patronizing sentimentality. Barnes (1992) showed how the vast majority of information about disability in books, films, on television and in the press is extremely negative, consisting of 'disabling stereotypes which medicalise, patronise, criminalise and dehumanise disabled people'.

Cumberbatch and Negrine (1992) identified three broad categories of disability stereotype in the cinema: the criminal, the subhuman and the powerless or pathetic character, while Barnes identified ten stereotypes that the media in general use to portray disabled people:

1 *As pitiable or pathetic* – characters that stir emotions and encourage pity in audiences, and programmes that treat disabled people as objects of charity, as is played on by TV charity telethons such as *Children in Need*.

2 *As an element of atmosphere or object of curiosity* – disabled people are sometimes included in the storylines of films and TV dramas to enhance a certain atmosphere, such as menace, violence or mystery, or to add character to the visual impact of a production.

3 *As an object of violence* – as victims, for example being helpless and vulnerable to bullying at school.

4 *As sinister or evil* – this is one of the most persistent stereotypes, portrayed in classic characters like Frankenstein or the Phantom of the Opera, or the nasty criminals in James Bond films, like Dr No with two artificial hands. Disability is often associated with evil and witchcraft in films and fairy stories, and with sexual menace, danger and violence. The tabloid red-top press frequently carry exaggerated stories of the alleged dangers posed to the public by the mentally ill, such as the (incorrect) *Sun* front-page headline on 7 October 2013: '1,200 killed by mental patients'.

5 *As the super cripple* – the disabled person is seen as brave and courageous, living with and overcoming their disability, or assigned superhuman, almost magical, abilities. For example, blind people are portrayed as visionaries with a sixth sense or extremely sensitive hearing.

6 *As laughable or an object of ridicule* – the disabled person as the fool, the 'village idiot' and so on.

7 *As his/her own worst enemy* – as individuals who could overcome their difficulties if only they weren't so full of self-pity or maladjusted, and started to think more positively.

8 *As a burden* – the view of disabled people as helpless and having to be cared for by others.

9 *As non-sexual* – disabled people are sexually dead and therefore their lives are not worth living. The exception to this, as Barnes notes, is the stereotype of the mentally ill sex pervert, which features quite regularly in the mass-circulation red-top tabloid press and in horror and crime TV and movie thrillers.

10 *As unable to participate in daily life* – this stereotype is mainly one of omission, as disabled people are rarely shown as anything other than disabled people. They are seldom represented as a perfectly normal part of everyday life, as workers, parents and so on.

How does media coverage of the Paralympic Games represent disability? Does it challenge stereotypes, or create new ones? How powerful do you think media representations have been in the case of disability and the Paralympic Games?

Shakespeare (1999) described the use of disability as a character trait, plot device, or atmosphere as 'a lazy short-cut', to provide hooks to engage the audience's interest, through sympathy or revulsion. He condemned these representations for not providing accurate or fair reflections of the actual experience of disabled people, and suggested such stereotypes reinforced negative attitudes towards disabled people, and ignorance about the nature of disability.

Disabled people, and those who have some personal experience of disability, may well ignore, resist, reject or reinterpret such general stereotypes. However, for the many who lack such experience, the media may have a role in forming distorted views and negative stereotypes of all those with impairments.

Activity

This activity could be divided up if working in a group, with people taking different media.
1 Drawing on media you use, such as websites, internet advertising, video games, films, TV programmes, newspapers and magazines and so on, list the types of disability/impairments you come across in a one-week period.
2 Identify the response you think each example is designed to evoke in the audience, such as horror, pity or fear.
3 Identify from your survey a range of examples to illustrate the ten stereotypes identified by Barnes.
4 Present your findings to the rest of the group, and discuss what conclusions might be drawn about the representation of disability in the contemporary media.

Practice questions

1 Outline and explain **two** ways in which media representations of some social groups may give a biased impression of those groups. **(10 marks)**

2 Read **Item A** below and answer the question that follows.

Item A

Most of us learn about disability as part of the socialization process, rather than as a result of personal experience. Popular views of disability are often formed through media stereotyping. Disabled people are seriously under-represented among those who work in the media industry, and media content very often portrays disabled people in negative ways, rather than as being deserving of support.

Applying material from **Item A**, analyse **two** differences between media representations of the disabled compared with those who are not disabled. **(10 marks)**

3 Read **Item B** below and answer the question that follows.

Item B

The media provide a range of stereotypical representations of social groups, based on characteristics such as their gender or social class. For example, working-class people are often represented in ways that devalue them relative to the middle class. Marxists suggest such stereotypical representations reflect the interests of the powerful, and promote a dominant ideology that justifies existing patterns of social inequality.

Applying material from **Item B** and your knowledge, evaluate the view that media representations of different social groups may promote a dominant ideology that justifies existing patterns of social inequality. **(20 marks)**

Topic 5

SPECIFICATION AREA

The relationship between the media, their content and presentation, and audiences

Much of this chapter has suggested that the patterns of ownership and control of the media, the influence of the media market, the social construction of the news, and the various ways that social groups are represented in the media have some effect on audiences. However, this cannot be taken for granted. People are conscious, thinking human beings, not mindless robots. They might not swallow everything they come across, and they might respond in a variety of ways to what they read, hear or watch on TV or see on the internet. In most cases, a media text (media content) is polysemic, meaning that it can be interpreted in different ways by different individuals. For example, they might dismiss, reject, ignore, criticize, forget or give a different reading to a media text from that intended by the producer, and this is likely to be influenced by factors such as their own social experiences, their ethnic group, social class, gender and so on. For example, a black person is likely to reject a racist message in a TV broadcast or newspaper report.

We also need to be aware that the media comprise only one influence on the way people might think and behave, and there is a wide range of other agencies involved in people's socialization. Families, friends, schools, workplaces and workmates, churches, social class, ethnicity, gender, disability, age and so on may all influence individual and group behaviour and attitudes. It is therefore very important to weigh the influence of the media alongside these other factors.

A **media text** refers to any media product which describes, defines or represents something, such as a movie or video clip, TV or radio programme, a newspaper or magazine article, a book, a poster, a photo, a popular song, an advertisement, a CD or DVD, a website, etc.

Polysemic means that a media text (such as a media message, picture or headline) can be interpreted in different ways by different people.

Methodological problems of researching media effects

1   It is difficult to establish whether it is actually the media, or other social factors, that cause any alleged effects. For example, if it is shown that those who watch more violence on television are more aggressive than those who watch less, this might be because people whose social circumstances have made them more aggressive choose to watch more violent programmes rather than because the media make them aggressive. This issue is discussed further at the end of this topic.

2   It is almost impossible to disentangle the effects of the media on audiences of things like violence, stereotypes, consumerism, prejudice or the influence of the dominant ideology, from the whole range of other factors influencing people, such as their social circumstances, experiences and knowledge. Even people exposed to the same media texts do not interpret and react to them in the same way, so there must be some influences on audiences other than the media.

3   It is hard to establish, with the spread of the new media, which particular media cause any alleged effects. For example, it could be television, newspapers, movies, any of a vast range of websites, YouTube clips, texts and videos on mobiles, and so on.

4   It is practically impossible to establish what people's beliefs, values and behaviour might have been without any media influence. For example, neo-Marxists like the GMG argue that the media encourages audiences to accept the cultural hegemony of the dominant class. But how can this media effect be proven? For example, might people have been racist or sexist or supported the dominant ideology anyway, even if they had never been exposed to media influences?

5   In a media-saturated society, everyone is exposed to some form of media, and for all their lives. This means it is almost impossible to compare different effects between those who have been exposed to the media and those who haven't. This is particularly the case with experimental situations, which are discussed at the end of this topic.

Media effects models

There is a range of media effects models, with the differences between them based around two key and related questions:

1 *How passive or active are the audiences?* This concerns the extent to which media audiences actively interact or engage with the media they consume: are they passive 'dopes' mindlessly consuming media texts, who accept everything the media throws at them, or do they actively interpret and criticize media texts, giving them different meanings and interpretations from that intended, or simply ignore or reject them altogether?

2 *How powerful are the media in affecting audiences?* How influential are the media, if at all, compared to other influences on audience behaviour, such as their own experiences or the influence of other agencies of socialization, like family, peer groups, schools and their local community?

Passive audiences

The hypodermic syringe model

The hypodermic syringe model, sometimes called the magic bullet theory, is a very simple model, and most commentators would now regard it as an old-fashioned and inadequate view of the relationship between media content and audiences of readers, listeners and viewers. This model suggests that the media act like a hypodermic syringe (or a bullet), injecting media texts into the 'veins' of media audiences. Audiences are seen as unthinking, passive receivers of media texts, who are unable to resist the messages that are 'injected' into them. In this view, media messages fill audiences with the dominant ideology, sexist and racist images, scenes of violence or other content, and the audience then immediately acts on these messages. It is like seeing violence on television, and then going out and attacking someone, or viewing pornography and then going on to abuse women, as radical feminists like Dworkin (1981) have suggested. It is a simple view of the media as causing immediate changes in people's behaviour. It is the hypodermic syringe model which lies behind many moral panics over the effects of the media on behaviour, and it was the model sometimes used to partly explain the Tottenham/London riots in August 2011, with some claiming social media like Facebook, Twitter and Blackberry Messenger were fuelling the riots.

The hypodermic syringe model suggests that the media inject messages into the 'veins' of media audiences, with an immediate effect on their behaviour

On rare occasions, people may react quite directly to what they see in the media, as in copycat crimes or urban riots where people copy what they've seen in the media. Advertisers also spend millions of pounds on advertising their products, and we might reasonably assume that these have some effect on consumers and the sale of the goods advertised.

Criticisms of the hypodermic syringe model

1   The model assumes the entire audience is passive and homogeneous (sharing the same characteristics) and will react in the same way to media content. However, people may well have a range of responses to media content, depending on their own social situation and the experiences they have had. Young people with limited life experiences of their own might react differently from older audiences, and middle-class people might react differently to media representations of social class from people in the working class. Violence in the media could have a variety of effects – people might be appalled and become determined to stamp it out; others might use it to work out their violent fantasies so it doesn't happen in real life; others might simply ignore it.

2   It assumes audiences are passive, gullible and easily manipulated – but people are active thinking human beings, who use media in a variety of ways for their own purposes. They have their own ideas, and interpret and give different meanings to media texts. They are therefore not simply the uncritical passive consumers of information that the model suggests.

3   It assumes the media have enormous power and influence, overriding all other agencies of socialization and people's own experiences.

4   There is little evidence that media content has the immediate effects on audiences the model suggests.

Active audiences

Active audience models of media effects see the media as less influential than the passive audience approach of the hypodermic syringe model. They believe that audiences are not homogeneous, and that they vary in terms of social characteristics like age, social class, gender, ethnicity, sexuality, disability, education and personal experiences. These factors will influence their choices in the way they use the media, what they use them for, and the ways they interpret media texts.

The two-step flow model

The weaknesses of the hypodermic syringe model are tackled by what is known as the two-step flow model, developed by Katz and Lazarsfeld (1955). This model of media influence suggests that the media still have quite strong effects on audiences, but they do not simply passively and directly react to media content, and will respond in a variety of ways to it. The key factor affecting these responses is the influence of 'opinion leaders' in the social networks (like contacts and friends in the family, at work, school or college, or in their peer groups) to which audiences belong. Opinion leaders are those respected members of any social group who get information and form views from the media, who lead opinion and discussion in their social groups, and whom others listen to and take notice of. It might, for example, be a sociology teacher or an assertive and popular student whose views others tend to take notice of.

The two-step flow model suggests that opinion leaders select, interpret and filter media texts before they reach mass audiences, and form their own opinions and interpretations of them (the first step). Opinion leaders then selectively pass on these messages, which contain their own opinions and interpretations, to others in their social groups (the second step). Audiences therefore receive and are influenced by *mediated* – or altered and interpreted – messages received from opinion leaders whose views and opinions they respect. Members of these groups may then, in turn, pass on their opinions to others, in a kind of chain reaction leading from one person or group to another. This model recognizes that media audiences are not a mass of isolated individuals, but that the social groups to which people belong influence the opinions they hold and how they respond to and interpret media content.

Limitations of the two-step flow model

1   There are probably more than two steps in the media's influence. Media content could be selected and interpreted by many different individuals in different groups. For example, parents (as opinion leaders) may have one view, an opinion-leading workmate another view, and a sociology teacher still another. This might mean ideas and interpretations of media content get bounced around in discussions in a variety of groups, creating many steps in the flow of media influence.

2   It stills rests on the basic assumption that the influence of the media flows from the media to the audience, and assumes that media audiences are more or less victims of media content, even if media messages are mediated first by opinion leaders.

3   It suggests that people are very vulnerable to influence and manipulation by opinion leaders. It does not recognize that people may have views, opinions and experiences of their own on which to base their views of media content.

4   It suggests the audience is divided into 'active' viewers/readers (the 'opinion leaders') and 'passive' viewers/readers who are influenced by the opinion leaders. It doesn't explain why opinion leaders are directly influenced by media content when others in the audience are not.

5   With the rise of the new media and social networking sites, the role of opinion leaders may be less influential, or replaced by a huge and diverse range of opinion leaders, as people receive a diversity of mediated messages from Facebook contacts, blogs, YouTube and so on.

The cultural effects model – the 'drip drip' effect

Like the hypodermic syringe and two-step flow models, the neo-Marxist cultural effects model suggests that the media do have an effect on the audience. However, it does not regard media audiences as simply passive consumers of media texts, with the media having the direct effects of the hypodermic model, and to a lesser extent of the two-step flow model, with direct effects mediated by opinion leaders.

Neo-Marxist cultural effects theory recognizes that the media are owned and heavily influenced by the dominant and most powerful groups in society, and their interests strongly influence the content of the media, as seen throughout this chapter. This content is mainly in keeping with the dominant ideology.

Although cultural effects theory suggests the media will generally spread the dominant ideology in society, it accepts audiences interpret the media they consume, and may respond in different ways depending on their social characteristics, such as their social class, gender or ethnicity, and their own experiences. While the majority are likely to support and agree with the content and 'slant' of media messages such as in TV and newspaper reporting, others might be critical of or even reject that content. For example, women might well resist gender stereotyping, and black people (and many white people) reject racist stereotypes. White British people living in multicultural communities might reject or modify negative media representations of ethnic minorities or of recent immigrants, because they have positive, first-hand experiences of minority ethnic group life or of newly arrived immigrants. Those without such experiences may well take for granted the media content, as they have no experiences of their own to judge media content by.

Nonetheless, the cultural effects model suggests that the media gradually influence the audience over a period of time – a sort of slow, steady, drip-drip effect – a subtle, ever-present process of brainwashing which gradually shapes people's taken-for-granted common-sense ideas and assumptions, and their everyday view of the world. For example, if we see minority ethnic groups nearly always portrayed in the context of trouble and crime, or women portrayed only as mothers, lovers and sex objects, over time this will come to form the stereotypes we hold of these groups, to the exclusion of other aspects of their lives. Through this process, media audiences come to accept that the dominant ideology is common sense, and the only sensible way of seeing the world, and what neo-Marxists refer to as cultural hegemony is therefore established and maintained.

There is a range of opinion, within the cultural effects model, of what exactly the balance is between the media's power and influence over audiences, and the extent to which audiences can resist and reinterpret media content. This discussion ranges from the encoding/decoding and reception analysis, and related selective filtering approach, on one side, which gives the greatest emphasis to active audiences and their ability to make their own interpretations or readings of media texts, to the work of Philo and the Glasgow Media Group on the other, who give greater emphasis to the power and influence of the media in shaping audience responses.

Encoding/decoding and reception analysis

The analysis of how audiences receive and interpret media texts, and therefore what effects they have on audiences, is known as reception analysis.

Hall (1980), from a neo-Marxist perspective, suggests media texts – the content of media messages such as television news and current affairs programmes – are 'encoded' by those who produce them, that is, they contain a particular intended meaning which they expect media audiences to believe. This meaning, or encoding, is what Hall called the dominant hegemonic viewpoint, which takes the dominant ideology for granted and accepts it as the normal, natural and only sensible way of viewing social events. This dominant hegemonic viewpoint is the one that is held by most media managers, editors and journalists, and reflects the interests, beliefs and values of media owners and advertisers, the pressures of market competition, and influences news values, the hierarchy of credibility, dominant media representations and so on.

Hall suggests most audiences will receive and interpret – or *decode* – media texts containing this dominant hegemonic viewpoint in the way they were intended or encoded, as the cultural hegemony of the dominant class means the dominant hegemonic viewpoint appears to audiences as the normal, natural and reasonable position. Other audiences, though, may decode or interpret the same media texts differently, relating to their social situations, such as their social class, gender, ethnicity and personal experiences.

Hall's approach was applied by Morley (1999 [1980]), in a study of how audiences responded to or decoded media texts in the popular *Nationwide* BBC1 news programme which ran from 1969 to 1983. Morley suggested people might read, or decode and interpret, media texts in one of three ways:

1 The *preferred or dominant reading*. Audiences interpret or decode media texts in the same way they were encoded in the first place, and in the way media producers would prefer their audiences to believe. This might be, for example, a preferred view that most welfare benefit claimants are workshy 'scroungers'.

2 A *negotiated reading*. Audiences generally accept the preferred or dominant reading, but amend it to some extent, like finding exceptions, to fit their own beliefs and experiences. For example, they might accept most benefit claimants are probably scroungers, but not all as they know of some really deserving cases.

3 An *oppositional reading*. Audiences reject the preferred or dominant reading. For example, they reject the media view of 'scroungers', which they see as creating a moral panic over one or two cases of benefit fraud to discourage people from claiming benefits, when most people in the communities they see around them are really deserving as they face unemployment or disability or other adverse circumstances.

Morley suggests that the particular reading that audiences adopt will be influenced by their own knowledge and experiences, the social groups to which they belong, and their social characteristics such as their social class, gender or ethnic group.

Selective filtering – an interpretivist approach

The way encoding/decoding and reception analysis might take place in practice is shown by the interpretivist selective filtering approach. Klapper (1960) suggested, like Hall and Morley, that people have experiences of their own, make choices, and interpret, or decode, and filter what they read, see or hear in the media. Klapper suggests there are three filters that people apply in their approaches to and interpretations of the media:

1 *Selective exposure*. This filter means people must first choose what they wish to watch, read or listen to in the media, and they may choose only media messages that fit in with their existing views and interests. For example, they might simply refuse to watch a programme exposing alleged benefit fraudsters.

A preferred (or dominant) reading is one where audiences read (or decode and interpret) media texts (messages) in the way that those producing media content intended, and which they would prefer their audiences to believe.

A negotiated reading is one in which media audiences generally accept the preferred or dominant meaning of a media text, but amend it to some extent, like finding exceptions that fit their own beliefs, values and experiences.

An oppositional reading is one in which media audiences oppose or reject the preferred or dominant or interpretation of media content.

Not everyone views the same media content in the same way.

2   *Selective perception.* This filter means people will react differently to the same message, and may choose to accept or reject a media message depending on whether or not it fits in with their own views and interests. For example, people may simply ignore aspects of news reports that suggest welfare claimants are largely undeserving fraudsters.

3   *Selective retention.* This filter means people will forget material that is not in line with their views and interests, and will tend to remember only those media messages with which they generally agree.

An example of the application of these filters might be the way people respond to party political election broadcasts, depending on which political party they personally support, as suggested in the cartoon. During the Iraq war of 2003, the *Daily Mirror* passionately opposed the war, yet half its readers were in favour of it. The *Daily Mail* was a strong supporter of the war – but one-quarter of its readers opposed it. This suggests people may form their own views beyond what the media tell them.

The Glasgow Media Group

Philo (2008) of the GMG is very critical of the suggestion in the encoding/decoding and selective filtering approaches that audiences can make their own readings or interpretations of media texts, and that they are polysemic and can mean whatever audiences interpret them to mean. He accepts that audiences are active, and can in some cases be critical of media accounts. However, he stresses that GMG research over many years shows that the media has a great deal of power in forming the way audiences view the world, and that most people accept the dominant media account unless they have access to alternative forms of information. In a study of the 1984/5 miners' strike in Britain, when TV news repeatedly showed images of miners and pickets in violent clashes with police, Philo (1990) found that people from different class and political backgrounds saw these images and interpreted them in the same way that was being shown, and believed the media account that the miners and pickets were responsible for the trouble. This was true even among those who were sympathetic to the miners. The only exception to this was among those who had actually seen a picket line, who, regardless of their class or politics, rejected the television account. Philo's study suggested that the decoding and selective filtering approaches within the cultural effects model underestimate the serious extent of the media's ability to mould public understanding of social issues like the miners' strike. Philo concluded that the media did have an effect on how audiences think about the world, and that the great bulk of the audience relies on very traditional news sources to form their beliefs and understanding.

While people can be critical of media messages, the work of the GMG shows the media play a key role in focusing public interest on particular subjects through agenda-setting (see page 204), which also influences what we do *not* think about by removing issues from public discussion. Philo (2012) points out that it can be very difficult to criticize a dominant media account if there is little access to alternative sources of information, and, in most cases, the media's role in agenda-setting means those alternative sources are simply not available to most people.

The work of the GMG emphasizes that we should not underestimate the power of the media, or overestimate the capacity of audiences to make alternative readings to the preferred or dominant reading of media texts, as, over a period of time, agenda-setting and the continual drip-drip effect of the media encourage people to accept the preferred reading as the only reasonable one.

In summary, the cultural effects model recognizes:

- The power of the dominant class to influence the content of the media, which transmits a dominant ideology which most journalists share
- That the media, although they generally present a biased, ideological view of the world favouring the dominant class, don't always have the same effect on media audiences, as audiences actively interpret media content
- That the way audiences respond to media messages will be affected by a wide range of factors other than the media message itself, such as their social circumstances, personal experiences, education, social class and their values and beliefs
- That the media, over a long period of time, are likely to be influential as a key shaper of people's views and the way they think and behave, as they gradually persuade most people to accept that the dominant hegemonic media view represents a mainstream, common-sense view of the world.

Limitations of the cultural effects model

1 *Reception analysis and selective filtering* exaggerate the active role of media audiences. Philo (2008) points out that, while audiences can sometimes be active and critical, much of the work of the Glasgow Media Group (GMG) has produced extensive evidence of the power and influence of the media in forming the social attitudes and beliefs of audiences, and limiting their ability to resist media messages.
2 *It assumes media personnel like journalists work within the framework and assumptions of the dominant ideology.* This fails to recognize that journalists have some independence in their work, and can sometimes be very critical of the dominant ideology and the existing arrangements in society.
3 *It suggests the audience can, through selective filtering, have some control* over their response to media output, but long-term socialization by the media through repetitive messages may limit the ability of audiences to filter those messages, or enable them to do so only within the framework laid down by the media itself, giving an illusion of choice rather than a real choice. For example, an individual may mock or walk out of a televised political debate, but not actually ask themselves why there are only three political parties represented, or why those parties are only discussing certain topics and not others. Even in apparently open questioning programmes, like BBC1's *Question Time*, the panel being questioned and the answers they give may themselves limit the boundaries of the debate.

The uses and gratifications model

Of all the media effects models, this model assumes the media have the weakest effects, and the audience is the most active. It asks not so much what the media do to influence and manipulate audiences, but changes the emphasis to what audiences do with the media or use them for.

The uses and gratifications model starts with a view that media audiences are thinking, active and creative human beings, who *use* the media in various ways for their own various pleasures and interests (*gratifications*).

Media audiences use the media in a whole variety of ways. McQuail (1972) and Lull (1990, 1995) suggest a variety of uses and gratifications of the media. They may be used for:

- *Diversion:* for leisure, entertainment and relaxation, to escape from daily routines.
- *Personal relationships:* to keep up with family and friends, or companionship, through identification with media communities like *Coronation Street* or *EastEnders*, or situations and characters in reality TV shows, or as a conversation starter in group situations; new media through social networking sites like Facebook or chatrooms may be used to establish relationships with people you've never even met.

- *Personal identity*: to explore and confirm people's own identities or to seek out new sources of identity, or explore interests and values, for example keeping up with contemporary trends in cooking, gardening or music, fashion changes and social attitudes.
- *Surveillance*: to access information about things that might affect users, to find out about the world or to help them do things, accomplish something or make their minds up about issues that may affect them. This might involve keeping up with the news and current affairs, or seeking out information, either through traditional media or through new media by surfing the internet, social networking sites like Facebook, blogs, Wikipedia, and so on.
- *Background wallpaper*: while doing other things.

Park et al. (2009) used the uses and gratifications model in a web survey of those who were members of Facebook groups. They found the online groups were used to satisfy multiple needs: for entertainment and amusement (*diversion*), talking and meeting with others to achieve a sense of community and peer support on the particular topic of the group (*personal relationships*), maintaining and seeking out their personal status, as well as that of their friends (*personal identity*) and to receive information about events going on related to the group (*surveillance*).

This variety of uses of the media, providing a range of pleasures, means people make conscious choices, select and interpret what they watch on TV or read in newspapers, magazines and websites, and use them for an array of needs which they themselves decide upon. These different uses mean the effects of the media are likely to be different in each case, depending on what people are using the media for. We therefore can't assume that the uses and effects even of the same media content will be the same in every case. The uses and gratifications of the media are likely to vary from one individual to the next, and these will be influenced by factors such as their age, gender, social class or ethnicity, and their previous experiences, attitudes and values. For example, a soft-porn cable TV channel or a programme about cars is likely to have rather different uses and gratifications for men and for women. It therefore becomes very difficult to generalize about the effects of the media, as people will be selective in their exposure to, and perception and retention of, media content.

The uses and gratifications model also recognizes that audiences have some power to decide media content: a failure by media companies to satisfy audience pleasures will mean no viewers, listeners or readers, hence no advertisers, and therefore the companies or the particular channel, radio station, website or newspaper or magazine will risk going out of business.

Limitations of the uses and gratifications model

1 The model overestimates the power of the audience to influence media content. It also underestimates the power and influence of the media and media companies to shape and influence the choices people make and the pleasures they derive from the media. Media companies set the choices, and the media may create the different pleasures themselves, through devices like advertising.

People will use the media for different uses and gratifications.

Table 3.6 The effects of the media on audiences: a summary

	Hypodermic syringe model	Two-step flow model	Cultural effects model (including encoding/decoding, reception analysis, selective filtering and GMG)	Uses and gratifications model
Effect of media content on audiences	Direct and immediate effect on people's behaviour.	Indirect effects, through role of opinion leaders who make interpretations and pass them on to others.	Effects vary from one individual/group to the next. Can't generalize about media effects. People will decode and filter media messages, and may make negotiated or oppositional readings of media content through selective exposure, selective perception and selective retention. Long-term effects, though, through continuous exposure into acceptance of the dominant ideology.	Effects vary from one individual to the next. Can't generalize about media effects – it depends what people use media for.
View of audience	Passive and easily manipulated.	Not completely passive, as influenced only indirectly through opinion leaders and through discussion in social groups.	Not completely passive, as people may respond according to their own interpretations, social circumstances, experiences and beliefs, though these may themselves be influenced by the media over a period of time.	Active, and make conscious choices, and select and use media for their own pleasures.

2   It focuses too much on the use of the media by individuals. It doesn't allow for the group aspects of media audiences, unlike the two-step flow and cultural effects models, which recognize that people often relate to the media in social groups, and it is these group settings which will influence their uses and gratifications.

3   The focus on individual uses and gratifications ignores the wider social factors affecting the way audiences respond. Common experiences and common values may mean many people will respond in similar ways to media content.

Table 3.6 summarizes approaches to the media's effects on audiences.

Conclusion on media effects

There is no easy way of assessing the effects of the media on audiences, and the issue is fraught with a range of methodological difficulties. Postmodernists like Baudrillard point out, as discussed in Topic 2, that we are living in a media-saturated society, in which everyone's view of the world is increasingly formed through media imagery and media interpretations rather than through personal experience. Nonetheless, for many of us, our gender, ethnicity, sexuality, age, social class, whether we are able-bodied or disabled, our experiences of school, college, work, friends and family, and our political or religious beliefs, are likely to have some influence on how we select, interpret and respond to the media. The media are but one part – albeit a very important one – of the range of socializing experiences making up the jig-saw of human behaviour. For some people, the media may have very significant effects, for others a significant effect other than that intended, and for still others, they may have little effect. This becomes even clearer as we examine the discussion over the effects of the media on violence.

Activity

1   Outline and explain **three** needs that people might satisfy by using the media.
2   Outline and explain **three** reasons why the media may not affect their audiences.
3   Suppose you wanted to study the effects of a TV programme on an audience. Suggest how you might go about researching this.

4 Carry out a short survey, finding out what use people make of the media in their daily lives (using ideas from the uses and gratifications approach outlined above). You might also ask them about how much and in what ways they think they are influenced by the content of what they see in the media.

5 In the previous topic, there was a discussion of media representations and stereotyping. Select **two** media stereotypes drawn from two of the following: age, social class, ethnicity, gender, sexuality or disability. Describe what each of the stereotypes is, and then apply each of the theories discussed above to explain what effects the media might have on audience perceptions of the two groups you have identified.

6 Outline **three** ways that you think you are influenced by the content of what you see in the media.

Violence and the media

Violence, including pornography, on the internet, in computer games, in TV news reports and dramas, in books, and in films and DVDs, is now part of popular culture, and more people are exposed to such violence than ever before. The new media mean that violent imagery is found everywhere, and people can access it whenever they want, and it is almost impossible to control. Digital technology means media violence is now also interactive – people not only consume violent images, but can also take part in that violence as they play computer games or upload violent imagery to YouTube and other websites.

Questions about media violence and whether the media cause violent behaviour have been a feature of media discussion for almost as long as mass media have existed. Every so often, there's a new moral panic about the effects of violent video games, television shows, movies, song lyrics and music videos, and internet pornography, with suggestions of a society that is slipping into violent depravity, and consequent calls to do something about it.

Such media violence is often blamed for increasing crime and violence in society. A high-profile example of this was the murder in 1993 of 2-year-old James Bulger by two 10-year-old boys. The judge in the case commented: 'I suspect that exposure to violent video films may in part be an explanation.' This view was disputed by the police, who said they could find no evidence that videos (*Child's Play 3* in particular) viewed by the family could have encouraged the boys to batter a toddler to death, or that the boys had even seen the films mentioned.

Assertions, like that in the Bulger murder case, that media violence generates real-life violence are commonplace. Masses of research has been done to investigate whether such a link really exists, particularly in relation to children. Typical of this was the report by Newson (1994), which opened with a reference to the James Bulger murder the previous year, and asserted that violent videos could lead to violent actions. Newson's review gained enormous media attention, and was reported as conclusively establishing a link between video violence and real-world violence, a link that was allegedly even stronger than the one established between smoking and lung cancer. Similarly, a review by Anderson et al. (2003) claimed that research showed indisputably that media violence increased the likelihood of aggressive and violent behaviour, both immediately and in the long term. Although much of the experimental research claims to have established some links between viewing violent TV and violent behaviour, such claims have been very strongly disputed.

Cumberbatch (1994), for example, heavily criticized Newson's report, arguing that its findings were nothing more than speculation fuelled by the popular press. A review by Newburn and Hagell (1995) of more than 1,000 studies concluded that the link between media violence and violent behaviour was 'not proven', and children displaying tendencies to violence may have had such tendencies regardless of television viewing. A 2003 report by the Broadcasting Standards Commission found that children are sophisticated media users and are fully aware that television production is a process and that they are not watching reality, with the report concluding: 'They are able to make judgements … they are not blank sheets of paper on whom messages can be imprinted'. A review of the research evidence by Cumberbatch (2004) for the Video Standards Council found the evidence for the view that violence on television caused violence in society to be quite weak. Cumberbatch cites a review that claims there are only around 200 separate scientific studies that directly assess the effects of exposure to media violence, and that this evidence does not support the view that media violence causes aggression. Ferguson (2014) conducted research into the effects of violent movies and video games in the United States. Ferguson was critical of previous laboratory studies (considered shortly) and studied instances of violence in films between 1920 and 2005 compared with levels of real-life violence (as measured by homicide rates) in society. In a second study, consumption of violent video games was measured against youth violence rates in the previous 20 years. He found no evidence of long-term links between media violence and real-life violence, and indeed in both cases more violence on screen and more people playing violent video games was associated with a decline in violence in wider society.

Some competing claims about the effects of violence in the media

The uncertainty of the effects of violence in the media on violence in real life, despite the mass of research that has been carried out, is shown by the range of different and contradictory conclusions reached, which are summarized below:

1 *Copycatting* or *imitation*. Like a hypodermic syringe injecting a drug, exposure to media violence causes children to copy what they see and behave more aggressively in the real world (as shown in Badura et al.'s 'Bobo doll' experiments, discussed in the box on page 251).
2 *Catharsis*. Media violence does not make viewers more aggressive, but reduces violence as it allows people to live out their violent tendencies in the fantasy world of the media rather than in the real world.
3 *Desensitization*. Writers like Himmelweit et al. (1958) and Newson (1994) have suggested that repeated exposure of children to media violence has gradual 'drip-drip' long-term effects, socializing audiences into accepting a culture of violence in which violence is seen as a normal part of life and a legitimate means of solving problems. This means people become 'comfortably numb' – less sensitive and disturbed (desensitized) when they witness real-world violence, have less sympathy for its victims and have an increased risk of aggressive behaviour as adults.
4 *Sensitization*. Exposure to violence in the media can make people more sensitive to the consequences of violence, and less tolerant of real-life violence.

Activity

1 Write an explanation of how each of the four effects models outlined earlier – hypodermic syringe, two-step flow, cultural effects, and uses and gratifications – might view the effects of media violence.
2 Suggest a range of different ways in which people might interpret and respond to seeing violent content in the media – for example, switching the television off, walking out of a film, or going out and beating someone up.
3 Suggest reasons why children might be more vulnerable to media violence than adults.
4 The preceding section outlines a number of claims about the effects of violence in the media. Look at each of them, and try to criticize them in as many ways as you can, as in the following example:

Effect of violent media content *Desensitization*: repeated exposure to media violence increases the risk of aggressive behaviour, as people become less sensitive and disturbed when they witness real-world violence, have less sympathy for its victims, and become socialized into accepting violence as a normal part of life.	**Criticism** Violent media content might so horrify people and sensitize them to violence that they become opposed to it in real life.

5 *Media violence causes psychological disturbance in some children.* Watching media violence frightens young children, causing nightmares, sleeplessness, anxiety and depression, and these effects may be long-lasting.

6 *The exaggeration of the fear of violence.* Even if what is shown by the media will not make people violent, it may lead people to believe that we live in a violent society. Gerbner (1988), for example, found that those who watch more television, and are therefore exposed to greater amounts of violence, have exaggerated fears about crime. They are more likely to overestimate their risk of being victimized by criminals, to believe their neighbourhoods are unsafe, to see crime as a serious personal problem, and to assume the crime rate is increasing, even when it is not.

Methodological problems of researching media violence

Research into the area of whether violence in the media generates real-life violence is fraught with difficulty. Even if agreement is reached on what violence is, how can the effects be measured? Livingstone (1996) points out that any link between media violence and violent behaviour does not mean media violence *causes* the behaviour. For example, having shown that those who watch more violent television tend to be more aggressive, researchers must resolve three questions:

- Whether more aggressive people choose to watch violent programmes (i.e. selective exposure)
- Whether violent programmes make viewers aggressive (i.e. media effects)
- Whether certain social circumstances both make people more aggressive and lead them to watch more violent television (i.e. a common third cause).

Livingstone and Ferguson (2014) each point out that media effects models have tried to resolve these issues by using the experimental method of research, with research exposing small samples to media violence in artificial laboratory conditions to see whether they then behave violently. Bandura et al.'s (1961) 'Bobo Doll' experiments are typical of a lot of this experimental research (see box below). Apart from the ethical issues related to deliberately exposing people, particularly children, to violent imagery to test their reactions to it, there are also several questions about the validity of

---

The Bobo doll experiments

In one range of experiments conducted from the 1960s onwards, Bandura et al. (1961) exposed three groups of children to violent scenes involving attacks with a mallet on a large, self-righting inflatable plastic doll. One group was shown the doll being attacked by an adult in real life, another group was shown the same adult attacking the doll in a film, and the third group was shown the same scene involving cartoon characters. A fourth group of children was not exposed to any violent scenes. When the first three groups were later placed in a room with a similar doll, they acted in the same violent ways they had observed earlier. The fourth group of children who had not been exposed to any violent scenes displayed no violent behaviour. The conclusion drawn was that exposure to violence causes violence among those who see it.

findings obtained by such experimental research, as well as other problems of research into the effects of violence in the media.

1 *There is a problem with how 'media violence' is defined in the first place.* Boxing and wrestling, fights, shootings and murders in TV dramas, mass shoot-outs, huge body counts and destruction in Hollywood blockbusters, parents hitting children, cartoon fights, police attacking protesters, and news film of warfare all depict violent scenes, but they may not be seen by researchers in the same way. There is a difference between scenes showing real-life violence, fictional violence and cartoon violence, and it is likely that people are able to distinguish between them, and react in different ways to them.

2 *The hypodermic syringe model of media effects underlies much of the research.* This doesn't deal with how people interpret what they see, with the context in which they view the violence (such as discussing with others or the uses they are making of the media), or with the wider range of influences on people's behaviour, apart from the media.

3 *It is almost impossible to avoid the Hawthorne effect* – whereby people who are aware they are the subjects of research change their behaviour. Gauntlett (1998) criticizes experimental studies, like Bandura et al.'s, on the grounds that people may behave quite differently in real life, and they may alter their behaviour or stated attitudes to media violence as a response to being observed or questioned, and the presence, appearance and gender of an observer can affect behaviour, particularly in children. Ferguson (2014) points out that, in experimental situations, aggressive behaviour appears to participants to have the approval of the researchers themselves, who actually provide the opportunity for aggression.

4 *Laboratory experiments last for only a short time,* and therefore can only measure the immediate effects of media violence in the experimental situation. This doesn't mean these effects are long-lasting. Even if there is violent behaviour in the long term, a laboratory experiment wouldn't prove it was the effects of violence in the media that caused this, rather than other social explanations such as being brought up in a violent family or neighbourhood.

5 *Laboratory experiments are necessarily small-scale, using small samples.* This raises questions over whether the results can be applied to, or generalized to, the whole population.

6 *It is difficult to separate out the effects of violent media imagery from other possible causes of people's reactions.* Wider issues of socialization or peer group influences might mean that people react in different ways to the same violent images, even in experimental conditions.

7 *It is almost impossible to find a group that hasn't been exposed to media violence.* To test whether media violence causes violent behaviour, it is necessary to compare a group that has been exposed to media violence with one that hasn't. Yet, in a media-saturated society where everyone is constantly bombarded by media imagery from across the globe, it is almost impossible to find anyone who has not been exposed to violent media imagery of some kind.

8 *The new media makes it almost impossible to test media effects.* Livingstone points out that audiences increasingly surf across different media and watch bits of programmes across multiple TV channels. The meanings of whole programmes, such as the causes of violence or the final punishment meted out to the violent bad guys, may not actually be watched. This makes it extremely difficult to know in the real world what media are watched, what violence people are exposed to, the context in which it occurs, and what meanings audiences give to what they see.

The **Hawthorne effect** is when the presence of the researcher, or the group's (or individual's) knowledge that it has been specially selected for research, changes the behaviour of the group or individual, raising problems with the validity of the research.

Conclusion on violence and the media

Despite all the research, combined with a range of methodological problems, there is little reliable and undisputed evidence about whether violence in the media leads to an increase in aggressive behaviour. The simplest answer to the question 'Does media violence cause violent behaviour?' is 'We don't really know.' Gauntlett (1998) suggests that one conclusion to be drawn from the failure to identify the direct effects of media upon people's behaviour, despite detailed analysis of hundreds of research studies, is that they are simply not there to be found.

Practice questions

1   Outline and explain **two** difficulties sociologists may face in assessing whether the media have an effect on audiences.   **(10 marks)**

2   Read **Item A** below and answer the question that follows.

Item A

The effects of the media on audiences are influenced by whether audiences are seen as mainly active or passive consumers of media content. The hypodermic syringe model, for example, suggests audiences are passive and the media have direct effects on their behaviour, while others argue that media audiences are more active, and may ignore, interpret, criticize or reject media messages.

Applying material from **Item A,** analyse **two** differences between passive audience and active audience approaches to the effects of the media on people's attitudes and behaviour.

                                                                                                       (10 marks)

3   Read **Item B** below and answer the question that follows.

Item B

Violence in the media is now a major part of popular culture, for example in computer games, in TV programmes and movies, and on websites, and more people are exposed to violent media imagery than ever before. Some have concluded that such media violence is responsible for more real-life violence in society, though the reliability of the evidence on which this conclusion is based is widely disputed by many sociologists.

Applying material from **Item B** and your knowledge, evaluate the view that exposure to media violence may make people behave in a more violent way and create more real-life violence in society.   **(20 marks)**

Topic 6

SPECIFICATION AREA

The new media and their significance for an understanding of the role of the media in contemporary society

The new media

'The new media' refers to the screen-based, digital (computer) technology involving the integration of images, text and sound, and to the technology used for the distribution and consumption of the new digitized media content which has emerged in the late twentieth and early twenty-first centuries. These include computers, tablets, smartphones and the internet, electronic e-books, CDs, DVDs and mp3, videos and music downloaded onto mobile phones and mp3 players, email, blogs (internet diaries/journals), user-generated media content through websites such as Facebook and YouTube, and interactive video/computer games on PlayStations, Wii systems and Xboxes. Digital cable and satellite TV now offer hundreds of channels, and consumers can customize television viewing to their own individual tastes, using digiboxes, DVD recorders, catch-up TV sites (like the BBC's iPlayer), internet downloads of films to hard drives, or downloads from sites such as iTunes.

While the traditional or 'old' media involve different devices for different media content – like printed format for books, newspapers and magazines, radios and mp3 players to listen to music and radio programmes, televisions to watch shows, and phones to make calls – the new media technology often involves technological convergence, where a single device combines various media technologies. For example, the latest media technology, such as smartphones and tablet computers, like the iPad, enable users, on a single device, to make phone calls, read books, send

The new media involve digital (computer) screen-based technology, often integrating many uses into a single device, as in Apple's iPhone and iPad shown here. Traditional print and TV are now competing with the internet, as shown by the BBC website pictured here

text messages and emails, take photos and record videos and send them to friends or upload them to internet sites, surf the internet, play music, watch films and TV, listen to the radio, consult maps, and hundreds of other applications. Likewise, businesses and advertisers are able to communicate with millions of people at the same time through a single device. Livingstone and Bovill (1999) suggest such converging screen technologies may be contributing to the blurring of boundaries between traditionally distinct activities such as gaining or searching for information, education, working and playing games and other forms of entertainment, as people constantly switch between these different activities, or combine them at the same time.

Jenkins (2008) argues that the process of technological convergence, bringing together multiple media in the same device, has led to a much more significant process of cultural convergence, whereby consumers are encouraged to seek out and share new information and make connections between dispersed contents from a range of media, which the new technology makes much easier than it ever was in the past.

Features of the new media

The features of the new media discussed below also outline their main differences from the traditional media. The traditional media, like the terrestrial TV channels (such as BBC 1 and 2, ITV 1, and Channels 4 and 5), radio stations and mass-circulation printed national and Sunday newspapers and magazines, delivered their content through separate media platforms, and communicated uniform messages in a one-way process to large mass audiences. These audiences were all assumed to be homogeneous (possessing many of the same characteristics and interests). It was basically media based on a 'take it or leave it' approach, with little consumer participation or control. The technological and cultural convergence considered in the previous section has changed the way people use or consume media, with consumer needs and interests driving media content, rather than it simply being in the control of media owners and editors.

Lister et al. (2003) suggest what distinguishes the 'new' from traditional forms of (mass) media are five main concepts – digitality, interactivity, hypertextuality, dispersal, and virtuality.

Digitality

Digitality essentially means 'using computers', where all data (text, sound and pictures) are converted into numbers (binary code), which can then be stored, distributed and picked up via screen-based products, like mobile phones, DVDs, digital TVs and computers.

Interactivity

Interactivity means consumers have an opportunity to engage or interact with a variety of media, and, because of convergence, to do this at the same time, creating their own material, customizing media to their own wishes, with much greater choice compared with the passive consumption and 'take it or leave it' features of the traditional media. This interactivity on the internet has been referred to as Web 2.0, to distinguish it from the original Web 1, where users were limited to the passive viewing of content that was created for them. In Web 2.0, users collaborate and interact with one another in information- and file/video-sharing, and user-generated content, such as Wikipedia and YouTube, and through other social media such as blogs and social networking sites like Facebook and Twitter. This interactivity is also found in new digital TVs ('press the red button'), and particularly those which are also connected to the internet.

Jenkins (2008) suggests this interactivity has led to:

- **Participatory culture**: where once the media was divided into the two separate roles of editors and journalists who produced media content, and passive audiences who consumed it, producers and consumers now interact with each other. Consumers produce media content which producers consume and then incorporate into new media texts. There has, in other words, been a shift from information-reception to information-production on the part of media audiences. Jenkins suggests this gives consumers more control over media content, and he emphasizes that the circulation of new media content depends heavily on consumers' active participation.

Cultural convergence refers to the way new media users engage with a range of media content delivered in a variety of ways, and the ways they seek out, share, and make connections between this content, and make sense of it.

Participatory culture refers to a media culture in which the public do not act as consumers only, but also as contributors or producers of media content. This new culture, as it relates to the internet, has been described as Web 2.0.

- **Collective intelligence**: Using the new media has become a collective process, with interactivity creating a 'buzz' between users. In the new interactive media with a vast range of information from across the globe at people's disposal, Jenkins points out that 'none of us can know everything; each of us knows something; and we can put the pieces together if we pool our resources and combine our skills' (2004: 4). He calls this 'collective intelligence', and suggests this is a new source of media power, which potentially represents an alternative to that of the media owners – the Lords of the Global Village – which was discussed in Topic 1.

> **Collective intelligence** refers to the way users of new media collaborate and share knowledge, resources and skills to build a shared or group intelligence that is greater than that of any one individual.

Web 2.0 combines these features of participatory culture and collective intelligence, whereby the internet becomes a global platform for the collaboration of a huge range of ideas and information. Very simple examples of this might be Amazon's user reviews, or TripAdvisor (www.tripadvisor.co.uk), where consumers participate in writing reviews and providing advice on hotels, resorts, flights, holiday rentals, holiday packages and travel guides they have used or visited. These build a collective intelligence about particular items or holiday services, and counter the power of the advertising companies. Websites of user groups who share similar interests or experiences – like heart disease, diabetes, etc. – and in the process build their knowledge and skills, provide further examples.

Hypertextuality

This refers to the links which form a web of connections to other bits of information, which give users a way of searching, interacting with and customizing the media for their own use.

Dispersal

This refers to the way the new media have become less centralized, more adapted to individual choices, with a huge growth of media products of all kinds, which have become a part of everyday life. The routine use of the internet for information, shopping and entertainment, email, laptop and tablet computers, interactive digital TV, social networking sites, downloadable content onto mobile phones, and podcasts to mp3 players all show how the media have penetrated into the fabric of everyday life. The production of media content itself is now becoming more generally dispersed throughout the population, rather than restricted to media professionals. For example, people are now making their own videos and posting them on the internet. In 2014, over an hour and a half of user-generated video was uploaded to YouTube every second, or 100 hours every minute, with over 6 billion hours of video viewed every month – the equivalent of almost an hour for every person on

---

Activity

1 Go to www.en.wikipedia.org and look up 'digital media', 'interactivity', 'hypertext' and 'virtual reality'. Follow the hypertext links given in Wikipedia and give two examples of contemporary media that use each of these.
2 Use Wikipedia to find out what a wiki is, and explain in what senses Wikipedia is an example of a wiki, and what problems this might pose for the validity of the information given.
3 Using Wikipedia, find out who Jean Baudrillard was, what he meant by a 'media-saturated society' and what he said about the first Gulf War.
4 Go to www.uk.youtube.com, do a search on sociology, and report your findings on any two sociology videos.
5 Explore the extent and significance of the blogosphere, by going to www.en.wikipedia.org/wiki/Blogosphere. Identify three different types of blogs, and what people use their blogs for. See if you can find any evidence for the use of blogging by large media businesses, either in the traditional or new media.
6 Go to www.news.bbc.co.uk and watch the UK news headlines online, making a note of the latest headline stories. Now do the same with www.sky.com. Compare the two sets of news stories, and whether they seem to be covering the same material. What might this outline to you about how the new media influence our views of the world?

The **blogosphere** is a collective term to describe all the online diaries or reports known as blogs.

Earth. Technorati (www.technorati.com) estimated there were 164 million blogs – internet diaries/ journals – in the blogosphere in 2011, and this didn't include those not in the English language, and blogs are beginning to rival traditional journalism as sources of information and news.

Virtuality

This refers to the various ways people can now immerse themselves in wholly unreal interactive experiences in virtual worlds created by new technology (as in computer games), and also create for themselves imaginary identities in online communication and networking sites, like Twitter, YouTube and Facebook.

Who uses the new media?

The new media are beginning to overtake the traditional media as a means of mass communication. Internet use across Europe is now around 14 hours a week per person, compared to around 12 hours a week of TV viewing, according to a Microsoft survey. In 2014 in the UK, around 84 per cent of households had internet access, and 80 per cent of the population used the internet; 48 per cent of all adults had a social networking profile, most of them on Facebook, which was the third most frequently used site after Google and Yahoo! sites. People spent most time on Google sites (mainly YouTube). People in the UK spend an average of about 27 hours a week watching TV, compared to around 8 hours a week online using a PC or laptop and a fixed internet connection, though this is an underestimate as many use devices other than a PC or laptop to access the internet, particularly those in younger age groups who are the higher users. On average, over half of adults' waking hours are spent using media and communications services. The traditional media, like newspapers and TV, have difficulty competing with the internet for advertising income, and advertisers now spend more on internet than traditional media advertising. Many national newspapers and TV stations now have their own websites, reaching millions more people than their printed papers or TV channels do. The importance of advertising income means that increasingly websites have to appeal to mass audiences to attract advertisers. Spam (unasked-for electronic bulk messages via texting or email) is becoming a cheap means for advertisers to reach masses of people.

Stratification in the new media

Users of the new media are not a homogeneous group, sharing the same social characteristics. As in most areas of social life, there is also stratification in cyberspace, with media users differentiated by social class, gender, age and location. Jones (2010) suggests that patterns in internet access and use tend to reflect and amplify existing inequalities, with particular concern regarding some of the more vulnerable groups, such as poorer families with young children, the unemployed, the physically and socially isolated, the elderly, disabled people and those living in rural and remote areas. Dutton and Blank (2011) found 91 per cent of those with higher education had used the internet, compared to 34 per cent of those with no formal qualifications. According to the Office for National Statistics, in 2014, more than 38 million adults in Great Britain used the internet every day, but 6.4 million adults had never used the internet, and about 16 per cent of households in Great Britain did not have home internet access. Helsper (2011) showed that it is the healthy, young, well-educated people with higher incomes and professionals who had taken up broadband and were the most likely to be frequent internet users, while those with health problems, the elderly, those without educational qualifications, low-income earners and those in manual occupations were left behind. Dutton and Blank show some of these differences in internet use between social groups, as illustrated in figure 3.2.

Social class inequalities

Broadly, the middle and upper classes are the biggest users of the new media, as they can more easily afford it. Figure 3.2 shows the rate of internet use decreased in line with socio-economic

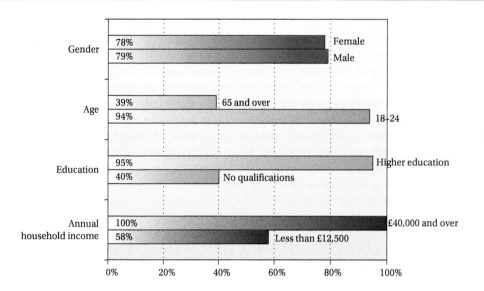

Figure 3.2 Internet users by socio-economic and demographic factors in 2013

Source: compiled with data from Dutton and Blank (2013)

status. Jones points out that around a third of the population, marked by socio-economic disadvantage intermingled with age, is more digitally excluded than the rest of the population. Those in the poorest social classes have the least access to the internet and other new media at home, as they are less able to afford it, and 65 per cent of those who are not online are in the bottom two social classes. Dutton and Blank (2013) point out that internet users remain disproportionately likely to be young, well educated and wealthy.

There is, then, evidence of a digital divide, between the information-rich digital haves, who have access to online information and services, and the information-poor digital have-nots. Helsper (2011) showed that a digital underclass was forming in Britain, with those who have lower education levels and no employment lagging far behind other groups in their access to the internet. She found such disadvantaged groups, even when they have managed to secure access, often lack the confidence and skills to fully engage with the opportunities available online. Livingstone and Wang (2011) suggest this situation may be worsening, as they found people's progress in acquiring digital skills had ceased to improve, with those from lower social classes particularly at risk. The internet is now such a normal part of life that those who lack internet access, or the skills and confidence to use it experience a form of social exclusion based on information and communication poverty which prevents them from participating in the normal activities of society.

This class difference in internet access extends across all the new media. For example, while most people now own a mobile phone, the middle class are more likely to have them on contracts than on pay-as-you-go (PAYG), and to have a smartphone, and that phone is more likely to be an Apple iPhone than any other make. BlackBerry handsets were until recently particularly popular among younger working-class adults and teens, partly because of the free BlackBerry Messenger service, and cheaper phone and network costs, with a PAYG BlackBerry costing around one quarter of the cost of a PAYG iPhone. Different social classes tend to use different social networks. For example, LinkedIn (http://uk.linkedin.com) is the social network of the elite, with nearly half of users saying they earn more than £50,000 a year, compared to about a quarter of Twitter users and a fifth of Facebook users.

> The **digital divide** refers to the gap between those people with effective access to the digital and information technology making up the new media and those who lack such access.

> A **digital underclass** is a group of people, mainly those from the lowest social classes, the least educated and the unemployed, who are increasingly disadvantaged in comparison to those who have full access to and use of the internet and other digital media.

Age differences

There is a substantial generation gap in access to and use of the new media. This is not surprising since, as Boyle (2007) points out, younger people have grown up with the latest developments in the new media, have learnt to use the internet at home, at school and from their peers, and are consequently more media-savvy than previous generations. They are, for example, more likely to consume media in a variety of formats, such as watching TV on their mobiles, laptops and iPads and tablets, rather than just on a TV set, and those aged 16–24 are over ten times more likely to go online via a mobile than those aged 55+. Young people have the highest levels of internet access and use, and this declines among older age groups.

However, there is also evidence of clear social inequality among young people. Jones (2010) points out that while young people have the highest levels of access and use, around 10 per cent of 16- to 24-year-olds from the most disadvantaged social backgrounds are likely to remain relatively infrequent users of the internet.

Ofcom (2012, 2014) found young people (16–24), compared to older people:

- Are greater internet users and spend more time online.
- Are more likely to have the internet at home.
- Are more likely to own and use a smartphone.
- Are more likely to use a mobile phone to go online.
- Are more attached to, aware of and confident in using new media technology.
- Tend to use the new media differently from older people: they are more likely to see the internet as a form of fun, relaxation and a pastime, through activities such as taking photos and videos, listening to music, playing games, watching video clips and webcasts, surfing the internet, and, particularly, social networking. They are also more likely to use the internet for work/studies information, entertainment and leisure information.
- Are more likely to get their news on mobile devices (rather than from TV, radio or newspapers).

Gender differences

There are some significant differences between men and women in the way they use and relate to the new media. For example, Ofcom (2011, 2012, 2014) found:

- Fixed games consoles and tablet computers are more popular among males than females, but e-readers are more popular among women for their reading
- Men spend three times as much time as women watching videos online
- There is a higher take-up of smartphones among males
- More females than males reported 'high addiction' to their mobile phones
- Young women make significantly more calls than young men and they also send and receive more texts
- Women are less likely to use the internet than men within a given three-month period, but women are slightly more likely than men to use social networking sites
- Women are less likely to use the internet to relax, or to keep up to date with news.

Li and Kirkup (2007), in a study of gender differences in the use of, and attitudes towards, the internet among Chinese and British students, suggested there are two global gender-based cultures with respect to the internet. They found that, although there are an increasing number of women going online and the gender gap in internet use may be narrowing, actual behaviour once online, such as the websites visited and reasons for searching, are still gendered. They found significant gender differences in internet experience, attitudes, usage and self-confidence. Men in both countries, compared to women, were:

- More likely to have positive attitudes towards the internet, spent more time on it, and used it more extensively
- More self-confident about their computer skills than women, and were more likely to express the opinion that using computers was a male activity and skill
- More likely to use email and chatrooms, and played more computer games
- Were less likely to use the internet for studying.

Li and Kirkup found women students underestimated their ability to use computers and the internet. For example, they more frequently reported that they had difficulty performing information-searching tasks, and that they were likely to get lost when searching the internet, although they actually performed in tests as well as their male counterparts. British women students were more likely than men to browse the internet for research and study. Li and Kirkup's research suggests that British women students still regard the internet more as a tool rather than as the toy for personal fun and pleasure that men do.

New media and rapid social change

It should be noted that many of the social class, age and gender differences in new media use identified above are in general diminishing rapidly each year. More and more households and people are getting connected and using new media every year, and the devices they are using to go online are forever changing and expanding. New media are penetrating so deeply into everyday life that it seems likely that in the near future almost everyone will be using new media technology, even if they are reluctant to do so, as an increasing number of services are only available online.

If you want to find contemporary data about the changing use of new media, who uses it and who doesn't, what they use it for and differences between users, it is worth taking a look at the Oxford Internet Surveys website (http://oxis.oii.ox.ac.uk) or at Ofcom's annual *Communications Market Report* (http://stakeholders.ofcom.org.uk/market-data-research/market-data/communications-market-reports)

Location, and the global digital divide

The most significant digital divide in terms of location is that between the information-rich and the information-poor countries, and the existence of a global digital underclass. The new media, and particularly the internet, are used most heavily and by the largest proportion of people in the Western world. Many of those living in the world's poorest countries lack access due to poverty. The poorest countries lack the resources to build the digital networks required, and private businesses

---

The digital divide

According to www.internetworldstats.com, between 2000 and June 2015 world internet usage grew by around 900 per cent, and, by the end of June 2015, around 3.2 billion people used the internet – only about 45 per cent of the world's population. Europe and North America made up 28 per cent of the world's internet users, even though these areas comprise just 16 per cent of the world's population. This contrasts with 9.5 per cent of the world's internet users in Africa, which makes up about 16 per cent of the world's population. This evidence suggests a clear global digital divide in terms of access to the new media.

Figure 3.3 shows the digital divide in internet access at the end of June 2014; even in Europe, there are divisions between the 95 per cent of people in Norway having internet access and the 51 per cent in Romania.

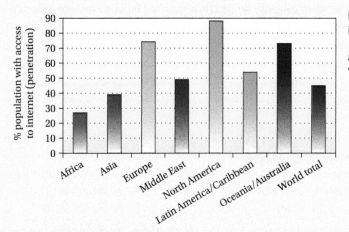

Figure 3.3 Worldwide internet access, June 2015

Source: compiled with data from www.internetworldstats.com.

won't provide them as there aren't enough customers willing or able to pay enough for them to make a profit. Language and cultural barriers can also be a problem, as about 85 per cent of websites are in English, and most web content is generated in the USA and Western Europe. This creates global inequalities, and a new digital underclass who are excluded from the new media. The box 'The digital divide' illustrates this.

The effects of new media and new technologies on traditional or 'old' media

All the traditional media companies, like News Corporation and the terrestrial TV and newspaper companies, are massively involved in the new media – part of the horizontal integration and cross-media ownership that was discussed in Topic 1. This means there is a form of *synergy* between the traditional and new media, as they support and interact with one another. Newspapers, for example, often refer readers to their websites and many printed newspaper reports now appear first on those websites.

The most obvious impact of the new media and new technologies on the traditional media is the huge decline in printed newspaper sales, and a general downwards trend in viewing of TV news bulletins. This contrasts with a huge increase in web traffic, and all the major TV channels, magazines and newspapers now have related websites, whose online readerships far exceed the circulation of their printed formats. There is therefore some convergence between the traditional and new media, as is explored further in this section.

Changes influencing traditional media

Some of the changes arising from the development and growth of new media which have had an impact on the traditional media include:

- Cheaper, more mobile and widely accessible digital technologies, such as smartphones, smaller video cameras, satellite video phones and the range of internet-based technologies like email and social networking sites
- Technologies expanding 'live' coverage, such as mobile phone picture and video recording at the scene of a news event, and their transmission to news organizations
- Use of the new media to form the content of the traditional media, with newspapers, magazines and TV using the internet, including the blogosphere and citizen journalism, for research and ideas, and bloggers and other citizen journalists publishing original news reports, commentary and criticism, which may get included in mainstream media reports
- Online criticisms of mainstream news output
- The development of online newsrooms in traditional media
- Engagement with the interactive aspects of new media, such as email, social networks, professional journalist blogs and online feedback on traditional media articles.

The effects of changes on traditional media

Bivens (2008) suggests the developments outlined in the previous section have led to three significant changes in the traditional journalism of the 'old' media:

1 *Shifts in traditional news flow cycles.* News production depends on a flow of reports of newsworthy items from individuals and groups. The rise of citizen journalism, whereby members of the public – rather than professional journalists and media companies – collect, report and spread news stories, has created not only a huge increase in the quantity of information, but also an increased speed of flow of news. An article or item posted by an online journalist or blogger in one part of the world immediately becomes part of a global system accessible to anyone with a laptop or smartphone. The traditional media (as well as new media organizations)

no longer control the flow of information, and need to respond regularly to this increased flow of news from citizen journalists. This increased flow means journalists have less time to process the news, particularly within the 24-hour cycles of traditional print media, and the much shorter cycles of TV rolling news.

2   *Heightened accountability.* Citizen journalism has made traditional media and media organizations much more accountable to the public, as their reports are scrutinized by the public, and responded to or criticized through online blogs or comments pages on online newspapers, or television web pages, or flak-producing campaigns if they produce distorted, biased or inaccurate reports. News organizations are now more aware of their accountability to audiences, and often use their related websites to offer more interactivity and transparency.

3   *Evolving news values.* Some important news values influencing what to report and what not to, include importance, interest, entertainment and proximity, along with the sense of immediacy (being there now – live!) reinforced by the impact of photos and video. In the highly competitive media market, all media need to give people the impression that they are, at all times, on top of everything that's going on around the world. The new media have enabled news organizations, including traditional TV media, to provide more immediacy through instantaneous live coverage, provided by citizen journalists from areas like battle-zones which traditional journalists might find hard to access, or through technology like video phones. News values may be changing, as traditional media are incorporating 'non-professional' material, like mobile phone and YouTube videos and citizen reports.

The Reuters Institute for the Study of Journalism (2015) suggested the growing use of new media technology like smartphones and tablets to access news has meant that traditional news outlets, like TV and printed newspapers, face an increasingly uphill struggle to make money, as many of those accessing news are via referrals from social media on smartphones and tablets. This leads to a growing concentration of power in the hands of the providers of new media technology platforms, giving corporations like Facebook, Google and Apple increasing control over news agendas at the expense of traditional news organizations.

The reduced power of ownership? Agenda-setting and a shift from top-down control to cultural chaos

McNair (2006) suggests the new media have meant that elite groups have less power to influence news agendas. Top-down control by media owners, managers and editors and by primary definers (see page 210), as discussed in Topics 1 and 3, is replaced by what he calls 'cultural chaos' – more anarchy, disruption, dissent, openness and diversity. The balance of power of media control is shifting, as citizen journalists – through blogging, tweeting, the uploading of videos to YouTube, through videos and photos sent to traditional media, and through social networks such as Facebook – have growing power to influence the news that is reported by traditional media. This has undermined the influence of media owners, and has given more power to ordinary people to spread their interpretations of events that happen in the world.

Agenda-setting, as Philo (2012) suggests, means the media can influence what we do *not* think about, by removing issues from public discussion by simply avoiding them. He points out that it can be very difficult to criticize a dominant media account – and most of these are still provided for most people by TV and newspapers – if there is little access to alternative sources of information. However, citizen journalism has a rising capacity to shape traditional news agendas. These online reports are potentially viewed by huge global audiences, and traditional media cannot afford to ignore items which are made newsworthy by citizen journalists. For example, Bivens cites BBC deputy editor Daniel Pearl's claim that the blogosphere had 'an immediate impact on Newsnight's running order'.

Bivens, though, suggests that this shift in power is only slight, and elite groups are adapting and will likely continue to find ways of shaping news output. She suggests news organizations retain the power to limit debate and preserve narrow news agendas, and points to the way dissenting views and radical critiques of both foreign and domestic policies remain rare among mainstream news accounts despite their popularity online. Philo's study of the way the traditional media responded to the global banking crisis from 2008 onwards (see pages 188 and 204) is a good illustration of this.

The rise of churnalism and infotainment

The rise of churnalism (see page 211) and infotainment (see page 190) in the traditional media is a consequence of cost-cutting by media owners, and their attempts to attract audiences and advertisers in a hugely competitive global media market. This is coupled with the time pressures arising from the intensity of 24/7 rolling news in the context of ever-expanding new media, and the changing news flow cycles discussed above.

Changing relationships with media audiences

As discussed above, the new media have forced traditional media to be more accountable and responsive to their audiences, allowing more interactive comment, feedback and complaints, and more personalized, customized content suited to their tastes. They have also had to become more responsive in the way content is delivered, such as through multiple delivery devices, like smartphones, laptops and tablets, and interactive/internet-enabled TVs, and for multiple formats – for example, Twitter, Facebook, SMS, and websites, with everything available, everywhere and at all times suited to their audiences. New media technology, such as smartphones and tablets, are increasingly becoming the preferred choice of readers and viewers, particularly younger ones, to consume news. They also want to 'snack' more, in terms of both the time they spend and the type of content they consume, and they want to do so more frequently throughout the day, rather than being dependent on fixed-time television and printed newspapers. This changing way consumers access content and news was reflected in the launching in the UK in 2015 of Apple News, a news app which aggregates digital news media, in partnership with fourteen UK newspaper and magazine publishers. This reflected the need for traditional media owners to ensure they adapted to the changing needs of consumers and how they consume content. The Reuters Institute (Newman and Levy 2014) found over one-third of 18–24-year-olds in ten developed countries say they now use smartphones as their primary means of accessing the news. This partly explains why traditional media are increasingly turning to infotainment, websites and apps to supplement their traditional printed or televised formats.

The significance of the new media in contemporary society

Curran and Seaton (2010) suggest there are two general views on the new media's significance in contemporary society:

1   The *cultural optimist view* – which sees the new media as playing a positive role in society. This is held by neophiliacs – those who like, rapidly embrace and adapt to new technology and are avid users of new media.
2   The *cultural pessimist view* – which has a more negative view of the impact of new media in society.

The cultural optimist/neophiliac view of the new media

More informed consumers, wider choices and more user participation

In July 2013, UK media audiences had a choice of over 500 digital terrestrial, satellite and cable TV channels, and, according to Netcraft (http://news.netcraft.com/), there were about 172 million active websites of all kinds in September 2015. News, information, shopping, a wide range of financial transactions and social networking are all now available online, and accessible through a range of different devices. Consumers can now access information, complaints and reviews about practically anything that interests them, making them better informed and offering them greater choice than ever before in history. Interactive digital TV, online news sites, blogging, tweeting and citizen journalism, video- and photo-sharing websites like YouTube, and social networking sites are all giving consumers more opportunities to participate in using and producing media content. User-generated sites like Blogger (www.blogger.com), WordPress (www.wordpress.com) or Trip Advisor (www.tripadvisor.co.uk) enable ordinary people, rather than just professional experts, to offer advice and make online reports and criticisms, and to learn from the experiences of fellow consumers in all spheres of life.

Greater democracy

Democracy here refers to two aspects:

1 *The narrower political aspect*, concerned with the empowerment of people – their rights and ability to control, influence, protest at and organize against governments, and their opportunities to initiate change in society.
2 *The wider conception of democracy* as the right to freedom of ideas and expression.

Neophiliacs argue that the new media can give more power to ordinary people, and have made positive contributions to building more democratic societies.

The new media have meant there is now a vast ocean of information available to all, and, as McNair (2006) says, 'information, like knowledge, is power'. McNair argues the internet means anyone – not just large media corporations – with a computer or smartphone and an internet connection can set up and maintain a blog or website, which can be visited and viewed by anyone, anywhere in the world, at any time. There are greater opportunities to report, criticize and comment than ever before. For example, ordinary people can now publish their thoughts on Twitter (www.twitter.com), attack those in power on Blogger (www.blogger.com) and report on events excluded from other mainstream media by sending their own news stories and photos to citizen journalism sites like Demotix (www.demotix.com), or uploading videos shot on mobile phones to YouTube.

Social movements and campaigns now use the new media to spread their ideas, build support and coordinate protests, like a kind of rolling conversation that can build up over time. Protest and campaigning websites – for example, Occupy (www.occupytogether.org), ROAR (www.roarmag.org), ALL OUT (www.allout.org), 38 degrees (www.38degrees.org.uk), Avaaz (www.avaaz.org/en), Wikileaks (www.wikileaks.org), the Coalition of Resistance (www.coalitionofresistance.wordpress.com) and numerous Facebook groups, such as Europeans against the political system (www.facebook.com/eatps) – have enabled protest groups to reach a worldwide audience very rapidly in ways never before possible, and have promoted a culture of questioning, challenging and holding to account elite hierarchies, and the power, authority and secrecy of governments and other organizations. For example, in 2014 Sheffield United Football Club were forced (on the club's own admission) by an intensive social media campaign and online petition to withdraw an offer to allow former player and convicted rapist Ched Evans to train with them. This has put more power into the hands of ordinary people and makes those holding power more accountable for their actions and decisions.

Public outrage can bring corporate and government websites to their knees, by 'denial of service' cyberattacks which flood websites with such huge amounts of traffic that they slow them down to such an extent that they crash and become unavailable to legitimate visitors.

Bloggers and other citizen journalists can exert a major influence on the mainstream media's content and agenda, by using social media to post their own reports or by responding to what might be seen as biased or distorted mainstream media output. This makes it increasingly difficult for mainstream newspapers, TV channels and websites to ignore stories they might have dropped in the past. For example, video shot on a mobile phone by a protester at a London demonstration in April 2009 provided evidence that it was police brutality that contributed to the death of an English newspaper vendor, Ian Tomlinson, which the police had tried to cover up before the video emerged. This forced the mainstream media to accept the protesters' version of events, rather than that of the police. As McNair puts it, 'neither editors nor proprietors call the shots on content any more'.

The new media, particularly the social networking media of Web 2.0, have become key tools in mobilizing people to fight against oppressive and corrupt regimes across the world, with some regimes toppled by revolutions driven in part by the fast-acting power of the internet, Twitter, YouTube and mobile phone technology. The mobile phone has become one of the most potent weapons in the hands of protesters, as images are uploaded and rebroadcast to a global audience of millions. For example, new media and new technology were crucial in the 'Arab Spring' – a series of uprisings against oppressive and dictatorial regimes in the Arab world which began in Spring 2011. Video and photos shot on mobile phones showing evidence of violent acts of repression, torture,

How might mobile phone technology be used to give more power to ordinary people, and expose wrongdoing by the already powerful?

atrocities and killing of protesters by the regimes were uploaded to YouTube and viewed by global audiences and the newsrooms of global media. Twitter and Facebook were also used to coordinate and publicize protests. These uprisings were consequently sometimes referred to as the 'Facebook revolutions'. In March 2012, *Kony 2012*, a 30-minute YouTube video exposing the plight of children in Uganda at the hands of the warlord Joseph Kony (http://youtu.be/c_Ue6REkeTA), rapidly went viral, and was viewed 100 million times in the first week. Such examples show how the new media can be used by those wishing to protest and receive coverage outside the control of established media and media organizations.

More access to all kinds of information

As seen in Topic 2, everyone now has access to huge amounts of information from all over the world, including access to high culture which was formerly limited to educated elites.

Social media sites enable news and information articles from a wide range of sources to be brought to the attention of others who may have missed them. This potentially gives people more power in society and in their daily lives, as they can gain access to information for themselves rather than relying on others for it. An everyday example might be people being able to gain more information about their health conditions by sharing information with online patient groups, or being able to check symptoms of illness online, through websites like NHS Choices (www.nhs.uk/Pages/HomePage.aspx), Netdoctor (www.netdoctor.co.uk) or Patient UK (www.patient.co.uk), and also to check any risks associated with prescribed medicines they have been given. This gives patients more power through information rather than them being solely dependent on doctors. Such information, and consequent empowerment of individuals, is available on practically all aspects of everyday life.

The world becomes a global village

As discussed in Topic 2, 'the global village' is a term used by McLuhan (1962) to describe how the digitized new media collapse space and time barriers in human communication, and allow users from around the world to connect and interact with each other instantaneously, making the world like one village or community. In this global village, the new media promote cultural diversity, national barriers are reduced, the boundaries between the local and the global are blurred, and different peoples and cultures are brought together, promoting greater understanding between different cultures.

Social life and social interaction is enhanced

Postmodernists see the new media as contributing to social diversity, and enabling people to share in globalized cultures, and to build and shape their identities and to make lifestyle choices in a media-saturated society.

The really significant change of social media is the way the web has enabled people to expand their personal boundaries beyond geographical area and immediate social connections. The new media have opened up new channels for communication and interaction, enhancing or supplementing existing face-to-face interactions. Factors like gender, age, ethnicity and social class, combined with separation by geographical distance, might once have meant some conversations in the real world might have been avoided or impossible to have, but alternative identities can be constructed in cyberspace or virtual worlds, and the media may become part of the means by which people express themselves. People can stay in touch via email, Facebook or Twitter when they are away, or meet anonymously in chatrooms or social networking sites, encounters which may develop into face-to-face meetings. Social networking and sharing sites, such as YouTube, Facebook and Flickr (www.flickr.com), and 'Googling' friends can enhance social networks, re-establish lost contacts between old friends, create online communities and bring people together from all over the world. Social networking accounts for more than a fifth of all time spent on the internet. According to Ofcom (2014), Facebook had around 36 million unique visitors per month in the UK in the year ending March 2014 – 56 per cent of the population and about two-thirds of the entire online audience – and more than five times as much time is spent on Facebook than on any other single internet site, equivalent to more than two-and-a-half hours a month for every person in the UK. In June 2013, there were around 24 million daily active users in the UK logging in to Facebook.

The cultural pessimist view of the new media

The cultural pessimist view is held by those who believe that the neophiliacs have exaggerated the benefits of the new media, and ignored or underestimated their negative aspects.

Problems of the validity of information

It is often difficult to know the source of messages in the new media – who they come from and who is sending them. It is therefore often hard to validate information – to know whether or not reports are true, and whether videos and photos are faked or doctored. For example, videos and images posted to Facebook or YouTube, or Twitter feeds (tweets), may appear to show the violent suppression of protest by repressive regimes. While this may be a good thing when protesters have no other means of publicizing their struggles, at the same time there may be no journalists, TV crews or independent witnesses on the ground to verify whether the images and tweets are real, faked or exaggerated, or to interview the people concerned. Similarly, much so-called 'factual' public information on the internet is often little more than disguised advertising for products. As suggested in the discussion of churnalism in Topic 3, such material is often recycled without checking the information or sources. The viral *Kony 2012* YouTube film mentioned above was criticized for, among other things, oversimplifying the issue, for deflecting attention away from atrocities committed by the Ugandan army, for failing to mention the fact that Kony had left Uganda six years before the film appeared, and for focusing too much on the views of white Western people and ignoring the views of local (black) people. Such criticisms are unlikely to have come to the attention of the millions of people who viewed the original video.

Cultural and media imperialism

Cultural and media imperialism is the idea that the new media, particularly the internet, satellite television and global advertising, have led to the imposition on non-Western cultures of Western, and especially American, cultural values, with the undermining of local cultures and cultural independence. This was discussed in Topic 2 (see pages 195–8), and you may wish to re-read those pages now.

A threat to democracy

The neophiliacs see the new media, and particularly the internet, as a means whereby millions of ideas can blossom and different schools of thought can debate, and see this as giving more information and power to the once powerless. However, critics suggest neophiliacs underestimate the threat to democracy posed by the new media corporations, and the impact of the digital divide, which restricts access to the new technology, particularly among the poorest and most oppressed people in the world.

The power of unelected commercial companies: the sovereigns of cyberspace

As the internet becomes more central to our lives, the power of the commercial companies providing the technology and web services increases. This poses a threat to democracy and enhances the power of the already powerful, as more and more of what we know is dominated and controlled by global corporations. MacKinnon (2012) uses the concept of what she calls 'sovereigns of cyberspace' to describe the power of giant multinational corporations like Amazon, Apple, Facebook, Google, Microsoft, Samsung and Vodaphone to control internet access, satellite channels, social networking and mobile technology. MacKinnon suggests such companies, among the largest and richest in the world, now hold the kind of power over us that was once held only by governments. These companies are now effectively part of our political system, but they are neither elected by nor accountable to the public in the way democratic governments are, and exercise what Curran and Seaton (2010) call 'power without responsibility'.

These private companies have enormous power to stifle free expression, and they actually use it. For example, in 2011 Amazon removed Wikileaks from its cloud computing servers without any justification that would have withstood a legal challenge, after Wikileaks released secret emails allegedly posing a threat to the US government, and other websites and finance companies attempted to starve Wikileaks of funds by blocking online donations from being made by Visa, Mastercard and Paypal. Facebook may be used to spread political and other potentially controversial views, but Facebook took down a page used by activists in the Arab Spring to co-ordinate protests on the grounds that they had violated the company's rules by not using their real names, which would have endangered the lives of those activists. Google has the power to render any website effectively invisible by blocking it in its search engine.

Censorship and control

MacKinnon (2012) demonstrates how some undemocratic, repressive regimes, like those in China and Iran, monitor and control new media use. The internet, and particularly social networking sites and email, face government censorship and surveillance using web filtering/blocking and surveillance technology often supplied by Western technology companies, which can monitor email and web traffic and block access to websites. For example, the majority of China's social networks employ content management teams to censor messages which might cause political problems with the government. Western democracies, such as the UK and the USA, are increasingly using the same surveillance technologies, with the British government in 2014 proposing more cyber-surveillance, with laws to monitor the content of emails, social networks and Skype traffic. In 2013, the US whistle-blower Edward Snowden revealed that the British government's eavesdropping agency, GCHQ, was conducting a secret surveillance operation – Project Tempora – involving a huge data-trawling of internet traffic, emails, phone calls and Facebook and other postings, including those of wholly innocent citizens, raising major concerns over privacy and illegal government surveillance activity.

As seen above, major corporations dominate the web, and despite all the claims of enhanced democracy by the neophiliacs, the vast majority of websites, and particularly those that get the most hits and the most advertising, carry mainstream material and online comments that are within the dominant ideology. The Reuters Institute (Newman and Levy 2014) found that in 2014 the majority of news consumed online still comes from established newspaper and broadcasting companies, and that much of the conversation in social media is driven by the work of mainstream journalists. Websites criticizing the status quo, calling for social and political change or promoting minority views are under-resourced, don't attract (or don't want) advertising, and are marginalized. They are swamped by the sheer extent of large, well-resourced websites filled with news, advertising, entertainment, sports and commercial sales run by corporations who seek to ensure that their view of the world, and their interests, are those that prevail. In many ways, the issues of ownership and control, government controls over the media, the social construction of the news and agenda-setting, which were discussed in Topics 1 and 3, are applicable as much – or more – to the new media as they ever were to the traditional or old media.

The lack of regulation

The global nature of the new media, such as the internet and satellite broadcasting, means there is a lack of regulation by national bodies like Ofcom. This means undesirable things like bias, internet crime, pornography (including child pornography), drug smuggling, paedophilia, people trafficking, identity theft, cybercrime, money-laundering, terrorism, violence and racism, and undesirable media representations like those discussed in Topic 4, including those which are illegal in the UK under equalities laws, can thrive virtually unchecked, alongside things like addiction to online gambling. In 2014–15, there were growing concerns about the way a terrorist group like ISIS (Islamic State), which had seized large areas of land in Syria and Iraq, could use new media to conduct a high-tech media jihad (holy war). ISIS was highly skilled and successful in using social media like YouTube, Twitter, Instagram and Tumblr to advertise itself globally. It was using techniques taken from movies, video games and news channels to spread its message and to create a network of militants recruited from all over the world (including the UK) and to frighten and intimidate people with uploaded videos of beheadings. Other undesirable effects include cyber bullying, in which individuals are bullied online through social networking sites or email or on mobile phones, and from which it is difficult for victims to escape, unlike other forms of bullying. Twitter, particularly, has come in for a lot of criticism as individuals and their families have faced vitriolic abuse, and rape and death threats from those disagreeing with their views.

Commercialization and limited consumer choice

For all the alleged benefits claimed by the culturally optimistic neophiliacs, the new media are essentially driven by consumerism and commercialization. The new media are about making money for the companies that produce the technology, who provide the internet connections, who provide the websites and services, and for those that advertise to sell their products and services. Internet and mobile phone advertising is now a bigger business than advertising in the traditional media. Social networking sites are not really about connecting people together, but are just a means of targeting advertising at people who spend extraordinary lengths of time freely giving away to advertisers detailed information about their lives and interests. This is a form of commercial surveillance, storing information about consumer preferences, through cookies left on their computers and mobiles, to bombard them with adverts offering products and other sites to visit based on their past browsing habits and online purchases.

There is no real increase in consumer choice

The digital divide means that there are still many people, both in the UK and worldwide, who are unable to access the alleged increased consumer choices made available via the new media. However, many cultural pessimists suggest there is no real increase in consumer choice. Preston (2012), for example, points out that, while digital media offer customers the choice of what they want to read or look at, they don't bring to their attention – unlike newspapers or TV – the stories that people didn't know they wanted to be informed about until they had seen them in newspapers or on TV. There may theoretically be more choice, but if people rely for their news, for example, on recommendations from like-minded friends and contacts on social media, it could mean they are consuming less news and that they are no longer exposed to a broader news agenda. Barnett and Seymour (1999) and Curran et al. (2009) showed how there is poorer-quality media content, with a 'dumbing-down' and tabloidization of popular culture to attract large audiences, much of the same content on different TV channels, and endless repeats. Celebrity culture has replaced serious programming, and 'infotainment' (information wrapped up to entertain) has replaced hard news reporting to encourage people to consume media. These issues have been discussed throughout this chapter, but particularly in Topics 1, 2 and 3.

Increasing surveillance

The new media have increased all kinds of surveillance in everyday life. Apart from the surveillance by advertisers mentioned earlier, there are endless examples of how the new media have operated to increase social control. For example, in 2012, a woman was jailed for twenty-one weeks for racially aggravated harassment and abuse after she was filmed on a mobile phone racially abusing fellow travellers on the London tube, which was uploaded to YouTube and viewed more than 200,000 times. In America, a teacher lost her job after a parent spotted a Facebook picture of her with a glass of wine in one hand and a beer in the other. A North Yorkshire police constable has used Twitter, Facebook and YouTube to post pictures and videos of graffiti and appeal to local residents for help in catching the culprits. The Metropolitan Police used a facial-recognition smartphone app to identify people suspected of committing crimes in the 2011 London riots, which allowed users who had the app to inform on people they saw by sending a name and address to the police.

While some might see these examples as a welcome use of the new media, such surveillance techniques can also be used by those with power to monitor and control social protesters, and to highlight and condemn all forms of non-conformist behaviour. Surveillance is actually an integral part of mobile phone technology, as the mobile signal can be used to locate mobile users, enabling the agencies of social control to find out where people are. These agencies also have the means of monitoring who is posting information online, and communications between individuals and groups.

The undermining of human relationships and communities

Social capital refers to the social networks of influence and support that people have.

There will be an increase in social isolation, with people losing the ability to communicate in the real world as they spend less quality time having conversations with family and friends, and more wrapped up in the virtual world of solitary electronic media. There will consequently be a loss of social capital or the useful social networks which people have, as they spend less time engaging with the communities and neighbourhoods in which they live.

Activity

1 Outline **three** ways in each case in which the new media may have (a) undermined, and (b) increased, the power and control of media owners and organizations.

2 Outline **three** ways in each case in which the new media may have (a) increased, and (b) decreased, consumer choice.

3 Visit some or all of the following websites, and describe the extent to which you think they present different views of the world from that found in the traditional media or in mainstream new media
   www.occupytogether.org
   www.roarmag.org
   www.38degrees.org.uk
   www.avaaz.org/en
   www.opendemocracy.net
   www.allout.org

Practice questions

1 Outline and explain **two** ways in which the new media have affected traditional newspapers and broadcast media. **(10 marks)**

2 Read **Item A** below and answer the question that follows.

> ### Item A
> New media technology has enabled a significant growth in citizen journalism, in which ordinary people rather than media professionals produce media content. This has taken some control of media content away from owners and editors, and made traditional media and media organizations more accountable to the public.

Applying material from **Item A**, analyse two ways in which the new media may have taken control of media content away from owners and editors, and placed it in the hands of media users. **(10 marks)**

3 Read **Item B** below and answer the question that follows.

> ### Item B
> The new media have enabled ordinary people to access and report, criticize, comment on and share more news and information than ever before. This has promoted a culture of questioning, challenging and holding to account the power, decisions and actions of elite hierarchies, governments and other organizations. Ordinary people consequently have more power in society.

Applying material from **Item B** and your knowledge, evaluate the impact of the new media on contemporary society. **(20 marks)**

CHAPTER SUMMARY AND REVISION CHECKLIST

After studying this chapter you should be able to:

- Explain what is meant by the media, and distinguish between the traditional and new media
- Identify formal controls on the media
- Identify a range of ways in which governments seek to influence and control media output
- Examine the view that the media reproduce an ideological view of the world
- Critically discuss the main features of media ownership and control, and how these influence the content of the media, including the strengths and weaknesses of the manipulative or instrumentalist approach, the dominant ideology or hegemonic approach, and the pluralist approach
- Consider competing views of the role of the mass media in relation to globalization and popular culture, including the meaning of media and cultural imperialism
- Explain and evaluate the postmodernist approach to the media
- Identify and discuss the influences on the content of the media, and the issue of media bias

- Discuss a range of ways in which the news is socially constructed, the significance of agenda-setting and gatekeeping, and the factors that make stories newsworthy
- Explain how the media can generate moral panics and amplify deviance
- Explain what is meant by 'infotainment', 'tabloidization' and 'churnalism', and why they have become significant features of the media
- Explain what is meant by the 'propaganda model' of the media
- Describe and critically discuss a range of media representations and stereotypes, including those related to age, social class, ethnicity, gender, sexuality and disability
- Critically discuss the effects of the media, including the methodological problems of researching these effects, and the strengths and weaknesses of the hypodermic syringe, the two-step flow, the cultural effects (including encoding/decoding, reception analysis and selective filtering) and the uses and gratifications models

- Discuss and evaluate the effects of violence in the media, including the methodological problems of researching this

- Discuss uses of the new media, stratification by social class, age, gender and location in new media access and use, how the new media and new technologies have affected the traditional media and consider a range of neophiliac and cultural pessimist arguments and evidence concerning the significance of the new media in contemporary society, including the extent to which these have reduced the power of media owners.

KEY TERMS

Definitions can be found in the glossary at the end of this book, as well as these terms being defined in the margin where they first appear in the chapter

agenda-setting	gatekeeping	impairment	polysemic
bias	glass ceiling	Islamophobia	primary definers
blogosphere	global culture	low culture	preferred (dominant)
churnalism	global village	male gaze	reading
citizen journalism	globalization	mass culture	popular culture
collective intelligence	Hawthorne effect	media gaze	sexual orientation
cultural convergence	hegemony	media imperialism	sexuality
cultural homogenization	heterosexuality	media representations	simulacra
cultural imperialism	hierarchy of credibility	media text	stigmatized identity
deviancy amplification	high culture	moral panic	social capital
digital divide	homosexuality	negotiated reading	social media
digital underclass	hybrid culture	neophiliacs	symbolic annihilation
disability	hybridization	news values	synergy
dominant ideology	hyperreality	norm-setting	tabloidization
elite	ideological state	oppositional reading	technological
false consciousness	apparatuses	participatory culture	convergence
folk devils	ideology	pluralism	

There are a variety of free tests and other activities that can be used to assess your learning at

www.politybooks.com/browne
You can also find new contemporary resources by following @BrowneKen on Twitter.

See also the revision guide to accompany this book:
Sociology for AQA Revision Guide 2: 2nd-Year A level

Please note that the above resources have not been endorsed by AQA.

PRACTICE QUESTION

Topic B3 The Media

Answer **all** the questions on this topic   **Time allowed: 1 hour**

1 9 Outline and explain **two** ways in which the media may have contributed to the emergence of a global popular culture.   **[10 marks]**

2 0 Read **Item A** below and answer the question that follows.

> **Item A**
>
> Many people spend more time on social media (networking) sites than any other online or internet-related activity. Social media have become an extremely significant form of the media in the twenty-first century, sometimes rivalling more traditional mass media in their ability to get their views across to large media audiences.

Applying material from **Item A**, analyse **two** ways in which social media may be changing traditional forms of the mass media.   **[10 marks]**

2 1 Read **Item B** below and answer the question that follows.

> **Item B**
>
> Rather than being a neutral record of events that have happened, media news is socially constructed by a range of complex social influences and processes of interpretation, selection and presentation. Some suggest media news is a series of socially manufactured propaganda messages produced within the context of the dominant ideology to protect the interests of the most powerful groups in society.

Applying material from **Item B** and your knowledge, evaluate the view that mainstream media news is socially constructed and protects the interests of the most powerful groups in society.   **[20 marks]**

Stratification and Differentiation

PAMELA LAW

- **Topic 1:** Stratification and differentiation by social class, gender, ethnicity and age
- **Topic 2:** Dimensions of inequality: class, status and power; differences in life chances by social class, gender, ethnicity, age and disability
- **Topic 3:** The problems of defining and measuring social class; occupation, gender and social class
- **Topic 4:** Changes in structures of inequality, including globalisation and the transnational capitalist class, and the implication of these changes
- **Topic 5:** The nature, extent and significance of patterns of social mobility

Contents

4 Stratification and Differentiation

Topic 1

SPECIFICATION AREA

Stratification and differentiation by social class, gender, ethnicity and age

Throughout the study of stratification and differentiation, you should remember the relative proportions of each of the groups being discussed as found in the UK today. Women comprise over half the population. About a quarter of the population have some kind of severe or activity-limiting disability. In the 2011 Census, over 10 million people out of a population of 63 million defined themselves as having a life-limiting condition but this is likely to be an underestimation. About 15 per cent of the population comes from an ethnic minority and we are totally uncertain about the proportions of people with different sexualities. In terms of class, about 5 per cent are in the upper class, with approximately 40–45 per cent in the middle classes and 50 per cent in the working classes, though, as we shall see later in Topic 3, this depends on definitions. In a global context, out of a world population of more than 7 billion people, 53 per cent are female, 15 per cent are disabled and the white Eurasian population is a definite minority, being 15 per cent of the total. Bearing all this in mind, we will now look at how stratification and differentiation affect all aspects of our lives.

Definitions

The concept of power

Underlying all known systems of stratification and differentiation is the concept of **power**: who has it and who does not? What kind of power is it – physical, economic or social? Is it seen as legitimate or not?

Physical power may involve violence or the threat of violence; economic power will involve control over scarce resources; and social power will involve some degree of the acceptance of power by others. When power becomes accepted or legitimated, it becomes **authority**.

Power is found in any relationship, whether two people are involved or many. Power within the family tends to rest with parents rather than children, and often with men rather than women. Power in the wider world is held by governments and large corporations rather than by individuals.

> **Power** is the capacity of individuals or groups to get their own way in any given situation.

> **Authority** is legitimate or accepted power, for example parents are said to have authority over children and governments over their citizens.

The concepts of stratification and differentiation

Differentiation is the way in which people perceive and treat each other as different, whereas stratification means using those perceived differences as a basis for power or authority. We look at the bases for these shortly. The concepts of stratification and differentiation have been crucial since the science of sociology began. In recent decades, it has been fashionable in the UK to deny that stratification or social differences are important, due to a perceived growth in individualism. However, research undertaken by the Department of Transport in 2008 showed that children under the age of 16 in the poorest areas of the UK are 4.5 times more likely to be killed and injured on the roads than those living in the richest areas. Research in 2014 demonstrated a strong link between poverty in early childhood, most likely to be found in the lower social classes, and obesity leading to chronic illness and early death. It would seem that income differences, at least, are still vitally important.

The concept of inequality

In recent times the concept of inequality has become more widely used rather than the terms of stratification and differentiation, and Platt (2011) draws distinctions between different types of inequality which mirror many of the concerns of previous writers about stratification and differentiation. She is careful to distinguish between 'inequalities of opportunity, inequalities of outcome, inequalities of access or inequalities of entitlement' and she points out that inequalities 'should be differentiated as to whether they are just or unjust, avoidable or unavoidable, "natural" or artificially sustained'. These distinctions within the concept of inequality can be applied to each and every form of stratification and differentiation.

Milanovic (2011), when looking at global inequality rather than just inequality within one society, suggests we need to consider three types of inequality:

1 *Inequality between individuals* in a single country
2 *Inequality of income between countries* as measured by the **Gini coefficient**
3 *Inequality among all the citizens of the world.*

> **Gini Coefficient** is a method of measuring one person's income against those of all other individuals in that society. A coefficient of 0 means all incomes are equal and there is no inequality; a coefficient of 1 means all income goes to one individual. Thus the nearer to 1, the more unequal the society.

He also suggests inequality can be good or bad. Good inequality is needed to create incentives such as those discussed by Davis and Moore (see pages 280–2 of this topic) but bad inequality occurs 'where, rather than providing the motivation to excel, inequality provides the means to preserve acquired positions'.

However, Wilkinson and Pickett (2009) and Platt (2011) have both noted there are vast inequalities of wealth and income in the UK and the USA, in particular . . . In *The Spirit Level*, Wilkinson and Pickett argue that a society with large differences in income is a society that is bad for everyone. Societies which have high levels of social inequality, compared to those which are more equal, have higher rates of imprisonment, lower literacy levels, worse health, more obesity and more mental illness, which affect not just the individual sufferers but the whole society in an adverse way. They look in great detail at these interconnections and find that the more divided a society is in terms of income and wealth distribution, the worse it fares in terms of social well-being.

The UK is a very divided society. Indeed Scambler (2013) among others, suggests that divisions are increasing, with the top 10 per cent of the population now 100 times more wealthy than the bottom 10 per cent: an inequality higher than in 1918. Sayer (2014) estimates that the richest 1,000 people in the UK had 15 per cent of the wealth of the whole country, and this had increased by more than 500 per cent between 1997 and 2014, and by over 15 per cent in 2013–14 alone. The £519 billion they hold could fund the total welfare bill for over four and a half years.

The bases for differentiation

People have always distinguished themselves from others in a variety of ways. When meeting for the first time, we classify others as either taller/shorter, more beautiful/ugly, or like us or not like us. Physical attributes are the easiest way of differentiating people, but other characteristics, such as accents, might be used too. Thus, subjective judgements are made and this subjective view becomes an objective inequality, or, as W. I. Thomas put it in 1928: 'What men believe to be real is real in its consequences' (Thomas and Thomas 1928). When A meets B, A will begin to act in ways that match what B instinctively feels about them, or A will begin to act out his or her beliefs about B. This might mean treating B with respect if A thinks of B as superior, or with disdain if A thinks of B as inferior. Person B will then respond in an appropriate way. In a short time, both A and B will be convinced that their original assessment of each other was correct. The original assessment has become a self-fulfilling prophecy. The ways in which these assessments become solidified create various systems of stratification.

It is irrelevant whether the differences are real or not. It is the perception of the differences that is important, and the way in which people respond. If women are constantly told they are inferior, they begin to believe it and teach their children that sons are more important than daughters. It then becomes the truth that boys are more important than girls and hence the differentiation becomes reality. The same can be said of any group perceived of as inferior or superior. Over time, the group itself comes to believe that its status is objective and justified, and stratification becomes seen as natural and inevitable. In this way even slaves accept their position as justified and natural.

The bases for differentiation may be physical attributes, such as:

- Sex/gender
- Age
- Ethnicity
- Disability.

Or they might be non-physical attributes, such as:

- Religion
- Economic bases – access to water, people, land and the means of production.

Stratification is the systematic ordering of these differentiations, so that some groups are seen as more important or as having more power than others. Members of each layer or stratum will have a common identity and culture, and similar interests, lifestyles and, usually, life chances. Some stratification systems are said to be open, and others closed. An **open system** is one in which it is possible to move from one social level to another (in the UK it is possible for the child of a shop-worker to become a Member of Parliament). This social mobility will be discussed in more detail in Topic 5. A **closed system** is one in which social position is fixed at birth, and nothing can alter it – such as the Indian **caste** system (see pages 299–300).

Before we look at each of these forms of differentiation, we shall consider general theories of stratification.

Theories of stratification

Many current theories of stratification were first considered in the nineteenth century but are still highly relevant today – many of those arguments are currently being reworked by politicians throughout the world.

Marxism

Marx and his associate Engels (1848) saw the basis of all stratification systems as the owner-ship and control of the means of production. In the past, this meant control of land, water or other scarce resources. Since the **Industrial Revolution**, when Britain changed from an agri-cultural society into a society based on manufacturing, it has meant ownership and control of manufacturing and the production of essential supplies. Society is divided into two groups: the **bourgeoisie** and the **proletariat**. The bourgeoisie, a minority group, own all primary production (such as mines, land, forests, etc.), the factories, and the banks and financial institutions. They employ the proletariat to work for them and they pay them the minimum needed to survive, selling

An **open system** is one in which it is possible for an individual to move from the social group in which he or she was born into a different social group.

A **closed system** is one in which there is very little social mobility between groups. Usually, members of such a society are likely to spend their whole lives in the class or group into which they were born. Status is therefore ascribed rather than achieved.

Caste: a system of closed social hierarchy based on the Hindu belief in reincarnation which determines one's social position during this lifetime.

The **Industrial Revolution** describes the process by which Britain developed from about 1750 onwards from an agricultural society into a society based on manufacturing.

In Marxist theory, the **bourgeoisie** is the class of owners of the means of production.

Proletariat is the social class of workers who have to work for wages, as they do not own the means of production.

the goods produced by the proletariat for a profit, thus growing richer and richer. The proletariat, forced to sell their labour in order to live, suffer from **alienation** as their social position cuts them off from shared interests with the rest of the human community. The capitalist system means they lose the right to determine their own futures and begin to define all relationships in terms of money and thus no longer recognize their own humanity. There is further discussion of the Marxist theory of stratification in Topic 1 of chapter 5 (see pages 375–9).

Neo-Marxism

Empirical evidence shows that there are different levels of pay within the proletariat, so Marxist ideas have been modified, but the basic idea remains. Neo-Marxists talk of different groups such as the 'petit bourgeoisie', the intellectual classes and the underclass, but, at heart, the distinction still remains: a few individuals own the means of production; the rest, the majority, do not. Classical Marxists regard the division of the non-bourgeoisie into separate groups as an example of false **class consciousness**, because emphasizing the differences between, say, skilled workers and teachers hides the fact that, essentially, they are all members of the proletariat and, as such, powerless compared to the bourgeoisie.

Exploitation

Wright (1978) suggested that a better distinction between the classes might be via exploitation: one class exploits the other. This allows distinctions to be made between different types of bourgeoisie, from the owner who does not work at all but employs many people, to the one-man business. The important point about exploitation is that the class *doing* the exploiting would be harmed if those *being* exploited were to stop working. Wright envisages a situation in which there is a gradation of classes dependent upon the skills and negotiating powers of different groups in the acquisition of scarce or desirable resources.

However, such distinctions are difficult to apply in practice, since the owner and the small businessman just cited may in reality have little in common. Edgell (1993) claims that mere skill in negotiating for scarce resources is not, in itself, an exploitative relationship.

Classic Marxist theories tend to ignore differentiation on the basis of sex/gender, ethnicity, disability and age, which has led to the appearance of sub-groups such as Marxist feminists to explain some of these aspects of stratification. These are discussed on page 285 (see also page 392 in chapter 5).

Can class be eliminated?

Marxism suggests that, by human action, it is possible to end stratification and create equality for all. Because Marx believed that all stratification systems are based on the economy, until there is a change in the nature of the economy, stratification into classes is inevitable. But the economic base could be altered if the subordinate class, the proletariat, became aware of their position and acted together to change society. This could only happen if they became class-conscious – that is, totally aware of their own position. But this is unlikely to happen, as all the institutions of society serve the interests of the bourgeoisie – directly, through laws on property ownership, or indirectly through ideology. Because the dominant ideology states that capitalism is best, class consciousness is more likely to be found among the bourgeoisie than among the proletariat. The bourgeoisie will realize that their best interests lie in acting together to keep wages down and increase profits. Although the proletariat forms a single class, it is blinded by the divisions within itself and cannot see its true position. As a result, the proletariat never acts in a concerted way as a class for itself – it suffers from **false consciousness**.

Marx thought that the unity of the bourgeoisie would eventually be destroyed as each individual strove to be bigger and better than the rest. See the box on 'The growth and effect of monopoly capitalism'. Competition leads to a **monopoly**, the monopolist would become over-powerful and the inequalities of the system would become so obvious that members of the proletariat class would realize their true position and revolution would occur. Thus, from a Marxist perspective, stratification may not be totally inevitable, but it will take a great struggle and requires action to remove it. In more recent years, neo-Marxists such as Althusser (1971) have concentrated on

Alienation refers to the lack of power and control, fulfilment and satisfaction experienced by workers in a capitalist society, where the means of producing goods are privately owned and controlled.

Class consciousness is awareness in members of a social class of their real interests.

False consciousness is a lack of awareness among people about what their real interests are, and the false belief that everyone benefits from the present organization of society, which is presented as fair and just.

A **monopoly** occurs when one person or company is the only possible provider of goods or services.

explaining why revolution has not occurred, examining the role of the state and other institutions in maintaining false consciousness through both **ideological** and **repressive state apparatuses**.

Ideological state apparatuses are agencies that spread the dominant ideology and justify the power of the dominant social class.

The growth and effect of monopoly capitalism

Modern industry has established a world market . . . [and] the bourgeoisie cannot exist without constantly revolutionising production, and the relations of society. Constant . . . disturbance of all social conditions, everlasting uncertainty and agitation distinguish the bourgeois epoch from all earlier ones. All old prejudices and opinions are swept away; all new-formed ideas are outdated before they become fixed . . . All that is solid melts into air . . . and man is, at last, compelled to face with sober senses his real conditions of life and his relations with his kind.

The need of a constantly expanding market for his products chases the bourgeoisie over the whole surface of the globe. He must nestle everywhere, settle everywhere, establish connections everywhere. Through this exploitation of the world market the bourgeoisie has given a cosmopolitan character to production and consumption in every country . . . All old-established national industries have been destroyed or are being destroyed . . . in place of the old wants, satisfied by the production of the country, we find new wants, requiring for their satisfaction the products of distant lands and climes . . . we have the universal interdependence of nations. And as in material, so also in intellectual production. The intellectual creations of individual nations become common property . . . and from the numerous national and local literatures there arises world literature.

Slightly adapted from Marx and Engels, *The Manifesto of the Communist Party*, 1848.

A repressive state apparatus is the parts of the state concerned with mainly repressive, physical means of keeping a population in line, such as the army, police, courts and prisons.

Functionalism

Functionalists see stratification as a necessary component of effective **role allocation** and believe it is based on a **meritocracy**, meaning that those who are at each level in the system deserve to be there because of their greater talents, abilities, qualifications and skills. Those at the top are superior in some way to those below them. This leads functionalists to see stratification as inevitable and necessary for the smooth running of society.

Role allocation is concerned with ensuring that the most suitable individuals fill the roles needed for society to function properly and maintain social consensus.

The functional necessity of stratification

Davis and Moore (1945) suggest that society needs to ensure that the right people are motivated to fill certain positions. They argue:

- That all social roles (occupations) must be filled by those best able to perform them
- That certain jobs are more important than others for society
- That these jobs will require more talent or training
- That not everybody has these talents or is prepared to undergo the necessary training.

Meritocracy is a social system in which rewards are allocated on the basis of merit or ability.

Therefore, in order for these functionally important jobs to be done, those people who are prepared to do them must be rewarded by:

- Material goods/access to scarce resources
- Extra leisure and pleasure
- Increased self-respect or status.

A position or job does not have great power and prestige just because it has a great income; rather, it has a high income because it is functionally important and the skilled people to fill it are very scarce. This argument is currently used by highly paid managers to justify their pay. If a job is functionally important but easy to fill (e.g. dustmen are important for public health but require little training), then high rewards are not needed. However, if a position is important and needs training (e.g. that of a doctor), then the rewards must be great to persuade the right people to undergo the training.

The ideas of Davis and Moore that inequality is both necessary and desirable continue to be espoused by current writers such as Marshall et al. (1997) and underpin much of the neoliberal

Schools and nurseries are examples of agencies controlled by the state to teach certain values. The media continue this work in the interests of their owners, the bourgeoisie. If children fail to learn the accepted values, they may later be subject to the repressive state apparatus of the police and the courts in order to control their deviant behaviour.

thinking of the current governments of both the USA and the UK. Platt (2011) summarizes some of these arguments as follows:

Defences of inequality

- It enables people to reach their potential.
- It enables people to feel that they deserve their different statuses.
- It values freedom, both to be successful and to fail, so that reward and failure are both justified.
- It values equality of opportunity, and outcomes can take care of themselves.
- It is intuitively sensible at an individual level as people think there are differences in talent and in application.
- It creates incentives.
- Fundamental freedoms are only achieved if inequality is allowed.
- The market will not operate successfully unless inequality is at least a potential outcome.

Criticisms of Davis and Moore

From within the functionalist school of thought, Tumin (1953) suggests that Davis and Moore are wrong for a number of reasons:

1 Some positions are functionally more important than they may appear to be in Davis and Moore's system. For example, in the 1900s, mathematicians were not highly regarded, yet, without their work, space exploration would not have occurred, and the internet would not exist.

Can training be considered a sacrifice? What positive aspects of professional training might Davis and Moore have overlooked in claiming that high salaries and status are rewards necessary to persuade people to undertake professional qualifications?

2 It is wrong to suggest that only a limited number of people have the necessary talent for important jobs. No society has ever known how great a pool of talent it has. Education systems are unequal, with children from higher classes doing disproportionately better than anyone else. The system of stratification itself prevents the pool of talent being larger.

3 Training is not a 'sacrifice' that needs rewarding. The costs are usually paid by parents or the state, and being a student can be pleasurable.

4 People do not need to be promised financial rewards in order to be persuaded to undertake training: money is not the only motivator. Not enough is known about the human psyche to assume that money and status are the only ways to reward people.

5 Far from being functional, Tumin argues that stratification may be dysfunctional because:

- It limits the possibility of discovering the full range of talent in a society
- It limits the expansion of a society that might occur if there was equality of opportunity
- It provides the elite group with enough power to dominate the ideology of their society and stifle change
- It limits the creative potential of many individuals
- It makes people feel less important to society, thus giving them less motivation to participate in society.

Tumin therefore concludes that stratification is not uniformly functional in guaranteeing that the most important jobs are filled by the most competent people.

Wilkinson and Pickett (2009) go further in criticizing the functionalist defence of inequality, pointing out that on almost every measure the more unequal a society is, the more it suffers from social ills such as greater unhappiness, higher suicide levels, more crime, more teenage pregnancies and greater social disharmony.

Functionalist writings, on the whole, suggest that stratification systems like those of industrialized nations are essentially meritocratic and open societies. Functionalism is not concerned explicitly with explaining differentiation on the basis of ethnicity or disability, although stratification by sex is seen as inevitable, as will be discussed on page 289.

Weberian theory

Max Weber suggests that stratification is somewhat more complicated than Marx indicated. Weber suggests that there is a need to distinguish between **class** (which has an economic base), **status** (which is based on esteem) and **party** (which is based on access to and use of power).

All three aspects of stratification are related to aspects of power as was discussed earlier (pages 276–7). By power, Weber meant the chance of one person, or a group of people, realizing their own will in a communal action, even when the rest of the population might not want the same thing. He distinguished between political power, which is realized through party – either a formal political party or

Class, for Weber, relates to an individual's market position, and how scarce and needed their skills are.

Status is the amount of prestige or social importance a person has in the eyes of other members of a group or society.

Party is a term used by Weber to describe the way in which political organization will appear in any group of individuals who work together because they have common backgrounds, aims or interests.

an informal clique within a group; prestige power, which is realized through status; and economic power, which is realized through class.

Class, for Weber, is the market situation of a person. If someone has a rare skill or one that is in much demand, then that person's worth to society will be greater than that of an unskilled person. For example, a highly trained doctor will command more money in the marketplace than an unskilled labourer unless there is a surplus of doctors, and few unskilled workers. If that situation were to arise, then the laws of supply and demand would mean that potential doctors might decide to remain unskilled in order to earn more as unskilled workers than they would as doctors. Different classes have different **life chances**, which are described by Weber (1947 [1920]) as access to things regarded as necessary and desirable in a society, such as food, housing, good health and access to healthcare, educational and occupational opportunities, police protection and social status.

> **Life chances** are chances to obtain those things defined as desirable and to avoid those things defined as undesirable in a society.

Status is honour accorded to certain individuals or groups. A person may have a low economic value but high social status. For example, a postman or woman may achieve a higher social status than is obtained from his or her occupation by being accepted for voluntary work as a magistrate (or Justice of the Peace); religious leaders, such as vicars, priests, rabbis and imams, often earn relatively little money, but are accorded prestige by the general public.

A political party, or organization for the pursuit of power, exists in any and every group. Wherever there are two or more people, then there will be a struggle for power. The amount of political power exercised by individuals is often linked to both their class and their status.

In many ways, the Weberian view of class underlies the model of class used by British governments since 1901 to categorize the population. The Registrar General later devised a schedule of class based on a mixture of occupation, education and social status for the 2001 Census. This will be looked at in more detail in Topic 3.

Unlike Marxism and functionalism, Weber's theory can be used to partly explain stratification by gender, ethnicity and age since these groups can be described in general terms relating to their market value, their status and their ability to organize in a party sense.

Feminism

Feminism developed as a response to what were seen as malestream tendencies in sociology pre-1970. This referred to sociological studies that were largely concentrated on men, were carried out mostly by men, and then assumed that what was true for men was true for women as well. Feminists see women's social experiences as different from those of men; women were seen as inferior and therefore their life was different from that of men. Some feminists think 'all men are bad', while others suggest that class elements might be involved and that only 'some men are bad'; another group suggests that men are merely misguided and that society could be changed.

> **Patriarchy** refers to power and authority held by males.

Feminism is sometimes described as falling into four main types: radical, Marxist/socialist, liberal and black. This distinction is not always helpful and many feminists cross boundaries, but all consider the concept of **patriarchy** as an important element in explaining women's position in society.

Patriarchy

Patriarchy is the belief that men are superior to women and therefore all institutions in society work for the benefit of men, rather than for the benefit of all. Most people would now agree that patriarchy/male superiority is merely a belief and not a biological fact. Millett (1970) and Walby (1990) have written in detail about patriarchy and its dimensions.

In *Sexual Politics* (1970), Millett explored the idea that politics occurs in every aspect of life and that patriarchy is the politics of the relationships between men and women. Men may be biologically stronger, but the strength of patriarchy lies in ideological control. Both sexes are socialized into their superior/inferior roles and the family is a key institution in this respect. As the main socializers, women are responsible for the continuance of patriarchal ideas. They are born to be inferior in this system and even class cannot completely cut across it. Women of all classes are subordinate to the men in their class (though they may be superior to men from a lower class). Other agents of socialization help to maintain this situation. Education is especially important because girls are treated differently from boys and are thus fitted for different parts of the workforce, which were,

How might patriarchy be experienced differently by women of different ages and ethnic groups?

and still are, lower paid despite the Equal Pay Act (1970). Millett suggested that men's patriarchal power over women is psychological, and ultimately physical. Few women commit sexual offences, and male violence against women (and other men) is much greater than female violence.

For Walby, the key elements of patriarchy are pay inequality, unequal household roles, sexuality, male violence and the state itself. Despite legislation, women's wages lag behind men's, even in the same occupation, and women are still less likely to be found in positions of power and influence. However, the position is gradually improving: the Welsh Assembly has more women than men, and women are now reaching high-level posts in medicine and surgery.

Work within the household remains largely gendered, although there is slow change. Male violence is still much in evidence. Walby argues that legislation like the Sex Discrimination Act (1975) has tried to reduce patriarchy, but that many state policies still suggest that women and men have different roles – for example, note the difference between maternity and paternity rights after the birth or adoption of a child. Statutory Maternity Pay for women far outweighs the ten days of Statutory Paternity Pay allowed to men. This would suggest that it is the role of the woman to be the main carer for a child. Although current changes to the law allow both partners to share the 'maternity pay' if they so wish, it is still expected that few men will take this opportunity.

Walby points out that patriarchy is experienced differently by different groups of women. In contemporary Britain, many younger women may experience it less than their mothers and grandmothers, though there are class variations here; some ethnicities experience it more than others. So patriarchy should now be seen as non-universal in its dimensions.

However, both Pollert (1996) and Bryson (1999) have pointed to the circular nature of the argument about patriarchy since it is used as both a description of and an explanation for the differences found between men and women. Pollert sees it as a metanarrative of little use in explaining the reality of women's lives, which she sees as best done by exploring individual stories.

Radical feminism

This strand of feminism is seen as being most 'anti-men', though this is not necessarily true. Firestone (1972) argues that biology is the basis for women's inequality and domination by men in all societies. Because women menstruate, give birth and breastfeed, they are, at certain times, physically dependent on others. This allows men to develop physical and psychological power and control, and men thus dominate the social world. Equality between the sexes can only occur when this psychological dominance is destroyed and the physical dependency of women is ended. Therefore, until human babies can be conceived outside the womb (now already possible) and brought to full gestation outside the mother's body, the inequality between the sexes will remain.

This theory has been criticized by other sociologists, both feminists and non-feminists, because it ignores other forms of inequality such as class and ethnicity, and fails to acknowledge that the dependency described by Firestone is both time- and society-dependent.

Ortner (1974) suggests that culture is the basis of differentiation between the sexes, because it is always valued more highly than biology and is controlled by men, whereas women are seen as being closer to nature because they give birth. However, Ortner fails to consider wide differences between societies and over time. There is little clear evidence that culture is always more highly prized than nature, or that women are not involved in the creation of culture. As mothers are the first point of socialization, women, it can be argued, have great control over the transmission of a society's culture and how it is shaped.

The connection between biology and inequality also occurs in the work of Rosaldo (1974), although she is more concerned with how biology places women within the domestic rather than the public sphere. Since most power lies in the public sphere, women are less likely to join in this aspect of social life because of being confined to the house looking after children. Again, the criticism is mostly that this is not true in all societies and that conditions change over time as shown in the work of Margaret Mead (see page 290).

Radical feminists tend to view men and the family as 'the problem' and suggest that women cannot be free until the family structure, as it now exists, is either abolished or greatly changed.

Current inequalities between the sexes in terms of both power and employment suggest that the situation remains the same. Discussions concerning the appointment of senior judges has shown that only when promotion was removed from the hands of the current judiciary and given to an independent committee did the number of female judges increase. It is believed that the 'old boy network' was the force that continued to influence promotion to the detriment of both women and ethnic minorities. Thus, radical feminists may be right to view men as the problem, or, at least, certain groups of men.

Marxist/socialist feminism

This strand of feminism suggests that, although men may sometimes be 'the problem', the class dimension is more important. Engels (1972 [1891]) suggested that in the past people lived in 'promiscuous hordes', where sexual relationships were not fixed and property passed from mother to child. As men became more determined to pass their property on to their own offspring, they began to demand fidelity from their womenfolk, thus leading to monogamous marriage and the power of men over women. Engels's theory has very little basis in known civilizations, though in some societies men who want to make sure their property passes to blood relatives leave it to the children of their sisters, since, as long as a man and his sister/s share the same mother, the genetic link is certain. With their own wives, they cannot be sure that the children bearing their name are actually blood relatives.

Coontz and Henderson (1986) attempted to link Engels's theory with other anthropological material, suggesting that patriarchy was more likely to occur in societies that were **patrilocal** rather than **matrilocal**. When a woman moved to live with her husband's family (patrilocality), she was more likely to lose control over the goods produced; as a result, men became more powerful. Historically, most societies appear to have been patrilocal.

Marxist feminists see the family as an important part in the maintenance of capitalism because:

- The family reproduces the next generation of workers for the owners of the means of production, at no cost
- The women and children act as a brake on revolutionary ideas – the men cannot afford to strike to improve their working conditions because their families would starve while the strike lasted
- Men come home from work stressed out and angry, and the wives and children calm them down, give them a reason for continuing to work and send them back the next morning, ready for another day's labour
- Women form a **reserve army of labour** which can be called away from the home when circumstances demand – for example, in times of war, or when there is a labour shortage.

Marxist feminists, however, feel that, given the right conditions and a higher level of class consciousness, this situation can be changed to achieve greater equality between the sexes.

Patrilocal describes family systems in which the wife is expected to live near the husband's parents.

Matrilocal describes family systems in which the husband is expected to live near the wife's parents.

The reserve army of labour is that part of the population who can be called on to work in times of need, but are otherwise not employed.

Liberal feminism

This strand of feminism is more optimistic about change and sees that progress has already been made, at least in the USA, the UK and Europe. Oakley's (1974a, 1974b, 1981b) work falls most easily into this tradition, though elements of her work come from other traditions.

Oakley points out that the position of women varies greatly between societies and over time. Women have always worked; with the Industrial Revolution, married women and mothers were taken out of the paid workforce. Before this time, both men and women worked inside and outside the home producing agricultural goods or cloth. During the 1800s, more and more people – men, women and children – began to work in factories, moving to towns from the countryside. But the Factory Act of 1819 banned children under the age of 9 from being employed, which meant that women were more likely to have to stay at home to care for them, leading to their role of 'housewife' as we know it today. Thus the family became reliant on the wages of the husband alone. Historically, this transfer of financial power to the husband was relatively short-lived, lasting only three or four generations, but the psychological effects are still being felt, as today's women are still socialized into the role of housewife as practised by their mothers and grandmothers. Whether their own daughters and granddaughters will take up this role is less certain.

Since the end of the Second World War in 1945, the position of women has been ambiguous. Oakley suggests that government policy and social norms imply that married women's primary care is their children, but that, at the same time, such women should work and help to support the family financially. Women in the UK therefore have a dual burden.

Liberal feminists suggest that the differences between men and women have lessened as a result of legislation such as the Equal Pay Act (1970) and the Sex Discrimination Act (1975) and may improve further as more laws come into force. Obviously, these Acts are now more than forty years old, and critics have pointed out that women are still paid less than men and treated as of lesser value. The '**glass ceiling**' prevents women from reaching top jobs. Issues such as the equalization of the age of retirement are having a profound effect. This, at least, will treat men and women as the same, although for women this has meant that their age of retirement has been raised.

There is optimism that sex stratification could be eradicated. But legislation does not change attitudes quickly. In defence of liberal feminists, it must be said that the life of most women in the UK has improved since the 1950s; but this may not be true worldwide. This universal dimension has been addressed by Oakley in her book *Gender on Planet Earth* (2002), which suggests that patriarchy has far-reaching consequences for the planet as a whole. She maintains that patriarchal ways of thinking and the desire to maintain patriarchal power lie behind most of the violence in the world and underpin most of the ideologies which she describes as delusional, such as postmodernism, psychoanalysis and even economics. Economics is especially delusional since it concentrates on such aspects as Gross Domestic Products and ignores all the unpaid labour, mostly undertaken by women, that allows the workforce to be able to work at all and thus produce the very thing economists measure.

Glass ceiling refers to an invisible barrier of discrimination which makes it difficult for women to reach the same top levels in their chosen careers as similarly qualified men.

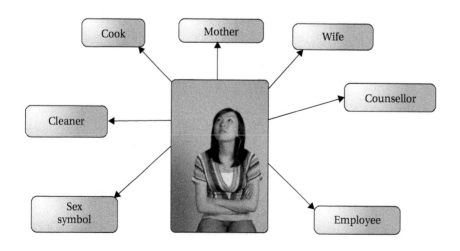

Figure 4.1 The multiple roles that patriarchy attaches to women

Black feminism

Ethnocentrism is the belief that one's own culture is the most important one.

Black feminism developed first in the USA as a response to what it saw as the **ethnocentrism** of feminism as a whole. Others have criticized feminism for being a middle-class concern, and black feminists also accuse it of ignoring the problems faced by ethnic minorities in the US and elsewhere. Black feminists argue that many of their problems have stemmed first and foremost from having to fight against racism, which blinded them to the problems they were facing as women in a patriarchal world. It was, therefore, essential to unpick these strands and understand in detail the forces that contributed to black women being at the very end of the queue when the good things in life are handed out.

Mirza (1992) has argued that, although black British women suffer many of the same problems as white British women, they have the added dimension of racism to contend with and thus their experience of life is different.

Black feminism is criticized for emphasizing the differences between women, rather than concentrating on the shared problems of all. It is a similar argument to that levelled against those who distinguish between the different classes in feminist analysis. These criticisms ignore the perceived, if not real, differences between the experiences of different ethnicities and different classes.

There is more discussion of a range of feminist theories of gender inequality and patriarchy in Topic 1 of chapter 5 (see pages 389–95).

Postmodernism

Postmodernists tend to regard class and, to some extent, gender and ethnicity as concepts that are no longer relevant in contemporary society. These dimensions, they argue, have been replaced by an individualistic society in which consumerism and choice are the key elements. What are now important are the choices that each individual consumer makes and which give them their identity. Allegedly, this is a pick 'n' mix society, in which each person can choose their own identity via what goods they decide to buy. At the same time, with choice also comes risk.

Consumerism as a form of differentiation

Pakulski and Waters (1996) discuss the decline of group solidarity, and the way in which individualism is now paramount and stratification is based on lifestyles. Individuals now belong to many different groups at different times, and hence have a multifaceted identity and are able to redefine themselves by changing consumption patterns. One of the reasons Pakulski and Waters give for this shift from class identity to a consumer identity is that wealth has become progressively more equally distributed and, because of the growth of education, there is now what they call a 'market meritocracy', based on an ability to buy a consumer identity.

One feature of postmodernism is that individuals are freer than ever to construct their own identities based on their consumer choices, rather than solely on features such as age, gender, ethnicity or social class.

However, it is actually not true that wealth has been redistributed. In the UK in the last twenty years, wealth remained in the hands of the same small proportion of the population and may even have become more concentrated within that group, as will be discussed in Topic 2. Pakulski and Waters's argument concerning the growth of education and professional skills leading to a 'market meritocratic' relationship is somewhat more plausible, but is still a major generalization; it might apply to Western, developed societies, but is not true across the globe.

Grusky (1996) noted that the postmodern focus on consumption is based on the ideas that there has been a decline in class-based identities as conflict in the workplace has diminished, and that cultural **globalization** has allowed people to sample different cultures and ideas. There is now a difference between the old Weberian idea of the life chance and what is termed 'life choice'. Life chance is usually beyond the control of the individual, whereas life choice suggests individual control and the right to take risks, either unconscious or conscious. Life choice in the field of education, for example, might involve choosing to stay on at school; the outcomes, both positive and negative, may not be fully known to the individual, but the choice is a risk to be taken in relation to future lifestyle, earning capacity, etc.

Objective and subjective differentiation

Postmodernists have explored consumerism in depth, and their writings concentrate on the subjective aspects of differentiation, especially class, rather than the objective aspects. Writers such as Strinati (1995) are concerned with the image people project through the choices they make as consumers. They speak of a pick 'n' mix identity in which the individual decides which aspects of culture s/he wishes to choose to utilize. Someone who wears designer labels and drives an Audi coupe is projecting an image of their worth which is different from someone who travels on the bus wearing clothes from the market stall. It would seem that the first is of higher status than the second and also, possibly, of higher wealth. Consumer choice, it is suggested, has now over-ridden the old divisions based on gender, ethnicity and class. It would seem that the image an individual projects is accepted by the rest of the society in which he or she lives.

Criticisms of postmodernism

Do individuals really have such power? Does the rest of society accept the self-image that individuals choose to portray? Bottero (2005) has argued that postmodernism ignores the very real constraints on behaviour caused by the inequalities in wealth, income and education, not to mention the constraints of gender, ethnicity and disability.

Although consumer choice says a lot about the subjective aspects of social differentiation, it cannot completely overshadow the objective dimensions. The image that one chooses to project should at least be plausible to the audience – that is, society at large. Not only is the working-class old-age pensioner probably unlikely to be able to support the lifestyle associated with driving a Porsche – also, such a projected image would not be plausible to the onlookers. Society reflects back not only the actors' view of themselves but also the perceptions of those surrounding them. Cooley's '**looking-glass self**' will affect their self-perception (see page 383).

Postmodernism also contains within itself some criticisms of how identity, ethnicity and racism interact. Some postmodernists see racism, and the inequalities that spring from it, as a product of **modernity**. As society became more rational and scientific, i.e. modern, it is argued, this led to explanations concerning the continuance of the inequalities found in society that essentially blamed traits in the working classes and other unsuccessful groups for their inability to become rich and successful. Class and ethnic differences came to be seen as inevitable. In postmodern society, as the number of ethnic identities multiply and hybridize, a type of radical multiculturalism develops and, according to postmodernist thinkers, inequality becomes part of one's identity. Goldberg (1993) says we should acknowledge all these differences and ensure that all have the opportunity to be heard, rather than suggest that assimilation will occur (see page 294). Malik (1996) says that this approach accepts difference and inequality as inevitable and a continuance of the racism of the past and therefore will do nothing to eradicate racism. He suggests it should be fought as racism prevents the creation of a fair society.

Globalization refers to the growing interconnectedness of societies across the world, with the spread of the same culture, consumer goods and economic interests across the globe.

Looking-glass self: the suggestion that our image of ourselves as a social being is built up by reflecting on the opinions of others, seeing ourselves as we think others see us.

Modernity refers to the condition of society from the Enlightenment of the seventeenth century to the middle of the twentieth century. It includes a rational outlook on social issues and highlights the role of science as a basis for understanding.

A plausible image, or a mismatch of stereotypes?

Bases for differentiation/stratification explained

Sex/gender as a basis for stratification and differentiation

This basis for differentiation appears in nearly all societies: men are seen as more powerful and important than women. Evolutionary biologists Tiger and Fox (1972) suggest that equality between the sexes is impossible, because men's genetics make them physically dominant, and they have a natural propensity to hunt, while women are predisposed to a nurturing role. However, others say that all differences between the sexes are, in fact, a product of society and can be eliminated. Cameron (2007) argues that the differences *between* men and women are much smaller than the differences *within* each of the two groups, and, therefore, it is incorrect to say that men are inherently superior. Employing a technique of **meta-analysis**, it can be shown that previous studies on differences between the sexes are unreliable. It may not be coincidental that the vast majority of the studies that argue in favour of men's natural superiority are written by men. Statistics from the United Nations estimate that 53 per cent of the total world population is female, with women doing three-quarters of the world's work but only earning 25 per cent of all earnings and holding 10 per cent of the world's wealth. In the UK, women in every economic group occupy a position below the men of that same group. Despite Equal Pay Acts, the situation remains the same.

In the UK, the Commission for Living Standards (2012) shows that the UK ranks fifteenth on the OECD scale of women in employment largely due to the underemployment of women in their early 30s. This suggests a main reason for this is the lack of affordable childcare.

Functionalist writers such as Parsons assumed the differences between the sexes were innate and biologically based, referring to differences between the **instrumental role** of the male and the **expressive role** of the female. Men are more fitted to go out to work, and physically or mentally more able to supply economic support for the women and children in their family; women are best fitted to remain in the domestic sphere, providing emotional comfort and physical support to the man – the worker – and the children. These roles were considered to be 'natural', though proper socialization was needed to ensure that all boys learned to be 'men', and all girls learned to be 'women'.

However, it is now argued that socialization leads to **gender** differences, and this is the explanation for the perceived differences between men and women in today's society. Indeed, in Britain, normal gender behaviour is learned from a very early age, starting at birth. To explain how this socialization is achieved, Oakley (1972) refers to the processes of manipulation – that is, boys and girls being encouraged to adopt behaviours regarded as appropriate and normal for

Meta-analysis is a statistical technique of collating many different research findings and testing the reliability of the results by controlling the variables within each individual study.

The **instrumental role** is that of the provider/breadwinner in the family, often associated by functionalists with men's role in family life.

The **expressive role** is a nurturing, caring and emotional one, often linked by functionalists to women's biology and seen as women's 'natural' role in the family.

Gender refers to the culturally created differences between men and women which are learnt through socialization.

Activity

Read the following passage:

In the last decade, the number of people living on less than $1 a day has fallen; the gender gap in primary and (to a lesser extent) secondary education has been reduced; and women enjoy greater participation in elected assemblies and state institutions. In addition, women are a growing presence in the labour market. However, the decline in overall poverty masks significant differences not only between but also within regions. Asia experienced the greatest decline in extreme poverty, followed by Latin America, but sub-Saharan Africa experienced an increase. Even where the numbers of extremely poor people have declined, notably China and India, poverty persists in different areas and social groups, reflected in rising inequalities (UN 2005). For women, progress, while steady, has been painfully slow.

Despite increased parity in primary education, disparities are still wide in secondary and tertiary education – both increasingly key to new employment opportunities. And while women's share of seats in parliament have inched up in all regions, women still hold only 16 per cent of parliamentary seats worldwide. Finally, although women have entered the paid labour force in great numbers, the result in terms of economic security is not clear. Women's access to paid employment is lower than men's in most of the developing world. Women are less likely than men to hold paid and regular jobs and more often work in the informal economy, which provides little financial security.

Strengthening women's economic security is critical to efforts to reduce poverty and promote gender equality, and decent work is basic to economic security. Data shows that:

- The proportion of women workers engaged in informal employment is generally greater than the proportion of men workers;
- Women are concentrated in the more precarious types of informal employment;
- The average earnings from these types of informal employment are too low, in the absence of other sources of income, to raise households out of poverty.

Unless efforts are made to create decent work for the global informal workforce, the world will not be able to eliminate poverty or achieve gender equality.

Adapted from UNIFEM (2006).

Answer the following questions:

1 Name *three* things the authors see as possible solutions to the inequalities currently suffered by women.

2 What do the authors see as the main causes of the inequality suffered by women?

their gender; canalization – for example, boys and girls being directed towards different toys and games; use of different verbal appellations – boys and girls being exposed to different language and praised or rebuked for different things, as in 'brave boy' and 'sweet girl'; and differential activity exposure, with boys and girls being exposed to and encouraged to carry out different activities.

Other societies treat the genders in other ways. In the 1930s, the anthropologist Margaret Mead (1935) examined differences among tribes in New Guinea. She discovered the differences to be entirely social, rather than based on sex. In one tribe, women were the traders, leaving home to work, while the men stayed in the domestic sphere and reared the children. Different tribes reared their offspring to have gender expectations that were distinct from those in neighbouring tribes, and were markedly different from the norms then prevalent in the USA and Europe. Thus, Mead concluded, gender is a learned response, not an innate difference.

Activity

Discuss the ways in which girls and boys are socialized through their early childhood and how this differs between groups or over time.

Many products are very effectively marketed at a specific gender from a very early age. What might be the consequences of boys and girls being encouraged to play with different toys? How significant do you think such socialization is?

Gender differences are complicated by the issues of both class and ethnicity. Studies on masculinity and on the rise of girl gangs and 'ladette'-type behaviour show that within each gender there are many subcultures. Swain (2007) discovered different attitudes to masculinity, sports and peer groups in three different schools which all had widely different social class intakes. Thus gender and gender expectations need to be considered alongside class when seeking to explain behaviour.

Theories about gender differences

Feminists would tend to see the explanation for these sex or gender differences as fully explained by patriarchy, though Marxist feminists would, obviously, stress the class element as well, whilst black feminists would stress the racial element. They are likely to discuss at some length the reserve army of labour and the **dual labour market**. The reserve army of labour is that part of the labour force which is hired in times of economic growth, or warfare, and is dispensed with when conditions change. The recession which started in 2008 has certainly affected women's employment more than men's employment. Although unemployment has affected all groups, the female workforce has suffered more redundancies, cuts in pay and short-time working than the male workforce.

The dual labour market suggests there are two distinct types of employment in contemporary societies: the first consists of secure jobs, nearly always permanent and full-time work, while the secondary labour market is mainly composed of temporary and/or part-time work. It is argued that women disproportionately appear in the secondary labour market. However, current employment figures for 2011–12 would suggest that the secondary market has grown in relation to the primary labour market and now involves men as well as women.

Functionalists do not try to explain such differentiation since they think of it as a natural state of affairs and a reflection of appropriate gender socialization. Marxists, with the obvious exception of Marxist feminists, appear more concerned with class and tend to consider the worry over gender as a mild form of false consciousness. Postmodernists have, as yet, offered no real explanation at all, other than individual traits and motivations.

> **Dual labour market**: the idea that there are two types of employment: the primary labour market with secure, permanent jobs and the secondary one with insecure, often temporary, part-time work.

Ethnicity as a basis for stratification and differentiation

Genetic theories

Theories concerning **ethnicity** and differentiation based on perceived ethnic differences have, mostly, a genetic or a biological base. Following Darwin's theory of evolution, social scientists such as Spencer (1996 [1885]) suggested that different human groups developed in isolation and were distinct from one another, and also that white races were inherently superior to others. These theories reflected the underlying beliefs of the British Empire, then at the height of its powers, and have since been discredited.

> **Ethnicity** refers to the shared culture of a social group which gives its members a common identity in some ways different from other social groups.

Criticism of genetic theories

Twentieth-century understanding of genetics, particularly the work of Jones (1994), has dispelled this idea. All human groups are capable of interbreeding, and the genetic differences that exist between so-called 'racial groups' are no greater than the range of genetic differences found within each of these populations.

In global terms, white European groups are an ethnic minority, or group of minorities, whereas in the UK they form the majority. In contemporary Britain, it would be difficult to deny that ethnicity still plays a part in stratification, given that ethnic minorities make up 15 per cent of the total population but are markedly absent from positions of power; they are also disproportionately represented in prison, among the unemployed, the under-educated and the low-paid. There are also differences between the various sub-groups described as minorities.

There are differences in the residences of such groups. For example the 2011 Census indicated that in Wales, the North-East and the South-West, 95 per cent of the population still define themselves as White British. In parts of London, notably Newham, that figure falls to 49 per cent. London as a whole remains 60 per cent white British with some areas, such as Kensington and Chelsea, being much higher. Since these definitions depend on people's own assessments, they may include some anomalies. For example, a third generation from a Polish background might still define themselves as 'White Other' whilst most of their neighbours would consider them to be British. The majority of those defining themselves as of ethnic minority origin are born in the UK.

The 2011 Census shows that, within the group of those defining themselves as not White British (nearly 20 per cent of the population), 6 per cent defined themselves as White Other, mostly Polish; 7.5 per cent, Asian British; 3.3 per cent, Black African or Black Caribbean (African Caribbean); and 3.2 per cent Other. Within these sub-groups there are many different groups. Indians were the

---

Activity

Read the following extract and answer the question that follows:

Poverty and ethnicity in the UK

This wide-ranging review of the literature, by Lucinda Platt at the University of Essex, summarizes the findings of poverty and ethnicity research since 1991. It describes differences in poverty rates and experiences by ethnic group. The study found that:

- There are stark differences in poverty rates according to ethnic group. Risks of poverty are highest for Bangladeshis, Pakistanis and Black Africans, but are also above average for Caribbean, Indian and Chinese people. Muslims face much higher poverty risks than other religious groups.
- The differences in poverty rates are found across poverty measures (income poverty, material deprivation) and across sub-populations (older people, children). The high rates of child poverty in some groups are of particular concern, both for their present welfare and for their future opportunities. Over half of Pakistani, Bangladeshi and Black African children are growing up in poverty.
- Evidence suggests that there is variation between ethnic groups in both the reasons for lower sources of income (for example, lower and less regular earnings, lower use of particular benefits) and in the numbers of people likely to need supporting from low income.
- Educational qualifications, employment sector, labour market experience, discrimination, location, disability, ill health and family form and structure all play a role in different poverty rates.
- When the contribution of individual characteristics (such as fewer qualifications) to employment disadvantage is analysed, there are some unexplained outcomes. For example, Black Africans have very high rates of higher education qualifications, but also suffer from high rates of unemployment and poor occupational outcomes. This 'ethnic penalty' includes the effects of discrimination.
- There also appear to be 'ethnic penalties' in access to social security benefits and other financial support.

Source: adapted from Platt (2007); from a report by the Joseph Rowntree Foundation. Further details can be found on www.jrf.org.uk.

Drawing on the data in the passage above, briefly describe the extent of **social exclusion** among ethnic groups in the UK.

Social exclusion occurs when individuals feel cut off from normal day-to-day life.

largest group among the British Asians, and West Africans the largest group among the African or African-Caribbean group.

Ethnic minorities, in any society, do not have to be among the downtrodden. The British Empire was a classic example of a minority group dominating large populations of different ethnic origins. However, in the UK today, membership of an ethnic minority tends, on the whole, to be linked to social exclusion and few advantages, though the dimensions of class and gender alter the situation – we shall see later that Indians, for example, are disproportionately represented in the medical field.

Stratification based on ethnicity

An **apartheid** system is where society is divided on the basis of ethnic grouping – more especially, skin colour. Found in South Africa until the mid-1990s.

Stratification based on ethnicity occurred in South Africa during the period of **apartheid**, when access to land, jobs and political power depended on having white skin. In many societies such as Jamaica and Brazil, the possession of light skin-colour is highly prized, and most of the ruling elites are drawn from this group. This is also true of India, where darker skin in any caste can lead to being seen as not quite belonging to the group. Perceived ethnicity was the basis for much of the 'purification' of the fatherland that took place in Hitler's Germany, where large numbers of non-Aryans, such as Gypsies and Jews, were sent to the gas chambers. Ethnicity was also given as a reason for the genocides and conflicts in the former Yugoslavia in the 1990s and for the genocide in Rwanda in 1994.

One example found in colonial Kenya shows how such stratification might operate. Milanovic (2011) shows that separation, in terms of social position and income, between the different groups was complete. He compares the life of Barack Obama's grandfather, Oyango, with that of Obama's father. In the 1920s and through to Independence in 1960, there were no high positions open to native Kenyans and no lower positions open to the settler white population. Whilst Oyango Obama worked as a domestic servant with a wage far above that of the bulk of the black population, being in the top 10 per cent of earners in the country, Kenyan Asians had an average income 14 times greater than his, whilst white settlers (0.33 per cent of the population) had average incomes 66 times greater than his. Until Independence, the opportunities for black Kenyans were very restricted – most being subsistence farmers, and very few rose to become domestic servants. After Independence, Obama's father was educated in the US and married a US citizen, and for Obama himself the path to the White House lay open.

Racism

Racism happens when people are treated differently on the basis of their ethnic origin.

Differentiating people on the basis of perceived ethnic differences can lead to both personal and institutional racism.

Racism occurs when people act in a way that discriminates against others on the basis of their ethnic origin and/or skin colour. **Institutional racism** occurs when aspects of society, especially the state or large institutions, have rules or procedures that directly or indirectly treat people differently. Direct racism would be, for example, not allowing non-whites to enter certain jobs. Indirect racism might occur if only qualifications gained in the UK were acceptable for a certain post, which would automatically disbar those who were educated outside the UK.

Institutional racism is when patterns of discrimination based on ethnicity have become structured into existing social institutions.

Dorling (2011) has pointed out that many of the current problems with racism and immigration have more to do with skin colour than actual immigrant status. He suggests that almost everyone living in the UK will have a great-, or great-great-grand-parent who was an immigrant, but until the 1930s most of these immigrants were white, and within a generation 'disappeared' into the general population. After the Second World War, Britain called on its old colonies to provide labour and these people were predominantly not white and hence found it more difficult to 'disappear'. Due to various anti-immigration laws from the 1960s onward, most current inflows are from the EU and most of the perceived non-white minorities are UK-born and not immigrants at all. He sums it up by suggesting that, when considering immigration, 'it is not the immigration that is of actual concern, it is who the potential immigrants might be'.

Dorling also points out that Britain has a long history of both inward and outward migration and there might well be twice as many grandchildren of British-born people living overseas as there are people living in Britain whose grandparents were born abroad.

Activity

Research the family trees of members of your group. Including migration from Wales, Scotland and Ireland into England, is Dorling's assertion correct?

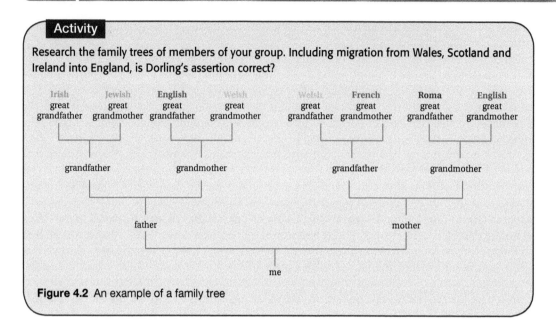

Figure 4.2 An example of a family tree

Theories about ethnic differences

Functionalist explanations of ethnic differences would tend to see them as a result of the meritocratic nature of society and suggest that differences are the result of different socialization or different educational achievement. Patterson (1965) introduced the **host–immigrant model**. This is sometimes referred to as the **assimilation model**.

In this model, the basically stable, consensus society of the United Kingdom was temporarily disrupted by waves of immigration. Such waves had occurred throughout history, with influxes from Europe, but now the incomers were from the Commonwealth and, Patterson argues, brought with them cultural norms which were dissimilar to those of the native population. Since the different cultures did not completely understand each other, these differences led to racial tension and discrimination. The white working-class group, who were competing with the newcomers for jobs, were particularly resentful. Patterson suggested that over time these differences would begin to disappear as the socialization patterns of the different groups merged into a British identity.

Both Marxist and Weberian explanations would consider the market aspect. The dual labour market and the reserve army of labour are both explanations which could be offered, as is the concept of the underclass. Whilst seeing these as explanations, Marxists might also view the existence of discrimination as a form of 'divide and rule'. Because of an existing ideology which suggests that ethnic minorities are somehow different and thus deserve lower levels of pay and employment rights, the possibility of class consciousness being fostered between all groups of workers is greatly reduced. It also allows **scapegoating** to occur.

Postmodernists suggest that ethnicity, and racism in particular, affect some groups differently. They tend to focus on culture and identity and suggest that globalization and consumption patterns are eroding ethnic identities. They introduce the notion of **hybrid identities** and say that racial/ethnic differences are now only a result of choice and no longer imposed by one's birth. However, evidence would suggest that ethnic identity is often imposed, not only by the response of others but by the very real factors of unemployment/poverty and racial discrimination and that the lives of many – but not all – ethnic minorities differ from those of their white neighbours.

Age as a basis for stratification and differentiation

Most societies distinguish between the rights of the very young, adults and the elderly. In Britain, children acquire more rights as they grow older, but in later adulthood they lose some control over portions of their lives. For example, from the age of 70, motorists have to declare their medical

---

The **host–immigrant/assimilation model** is a view of race relations which sees the host community as homogeneous and expects the immigrant groups to be absorbed into this community by adapting their culture to that of the original population.

Scapegoating is blaming an individual or group for problems which are not necessarily their fault.

Hybrid identities are ones created by a mixing of different cultural identities – for example, British Asian.

conditions and renew their driving licence every three years. Discrimination on the basis of age, in employment and other areas, is now illegal under the Age Discrimination Regulations, which came into force in October 2006.

In the UK, different ages are marked by semi-ritualized responsibilities or rights, such as being allowed to smoke tobacco, drive cars, borrow money and vote.

The social construction of age

Social construction means the way something is created through the individual, social and cultural interpretations, perceptions and actions of people. Official statistics, notions of health and illness, deviance and suicide are all examples of social phenomena that only exist because people have constructed them and given these phenomena particular labels.

If other forms of stratification and differentiation rely on people's perceptions, this is certainly true of childhood, the teenage years and old age. It is said that childhood is not a biological time span, but a **social construction**. This means that what is thought of as childhood or old age changes through time and between societies.

Childhood

Ariès (1973), writing of pre-industrial European societies, said that childhood then consisted of a very short period of time when a child was dependent on his or her parents. After the age of 4 or 5, children were treated as small adults and took part in all aspects of life. Postman (1994) dated the emergence of contemporary childhood to the invention of the printing press and the spread of literacy among the general population. Once knowledge could be written down, rather than spread only orally, it became possible to keep information secret from certain groups, most notably from those who could not read. Postman maintains that this led to an idea of childhood as a time of innocence. However, the growth of the mass media, especially the internet, is now allowing children access to knowledge far greater than that experienced by their parents at a similar age and so this notion of childhood is disappearing. Lee (2005) suggests that there has been a marketization and sexualization of children, which has made the difference between childhood and adulthood less distinct.

Teenagers

Teenagers are young people at a time of life between childhood and adulthood – in their 'teen' years. The teenager's status is often ambiguous and changes from one situation to another, which reflects the confusion felt by teenagers themselves as to their exact status.

The term **teenager**, to describe a separate group, did not occur in the UK until the late 1940s/early 1950s. In other societies, the transition from child to adult is mapped out with specific staging posts, but this is not generally true of Western societies, where there is a grey area between childhood and adulthood. This period of time is not a fixed number of years, and changes in society have added to the blurring of the edges between one stage and the next. For example, the age at which sexual activity, tobacco-smoking, marriage (with parental consent) and work are permitted have all changed radically over the years, often arbitrarily. In the early nineteenth century, there was no age bar to any of these activities, except marriage; today, there are regulations concerning many activities, and in most countries there is an official 'age of consent' before which sexual activity is illegal. Changes to education policies and welfare benefits have increased the age of dependency in the UK up to 18, whilst at the same time adult behaviour is expected and adult activities, such as consuming tobacco and alcohol and having sex, are allowed. Clearly, being a teenager is a rapidly changing condition.

Hobbs et al. (2003) suggested that, even as late as the 1950s, specifically teenage problems, such as binge drinking, did not occur, because drinking took place in the local pub or club, where the young, usually boys, learned to drink in a responsible fashion surrounded by relatives and workmates who had some control over their behaviour. Girls learned to drink responsibly in a similarly closed environment. However, as family sizes have declined, and local communities have been dispersed, these social constraints have disappeared and young people now learn to drink alcohol within their peer group. This, it is argued, has led to the greater incidence of binge drinking.

Old age

British society tends to think of the elderly as somehow different – as less capable, likely to be frail or suffering from dementia and in need of help and support. However, it is unclear what constitutes being elderly: old age is also a social construct.

As the chance of long life increases, social perceptions of old age change. Novels of the 1930s refer to 60-year-olds as 'old', but most of today's 60-year-olds do not think of themselves as elderly. Questionnaires concerning social attitudes to age have found that most of those under 60 think of old age as beginning at about 65, although, by the time they actually reach 65, most people tend to

Table 4.1 Two experiences of being a teenager

Nineteenth century	Twenty-first century
Legal aspects	
I can work	I am still at school
Work involves a twelve-hour day	If I have a job, it's only part-time
I can have sex	I can't have sex until I'm 16
I can smoke	I can't smoke until I'm 18
I can drink alcohol	I can't drink alcohol until I'm 18
I have a 50:50 chance of dying before I'm 50	I am likely to live to 80
I won't ever be able to vote	I can vote when I am 18
Social aspects	
The money I earn will not be my own	I can have my own bank account
I [if female] cannot associate with men outside of my family, and very soon it is likely my parents will choose a husband for me	I am freer to express my sexuality as I wish
If my parents are poor, I will only have had a few years of education and will have had to work from a young age	I have the right to a free education until I am 18 and I am protected from exploitative child labour by law

place the onset of old age as later than this. In addition, the experience of old age can vary widely, depending on a person's class, ethnicity and gender.

The growth in numbers of the group referred to as 'grey panthers' illustrates this. The phrase was coined to describe the wealthy, retired population who can afford to travel widely and spend extravagantly. They are also tending to flex political muscle and demand that their living standards are not diminished. Since politicians are aware that they are the group most likely to vote, they have disproportionate power as evidenced by the promise by the Coalition government of 2010 that pensioners' incomes would be protected for the life of their first Parliament.

Implications of changes in the age structure of the UK

In 1970, approximately 50 per cent of the world population was under the age of 20, and nearly as many were aged 20–64 with less than 5 per cent over 65. Today, worldwide, 25 per cent are under 20, approximately 58 per cent are between 20 and 64 with 17 per cent being over 65. But in Britain, there are now more people over the age of retirement than there are under the age of 16. The chances of achieving old age are affected by both sex and class. Women are still more likely than men to have a long retirement, though the gap is narrowing, and higher social classes have greater life expectancy. The implications of this for the future are profound, and probably underestimated. The potential of the over-50s to live to their hundredth birthday is increasing every decade and has important ramifications in terms of healthcare, housing and the funding of pensions.

These women are all of a very similar age. However, their levels of physical activity, independence and knowledge of the latest technology are very likely to determine which one you consider to be the 'oldest'.

Governments have partially recognized this fact by raising the age at which State Retirement Pensions are paid, and by setting up compulsory additional pensions for everyone earning above a specific, relatively low, limit: the so-called NEST pensions. Previous systems such as SERPS and, before that, Graduated Pensions, for middle- to high-income earners have created vast differentials in the State Pensions paid to different groups within the retired workforce. Most of the beneficiaries of previous systems tended to be men rather than women, and men are more likely to be in receipt of an occupational pension, but such pensions are also linked to class, with professionals more likely to have them than manual workers. Again the picture is affected by sex and class.

Theories about age differences

Functionalists tend to consider age at the two extremes: childhood and old age. Childhood is considered in terms of the socialization of the young to enter the workforce and find their appropriate place in the meritocracy. The elderly, as they grow older, allegedly diminish in their ability to work and thus retire to make way for the new, younger workforce to the advantage of the whole society. A criticism of this is that the skills and expertise of the older worker are thus lost to the economy and the evidence for declining capacity is somewhat uncertain.

Feminists tend to explain the differences between male and female children and elderly men and women in terms of patriarchy. Marxists, however, suggest that capitalism will use the young as a cheap form of labour and dismiss older workers as are more expensive. Stripped of their earning capacity, the elderly are then seen as a drain on the economy and their social status declines as their spending power decreases. But there are differences between groups of the elderly. Those with pensions above the average wage, usually earned from higher-class jobs in their working life, have buying power beyond that of the average family and thus it could be that class, still, is more important than age in defining one's life chances and standard of living. Postmodernists might decide that the wealthy elderly have more chance than most to create their own social identity through their consumption.

Disability as a basis for stratification and differentiation

While there are no existing stratification systems which openly use physical attributes other than age, gender and ethnicity as a basis for stratifying populations, in the past, notably in Hitler's Germany, physical and/or mental disability were used as a reason not to grant full citizen rights to certain sectors of society, or to send them to closed asylums or the gas-chambers. Evidence from both the USA and Sweden suggests that some forms of sterilization were used on the 'mentally and physically disabled' as late as the 1980s to prevent them from having children.

Most commentators tend to think of disability as a physical or mental condition, which prevents an individual from leading what is seen as a 'normal' life. However, Oliver (1990) suggests that physical/mental impairment (or an inability to carry out certain physical activities) only becomes a disability when society fails to make provision for the individual concerned to live a normal life. In theory, almost any physical difference could be made into a disability if society were to act in certain ways. For example, left-handed people sometimes argue that, in many ways, the UK is a right-handed society; and shorter people have difficulty reaching high shelves in supermarkets. With a little bit of social engineering, both these conditions could be transformed into full-scale disabilities. For example, if all food were to be placed on shelves above 5 feet high in supermarkets, then shorter people would become disabled, needing help from able-bodied tall people before they could do their shopping.

Finkelstein (1980) has dated the perception of the physically impaired as a distinct disabled group to the arrival of industrialization and the need for factory hands to work. It is argued that until that point they were merely one of several marginal groups in society, but not seen as distinctly different. Shakespeare (1994) has argued that prejudice against the physically impaired has a long history and existed before industrialization. Degrees of prejudice and discrimination may well be linked to the level of disability and how far it affects day-to-day living and working. People who are deaf say they are frequently treated as if they are also stupid, since it is, mostly, an invisible impairment and therefore frequently not recognized as existing, whereas those in wheelchairs report being ignored by people standing around them who see them only as disabled or impaired and not as people at all. Disability is increasingly a basis for **hate crimes**.

Disability, therefore, is a concept that is hard to define, since it is relative. It implies a level of exclusion and is widely used to suggest that the individual is precluded somehow from leading life in the

Hate crimes are criminal offences which are perceived by the victim or any other person to be motivated by hostility or prejudice based on a person's ethnicity, religion, sexual orientation or disability.

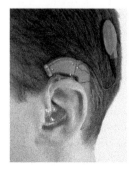

Which of these people would you say has a disability?

same way as the majority of the population. Since estimates of the number of disabled people vary widely – some suggesting that up to half the population is disabled in one way or another – it might be said that the usefulness of the concept is limited. In official statistics, it is often left to respondents to define themselves as disabled or as suffering from 'a limiting condition'. In the 2011 Census, 10 million people in England and Wales defined themselves as having a 'life-limiting condition', but since this is a self-diagnosis such statistics are often less useful than they might at first appear.

In theory, disability is not a bar to access to the highest levels of power in the UK. In reality, there are very few politicians or controllers of large businesses and financial institutions who have noticeable disabilities, though it is suggested that the incidence of bipolar disorder may be higher in this group than in the general population. However, since the stigma of mental illness is still great in British society, many people keep this aspect of their lives completely hidden, making it difficult to investigate this point. It is known that various types of disability are more likely to be found among the unemployed or those on exceptionally low wages than in the general population. The 'social selection' explanation suggests that certain forms of disability lead to a lower-class position rather than that the class of the individual caused the disability.

There may be class dimensions to how a condition is labelled. For example, children from professional-class families who suffer from dyslexia are more likely to be diagnosed and given help than those from working-class backgrounds. In Topic 2, we will see in more detail how disability affects working life.

Theories about disability

Like Finkelstein, Marxists tend to see disability more as a social factor partly created by industrial capitalism. In agricultural societies, most people are able to do some form of work and are thus integrated into their community. However, the growth of the factory led to people being assessed on their ability to work in those conditions, and thus some became labelled as disabled since they could not meet the needs of the employers. Feminists and functionalists have little specific to say about disability. Interactionists tend to concentrate more on self-perception and images of disability and the scapegoating of certain groups, which ties into the Marxist theory of divide and rule. Whilst there are other people to blame, class consciousness is unlikely to occur.

Religion as a basis for stratification and differentiation

A powerful example of a society with a stratification system based on religion is contemporary India. Other examples exist, but are not always recognized as based on religion. In the Middle East, religion could be seen as of paramount importance in explaining current conditions – for example, in Israel and Palestine, and, as we shall see later, religion is still influential in the UK.

The caste system

India still has a system based on castes, despite several Acts of the Indian Parliament to abolish it. Technically, it does not exist but, in reality, it still shapes the lives of hundreds of millions of people. Although the caste system is based on Hindu beliefs, the influence of caste affects not only Hindus but other groups too – such as Sikhs, Muslims, Jains and Parsees. It is centred on a belief in reincarnation: that one life is followed by another until a state of perfect knowledge and harmony is reached and the individual dies for the last time to become part of the universe – the state of Nirvana. Birth into a high or low caste is dependent on the purity of one's previous life. Caste is fixed at birth and one lives throughout life within that caste, working at the same job as one's father, and marrying within the caste. It is essentially a closed stratification system. The only mobility that can take place is when someone is excluded from the caste – becomes an outcast – for breaking the rules that govern it. In other words, the only possible mobility is downward. Since complete purity and Nirvana can only be attained after seven lifetimes as a Brahmin, Brahmins are deemed to be the most holy, have the highest esteem and, traditionally, have controlled the state and had great wealth.

In modern India, caste is still a great determinator of both political and economic position despite the fact that caste discrimination was outlawed in 1950. In the villages of India, in particular, caste still dictates marriage, rituals concerning birth and death, and, most importantly, occupation.

A Dalit in India, a member of the lowest caste. The caste system would have made it impossible for this man, or his child, to escape poverty. Even though the caste system is now officially outlawed, there are still great obstacles to social mobility for those traditionally from the Dalit caste.

Dalits, the untouchables, are still excluded from many posts in rural areas. The impact is tremendous although subtle. It is thought that in cities the situation is less rigid but Dalits are rarely found in prestigious occupations.

Caste considerations persist overseas. In the UK, 2012 saw the first case to come before an industrial tribunal claiming unlawful discrimination on the basis of caste differences.

Contemporary society and religious differences

In the UK, religion still is a factor in the stratification system, especially in Northern Ireland. In the late 1960s, one of the main complaints of the Catholic population was that certain jobs were closed to them and they were thus denied a chance of higher standards of living. In addition, religion is an intervening variable in the study of ethnic minority groups in the UK. It is sometimes argued that Islam acts as a unifying force between different ethnicities, such as Arabs, Palestinians, Bangladeshis and Pakistanis. Religious differences between Sikhs, Muslims and Hindus divide those coming from the Punjab or Gujarat, who might be thought to have a geographic link, into different groups. The same is possibly true also of those coming to the UK from Ulster, as whether they are Catholic or Protestant seems to be of greater importance than the town where they were born, in creating links between people. Despite the apparent unity of Islam as portrayed within the UK media, it is worth remembering that Islam, like Christianity, has different strands, so Sunnis and Shias may have less in common than appears superficially.

In the UK there is a connection between Islam and poverty, and Muslims face much higher risks of being in poverty than other religious groups, but it is not currently known whether there is a causal connection; maybe the link is coincidental. But it is possible there is discrimination on the basis of religion, just as much as on the basis of race and ethnicity. For some commentators, the two are intertwined, and discrimination must be considered when looking at religion as a form of stratification.

> A **hydraulic society** is one in which power is related to the control of access to water.

> **Bureaucracy** is a term derived from the works of Weber and means a system of organization in which there is a hierarchy of officials, each with different levels of authority.

Economic bases for stratification and differentiation

The economic bases for differentiation are to do with the control of essential resources, usually water, people and land, or the means of producing desired goods.

Hydraulic societies/control of water

Where control of water is the basis for power, and the way of distinguishing between groups, the society is known as a **hydraulic society**. Wittfogel (1957) described how complex irrigation works in Asia needed an organizational structure in order to maintain them. The state had to attract labour from the population at large, and this required a large **bureaucracy** staffed by competent and literate officials. These bureaucrats controlled all the wealth and power of the country, and became rich and powerful themselves. China, and much of Asian society, as well as the early empires of the Middle East, were – and to some extent still are – hydraulic societies.

Water is both a powerful destroyer as well as a giver of life, and controlling the supply is therefore essential for all societies, even where it is no longer the sole basis for power. The future of the Middle East may depend as much on who controls the water as on who controls the oil. Some commentators suggest that Israeli incursions into neighbouring countries are as much about water as about security.

Slavery/control of people

The classic view of slavery mostly concentrates on the ancient world of Greece and Rome, with the notion that **slavery** was also prevalent in the West until its abolition both in the UK and the USA in the nineteenth century. Certainly, the trade in slaves to the sugar and cotton plantations in the Americas made Britain very wealthy.

However, slavery, in many forms, still exists today – for example, bonded labour, whereby someone borrows money and is forced to work for the creditor for no pay until the debt is repaid. Since they are receiving no pay, they can never repay the loan. It is unknown how many people are affected by this. The Anti-Slavery Campaign (www.antislavery.org) also considers **people trafficking**, **forced labour**, early **forced marriages** and much **child labour** as forms of modern slavery since the individuals involved have no control over their lives. In 2014 the WalkFree Foundation estimated that worldwide 35 million people are trapped in modern forms of slavery. Bonded labour accounted for approximately 14.5 million, mostly in India and Pakistan, and people trafficking for sexual exploitation was found in most countries in the world. In 2012, the Thomas Coram Foundation reported that the number of children trafficked into the UK has rapidly increased. The National Referral Mechanism for trafficking victims dealt with 234 children in 2011. But, according to a 'baseline assessment', calculated using a broader range of data, it is more likely that the actual number of children trafficked into the UK was more than double that. Of the 234 young 'trafficking victims', 11 per cent were under the age of 10, the majority of whom were trafficked for domestic servitude or forced labour. In total, 56 per cent were aged 16 to 17 years old. Around half of this group were trafficked for sexual exploitation.

Control of land

Feudal/estate system

Control of land has been, and is, at the heart of many systems of stratification. In medieval Europe, the **feudal (or estate) system** depended on ownership of land, which was the basis of all power. The king owned all the land, often acquired by the right of conquest. The nobility held and administered large areas of the country, but owed allegiance to the king, providing an army when required. The nobles, in turn, granted land to lesser nobles who provided the actual fighting men. Each piece of land was worked by the peasants and serfs, who were owned by the lords. Peasants and serfs had no, or very few, freedoms and were called upon not only to farm the land held by their lord, but to go to fight when required.

Society was therefore broadly divided into what were called Estates of the realm: the First Estate was the Church or Spiritual Estate, the Second Estate was the nobility and the Third Estate was the commoners, who made up over 90 per cent of the population.

The First Estate had gradations: the pope, cardinals, archbishops, bishops, priests, curates, etc., alongside a monastic tradition. The monasteries were often large landowners. Everyone paid taxes to the church – the tithe, or one-tenth of one's income – and the Third Estate also owed tax or labour to the Second Estate. The idea of tithes still exists in some religions today, though the legal obligation to give it to the Church of England finally died out completely in the 1930s. Groups such as the

Slavery is when people are sold like objects, forced to work for no pay and have their whole lives controlled by their owners.

People trafficking is where individuals are traded across national boundaries and often sold into prostitution, frequently becoming slaves.

Forced labour is where individuals work for another person with no control over any aspect of their lives, but do get paid, usually a very small amount.

Forced marriage is a marriage in which at least one party, usually the woman, has no chance to refuse. Often involves the exchange of money.

Child labour is where children, usually under the age of 10, are employed, often for very low wages.

A **Feudal/estate system** is a system of society in which the hierarchy of power and prestige is closely tied to the ownership of land.

Unification Church (the Moonies) and Jehovah's Witnesses still expect such payment from their followers.

The estate system survived, in great part, in Russia until the emancipation of the serfs in 1861, and it could be argued that it still persists in some ways in Britain and the rest of Europe today, through the ownership of large areas of land by aristocratic families.

Industrial capitalist societies

Since the Industrial Revolution, which started in Britain around 1750 and has now spread to most of the planet, control of land and land ownership are considered less important. Instead, control of industry and commodity production is, in much of the world, a basis for stratification systems, although remnants of previous systems still remain in place. In the UK, the aristocracy still hold some power and the church still has a voice in Parliament in the House of Lords. But people are now more likely to talk of class rather than caste or estate; the notion of peasants and nobles no longer exists. Class was considered by both Marx and Weber to be a defining characteristic of society and central to an understanding of it. We now turn to look at class in more detail.

Practice questions

1 Outline and explain **two** reasons why some sociologists see stratification as inevitable. **(10 marks)**

2 Read **Item A** below and answer the question that follows.

> **Item A**
>
> Racism has often been given as a reason for the historic position of ethnic minorities. As the UK became a more diverse culture and assimilation occurred, it was hoped that differences between groups would become less marked and all would be treated equally. However, figures for poverty and unemployment show this has not happened.

Applying material from **Item A**, analyse **two** reasons why ethnic minorities still tend to be treated less equally than the majority population. **(10 marks)**

3 Read **Item B** below and answer the question that follows.

> **Item B**
>
> Despite greater equality of opportunity between young women and men, gender inequalities still exist in employment and earnings. Functionalists see this as a 'normal' state of affairs and as the result of correct socialization, whilst Marxists suggest that class affects different groups in different ways.

Applying material from **Item B** and your knowledge, evaluate the usefulness of functionalist and Marxist theories in understanding the position of women in society today. **(20 marks)**

Topic 2

SPECIFICATION AREA

Dimensions of inequality: class, status and power; differences in life chances by social class, gender, ethnicity, age and disability

We have already looked at how gender, ethnicity, age and disability affect people's lives in Topic 1, and the major theories to explain these factors. We are now going to look at social classes in the UK and how these interact with gender, ethnicity, age and disability in shaping people's lives. We shall consider major changes and whether we still live in a class society in Topic 4. It should be pointed out that the groups we are looking at have what Weber would describe as differing amounts of status and power (see Topic 1).

Life chances are originally a Weberian concept that considers the ways in which people's class, status and power affect many aspects of their lives, from their life expectancy to education, income, degrees of health and causes of death. The term is not used to describe the lives of individuals, rather the statistical likelihood of particular occurrences happening to different groups. As we shall see, the dimensions of social class, gender, ethnicity, age and disability are very tightly intertwined. The higher social groups are given status in the eyes of society and have great power to defend their position from slipping from their grasp or that of their children. Although we shall not look at definitions of class until Topic 3, we will assume basic boundaries between higher professional/managerial positions, routine administrative positions and manual work as basic class differences. In what follows, different tables and commentators have used slightly different definitions but they are all based on occupation and income. We will now consider how class interacts with gender, ethnicity, age and disability in terms of life expectancy, education, employment/income, and causes of death. Since many of the tables and figures overlap they will not be repeated.

UK social classes

Social class and health

Social class and life expectancy

From birth onwards, the social class of your parents has a marked effect on your life chances. The chance of surviving birth itself is lower in the unskilled working class than in the professional/managerial class, as seen in table 4.2.

Table 4.2 Infant mortality:[1] by socio-economic classification, England and Wales, 2007		
	Rates per 1,000 live births	
	Inside marriage	Outside marriage[2]
1.1 Large employers and higher managerial	2.7	3.3
1.2 Higher professional	3.1	3.9
2 Lower managerial and professional	3.3	3.5
3 Intermediate occupations	4.5	3.9
4 Small employers and self-employed	3.9	4.0
5 Lower supervisory and technical	3.8	4.1

Table 4.2 (continued)

	Rates per 1,000 live births	
	Inside marriage	Outside marriage[2]
6 Semi-routine occupations	6.0	6.0
7 Routine occupations	6.3	5.5
All	4.2	5.0

[1] Deaths within one year of birth.
[2] Jointly registered by both parents.

Source: Office for National Statistics 2011

Table 4.3 Life expectancy at birth by socio-economic classification and gender, England and Wales, 2007–2011

	Men	Women
1 Higher managerial and professional	82.5	85.2
2 Lower managerial and professional	80.8	84.5
3 Intermediate occupations	80.4	83.9
4 Small employers and self-employed	80	83.5
5 Lower supervisory and technical	78.9	81.9
6 Semi-routine	77.9	81.7
7 Routine	76.6	80.8
All	79.1	82.4

Source: Office for National Statistics 2015

Table 4.3 shows that there are clear advantages, in terms of longer life, in being born into families with higher managerial employment. You will also notice that gender differences exist.

Life expectancy for males by NS–SEC (National Statistics Socio–economic Classification), 1982–2011

- Inequality of life expectancy by socio-economic status widened overall from 5.6 years to 6.7 years but has shown a slight decrease from the highest difference of 7.5 in 2001
- Improvements in life expectancy varied by class with the Intermediate class gaining 7.1 years whilst the Routine class gained 5.8 years
- Despite significant growth in life expectancy at birth for all classes, the life expectancies of the Routine class in 2007–11 were still only similar to that enjoyed by the Higher Managerial and Professional Class in 1982–6
- At the age of 65, men in the Higher Managerial and Professional class could expect to live a further 20.3 years, whilst men from the Routine Class could expect to live a further 16.4 years.

Life expectancy for females by NS–SEC, 1982–2011

- Inequality of life expectancy at birth by socio-economic status widened from 3.8 years to 5.3 and was widest in the period 2007–11
- Improvements in life expectancy varied by class and was 4.8 years for the Lower Managerial and Professional class and 3.3 years for the Lower Supervisory and Technical class

- Like men in the same class, women in the Routine class had similar life expectancies to those enjoyed by the Higher Managerial and Professional class in 1982–6
- At the age of 65, women in the Higher Managerial and Professional class had a life expectancy of 22.5 years whilst those in the Routine class could expect to live another 19.4 years, both outliving men in the same class
- However, overall there is a trend for the gap between the sexes of all classes to diminish as women's lifestyles change, especially in relation to paid employment and activities such as increased smoking and alcohol consumption.

Drawn from ONS Statistical Bulletin (October 2015) *Trend in Life Expectancy at Birth and at Age 65 by Socio-economic Position based on the National Statistics Socio-economic Classification, England and Wales, 1982–1986 to 2007–2011*

Social class and the causes of death

The chances of early death are clearly linked to class. We saw earlier that life expectancy varied by class, but what kills you also has a class dimension. Accidents and transport accidents might be expected to show no class distinction but, among men aged under 64, those in Social Class V (unskilled manual workers) are twice as likely to die in a transport accident and four times more likely to die in other accidents than men in Social Class I (professionals). Figure 4.3 shows different causes of premature death (that which occurs before 65) for different social classes. All the causes of death listed here are more likely to occur among the working class than among the managerial class. The idea of heart disease being a rich man's problem is not borne out by these figures. Causes of death among the over-65s are more difficult to quantify due to many death certificates not adequately identifying the deceased's social class, simply putting 'retired' under the occupation section of the form, but we know from table 4.3 that life expectancy is higher in the managerial class than in the working class.

There is further detailed discussion of social class and health inequalities on pages 385–96 in the accompanying Volume 1 (Browne (2015)) covering the first year of the course.

Figure 4.3 Mortality of men in England and Wales aged 25–64, by selected causes of death and by social class, 2001–2003 (rates per million)

Source: compiled with data from *Health Statistics Quarterly* 38, Office for National Statistics 2008

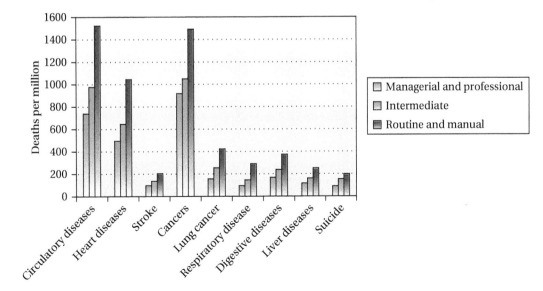

Social class and education

The advantages of coming from higher classes also apply to education, with children from higher classes tending to achieve more educationally. By the age of 18, different outcomes are apparent for different social classes. Table 4.4 shows the proportion of students in full-time education at age 18, compared to those either in some employment/apprenticeship or not in employment, education or training (**NEETS**) by social class and parental educational achievement. The differences are quite marked. The children of the lowest two classes are twice as likely to be NEETS as are the children of higher professionals, and less likely to stay in full-time education.

It is also worth noting the link between parental education and the likelihood of a student staying in education. Since, historically, graduates have earned more and been in the higher classes, it might suggest that in order to stay in the same social class as their parent(s), children in the higher professional classes have to remain in education.

NEETS are people between the ages of 16 and 25 who are not in education, employment or training.

Table 4.4 Main activity at age 18, by class and parental education, for year 2009 (%)

	Full-time education	Job with training	Job without training	Government-supported training	Not in employment, education or training
Parental occupation					
Higher professional	56	12	17	6	10
Lower professional	52	11	20	6	11
Intermediate	42	12	24	8	14
Lower supervisory	34	15	28	9	14
Routine	34	12	25	8	21
Unclassified	42	8	18	5	28
Parental education					
Degree	62	8	15	4	11
At least 1 A-level	45	13	21	8	12
Below A-level/not sure	38	12	25	7	18

Source: adapted from *Youth Cohort Study and the Longitudinal Study of Young People in England: The Activities and Experiences of 17 year olds: England 2010*, Department for Education

You should have studied social class differences in education in the first year of your A level studies, and there is further detailed discussion of this on pages 52–66 in the accompanying Volume 1 (Browne (2015)) covering the first year of the course.

Social class inequalities in income and wealth

Since social class definitions, which we shall consider in Topic 3, are mostly based on employment/occupation, this section will look at **income** and **wealth** differences between sectors of the population. The UK is a society with great inequality of both income and wealth.

Income refers to an inward flow of money over time. For most people this consists of wages/salary, but other sources are benefits, pensions, interest on savings and dividends from shares.

Income

Income, both in the UK and worldwide, shows great disparities. In the UK in 2014, the median wage (the wage at which half the wage-earners are above and half are below) was approximately £22,000 per year. Certain Premier League footballers were earning more than three times that amount per week.

Wealth refers to the total value of the possessions held by an individual or society.

Figure 4.4
Distribution of
household wealth:
Great Britain,
2010–12

Source: Browne (2015)

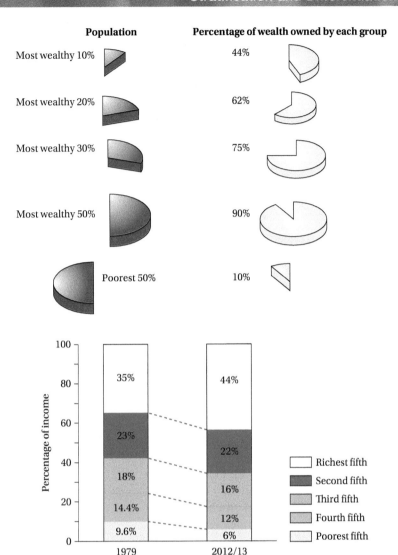

Population   Percentage of wealth owned by each group

Most wealthy 10%   44%

Most wealthy 20%   62%

Most wealthy 30%   75%

Most wealthy 50%   90%

Poorest 50%   10%

Figure 4.5 Changes
in the distribution
of income, by fifths
of the population:
United Kingdom,
1979–2012/13

Source: Browne (2015)

Percentage of income

1979: 35%, 23%, 18%, 14.4%, 9.6%

2012/13: 44%, 22%, 16%, 12%, 6%

Richest fifth
Second fifth
Third fifth
Fourth fifth
Poorest fifth

Wealth

Attitudes to wealth will differ between those who inherit it and those who earn it. There are of course, different forms of wealth:

- Land and property, including mining rights
- Industrial ownership
- Finance and banking
- Ownership of stocks and shares.

All these forms of wealth can be passed from one generation to another.

Figures 4.4 and 4.5 show the division of wealth, in 2010–12, and in income in the period 1979–2012/13 in the United Kingdom, and table 4.5 shows what this means in real terms, the actual amount of money this wealth represents.

It is worth noting that the figures in table 4.5 exclude money or assets held in trust funds. The very wealthy in our society hold their assets in this way in order to avoid inheritance tax and other fiscal measures which might deprive them of their assets, so these figures probably underestimate the wealth of the very richest. Not only do they have high status because of their wealth, but this status gives them the power to hide the exact extent of their assets. If we exclude housing from the picture the bottom half of the UK population owned just 1 per cent of the total wealth, and the top 1 per cent owned more than the bottom 75 per cent put together.

Table 4.5 Household total wealth (banded): 2010/12 (Great Britain)	2010/12
	Percentage of households'
< £12,500	10
> £12,500 but < £40,000	11
> £40,000 but < £100,000	12
> £100,000 but < £150,000	8
> £150,000 but < £250,000	13
> £250,000 but < £300,000	6
> £300,000 but < £450,000	12
> £450,000 but < £600,000	8
> £600,000 but < £1 million	11
£1 million or more	9

Source: *Wealth and Assets Survey*, Office for National Statistics 2014

This inequality has grown and this growth is not just a UK phenomenon. Figures from the USA are similar. Frank (2007) shows that, whilst all groups in the USA saw a rise in living standards between 1979 and 2003, the poorest 20 per cent saw a rise in income of just 3.5 per cent whilst the top 5 per cent saw an increase of 68 per cent in their income, so the rich are growing richer at a far faster rate than their compatriots. This is also true throughout the developing world.

Dorling et al. (2007) showed how wealth and poverty have polarized in the UK in the latter part of the twentieth century. Not only is wealth (and poverty) increasingly concentrated in particular social groups and classes, but it clusters geographically as well. Dorling et al. point, in particular, to the fact that poverty is clustered in urban areas, while wealth is more concentrated in the country-side and in the south-east of the country. Thus the classes based on these differences in wealth are also clustered in different areas.

Worldwide, the situation is similar. In 2006, the World Institute for Development Economics Research found that the richest 1 per cent in the world owned 40 per cent of the planet's wealth. The richest 10 per cent owned 85 per cent, while the poorest 50 per cent owned just 1 per cent of this wealth. Even within this bottom half, there will be vast discrepancies between the wealth of individuals. Within these groups we know that women will own less than men, and children less than adults. We will consider this further in Topic 4.

Gender

Gender and health

Gender and life expectancy

Despite many of the arguments of feminist sociologists (see Topic 1), the differences between the classes are as great, or greater, than the differences between the genders. Statistics for mortality and life expectancy, as seen in table 4.3 and figure 4.6, all show that the higher the social class, the greater the chance of a long and healthy life, regardless of one's sex. Whilst it is now true that women in all classes outlive men, this trend seems to be declining over time as women take a greater role in the workplace and indulge in more hazardous lifestyle choices, such as tobacco smoking and alcohol consumption.

Figure 4.6 Life expectancy at birth and age 65 by sex and social class

Source: compiled with data from *Health Statistics Quarterly* 49, Office for National Statistics 2011

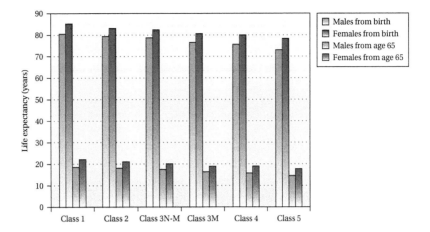

Gender and premature death

Social inequalities in mortality among men have been studied continuously since the early twentieth century. Corresponding studies of female mortality have been rarer, as a result of women's historically weaker ties to the labour market and the related difficulties in accurately classifying women to a socio-economic class based on occupation. However, some studies did measure inequalities in mortality among women. The *Black Report* (Black 1980) estimated that the premature death rate for women in the most disadvantaged social class was two and a half times higher than the comparable rate for women in the most advantaged social class. Table 4.6 brings the figures more up-to-date and shows that, whilst premature death rates have been falling in all social classes, the decline is uneven over the years and is more marked for the Managerial and professional group than for the Routine and manual group.

Although fewer women than men die prematurely whilst still of working age, class has a fairly major effect on their chances of reaching retirement age. The class aspect for both men and women shows a similar trend: those in the higher classes are less likely to die young and also have a longer life expectancy.

There is further detailed discussion of gender and health differences on pages 396–9 in the accompanying Volume 1 (Browne (2015)) covering the first year of the course.

Table 4.6 Age-standardized mortality rates by condensed NS-SEC of women aged 25–59 from 2001 to 2008, rate per 100,000

Year	NS-SEC ANALYTIC CLASSES		
	Managerial and professional	Intermediate	Routine and manual
2001	130	164	242
2002	127	164	235
2003	121	168	247
2004	116	161	240
2005	117	161	238
2006	111	161	238
2007	111	157	237
2008	109	164	234

Source: adapted from *Health Statistics Quarterly* 52, Office for National Statistics 2011

Gender and education

Since the early 1990s, girls as a group have been out–performing boys at both GCSE and A–level. Girls are more likely than boys to stay in education post-16 – 48 per cent compared to 42 per cent for boys – and are slightly less likely to be NEETS – 14 per cent as compared to 16 per cent.

When we turn to look at university education, we see in table 4.7 that in nearly every ethnic group, except for the Asian/Asian British group, more females than males undertake higher education. Unfortunately, this does not necessarily lead to the same level of well-paid jobs for the two genders. It is worth noticing that female participation is not evenly spread between all groups: the females from all the ethnic minority groups are more likely to go on to higher education than white women.

You should have studied gender differences in education in the first year of your A level studies, and there is further detailed discussion of this on pages 67–77 in the accompanying Volume 1 (Browne (2015)) covering the first year of the course.

Table 4.7 Higher education initial participation rates (percentage of each group participating)

Ethnic Group	Male	Female	All
White	34	41	38
All minority ethnic	55	58	56
Asian or Asian British	62	59	60
Black or Black British	55	66	61
Chinese or Other Ethnic	47	50	49
Mixed ethnic	35	44	40
All (with known ethnicity)	37	43	40

Source: Stijn Broecke and Tom Nicholls, *Ethnicity and Degree Attainment*, Department for Education and Skills Research Report RW92, 2007

Gender and employment

Paid work

Women as a group are less likely to be in full-time work, or in highly paid occupations. Platt (2011) has noted that the employment gap between men and women is substantial. About 79 per cent of working-age men but only 70 per cent of working-age women were in employment in 2008, and over half the jobs taken by women were part-time rather than full-time. Hakim (2000) has suggested that this may be due to preference, but preference theory cannot really explain the class differences that exist. Hills et al. (2010) point out that a fifth of women from a professional household have a full-time job, compared with over half of women from 'routine' or 'semi-routine' households. (For more detail on this typology see Topic 3.) However, some ethnic minority women are more likely to work full-time, possibly because of greater need for income and/or more available childcare from within the household.

Many occupations are gendered, with women found in personal service, administration or sales, with men predominating in managerial positions and skilled trades. The reasons for this may be wide-ranging and interwoven. When women take a career break to have children there are long-reaching consequences, such as in their career trajectory, the reduced likelihood of promotion and reduction in relative pay, and then later, into old age, a reduced pension entitlement and hence the greater likelihood of poverty. When looking at gender and poverty, Platt (2011) has shown that, whilst 21 per cent of single male pensioners are in poverty, 30 per cent of single female pensioners are. Single men and women without children are both similar in poverty risk, but single people with children have a 35 per cent chance of being in poverty. The vast bulk of these are women, and usually women from the lower social classes.

We will look in more detail at gender differences in terms of employment and pay when we look at ethnic dimensions in employment in figure 4.9 and Table 4.12. They show women earning less than men and being employed part-time rather than full-time. Most feminists argue that the status of women is lower than that of men and their power is also less. Despite the changes in women's lives in the last forty years, it is still true that very few women enter the boardrooms of major companies as executives rather than secretaries, and therefore, on that measure, their power still seems to be low compared to that of men. Part of the reason for this may lie in the theories of the dual labour market and the reserve army of labour which were considered in Topic 1.

Unpaid work

There are marked differences in the amount of unpaid work – household labour – undertaken by men and women, with the bulk being done by women, though the higher the social class the smaller the difference, as noted by Oakley (1974b). But within these family differences, there are also ethnic differences. For example, within African Caribbean families, according to Reynolds (2001), 51 per cent are lone-parent mothers who work full-time and rely on honorary or natural grandmothers to help with childcare. Within South Asian families, Beishon et al. (1998), Bhatti (1999) and Brah (1992) have noted a more extended family network with household chores shared between generations of women, mixed with full-time work for some of the female members, depending on the financial needs of the household, while Asian women were more likely than white women to experience the dual burden of paid and domestic work.

Power within households as described by Pahl (1993) and Edgell (1980), concerning finance control and decision, suggest that men are more likely to be in control but that the higher the social class, the less this occurred. Also, when women's wages equalled or exceeded those of the man, the power relationship altered. Whilst Brah noted the public subservience of Asian women to their men-folk, she noted that within the domestic sphere women control the economy, and decision-making is largely shared.

One of the largest ethnic minorities in the UK is the Irish community and here the role of women is central to the family. More women than men migrated to the UK, but they are also called upon to return to Ireland to nurse or care for elderly relatives. The extended kin network is very strong, and Ryan (2004) notes the way in which family provided accommodation, jobs and financial assistance for newcomers migrating to England. In many ways the immigrant Irish family with its extended family pattern reflects the findings of Young and Willmott's (1962) work in East London in the early 1950s, and this migration pattern was followed by immigrants from the Indian sub-continent.

One area in which change might have occurred is in childcare, and it was hoped that with **paternity leave** men would be more involved with this. However, Miller (2011), studying middle-class men at the birth of their first child, found that their good intentions of sharing childcare with the mothers lasted only a short while until the demands of balancing work and childcare collided. Although these men are more actively involved in childcare than their own fathers were, they find that 'whilst taking turns in aspects of caring, for the most part it is the mother who is left holding the baby'.

Paternity leave is where men are given time off from work, with pay, to be with their partner and child during a short time in the first six months of the child's life.

Ethnicity

We saw earlier in Topic 1 some links between ethnicity and poverty. Ethnicity also has a great effect on family life – as seen earlier, it affects educational chances, employment opportunities and causes of death. However, there are many differences between ethnic minority groups in the UK, depending on such factors as:

- The country of origin
- Whether they were born here
- The time period when they arrived
- Their fluency in English

- Their family structure
- Their age
- The amount of racism they have encountered.

Platt (2011) shows that over 90 per cent of children from Pakistani, Bangladeshi and African Caribbean (Black Caribbean) backgrounds were UK-born. For these groups, fluency of language may not be a problem, but racism probably is.

Rollock et al. (2012) look at how the black middle classes attempt to overcome this racism by adopting a set of what Bourdieu would call '**cultural capitals**' which include 'accent, language and comportment to signal their class status to others'. They conclude that it is evident that racism persists and even middle-class blacks are judged on the colour of their skin, but 'they have at their disposal relative power and privilege . . . by deployment of cultural capital that is not available to their black working class counterparts'.

> **Cultural capital** is the knowledge, education, attitudes and values usually associated with the upper social classes.

Ethnicity and health

Ethnicity and life expectancy

Figures in table 4.8 show that ethnic minorities in the UK have broadly similar life expectancies to the majority White British population and, like them, the differences are between men and women rather than different ethnicities. However, at present, there are relatively low numbers of older people in ethnic minority communities since the vast bulk of migration was of young people from 1948 to 1970. They are just now beginning to reach retirement age.

Ethnicity and causes of premature death

At the present time, the wave of immigrants who arrived from the late 1950s onwards are just entering retirement, and figures are now becoming available for causes of premature death. Because the numbers involved are relatively small, many of the rates lack rigorous statistical validity. However, an interesting study of heart disease seen in table 4.9 shows that, whilst ethnicity may play a part in early death, class is probably a greater determinant.

Table 4.8 Ethnicity and life expectancy at birth, United Kingdom 2001

Ethnic group	Male	Female
All	76.2	82.2
White British	76.2	80.6
White Irish	75.6	80.5
White Other	77.1	81.2
Mixed	75.1	79.9
Indian	76.3	79.6
Pakistani	74.6	78.3
Bangladeshi	74.4	78.5
Other Asian	75.9	79.7
Black Caribbean	75.5	79.5
Black African	77.1	80.7
Chinese	78.6	82.2

Source: adapted from Rees and Wohland, *Estimates of Ethnic Mortality in the UK*, University of Leeds School of Geography, Working Paper 08/04 Version 1, 2008

Standardized Mortality Ratio is a measure of actual deaths against expected deaths. Figures below 100 suggest fewer than expected, and those above 100 indicate a higher-than-expected death rate.

Table 4.9 Standardized Mortality Ratios, for men born in India, Pakistan Pakistan and Bangladesh and living in England and Wales, aged 20–64, by social class, for coronary heart disease, 1991–1993

Class	All in England and Wales	India	Pakistan	Bangladesh
I/II	71	126	151	177
IIIN	107	157	233	291
IIIM	125	180	181	232
IV/V	137	188	249	309
Non-manual	78	133	170	227
Manual	130	184	220	282
All	100	140	163	184
Deaths	49,845	908	418	221

Source: derived from Seroomanie Harding, 'Examining the Contribution of Social Class to High Cardiovascular Mortality among Indian, Pakistani and Bangladeshi Male Migrants Living in England and Wales', Health Statistics Quarterly 5, 2000

For all three groups, it is clear that death rates are higher than should be expected and especially so among the manual groups. The author concluded that these ethnic differences 'are more likely to be due to social and environmental factors than genetic factors. The lowering of coronary heart disease death rates in south Asians in Canada, and the rise in diabetes in a similar group in England and Wales suggest factors in the current environment are important.' Other ethnic groups show similar class gradients in the death rates from genetically pre-disposed conditions such as sickle-cell anaemia. So it could be argued that, regardless of ethnicity, class determines the likelihood of premature death.

There is further detailed discussion of ethnicity and health differences on pages 400–2 in the accompanying Volume 1 (Browne (2015)) covering the first year of the course.

Ethnicity and education

There seem to be marked differences between ethnic minority communities when it comes to education, both in terms of participation at various levels and in achievement, as table 4.10 shows. The box below contains findings from a Department for Education report from 2005. Table 4.11 shows

- In 2004, 17 per cent of the maintained school population in England was classified as belonging to a minority ethnic group.
- Indian, Chinese, White/Asian and Irish pupils are more likely to gain five or more A*–C GCSEs, compared to other ethnic groups.
- Gypsy/Roma pupils, Travellers of Irish Heritage, Black Caribbean and White/Black Caribbean pupils are amongst the lower achieving pupils at Key Stage 4.
- Only 23 per cent of Gypsy/Roma pupils achieved 5+ A*–C GCSEs in 2003 (compared to the 51 per cent national average).
- Attainment data on Mixed Heritage pupils shows that White/Asian pupils are amongst the highest-achieving ethnic groups (with 65 per cent attaining 5+ A*–C GCSEs, compared to the 51 per cent national figure), and that White/Black Caribbean pupils have lower achievement than the average (40 per cent attaining 5+ A*–C GCSEs).

- Black Caribbean and Black Other boys are twice as likely to have been categorized as having behavioural, emotional or social difficulty as White British boys.
- Pakistani pupils are two to five times more likely than White British pupils to have an identified visual impairment or hearing impairment (identified as a special educational need of School Action Plus or statement).
- Permanent exclusion rates are higher than average for Travellers of Irish Heritage, Gypsy/Roma, Black Caribbean, Black Other and White/Black Caribbean pupils.
- Black Other pupils have higher rates of unauthorized absence than other pupils. White pupils have higher rates of authorized absence than Black Caribbean, Indian, Bangladeshi, Black African or Chinese pupils.
- Just over half (53 per cent) of parents/carers of minority ethnic children reported feeling very involved with their child's education, a much greater proportion than the 38 per cent of a representative sample of all parents who reported this.
- Of all teachers teaching in England, 9 per cent are from a minority ethnic group. In London, this figure rises to 31 per cent.

Taken from *Ethnicity and Education: The Evidence on Minority Ethnic Pupils*, Department for Education and Skills: Research Topic Paper RTP01–05, January 2005

the proportion of different ethnic groups who stay in education after 16, enter employment or training, or become NEETS. There are quite wide differences between the groups. Explanations tend to focus on parental attitudes to education in explaining these differences, particularly in relation to staying on after compulsory education ends.

If we use poverty as a crude indicator of social class and use the number of children receiving free school meals as an indicator of poverty, as shown in figures 4.7 and 4.8, then the connection between ethnicity and educational achievement takes on a distinctly class dimension. It could be argued that it is the child's class as much as their ethnicity that affects their achievement levels.

Being poor and in receipt of free school meals (FSM) affects educational attainment, as figure 4.7 shows. The decision to give free school meals to all children in the first three years of their primary education from September 2014 means that this indicator of poverty will not be so easily seen in future statistics. Of those pupils known to be eligible for FSM, there are variations in achievement by gender and ethnic group – for example:

- in 2010–11, of White British boys eligible for FSM, 22.8 per cent achieved 5 or more A*–C grades at GCSE or equivalent, including English and mathematics, compared with the overall national level of 54.8 per cent.

Table 4.10 Key Stage 4: proportion of pupils achieving 5 or more A*–C grades at GCSE or equivalent, including English and mathematics GCSEs, by selected ethnic groups, 2009/2010

Ethnicity	% gaining 5 or more GCSEs
White British	55
Black Caribbean	45
Indian	70
Pakistani	50
Bangladeshi	55
Chinese	75

Source: adapted from *GCSE and Equivalent Attainment by Pupil Characteristics in England*, Department for Education 2010

Table 4.11 Main activity at age 18 by ethnicity (%)

Ethnicity	Full-time education	Job with training	Job without training	Government-supported training	Not in employment, education or training
All groups	45	11	22	7	15
White	41	12	24	7	16
Mixed	48	11	21	4	16
Indian	78	5	8	1	9
Pakistani	67	5	10	3	16
Bangladeshi	63	3	13	3	18
Other Asian	79	2	8	3	8
Black African	85	2	5	2	7
Black Caribbean	57	8	15	4	16
Other	62	3	16	1	18

Source: adapted from *Youth Cohort Study and the Longitudinal Study of Young People in England: The Activities and Experiences of 17 year olds: England 2010*, Department for Education

- In 2010–11, of Black Caribbean boys eligible for FSM, 27.6 per cent achieved 5 or more A*–C grades at GCSE or equivalent, including English and mathematics, compared with the overall national level of 54.8 per cent.

In table 4.11, we saw the figures for ethnic minority participation in higher education (HE). However, despite high HE participation rates, a number of studies have found that students from minority ethnic communities perform less well than their White peers and obtain fewer upper-second- or first-class degrees (so-called 'good' degrees). This has serious implications, as having a good degree has a premium in the labour market. It should be noted, however, though students from minority ethnic communities are less likely to perform well than their White counterparts, men from these groups perform significantly less well than the women.

But there are variations – for example, when looking at entry to medical school, Dorling (2011) found that, in 2004, the group most likely to be studying medicine were Asians from Social Class I – whose parents were professionals or owners of big businesses. They were forty-two times more

Figure 4.7
Percentage of children eligible for free school meals by ethnic group, 2004

Source: Ethnicity and Education: The Evidence on Minority Ethnic Pupils, Department for Education and Skills: Research Topic Paper RTP01–05, January 2005

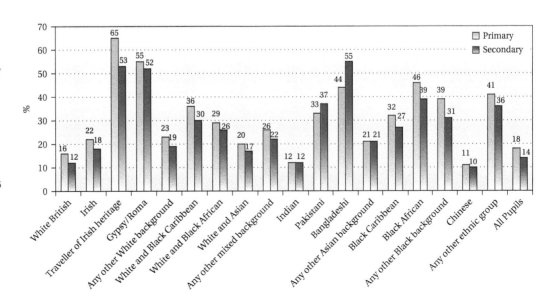

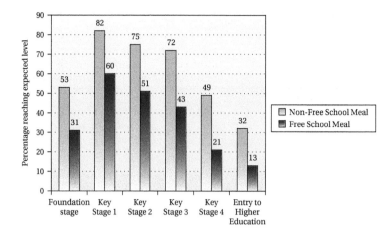

Figure 4.8 Free school meals and educational attainment at different stages

Source: Hills et al. (2010)

likely to be in medical school than the average young white person, and 600 times more likely than black students from Social Class IV. Since there were no black students from Social Class V enrolled in medical school between 1996 and 2000, it was impossible to work out a ratio comparing this group. Interestingly, there were more girls than boys among this Asian group.

Thus we can see that the variables of class and gender have an effect on educational attainment, as well as ethnicity. This is later reflected partly in the different earning power of men and women from different groups.

You should have already studied ethnicity and education in the first year of your A level studies, and there is further detailed discussion of this on pages 78–86 in the accompanying Volume 1 (Browne (2015)) covering the first year of the course.

Ethnicity and employment

The statistics in table 4.12 and figure 4.10 show that there are clear employment and pay differences between groups and between minority groups and the majority white population. The chances of working full-time vary between groups and between genders, and the pay rates for full-time workers also vary widely, with all groups of women being lower-paid than men in the same group – but some ethnic minorities do better than the white group, whilst others do not. Platt (2011) points out that the white group of women has a higher proportion of older workers, who, due to a discontinuous work history, may not be able to command higher rates of pay. The picture cannot be explained simply in terms of just ethnicity or gender, though racism and sexism probably play their part. The dimensions of age and class may also be factors. The situation is complex and there are no simple explanations.

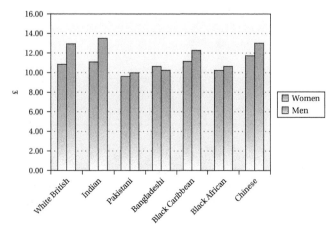

Figure 4.9 Pay of men and women in full-time work by ethnic group, 2007

Source: compiled with data from Longhi and Platt (2008)

Table 4.12 Employment status by sex and ethnicity, Great Britain 2004–2007 by percentage (to the nearest whole number)

	Employed full-time	Employed part-time	Self-employed	Un-employed	Other / inactive
White British men	60	5	13	4	18
Indian men	58	6	12	6	18
Pakistani men	37	7	19	7	30
Bangladeshi men	36	19	10	10	25
Black Caribbean men	50	6	10	12	22
Black African men	55	10	6	9	20
Chinese men	36	9	12	7	36
White British women	39	27	4	3	27
Indian women	38	18	3	3	38
Pakistani women	13	7	2	5	73
Bangladeshi women	10	8	3	7	72
Black Caribbean women	44	15	3	6	32
Black African women	38	13	2	7	40
Chinese women	30	18	7	5	40

Source: adapted from Longhi and Platt (2008: fig. 2.1)

In attempting to explain the rates of part-time work and self-employment, which show differing levels in the groups, Platt (2011) suggests that the high level of part-time work amongst Bangladeshi men may be a reflection of their higher rates of disability, making it harder for them to find full-time work. She also suggests that the high level of self-employment among Pakistani men, rather than being seen as positive and a sign of being small businessmen, may reflect the work these men do, with a high concentration of taxi work and chauffeuring, neither of which can be seen as either well-paid or high in status.

Age

We saw earlier, in Topic 1, that class affects the way you are socialized as a child. It also affects your education chances, your family life, the work you do and hence many other parts of the ageing process. As you age, your pay first rises and then falls, and as you reach retirement your likelihood of being in poverty rises, though there will be marked class differences here as well. With ageing, your chance of becoming disabled increases. Berthoud (2006) estimates that, at age 20, about 5 per cent of the population are disabled; at age 60, it is nearer 28 per cent. We look at class and disability in more detail later.

Age and wealth and poverty

Being young or being old are both conditions with a high chance of being in poverty. Current estimates for 2010/11 from the Department for Work and Pensions suggest that 2.3 million children in the UK – which represents 18 per cent of the under-16s – live in families whose income is inadequate to meet their basic needs. In most cases, the parents are working, but their pay is so low that it is supplemented by various state benefits. When housing costs are taken into account, the figure rises to 3.6 million children, which equals 27 per cent of children. Poverty, as we saw earlier, is found in the lower social classes not the higher.

When it comes to later age and income, Aldridge et al. (2011) found that, although in the age-group 55–59 about 30 per cent earn in the top fifth of income distribution, by the age of 70, more women are in the bottom fifth than in the top fifth. For men that point is reached at age 80. However, this makes clear that not all elderly are poor, but that there is a greater likelihood of so being. In 2009/10, 1.1 million pensioners had no income other than the State Retirement Pension and/or state benefits. In 2009/10, around 9.2 million people living in households headed by people aged 55 or above had household savings of less than £1,500. More detailed analysis of this shows that 80 per cent of those with household savings of less than £1,500 had no savings at all.

On the whole, women earn less than men during their working life and suffer greater poverty in retirement. Women are more likely than men to be in receipt of social security benefits such as Income Support or Working Tax Credits during their 'working' life, and Pension Credits in their retirement. This becomes doubly true if they are from an ethnic minority, and even more true if they are disabled or in ill health.

Poverty and **social exclusion** are similarly linked to forms of differentiation such as age, gender, ethnicity, disability or locality. An elderly, childless widow living in a country village with no post office, bus service, doctor or shop may be socially excluded even if she is relatively wealthy, whereas her counterpart in a big city may be less socially excluded because she has access to many services.

Social exclusion occurs when individuals feel cut off from normal day-to-day life.

Putnam (2000) has suggested a link between social exclusion and **social capital**. Social capital refers to a person's social networks of friends and relatives. High social capital can, to some extent, lessen the problems of social exclusion experienced by different groups. For example, a newly arrived Bangladeshi woman speaking little English, living as part of the only Asian family in the village, will have less social capital and experience higher social exclusion than if she lives in a multi-cultural town with an enclave of other Asian families.

Social capital refers to the social networks of influence and support that people have.

So it can be seen that class (as measured by poverty) affects life in both youth and old age, but gender, ethnicity and disability are also tightly interwoven. Due partly to the dependency of the young and some elderly people, their status in society is not great. Their power, particularly for children, is very limited due to the controls that their parents and/or wider society place upon them. It is invidious to suggest that all old people lack power, since among the wealthy elderly the strength of the grey pound is immense, but for the poor, group action seems to be the only way to effect changes. There is now a growing Pensioner Voice, championed by the TUC and other bodies, to give the elderly more of a say in their lives.

Disability

Disability takes many forms, both physical and mental, and we saw earlier that Berthoud (2006) showed how it increased as people grew older. Disability has far-reaching consequences in terms of education, employment and earnings. This is especially true for mental illness/disability. We will look at these aspects in turn. Longhi et al. (2009) show that, compared to the non-disabled, those with physical or mental disabilities are less qualified, more likely to be working part-time rather than full-time, more likely to be found in manual than non-manual jobs, and to earn significantly less. What it is difficult to do is to disentangle cause from effect. Is disability being discriminated against in the workplace or are the low qualifications a result of the disability? Disabled people are disproportionately found in the lower social classes, but is this because of their disability or is being lower-class more likely to lead to disability? The Office for Disability Issues has demographic details of the level of disability, and some of its effects are discussed in the box below.

Some general points concerning disability in Great Britain

- There are over 11 million people with a limiting long-term illness, impairment or disability in Great Britain.
- In Great Britain, the most commonly reported impairments are those that affect mobility, lifting or carrying.

- The prevalence of disability rises with age. Around 6 per cent of children are disabled, compared to 15 per cent of working-age adults, and 45 per cent of adults over state pension age in Great Britain.
- A substantially higher proportion of individuals who live in families with disabled members live in poverty, compared to individuals who live in families where no one is disabled.
- 22 per cent of children in families with at least one disabled member are in poverty, a significantly higher proportion than the 16 per cent of children in families with no disabled member.
- 20 per cent of working-age disabled people do not hold any formal qualification, compared to 7 per cent of working-age non-disabled people.
- 14.5 per cent of working-age disabled people hold degree-level qualifications compared to 26.8 per cent of working-age non-disabled people.
- According to the Labour Force Survey, disabled people are now more likely to be employed than they were in 2002 – the employment rate gap between disabled and non-disabled people has narrowed slightly by 5.8 percentage points and stood at 29.9 per cent in 2012.
- However, disabled people remain far less likely to be in employment. In 2012, 46.3 per cent of disabled people were in employment, compared to 76.2 per cent of non-disabled people.
- Disabled people are significantly more likely to experience unfair treatment at work than non-disabled people. In 2008, 19 per cent of disabled employees experienced unfair treatment at work, compared to 13 per cent of non-disabled employees.
- Around a third of disabled people experience difficulties related to their impairment in accessing public, commercial and leisure goods and services.
- Disabled people are less likely to live in households with access to the internet. In 2010, 58 per cent of disabled people lived in households with internet access, compared to 84 per cent of non-disabled people.
- Disabled people are significantly more likely to be victims of crime than non-disabled people.

Taken from *Key Facts from the Life Opportunities Survey Interim Results, 2009/10*, from the Office for Disability Issues 2012

Disability and education

The *Youth Cohort Study* examined in tables 4.4 and 4.11 also reveals that, although the proportion of disabled students staying on in education at age 16 was the same as the national average, they were less likely than the non-disabled to have any kind of job or training and were more likely to be NEETs, with 22 per cent fitting into this category. Figure 4.10 shows the levels of education reached by disabled people, which are lower, in every area, than the achievements of non-disabled students.

Figure 4.10 Summary of educational attainment of adults with impairments, 2009/2010

Source: Office for National Statistics 2012

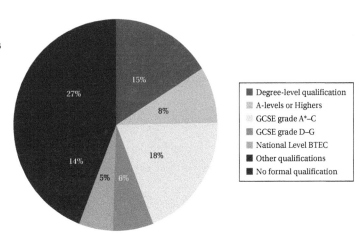

- Degree-level qualification
- A-levels or Highers
- GCSE grade A*–C
- GCSE grade D–G
- National Level BTEC
- Other qualifications
- No formal qualification

Table 4.13 Degree-level qualifications by percentage of total population, aged 16–64 (males) and 16–59 (females), Great Britain

	2002	2003	2004	2005	2006	2007	2008	2009	***	2010	2011	2012
Disabled	8.2	8.4	9.7	9.9	10.8	11.2	11.4	12.7		13.4	14.5	14.9
Non-disabled	17.4	18.0	19.0	19.6	20.7	21.5	22.1	23.2		24.8	26.8	28.1

*** Gap in data due to changes in reporting disability.
Respondents who report a current disability consistent with the Disability Discrimination Act (DDA) are defined as disabled. From 1 October 2010, provisions in the Equality Act 2010 replaced the majority of provisions in the DDA.

Source: Office for Disability Issues, *Disability Indicators*, derived from Labour Force Survey, Quarter 2, 25 October 2012

Whilst the proportion of disabled people getting degree-level qualifications has improved in the last ten years, so has the proportion of non-disabled people. Table 4.13 shows the gap has not actually decreased. Explanations for this will obviously include such aspects as discrimination, difficulty of access and, possibly, funding.

Disability and employment

We saw earlier that disability is linked to levels of unemployment higher than the national average, with only 46.3 per cent of disabled people being employed, compared to 76.2 per cent of non-disabled people, in 2012. Within these figures, and in employment/unemployment figures generally, where disabled people are concerned, there are also differences by gender as seen in figure 4.11. This shows that women with disability are less likely to be employed full time than men with disability.

One explanation for these gender differences might be found in the feminist and Marxist arguments about the reserve army of labour which we discussed in Topic 1. If we then add ethnicity into the equation, the picture becomes more difficult. Part of the problem with figures for disability lies with the fact that, to some extent, disability is partly a matter of self-perception and self-reporting. Whilst blindness or wheelchair use may be self-evident other levels of disability are not so clear-cut, so often the disability is self-reported. The figures for reporting a long-term limiting illness, which would prevent normal life, show there are ethnic differences: 15 per cent of White British claim to be affected by this, but only 11 per cent of Chinese and 16 per cent of Black Africans do, with Black Caribbeans and Indians at 18 per cent, and Pakistanis and Bangladeshis reporting levels at about 24 per cent. Within these groups, there are differences between men and women. Because it is self-reported, it is difficult to know how much cultural expectations play their part in deciding to label oneself as having a limiting illness.

When we come to look at class and disability, occupation and earnings, Longhi et al. (2009, 2012) found that disabled people generally earn less than non-disabled people: the earnings for physically

Figure 4.11 Employment status and disability, men and women 2006–2008

Source: adapted from the Labour Force Survey 2009

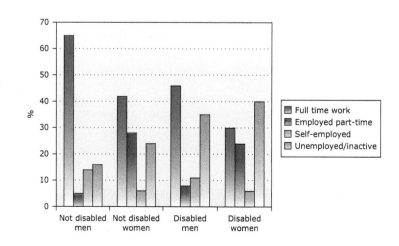

Table 4.14 Occupations of disabled and non-disabled men (aged 23–64) in paid work, 1997–2008 (pooled data), UK (percentages)				
Occupation	Non-disabled	All disabled	Physical disability	Mental disability
Managers & senior officials	21.7	16.7	16.9	12.7
Professional, associate professional, and technical	27	21.3	21.3	21.4
Administrative and secretarial/clerical	5.6	7.1	6.6	11.1
Skilled trades	16.2	15.6	16.2	12.3
Personal service, sales and customer services	7.4	8.6	8.3	12.7
Process, plant and machine operators	13.9	17.7	18.6	10.4
Elementary occupations	8.2	13	12.1	19.4
TOTAL	100	100	100	100

Source: adapted from Longhi et al. (2009: table 8), and Longhi et al. (2012: table 2)

disabled men are on average about £1 per hour lower than those for the non-disabled, with the figures for those with mental disability being approximately 75 per cent of the earnings of the non-disabled. Longhi et al. also found that the disabled are more likely to be found in the lower social classes. As shown in table 4.14, compared to the non-disabled, disabled men are under-represented in the two highest classes, and in general are over-represented in the lowest classes. Longhi et al. also show that disabled people are less likely than the non-disabled to have higher-level qualifications. Since class is largely based on occupation and income, there is a class dimension to disability. However, it is impossible to say that class caused the disability – rather, it is likely that the disability affected the class the person ends up in.

Disability and health

The **inverse care law** means that those whose need is least get the most resources, while those in greatest need get the fewest resources.

How disability is both diagnosed and treated may well be affected by access to the health system, which is known to be class-linked. Tudor-Hart's '**Inverse Care Law**' (1971) states that those living in areas with the greatest need receive the least care, and those with the least need receive the greatest provision of health facilities. Working-class access to GPs may be affected adversely by their working hours and, when access is achieved, consultation times are shorter for working-class patients than for middle-class patients. The latter are also more likely to be referred for further specialist treatment. The middle classes are more likely to be able to gain access to private healthcare, either through their employer or through their own insurance provision.

Other physical factors must also be taken into account when looking at the limiting effects of disability. Inappropriate housing and poor diet caused by lack of money, or having reduced access to shops that sell fresh fruit and vegetables, also have an effect. Such factors are more likely to be experienced by the working classes than by the middle classes and make the effects of certain disabilities worse. Whilst this is clearly not true of all disabilities or disabled people, evidence does seem to show levels of social exclusion are higher among the disabled population than the general public. When age, and thus dependence on others, is added to the equation, the effects are more pronounced.

Ethnic minorities often have problems with access to National Health Service facilities and hence the treatment or alleviation of their disability. Even the diagnosis of a disability may be affected by access to healthcare. The reasons for the problems with access include:

- Cultural reasons, the need for Muslim women to see female doctors or be chaperoned by a male relative when visiting the doctor
- Language barriers
- Racism in health provision.

As the number of Asian doctors born and trained in Britain grows, it is to be hoped that many of these problems will disappear.

The status of the Paralympics in 2012 allegedly raised the profile of disabled people. Disability rights groups remain sceptical about these claims and point to the increasing government curbs on welfare benefits aimed at the disabled. The introduction of Personal Independence Payments in 2013 is apparently designed to empower the disabled person by enabling them to purchase care in the marketplace to meet their own specific needs. This would seem to give more power to them. However, the rules are complex and the intricacies of arranging your own care may be beyond the capability of many people, so whether it will give them greater power remains to be seen.

Conclusion

It seems clear, therefore, that class dimensions are affected by gender, ethnicity, age and disability, whilst at the same time class cannot be ignored when looking at these other dimensions. The status of many groups in our society is not high, and there remains little doubt that white men born into the top Social Class 1 have higher status and better life chances than other groups. They also appear to have more power in society as a whole. There may not be a single cause for the situation, but many causes combine to create the society in which we live. The complexity must never be ignored.

Practice questions

1 Outline and explain **two** reasons why those with disabilities are more likely to have lower occupational status than other groups. **(10 marks)**

2 Read Item A below and answer the question that follows.

Item A

Class as measured by poverty affects life in both youth and old age, but gender, ethnicity and disability are also tightly interwoven. This may be due to factors such as social exclusion and the social capital of these two groups, or may merely be due to the fact these groups are less likely to be employed.

Applying material from **Item A**, analyse **two** reasons why the very young **or** the elderly face a higher risk of living in poverty. **(10 marks)**

3 Read **Item B** below and answer the question that follows.

Item B

It is claimed by some sociologists that the social class of birth is the key determinant of many aspects of an individual's life, such as their health, educational achievement, employment prospects and even the likely cause of death. Others, such as feminists, suggest that factors such as gender play an equally important part, particularly in explaining the differential position of women in contemporary society.

Applying material from **Item B** and your knowledge, evaluate the usefulness of feminist approaches in explaining the position of women in society today. **(20 marks)**

Topic 3

SPECIFICATION AREA

The problems of defining and measuring social class; occupation, gender and social class

There have been many difficulties in trying to define and measure class. Most sociologists have relied on something tangible and easy to see. Apart from income and wealth, occupation has long been the most widely used aspect of life since it is an objective fact that most can agree on. It does, of course, ignore those who do not work, either because they do not need to, they cannot, or they do not wish to. Later studies have attempted to look at consumption patterns as indicators of class, but they are, essentially, based on levels of disposable income, which is, of course, related to occupation, among other things.

The Registrar General's Scale

The categories that are still widely used in old government statistics were first devised by the Registrar General in 1901 (see table 4.15). There have been alterations to some categories as society has changed, but the basis has remained relatively constant, which allows comparisons to be made between various eras of the twentieth century. Problems begin to arise when trying to compare current statistics with those of 100 years ago, as the categories recently underwent change when, in 2001, the NS-SEC model was adopted (see the next section for details).

Table 4.15 The Registrar General's classification of class

Class	Typical occupations
Class I Professional	Accountants, dentists, doctors, lawyers, university teachers, vets, vicars
Class II Intermediate	Actors, airline pilots, chiropodists, diplomats, MPs, teachers, journalists
Class III Skilled	
N = non-manual	Bank clerks, police officers, secretaries
M = manual	Bus-drivers, miners, plumbers, printers
Class IV Semi-skilled	Farm labourers, gardeners, postal delivery workers, bar staff
Class V Unskilled	Builder's labourers, ticket collectors, chimney sweeps, porters, office cleaners

Criticisms of the Registrar General's (RG) Scale

Problems with the Registrar General's Scale are:

- It became inaccurate as certain occupations changed their social status over time.
- Some occupations became deskilled, and others disappeared altogether.
- It also classified whole families by the occupation of the male head of household.
- It ignored people who did not work, whether it was because they had enough wealth to live on or because they were unemployed or retired.

Feminists, in particular, objected to the false picture this produced, especially in those households where the woman's job was of a higher status or more highly paid than that of the man.

National Statistics Socio-economic Classification: NS-SEC

For government purposes, the National Statistics Socio-economic Classification (NS–SEC) scale has been used since 2001 (see table 4.16). This scale recognizes women as a distinct group of wage earners and categorizes them according to their own occupation rather than that of their father or husband. It considers occupation, security of income, prospects of advancement, and how much authority or control the occupation in question has over other people/employees. In order to assign an occupation to a particular rank, certain questions are asked, such as:

- What education or training is required?
- Does the post involve supervising others?
- How much autonomy or control over their own actions do post-holders have?

Table 4.16 The National Statistics Socio-economic Classification

Occupational classification	Percentage of working population	Common name	Examples
1 Higher managerial and professional	11	Upper middle class	Company directors, doctors, clergymen, barristers, solicitors, accountants, dentists, university lecturers
2 Lower managerial and professional	23	Middle class	Teachers, nurses, police inspectors and above, physiotherapists, journalists, authors, sportspersons, musicians
3 Intermediate	14	Lower middle class	Secretaries, clerks, computer operators, travel agents, nursery nurses, ambulance staff, fire officers, lower police officers
4 Small employers and self-accountable workers	10	Lower middle class	Taxi drivers, publicans, self-employed one-person businesses, child-minders, plasterers
5 Lower supervisory, craft and related	10	Skilled manual/ upper working class	Train drivers, printers, plumbers, motor mechanics, electricians, TV engineers
6 Semi-routine	18	Semi-skilled manual/working class	Traffic wardens, shop assistants, call-centre workers, scaffolders, forklift-truck drivers, farm workers, shelf-fillers, security guards
7 Routine	13	Unskilled manual/lower working class	Cleaners, road-sweepers, carpark attendants, labourers, van drivers, bar staff
8 Long-term unemployed or the never-worked		The poor/ underclass	

Four professions that fall into the same class, according to the NS-SEC scheme. How helpful is it to place teachers, musicians, pharmacists and sports people in the same class group? Would these people necessarily share the same leisure pursuits, social backgrounds, political attitudes and tastes just because they fall into the same NS-SEC class?

- How much security of tenure is attached to the post?
- How much job advancement exists in the post?
- How much money is paid, and is it a pensionable post?

It is hoped through this mechanism to have a more specific and accurate ranking of occupations, so that those found in the same level could be said to have much in common with each other.

NS-SEC condensed scale

NS-SEC can also be collapsed into three analytic classes. This is known as 'condensed' NS-SEC and comprises:

1 *Professional and managerial* (consisting of analytic classes 1 and 2 in table 4.16)
2 *Intermediate* (consisting of analytic classes 3 and 4 in table 4.16)
3 *Routine and manual* (consisting of analytic classes 5, 6 and 7 in table 4.16)

Hope-Goldthorpe scale

Originally designed as a tool for the Nuffield Mobility Study (see Topic 4), this scale was derived from a survey of the social standing of occupations, so jobs are ranked in terms of their social desirability and status in the marketplace, a Weberian aspect taken into consideration.

Like the NS-SEC scale, this looks at autonomy in the workplace, how much the individual is in control of their own work and that of others. It dispensed with the RG scale's distinction between manual and non-manual occupations and created an intermediate class. This scale was also based on the position of the male head of household.

> ### Table 4.17 Hope-Goldthorpe scale
>
> *Service class*
>
> 1 Higher Professionals: high-grade administrators, managers of large enterprises and large proprietors
>
> 2 Lower Professionals: higher-grade technicians, supervisors of non-manual workers, administrators in medium-sized enterprises, small business managers
>
> *Intermediate class*
>
> 3 Routine clerical and sales [non manual]
>
> 4 Proprietors of small businesses, self-employed craftspeople
>
> 5 Lower-grade technicians, supervisors of manual workers
>
> *Working class*
>
> 6 Skilled manual workers
>
> 7 Semi- and unskilled manual workers
>
> *Source*: adapted from Goldthorpe (1980)

The Great British Class Survey (GBCS) or the Savage-Devine Scale

This scale was drawn up by asking members of the public to answer a raft of questions in a BBC internet survey known as the Great British Class Survey (GBCS) (2014). It recognized that **economic capital**, **cultural capital** and **social capital** (see glossary boxes) are resources that can give people the opportunity to do things they would not otherwise be able to do. This scale attempted to move from mere employment to look at other aspects of life in defining class boundaries. It produced seven groups:

- **Elite**: This is the most privileged class in Great Britain who have high levels of all three capitals. Their high amount of economic capital sets them apart from everyone else.
- **Established Middle Class**: Members of this class have high levels of all three capitals although not as high as the Elite. They are a gregarious and culturally engaged class.
- **Technical Middle Class**: This is a new, small class with high economic capital but its members seem less culturally engaged. They have relatively few social contacts and so are less socially engaged.
- **New Affluent Workers**: This class has medium levels of economic capital and higher levels of cultural and social capital. They are a young and active group.
- **Emergent Service Workers**: This new class has low economic capital but has high levels of 'emerging' cultural capital and high social capital. This group are young and often found in urban areas.
- **Traditional Working Class**: This class scores low on all forms of the three capitals although they are not the poorest group. The average age of this class is older than the others.
- **Precariat**: This is the most deprived class of all with low levels of economic, cultural and social capital. The everyday lives of members of this class are precarious.

Economic capital refers to people's wealth, earnings, assets and savings.

Cultural capital refers to the extent and nature of people's cultural interests and their participation in cultural activities.

Social capital refers to the social networks of influence and support that people have: the number and status of the people they know.

Criticisms of the Great British Class Survey

Mills (2014) points out that the internet survey of over 160,000 people was a self-selecting and therefore biased unrepresentative group, that the data collected was of poor quality, and he suggests that the seven 'classes' are not social classes at all, but reflect people's different ages and are more lifestyle groups based on cultural preferences. He believes that the survey findings show that cultural consumption (cultural capital) is related to more conventional measures of social class, such as those of the NS-SEC model which has been extensively validated. Bradley (2014) points out that the emphasis placed on social contacts (social capital) and cultural activities (cultural capital) means that people with the same occupation are placed in different classes, and she questions whether there is anything which really binds these 'classes' together into coherent groups of people. Bradley argues the GBCS underplays the importance of economic capital, and that traditional Marxist and Weberian conceptions, in which classes are defined by their economic position, remain at the heart of class relations. She suggests such a class structure involves the broad classes of the elite, defined by their ownership of wealth (the upper-class owners of wealth in the form of ownership of the means of production), the middle and working classes defined by their income, and the 'Precariat' defined by its marginal and insecure temporary and part-time employment. Bradley also rejects the suggestion that the 'Precariat' is the same as the Underclass, and she points out that many people currently in the Precariat do not have the same low or non-existent levels of social and cultural capital as some suggest is found in the Underclass.

Problems with using occupation to measure class

All systems based on occupation have problems for sociologists, for the following reasons.

1 They always exclude the very wealthy who do not need to work, and thus hide some very real differences that exist in society.
2 Unpaid workers, such as houseworkers/housewives, voluntary workers, and those never employed and the long-term unemployed are also excluded.
3 They tend to be based on the occupation of the highest earner in a household, ignoring households with two incomes, whose class position may well be different from that of a single-earner household.
4 Occupational scales can be very broad and include within them people whose interests might be seen as very different – for example, a headteacher and a classroom teacher fall in the same category, though their responsibilities and powers are very different.
5 They assume a similarity of tastes and attitudes amongst people in the same occupation or ranking. This may be untrue, given that personal interests are formed in many ways. Also, those who are born into and remain in the same class may well have different attitudes from those who have entered the class through **social mobility**. We will consider this in more detail in Topic 5.

> **Social mobility** is the movement of individuals or groups from one social class to another, both upwardly and downwardly.

Feminist alternatives

There have been several attempts at classification by feminists such as Arber et al. (1986), who drew up the Surrey scale, which attempted to reflect more closely the types of work women did and to include them in the scale, and classified women and men separately based on their occupation. Because of women's disjointed work careers, as they are more likely to take career breaks for motherhood and other caring roles, it was difficult to know how useful this scale would be in projecting data concerning life experience as a whole. Similar work undertaken by Martin and Roberts in 1984, which was a modification of the RG scale with emphasis on women's occupations, was eventually subsumed into the NS-SEC model currently used by the government.

IPA scale – Institute of Practitioners in Advertising Social Grade

This scale is widely used in the advertising industry and by some government departments who are attempting to inform the public or change public attitudes. It defines target markets and discriminates

Table 4.18 The Institute of Practitioners in Advertising (IPA) scale

Social class	Commonly called	Examples of occupations
Class A Higher managerial, administrative or professional occupations	Upper middle class	Opticians, judges, solicitors, senior civil servants, surgeons, senior managers (in large companies), accountants, architects
Class B Intermediate managerial, administrative or professional occupations	Middle class	Airline pilots, MPs, teachers, social workers, middle managers, police inspectors
Class C1 Supervisory or clerical and junior managerial, administrative or professional occupations	Lower middle class	Clerical workers, computer operators, receptionists, sales assistants, secretaries, nurses, technicians
Class C2 Skilled manual workers	Upper working class	Carpenters, bricklayers, electricians, chefs/cooks, plumbers
Class D Semi-skilled and unskilled manual workers	Semi-skilled and lower working class	Postal workers, bar workers, office cleaners, road sweepers, machine minders, farm labourers
Class E Those on the lowest levels of income	The poor	Pensioners (on state pensions), casual workers, long-term unemployed, and others on income support and the lowest levels of income

Source: Browne (2011)

across markets and products. It contains six grades which cover a wide range of occupational groups as well as people on state benefits and pensions. It, like most scales, is based on employment status, current or previous occupation with consideration given to grade, size of employer, supervisory capacity and qualifications. However, it is not widely used in academic sociology.

Advertisers are mainly interested in selling things to people, so their scale ranks occupations primarily on the basis of income. They obviously want to know how much money people have so they can target their advertising at the right people. This scale is very widely used in surveys of all kinds.

Non-occupational measures of social class

Various attempts have been made in academic circles to find measures of class that avoid occupation. As seen earlier (see page 279), the neo-Marxist Wright thought that exploitative relationships might be a way to measure class. The difficulty in how this might be measured has not really been addressed. Runciman (1990) has also suggested that we need to look at the sets of roles held by each individual based on three elements – ownership, control and marketability of skill – whilst those who have no job should be assigned a role dependent on their economic power. However, at no point does Runciman explain how easy it would be to collect the information needed to assign people to their role and he himself has never carried out such research.

It has been suggested that, since the Census now includes questions about housing tenure and car ownership and other consumption variables, as well as educational achievement, this might form the basis of classification. This might help, for example, to give a more accurate picture of the population over 65. In response to this, it should be noted that consumption variables, whilst interesting, are again reliant upon income, and income is heavily reliant upon occupation, or lack of it. The GBCS/Savage-Devine Scale also attempted to use non-occupational measures of social class, employing the concepts of economic, cultural and social capitals (see page 326) to categorize people into social classes, based on data gathered from a very large (though unrepresentative) survey of over 160,000 people.

Problem of defining and measuring each of the main social classes

We have just seen the problems with using occupation as a basis of measurement, due to the lack of agreement over which occupations should be considered part of each class, where women should be placed, and so forth. For some theorists, such as Marx, this whole discussion is, essentially, irrelevant, since it merely reflects the false consciousness of the vast majority of the population: that section that is not the bourgeoisie. Weberians pay great attention to the market situation of individuals and it is this theory which underlies most of the British work in this field. As markets change, so the social class system changes and membership of classes changes.

One possible problem with all occupational categorizations of class is that they are essentially snapshots in time, and those currently in what are regarded as middle-class jobs may have been born and raised in a working-class household. Others now in manual occupations may have been born into managerial families – though this is rarer, as we shall see in Topic 5. Such groups are more likely to define themselves as belonging to their class of origin, though this is partly dependent on the links they have kept with their family of socialization.

We will look in more detail in Topic 4 at who makes up these social classes and how things may or may not have changed. At present it is probably true to say that most people can agree on who are members of the upper class and who are members of the underclass. In-between these two extremes lies the great mass of the population. We have tried to classify them objectively, but what do they themselves think about their own class position?

Objective and subjective views of class

Whatever scale is used, it consists of objective views of people's social class. An individual's own view of his or her social class may well be different. Few people are likely to say 'I belong to social class seven', but they may well say 'I am working class.' Subjective classifications need to be considered, especially when attitudes to and relations between classes are examined. Giddens (1991), considering the subjective aspects of class, suggested that employment/occupation is being replaced by patterns of consumption as an indicator of the group one sees oneself as belonging to, an idea much espoused by postmodernists, as we saw in Topic 1.

In 'Class, Mobility and Identification in a New Town' (2002), Southerton showed that **consumption patterns** were important in people's minds when describing *other* inhabitants of the new town as 'them' or 'us'. Thus, class identification has been replaced by consumption patterns as a way of identifying others' as well as one's own social position.

However, Savage et al. (2001) used in-depth interviews to discover how people classified themselves. They found a marked reluctance to assign oneself to a class in a specific way. Most people valued being normal and 'just like everybody else' above a specific class label for themselves. A proportion wished to be considered as individuals rather than accepting a class designation and were more likely to say what they were *not* rather than what they thought they were. Postmodernists might regard this as proof of the rise of the pick 'n' mix society and thus of their belief that class is an individual choice.

When people consider themselves as belonging to a class to which others might not objectively assign them, and attempt to live out the lifestyle which they believe is appropriate for that group,

Consumption patterns describe the ways in which people spend their money – some sociologists, such as Giddens, suggest this is as important as class in demonstrating identity.

reality – in the form of other people's responses and their own previous socialization – may well prevent them living out their fantasy: Cooley's 'looking-glass self' (see page 383) will affect their self-perception.

Conclusion

Because of the difficulties of classifying groups, and also because of the vagueness of people's own self-assignment to class, it has been suggested that maybe class is dead and we now live in a postmodern world of consumption patterns and hybrid, pick 'n' mix identities. We shall look at the evidence for this in Topics 4 and 5.

Activity

1 As a group, devise a questionnaire to discover how people define their own social class. Do not forget to include questions that can help you identify people's objective class, as well as questions asking them how they would describe themselves and why.
2 Administer the questionnaire to a range of relatives/friends.
3 Compare people's subjective class with their objective class.
4 From your evidence, do you think that consumption patterns have replaced occupation as a way of defining one's own class position? Give reasons for your answer based on your findings.

Practice questions

1 Outline and explain **two** problems with using the occupation of the father to explain the social class position of the whole family. **(10 marks)**

2 Read **Item A** below and answer the question that follows.

Item A

Postmodernists suggest that subjective class is as important as occupation in defining a person's social class, as in our fluid occupational structure an individual may change jobs many times, thus changing their identity. Consumption patterns may play a part in their self-classification. Marxists, however, would suggest that objective social class is the most important aspect of an individual's position in society.

Applying material from **Item A**, analyse **two** problems with using subjective class as an indicator of an individual's position in society. **(10 marks)**

3 Read **Item B** below and answer the question that follows.

Item B

Marxists suggest that occupation is still the most efficient way of describing the social class of both an individual and the family they belong to at any point in their lives. Most studies have concentrated on the occupation of the man in the household. Some feminists would argue that to fully understand the class position of a family the occupation of both parents should be considered.

Applying material from **Item B** and your knowledge, evaluate the extent to which occupation is a useful indicator of an individual's social class. **(20 marks)**

Topic 4

SPECIFICATION AREA

Changes in structures of inequality, including globalisation and the transnational capitalist class, and the implication of these changes

It is frequently argued that class is becoming less important in the UK but in the following pages we will consider what, if anything, has changed. We will look in detail at the various social groups in terms of class, gender and ethnicity and look at changes. Postmodernists argue that consumption and lifestyle choices have changed our class identities. We will now look at the evidence for and against this view. Others argue that class has fragmented, whilst Marxists consider class to still be the most dominant factor in life.

Social groups in modern Britain

The upper class

One aspect of the upper class is the amount of wealth and income its members possess. There are different sources of wealth and income. Some people inherit their wealth and the income that derives from it; others earn both their wealth and their income. However it is gained, the upper class is wealthy and this wealth leads, in Weberian terms, to both status and political power – which he called 'party'. This has led, in some cases, to the formation of political and financial elites. However much postmodernism suggests that individuals can choose their identity, it is not possible just to choose to be rich.

Ruling elites

Elite theory suggests that a small group in the UK has maintained its position through control of the political life of the country, and indeed, until the extension of voting rights to all people over 21 in 1929, this may have been true. Now it is suggested that their power is somewhat more diffuse.

Writing from a Marxist perspective, Westergaard and Resler (1975) have suggested that the private ownership of capital provides the key to understanding class divisions in the UK. Since the whole ideology of the UK is a capitalist one, the system will work in favour of those who own the means of production or who control the financial institutions that make the major decisions concerning life in the UK. This group makes up the **elite**.

> The **elite** consists of a small group that holds great power and privilege in society.

However, Saunders (1990), writing from a New Right perspective, has disputed this notion of a wealthy ruling elite. He maintains that much wealth is now bound up in pension funds: anyone with a private or work pension is bound to have an interest in the workings of capitalism since their hard-earned pensions are invested in the stock market. Therefore, he argues, the capitalist class has 'fragmented into millions of tiny pieces' spread across society. Nevertheless, this ignores the role played by financial institutions in controlling these pension funds, and the large incomes of the managers and chief executives of such institutions.

Evidence from the Sutton Trust reveals that political and economic power is, on the whole, maintained across generations through the class system. There is a tendency for members of these elites to intermarry and then to educate their children at fee-paying schools, send them to Oxford or Cambridge University, and encourage them to marry within the group. The Conservative government of 1959 and the Conservative-led Coalition government of 2010 show remarkably similar characteristics in this regard. Work by Bond (2012), looking at the current House of Lords, would suggest that these elite characteristics are still prevalent in today's society.

The establishment

Jones (2014) suggests that these old elite groups have been replaced, in Britain at least, by what he refers to as the **establishment**. Whilst containing many of those previously thought of as the elite, what binds it together is no longer family or education but a political ideology, a deep belief in the free-market economy. This leads them to maintain that the only way that the UK can hope to compete in an increasingly competitive and globalized world is by reducing the role of the state and cutting down on welfare provisions. However, Jones maintains, the reduction in welfare only applies to the working class. Big business continues to enjoy subsidies from the tax-payer and he cites the examples of the bank bail-outs of 2008 and the continuing subsidies to the privatized rail companies. Indeed, it could be argued that even such apparent welfare benefits as working tax credit help the employer rather than the employee since they allow the employer to pay minimal wages whilst knowing that the state will provide this top-up. Even the proposal in 2015 to raise the minimum wage to the living wage included tax breaks for large employers who would be affected by the change, though small employers were offered no such safeguard.

This elite group consists not only of big business, bankers and politicians, but also media owners, accountancy firms, the arms trade, the lobbying industry and many foreign oligarchs who have found in Britain a safe tax haven for their wealth. Shared interests are more important than shared backgrounds.

> The **establishment** refers to an elite group of people with a belief in the free-market economy whose shared beliefs and financial interests bind them together.

Activity

1 Working in pairs, and using the internet and a source such as *Who's Who*, see how much you can find out about the directors of the major pension funds. (Start with the directors of groups such as the Prudential, Standard Life, and Aviva – all of which provide personal pension plans.)
2 Do your findings lend credibility to Saunders's theory, or do the directors still tend to come from the privileged social groups which make up the majority of top earners in financial institutions?

The middle class

In the past, the distinction between middle and working class was the distinction between non-manual and manual work. However, how are jobs defined? Is typing, or inputting data at a computer, manual or non-manual? In so far as hands are needed, it is manual; in terms of working conditions, it is far removed from working on a building site or other traditional manual work.

Weber suggested that it is probably more useful to consider life chances in distinguishing between the two groups. On the whole, non-manual work tends to take place indoors, in pleasant working conditions, with shorter hours, more job security, more fringe benefits and better promotion prospects. Non-manual workers also enjoy better health and better standards of health-care, live longer, are less likely to be convicted of a crime, own their own home and retire earlier than manual workers. There has also been a consistent gap between the earnings of manual and non-manual workers throughout the twentieth century.

However, during the course of the twentieth century, this very diverse group of non-manual workers, whose occupations range from university professors to routine call-centre workers, have become divided into different groups with different interests. Many of these jobs have lost skills which they once had and, it could be argued, have become **proletarianized** (see page 334). It now makes more sense to talk of the **professions** and the lower middle class as two quite distinct groups.

> **Proletarianization** is the process whereby other groups take on the attributes and characteristics of the proletariat.

> The **professions** are those types of occupation which are self-governing and generally of relatively high status.

The professions

Professional groups grew in numbers throughout the twentieth century, from 4 per cent of the working population in 1901 to more than 20 per cent by 2011. Most commentators divide professionals into two groups: higher professions, such as judges, barristers, solicitors, architects, doctors, dentists, accountants, university lecturers, scientists and some engineers; and lower professions, which include schoolteachers, nurses, social workers and librarians.

Higher professionals, such as lawyers, medics and chartered accountants, have mostly been rewarded with relatively high levels of pay. Explanations for this depend on the theoretical perspective of the commentator. Functionalists such as Parsons (1967) and Barber (1963) contend that professionals have four attributes that distinguish them from other workers and thus justify higher rewards:

1 *They hold a body of knowledge* about their field of work which can be applied to any situation that arises.
2 *They have a concern for the interests of the community* rather than self-interest. The primary motivation of all professionals is to serve the public, not to get rich.
3 *Professionals' conduct is always guided by a code of ethics*, which is maintained and upheld by a professional body to which they must belong if they wish to continue to practise. Should they break the code of ethics, they may be barred from practising their skill.
4 *The high rewards are a result of their prestige* and the high regard they are held in by the community they serve.

Critics of the functionalist view argue it makes huge assumptions about professionals – for example, in the claim that they serve the whole community rather than just a section of it, and that they are public-spirited rather than in it for the money. Weberians would suggest that professions are occupational groups that have succeeded in controlling the labour market to their own advantage.

Parry and Parry (1976) argue that professionals and professionalism have the following attributes.

1 By controlling the training and entry requirements necessary for membership, professionals control the supply of qualified practitioners at a level that will guarantee high fees. Rarity means they can charge more.
2 By forcing all members to belong to the professional association, the group can claim to be maintaining the highest public standards; by demanding the right to investigate and punish their own members, they make it difficult for outside scrutiny to take place.
3 Professionals have, on the whole, managed successfully to claim that only their members are qualified to carry out this work. The monopoly enjoyed by lawyers and doctors, for example, is backed by law; it is a criminal offence to impersonate a doctor, and only solicitors have the right to carry out certain legal procedures.

Because of this market strategy – that is, closing access to the group and restricting their numbers – professionals have become wealthy and secure. Lower professionals, such as teachers, are, in the eyes of Parry and Parry, not really professionals at all, since they do not have the market control enjoyed by doctors.

Activity

1 From the list of occupations below, pick out the ones that Barber would regard as professionals, and the ones that Parry and Parry would regard as professionals:
- *University lecturers*
- *Nursery nurses*
- *General medical practitioners*
- *Surgeons*
- *Solicitors*
- *Primary school teachers*
- *Bank clerks*
- *Nurses*
- *Airline pilots*
- *Army officers.*

2 From your own experience, which of the above groups would consider themselves to be professionals?

3 What does the difference in the three lists you have compiled tell us about the status of professionals in the UK today? Give reasons for your answer.

The lower middle class

The lower middle class consists of routine white-collar workers, such as clerical workers, secretaries and call-centre workers. Their jobs have changed so much, however, that some sociologists speak of proletarianization, others claim they are still part of a distinctive middle class, and a few suggest they are now a distinct group somewhere between the middle and the working class.

The theory of proletarianization is most associated with Marxists such as Braverman (1974), who suggested that, although the number of white-collar jobs has grown enormously, the skill needed to do the job has declined. Early clerical workers were able to run all aspects of the small company that employed them. As companies grew larger, each clerical worker took over one part of the operation and specialized in it. However, workers were only able to carry out that one specialism and, if the need for it disappeared, they became redundant. That is to say, they had become deskilled. Automation and computerization have both continued the process of **deskilling**. Braverman says that, in an age of mass literacy and numeracy, the work of white-collar workers can be done by almost anyone, and they are no better-off, in bargaining terms, than manual workers. Computerization has now entered every sphere of work – even in personal care settings, records are kept on computers, so literacy and keyboard skills have become an essential element for working in many occupations.

Stewart et al. (1980) found that there is a high rate of turnover and promotion amongst male clerical workers. By the age of 30, 51 per cent of men who started out as clerical workers have been promoted into management, and 30 per cent leave clerical work altogether before they are 30. For men, clerical work is merely a stage in a career path. However, Crompton and Jones (1984) show that, although this may be true for men, the vast majority of clerical workers are now women. In their study of three workplaces, they concluded that, for the women employed there, the work was lacking in skill, they had no control over their work and that, therefore, the female clerical workers could be labelled a white-collar proletariat.

> **Deskilling** is the situation in which the skills and knowledge previously needed to do a job are no longer required. A good example would be in printing photographs which used to need four specialized workers, but can now be done by a computer operated by a relatively unskilled person.

The middle class or the middle classes?

Sociologists disagree about whether it is accurate to talk about the middle class or the middle classes. Giddens (1973) argues that there is one middle class whose members are distinguished from those in the upper class because they do not own 'property in the means of production'. They are also distinguished from the working class by the fact that they can sell their mental labour power rather than just their manual labour power because they possess educational or technical qualifications. However, groups such as electricians and plumbers also increasingly have technical qualifications, but are still considered by most to be manual workers.

Mechanization and automation have led to widespread deskilling and the loss of many jobs. In such a situation, who stands to lose and who stands to gain?

Here for life? It can be harder for women in clerical jobs to move onwards and upwards.

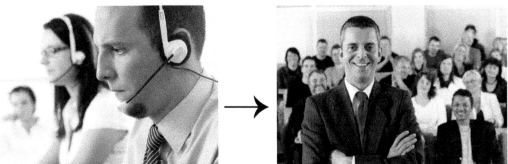

A male clerical worker has only a 25 per cent chance of staying in that position for life. For most men, it has historically been the starting point of an upward career.

Savage et al. (1992) argued that the middle class consists of three distinct groups:

- Those with property assets, which includes self-employed and small employers
- Those with organizational assets, who hold important positions in large organizations
- Those with cultural assets deriving mainly from educational qualifications.

In the twentieth century, the fates of these three groups began to vary. Those with property assets still have the ability to pass these on to their children. However, those with organizational assets gradually declined in importance as industry entered more specialized areas demanding greater flexibility. In this situation, those with educational qualifications and potential flexibility have become more valuable to owners of industry. However, a major flaw with this theory is that it ignores a great part of the traditional middle class – it fails to consider the routine white-collar workers.

Functionalists would see the gradations in the middle classes as reflecting the need of the economy for various jobs. The pay differentials now found reflect these needs, and the amount of ability available in the society to carry out this work. Marxists of course continue to regard these differences in pay and status as a smokescreen to hide the basic division between proletariat and bourgeoisie.

Activity

1 List **three** reasons why clerical workers could be considered to be part of the middle class.
2 List **three** reasons why clerical workers might not be considered to be part of the middle class.
3 Suggest **three** reasons why women are less likely than men to be promoted from routine clerical work to higher positions.

The working class

Again, the question has to be asked: is there a single working class, as classical Marxism would suggest, or is it more accurate to speak of the working classes? Marxist sociologists argue that, in order to be considered part of a social class, people must at least recognize themselves as having similarities. It has been found that most manual workers will define themselves as working class. It is assumed that there will be a similarity of lifestyle, norms and values – that is, a common culture – amongst the members of this group, and that they will show a tendency to mix socially with members of the same group rather than with members of other groups/classes.

Proletarian traditionalists

While there may be differences within the working class, and therefore a number of working-class subcultures, Lockwood (1966) has drawn up what could be described as an **ideal type** working-class subculture, made of those he labelled 'proletarian traditionalists'. This group was based on a range of studies of working-class life and is frequently used as a basis for comparison when considering other working-class groups.

Among other traits, proletarian traditionalists display the following characteristics:

* Living in close-knit working-class communities often based on long-established industries such as mining, dock-work, steel, etc.
* Having a strong sense of **social solidarity**
* Workmates are often neighbours and friends, and leisure time will be spent in each other's company
* Little geographical or social mobility
* Tendency to seek collective goals rather than individual ones, often linked to **trade union** membership
* An approach to life based on **fatalism**, with an emphasis on **present-time orientation** and **immediate gratification**
* A tendency to see the world divided into 'us' and 'them'.

Is this an accurate picture of working-class life in the early twenty-first century? There has been a marked decline in the industries that formerly employed the proletarian traditionalist. Mining as a way of life has all but disappeared, as deep mines have been replaced by open-cast mining; steel is now a minority industry; dock-work has been replaced by containerization. This trend continued so that manufacturing is now a minority occupation and the overall figure of those who could be considered traditional working class from their occupations has declined, and continues to decline. Lockwood also points out, however, that the jobs in hotel and catering are often themselves essentially manual, boring and repetitive, as are the new jobs in call-centres.

Fulcher and Scott (2002), however, found that Lockwood's proletarian traditionalist still existed, with a keen sense of the unfairness of society and an 'us and them' attitude to employers. The feeling of exploitation persisted. MacKenzie et al. (2006) found that even when the steelworks of South Wales closed and the steelworkers were dispersed to other jobs or were made unemployed, they still took their identity from being steelworkers, and felt a strong sense of solidarity with their former workmates. The authors concluded that the decline of the traditional working-class occupations, mostly undertaken by men and generally attached to a trade union, did not necessarily lead to a difference in the way they were identified, or identified themselves.

However, others, such as Cannadine (1998), argue that there is little evidence either that the collective consciousness described by Lockwood existed in the past or that it exists today in a consistent fashion. He suggests instead that collectivism occurs at particular times and in specific contexts, but usually unites a small part of the working class rather than the whole group. Thus, groups may join together to defend their work, for example in strikes to protest about redundancy, but it rarely involves other groups beyond those directly affected.

The new working class

While the number of working-class jobs was falling, the average living standards for those manual workers in regular employment improved. Their increased affluence led many political commentators to suggest that the attitudes of the working class would wither away and that most people would form a single homogenized mass. These ideas started from as early as the election slogan of 1959 – 'You've never had it so good' – through to 1992 and the claim of prime minister John Major that 'We are all middle class now.' It was argued that, rather than middle-class employees becoming

Ideal type refers to a view of a phenomenon built up by identifying the essential characteristics of many factual examples of it. The purpose of an ideal type is not to produce a perfect category, but to provide a measure against which real examples can be compared.

Social solidarity refers to the integration of people into society through shared values, a common culture, shared understandings and social ties that bind them together.

A **trade union** is an organization of workers whose aim is to protect the interests of its members and improve their life chances.

Fatalism is a state of mind in which someone believes there is nothing they can do to alter their situation or circumstances.

Present-time orientation involves a concentration on today without much consideration for the future or the past.

Immediate gratification is a desire to have rewards now rather than waiting to acquire them in the future, which is known as deferred gratification.

deskilled and proletarianized, the opposite was occurring, and the working class was becoming more like the middle class, through a process of **embourgeoisement.**

In 1962, Goldthorpe et al. began work on what was later published as *The Affluent Worker in the Class Structure* (1969). They set out to test the theory that the working classes were becoming more middle-class, by focusing on the town of Luton, where they felt such a transformation was most likely to occur, arguing that if they failed to find the tendency there, it would be reasonable to assume that it was not happening anywhere. Luton was chosen because of the absence of long-established industries, the decline of a closely knit community, higher than average home-ownership and, above all, higher wages, which together, they felt, were the circumstances most likely to foster the process of embourgeoisement. The study looked at four aspects of class:

Embourgeoisement refers to the idea that working-class manual workers were adopting more middle-class norms and values.

1   *Attitudes to work*: assuming that affluent workers would enjoy their work and have an instrumental relationship to work (i.e. work for money) rather than working to make friends and build a sense of community
2   *Political views*: assuming that embourgeoisement would mean more people voting for the Conservative Party
3   *Aspirations and perspectives on society*: or how workers themselves defined the various social classes
4   *Social interaction* between groups from different social classes in the communities in which they lived

The authors argued that, if embourgeoisement was occurring, there would be few discernible differences between the various groups of workers. However, they concluded that embourgeoisement was *not* taking place, but, rather, that a new working class was being formed with a privatized family lifestyle and an **instrumental orientation** to work and politics.

An **instrumental orientation** is an attitude in which wages/money are the most important aspect of work.

Later studies by Hill (1976) on the London dockers suggested that this new working class was more widespread than originally thought. In the 1980s, Devine (1992) returned to Luton to see whether there had been further changes. Her findings suggest that the employment insecurities of the 1970s and 1980s had affected some attitudes, but, in the main, the affluent workers remained instrumental in their attitudes to work, concerned about their consumption patterns but also keen to see a more egalitarian society.

A study that has brought the picture of one working-class community more up to date is by Dench et al. (2006), which looks in detail at how the close-knit networks of the old docklands of East London have gradually disappeared as work was transferred elsewhere and no other obvious employment took its place. The reliance on neighbours has all but disappeared, extended families have been priced out of the neighbourhood, and new housing in Essex took the younger generation away, leaving the older members to cope in an increasingly unrecognizable world. The role of the working-class family as a source of status, solidarity and support has gone, and with it the traditionalist solidaristic community that was so important in the lives of the many people who worked in the London docks, loading and unloading cargoes – a job now replaced by large cranes and container ships and lorries. Here, the traditional proletarian lifestyle described by Lockwood no longer exists.

The **underclass** is a concept developed by Murray to describe a group considered to be outside the mainstream of society, below the working class.

Such evidence has been used by some commentators to suggest that we must now speak of working classes rather than one working class. Traditional Marxists continue to point out the element of false consciousness this implies. These apparent 'class fractions', they suggest, still have the alienation and exploitation caused by a capitalist mode of production, and thus should be regarded as one class.

The underclass/poor

Lumpenproletariat is a term used by Marx to describe the group of unorganized working-class people. It is now seen by many commentators as being synonymous with the underclass.

It is argued that there is a stratum below the working class. It has been given many names. At present, the most common one is the term **underclass**. Marx referred to this group as the **lumpenproletariat**. The underclass is described either in *economic* terms: those within its ranks are unemployed, dependent on benefits and poor; or in *normative* terms: they have a different culture and subculture from the rest of the population. Some commentators, most notably Murray (1984), would suggest that both economic and normative differences exist.

According to Marx, the main problem facing the lumpenproletariat was the diverse nature of the group – its fluctuating population, which would prevent it from developing class consciousness. Its very presence might also hinder the formation of class consciousness within the proletariat, since the fear would always exist that employers could recruit a new labour force from within the lumpen-proletariat. This led Marx to describe this group as the 'reserve army of labour' – a group of people not normally in the paid workforce who can be called on in times of need – a concept that has been widely used by feminists to describe the role of women in the twentieth century.

A study by Coates and Silburn (1970) showed that the poor are no different from the rest of us: they have the same hopes and aspirations, the same coping strategies and do not consider them-selves different in any great way. The study group referred to others, worse off than themselves, as 'poor' and did not regard their own position as poverty-stricken at all. Later pan-European studies in 2001 and 2004, have come to similar conclusions – poverty is a relative concept, even to those whom others would regard as poor.

Writing originally about the USA, Murray (1984) argued that the poor and the underclass have traits and characteristics that distinguish them from the rest of society and suggested this is a growing group which was a threat to the stability of society. Government policies are increasing the numbers of people who no longer work and who rely on government welfare for their subsistence; this discour-ages self-sufficiency and this group then turns to crime, delinquency and other forms of anti-social behaviour. In 1989, Murray visited the UK and declared that here too an underclass flourished.

Murray's definition is not economic, but, rather, normative or cultural. The underclass is distinguished by:

- High levels of illegitimacy
- Absent fathers, or fathers who are incapable of keeping a job
- An unwillingness to work, particularly among the young
- Drunkenness
- Poor education
- Delinquency.

Murray says that, in certain neighbourhoods, traditional values such as honesty, belief in family life and the virtue of hard work have been so seriously undermined that generations are being born with no such ideas or access to them. He blames the underclass for the situation they are in, paying no attention to any structural causes and making no attempt to see any coherent solutions other than to cancel all benefits. This theory concerning poverty lies beneath the welfare reforms of the Coalition government of 2010–15 and the Conservative government elected in 2015.

Dahrendorf (1959) explains how such an underclass has been formed through changes in the economic structure of society. Technology now allows for more production with fewer workers, thus creating unemployment. In the USA, moreover, wages are kept so low in some industries that the workers concerned cannot rise out of poverty. Even better-paid workers are increasingly employed on short-term or part-time contracts. Education is the key to a successful job, but the education system fails members of the underclass; thus, argues Dahrendorf, 'those who are in, by and large, stay in, but those who are not, stay outside'.

There is clearly an economic base to the underclass, but fragmentation will prevent class consciousness. Members of the underclass have little security and do not feel like full citizens of their societies. The group includes newly arrived immigrants and those who either have not gained a job at all, or have lost their job. As they have no real stake in society, they feel no need to conform to mainstream values, and this lack of conformity will be passed on to their children. Their frustra-tions often come to the surface through rioting and violent crime, which affects the lives of other citizens, but because of the different strands in this group, Dahrendorf does not regard them as a class in itself, but rather as a group of people who are not needed by society and whose presence is a challenge to dominant values.

Gallie (1988, 1994) argues that certain groups within the so-called 'underclass' are really members of the working class. Among these, most particularly, are the unemployed or those on very low wages. Groups drift in and out of employment and thus have similar class interests. The only people for whom this might not be true, according to Gallie, are the very long-term unemployed,

The living conditions of members of the underclass can lead to them feeling excluded from society. Such frustrations can occasionally explode to the surface, for example in urban riots.

but most of these were formerly manual workers or came from such a background. Whether this is also true of people who have never been able to find a job is left unconsidered. However, despite the claims of politicians, the number of families in which unemployment has been present throughout even two generations is extremely small.

The term 'ghetto poor' has been used by some US commentators to describe the group that exists as the lowest stratum of capitalist societies. They are considerably worse-off than manual workers in regular employment. Whether they form a separate class is still undecided.

Transitory residents/stateless persons/undocumented persons

With the constant movement of people across borders in search of work and a better life for themselves and their families, there are a growing number of residents who are not legally citizens of the country where they live. This group has a very unusual position in the class structure. Some, who may have false documents, manage to rise to positions in the semi-professional classes and routine clerical class, but do not, on the whole, appear in official statistics, as they are reluctant to draw attention to themselves. Others find themselves working in the **black economy**, paying no tax or national insurance, prey to unscrupulous employers and landlords, with no chance of escaping from this semi-slavery. The exact numbers cannot be known, but raids by various branches of the police routinely uncover cases every week. Their position in the class structure is impossible to determine.

Black economy: running parallel to the official economy, the black economy is informal and most people in it work for cash-in-hand which thus avoids payment of various taxes. It is illegal.

In 2012 the BBC reported that Oxford University Centre on Migration Policy and Society found that approximately one in ten of London's children have uncertain immigration status. They had arrived legally with parents or guardians when they were minors but failed to be officially registered as documentation was missing. Without this documentation they are unable to stay in education after 16, work or use the NHS. They are now officially stateless but have known no other country. Again their class position is nebulous.

Children born in the UK are not necessarily citizens, since the law changed in 1982. If their parents were here illegally, then they too are treated as illegals, but they have no obvious alternative homeland. Current estimates suggest there were at least 120,000 such people in 2012. The figure is likely to grow.

Does class still exist?

We saw earlier in Topic 1 that postmodernists such as Pakulski and Waters claimed that class no longer offered an identity since people now saw themselves as individuals rather than members of a group. They suggest that consumption of goods and services shapes identity, but fail to recognize the role that income and occupation play in framing those consumption patterns. Since income and occupation are largely class-determined, it would seem premature to completely ignore class as a factor in modern-day life.

Globalization and inequality

Globalization and the transnational capitalist class (TCC)

It has been argued that since the 1990s there has been a major change in the globalized class structure with the growth of a new global power elite or ruling class: the **transnational capitalist class** (TCC).

Sklair (2000) suggests the TCC is made up of four main groups:

- The owners and controllers of transnational – global – corporations
- Globalizing officials and politicians, who operate on a world stage
- Globalizing professionals, who have high skill and education levels, speak foreign languages, travel internationally, are highly paid, think in global rather than national terms, and advise and develop proposals on issues of global concern, and particularly global business and trade
- Consumerist elites of the media, and merchants (business people) trading globally in consumer goods.

Sklair argues the TCC is transnational (or globalized) in that its economic interests are globally linked rather than being exclusively local or national in origin. It seeks to exert economic control in the workplace, and political control in domestic, international and global politics, and to promote a global ideology of consumerism. The TCC is linked by shared lifestyles, with consumption of luxury goods and services, and ultra-expensive exclusive clubs, restaurants and holiday resorts on all continents, and private, as opposed to mass, forms of travel and entertainment, and is residentially segregated in gated communities for the very rich in many countries of the world. Members of the TCC seek to project images of themselves as citizens of the world, as well as of their places or countries of birth.

The TCC represents the culmination of a rapid increase in global inequality. Piketty (2014) shows that the number of dollar billionaires has risen ten-fold from 140 in the late 1980s to 1,400 by 2010, by which time their total wealth exceeded a staggering $5,400,000,000 – a twenty-fold rise in less than thirty years. Savage (2014) suggests that 'future historians will look back at these last two decades as witnessing a process of astonishing class formation at the top reaches of the social hierarchy'.

Oxfam (2014) has shown that it is national inequality that matters most to people's lives, and this is rising rapidly almost everywhere. Seven out of ten people on the planet now live in countries where economic inequality is worse than it was thirty years ago. Today, the rich are earning more, both in absolute terms and relative to the rest of the population. For example, in India, China and Nigeria, which are three of the world's fastest-growing, and most populous, developing economies, the benefits of economic growth have gone to the richest members of society: the share of national income held by the richest 10 per cent has risen, whilst the income of the poorest 40 per cent has fallen. In just these three countries, more than 1.1 billion people – 16 per cent of the world – are getting an increasingly smaller share.

Millionaires, even billionaires, are no longer social oddities, but are central to the dynamics of global society today. In the past, millionaires were mostly found in the USA and Europe, or in European holdings overseas. Today the range of millionaires and billionaires is truly transnational with examples from nearly every country in the world. For instance, the Tata family of India hold a vast empire of interests from steel production, to car manufacture, to hotels, banks, food and mining, whilst the Hinduja family have holdings in thirty-seven countries and employ 70,000 people.

Added to this potent mix are the Sovereign Wealth Funds and Pension Funds which also control huge assets, and are sometimes controlled by very small groups of people – often, as in the case of the Qatari Sovereign Wealth Fund, billionaires and members of the ruling family.

There is a major problem when talking about these very rich, international holders of wealth. Do we simply call them the 'super-rich'? Savage (2014) suggests this is too simplistic as it fails to distinguish different sources of wealth: rentier income, fortunes from inheritance, extremely high earnings, and so on. Also, there are some fairly wealthy individuals, such as football players, who,

The **transnational capitalist class** (TCC) is a global power elite or ruling class made up of the owners and controllers of transnational corporations and the globalized media, top officials, professionals and politicians who operate globally, and top business people who trade in global markets.

arguably, have earned their wealth due to a specific talent rather than having merely inherited it, which only demands being born to the right parents. Piketty (2014) focuses on the process of wealth accumulation, as those who are already extremely wealthy are able to accumulate proportionally more than others and thus become even more wealthy.

This group does not appear to have the same social connections as can be traced among the British elites (see page 331) but closer inspection finds certain common traits. Usually they have been educated in elite universities, frequently in the USA or the UK, they have often inherited at least part of their wealth and it is now spread throughout the globe, and they employ accountants and lawyers to minimize the amounts they pay in tax, often claiming non-resident status in every country in which they have assets. Another trait is to marry others like themselves and to ensure that their own children are well employed within the family businesses.

The old European and American version of elites is now international or transnational with a very distinct capitalist culture, having a tendency towards monopoly capitalism.

Activity

Read the passage below and have the discussion outlined beneath:

Between 1980 and 2002, inequality between countries rose rapidly reaching a very high level. It has since fallen slightly due to growth in emerging countries, particularly China. But it is inequality within countries that matters most to people, as the poorest struggle to get by while their neighbours prosper, and this is rising rapidly in the majority of countries. Seven out of 10 people live in countries where the gap between rich and poor is greater than it was 30 years ago. In countries around the world, a wealthy minority are taking an ever-increasing share of their nation's income.

Worldwide, inequality of individual wealth is even more extreme. At the start of 2014, Oxfam calculated that the richest eighty-five people on the planet owned as much as the poorest half of humanity. Between March 2013 and March 2014, these eighty-five people grew $668m richer each day. If Bill Gates were to cash in all of his wealth, and spend $1m every single day, it would take him 218 years to spend it all. In reality though, he would never run out of money: even a modest return of just under 2 per cent would make him $4.2 million each day in interest alone. Since the financial crisis, the ranks of the world's billionaires have more than doubled, swelling to 1,645 people.

And extreme wealth is not just a rich-country story. The world's richest man is Mexico's Carlos Slim, who knocked Bill Gates off the top spot in July 2014. Today, there are sixteen billionaires in sub-Saharan Africa, alongside the 358 million people living in extreme poverty. Absurd levels of wealth exist alongside desperate poverty around the world.

Some inequality is necessary to reward talent, skills and a willingness to innovate and take entrepreneurial risk. However, today's extremes of economic inequality undermine growth and progress, and fail to invest in the potential of hundreds of millions of people.

Source: adapted from Oxfam (2014)

In groups discuss:
1 How far the facts in the passage support the view that a transnational capitalist class exists.
2 What evidence might prove or disprove the idea that these people form and act as a coherent class group.

Globalization, migration and stratification

Migration has been a feature of nearly all societies. It occurs because of various 'push' and 'pull' factors. 'Push' factors are those that may encourage someone to leave their home country, and 'pull' factors are those that may attract them to a new country.

- *Push factors* include things like escaping from natural or socially created circumstances such as earthquakes, famine, the effects of wars, poverty, lack of jobs and unemployment, and political and religious persecution.
- *Pull factors* include things like better opportunities for jobs, study, a higher standard of living, better healthcare and education, more political and religious freedom, and joining relatives.

Worldwide industrialization has long been a pull factor taking people from the countryside to the towns, and in the European Union, migration between nation-states is commonplace as people move for better jobs and higher standards of living in other member states.

In the twenty-first century, Europe has experienced one of the most significant influxes of migrants and refugees in its history, pushed by civil war and persecution – particularly from the Middle Eastern countries, Afghanistan and Africa – and pulled by the prospects of a better life, often risking their lives along the way.

However, the increasing interconnectedness of societies across the world that has accompanied globalization, and growing inequality on a global level, have generated economic migration between countries on a hitherto unprecedented scale, as people are pushed from poorer countries to more affluent Western ones in search of better job opportunities and a higher standard of living.

Such migration affects stratification in several ways.

Migrants, and particularly economic migrants are, on the whole, better educated and often more ambitious than those who do not migrate. This strips the country they leave of valuable resources in terms of trained personnel, but at the same time this may provide more opportunities for upward social mobility for some of those remaining. It may also skew the skill base of the new host country, potentially driving down wages if there becomes a glut of certain skills, thereby blocking opportunities for upward mobility for those already living there. This may cause resentments and divisions within existing social classes, as they see their wages being cut by competition from cheaper migrant workers, and reduced opportunities for themselves. This may lead to greater instability in the stratification system.

Migration may cause two further problems. Firstly, the country of origin has lost valuable resources, which might affect its development and make inequality and poverty worse. Secondly, if the economic position in the country of origin improves, these migrants may return to those countries, leaving a shortage of labour behind them. For example, in 2014, it was estimated that 11 per cent of all professionally trained NHS staff in the UK were overseas nationals, with the figure rising to 26 per cent for doctors. Should these staff choose to leave the UK in the future, the healthcare system as we know it would be unsustainable.

A further effect is that there will be more undocumented workers, who come and stay in countries illegally (also known as illegal immigrants). These are 'pulled' by the prospects of better living standards, and often 'pushed' by poverty and the lack of opportunities in their own countries, but they lack the skills or wealth which would allow them to enter the country legally. There is a growing influx of undocumented workers in the UK – Home Office estimates suggest there are between 500,000 and 800,000, but the fact that these don't officially exist means estimates are very difficult to substantiate. Such undocumented workers swell the poor underclass which was discussed on pages 337–9. They are exploited by UK employers, and often by people-traffickers as well, who smuggle them into the country by various means, and keep them in conditions of semi-slavery. Such super-exploited workers lack the safety nets available to other workers, such as health and safety laws and access to the benefits and healthcare of the welfare state, but they can cause divisions among the most disadvantaged in society, as they often work for less than the legal minimum wage, and cause resentment among other workers as, by taking up employment at cheap rates offered by ruthless employers, they undercut the wages and job opportunities of those who seek to work legally.

Changes in the treatment of gender differences

Since the passing of the Equal Pay Act (1970) and the Sex Discrimination Act (1975), it might be hoped that gender differences would have shown a steady decline. Whilst the situation is far better

Table 4.19 Median full-time gross weekly earnings by gender, UK, for selected years 1997–2015		
	Men £	Women £
1997	357	265
2000	398	298
2004	460	357
2007	498	395
2010	538	439
2015	567	471

Source: *Annual Survey of Hours and Earnings, 2015 Provisional Results.* Office for National Statistics

than it was in the 1960s when married women had to have their husband's permission to sign a hire purchase agreement and other legal documents, it is far from equal.

We saw earlier in Topic 2 that girls outperform boys right up to university entrance level, but earnings do not reflect this and changes in full-time earnings, as shown in table 4.19, indicate that gender differentials still exist and have hardly changed in the last seventeen years or so.

If we take into account that women are more likely to work part-time than men, the picture is slightly different. Part-time pay rates are more equal due to the Equal Pay Act, but men who work part-time tend to work more hours than women so their take-home pay stays higher.

Women's employment position still seems to be affected by the glass ceiling, an invisible barrier of discrimination which makes it difficult for women to reach the same top levels in their chosen careers as similarly qualified men, and few women are found in very high-paying posts. However, there have been improvements in many of the professions: women are now more likely to be found as headteachers – though of primary schools more than secondary schools – and more hospital consultants are women than in 1990. More members of the legal profession than previously are now women, and in nursing and midwifery more men are found than before. Women are now allowed in all branches of the armed forces, though mining is still a prohibited occupation for women.

When women do break through the glass ceiling, figures from the Chartered Management Institute in a report from 2012 show that 'A lot of businesses have been focused on getting more women on boards but we've still got a lot to do on equal pay and equal representation in top executive roles. Women make up almost three out of four at the bottom of the ladder but only one out of four at the top.' The report also noted that 'The figures show that the percentage of women in the executive workforce now stands at 57 per cent. However, while at junior level the majority (69 per cent) of executive workers are now female, a much smaller percentage have made it into top roles – just 40 per cent of department heads are female and only one in four chief executives (24 per cent).' Even when women do get into executive positions,

> female directors earn an average basic salary of £127,257 – £14,689 less than the male director average of £141,946 . . . The gender pay gap extends to annual rewards. At the 91 participating employers providing data on the payment of bonuses, women receive less than half what men are awarded in monetary terms – the average bonus for a male executive was £7,496, compared to £3,726 for a female executive. This picture gets worse as women and men progress in their careers with 50% of males at director level receiving bonuses compared to 36% of females. At £65,000, the average bonus paid to a male director was £7,000 more than that awarded to a female director.

It would seem that women are still unequal in many aspects of life today.

Changes in the treatment of ethnic differences

In the late 1960s it was not an uncommon sight to see notices on rented accommodation which said 'no dogs, no Blacks, no Irish'. Such overt racism was outlawed by various Race Discrimination Acts of 1965, 1968, 1976 and 2000, but as late as 2003 signs appeared in rural Northamptonshire saying 'No Gypsies'. Such signs are quickly removed but they reflect a deep-seated attitude in some sections of the population. During the last fifty years, there have, however, been many changes, not least in the composition of the ethnic minorities themselves.

This composition has changed since the EU Accession Treaties of 2003 and 2005 which allowed people from the Czech Republic, the Republics of Estonia, Cyprus, Latvia, Lithuania, Hungary, Malta, Poland, Slovenia and the Slovak Republic (2003) and from Romania and Bulgaria (2005) to settle in any part of the EU, including the UK. Whilst the number of non-white citizens has continued to rise, this is due to natural increase in family size as second and then third generations marry and procreate, rather than to continued immigration. The number of EU immigrants has also risen as workers from the accession states, particularly Poland, Latvia and Lithuania, have found work here and brought their families with them. Between 2004 and 2007, 500,000 Poles registered for work permits in the UK. The majority of these workers have remained and more have followed, but actual figures are unclear since registration to work is no longer a legal requirement. These immigrants tend to be more highly educated than the indigenous population and frequently speak more than two languages. However, they are not immune to discrimination of the same kind faced by previous immigrants, though their chances of assimilation may be higher since they share the same skin colour as the majority population.

Ethnicity, gender and earnings

We saw earlier that women still earn less than men, and Nandi and Platt (2010) have shown that earnings for ethnic-minority women are lower than for white British women, and that this situation does not appear to have improved in the last ten years. This leaves postmodern ideas about being able to choose identity just as doubtful for these groups as any other.

Ethnicity and employment/unemployment

Has the UK improved as a place to live for non-white citizens? Unemployment figures would suggest that there is still an ethnic bias. Whilst in 2010 the Department of Work and Pensions recorded an unemployment rate for White British people of 7.7 per cent, the rate was lower for non-British white people, possibly because they would return to their country of origin if unemployment lasted for any length of time. Ethnic-minority groups by contrast had an unemployment rate of 13 per cent, but this hid variations between groups. For Indians, the rate was 8 per cent, but for Pakistanis it was 18.5 per cent; Bangladeshi 18 per cent; Black Caribbeans averaged about 15 per cent, with Black Africans about 16.5 per cent, whilst the Chinese had a rate of just over 8 per cent. Within these groups the gender differences show an inconsistent pattern. Whilst the white groups of women were less likely to be unemployed than men, for the non-white groups the unemployment figures for women were significantly higher than those for men. Whether this is as a result of different attitudes to signing on as unemployed or whether it reflects some other explanation is not clear. It would seem, however, that work for some ethnic minorities is not as secure as for the ethnic majority.

Ethnicity and the law

Other aspects of life suggest some improvements. The Home Office claims that there are fewer stop and searches carried out on Asian and African-Caribbean males, but the actual numbers of stop and searches being carried out has continued to rise, and in 2011 46 per cent of all stop and searches were made by the Metropolitan Police. The Home Office reports:

Self-classifications of persons stopped and searched in 2010/11 were of similar proportions across all ethnic groups as compared to the previous year. In 2010/11, 66 per cent of the persons defined themselves as White, 15 per cent as Black and ten per cent as Asian. Smaller proportions defined themselves as Chinese or Other (1 per cent) or Mixed (3 per cent). The ethnicity for four per cent of persons was not stated. However, a large proportion of these stops and searches were conducted by the Metropolitan Police Service, and these have had considerable effect on the proportions for England and Wales as a whole. Excluding stops and searches by the Metropolitan Police Service, the vast majority of persons searched in England and Wales were White (84 per cent); very small proportions were Asian (6 per cent) or Black (4 per cent). In contrast, of the persons searched by the Metropolitan Police Service, 43 per cent defined themselves as White, 30 per cent as Black and 16 per cent as Asian. Proportions of persons searched by the Metropolitan Police Service who defined themselves as Mixed (4 per cent) or Chinese or Other (3 per cent) were similar to those seen in other forces in England and Wales (2 per cent and 1 per cent respectively). Fifty-two per cent of the stops and searches conducted by the Metropolitan Police Service were on Minority Ethnic persons, compared to 13 per cent across all other forces. This in part is explained by both the high population density and the high Minority Ethnic populations (resident and visitor) within the Metropolitan Police Service area.

> **Race hate crimes** are criminal offences which are perceived by the victim or any other person to be motivated by hostility or prejudice based on a person's ethnicity or religion.

These figures are a small but limited decrease on the situation at the time of the Macpherson Inquiry into the murder of Stephen Lawrence (see page 485 for more on this).

Race hate crimes, that is crimes directed against a specific group because of their ethnicity or religion, show mixed figures on current trends – whilst incidents reported to the police are falling, levels reported in surveys have fluctuated.

Ethnicity and the media

Ethnic minority representation in the media has increased to the point that it could be argued that news readers on the terrestrial TV channels over-represent ethnic minorities. However, ethnic representation in comedy shows, or on quiz shows and other forms of entertainment, does not show representation at a level that should be expected. Less than 8 per cent of such participants come from ethnic minority groups. So the situation is not clearly changing only in one direction.

There is a full discussion of ethnicity and the media on pages 221–6.

Conclusion

Whilst there have been changes in the class structure and in the position of women and ethnic minorities, they have not, on the whole, been of great extent. However, there have been improvements, and legislative changes such as the Equalities Act of 2010 may well bring more. Changing attitudes takes time, probably a generation or more when dealing with such aspects as sexism and racism. Liberal feminists have always been fairly optimistic about change and there is no reason to doubt that change is possible.

The Equality and Human Rights Commission's First Triennial Review, *How Fair is Britain? Equality, Human Rights and Good Relations in 2010*, summed the current position up by saying:

> (Legal) changes, and more besides, have made a meaningful difference in the lives of many people who may be subject to disadvantage because of who or what they are. More importantly they have transformed the expectations of most British people about what constitutes reasonable behaviour and what a decent society should look like. Yet even a summary investigation reveals that in many instances, what happens in the real world falls short of the ideals of equality – from the harassment of disabled people, to homophobic bullying in schools, to stereotypes and arbitrary barriers that prevent older people from giving of their best in the workplace. (page 13)

> In short, we twenty-first century Britons are a largely fair-minded people. But we are not yet a fair society. And we know that no individual can be truly free to realise their potential, or to exercise their inalienable human rights as long as they are imprisoned by the invisible, many-stranded web of prejudice, inertia and unfairness that holds so many back. (page 7)

As the Triennial Review noted, 'The fact is that we are still not, as a society, as fair as we would like to be' (page 13).

On a global level, it is argued the situation may be even more grim. Piketty (2014) argues that the apparent class convergence noted in the late twentieth century was accidental and temporary rather than a long-term historical trend and that the old industrialized nations are returning to regimes based on inherited wealth and rigid hierarchy. Those who are currently rich may have taken risks to achieve their initial wealth but rapidly invest it in such a way that they become rentiers and thus their fortunes continue to grow, and with it the power to control the economy to their advantage. They thus become an oligarchy and control the destiny of their fellows, and the dream of democracy and an equal society is thus an illusion.

Practice questions

1   Outline and explain **two** reasons why consumption may not have replaced class as an indicator of status. **(10 marks)**

2   Read **Item A** below and answer the question that follows.

> ### Item A
> Due to the deskilling of many occupations, both those formerly considered middle class and those considered working class, it no longer makes sense to speak of the UK as being divided into upper, middle and working class but rather as having a multitude of classes. Marxists would disagree.

Applying material from **Item A**, analyse **two** reasons for suggesting that class definitions based on occupation are no longer relevant to the UK today. **(10 marks)**

3   Read **Item B** below and answer the question that follows.

> ### Item B
> Worldwide, the rich have got richer, even when the world economy slumped into recession, and the poor have got poorer. At the start of 2014, Oxfam calculated that the richest eighty-five people on the planet owned as much as the poorest half of the world's population. Marxists might explain this as the rise of a transnational capitalist class, while functionalists might explain it in terms of meritocracy.

Applying material from **Item B** and your knowledge, evaluate the usefulness of Marxist theories in explaining growing global inequality. **(20 marks)**

Topic 5

SPECIFICATION AREA

The nature, extent and significance of patterns of social mobility

Social mobility

Social mobility is the movement of people from one class to another. It has long fascinated sociologists, and raises a number of interesting questions, for example:

- Why is it important?
- Are there different types of mobility?
- How is social mobility measured?

How much social mobility exists within a society, and who is mobile, can be affected by several variables.

1 *The occupational structure of a society at a given time*: are all jobs open to all members of society? How easy is it to gain the qualifications necessary for a professional position, such as being a doctor?

2 *Fertility differences between groups within society*: if women from higher social classes have fewer children, then not all professional jobs can be 'inherited' and some positions will need to be filled from people lower down the class scale.

3 *The structure and availability of education*: is education freely available to all, or do hidden barriers exist, such as expensive uniforms, or the need to belong to a certain faith? Will universities favour those from private schools, or will government policies mean that universities are more likely to encourage working-class students to apply?

4 *The distribution of opportunities*: in London, for example, there is a wider array of job types than in rural areas, making upward and downward mobility much easier. Children of professionals may also be more aware of what opportunities exist in society, as opposed to children who have grown up in a working-class community.

5 *The distribution of motivation*: in some working-class communities, there may be pressure on boys to resist upward mobility and to link working-class jobs to their masculine identity.

Why is social mobility important?

Sociologists have argued that a study of social mobility tells us a great deal about a society, for example:

1 High rates of mobility, both up and down, would suggest a society in which status might be awarded on merit.

2 High upward rates with little downward mobility would suggest an economy that is expanding.

3 A society with a low rate of mobility is likely to lead to higher levels of class consciousness, solidarity and class cohesion, as people are born into and stay in one class which they then pass on to their children, creating a distinctive culture.

4 A fluid system that allows people to move easily from class to class will lead to a free exchange of ideas and be more open to change, while a closed system, such as the caste system, will be less likely to experience great social change.

It is important to understand what effect mobility has on those who are mobile: do they hold on to the norms and values of their original class, or do they adopt those of their new class? What effect does this have on their children? Maintenance of class attitudes from a previous class might explain certain voting patterns – for example middle-class Labour voters who came from a working-class background, and working-class Conservatives who may have been born into the middle class and been downwardly mobile.

High levels of social mobility can lead to dissatisfaction in society. Dorling et al. (2007) examined the tenfold increase in the number of university graduates between 1968 and 2002 in their study of the geographical dimensions of wealth and poverty. They suggest that those who have been educated to a level undreamt of by their parents will have aspirations that society may be unable to meet if, in reality, there are only a few jobs that require a university education. This failure to attain greater status and income within a new class may lead to resentment.

> **Activity**
>
> 1 In your own words, give **four** reasons why sociologists consider mobility to be worth studying.
> 2 Assess the importance of mobility in maintaining social order.

Types of social mobility

Social mobility can be considered in many forms. An important distinction is that between individual and group mobility. Group mobility occurs when a specific occupation alters its status, such as farm work. As agriculture has become more mechanized, farm workers have acquired other skills, whereas computerization has deskilled the printing industry and printers have, as a group, been downwardly mobile.

Perfect social mobility is a situation in which every position in a society is filled on merit and the society is constantly changing. This is perhaps what Davis and Moore (1945) claimed to be describing – as discussed earlier in this chapter (Topic 1).

An **absolute rate of mobility** is the total number of movements of individuals up and down the class structure within a given time period. For example, between 1945 and 2000 there was a high rate of absolute mobility, mostly upward. It should not be confused with the **relative rate of mobility**, which concerns the amount of mobility in the class structure, taking into account the changes there have been in the occupational structure of a society, which would provide more opportunities or fewer in particular occupational groupings. For example, in the UK, the years after 1945 saw a major shift from primary industry such as mining and agriculture to secondary/ manufacturing and then to tertiary/service-sector jobs. Since the possibility of entering the service class grew as that sector expanded, the relative chances of movement have remained much the same.

It is also necessary to distinguish between **intragenerational** social mobility and **intergenerational** social mobility. Intragenerational social mobility is that which occurs within an individual's own lifetime – for example, when someone starts by working in a factory, then goes to teacher training college and finally becomes a teacher, thus moving from manual work to professional work, or starts as a doctor and drops out to become a call-centre worker.

Intergenerational social mobility is when there has been movement between the adult occupation of a child and that of his or her parents – for example, if the father is a white-collar clerical worker and the son becomes a dustman, he is downwardly mobile; if, instead, he becomes a teacher, he is upwardly mobile. It is worth noting that, until now, all studies of social mobility have considered fathers and sons rather than mothers and sons, fathers and daughters or mothers and daughters.

> **Activity**
>
> 1 How might you measure each form of social mobility using interviews? What questions would you need to ask?
> 2 What are the difficulties of using questionnaires to measure intergenerational social mobility?
> 3 If measuring the social mobility of women what advantages might there be in comparing them to their mothers rather than their fathers?

Perfect social mobility occurs where every position is filled on merit and individuals move easily between the class of birth and the class of achievement based on their ability and nothing else.

Absolute rate of mobility is the total number of movements within a class structure within a given period of time

Relative rate of mobility is the actual number of movements within a class structure adjusted to take account of changes in the occupational structure of a society.

Intragenerational social mobility occurs when an individual moves from one class to another during their own working life. It can be either upwards or downwards.

Intergenerational social mobility occurs when the class of the child is different from the class of the parent. The move can be either upwards or downwards.

Measuring social mobility

Studies of social mobility, like most studies of class, have been based on employment, as this is easily measurable. They tend to concentrate on absolute rates of mobility. Of the approximately 60 million people in the UK, about 30 million are in employment. How can we classify the others? The retired could be assigned a class based on previous employment, and children on the basis of their parents' occupation. Mothers raising children were traditionally assigned a class based on the occupation of their partner. But what if they have no partner, and have never worked themselves? In the past, they have been assigned a class based on their father's occupation. Feminists, among others, have suggested that this is not a very satisfactory or accurate measure. This dilemma has led to three main positions on how to measure class and thus how to measure whether social mobility has occurred:

1 *Goldthorpe* (1980) suggests staying with convention and counting the person in the family with the most direct link to the labour market.
2 *Heath and Britten* (1984) suggest still using the family, but taking the labour position of both the adult male and the adult female to give a class position for the whole family.
3 *Stanworth* (1984) suggests that the family is left out of the equation, and that individuals should be the unit of stratification.

However, the class system of the UK remains very heavily gendered and there is an uneven distribution of men and women in the different classes. For example, following the Registrar General's classification of class (see Topic 3), Goldthorpe found that Class I consisted mostly of men, while Class IV contained more women than men. In addition, there are different mobility chances for men and women, and within any one class men are advantaged. At any specific skill level, men with that skill are higher placed than women with the same skill; for example, with a teaching qualification, men are more likely to be found in education management than women.

The causes of social mobility

In this section, most of the emphasis will be on the UK, but many of the causes of change and hence of social mobility will apply to other societies. The major causes could be said to be:

- Changes in the economy
- Changes in patterns of education
- Changes in fertility and death rates
- Global changes
- Migration

The economy

Historically, the stratification system seemed relatively rigid, with people being born into one class and staying there for life, but some social mobility did exist. When servants were more commonplace, employment in a rich man's house often led to social advancement. For those who had learned to read and write, the future was promising. The chances altered with the Industrial Revolution, as the economy shifted from an agricultural to an industrial base. People moved from countryside to town. Similar changes are occurring in the developing world today, with urbanization occurring everywhere.

In the twentieth century, the pace of change increased, though it will be seen later that upward social mobility is slowing down in the UK as **social closure** becomes more rigid in the higher social groups.

Employment has changed in many ways. There is now a more service-based economy, dependent on international trade and transnational employers. This inevitably alters the power of the state to control events within its own borders. Even employment law is now international. The growth of women's rights has led to a feminization of the workforce. Although women have always done the bulk of the world's work, now they are being paid for some of it. This has led to a major shift in

Social closure
applies in a system whereby members of a group can act to prevent others from joining them.

power within family relationships, as women have income, and the power of the patriarch to dictate to the family is severely diminished.

Activity

1 Pick an older member of your family and ask questions about their family history to discover what class movement there has been in the last two or three generations (or as far back as the respondent can remember).
2 Report your findings to the whole class, to compare just how much class fluidity there has been.
3 List the advantages and difficulties of this kind of in-depth interviewing and empathetic research.

Education

Universal education has opened up many occupations. In the UK, this began towards the end of the nineteenth century. However, the changes to the education of women, to an equal footing with men, did not really occur until the 1970s, with the Equal Pay and Sex Discrimination Acts. This has had a major impact on the ability of women to compete with men for higher positions. The full effect is now being felt, as women enter the higher professions in larger numbers.

Worldwide, the importance of education is widely recognized by many governments. One of the United Nation's Millennium Development Goals was free universal education for all – girls as well as boys. This is likely to change the position of women greatly: as they achieve more equality with men in one field, they are unlikely to accept lower positions in terms of power in the home or in the public sphere. Patriarchy may become a thing of the past.

Fertility and death rates

Changes in women's fertility rates have had major impacts on class and social mobility throughout the world. As the number of children a woman has falls, populations grow smaller, thereby leading to labour shortages. When women achieve educational success, the first effect is a reduction in the number of children they have, partly because the age of marriage is delayed in many societies, but also because they learn about the medical dangers of too many pregnancies. Their aspirations for their children also rise and having fewer children makes it easier to achieve those aspirations.

Until the mid twentieth century, high death rates in the UK before the age of 20 meant that in certain groups there was a shortage of labour. This resulted in a fairly fluid workforce as people moved from one social class to another. Historically, one of the greatest shifts in stratification in Europe followed the Black Death in the mid fourteenth century. Currently, in sub-Saharan Africa and elsewhere, HIV/AIDS is having a similar effect, as whole generations are often halved in size.

Global changes

One major global change, particularly in the past fifty years, has been the rise of the transnational corporation (TNC); the owners of an industry may be resident in one country and have the factories that produce the goods and services spread throughout the world. This means national governments may no longer have control over the economic structure of their own society. For example, when the Ford Motor Company decided to move car production from the UK to India, to cut costs, the UK government was unable to prevent this, and skilled and semi-skilled jobs were lost to the UK economy. As this happens more frequently, the whole structure of the economy and employment changes. A country could easily go from having a highly trained workforce, earning good wages, to one where there is mass unemployment, as the jobs move.

Migration

Labour shortages in the UK have already led to migration within the country, and immigration from outside the country. Internal migration from north to south, in particular into London, has been a feature of British society for centuries. In the past, the British Isles, and in particular Wales, Scotland and Ireland, have been exporters of people. That situation has now been reversed, and immigration into the UK, particularly of certain sections of the workforce, is commonplace.

Many of the migrants are here on a temporary basis and return home after only a brief spell. If economic situations in their home country improve, or if the scarcity of labour that their emigration has created pushes up wages in the mother country, they are more likely to return home. This has certainly been the case with migrants from Poland, since that country joined the European Union in 2004. Other migrants return to their motherland as they retire – something that is particularly common among the African Caribbean (Black Caribbean) population.

At present, the UK economy needs more people of working age, and in the future, with a growing elderly population unable to work and requiring support, this need could become even greater. This will have an effect on the stratification system. As workers become more scarce, their status will increase, and this, in turn, will have great consequences for all kinds of government planning and policies, such as health, education, housing, etc.

There are both benefits and problems involved in the migration of labour. Maybe the greatest problem – and one that Britain has yet, as a society, to consider in detail – is that migrants can leave as well as arrive. They owe no particular loyalty to their new home and, if conditions are better elsewhere, they are likely to leave.

This is also true of people born in the UK. Many countries – notably Australia, New Zealand, Canada and South Africa – have all experienced, and are still experiencing, immigration from the UK, while Spain is home to a large English expatriate community, amongst them many retired people.

> **Activity**
> 1 List and explain in your own words *five* possible causes of change in the stratification system.
> 2 Identify *two* pieces of evidence that would suggest that each of these causes might be occurring.

Studies of social mobility

There have been many studies of mobility since the 1930s, both in the UK and worldwide. Here, studies concerning the UK will be considered.

The Glass Study

Using the Hall-Jones scale of social class, which graded occupations according to their prestige, Glass (1954) compared the occupations of men over 21 with that of their fathers. Two-thirds of the men interviewed were in a different social class from their fathers (one-third went down, one-third moved up). Most movement was to a class adjacent to that of the father. Long-range mobility from top to bottom or bottom to top was very rare. The figures, however, disguised the high degree of self-recruitment, where those in the top social classes closed ranks to those from lower down the hierarchy and recruited the offspring of others like themselves to its privileged positions. In general, Glass discovered a high degree of social closure.

Criticisms of the Glass study

Critics have suggested the following problems with this study:

- Much of the evidence was based on people's recollections of their father's occupations, which may have been faulty

- Many of the fathers had been working, or perhaps not working, through the Great Depression of the 1930s, which may also have led to inaccurate data as to their real occupational level
- This was a snapshot in time, and the men interviewed in 1949 probably went on, through the expansion of the 1950s, to higher and better positions: they were intragenerationally socially mobile.

However, other studies done at a similar time, in the UK, USA and other societies, suggested that intragenerational social mobility, too, was relatively short-range, from manual to routine clerical rather than from manual to managerial.

The Oxford Mobility Study

The next major British study was started in 1972 by Goldthorpe (1980) at Nuffield College, Oxford. It is sometimes referred to as the Nuffield study and sometimes as the Oxford Mobility Study. It is almost impossible to compare this study with the one by Glass, since different criteria were used for the various strata. Glass had used groups based on occupational prestige; Goldthorpe used his own classification based mainly on market rewards. However, this study seemed to show higher rates of long-range mobility (and more upward than downward), and fewer than half of the people surveyed were still in the social class into which they were born. Goldthorpe therefore concluded that the chances of upward movement, particularly from the manual classes, had improved during the twentieth century.

Criticisms of the Oxford Mobility Study

Later work by Kellner and Wilby (1980) shows that the claim made by Goldthorpe was not equally true for all social classes. They drew up a 1:2:4 rule of relative hope which shows that, over the period covered (the middle to latter part of the twentieth century), whatever the chance of a working-class boy reaching the service class, a boy from the intermediate class had twice the chance, and one from the service class itself had four times the chance. Therefore, they concluded that UK society has seen no significant increase in openness. That is to say, although the level of absolute mobility had increased, relative mobility had not.

Another major problem with Goldthorpe's study is that, although it suggested easier entry to the service class as a whole, it did not explore what might be called elite self-recruitment. Also, feminists would rightly argue, the study ignored a large part of the workforce – namely, women. In a later work, Goldthorpe and Payne (1986) attempted to address this issue. They found that, however women were included in the study (whether by including them in their husband's class, by assigning the family a class based on the higher wage-earner, or by assigning women their own class), very little difference was made to relative mobility rates.

The Essex Study

The Essex Study of social mobility in the 1980s attempted to consider both male and female mobility, and both inter- and intragenerational mobility. Marshall et al. (1988) found that, as a result of the expansion of white-collar work, there had been fairly high rates of upward mobility, but the rates were lower for women. This study found that the class of origin has a strong effect on subsequent job opportunities. They interviewed people who had begun their working careers in the service class and looked at how many of them had managed to stay in this class over a period of time. Of the men who had been born into the service class, 84 per cent were still there at the time of being interviewed (that is, there had been no inter- or intragenerational mobility). However, only 64 per cent of the men born into the working class were still employed in the service class. For women, the figures were 77 per cent and 43 per cent. It could be argued that even when some social mobility is achieved early in life, it is not always maintained, and that life chances at birth may have a part to play in the ultimate destination of an individual.

Goldthorpe and Jackson (2007) argue that because service-sector jobs have probably now reached a peak, the chances of upward mobility from the working class are now very low. The levels of mobility found in Goldthorpe's earlier work are unlikely to be repeated over the next decade, and social mobility patterns are likely to be much more static. Relative mobility is low, even though in the past absolute mobility has seemed high. Goldthorpe and Jackson are now implying that absolute mobility also may be declining.

The National Equality Panel Report

In 2010 the National Equality Panel produced a far-ranging report on current inequalities in the UK. Among other findings they discovered an increasing tendency for parental income to be mirrored in the earnings of their adult children, suggesting that boys born into the poorest 25 per cent of the population in 1970 were three times more likely to stay there than to rise, in income terms, to the top 25 per cent, and that this entrenchment of the class divide had increased since the 1950s. The box below gives details of these findings.

An anatomy of economic inequality in the UK: Relative intergenerational income mobility

Table 4.20 compares where children came in the ranking of their earnings in their early 30s with their parents' income group when they had been teenagers. So in the upper panel, it can be seen that 30 per cent of men born in 1958, whose parents were in the bottom quarter of incomes when they were teenagers, ended up in the bottom quarter of earnings themselves; only 18 per cent of them ended up in the top quarter of earnings. For their equivalents born twelve years later, more (37 per cent) ended up at the bottom, and fewer (13 per cent) at the top. The stickiness of high income strengthened even more – 45 per cent of those born in 1970 with the most affluent parents ended up highly paid themselves, compared with 35 per cent for the earlier cohort. The lower panel shows a similar strengthening of the links between daughters' earnings and parental income.

Table 4.20 Intergenerational income mobility, Great Britain	Parents' Income Group	
	Bottom 25%	Top 25%
Sons' earnings at 33–34 (%)		
In bottom 25%:		
Born 1958 (at 33)	30	18
Born 1970 (at 34)	37	13
In top 25%:		
Born 1958 (at 33)	18	35
Born 1970 (at 34)	13	45
Daughters' earnings at 33–34 (%)		
In bottom 25%:		
Born 1958 (at 33)	27	18
Born 1970 (at 34)	32	16
In top 25%:		
Born 1958 (at 33)	18	37
Born 1970 (at 34)	14	41
Source: Blanden and Machin (2007)		

Taken from National Equality Panel Report 2010

The Sutton Trust and the Social Mobility and Child Poverty Commission

The Sutton Trust, founded in 1997, has the aim of helping 'highly able children from disadvantaged backgrounds' to reach their full potential. It believes that this may aid the upward social mobility of such groups, to the benefit of the wider society. The Social Mobility and Child Poverty Commission (SMCPC) was set up in 2010 'to act as an advocate for social mobility' and has a wider remit than the Sutton Trust. However, when considering the evidence produced by these two sources we should not forget these aims.

Much attention has been paid to the declining levels of mobility in the last forty years, especially the lack of upward social mobility for apparently bright children from a lower-working-class background and the similar lack of downward mobility for less bright children from the higher social classes.

The Sutton Trust has looked in detail at the education system and particularly at the pupil premium set up in 2011 – extra money given to schools for pupils who were seen to be disadvantaged because they were from poorer homes, as measured by their entitlement to free school meals.

This pupil premium, like other previous measures, was expected to improve the qualifications of this group. So far, according to the Sutton Trust (*The Pupil Premium: Next Steps*, July 2015), if we measure attainment by GCSE results, the percentage gap between disadvantaged children and the national average has remained static since the introduction of the pupil premium. Allen (2015), in a study of missing talent, discovered that every year high achievers at Key Stage 2 fail to reach their expected potential at GCSE, and that pupils – especially boys – attracting the pupil premium are most likely to be in this group. They are also less likely to be taking those subjects highly regarded by universities and employers, namely triple science, languages, history and geography. This means that disadvantaged pupils may lack the qualifications to enable upward social mobility. However, this might be reversed over time as the pupil premium scheme has been running for a very short period and may not have full effect for at least eleven years.

Opportunity hoarding and the glass floor

However, findings from the SMCPC show that such upward mobility may be blocked not only by the lack of qualifications of aspirants, but also by the failure of children born into higher groups to become downwardly mobile.

In a study based on a cohort born in 1970 and followed throughout their lives so far, McKnight (2015) separated out two distinct groups. One was from the lowest income group and one from the highest, and each contained two subgroups of children who, at age 5, were deemed to be either high or low attainers based on cognitive tests. Other factors such as self-motivation, social and emotional skills in childhood, parents' highest qualification, school attended, and whether or not the child acquired a degree were also considered. The study then looked at the chances of group members being in the highest-paid jobs at the age of 42, as this was the age the cohort had reached when the study was undertaken. The results can be seen in table 4.21.

Both low- and high-attaining children at age 5 from high-income backgrounds were more likely to be high earners at age 42 than their peers from less advantaged backgrounds. Those from the lowest income group who were initially high attainers did not manage to convert their early potential into high earnings at age 42 with the same degree of success as children from more advantaged family backgrounds. McKnight concludes that more advantaged parents are able to protect children from downward social mobility through a range of measures such as private schooling or by getting access to the remaining grammar schools, or simply by having a better understanding of the workings of the education system. They will also use their social networks to get unpaid internships for their children and use other similar techniques to ensure access to higher-paid jobs. This she calls **opportunity hoarding**.

For example, private schooling not only has educational advantages, it also sets up social and cultural networks – 'old-boy networks' – that are crucial in accessing certain highly paid jobs. It also bestows soft skills such as self-presentation, conduct in social settings, accent and self-confidence, which have little to do with productivity but influence recruitment to elite professions. These are all examples of opportunity hoarding.

Opportunity hoarding refers to the ability of more socially privileged groups to manipulate situations, organizations and opportunities to prevent their own children from losing advantages over other children from more disadvantaged backgrounds.

Table 4.21 Predicted probability of being in the top fifth of hourly earnings at age 42 associated with key characteristics

		Low attainers		High attainers	
		Male	Female	Male	Female
Family income	Lowest income group	14%	6%	25%	12%
	Highest income group	16%	7%	35%	19%
Parents' highest qualification	No qualification	13%	5%	26%	12%
	Degree	22%	10%	29%	14%
Secondary school	Comprehensive	15%	6%	28%	14%
	Private	33%	18%	43%	25%
Highest qualification gained	No qualification	12%	5%	19%	9%
	Degree	40%	23%	52%	33%

Adapted from McKnight (2015)

Not only do children from better-off families hoard opportunities in the education system – their increased chances of gaining degrees lead them to hoard opportunities in the workplace as well.

This opportunity hoarding applies also to the low-ability children of the highest income group, who are protected from downward mobility even when, on the evidence of their skills, it would be predicted that they should occupy a lower socio-economic position. This is known as the '**glass floor**'.

The **glass floor** is the opposite of a glass ceiling – an invisible baseline below which more advantaged groups prevent their children from falling.

High achievers from the lowest income group, especially where parents have low education levels themselves, do not have such help and consequently are less likely to be successful. It can therefore be said that, rather than there just being a 'glass ceiling' to upward mobility from below, there is also a 'glass floor' preventing downward mobility from above.

It could be argued that, since this study relates back to events over the last forty years, its findings may no longer be true for groups in the future. However, the work from the Sutton Trust (see above) is not overly optimistic, and there is no reason to suppose that parents who have themselves been advantaged by such things as private education and so on will forgo these advantages for their children.

It would then appear that the argument that we live in a meritocratic society is far from true. In order for that to occur, not only must barriers to upward mobility be removed but so must the advantages that prevent downward mobility. Whilst it might be relatively simple, through changes in the education system, to ensure that the qualifications needed for high posts are open to all, the changes needed to prevent opportunity hoarding are far more contentious and difficult to achieve since they might include strategies such as disallowing private education or extra tuition, which are not likely to be popular with certain highly placed and influential groups. See the activity below for the suggestions for tackling this problem made by the Social Mobility and Child Poverty Commission.

Activity

The research from the SMCPC makes several key policy recommendations, including:
- Educating parents to improve their skills and perspectives – reduce inequalities in parental education through adult skills programmes, given there appears to be a direct link between parental education and child outcomes
- Ensuring children from less advantaged backgrounds have access to the support and opportunities available to their peers – give opportunities for them to build non-cognitive and

'soft' skills, provide good careers information and guidance, mentoring and a rich set of opportunities to understand the world of work
- Tackling material deprivation and the financial pressures on parents that undermine their efforts to give their children the best possible start in life
- Dealing with the institutional barriers to aspiration – improve school quality in disadvantaged areas, broaden access to high-quality schools and universities (for example, via admissions procedures), and remove financial barriers to higher education
- Taking action to reduce 'opportunity hoarding' – for example, tackle unpaid internships, encourage employers to remove barriers in the recruitment process that inadvertently prevent those with high potential from disadvantaged backgrounds being successful, and ensure school selection procedures don't unintentionally skew access towards those from advantaged backgrounds who can afford extensive private tuition.

As a group, discuss how likely it is that each of these ideas will be implemented, and what the effects might be on social mobility if they were.

Social mobility and women

Works by Stanworth (1984), Heath (1981) and Payne and Abbott (1990) suggest that women from all social classes are more likely to be downwardly socially mobile and less likely to be upwardly socially mobile than men, and that women born into Classes 1 and 2 were very likely to fall to Class 3. Of the number from the lower classes who were socially mobile, very few ended up in the top two classes. It could be argued that, by ignoring women, the picture of social mobility in the UK is inaccurate and incomplete. The study of women would suggest that mobility is somewhat less than previously thought and that, for women, downward mobility is as likely as upward mobility. McKnight (2015) attempted to overcome the lack of women in social mobility studies by assigning children to their class at birth based on the higher earner in the household, so for that study the class at birth was sometimes based on the mother's status. However she still found lower mobility rates for women than for men.

Social mobility and ethnic minorities

Platt (2005) argues that longitudinal studies concerning the social mobility of ethnic minorities show that some groups have been more upwardly mobile than others, particularly African Caribbean, Black African, Indian and Chinese people. Their mobility patterns appeared to be linked to their educational success. She distinguished between migrants and non-migrants, looking at how subsequent generations had fared since the arrival in the UK of the first generation. Migrants were less likely than non-migrants to be upwardly socially mobile, with 70 per cent of migrants and 60 per cent of non-migrants remaining in the same social class as their parents. Middle-class migrants were more likely to suffer downward mobility than upward, though their children had a relatively high chance of returning to their parent's class position. There were religious differences within ethnic groups, with Hindus more likely to be upwardly mobile than Muslims or Sikhs. Gender also affected mobility, with women more likely to remain in the same social class throughout their lives.

The chances of social mobility

Measuring social mobility is difficult since there has to be a time lag. However, some figures are available demonstrating the chances of such mobility in selected European countries. They show that, between the 1970s and the 1990s, there was some increased intergenerational mobility for

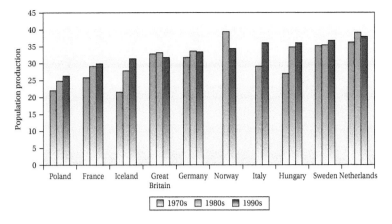

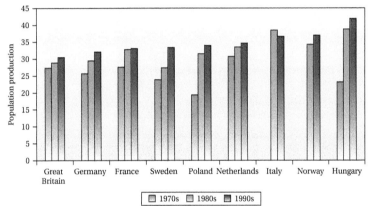

Figure 4.12 Absolute social mobility in different countries, for men and women: proportion of men or women getting better jobs than their parents (%)

Source: National Equality Panel Report 2010

both men and women. It is impossible, as yet, to say whether this trend has continued. Recent figures concerning youth unemployment, especially among young black men, suggest that upward mobility may no longer be occurring. Figures for downward mobility do not appear to exist. In many ways these might be more interesting as a measurement of the openness of a society, since a system based solely on meritocracy should have losers as well as winners. Figure 4.12 shows the likelihood of absolute mobility across Europe. Nearly all countries have shown an increase for men between 1970 and 1980, but thereafter Great Britain and Norway show a decrease. For women there is a steady increase in upward mobility except for in Italy. Thus, continuing social mobility in an upward direction cannot be seen as certain; as economies contract, downward social mobility is likely to occur. The implication of this for society as a whole will need careful thought. When people's expectations of an increasingly better life are not met, social unrest is likely to follow.

Social mobility and the maintenance of class differences

When looking at whether social mobility matters in the formation of class solidarity or of class consciousness, different arguments will have to be made for different classes. It would appear that those members of the working class who are not upwardly mobile might develop a form of solidarity, since, for the past fifty years or so, there has been relatively little downward mobility into that class.

However, for those classes in which there has been much inward and outward mobility, the chances of class consciousness would seem slight. For Marxists, it could be argued that this talk of increased social mobility is nothing but a smokescreen, since, as has been seen, social closure at the top means that mobility is only within the ranks of the proletariat and merely serves to disguise the fact that none of these people own or control the means of production.

Activity

Ethnicity

Age

Disability

Adherence
to
particular
religious
practices

Sexuality

What inequalities still persist in each of these areas of life?

Conclusion

From the discussions above, it would seem that, whatever politicians and other social commentators may say about the inherent fairness of contemporary society, in which all are treated equally, the reality is somewhat different. The life chances enjoyed by an individual are determined by his or her social class of birth, sex or gender, ethnicity, disability, status. Moreover, being born in an affluent country such as the UK is far preferable to being born in, for example, sub-Saharan Africa.

Despite the recent tendency of sociologists and social commentators to suggest that social class is dying, Chapman (2008) and Reay (2007), amongst others, would suggest that it is still the major determinant of life chances in the UK and this is unlikely to change in the immediate future.

Dorling (2011) sums it up best:

> we know we have returned to inequalities as great as those last seen [in the UK] in 1918 because we can compare . . . then and now. We can see that both before and after they have paid tax, the rich are again so very rich that in terms of social inequality we are all back almost to the Edwardian era of great socio-economic injustice. We know we have returned because our voting patterns reveal how geographically and politically segregated we now are. We know that polarization is still on the rise because we can measure it.

Practice questions

1 Outline and explain **two** reasons for changes in the rates of social mobility.   **(10 marks)**

2 Read **Item A** below and answer the question that follows.

Item A

Social mobility is often seen as an indicator of an open society where meritocracy and individual hard work are of more importance than the accident of birth into a particular class. Yet, in the UK today, a child born into Social Class V is as likely to stay there as to reach even Social Class III.

Applying material from **Item A**, analyse **two** reasons why the UK still remains a relatively closed society in terms of social mobility.   **(10 marks)**

3 Read **Item B** below and answer the question that follows.

Item B

Functionalists maintain that stratification is inevitable and necessary, but it is accompanied by meritocracy and, by implication, involves a high degree of social mobility as those most capable achieve the highest rewards and status. Marxists and feminists would disagree that this in any way describes reality.

Applying material from **Item B** and your knowledge, evaluate sociological explanations of the extent of social mobility in the UK.   **(20 marks)**

CHAPTER SUMMARY AND REVISION CHECKLIST

After studying this chapter, you should be able to:

- Describe the different forms of differentiation, inequality and stratification.
- Describe the different theories of stratification, by social class, by ethnicity and by gender.
- Explain and criticize the different theories of stratification such as functionalist, Marxist, interactionist, feminist and postmodernist.
- Explain the problems in defining and measuring class.
- Explain and criticize theories concerning the defining and measuring of class.

- Use evidence about different classes to assess theories of stratification.
- Describe changes in the structure of inequality and stratification.
- Describe global patterns of inequality, their consequences, and the transnational capitalist class.
- Describe the patterns of social mobility.
- Explain and criticize theories about social mobility, what it signifies and whether it exists.

KEY TERMS

Definitions can be found in the glossary at the end of this book, as well as these terms being defined in the margin where they first appear in the chapter.

absolute rate of mobility
alienation
apartheid
authority
black economy
bourgeoisie
bureaucracy
caste
child labour
class
class consciousness
closed system
consumption patterns
cultural capital
deskilling
dual labour movement
elite
embourgeoisement
establishment
ethnicity
ethnocentrism
expressive role
false consciousness
fatalism
feudal estate/system

forced labour
forced marriage
gender
Gini coefficient
glass ceiling
glass floor
globalization
hate crimes
host immigrant/
    assimilation model
hybrid identities
hydraulic society
ideal type
ideological state apparatus
immediate gratification
income
Industrial Revolution
institutional racism
instrumental orientation
instrumental role
intergenerational social
    mobility
intragenerational social
    mobility
inverse care law

life chances
looking-glass self
lumpenproletariat
matrilocal
meritocracy
meta-analysis
modernity
monopoly
NEETs
open system
opportunity hoarding
party
paternity leave
patriarchy
patrilocal
people-trafficking
perfect social mobility
power
present-time orientation
professions
proletarianization
proletariat
race hate crimes
racism
relative rate of mobility

repressive state
    apparatus
reserve army of labour
role allocation
scapegoating
slavery
social capital
social closure
social construction
social exclusion
social mobility
social solidarity
Standardized
    Mortality Ratio
status
teenager
trade union
transnational capitalist
    class
underclass
wealth

There are a variety of free tests and other activities that can be used to assess your learning at

www.politybooks.com/browne
You can also find new contemporary resources by following @BrowneKen on Twitter.

See also the revision guide to accompany this book:
Sociology for AQA Revision Guide 2: 2nd-Year A level

Please note that the above resources have not been endorsed by AQA.

PRACTICE QUESTION

Topic B4 Stratification and Differentiation

Answer **all** the questions on this topic   **Time allowed: 1 hour**

| 2 | 2 | Outline and explain **two** reasons why the occupational status of disabled groups may not offer a satisfactory understanding of their social class position.   **[10 marks]**

| 2 | 3 | Read **Item A** below and answer the question that follows.

Item A

Where and to whom a child is born in Britain today is more important than ever in determining that child's life chances, particularly his or her chances of survival. For instance, an infant girl in industrial Leeds is now more than twice as likely to die in the first year of life as an infant girl growing up in rural Dorset. A child born in the underclass is more likely to die in the first year of life than a child born to parents in the professional class.

Applying material from **Item A**, analyse **two** reasons for social class differences in mortality rates.   **[10 marks]**

| 2 | 4 | Read **Item B** below and answer the question that follows.

Item B

Functionalists maintain that those who are most needed in society are most likely to be the best rewarded. Currently it is estimated that less than 2,000 people own over half the world's wealth. It is difficult to reconcile these two statements.

Applying material from **Item B** and your knowledge, evaluate the usefulness of functionalist theory in understanding global inequality.   **[20 marks]**

Theory and Methods

KEN BROWNE

Contents

Theory and Methods

Theory and Methods – an introductory note to students

This chapter assumes you are familiar with the research methods, and their various practical, ethical and theoretical strengths and weaknesses, you may have studied during the first year of your course. These are covered in chapter 3 of the companion volume to this book: Ken Browne's *Sociology for AQA Volume 1: AS and 1st-Year A Level*.

Throughout your A level course, a key aim is to develop a good knowledge and understanding of sociological theories and research methods. This chapter should enable you to provide a stronger theoretical basis for applying, analysing, interpreting and evaluating the research methods you studied during your first year, as well as introducing a range of new sociological theories and related issues. The material in Topic 4 of this chapter (pages 416–23) re-examines some issues covered in Volume 1, but in more depth. There is an expectation that students doing the full A level at the end of a two-year course will be able to evaluate research methods and methods-in-context issues in greater depth than students who study only for the AS examination.

Several of the sociological theories and other issues discussed in this chapter will have been considered already during your first year, such as in the study of the topics of Education, Culture and Identity, Families and Households, Health, or Work, Poverty and Welfare. They are also discussed in the other chapters of this book. It would be wise to refer to some of these areas in the Theory and Methods questions in the exam, when appropriate, to illustrate how, for example, functionalist, Marxist, interactionist and feminist theories are applied to particular social issues and the workings of social institutions, and contribute to our understanding of contemporary society.

Theory and Methods in the examination

Theory and Methods makes up 25 per cent of your total A level marks, and is examined in specific questions in Paper 1 and Paper 3. In Paper 1 (Education with Theory and Methods), 30 out of 80 marks are awarded for Theory and Methods: 20 marks for a question on the application of research methods in the context of education (the 'Methods in Context' question) and a further 10 marks for a free-standing question on Theory and Methods. In Paper 3 (Crime and Deviance with Theory and Methods) there are two questions on Theory and Methods: one worth 10 marks, and the other (with a stimulus item) worth 20 marks. This emphasis on Theory and Methods means it is important you have a good grasp of the research methods covered in your first year, including the way these methods might be applied in the context of education, and the more developed theoretical issues considered in this chapter.

Unlike the other chapters, there is no practice question at the end of this chapter, but at the end of each topic there are practice questions which are similar to those you might expect in the Theory and Methods sections on Papers 1 and 3; and at the end of chapter 6, there is a full example of a Paper 3 practice question on Crime and Deviance with Theory and Methods. Examples of the Methods in Context question on Paper 1 are found in Volume 1.

Topic 1

SPECIFICATION AREA

Consensus, conflict, structural and social action theories

The development of sociology and sociological theory

Modernity refers to the period of the application of rational principles and logic to the understanding, development and organization of human societies.

The development of sociology as a subject, and many related sociological theories of society, are linked to what is known as **modernity**.

Modernity (discussed further in Topic 2) refers to the period from the mid seventeenth to the mid twentieth centuries, during which there was a growth of rational scientific understanding and explanations of the world, which were seen as a means of increasing human knowledge and control of both nature and society, and thereby the means to improve the world. Sociology, as developed by some of the key early figures such as Auguste Comte (1798–1857), Emile Durkheim (1858–1917), Max Weber (1864–1920) and Karl Marx (1818–83), was an attempt to apply similar scientific principles to those being developed in order to understand the natural world to the development and organization of human societies.

This topic focuses on a range of sociological theories which first emerged in this period of modernity, which were grounded in the belief that, by explaining society and the patterns of social life, sociology could also develop the means for improving human lives. The underlying belief was that sociological research could help to achieve a more secure, stable and prosperous society by eliminating social problems like poverty, homelessness, ill-health, crime and the resentments and conflicts caused by social inequality.

Auguste Comte (1798–1857)

Karl Marx (1818–83)

Emile Durkheim (1858–1917)   Max Weber (1864–1920)

Social order

Sociological theory and research have traditionally been concerned with the problem of **social order** – how large groups of individuals manage to live together and relate to one another in such a way that society does not descend into chaos and anarchy. How does society manage to form and maintain social structures like the family, the education system, the law and religion, and establish some orderly patterns in everyday life? How is society built and maintained, how does it operate and how do people make sense of everyday life?

Social order refers to a relatively stable state of society, with some shared norms and values which establish orderly patterns that enable people to live together and relate to one another in everyday life.

Themes in sociological theory

Much sociological theory in the modernist tradition has developed large-scale theories providing general explanations for how society works, how it is maintained and whether it is fundamentally stable, based on consensus, or marked by instability and conflict.

There are two broad themes in sociological theory:

1 *The extent of consensus and conflict in society*: how is social order maintained, and how do people manage to live together with some degree of relative harmony and stability despite any differences they may have?
2 *The problem of* **determinism** *and choice*: how much freedom and choice do people have to influence society? Are the identities and lives of individuals moulded or determined by social forces outside their control, or do individuals have control over the factors that influence their lives?

Determinism is the idea that people's behaviour is moulded by their social surroundings, and that they have little free will, control or choice over how they behave.

Consensus and conflict theories

The **dominant ideology** refers to a set of ideas which justifies the social advantages of wealthy, powerful and influential groups in society, and justifies the disadvantages of those who lack wealth, power and influence.

Consensus theory assumes that society is primarily harmonious, and social order is maintained through a widespread agreement (consensus) between people on the important goals, values and norms of society. Consensus theory is primarily associated with functionalist theory (see pages 370–5), which has its origins in the work of Durkheim.

Conflict theory has its origins in the work of Marx and Weber. Conflict theory takes the opposite view to that of the consensus theorists, and rather than seeing society as mainly harmonious and stable, it sees it as primarily conflict-ridden and unstable, and emphasizes social differences and conflicts between groups. It is concerned with issues such as social inequality and the conflicts it produces; the power and control of dominant groups and classes; the role of the education system in reproducing and legitimizing (justifying) inequality; elite rule and the **dominant ideology**. This is illustrated below in the discussion of Marxist theories, but it is also worth mentioning here the conflict approaches of Weber and of feminist writers.

Weber – class, status and party

Weber was concerned, like Marx, with the unequal distribution of power in society, and he saw conflicts in society arising between social classes pursuing economic interests; between status groups pursuing social honour, prestige and respect (shown in lifestyles and consumption); and between parties, which are groups specifically concerned with exercising power, making decisions and influencing policies in the interests of their membership. Society was therefore fundamentally unstable as individuals and groups struggled with one another as they pursued their competing interests (see pages 282–3 for a discussion of Weber's ideas of class, status and party). Other aspects of Weber's sociology are discussed later in this topic (see page 387)

Feminism

Feminists view society as fundamentally patriarchal, with men in positions of power and dominance over women in many areas of social life. There are a number of different feminist theories which are discussed later in this topic (and in chapter 4 on Stratification and Differentiation), but they all share a recognition of the essential conflicts between men and women that gender inequalities create in society. Feminist theories in sociology are therefore also conflict theories.

Determinism and choice

The second theme in sociological theory is concerned with the problem of determinism and choice – the extent to which the individual has control over, or is a passive victim of, social forces.

There are three main sociological approaches in this debate:

- *Structuralism* – the sociology of system or structure
- *Social action* or *interpretivist approaches* – the sociology of action
- *Integrated approaches* – combining the structure and action approaches. This includes Weber's sociology and Giddens's theory of structuration.

Structuralism

Structuralism is a perspective which is concerned with the overall structure of society, and sees individual behaviour moulded by social institutions like the family, the education system, the media and work.

Structuralism is concerned with the overall social structure of society, and the way social institutions, like the family, the education system, the media and the economy, act as a constraint on, or limit and control, individual behaviour. Structuralist approaches have the following features:

1 *The behaviour and values of individual human beings*, and the formation of their identities, are seen as being a result of social forces which are external to the individual. Individuals are determined, or moulded, shaped and constrained, by social forces acting upon them, like socialization, positive and negative sanctions, and material resources like income and jobs.

Structural approaches see individuals formed by the wider social forces making up the social structure of society

They have little control or choice in how they behave. According to the structuralist approach, the individual is like a puppet, whose strings are pulled by social institutions like the family, the education system, the media and the workplace, as suggested by the cartoon on this page.

2 *The main purpose of sociology is to study the overall structure of society*, the social institutions which make up this structure, and the relationships between these social institutions, such as the links between the workplace and the economy, the economy and the political system, the family and the education system, and so on. The focus of sociology is on the study of social institutions and the social structure as a whole, not on the individual. This focus on large-scale social structure is sometimes referred to as a **macro approach**.

3 *Positivism is the main methodological approach*, using quantitative research methods, as individual behaviour is seen as a response to measurable social forces outside individuals, acting upon them to control their behaviour. The focus of sociological research should then be on these social forces. The individual states of mind and meanings of individuals are seen as a reflection of these external forces, and so are not seen as worth studying in their own right.

There are two main varieties of structuralism:

- Functionalism (consensus structuralism)
- Marxism (conflict structuralism)

A **macro approach** is one that focuses on the large-scale structure of society as a whole, rather than on individuals.

Positivism is the view that the logic, methods and procedures of the natural sciences, as used in subjects like physics, chemistry and biology, can be applied to the study of society with little modification.

Functionalism (consensus structuralism)

Functionalism is a modernist structuralist consensus theory rooted in the work of Durkheim, and refined by Parsons (1902–79) and Merton (1910–2004). It was a very popular approach in the 1950s and 1960s, but is now generally regarded as an inadequate and old-fashioned approach to understanding society. Functionalism regards society as a stable, harmonious integrated social system, with social order and cohesion maintained by a fundamental value consensus.

Society as a system

Functionalism views society as a system – a structure of interconnected parts which fit together to form an integrated whole. The basic unit of analysis is the social system as a whole, and social institutions such as the family, religion and education are analysed in relation to the contribution they make to the maintenance of this system.

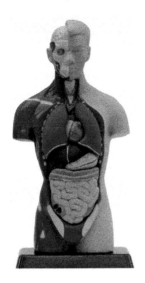

Functionalists view society as working much like the human body, with all the parts having a function and working together harmoniously to maintain the system as a whole.

Functionalists often draw an analogy between the workings of society and the human body. For example, understanding the workings and importance of the heart, lungs and brain involves understanding what function or purpose each carries out and how they work together to satisfy and maintain the needs of the human body as a whole, such as the role of the heart and lungs in refreshing and pumping blood around our bodies. Similarly, functionalists argue that, just like the human body, any society has what Parsons (1951) called **functional prerequisites** – basic needs or requirements that must be met if society is to survive. These include the production of food, the care of the young and the socialization of new generations into the culture of society. Social institutions like the family, education and the workplace exist to satisfy these basic needs, and, as in the human body, the various social institutions are connected and work together to meet functional prerequisites for the benefit of society as a whole.

> **Functional prerequisites** are the basic needs that must be met if society is to survive.

All social phenomena are regarded by functionalists as having some function in society, just as all parts of the human body have specific functions. For example, pain in the human body may be very unpleasant, but serves a valuable function in alerting us to something wrong. Similarly, parts of society also sometimes malfunction, such as families breaking up, people rioting, workers going on strike, or people committing crime. Deviance (rule-breaking) is a sign of disorder, but can act as a useful warning that something is wrong in society, and people's reaction of disapproval encourages action to prevent further rule-breaking and also helps to strengthen the rule. For example, the occasional incident of child abuse functions to remind us all how we should *not* treat children, reinforces our values around the protection of children, and strengthens sanctions against potential future offenders.

Functional prerequisites: Parsons's GAIL model

Parsons suggests that, to survive in a healthy state, all societies have to resolve two sets of problems, instrumental and expressive, and satisfy four functional prerequisites which are met by four related sub-systems. This has come to be known as the GAIL (**G**oal attainment, **A**daptation, **I**ntegration and **L**atency) model, and is shown in table 5.1.

The establishment and maintenance of social order: value consensus and social integration

> A **collective conscience** means shared beliefs and values, which form moral ties binding communities together and which regulate individual behaviour.

Durkheim (1982 [1895]) suggested that people are basically selfish, and that society would soon fall into chaos and disorder unless they learned to share some common values and show commitment to cooperation in society. Durkheim therefore placed great importance on the role of social institutions, such as the family and the education system, in socializing people into what he called a value consensus or **collective conscience**. This is a widespread agreement on values, norms and moral beliefs, which binds people together, builds social solidarity or social cohesion, and regulates individual behaviour.

Table 5.1 Parsons's GAIL model

Instrumental problems	Setting and achieving social goals; adapting to and achieving basic needs for survival	
Prerequisite or system need	**Description/explanation**	**Sub-system**
Goal attainment	The selection and definition of a society's priorities and aims/goals, and providing the means of achieving them. For example, Parliament and the government set the goals by making and carrying out policy decisions, and provide the means of achieving them by allocating resources raised through taxation.	Political system For example, political parties, pressure groups, government, Parliament and state agencies.
Adaptation	Adapting to the environment and providing the basic material necessities for continued human existence, and sufficient resources to achieve valued social goals.	Economy For example, organizations like factories, financial institutions and shops concerned with economic production.
Expressive problems	**Maintaining efficient cooperation and social solidarity; managing conflicts and tensions between individuals**	
Prerequisite or system need	**Description/explanation**	**Sub-system**
Integration	Coordinating all parts of the system to achieve shared goals, with people having a sense of belonging to society. Socialization into shared values, beliefs and goals promotes social harmony and solidarity, with social control to prevent deviance.	Cultural/community organizations For example, the media, education and religion socialize individuals into conformity to social norms and values, and the criminal justice system and other social control agencies restrict any threats to social order.
Latency (or pattern maintenance)	Minimizing social tensions and interpersonal conflicts which might prevent individuals and society working efficiently, and preserving/maintaining commitment to culture and pattern of values.	Family and kinship For example, the family is a key agency of socialization and social control: a place to recharge batteries, let off steam and escape and recover from the stresses and destabilizing influences of daily life outside the family.

Functionalists see the agencies of socialization integrating individuals into society with shared values and goals enabling social life to become stable, orderly, predictable and harmonious, without much conflict between people and groups. Parsons (1951) shared Durkheim's view on the importance of the agencies of socialization in building value consensus, and as sources of social control to maintain social order and prevent deviance, but he particularly emphasized the importance of primary socialization in the family in passing on norms and values between generations, which he saw as becoming internalized as part of an individual's personality.

Social change and social evolution

Functionalists regard social change as occurring when new functions emerge or society needs to adapt. They regard change as a slow process of social evolution, as gradual shifts occur in social values and people adapt to changes and reaffirm their commitment to them. As all the parts of society link together, a change in one part will result in changes elsewhere, but the system will remain balanced and stable. Parsons explains this in terms of **structural differentiation**. This means that as societies evolve and new needs arise for both society and individuals, institutions become more specialized, and functions they once performed are lost to new institutions. For example, the family used to be responsible for work training and education, but these gradually transferred to a specialized education system and work-based training, as the family (as individuals within it gradually realized) was no longer able to provide the work skills and education necessary for a more complex industrial society.

Manifest and latent functions and the concept of dysfunction

Merton (1968 [1957]), who was also a functionalist, criticized Parsons for his assumption that all social institutions performed beneficial, positive functions for society and individuals. Merton recognized that, in a highly complex interdependent social system, there is plenty of scope for things to go wrong, and there may be unforeseen consequences when some apparently beneficial functions are performed. Merton introduced the idea of **dysfunction** to describe the situation whereby some parts of the social structure don't work as intended, and there can sometimes be negative consequences, with harmful effects for society, or for some individuals.

For example, the growth of new technology may have been functional in so far as it made possible huge leaps in scientific progress and the production of cheaper and better-quality products, but at the same time it had the dysfunctions of generating environmental pollution, climate change, and industrial diseases among workforces. To this extent, Merton recognizes that there were, potentially, conflicts within the functionalist view of all parts of society working for the benefit of all. As part of an integrated system, these dysfunctions can affect all other parts of the system. For example, just as a diseased heart can weaken the whole human body, so dysfunctional families can have consequences beyond the family, such as on mental health, educational attainment, crime and anti-social behaviour.

Merton suggested there were **manifest functions** of an institution, with intended and recognized consequences, but that there were also **latent functions** alongside them, with unintended or unrecognized consequences. For example, a hospital has the manifest function of dispensing healthcare, but a latent function is that it provides a means for those who work there to meet partners with whom they can form married or cohabiting relationships. Similarly, a manifest function like a hospital providing healthcare can also have a dysfunctional side, providing a locus for the spreading of infection through antibiotic-resistant 'superbugs' like MRSA and *C. difficile*.

Evaluation of functionalism

Strengths

1 It is, along with Marxism, a reasonably successful attempt to produce a general theory of the workings of society.
2 It recognizes the importance of social structure in understanding society, how it constrains individual behaviour, and how the major social institutions, like the family, education and the economy, often have links between them.
3 It provides an explanation for social order and stability, and why most people generally conform to the rules of social life.

Weaknesses

1 Action theorists, discussed shortly, see it as too deterministic, as it sees individuals as simply passive products of the social system, which socializes them into conformity and controls their behaviour. It doesn't allow for individual choice, and pays no regard to the action, interpretations and meanings individuals give to situations, as the social action theorists do.
2 It is a metanarrative or grand theory that tries to explain everything from a single perspective. Postmodernists emphasize such metanarratives can no longer explain contemporary societies,

Structural differentiation refers to the way new, more specialized social institutions emerge to take over functions that were once performed by a single institution.

Dysfunction refers to a part of the social structure which does not contribute to the maintenance and well-being of society, but creates tensions and other problems.

A **manifest function** is the recognized and intended outcome of the action of an individual or institution.

A **latent function** is the unrecognized or unintended outcome of the action of an individual or institution.

where social life is essentially chaotic, values diverse, and social structures fragmented. The functionalist metanarrative has no more validity in explaining social life than any other.

3   It does not explain social change very effectively, as socialization, value consensus and social control contributing to social stability and conformity should limit social change. Functionalists can't explain periods of very rapid social change.

4   It over-emphasizes the beneficial aspects of functions performed by social institutions, and (with the exception of Merton) ignores harmful dysfunctions. For example, Davis and Moore's functionalist theory of stratification (see chapter 4, pages 280–2) sees only the benefits of inequality, while ignoring the resentments, divisions and conflicts it can generate. Similarly, Parsons's view of the functions of the family and women's role within it ignores the harmful consequences these may have for women's lives and careers.

5   It takes for granted there is a value consensus in society, and that this will provide social stability. However, value consensus in itself does not provide stability – it depends what those values are. For example, a consensus on aggressive individualism in which dog-eats-dog, the winner takes all and losers are cast aside is more likely to generate conflicts and resentment than social stability and harmony. Conflict theorists would argue the value consensus that functionalists assume is not a consensus at all, but just the ideas of the dominant social class imposed on the rest of society through institutions like the education system, religion and the media. Postmodernists would argue there is a wide diversity of values in society, and no consensus at all.

6   It over-emphasizes harmony and consensus and ignores or downplays the extent of conflict and the unequal distribution of power in society, with which Marxist and feminist conflict theorists are concerned.

7   It tends to be very conservative, supporting the status quo – the way society is presently organized – which it generally sees as desirable and unavoidable. It sees society as working more or less harmoniously for the benefit of all, and therefore there is no fundamental need to change it. It has no sense of inequalities in life chances and power, and how these might generate social conflict and social problems needing fundamental changes in society.

Activity

1   Suggest how functionalists might explain how (a) social inequality and (b) crime perform necessary functions for the benefit of society.

2   Using Parsons's GAIL model (see table 5.1 on page 372), explain in your own words what is meant by society's:
- Expressive problems
- Need for integration
- Instrumental problems
- Need for adaptation

3   Explain in each case above which sub-system(s) deal with these problems and needs, and, taking one example of your own, explain carefully how it does this.

Functionalism and the New Right

Functionalist theory is often associated with approaches adopted by the **New Right**, which you will have come across in your AS course, such as in New Right approaches to the family, poverty and the education system. The New Right is more a political ideology and an approach to social and political policies than a sociological perspective, and its emergence in Britain is associated mainly with the years of the Conservative government between 1979 and 1997. New Right ideology shares much in common with functionalist theories of society, with its emphasis on the importance of socialization into shared core values for the maintenance of social stability. It lays great stress on the role and importance of traditional institutions in building shared values, such as conventional marriage and family life and traditional education, and condemns anything that it sees as threatening these values, or undermining the core functions of social institutions in maintaining social stability.

The **New Right** is a political ideology and an approach to social and political policies that stresses individual freedom; self-help and self-reliance; reduction of the power and spending of the state; the free market and free competition between private companies, schools and other institutions; and the importance of traditional institutions and values.

For example, New Right theorists like Murray (1989, 1990) and Marsland (1989) argue that the welfare state has undermined personal responsibility and self-help, and devalued the importance of support from families, and the traditional functions families have carried out. They see the decline of the traditional family, and especially growing numbers of female-headed lone parent families, as threats to the adequate socialization and disciplining of children, particularly because of the lack of male/father role models. They view the interference of the welfare 'nanny' state and the decline of traditional family life as contributing to the emergence of a **dependency culture** and a culture of laziness, with the emergence of a deviant workshy underclass which wants to avoid work by living off welfare benefits, and which is associated with high levels of illegitimacy, lone parent-hood and family instability. The New Right sees the decline of the conventional nuclear family unit and an over-generous welfare state contributing to wider social problems, such as immorality, the lack of a work ethic, alcohol and drug abuse, anti-social behaviour and 'yob culture', crime, fiddling of the benefit system and exclusion from school and educational failure. Functionalist theories are also reflected in the New Right view of the need for strong social control, such as cracking down hard on criminals and deviants, as suggested by Right Realist approaches to crime prevention (see pages 534–7). These New Right views echo functionalist concerns with the maintenance of social order through socialization, reinforcement of a value consensus and the prevention of deviance.

A **dependency culture** is a set of values and beliefs, and a way of life, centred on dependence on others. It is normally used by New Right writers in the context of those who depend on welfare state benefits.

Classical Marxism (conflict structuralism)

Classical Marxism comes from the work of Marx, who founded the political creed known as communism (discussed on pages 377–8). Marxism, like functionalism, is a modernist theory that believed that a scientific analysis of society, and the discovery of the laws of its development, would provide the means for improving it, in this case through eventual revolution and the establishment of a communist society.

Base and superstructure

The **means of production** are the key resources necessary for producing society's goods, such as land, factories and machinery.

Marx believed that the economy was the driving force in society, and it was this that determined the nature of social institutions, and people's values and beliefs. Marxism sees the structure of society divided into two main parts, illustrated in figure 5.1.

1. The *economic base*, or *infrastructure*, which underpinned and determined everything else in society. This consisted of:
    *   The **means of production** like the land, factories, raw materials, technology and labour necessary to produce society's goods
    *   The **relations of production** – the relations between those involved in production, such as shared ownership or private ownership, who controls production, and the relationship

The **relations of production** are the forms of relationship between those people involved in production, such as cooperation or private ownership and control.

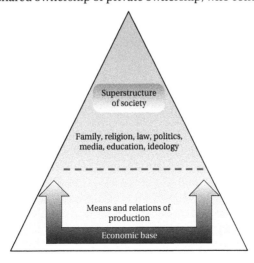

Figure 5.1 The base and superstructure in classical Marxist theory

between owners and non-owners, e.g. whether people are forced to work, like slaves, or paid for their work.

2. *The superstructure*, which includes society's social institutions, such as the family, education, the media, religion and the political system, and beliefs and values (ideology), which Marx saw as primarily determined (or influenced) by the economic system.

Private ownership and social classes

Marx argued that work (labour) is the sole source of wealth. In simple societies, when society produced only enough for its own essential needs, everyone had to work in order to survive. As a result, all people were producers on the same economic level. However, as soon as society began to produce more than was necessary for mere survival, it became possible for a section of society not to work, and to be supported by the labour of others. It was at this stage that Marx saw private ownership of the means of production emerging, and he argued that, since the simplest societies, the means of production have been privately owned with most people dependent on the owners for employment. Society is then divided into two fundamental social classes – the owners and non-owners of the means of production. For example, slave-owners and slaves in Ancient Rome, landowners and serfs in medieval feudal society, and capitalists and workers in contemporary societies. Marx argued that as the means of production developed – for example as production became more sophisticated and technologically based – so new relations of production would emerge, and society would evolve through revolutionary changes arising from conflicts between the owners and non-owners, from slavery, to feudalism, to capitalism and eventually to **communism**.

Exploitation

Marx argued that the workers (non-owners) produce more than is needed for employers to pay them their wages – this 'extra' produced by workers is what Marx called **surplus value**, and provides profit for the employer. For example, in a burger chain in contemporary society, it is the workers who make, cook, package and serve the burgers, but only half the burgers they sell are necessary to cover production costs and pay their wages. The rest of the burgers provide profit for the owners of the burger chain. This means the workers who produce the burgers do not get the full value of their work, and they are therefore being exploited.

Capitalists and workers

Marx argued that there were two basic social classes in capitalist industrial society: a small wealthy and powerful class of owners of the means of production (which he called the **bourgeoisie** or **capitalists**) and a much larger, poorer class of non-owners (which he called the **proletariat** or working class). The proletariat, because they owned no means of production of their own, had no means of living other than to sell their labour, or **labour power** as Marx called it, to the bourgeoisie in exchange for a wage or salary. The capitalists exploited the working class by making profits out of them by keeping wages as low as possible instead of giving the workers the full payment for the goods they had produced.

Class conflict

Marx asserted that exploitation of the non-owners by the owners created major differences in interest between the two classes, and this created conflict. For example, the workers' interests lay in higher wages to achieve a better lifestyle, but these would be at the expense of the bosses' profits. The bosses wanted higher profits to expand their businesses and wealth, and to be able to compete with one another and beat their opponents, but this could only be achieved by keeping wages as low as possible and/or by making the workers produce more by working harder. The interests of these two classes are therefore totally opposed, and this generates conflict between them (class conflict). Marx believed this class conflict would affect all areas of life.

Communism is an equal society, without social classes or class conflict, in which the means of production are the common property of all.

Surplus value is the extra value added by workers to the products they produce, after allowing for production costs and the payment of their wages, and which goes to the employer in the form of profit.

The **bourgeoisie** (or **capitalists**) is the class of owners of the means of production in industrial societies, whose primary purpose is to make profits.

The **proletariat** is the social class of workers who have to work for wages as they do not own the means of production.

Labour power refers to people's capacity to work. In capitalist societies, people sell their labour power to employers in return for a wage, and employers buy only their labour power, but not the whole person as they did, for example, under slavery.

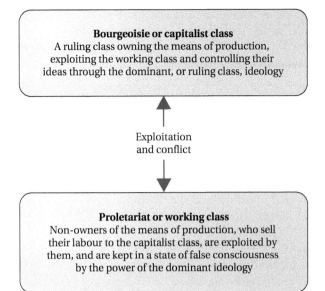

Figure 5.2 A summary of the Marxist view of capitalist society

Bourgeoisie or capitalist class
A ruling class owning the means of production, exploiting the working class and controlling their ideas through the dominant, or ruling class, ideology

Exploitation and conflict

Proletariat or working class
Non-owners of the means of production, who sell their labour to the capitalist class, are exploited by them, and are kept in a state of false consciousness by the power of the dominant ideology

The ruling class

Marx argued that the owning class was also a ruling class. For example, because they owned the means of production, the bourgeoisie could decide where factories should be located, and whether they should be opened or closed down, and they could control the workforce through hiring or firing. Democratically elected governments could not afford to ignore this power of the bourgeoisie, otherwise they might face rising unemployment or other social problems if the bourgeoisie decided not to invest its money. Marx believed the state, through institutions like the law, the police and the criminal justice system, was fundamentally concerned not with protecting everyone, but with protecting the interests of the ruling class.

Dominant ideology

> **False consciousness** is a lack of awareness among people about what their real interests are, and the false belief that everyone benefits from the present organization of society which is presented as fair and just.

Marx believed the ruling or dominant ideas in any society – what he called the dominant ideology – were those of the owning class (hence it is sometimes also called ruling class ideology) and the major institutions in the superstructure of society reflected those ideas and the bourgeoisie's interests. For example, the law protected the interests of the owning class more than it did those of the workers; religion acted as the 'opium of the people', persuading the working class to accept their position as just and natural (rather than rebelling against it), by 'drugging' them with promises of future rewards in heaven for putting up with their present suffering; and the mass media were owned by those in the ruling class, so only their ideas were put forward. In this way, the workers were almost brainwashed into accepting their position. They failed to recognize they were being exploited and therefore did not rebel against the bourgeoisie. Marx called this lack of awareness of their own interests **false consciousness**.

Revolution and communism

> **Class consciousness** is an awareness among members of a social class of their real interests.

However, Marx thought that one day the circumstances would arise in which the workers did become aware of their exploitation. Wealth and power would become ever more concentrated in the hands of the few, and, on a global scale, the workers would become poorer and remain relatively poor. This contrast between wealth and poverty and growing inequality would lead the working class to develop **class consciousness** (an awareness of their real interests and their exploitation) and the population would become polarized into two opposing and hostile camps of capitalists and workers, with the battle lines clearly drawn between them. The working class would join together to act against the bourgeoisie through strikes, demonstrations and other forms of protest. This would eventually lead to a revolution against, and overthrow of, the bourgeoisie. The means of production would then be put in the hands of the state and run in the interests of everyone, not just of the bourgeoisie. A new type of society – communism – would be created, which would be without exploitation, without classes and without class conflict.

Evaluation of classical Marxism

Strengths

1 It recognizes the importance of the economy and how economic changes can influence a wide range of other social institutions.
2 Its focus on private ownership of the means of production provides an explanation for the extreme social inequalities in wealth, income and power that persist in contemporary societies, and for the conflicts and upheavals that periodically surface, many of which are rooted in social class inequalities.
3 It recognizes the importance of society's social structure, and links this to the ideas, consciousness and behaviour of individuals and groups.
4 It remains a highly influential theory, which has had a significant influence on a range of other sociological theories, such as those of Weber and of Marxist feminists.

Weaknesses

1 Marx's predictions have not come true. Far from society becoming polarized and the working class becoming poorer, almost everyone in Western societies has far higher living standards than ever before. The collapse of the so-called 'communist' regimes of the Soviet Union (now Russia and the surrounding countries) and Eastern Europe, and growing private ownership and continuing extreme inequality in communist countries like China, casts some doubt on the viability of the practical implementation of Marx's ideas. Harvey (1990) points out that, with globalization, national governments have less power, and more power lies with transnational corporations which exist outside national boundaries. Such corporations, like Apple and Nike, reap huge profits producing goods cheaply in countries where wages are low and selling them in Western markets where prices are high. Capitalism and Western capitalist culture is now spread throughout the world, possibly making capitalism stronger than ever before.
2 Classical Marxism over-emphasizes the extent of conflict in society. Functionalists would argue society is primarily stable, and there must be some shared values for social life to be possible. That Marx's predicted revolution has not succeeded in any Western society reflects this.
3 Marx's two-class model of inequality is inadequate. There has been the growth of a new middle class of managerial, professional and clerical workers between the bourgeoisie and proletariat, and Marx's theory cannot account for all the differences in power, rewards, consciousness and status within the mass of the population who are not capitalists, such as between manual and non-manual, and male and female, workers.
4 It over-emphasizes social class as a source of inequality and conflict, and pays little attention to other sources such as ethnicity, age and gender.
5 The economic base and superstructure model is too deterministic, giving too much importance to the economy. Classical Marxism doesn't allow for the possibility that the ideas and institutions of the superstructure may themselves influence behaviour and cause social change independently of the economy, as Weber (2001 [1904]) saw in the ideas of the Protestant ethic generating change in early capitalism (see pages 26–7 and page 387 for a discussion of Weber's Protestant ethic).
6 Classical Marxism is too deterministic, and sees individuals as simply passive products of the social system, which socializes them into conformity and controls their behaviour. It doesn't allow for individual choice, as the social action theorists do.
7 It is a metanarrative or grand theory that tries to explain everything from a single perspective. Postmodernists emphasize such metanarratives can no longer explain contemporary societies, where social life is essentially chaotic, values diverse, and social structures fragmented. The Marxist metanarrative has no more validity in explaining social life than any other.

8   Postmodernists suggest the economy is not the key factor influencing people's ideas; instead, in what they regard as a media-saturated society, it is the media that form and dominate people's consciousness and view of the world.

9   Postmodernists argue that the metanarrative (or large-scale all-embracing theory) of class is no longer important, and the main social divisions are now around individual choices in consumption patterns and lifestyle.

Neo-Marxism

Neo-Marxists are those who have further developed and modified the ideas of Marx's classical Marxism, partly due to some of the criticisms made above.

Humanistic neo-Marxism: Gramsci's concept of hegemony

Relative autonomy is the idea in neo-Marxist theory that the superstructure of society has some independence from the economy, rather than being directly determined by it.

The Marxist Gramsci (1893–1937) thought Marx was mistaken in giving such over-riding importance to the economy, and he saw ideology and people's ideas having **relative autonomy** from the economic base.

Gramsci's concept of **hegemony** placed much more emphasis than Marx did on the role of ideas (ideology) rather than just the economy in maintaining ruling-class power and in influencing people's behaviour. Gramsci (1971) emphasized that people's ideas underpin the actions they choose to make. He stressed the importance of people's ideas, choices and action in bringing about change, and not just economic conditions like poverty, homelessness and unemployment. By hegemony, Gramsci was referring to the dominance in society of the ruling class's set of ideas over others, and acceptance of and consent to them by the rest of society. He saw this control of people's minds by the dominant ideology, rather than simply control by the police, prisons and other repressive agencies of the state, as one of the main reasons why the working class had rarely rebelled against the ruling class, as they had failed to develop their own alternative vision of how society might be. The concept of hegemony meant Gramsci's neo-Marxism was leaning more towards a social action approach to society, with a greater emphasis on people's ideas, meanings and actions in bringing about revolutionary change, and less on the structuralist approach and economic determinism of classical Marxism.

Hegemony refers to the dominance in society of the ruling class's set of ideas over others, and acceptance of and consent to them by the rest of society.

Structuralist neo-Marxism: Althusser and the economic, political and ideological levels

Althusser (1969, 1971) argued that the structure of capitalist society consists of not just the economic base and superstructure, but of three levels.

The **repressive state apparatus** refers to those parts of the state which are concerned with mainly repressive, physical means of keeping a population in line, such as the army, police, courts and prisons.

1   *The economic level*, consisting of the economy and the production of material goods.

2   *The political level*, consisting of the government and organizations involved in the political organization and control of society, including what he called the **repressive state apparatus** (RSA). The RSA refers to those parts of the state which are concerned with mainly repressive, physical means of keeping a population in line, such as the army, police, courts and prisons.

3   *The ideological level*, concerned with ideas, beliefs and values. This consists of the **ideological state apparatuses**, which are a series of institutions which spread the dominant ideology and justify the power of the dominant class. These include the media, the education system and religion.

Ideological state apparatuses are agencies that spread the dominant ideology and justify the power of the dominant social class.

While the economy remains of overall importance, and all three levels ultimately preserve and justify the power of the dominant class, the political and ideological levels can affect society independently of the economy. Each level has relative autonomy and *some* independence from the economic base – distinguishing this from classical Marxist theory – while still retaining some link to it. Figure 5.3 illustrates this idea. Despite this concept of relative autonomy, Althusser still retains the structuralist emphasis of classical Marxism on the way social structures, and particularly the economy, are still the key influences on people's ideas, and he does not share Gramsci's view that

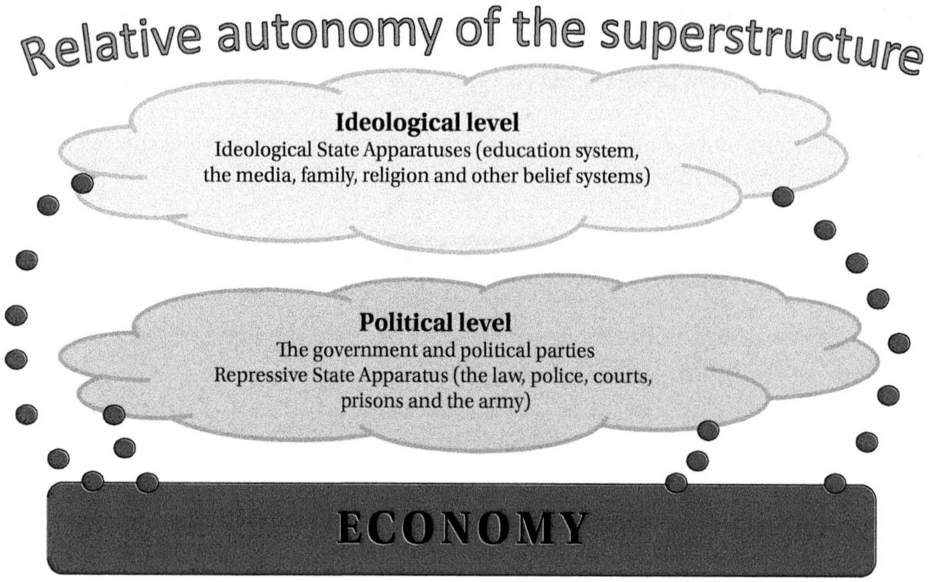

Relative autonomy of the superstructure

Ideological level
Ideological State Apparatuses (education system, the media, family, religion and other belief systems)

Political level
The government and political parties
Repressive State Apparatus (the law, police, courts, prisons and the army)

ECONOMY

Figure 5.3 The relative autonomy of the superstructure in neo-Marxist theories

people have more free will and choice than Marx suggested, and that political ideas and action are more important than economic factors in bringing about revolutionary change.

Evaluation of neo–Marxism

Neo-Marxists have tried to overcome some of the weaknesses of classical Marxism, and particularly its economic determinism in which everything is explained by the operation of the economic base. The concept of hegemony (Gramsci) recognizes the importance of people's ideas and actions, and Althusser's concept of relative autonomy suggests that institutions in the superstructure can impact on the economy, and not simply the other way round. However, some classical Marxists would argue that Marx himself did recognize the importance of ideas and meanings, with his discussions of class consciousness, and they also suggest that neo-Marxists can underplay the importance of the economy in shaping social reality. Gramsci has been criticized for over-emphasizing the role of ideas, and for under-emphasizing the role of material factors, like economic crisis and collapse, fear of poverty and unemployment, and state repression in preventing revolutionary action by the working class.

> **Activity**
>
> 1 To what extent do you agree with Marx's view that the dominant ideas in Britain today are those of a wealthy and powerful ruling class?
> 2 Do you think an analysis of Britain today fits more closely the consensus perspective of functionalism or the conflict perspective of Marx? Explain your view, with examples.
> 3 What evidence might you use from contemporary Britain to suggest that Marx's ideas are: (a) still relevant today; (b) out-of-date?
> 4 Explain in your own words what you understand by the following concepts, giving examples to illustrate them: relative autonomy; base and superstructure; hegemony; class consciousness; exploitation; class conflict.

Marxism as a political ideology

Marxist theory is an important influence in sociology, as you will know from your studies on, for example, Marxist theories of the family, education, poverty, religion and, later, crime and deviance

As well as being an important modernist social theory, Marxism is also a political ideology, which has had and continues to have enormous influence across the world. Although its influence has declined in contemporary Britain, Marxist-inspired groups are still common in this country, albeit small in numbers, as in the Socialist Workers and Communist Parties, shown here in a demonstration in London in October 2012.

and stratification and differentiation, and the theories discussed in this chapter. However, not only is Marxism a sociological perspective which tries to understand and explain how societies work and change, but also it has been a highly influential political ideology.

While Marx was a social scientist concerned with the systematic study of society in the modernist tradition, he regarded this very much as also providing the means for changing and improving the world through the establishment of communist societies. Marx summed this up when he wrote that 'The philosophers have only interpreted the world in various ways; the point is to change it.' Marxist-inspired politicians have had, and continue to have, enormous impact in the world. By the 1980s, around a third of the world's population lived under communist regimes which claimed (somewhat dubiously) to be inspired by Marx's ideas. Although many communist regimes collapsed in the 1980s and 1990s, even today contemporary China, Cuba, Laos, Vietnam and North Korea all profess allegiance to Marxist beliefs, and around a fifth of the world's population still live under communist governments. Communist parties are also found in several coalition governments around the world.

Social action or interpretivist theories

Interpretivism is an approach emphasizing that people have consciousness involving personal beliefs, values and interpretations, and these influence the way they act. People have choices and do not simply respond to forces outside themselves. To understand society it is therefore necessary to understand the meanings people give to their behaviour, and how these are influenced by the behaviour and interpretations of others.

The main focus of social action or **interpretivist** theories is on individual behaviour in everyday social situations. These theories are concerned with discovering and thereby understanding the

Social action or interpretivist theories emphasize the free will and choice of individuals, and their role in creating the social structure

processes by which interactions between individuals or small groups take place, how people come to interpret and see things as they do, how they define their identities, and how the reactions of others can affect their view of things and their sense of their own identity.

Social action or interpretivist theories include the following features:

1   Society and social structures/institutions are seen as socially constructed creations of individuals, not something separate from and above them.
2   An emphasis is placed on the voluntarism, or free will and choice, of people to do things and form their own identities, rather than them being formed by external social forces as suggested in the determinist approach of structuralism.
3   The focus of sociological research is placed on the individual or small groups of individuals rather than the overall structure of society. Rather than studying general trends and the wider causes of crime, for example, interpretivists are more likely to study a juvenile gang, to see how they came to be seen and labelled as deviant, and how they themselves see the world. This is sometimes referred to as a **micro approach**.
4   People's behaviour is viewed as being driven by the beliefs, meanings, feelings and emotions they give to situations: their definitions of a situation, or the way they see things and therefore behave, become very important. For example, a parent might interpret a baby crying as a sign of tiredness, hunger, fear or illness. The action the parent takes – putting the baby to bed, feeding her, comforting her or taking her to the doctor – will depend on how the parent defines the situation, and to understand the parent's behaviour we have to understand the meaning he or she gives to the baby's crying. In turn, how the parent acts in response to the meaning given to the baby's behaviour is likely to affect the baby's behaviour – whether it stops crying because it is no longer tired, hungry, afraid or ill.
5   The main methodological approach is *interpretivist*, using qualitative research methods, as the purpose of sociology is to study, uncover and interpret the meanings and definitions individuals give to their behaviour. The best means of doing this is, as far as possible, through empathy – seeing the world through the eyes of those they are studying.

> A **micro approach** is one that focuses on small groups or individuals, rather than on the structure of society as a whole.

There are two main branches of social action theory – symbolic interactionism and ethnomethodology. Weber is often regarded as the first sociologist to place an emphasis on social action, but will be considered later as he really combines both structure and action approaches.

Symbolic interactionism

Mead (1863–1931) was the founder of symbolic interactionism, though it was Blumer (1969), a follower of Mead, who actually first used the term. Symbolic interactionism sees society as built up by interactions between people which take place on the basis of meanings held by individuals. Blumer suggests interactionism has three basic features.

1   People act in terms of **symbols**, which are things, like objects, words, expressions or gestures, that stand for something else and to which individuals have attached meanings, and they act towards people and things in accordance with these meanings.
2   These meanings develop out of the interaction of an individual with others, and can change during the course of interaction.
3   Meanings arise from an interpretive process, as people try to interpret the meanings others give to their actions by imagining themselves in their position and taking on their role. Individuals can only develop a conception of themselves by understanding how others see them, and they will be unable to interact successfully with others unless they can do this. Successful interaction involves correctly interpreting what sort of person you're dealing with, how they see you, what they expect from you and what you expect from them. This contrasts with structuralist approaches which see people simply acting out roles handed down by the social structure, as people are in a constant process of forming and negotiating roles and how they interact with others, and making choices about how they do this. For example, teachers

> A **symbol** is something, like an object, word, expression or gesture, that stands for something else and to which individuals have attached some meaning.

Cooley thought our view of ourselves was formed not by the social structure, but through the responses of other people reflecting back to us in the course of interaction.

The Looking-glass Self

How my mum and dad see me.

How my girlfriend sees me.

How my older brother sees me.

How my ex-girlfriend sees me.

may have a role as educators handed down by the social structure (such as the government, the education system and the demands of the economic system), but there is huge diversity in how teachers choose to perform this role.

The 'looking-glass self'

Cooley (1998) writing in 1902, developed the concept of the 'looking-glass self' to describe this process of negotiated interaction. The 'looking-glass self' is the idea that our image of ourselves is reflected back to us (like a mirror) in the views of others. As we consider the image of ourselves reflected in the reactions of other people to us, we may modify and change our view of ourselves and our behaviour, as illustrated in the cartoon shown. Cooley is alleged to have described the looking-glass self in these terms: 'I am not what I think I am and I am not what you think I am; I am what I think you think I am.'

An individual, for example, might see her- or himself as outgoing, friendly and sociable, but if others see them as introverted, unfriendly and stand-offish, then they might adopt a new self-identity in accordance with how others see them, or modify their behaviour and try to change people's views of them. Our self-concept and social role are not therefore simply handed down by the social structure, but socially constructed and subject to constant change through the process of interaction.

Smiling is a useful way of illustrating this process. A smile is an object that is just a physical contortion of the face, but people have learnt through interaction with others to attach to smiling the symbolic meaning of warmth and friendliness. When interacting with someone who is smiling, individuals may, because of this meaning, be encouraged to smile back, particularly if they interpret this as a gesture of warmth and friendliness by the other person. If someone smiles and the other individual doesn't respond to this symbol by smiling back, this is likely to influence how the first person sees that individual (as perhaps cold, rude or unfriendly) and if the non-smiling individual doesn't realize this by putting themselves in the other person's position, then interaction is likely to end or become fraught. Language is one of the main ways humans negotiate meanings, and language – words – are symbols carrying meaning: 'little honey', for example, carries a rather different meaning from 'cheating bastard'.

Symbolic interactionism therefore sees society and social order made possible by and based on shared meanings which are developed and learned through the process of interaction. The task of sociology is to understand:

These pictures show some common symbols that are used in everyday social interaction. What do these symbols stand for, and what consequences might follow if someone misinterpreted or did not understand their meanings?

- How the meanings individuals give to situations are constructed in face-to-face interaction
- How individuals and situations come to be defined or classified and labelled in particular ways
- The consequences for individual behaviour of such definitions, as people will behave according to the way they and others see situations.

Labelling theory

Symbolic interactionism has been applied in labelling theory, which suggests that people label or define individuals and situations in particular ways, which will affect the way those so labelled behave. For example, the sociologist's task might be to understand the point of view and experience of the disillusioned black youth who is very hostile to the police, and feels 'picked on' because of misleading stereotypes and racist assumptions held by the police about black people. Sociologists should try to understand how and why the police label some black youth as deviant, and what happens to the behaviour of those young people once they have been classified in that way, and whether it amplifies deviance and generates deviant careers (these issues are discussed in chapter 6 – see pages 459–63). Interactionists might also study the way teacher attitudes, streaming and labelling can influence educational achievement and lead to self-fulfilling prophecies, as students bring their behaviour into line with the label attached by the teacher. Another example might be the consequences which flow for those labelled as mentally ill, whereby the attachment of the label may make the condition worse.

Goffman and impression management

Goffman (1990b [1963]) studied the ways people construct meanings and interpretations in the process of interaction, using what has been described as a dramaturgical model, based on the idea of society being like a stage, with people acting out performances like actors do in a play or TV drama. Like actors on a stage, people in society are constantly engaged in managing the impressions they give to other people by putting on performances or a 'show' to try to convince others of the identities they wish to assert. Goffman calls this **impression management**. This is often achieved by the use of symbols of various kinds, like styles of clothing or choices in music, to demonstrate the kind of person they want to be seen as. Goffman says everyone is engaged in this process of manipulating others and being manipulated by them to give the best possible impression of themselves.

Symbolic interactionism, through concepts such as labelling, the looking-glass self and impression management, suggests that structural approaches are completely inadequate for explaining society. This is because they do not penetrate the multiple micro interactions and the generation and interpretation of meanings that people attach to their behaviour and that of others, which influence their everyday behaviour.

Impression management is the way individuals try to convince others of the identity they wish to assert by giving particular impressions of themselves to other people.

Ethnomethodology

Ethnomethodology is associated with the work of Garfinkel (1984 [1967]), and refers to the description of the methods or interpretive procedures which people use to make sense of and construct order in their everyday social world.

Ethnomethodology differs from most other social theories, including interactionism, as it rejects the view that society has any kind of social structure, social order or patterned interaction that exists outside of individuals' consciousness. Social order is an illusion, and only appears to exist because members of society create it in their own minds and impose a sense of order using their own common-sense procedures and culturally embedded rules and assumptions; society only retains some semblance of stability and order because people share these assumptions. Social reality is simply a social construction. For example, Atkinson's (1971, 1983) study of suicide suggested that classifying a sudden death as a suicide was simply a social construction of meaning – a corpse is simply a lifeless body, and remains so until people decide to construct or label it as, for example, a 'suicide', an 'accident', a 'murder' or a 'natural death'. Suicide therefore doesn't exist 'out there' as something to go and find the causes of, which would be impossible as the people concerned are dead so we can't ask them why they killed themselves. All that can be done is to find out why some unexpected sudden deaths get classified as suicides, while others don't. This involves looking at the methods or procedures coroners use to make sense of and impose their classifications of suicide.

Garfinkel was interested in discovering how individuals make sense of the social world, and impose some sense of order in their daily lives. He sought to expose people's taken-for-granted assumptions and the rules they imposed on the world by experimental techniques known as 'breaching experiments'. These aimed to examine people's reactions to the breaching or disruption of their taken-for-granted everyday assumptions embodied in commonly accepted social rules or norms. For example, one of Garfinkel's experiments involved asking students to behave as visitors or lodgers in their own homes, and to record how their parents reacted to the sudden change in the taken-for-granted relationship they had with their children. Their reactions of concern, bewilderment, anger and confusion revealed not only how people create social order through assumptions and meanings shared with others, but also how fragile the social order they create around these shared assumptions really is.

Activity

1 The way ethnomethodology tries to explore the taken-for-granted rules which people use to make sense of the world can be illustrated by language. Understanding language involves a whole host of taken-for-granted rules, which is why learning a new one can be quite difficult, and why we can't make sense of it until we do learn the rules. In the following passage, the accepted rules of the English language have been removed, and the text therefore appears meaningless. Try to re-apply the rules of the English language to rediscover its meaning.
Ethn omet hod olo gyis asoci olog icaldis cipl inew hich stud iest heways inw hich peo plem akes enseof the irwor lddisp layt hisun derst an dingtoo the rs a ndp roduce themu tuallys har edso cia lor derinw hichth eylive thete rmw asin iti ally co ined byh ar old gar fink elin 1954 (the answer to this activity is at the end of the chapter)

2 Try a bit of 'Garfinkeling' and apply Garfinkel's breaching experimentation yourself. Think of an everyday encounter in a familiar situation – perhaps your next sociology class? – and how you might alter it in some way to disrupt taken-for-granted rules, such as behaving or speaking in unexpected ways. For example, if someone asks 'How are you today?', give them a full, blow-by-blow detailed and lengthy report on the state of your health, or ask them what they mean by 'how are you?' In what sense? Your health? Your financial situation? – and so on. Be careful not to cause too much offence. Describe what happens, and analyse the rules you have exposed, and explain how this shows the way social order and reality are socially constructed.

Evaluation of social action theory

Strengths

1 It shows that human beings create and negotiate meanings, and make sense of the world either through interaction with others (symbolic interactionism) or by drawing on their own common-sense understandings (ethnomethodology). In recognizing that people have reasons and motives for what they do, and by focusing on the creative role of individuals in forming meanings, through devices like impression management, it suggests people are not simply puppets moulded by the social system. It therefore overcomes the determinism of structuralism found in functionalist and classical Marxist theories.
2 It recognizes that, unlike in structuralism, to fully explain people's actions and the creation of social order it is necessary to understand the motivations and meanings people attach to their behaviour, and how they come to share these with others through everyday interaction.
3 It provides real insights into how the social construction of meanings through interaction has consequences for individuals – for example, how the processes of streaming and labelling in education can generate self-fulfilling prophecies of success or failure, and how the labelling of deviance can lead to deviant careers (see pages 459–63).
4 The interpretivist approach and the use of qualitative methods mean research findings often have high levels of validity. For example Atkinson's qualitative research on suicide, through detailed interviews with coroners and observations of them at work, gained a highly valid in-depth understanding of how coroners came to classify some sudden deaths as suicides.

Weaknesses

1 It doesn't pay sufficient attention to the structures of society, such as power, social class, gender and ethnic inequalities, and the constraints on individual behaviour that come from these with which structural theorists are concerned. People do not have free choices, and structures and differences in life chances are real, not simply social constructions in the consciousness of individuals. For example, poverty is a real phenomenon, affecting people's health and life expectancy, and their opportunities for choice.
2 It does not really explain people's motivations – the reasons for what they do, and what they hope to achieve by their actions. Where do people get their meanings and goals from?
3 It tends to under-estimate or ignore the distribution of power in society. Not everyone has the same chance of getting their definition or classification of others to 'stick'. For example, the interaction between young people and a police officer who seeks to define their behaviour as deviant does not take place on equal terms.
4 Postmodernists would suggest that action theory is as much a metanarrative as any other theory that claims to provide a full explanation of social life. Action theory is just one of many competing points of view, all of which provide equally valid insights into society.

Integrated approaches – combining structure and action

A third or middle way between structuralism and action theories recognizes the importance of both the constraints of social structure and the possibilities for choice. In real life, society is probably best understood using a mixture of both structural *and* action approaches. In other words, constraints from social structures, like the family, work (and the income it does or doesn't produce), the law and education, limit and control the behaviour of individuals or groups, and have important influences on the formation of individual and group identities. However, individuals can, within limits, make choices within those structures and thereby change them. Two theorists operating within this integrated approach are Max Weber and Anthony Giddens.

Weber's sociology

Weber's sociology does not fit neatly into either structuralist or action approaches. He is often regarded as the original social action theorist, and he was the first sociologist to emphasize the importance of understanding the subjective meanings people held and how they viewed the world. This was reflected in his concept which he termed, in German, **Verstehen** (pronounced *fair-shtay-en*), which literally means 'understanding'. This involves researchers trying to put themselves in the position of those they are studying in an attempt to see the world through their eyes, and thereby discover the meanings behind their actions. Weber rejected what he regarded as the crude determinism of structuralist theories, and particularly Marx's economic determinism, and recognized that people had choice and could act to change structures, and were not simply puppets controlled by them. At the same time, he recognized that people did not have a completely free choice in how they behaved. Weber did not dismiss the importance of social structures, particularly the structures of inequality, with his concepts of class, status and party, and how these influenced people's ideas, shaped their lives and life chances, and limited the choices available to them. In many ways, therefore, Weberian sociology combines both structure and action approaches, with a full understanding of society and human behaviour involving both an analysis of structural factors *and* the role of subjective meanings people attach to their behaviour.

This was illustrated in Weber's study of the emergence of capitalism in Western Europe, *The Protestant Ethic and the Spirit of Capitalism* (2001 [1904]). In this he identified the significance of the religious ideas (the Protestant ethic in the Calvinist religion) that people held in generating changes in the social structure (see pages 26–7 in chapter 1 for more on the Protestant ethic). He saw these ideas as a major reason why capitalist industrialization developed first in Western Europe, even when other societies had similar levels of technological and economic development. This illustrated well Weber's view that explaining society involves understanding the meanings and motives for people's actions, such as the meaning of Protestantism to Protestants, by the process of *Verstehen*, as well as the influence of social structures such as the level of development of the economy.

Giddens's theory of structuration

Giddens's (1986) theory of **structuration** is an attempt to combine both structure and action, which he regards as two parts of the same process. Structure and action depend on one another, and structures only exist because of people's action, and people can only act because the structures enable meaningful action to take place. Giddens referred to this link between structure and action

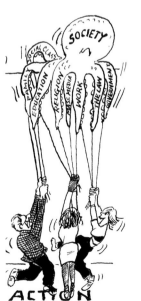

Structuration theory refers to the two-way process by which the actions of individuals shape their social world, but they are themselves shaped by society

as the *duality of structure*. Structuration and the duality of structure refer to the two-way process by which people are constrained or shaped by society and social institutions, but these structures can only exist as long as people continue to take action to support them, and they can at the same time take action to shape and change them. This change occurs through **reflexivity**, whereby people are constantly reflecting on the things they do and how they do them as they live their daily lives (there is more on reflexivity on pages 401–2).

Giddens's theory suggests that the existence of the social structure, including social institutions, beliefs, values and traditions, provides people with a framework of rules and established ways of doing things that enable them to live in society, and by doing so they are at the same time reproducing that structure. At the same time, individuals can change this structure by ignoring, modifying or replacing rules or conventional ways of doing things. So people are shaped by society, but at the same time can act to shape society. Structuration theory can be illustrated by the legal system.

The legal system is part of the social structure, and the law has an existence separate from and above the individuals living in society at any one time. People are constrained (forced) by the law to behave in particular ways, and this allows people to go about their daily lives – to act – in some orderly fashion, as most people generally abide by the same rules, and the action of people in conforming to the law enables it to continue to exist from one generation to the next.

However, the law can continue only as long as people continue to support and conform to it. Giddens suggests people are constantly reflecting on their everyday behaviour and they may, for example, decide some laws are outdated and no longer relevant to the way they live their lives, and so choose to break them. For example, laws might prohibit the use of cannabis, and those who disobey this law risk punishment by the criminal justice system. But people may gradually reflect on their lifestyles, and choose to start using cannabis as part of their leisure lifestyles, and choose to break the law. If there is very widespread use of cannabis, the law would either have to be enforced despite the wishes of the majority of the population, risking it becoming treated with widespread contempt, or the law would cease to be an effective social structure and have to be abandoned or changed. This shows human beings can create and reinforce, or can change or destroy, structures. The cannabis laws are a good example of this, as attitudes to the law and the use of cannabis have changed dramatically over the years as people acted in defiance of the law and campaigned to change it, and it became clear that the social structure (the law and punishments) needed to change to reflect changing attitudes.

This shows that social structures, like the law, while constraining human action, also enable human action to take place in an orderly way, and people constantly reproduce these structures by their actions in supporting them. At the same time, people can also act to change that social structure. This doesn't mean that people can act in any way they like, as the reactions and expectations of others will limit their possibilities of doing so, and often even minor infringements of social rules can shock people, as you may have found in the earlier Garfinkel activity of 'how are you today?' (see the activity on page 385).

> **Reflexivity** refers to the way the knowledge people gain about society can affect the way they behave in it, as people (and institutions) reflect on what they do and how they do it.

Evaluation of integrated approaches

Integrated approaches which combine structural and action approaches have been criticized by structuralists for overstating the capacity of individuals to change society's social structures, and for under-estimating the constraints on individual choices of action. Action theorists tend to regard them as perhaps under-stating the capacity of individuals to change society, and over-estimating the constraints of the social structure on individual choices of action. This probably means integrated approaches have got it about right.

Structure, action and integration: a conclusion

It is easy to get the impression that sociological theory and research is divided into two opposing camps, with structuralists focusing on macro social structural forces, using positivist research methods generating quantitative data, and action theorists focusing on micro group or individual action, using interpretivist research methods generating qualitative data. In the real world of practical research, most sociologists will combine both structural and action theoretical approaches – a kind of real-world Weberian or structuration approach. There is often a process of theoretical pluralism and triangulation similar to the methodological pluralism and triangulation found in combining quantitative and qualitative research methods. Sociologists are in most cases interested in explaining the social world, and they will use whatever theories and methods seem most suited to achieving this.

Feminist theories

Feminist theories have revolutionized sociology, and have put women and gender at the heart of sociological thinking and research. Most of these theories are part of the modernist tradition, in the sense that they seek not only to understand and explain society, and women's unequal position in it, through the application of reason and scientific evidence, but also to enable an improvement in the lives of women.

The challenge to malestream sociology

Malestream is a word coined by feminists to describe the type of sociology that concentrates on men, is mostly carried out by men and then assumes that the findings can be applied to women as well.

Before the 1970s, women were often marginalized and ignored in sociological research, and areas of interest to women – such as domestic labour, the domestic division of labour, domestic violence, women's health, female criminality, and the significance of gender differences and inequality – were largely ignored. Feminist sociological theory emerged as a challenge to a mainstream sociology that was seen as '**malestream**': as male-dominated; that viewed the world from a male perspective; that generalized research on men to the whole population; and that neglected and undervalued the roles, views and experiences of women. Sociology had therefore provided distorted, inadequate and incomplete descriptions and explanations of social life. Feminist theory set out to correct this male bias, by exploring and explaining women's subordinate position to men in society, making heard the voices of the neglected 50 per cent of the population, and putting women at the centre of sociological research.

The contribution of feminist theory

Since the 1970s, feminist contributions have sensitized sociology in all research areas to the experiences of women in contemporary societies. Feminist theories have succeeded in bringing the wider issues of gender identity, the social construction of gender differences and gender inequality into the centre of sociological theory and research. This has also led not only to gender becoming considered as a major part of existing topic areas, but to the development of new areas of research, such as masculinity and sexuality (including homosexuality). For example, feminism has introduced new areas into the study of the family, such as housework and its contribution to the economy, the domestic division of labour, domestic violence, the negative effects of family life on women's careers in paid employment, the experience of motherhood and childbirth, and the continuing inequality between men and women in the family. In education, examples include the issues of gender and achievement, and the construction of gender identities through schooling. Later in this chapter (Topic 4), it will be seen that feminist theory also influenced the research methods sociologists use to carry out their research.

Debates between the different strands of feminist theory (discussed below) have led to rapid theoretical developments, and, just as feminism exposed 'malestream' sociology, so intersectional feminism (see page 393) has exposed the limitations of the early white middle-class feminist perspective, and its inadequacy and neglect of issues like ethnicity and class. As you will have found during your sociology course, feminist approaches now feature in most topics studied on AS and A level Sociology courses, yet such courses were until fairly recently predominantly malestream, and feminist theories only appeared for the first time in the early 1980s. This perhaps illustrates in some measure the success feminist sociology has achieved.

Figure 5.4 Walby's six structures of patriarchy

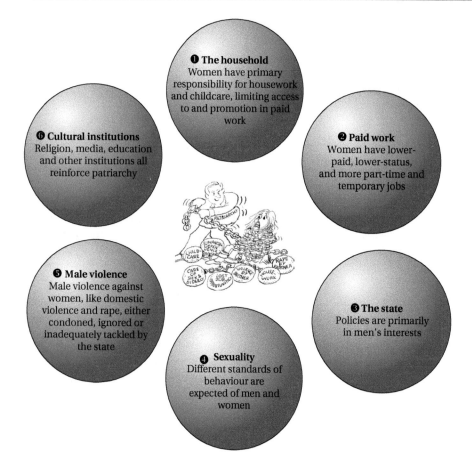

❶ The household
Women have primary responsibility for housework and childcare, limiting access to and promotion in paid work

❷ Paid work
Women have lower-paid, lower-status, and more part-time and temporary jobs

❻ Cultural institutions
Religion, media, education and other institutions all reinforce patriarchy

❺ Male violence
Male violence against women, like domestic violence and rape, either condoned, ignored or inadequately tackled by the state

❸ The state
Policies are primarily in men's interests

❹ Sexuality
Different standards of behaviour are expected of men and women

General features of feminist theory

Although there is a range of feminist theories, they all share the following basic features.

- There are inequalities in power and status between men and women, with women dominated by men and subordinate to them in most areas of social life.
- These inequalities generate differences of interest and conflict between men and women. Feminist theories are therefore conflict theories.
- Gender roles and inequalities are primarily socially constructed, and not based on innate (inborn) biological differences between men and women. As they are socially constructed, they can therefore be changed by human action.
- A recognition of the importance of the concept of patriarchy. Walby (1990: 20) defines patriarchy as 'a system of social structures and practices in which men dominate, oppress and exploit women'. She sees patriarchy as embedded in six structures, shown in figure 5.4, which combine to keep women in a position of subordination.

Activity

1 Explain what is meant by 'malestream sociology'.
2 Refer to figure 5.4 and suggest some examples of how patriarchy is maintained by any **two** of the patriarchal structures identified by Walby.

Liberal feminism

Liberal feminists suggest women's inequality arises primarily from factors like sexist stereotyping; gender role socialization; women's primary responsibility for housework and childcare; a lack of positive role models; and sex discrimination through outdated laws and attitudes. These generate a lack of equal opportunities for women, and keep women in lower-paid, lower-status occupations.

Liberal feminist research, such as the pioneering research by Oakley (1974a) on housework, and Sharpe (1994) on gender socialization and education, documents these inequalities. Legal, economic and social equality for women will come through a gradual process of reform, enabling women to take a full part in existing society on equal terms with men. Such reform measures include things like: better – high-quality and free or more affordable – childcare; men taking on more responsibility for housework and childcare; equal pay; anti-discrimination and equal opportunity laws; challenges to male prejudice, sexist attitudes and discrimination, and to gender stereotyping in institutions like the family, the media, the criminal justice system and education.

Evaluation of liberal feminism

Strengths

- Liberal feminist research has produced much evidence demonstrating that gender differences are socially constructed, through prejudice and discrimination generated by the socialization process and the legal and political system.
- It has had important effects on social policy, with the passing of anti-discrimination laws like the Equal Pay Act (1970), the Sex Discrimination Act (1975) and Equality Act (2010), and has done much to change traditional attitudes and improve women's lives and opportunities.

Weaknesses

- Liberal feminism merely deals with reducing the *effects* of women's subordination, rather than challenging the fundamental *causes*. Radical, Marxist and dual systems feminists suggest these lie in the structures of patriarchy and/or capitalism, and women's equality can only be brought about by revolutionary changes that overthrow these.

Radical feminism

Radical feminists regard patriarchy as the most fundamental form of inequality, with the world divided into two 'sex classes' of women and men, with men dominating women in all areas and from which all men benefit. All women, whatever their social class or ethnicity, have shared interests in challenging men, who are the enemy who strive to dominate and control women through violence, fear and intimidation, and turn women into sex objects for their own pleasures. Men are the key instruments of women's oppression, and all personal relationships with men, including the most intimate personal and sexual relationships, involve sexual politics – power struggles whereby men try to dominate and control women – and the personal is therefore political. Patriarchal power inequalities are found in all public (outside the home) and private (family and personal relationships) spheres of life, such as the six structures that Walby identified above.

Firestone (1972) and Ortner (1974) link women's subordination to women's biology (pregnancy and childbirth) which makes them dependent and vulnerable, and enables men to develop physical and psychological control over them (see pages 284–5).

Radical feminists propose the complete destruction of patriarchy, and for childbirth to be carried out independently of men. Women should begin to free themselves from oppression by living their lives separately and apart from men, through separatism (living apart) and lesbianism.

Criticisms of radical feminism

- It assumes all women share common interests. It fails to recognize, as Marxist and intersectional feminists do, that other factors like social class and ethnicity are also important sources of inequality. Women may have more differences between them than things they share – for example, poor, black working-class women may have little in common with rich, upper-class white women.

- It fails to recognize that gradual reform has improved women's opportunities and weakened the significance of patriarchy without revolutionary change, as liberal feminists argue.
- It doesn't really offer any explanations or solutions for how patriarchy might be abolished. The separatism and lesbianism radical feminists advocate are personal lifestyle choices, which are means of escaping patriarchy, rather than challenging it, and are unlikely to appeal to all women.
- It sees men as 'the enemy', but all men may not be engaged in the domination of women, and working-class or black women may find they have more in common with men in the same social class or ethnic group than they have with women outside these groups.
- It is capitalism, not patriarchy, which is the main source of women's subordination, and it is capitalism, rather than men, who benefit from it, as Marxist feminists argue.

Marxist feminism

Marxist feminists argue gender inequality arises primarily from the nature of capitalist society, not from an independent system of patriarchy. Capitalism intensifies patriarchal inequalities in pursuit of its own interests. Women are used as a cheap labour force, as a reserve army of labour which can be sacked and returned to the home during periods of economic recession, and re-employed during periods of prosperity, or as free labour in the form of women's unpaid domestic labour and childcare, which reproduces labour at no cost to the capitalist. Women's expressive role is to absorb men's anger at their exploitation at work – what Ansley (cited in Bernard 1982: 220) called women's role as 'takers of shit' – and this helps to keep capitalism stable. Barrett and McIntosh (1982) argue that the ideology of the idealized 'cereal packet' family is patriarchal and harmful to the interests of all women, but it is working-class women who suffer the greatest degree of subordination. Improving the position of women involves a fundamental challenge to capitalism and class inequality, and to the patriarchal ideology which is used to support it. Capitalism is the root cause of women's oppression, not men (as radical feminists suggest), nor simply outdated attitudes, stereotypes and so on as the liberal feminists believe.

Criticisms of Marxist feminism

- Marxist feminists don't explain the fact that patriarchy has existed in all known societies, not just capitalist societies, as radical feminists point out.
- It is men, not just capitalism, who benefit from women's subordination, and who enjoy positions of power, high status and pay, and it is men who are the instruments of oppression. For example, as radical feminists argue, it is men who discriminate, who commit sexual and physical violence against women, and view them as sex objects in cultural institutions like the media.

Dual systems feminism

Dual systems feminists, like Walby, blend Marxist and radical feminist theories. Capitalism and patriarchy are seen as two (dual) separate systems that interact with and reinforce one another in the form of 'patriarchal capitalism'. This generates dual roles for women as both homemakers/child-rearers and as paid workers outside the home. For example, patriarchy creates women's primary responsibility for housework and childcare, and related economic dependence on, and subordination to, men. This, as Marxist feminists contend, at the same time serves the needs of capitalism for a cheap and expendable paid labour force of women, and the free reproduction of labour power. Patriarchal and capitalist structures combine with other related factors like social class and ethnic inequalities to generate multiple causes for the subordination of women. It is these structures, rather than men, that are the source of women's inequality. Unlike radical feminism, all men are not necessarily or always seen as 'the enemy'.

Lasting solutions to women's inequality ultimately lie in removing the twin structures of patriarchy and capitalism, but dual systems feminists also support reform measures like those proposed by liberal feminists. These include tackling both the patriarchal nature of male/female relations in the private sphere of the home and family, and the patriarchal/capitalist exploitation of women in public spheres, such as the labour market, business, government and the media, and wider areas of social life, such as physical and sexual violence and intimidation of women by men.

Dual systems feminism has been criticized for its primarily theoretical approach, and for not offering many solutions to the problems of women's subordination that have not been already considered by other feminist theories.

Intersectional feminism (including black feminism)*

Black feminism (see page 287) originally emerged as a result of concerns that many early feminist theories ignored the different experiences of patriarchal subordination found among black women and others from minority ethnic groups. This concern has now been broadened to include a range of other groups, and is considered here under the broader heading of 'intersectional feminism'.

Intersectional feminists suggests that other variants of feminism, particularly in the early days of feminism in the 1960s and 1970s, viewed women's subordination through the eyes of white middle-class women. They emphasize that, while all women suffer many of the same problems, not all women are in the same position. The subordination of women and women's experiences of oppression can take very diverse forms in different contexts and among different social groups. This is particularly the case in postmodern societies, in which postmodernists claim there has been a weakening of structures like gender, social class and ethnicity as sources of identity, and people pick 'n' mix and choose identities and lifestyles from the wide range of choices available in a media-saturated, consumer-based society. This is reflected in a diversity of meanings attached to being a woman in contemporary Western societies.

Intersectional feminists emphasize that different forms of discrimination can become intensified when they combine, overlap or intersect (or interconnect). For example, there are substantial differences in the experiences of women from different social classes and from different ethnic groups, and between non-disabled and disabled women, between lesbian, transgender, bisexual and heterosexual women, and between women living in different areas, such as in working-class communities in the north of England and southern middle-class communities. Specific groups may face multiple intersecting/interlocking oppressions, such as racism and homophobia (an irrational fear of or aversion to homosexuals), which may be intensified by patriarchy, so that, for example, black working-class lesbians may experience patriarchal oppression in different ways to white, middle-class heterosexual women. Different groups of women may also have different conceptions of what the meaning of oppression is. For example, many white feminists regard the wearing of the hijab (headscarf) or burqa (full body covering) by British Muslim women as a sign of oppression, but Muslim women themselves may see this as a symbol of female and ethnic identity, as a sign of Muslim pride, and as a form of resistance to patriarchy – enabling them to free themselves from the male gaze and sexual harassment in a patriarchal Western culture which treats women as sex objects. The strength of intersectional feminism is that it recognizes that generalized 'broad brush' feminist theories do not take into account this diversity in the nature and experience of women's subordination, and that it is necessary to explore patriarchy and women's subordination in this increasingly complex and fragmented context. However, liberal and radical feminists are critical because, by emphasizing the differences between women, intersectional feminism deflects attention away from those problems shared by all women.

Feminism as a political ideology

Feminist sociologists are primarily social scientists, and operate in the modernist tradition in that they see their work not simply as an abstract academic exercise, but as a means of changing the world to improve the position of women by careful and systematic research.

However, feminism has had a much longer history as a political ideology and as a social and

*In previous printings of this book, this was incorrectly referred to as 'Difference feminism'.

Activity

1 Go to the two following contemporary feminist campaigning websites (or others you may be familiar with):

www.fawcettsociety.org.uk (the Fawcett Society)

www.ukfeminista.org.uk (UK Feminista)

a) Outline what the aims of the website/campaigning organization are.

b) Outline three issues that contemporary feminists are currently campaigning on.

c) Suggest what feminist perspective the websites seem to be most closely aligned with (if any) and give your reasons.

2 Return to one of the topic areas you have studied during your sociology course, and make a brief summary of the feminist contributions to that area, attempting to link them to some of the feminist theories just discussed (keep this in your notes for revision purposes).

3 Look at the following feminist slogans and statements, and suggest which feminist theory or theories (they may fit more than one) they are most likely to be associated with, and explain why.

a) A woman needs a man like a fish needs a bicycle.

b) Class war feminist (slogan on a T-shirt).

c) The family is a patriarchal and unequal institution controlled by and for men.

d) Women's role in the family is to do housework, to care for children, the sick and the elderly, and to flatter, excuse, sympathize with and pay attention to men. This often disadvantages women in many aspects of their lives.

e) Every mother is a working mother.

f) The family always benefits either men or capitalism.

g) I like to think of 'men' as the diminutive of 'women'.

h) The family exists primarily to pass on private property from one generation to the next, and to prepare a submissive and obedient workforce.

i) When wives play their traditional role as 'takers of shit', they often absorb their husbands' anger and frustration at their own powerlessness and oppression in the world of work, and stop rebellion in the workplace.

j) Think we're equal? Think again! Across the UK today, inequality between women and men is alive and kicking. Policies like equal pay and anti-discrimination laws, improved educational opportunities and paid maternity leave have improved women's prospects in paid employment, but the gender pay gap remains and is a persistent thorn in the side of workplace equality. We need to strengthen laws and government obligations to translate formal equality into reality for women, so women are placed on an equal footing with men. We need to campaign for an end to gender stereotyping, to violence against women and girls, strengthened democracy with improved representation of women across society and in leadership roles, and equality in the economy, in work, in the family, in justice and in rights for women.

k) Women's unpaid domestic labour reproduces the workforce at no cost to the capitalist.

l) There is no revolution without the liberation of women. There is no liberation of women without revolution.

political movement. There have been three 'waves' of feminism, which have focused on changing women's lives. The first wave was the campaign in the late nineteenth and early twentieth centuries for women to gain the right to vote (the suffragette movement) and for improved working conditions and educational rights.

The second wave was the Women's Liberation Movement of the 1960s to the early 1980s, which sought to challenge patriarchy and raise the consciousness of women to fight for new roles beyond the home, for equal rights in a wide range of legal and cultural institutions, and to reject sexism and their position as sex objects for men's pleasure. This set in train many of the gains in improved equality of opportunity and equality and anti-discrimination laws contemporary women now have.

Feminism has a long history as a vibrant social and political movement which continues to this day. For example, in 2011, a 'SlutWalk' protest in Toronto, Canada, against patriarchal attitudes that suggest rape victims are partly responsible for rape because of the 'sexualized' way they dress, inspired similar protests around the world.

There is a third wave which is still going on now, which continues the struggles begun in the second wave, but also embraces much more the issues like those raised by intersectional feminism, reflecting the diversity of women's lives and experiences in contemporary societies, not just in the UK but across the world.

Practice questions

1 Outline and explain **two** ways in which structuralist theories of society differ from social action or interpretivist theories. **(10 marks)**

2 Outline and explain **two** arguments that suggest functionalist theories may have little to contribute to an understanding of society today. **(10 marks)**

3 Read **Item A** below and answer the question that follows.

> **Item A**
> Before the 1970s, women were often marginalized or ignored in sociological research. Areas of interest to women, such as gender differences and inequality, were largely ignored. Feminist sociological theories emerged as a challenge to male-dominated 'malestream' sociology. Feminist theories have since revolutionized sociology, and put women and gender at the heart of sociological thinking and research.

Applying material from **Item A** and your knowledge, evaluate the usefulness of feminist approaches to a sociological understanding of contemporary society. **(20 marks)**

Topic 2

SPECIFICATION AREA

The concepts of modernity and post-modernity in relation to sociological theory

The terms 'modernism' and 'postmodernism' refer to the beliefs and theories which are associated with two periods in human society known as 'modernity' and, following it, 'postmodernity'. Modernity began roughly around the 1700s, and postmodernity in around the 1980s. The features of modernity and postmodernity are contrasted in table 5.2 on pages 397–8), which you should study carefully as it covers a lot of important material.

What are modernity and modernism?

The main features of modernity and modernist views are shown in table 5.2., but these include:

- Industrialization and the manufacture of standardized goods for a mass market
- work and social class are the main forms of social division and social identity, and both culture and politics are social class-related
- Life is fairly orderly and predictable, and people have a fairly stable and clear idea of their position in society and where they are heading
- Societies are based on independent nation-states, national economies and national identities
- One-way mass media more or less reflect social reality
- An optimistic view that the application of rational thought, science and technology could provide a means of controlling and improving the natural world
- A view that sociological theory and research could provide insight into and explanations of the social world, and could be used to improve it.

The move from modernity to postmodernity

The (alleged) transition from modernity to postmodernity emerged around the 1980s. Postmodernists argued that society was changing in such a way that modernist social theories, such as the dual structure/action approaches to understanding society, and modernist sociological theories like functionalism, Marxism, interactionism and many feminist theories were no longer able to provide adequate explanations of society. Factors like the rise of the new media, rapid technological change and the growth of service and knowledge-based industries that didn't actually make anything, globalization and consumer culture meant traditional sources of identity, such as class, gender and ethnicity, were becoming irrelevant to people's lives, and structures like the family and work, and the power of the nation-state, were disintegrating. People were no longer relating to the political parties of the past, which were rooted in the old structures of class, economy and community, but to new social and political movements focused on single issues concerning culture, identity, lifestyle and quality of life. These reflected their personal interests, such as the environment, climate change, sexuality and sexual orientation – as in the LGBT (lesbian, gay, bisexual and transgender) movement – world peace, human rights, globalization and the interests of marginalized and excluded groups like the disabled. Social change meant people's lives were becoming more insecure and unpredictable. These changes were accompanied by a decline in faith in science, and science came to be seen as the cause of problems rather than necessarily the solution. These changes challenged traditional modernist theories, and led to a view that society was moving from modernity to a new stage of postmodernity, and new approaches and theories were needed to understand this changing world.

Table 5.2 Modernity and postmodernity compared

Modern society or modernity	Postmodern society or postmodernity
Industrialization and the use of technology for the manufacture of standardized goods for a mass market, usually produced by manual workers in full-time (5 days a week) lifetime jobs.	Rapid and continuous introduction of new goods and services, with much wider consumer choice. Manual work and mass manufacturing replaced by service economy, like finance, telecommunications, various kinds of information processing, and customer service. Jobs for life disappear, with more job changes, job-sharing, more flexible, 24/7 and part-time working.
Central importance of work and social class as the main form of social division and source of identity. Bradley (1996) saw identity as fairly predictable, unchanging and stable, formed by social structural factors, like family life, work, social class, gender, ethnicity and community.	Media images, consumption and lifestyle become the major sources of identity. Bradley suggests identities become less certain and less predictable, more fluid and fragmented, and based more on choice than constraints of social structural factors. People can now have pick 'n' mix multiple identities and change them at will. There is a fragmentation of identities even among people in the same social groups, reflecting the fragmentation of classes and other social structures. Bauman (1996) suggested lives now gain meaning through consumption choices, influenced by designer labels, lifestyles and images gained from the global media in a media-saturated society.
Culture reflects the class structure, with clear distinctions between high and low/mass/popular culture.	Culture becomes more diverse and fragmented, and people pick 'n' mix elements from an increasingly diverse global culture which becomes just another product to consume. The distinctions between high and low/popular/mass culture dissolve.
Politics centre around social class interests, focused on political parties and government.	Politics become more personalized and linked to the diversity of consumer, lifestyle and identity choices. Party politics are displaced by identity politics, such as gay, lesbian, feminist, ethnic and religious (e.g. Islam) politics. New social movements emerge based on personal concerns rather than structural influences, such as the peace movement and environmental campaigns. The macro politics of political parties and government decline, and are replaced by micro politics of single-issue more localized campaigns and locally based transnational, global campaigns.
Nation-states, national economies and national identities predominate.	Nation-states and national identities are displaced by globalization. Supranational bodies, like the European Union and the United Nations, and multinational companies producing global products, like Apple, Google, Starbucks, McDonald's, Microsoft, Ford, Sony and Samsung, eclipse national and local identities. Global media and global marketing in a media-saturated society turn the world into a global supermarket.
Mass media concerned with one-way communication, more or less reflecting or mirroring a basic social reality, through media like terrestrial TV, newspapers and magazines.	Society becomes dominated by global interactive digital media, social networking and electronic communication, including the internet. Media become more removed from reality. Strinati (1995) suggests media imagery becomes a source of individual identity, and the media now dominate and create our sense of reality, generating what Baudrillard called *hyperreality* in a media-saturated society.
Tradition, religion, magic and superstition are displaced by rational thought and scientific theories which are seen as superior forms of knowledge for discovering the truth about and understanding the world and therefore improving it.	Objective truth is undiscoverable. Lyotard (1984) argues that individuals have lost faith in progress and in metanarratives – the all-embracing 'big stories' like the natural and social sciences which try to produce all-embracing explanations of the world. Metanarratives are just myths, and there are no certain or absolute truths about the world. Every question has an infinite number of answers, and all forms of knowledge are equally valid. For example, scientific theory is no more valid than knowledge provided by New Age beliefs and religions. There is a loss of faith in the certainty, rational thought, and scientific and technological progress of modernism. These are replaced by risk, doubt, uncertainty and anxiety.

Table 5.2 (continued)	
Modern society or modernity	Postmodern society or postmodernity
Scientific knowledge and scientific and technological progress are forces for good, providing the means to understand and solve the world's problems and make the world a better place.	Science and technology often cause rather than solve problems, such as climate change, pollution, nuclear weapons and nuclear accidents, and antibiotic-resistant superbugs. There is growing scepticism about the idea of progress, and science as a force for good and its ability to explain and improve the world. Science is no longer a source of truth and progress, but just another failed metanarrative.
Sociology developed to try to understand and explain society in a scientific way, with rationality and scientific methods providing the tools to understand the workings of society in order to improve it. The development of positivist structural theories like functionalism and Marxism reflected the modernist concern with using the same scientific methods used in the natural sciences to explain society.	Everything is in a permanent state of flux. Society is changing so constantly and rapidly, with social structures breaking down, that there is chaos and uncertainty. Societies can no longer be understood through the application of metanarratives like Marxism or functionalism which seek to explain society as a whole. Such metanarratives are inadequate to explain the changing world, because society has become fragmented into so many different groups, interests and lifestyles that are constantly changing, that society is essentially chaotic. There are few of the social constraints on people that structuralist approaches identify, and society and social structures cease to exist – there is only a mass of individuals making their own personal lifestyle choices. Sociological theories are just one set of ideas competing against other equally valid ideas, and provide no basis for improving society.

What are postmodernity and postmodernism?

Chaos, uncertainty and the collapse of social structures

Postmodernists like Bauman (1992) stress that society is now in such a state of constant change that it is unpredictable, and is marked by chaos and uncertainty – a state he referred to as 'liquid modernity' – in which social structures like the nation-state, the family and social class are breaking down. Postmodernists argue that it is nonsense to talk of an institution called the family, for example, as people now live in such a wide range of ever-changing personal relationships. Gay and lesbian couples, cohabiting heterosexual couples who do not marry, multiple partners, high rates of divorce and remarriage, lone parents, stepparents and stepchildren, dual-income families with both partners working, people living alone, people living in shared households with friends, couples who have differing arrangements for organizing household tasks – all mean that any notion of the 'typical family' or 'the family as an institution' is absurd.

Globalization

Globalization means that the nation-state and national differences are becoming less significant in people's lives, and the world is becoming increasingly interconnected. People's lives are no longer rooted (embedded) in and confined to local contexts, but are lived in and influenced by the global framework (whether they realize it or not), unlimited by time and place. Giddens (1990) (from a late modernist perspective, discussed on pages 401–2) calls this **disembedding**. An example is the internet, where we might interact with others or do online shopping regardless of physical location or time.

Technological changes like the internet, satellite TV and the other new media, instantaneous electronic communication, the increasing globalization and interconnectedness of economies, and the growth of supranational bodies – like the European Union and transnational corporations, like Coca-Cola, Microsoft, Apple, Amazon and McDonald's – are displacing nation-states and national identities. Tourism and travel, immigration and emigration, migrant labour, undocumented

> **Disembedding** refers to the way social relations are lifted out of local contexts, and are no longer confined by time and space.

workers (illegal immigrants), and asylum seekers undermine national identities, and national cultures are diluted, as they increasingly become global cultures. The same consumer goods, films, TV shows, music, fashions and foodstuffs are now found in most countries of the world, largely based on Western cultures. People now form identities around images and consumer lifestyles drawn from this global culture, such as through global TV networks and the internet, rather than ever-fragmenting traditional sources of identity like their local community, or social class, gender and ethnicity. Globalization has meant that modernist sociology, formed around concepts such as structure/action and social class, gender and ethnicity within the framework of the nation-state, needs to be rejected or reformulated to take into account the new contexts of globalization and global interconnectedness.

Metanarratives and the 'myth of truth'

Lyotard (1984) described postmodernism as 'an incredulity towards metanarratives' and argued people no longer believed in the 'myth of truth'. Because society is now changing so constantly and so rapidly, societies can no longer be understood through the application of general theories or metanarratives. Metanarratives are 'big' theories like Marxism or functionalism, which seek to explain society as a whole, but these no longer apply according to postmodernists because society has become fragmented into so many different groups, interests and lifestyles that are constantly changing that society is essentially chaotic. All knowledge of any kind is now equally valid.

There has been a loss of faith in the superiority of rational thought and science as a means of progress and improvement of the world. Science and technology often cause rather than solve problems, such as climate change, pollution and antibiotic-resistant superbugs.

Choice, identity and consumption

Postmodernists believe that there are few of the social constraints on people identified by structuralist approaches, and that society and social structures have fragmented, weakened or ceased to exist. Lyotard suggests postmodern societies are characterized by growing individualism; there is now only a mass of individuals, with few social bonds connecting them, forming their identities through individual choices in education, health, their personal relationships, lifestyle and the consumer goods they buy. Baudrillard called this 'the end of the social'. People can now form their own identities – how they see and define themselves and how others see and define them – and they can be whatever they want to be. Postmodern society involves a media-saturated consumer culture in which individuals are free to pick 'n' mix and transform identities and lifestyles chosen from a limitless range of constantly changing consumer goods and leisure activities, which are available from across the globe.

Simulacra are images or reproductions and copies which appear to reflect things in the real world but have no basis in reality.

A media-saturated society

Baudrillard (2001) sees life in the postmodern era so dominated by media imagery that it has become what he calls 'media-saturated'. The mass media used more or less to reflect some basic reality, but media images now dominate and distort the way we see the world. Baudrillard suggests the media present what he calls **simulacra**, images which appear to reflect events in the real world but have no basis in reality, and which are viewed simultaneously across the globe. Even images of real events are so distorted and distanced from reality that they actually replace reality. For example, the reality of a missile hitting its target is not shown to a viewer, but a simulacrum of the real event. Laser technology and video reportage have eliminated the blood, the suffering and the corpses from war, and the TV news presents a sanitized version of conflicts. Wars become media-constructed spectacles, which have such an air of unreality about them that we are unable to distinguish them from Hollywood movies or video games. Baudrillard calls this distorted view of the world which is actually created and defined by the media **hyperreality**, with the media image of an event becoming more real than the reality it is meant to be depicting, as it tries to make viewers feel

Hyperreality is a view of the world which is created and defined by the media, with the image of an event more real than the event it is meant to be depicting.

To what extent do you think contemporary society is media-saturated and both distorts reality and creates the way people see the world?

they are experiencing an 'event'. Some celebrities, for example, are famous, not for doing anything, but for no other reason than being made famous by the media. All this means, as Giddens (2006) puts it, 'much of our world has become a sort of make-believe universe in which we are responding to media images rather than to real persons or places', as shown by people who write to characters in television soaps, imagining they are real. For example, in *Coronation Street* in 1998, the character Deirdre Barlow was sent to prison *in the show* for a crime she did not commit. A media-fuelled grassroots campaign began, pleading with Granada Television to 'free the Weatherfield One'. The real-world home secretary even involved the prime minister, who, with only a touch of irony, attempted to intervene in this unreal world on Deirdre's behalf.

Pick 'n' mix identities

Baudrillard (2001) sees life in postmodernity involving the search for satisfaction of media-created desires, and pressures to consume, with individual identity and behaviour no longer formed predominantly by factors such as class, ethnicity or gender, but by information, images and signs like designer labels gained from the media. In a globalized popular culture, the media present to us a massive choice of lifestyles, images and identities drawn from across the world. Bradley (1996) argues that new identities are created by globalization, bringing different cultural groups into contact. People now adopt different identities based on consumer lifestyles to meet the diversity in their lives – they no longer identify with class alone, but with ethnicity, gender, disability, race, religion, nationality, music, fashion designer labels, dress, sport and other leisure activities – they can pick 'n' mix to create whatever identities they wish.

You are what you buy

Bauman (1996) argues that life in postmodern society resembles a shopping mall, where people can stroll around consuming whatever they like – trying out, constructing and changing whatever identities they choose. People buy goods not for their usefulness, but as identity symbols for the image and the impression of themselves they wish to project to others. In this postmodern pick 'n' mix consumer society, people can become whatever they want to be, adopting lifestyles and identities built around the almost unlimited choice of leisure activities and consumer goods available in what has become a globalized consumer market.

> **Activity**
>
> Refer to table 5.2 and the sections on postmodernism, and answer the following questions:
>
> 1 Identify the following statements about postmodernism as true or false:
>   a) The mass media reflect reality.
>   b) Individual identity is formed by the social structure.
>   c) Scientific knowledge is superior to common sense.
>   d) Politics is based around social class interests.
>   e) Science can solve the world's problems.
>   f) The social structure has become fragmented.
>   g) You can be whatever you want to be.
> 2 Suggest whether each of the following statements is more likely to be regarded as true by a modernist or postmodernist, and explain your reasons in each case:
>   a) There is no such thing as society, only individuals.
>   b) Philosophers have merely interpreted the world, the point is to change it.
>   c) If there is one thing we should have learned by now, it is the total obsolescence of any idea that it is possible to distinguish truth from falsehood, or science from ideology.
>   d) People trip on pavements because they walk under ladders.
>   e) Industrialization and urbanization, the growth of science and religious beliefs as a means to understand the world gave way to the need for new ways of understanding and explaining society.
>   f) A rational understanding is an understanding of reality which is valid because it starts from valid premises.

Evaluation of postmodernism

Strengths

1 It has highlighted some important cultural changes, particularly in the areas of the media, culture and identity.
2 It emphasizes that the construction of identity has become a more fluid and complex process, with people having more choices to pick 'n' mix identities based on consumer lifestyles and global media imagery – and cannot be reduced to simply a response to social structural factors.
3 It provides insight into most contemporary social changes, such as growing risk and uncertainty, globalization, and the growing power of the media.
4 In challenging sociological metanarratives, it has perhaps encouraged sociologists to reflect more on some of their assumptions, how they set about their research, and the meaning of some contemporary social changes. This is reflected, for example, in the intersectional feminism (postmodern feminism) discussed in the previous topic (see page 393).

Critical views of postmodernism

Giddens: late modernity and reflexivity

Giddens (1991, 2006; Giddens and Sutton 2013) doesn't dispute that the changes in society that postmodernists identify have occurred – such as globalization, the declining power of nation-states and the growing diversity of identities, social movements, cultures and ways of life. He accepts we live in what he calls a 'runaway world' and a 'risk society' marked by new risks and uncertainties, and growing individualism, in which neither people nor institutions can any longer take for granted traditional ways of doing things. However, he says that these changes are a continuation of modern society in an intensified form, and have not brought us into a new era of postmodernity, but into what he calls late modernity or high modernity, which requires us to adapt, but not abandon, traditional sociological theories. Giddens sees late modernity as characterized by what he calls social reflexivity. This means the knowledge we gain from society can affect the way we act in it (much as the interpretivists say). In late modernity, reflexivity grows in importance, as individuals and social institutions face greater uncertainty in a world in which traditional established customs and values have weakened, and no longer provide clear guidance on behaviour and life choices. Everything is unstable and changing rapidly, and life becomes full of risks, like nuclear accidents, economic crisis, climate change and environmental pollution. People are constantly having to reflect on and reassess what they do and how they do things, and to think about or reflect on the circumstances in which they live their lives, and weigh up the risks they face when they make their choices.

In late modernity, reflexivity for individuals focuses on personal freedom and fulfilment as people establish goals for what Giddens calls their 'life projects'. This social reflexivity gives people and institutions a greater capacity to act and plan rationally to change and improve the world, which is an element of modernity.

Beck: 'risk society' and reflexive modernity

Beck (1992) is another theorist of late modernity, who suggests there is a new phase of modernity – 'the second modernity' – which he calls 'reflexive modernity', in which there are high levels of uncertainty and risk in what he calls 'risk society'. These risks occur in rapidly changing everyday life in social institutions like the family, as seen in things like rising divorce rates and the growing diversity of personal relationships; they can also be seen in the failings or abuse of so-called 'scientific and technological progress' in modernity, such as environmental pollution, climate change, nuclear accidents, genetically modified crops and foods, avian flu, *E. coli*, MRSA, *C. difficile* and other antibiotic-resistant superbugs. These risks from science are different from the natural disasters and plagues of the past which were beyond human control, as many are generated by progress itself. In late modernity these risks have higher chances of spinning out of control, for example climate change; the unsustainability of the wasteful throwaway society; the safe disposal of hazardous waste; nuclear accidents and risks of nuclear warfare; nuclear, chemical and biological weapons used by terrorist groups; and global crime networks. Such risks are often beyond the control of individual nation-states. While Beck recognizes science still carries risks of making things worse, it also has the capacity to make things better and control or reduce these new risks – and that is a feature of modernity.

Beck shares with Giddens the idea of reflexivity, and suggests we are living in a period of reflexive modernity, as people, institutions and governments need to think and reflect more about risks today, work out how to resolve problems, and therefore change society. People have lost trust in the capacity of governments and scientists to manage risks, and they consequently make more individualized choices and take decisions about the identities and lifestyles they wish to adopt formed around awareness of the risks their choices involve. This reflexivity carries within it the modernist hope of improving society and the lives of individuals, albeit with greater risks than ever before.

Harvey and Marxism

Harvey (1990), from a Marxist perspective, suggests many of the changes claimed by postmodernists to be evidence of postmodernity can be explained by modernist theories like Marxism. Harvey claims, for example, that changes like globalization, rapid cultural change, the growth of consumerism and the individualization of identity reflect capitalism opening up new markets and new sources of profits in a global economy.

The work of Giddens, Beck and Harvey suggests that, though there has been a lot of very rapid social change, and everyday life is breaking free from tradition and custom and is more fluid and chaotic today, the distinction between modernity and postmodernity is exaggerated. What is called 'postmodernity' is little other than the latest developments within modernity, and the changes can be explained by adapting existing sociological theories like Marxism, and developing more sophisticated new ones, as in Giddens's theory of structuration, or Beck's and Giddens's ideas of reflexivity. These changes do not mean that knowledge is always relative as the postmodernists contend, and that rational thought and research cannot explain society and find solutions to its problems. It is still possible to develop general theories of the social world, and such theories can help to shape society in a positive way, and governments still have the power to intervene to improve society.

Other criticisms of postmodernism

1 *It is all criticism*, and since it sees no knowledge or vision as any better than any other, it lacks any values or vision for improving society; it undermines any idea of progress, and in a world with widespread poverty, inequality and injustice, this is in effect ignoring a range of diverse and serious social problems.
2 *It over-emphasizes the influence of the media*, and tends to assume people are passive, and easily duped and manipulated by them. People are perfectly able to make judgements about what is real and what is not, and are aware that the media do not always, or even often, provide the truth about the world.
3 *It exaggerates the scale of social change*, such as that cultural distinctions are blurred, and that there is a global culture. Cultural tastes are still strongly influenced by class, gender and ethnicity, and national cultures and identities are still strong.
4 *It is too voluntaristic* in that it assumes that all individuals are free to act as they wish and can create, pick and choose and change identities at will. It ignores differences in power, and the existence of widespread social inequality. Such social structural factors still exert major influences. For example, people are still constrained by economic factors, which influence their consumption and related consumer lifestyles. Class, gender and ethnicity are still major defining characteristics in contemporary societies.
5 *Postmodernism is itself a metanarrative*, and if metanarratives and absolute truths are dismissed by postmodernists, then it has, in effect, dismissed itself as having anything to say that is any more valid than anything else.

Practice questions

1 Outline and explain **two** ways in which modernist approaches differ from postmodernist approaches to the study of society. **(10 marks)**
2 Outline and explain **two** arguments that suggest that society may have moved beyond modernity to a new stage of postmodernity. **(10 marks)**
3 Read **Item A** below and answer the question that follows.

> **Item A**
> Postmodernists believe that society is now changing so constantly and rapidly that social life has become unpredictable and is marked by growing uncertainty. Social structures like the family and social class are disintegrating and becoming less significant in people's lives. The application of sociological metanarratives or 'big theories' like functionalism or Marxism is consequently no longer adequate to explain contemporary societies.

Applying material from **Item A** and your knowledge, evaluate the usefulness of postmodernist approaches to a sociological understanding of contemporary society. **(20 marks)**

Topic 3

SPECIFICATION AREA

The nature of science and the extent to which sociology can be regarded as scientific

Science as a product of modernity

As discussed in the previous topic, science as we know it today was part of modernism. In modernity, explanations for events as arising from the actions of spirits, gods or other supernatural beings are displaced by rational scientific explanations based on **empirical evidence** derived from observation and experimentation, logical thought and reasoning. Deciding whether a particular understanding of the world was true or not would no longer be based on appeals to religion, faith, intuition, tradition and superstition, but on evidence and rational argument based on the scientific method. Through the application of rational principles and the use of empirical evidence, it was thought that the scientific method could contribute to the understanding and control of the natural and social worlds, and thereby improve them. Because of the scientific method, science came to be seen as superior to other forms of knowledge.

> **Empirical evidence** is observable evidence collected in the physical or social world.

The scientific method

Popper (2002 [1935]) suggests that science involves the hypothetico-deductive method. This involves drawing up a specific question, idea or possible explanation (a hypothesis), which is based on previous research, observation and hunches, to test through research. For example, a researcher looking at official crime statistics might deduce that young people have a greater involvement in crime, leading to the formation of a hypothesis for investigation and testing that this might be due to status frustration. Popper's features of the scientific method include:

1 *Hypothesis formation*: forming ideas or informed guesses about the possible causes of some phenomena.
2 *Falsification*: the aim of testing hypotheses against the evidence is to try to prove them wrong, as just one exception can prove a hypothesis false (this is discussed further shortly).
3 *The use of empirical evidence*: no hypothesis can be regarded as a scientific hypothesis unless it is capable of being falsified (proven wrong) by testing against empirical and measurable evidence derived from systematic observation and/or experimentation.
4 *Replication*: testing against empirical evidence is capable of being checked by other researchers who can repeat (or replicate) the research to verify the accuracy of the findings.
5 *The accumulation of evidence*: scientific knowledge is cumulative – that is, it builds up over time, through a constant cycle of hypothesis formation, falsification through testing against empirical data, and new hypothesis formation, until the hypothesis seems to be robust and accurate.
6 *Prediction*: through establishing cause-and-effect relationships rooted in evidence, precise predictions of what will happen in the same circumstances in future can be established.
7 *Theory formation*: if the hypothesis is capable of being tested against evidence and cannot be shown to be false, and predictions appear sound, then there can be some confidence that the hypothesis is probably true. This may then become part of a scientific theory.
8 *Scrutiny*: a scientific theory will be scrutinized by other scientists, and will stand only until some new evidence comes along to show the existing theory is false.

Popper argues that a proposition like 'all swans are white' is a scientific hypothesis because it can be tested by empirical research; but it can never be finally proven true as there is always the possibility of finding an exception. So scientists should hunt for the exception, or the non-white swan, to falsify their hypotheses, rather than for evidence to prove them true.

Popper's principle of falsification

Popper suggests no hypothesis can ever finally be proven true, as there is always the possibility of some future exception. However, a hypothesis can easily be proven false, as just one observation to the contrary can disprove it. Popper used the famous case of the 'white swan' to make his point. He argues that the hypothesis that 'all swans are white' can never be finally proven true as there is always the possibility of finding an exception, but it can easily be proven wrong or falsified by finding just one example of a non-white swan. So Popper argues that researchers should aim, not to prove their hypotheses true, for example by counting all the white swans, but to falsify them by looking for the non-white swan. The more a hypothesis stands up to such attempts, the more likely it is to be a 'scientific truth' – though it will remain only a probability and not a proven fact, as an exception may always come along. Popper suggests that much of sociological theory is not scientific as it can't actually be falsified by empirical research, and will only become scientific when it produces testable and falsifiable hypotheses.

Objectivity means approaching topics with an open mind, avoiding bias and being prepared to submit research evidence to scrutiny by other researchers.

Objectivity and value freedom

Objectivity is an important part of the scientific process, and the data collected are seen as objective facts, not distorted by the value judgements and personal beliefs of the scientist. Objectivity involves three main aspects:

Value freedom is the idea that the beliefs and prejudices of a researcher should not influence the way research is carried out and evidence interpreted.

- Open-mindedness on the part of the researcher, and a willingness to consider all possibilities and evidence, to demonstrate 'fair play' and act in good faith;
- **Value freedom** – keeping personal prejudices, opinions and values out of the research process (the difficulties with this are discussed in Topic 5);
- Findings should be open to inspection and criticism by other researchers: the 'community of scientists' should have the opportunity to scrutinize and check findings, and criticize them.

Science and the study of society

Positivism

Positivism is the view that the logic, methods and procedures of the natural sciences, as used in subjects like physics, chemistry and biology, can be applied to the study of society with little modification, and that human behaviour is a response to external forces – such as the agencies of socialization – in much the same way as events in the natural world. Such claims were made by many of the founders of sociology. Comte, for example, argued that the application of natural science methodology to the study of society, based on empirical evidence and objectivity, would produce a 'positive science of society', showing that behaviour in the social world is governed by laws of cause and effect in the same way as the behaviour of objects in the natural world. Marx similarly claimed his theories of class struggle, revolution and the transition to communism were based on cause-and-effect theories established by the application of the scientific method to historical and contemporary empirical data. In keeping with the modernist tradition, and the aims of natural science, such a 'science of society' was seen as a means to solving social problems, improving the quality of human lives and making the world a better place to live in.

Durkheim, in *The Rules of Sociological Method* (1895), argued clearly for a positivist approach in sociology, with his fundamental rule: 'Consider social facts as things'. Sociology rarely produces results that are as precise and repeatable as those produced by natural scientists (although this is not seen as a major problem by positivists). This is partly because sociologists are unable to control all the variables in the situations they study, as natural scientists are able to do under laboratory conditions. Nonetheless, positivists argue that applying the procedures of the natural sciences to the study of society enables an objective and value-free science of society.

Social facts

Positivists believe that, just as there are causes of things in the natural world, so there are **social facts** that cause events in the social world. Durkheim said the aim of sociology should be the study of these social facts, which should be considered as things, like objects in the natural world, and could in most cases be observed and measured quantitatively – in number/statistical form. By social facts, Durkheim meant social phenomena which exist outside individuals but act upon them in ways that constrain their behaviour. These include customs, belief systems and social institutions, such as the family, law and the education system. For example, social classes are social facts, with clear measurable differences between them, such as in income, crime rates, housing, health and educational achievement; although social classes exist independently of individuals, they shape the way they act. For positivists, society has a reality external to individuals, and social facts – for example, customs and norms – although independent of the individual, exercise constraint on and limit the options of individuals. Simply put, individuals cannot do exactly as they wish without coming up against a whole range of social sanctions which curb the opportunities for anti-social behaviour.

> **Social facts** are phenomena that exist outside individuals and independently of their minds, but which act upon them in ways which constrain or mould their behaviour.

The main features of positivism in sociology

Positivists argue that sociology should be a science, and that this is made possible by following the scientific approach using the hypothetico-deductive method. This positivist view consists of the following features.

1 A view that human behaviour is a response to observable social facts, and can be explained in terms of cause-and-effect relationships.
2 Direct observation and the use of quantitative, statistical methods of data collection should be used to study society. Only those factors which are directly observable and can be statistically measured form acceptable data: the feelings, motives and mental states of individuals cannot be observed, and are therefore inadmissible evidence. Without quantification, sociology will remain at the level of insight, lacking evidence, and it will be impossible to replicate (or repeat) studies to check findings, establish the causes of social events, or make generalizations and predictions.
3 Research should focus on the search for the social causes of events in society. Examples might be to establish hypotheses about why people in some social classes suffer poorer health, or are more likely to commit suicide or get involved in crime than those in other classes, and look for causes by studying official statistics or carrying out surveys. This is what Durkheim tried to do in his 1897 study *Suicide*, in which he suggested the causes of suicide were imbalances in the degrees of **social integration** and **moral regulation** in society.
4 The focus of sociology is on the study of social institutions and the social structure as a whole, not on the individual, as it is these external structures which shape and mould individuals.

> **Social integration** refers to the integration of individuals into social groups, binding them into society and building social cohesion.

> **Moral regulation** refers to the regulation or control by social values of the actions and desires of individuals.

How does studying society differ from the procedures used in the natural sciences?

Can sociology be scientific?

There are disagreements within sociology as to how far the logic, methods and procedures of the natural sciences can be applied, as positivists suggest, to the study of society. Many sociologists argue that such methods – for example, the laboratory experiment and the use of observable, quantitative data – are inappropriate or insufficient for the study of society. This is because there are fundamental differences between the social world and the natural or physical world, and sociology therefore cannot simply copy the approach and methodology of natural science, as the following points suggest:

1 *The problem of prediction.* In natural science, experiments can be carried out to test ideas and it is possible to isolate causes in laboratory conditions; therefore, natural scientists can accurately predict what will happen in the same circumstances in the future. Human beings, however, might behave differently in an experiment, knowing they are being observed. Human behaviour cannot be predicted with certainty: people have free will and choice, and might react differently to the same circumstances on different occasions – for example, not everyone facing the same set of circumstances will commit suicide.

2 *Artificiality.* Sociology wants to study society in its *normal* state, not in the artificial conditions of a laboratory experiment.

3 *Ethical issues.* Human beings might well object to being boiled, weighed, wired, prodded with sticks, interrogated or observed in laboratories.

4 *The Hawthorne effect.* In the natural sciences the presence of the scientist does not usually affect the behaviour of chemicals or objects. However, sociologists studying people may themselves change the behaviour of those being studied. When people are being interviewed or observed, they may become embarrassed, be more defensive and careful about what they say, or act differently because they have been selected for study (this is known as the 'Hawthorne effect'). If this happens, then the results obtained will not give a true picture of how people behave in society.

5   *Validity.* The natural scientist does not have to persuade objects, chemicals or (usually) animals to take part in research, but people may distort and conceal the truth, refuse to answer questions or otherwise cooperate, making sociological research difficult or impossible. Those who have attempted, but failed, to commit suicide may, for example, later invent reasons for their suicidal behaviour which might be quite different from their real motives at the time. This raises the possibility of obtaining invalid or untruthful evidence.

6   *Empirical observation.* Popper suggests scientific hypotheses must be capable of being tested against evidence derived from systematic observation and/or experimentation. However, not all social phenomena are observable or quantifiable, such as the meanings and motives people have for their behaviour. The realist view of science, on the other hand, suggests this is also true in the natural sciences (see pages 409–10).

Interpretivism

Interpretivists argue that sociology cannot be a science either in the same way as natural science or in the way positivists suggest. Interpretivism emphasizes the difference between studying society and studying the natural and physical world. Interpretivists argue people do not simply respond to external forces, as positivists claim: they interpret and give meaning to a situation before responding to it. It is therefore impossible to predict human behaviour or to establish simple cause-and-effect relationships through simple observation, experimentation and the collection of empirical, quantitative data obtained through surveys or official statistics. In order to understand and explain human society it is necessary to discover and interpret the meanings people give to situations. This is achieved by letting people 'speak for themselves'. Weber argued that this is a process of 'understanding', which he termed (in German) *Verstehen* (pronounced *fair-shtay-en*). This involves a recognition that people give meaning to their actions, and researchers can only understand these meanings if they try to put themselves in the position of the people whose actions they are trying to understand.

Interpretivists emphasize that meanings do not exist independently of people. For example, social phenomena such as suicide, crime and social class are not social facts, but social constructions that have no reality outside the meaning given to them by people. A tree or mountain exists whether people are there or not. A sudden unnatural death only becomes a 'murder', a 'manslaughter', an 'accident' or a 'suicide' because people define it as such, and these definitions can

How might positivists and interpretivists differently explain the fact that (most) people conform to the norm of stopping at a red traffic light?

change from place to place and from person to person. There can be no laws of human society, and no possibility of prediction as human behaviour is variable and changeable. Sociologists cannot hope to explain anything without moving from quantitative, empirical data towards a more qualitative understanding of peoples' own subjective views of the world. In order to understand society, the principles of objectivity and detachment associated with the natural sciences and positivism are completely inadequate, as involvement, closeness and empathetic understanding (*Verstehen*) are necessary to understand the meanings which drive people's behaviour in society.

Is science really as scientific as it claims to be?

The discussion of positivism and interpretivism above highlighted different approaches to the study of society, with the positivists taking the view that 'good sociology' can and should model itself on the procedures of the natural sciences, while the interpretivists suggest sociology cannot follow such procedures because of the fundamental differences between the natural and social worlds.

Sociology as a whole (including positivist research) is often seen as inferior to the natural sciences, and made out to be sloppy and less scientific than natural science research. This is because sociology rarely produces results or is able to make predictions that have the same kind of precision as those of natural scientists, and sociological research, particularly interpretivist research, is often difficult to replicate to check findings. However, this comparison rests on assumptions that natural scientists are wholly objective and value-free, remorselessly engaged in the pursuit of scientific truth as they attempt to falsify their hypotheses through the scrupulous and detached collection of observable empirical data, and are able to make accurate predictions based on scientific laws. However, there are two general reasons to doubt this view of natural science.

1 It is based on mistaken assumptions about what natural science and scientific method are really like, as the realists suggest.
2 It ignores the way scientific knowledge is socially constructed.

These suggest that, when considering whether or not sociology is or can be a science, a starting point could well be to ask whether the natural sciences fulfil their own criteria of being as neutral, objective, detached and based on empirical evidence as natural scientists might claim them to be. These issues are discussed in the next sections.

The realist view of science

Realism is the view that events in both the social and natural worlds are produced (caused) by underlying structures and processes, which may be unobservable.

Bhaskar (1998) adopts a realist view of science. **Realism** suggests that not all phenomena are material objects or (for positivists) social facts capable of observation and measurement, but there can be underlying, unobservable structures that cause events. Part of 'doing science' is the discovery and explanation of what these structures are. Bhaskar argues that these underlying structures are a feature of both the natural and social worlds, and the positivist view is based on an incorrect assumption that natural scientific method, as Popper suggests, is based only on that which can be observed. For example, many of the greatest scientific discoveries have not been directly observed, but inferred or worked out from their effects. These include things like sub-atomic particles, viruses, germs, energy and solar fusion. The view that the Earth is round has been an accepted view of science for hundreds of years, yet it was only physically observed in the 1960s, with the start of space exploration. Sociology operates in much the same way. We can't see or observe structures like social classes or belief systems, but we can discover them by their effects, such as by large numbers of people sharing similar incomes, education and housing, or by full or empty churches, mosques and temples.

Even Durkheim, who as a positivist claimed to use natural science methodology, used the twin social forces of social integration and moral regulation to explain suicide, though neither were observable or quantifiable. So natural science is not simply limited to the observable, as Popper suggests.

That the Earth is round has been an accepted scientific fact for hundreds of years, yet it was only physically observed last century with the start of space exploration. Studying the social world also includes many things that aren't observable, but does this make it any more 'unscientific' than natural science?

Open and closed systems

Realists such as Sayer (1992, 2000) and Keat and Urry (2010 [1975]) point out that prediction is often not as precise a process in natural science as Popper claims. Natural science has an advantage over social science in predictive powers when it can study events in what Sayer calls *closed systems*, when all the potential causal factors are under the control of the researcher and precise measurements are possible, as in the closed environment of the laboratory experiment. However, much natural scientific research, like most sociological research, takes place in much more *open systems* where these factors can't be controlled, and prediction is much more difficult and imprecise. Examples might be weather forecasting and seismology (the study of earthquakes). Although natural science might be able to predict general weather trends or identify areas at risk of earthquakes, it still often fails, despite a huge range of sophisticated technology and scientific knowledge, to give accurate predictions of whether or not it will rain tomorrow, or if and when our house may collapse around us through an earthquake.

In short, the claim that sociology is unscientific because it is unable to predict human behaviour, and shouldn't aim to copy natural scientific methods as all the factors necessary to explain human behaviour are not observable, as the interpretivists suggest, is based on a mistaken view of what real natural scientific research is like. Researching the social world and the natural world therefore may have more in common than might first appear, as they both study unobservable phenomena, and they both operate in open systems where they are unable to control all potential causes.

From a realist perspective, positivists and interpretivists both misunderstand what natural science is really like, and both positivists and interpretivists are using scientific approaches. Positivists are focusing on the observable, and interpretivists on the unobservable, but both are engaged in 'doing science' as much as any natural scientist. From a realist view, sociology is, then, a science.

The social constructionist approach: the social construction of scientific knowledge

The social constructionist view suggests that science, scientific method and scientific knowledge are not neutral, objective things, but that they are produced within a specific social context. They are created by the actions and interpretations of scientists themselves and influenced by a wide range of social factors. In other words, science is socially constructed.

Kuhn, the influence of paradigms and 'scientific revolutions'

Kuhn (2012 [1962]) questions whether scientists really do in practice set out to collect evidence with the specific aim of trying to falsify their hypotheses, as Popper suggests they should. Kuhn argues that, on the contrary, scientists work within **paradigms** – frameworks of scientific laws, concepts, theories, methods and assumptions – with which they approach the various puzzles they seek to understand and investigate, which are not called into question until the evidence against them is overwhelming.

A paradigm acts like a pair of coloured lenses through which scientists look at the 'puzzles' they are investigating, and these influence what they think they should look for, what sort of questions they ask, the approved methods which they follow to investigate these puzzles, and what they count as proper and relevant scientific evidence. The paradigm also provides what is likely to be seen as a correct or approved answer to the original puzzle being investigated. Paradigms are learnt by scientists in their training, during which they are socialized into the accepted view of 'normal science', based on the values of the scientific community at the time. This is just like sociologists learning different methodological approaches such as positivism or interpretivism, and what counts as 'good sociology'.

Kuhn argues that most scientists in their experimental work rarely question the paradigm, and the paradigm acts like blinkers which encourage scientists to try to fit observations into the paradigm, rather than actually attempting to falsify their hypotheses as Popper suggests. The more an idea challenges the dominant paradigm, the more experimental work is scrutinized for error; and the more findings do not fit into the existing paradigm, the more likely they are to be dismissed and the blame laid on experimental errors or freak conditions: the adequacy of the paradigm itself is largely unquestioned. Only when there are many anomalies, or things that the existing paradigm can't explain, will the established paradigm change, as scientists begin to question their basic assumptions and produce a new paradigm – a revised set of theories – that explains research findings that cannot be fitted into the old paradigm.

In other words, scientific paradigms change radically only when a series of discoveries cannot be explained by the dominant paradigm, and there is in effect a scientific crisis. Kuhn therefore argues science changes, not through the gradual accumulation of research as hypotheses are tested and falsified as Popper suggests, but in dramatic leaps – what he calls 'scientific revolutions' – when one scientific paradigm breaks down and another comes along to take its place.

Because hypotheses and experiments to test them are fitted into the existing paradigm, it can be argued that scientific method and scientific knowledge are therefore socially constructed products, produced by the community of scientists in terms of agreed, taken-for-granted assumptions and methods.

> A **paradigm** is a framework of scientific laws, concepts, theories, methods and assumptions within which scientists operate, and which provides guidelines for the conduct of research and what counts as proper evidence.

Activity

Try to think of times in your own science lessons at school when you got the 'wrong' result. Did you immediately question the validity of the theory or just assume that you had, for example, a dirty test-tube or did something wrong? Did you investigate the new finding – or stick with the paradigm, and keep trying until you got the 'right' result?

Do scientists cheat? Reconstructed logic and logic-in-use

Much of the 'science debate' concerns the methods and procedures scientists should use and, indeed, claim to use. However, there may be a large gap between the methods scientists claim they use, and those they really do use. Kaplan (1973) suggested that scientists write up research using what he called *reconstructed logic* – the formal scientific method they are meant to use as scientists, and which is essential for the scientific community to accept their results as good science. However, in practice, scientists depart from these procedures, and the research process is much more haphazard, unsystematic and ad hoc (made up as they go along) than the ideal suggests. Kaplan calls this *logic-in-use*. There is, then, no guarantee that scientists will actually follow the rules of good scientific practice they might publicly claim to support. This is, in effect, a form of scientific cheating. Surveys show that only about one in four scientists is prepared to provide original data for checking by others, and this suggests there may be something to hide and that cheating is common in natural science.

One form of cheating is to keep re-running an experiment until the desired result is obtained, and then publish it, ignoring the failed experiments. Evidence suggests that only experiments that confirm hypotheses get written up, while the negative results are ignored. In 1998, the editor of the *British Medical Journal* said that only 5 per cent of published articles reached minimum standards of scientific soundness. Many clinical trials were too small to be relevant, and most of the published studies were the positive ones and a lot of negative evidence was being concealed.

There is little prestige or career progress to be gained by replicating (repeating) other scientists' work to check their findings, so scientific research is not really scrutinized as carefully as it should be. Acceptance of findings by the scientific community may therefore all too often be more an act of faith in scientific values than of scientific rigour.

Scientists may get things wrong, simply because the power of the paradigm may mean scientists focus on what they are looking for, and overlook or fail to see evidence which doesn't fit the paradigm. Sociologists may well face similar problems when they are trying to decide on the significance of observations and their interpretations of them.

Activity

Go to www.theguardian.com/science/series/badscience.
Examine one of the stories of dodgy so-called 'scientific' research there, and suggest three ways that scientists in effect cheat, and do not live up to their claimed scientific principles.

Social influences on the nature and direction of scientific research

There is a range of other factors that contribute to the social construction of scientific knowledge and undermine objectivity and introduce values into scientific research, which are summarized in figure 5.5, with some discussed in this section.

The values and beliefs of researchers will inevitably influence whether they think issues are important or unimportant and therefore worthy of studying or not. Scientists are professionals with careers and promotion prospects ahead of them, and they face a constant struggle to get money to fund their research. They therefore have an understandable desire to prove their own hypotheses right, and for their experiments to succeed. The desire for promotion may influence which topics are seen as useful to research, as will the current state of knowledge and what constitutes a cool or lucrative research area. The search for funding may determine which research is carried out and how it is approached. For example, as Marxists point out, research for military or defence purposes, or that helps private businesses to sell products and make profits, might attract funding more readily than research into help for disabled people. Government-backed research is likely to open more doors to researchers and produce more sponsorship than private individuals or small research departments are able to achieve by themselves. Objectivity may be limited by the institutional or funding constraints within which the scientist is working; for example, medical research on the effects of smoking funded by the tobacco industry, or research on genetically modified crops funded by the biotechnology industry. Publication of scientific papers is an important aspect of a scientific career, particularly in academic circles. Publishers' deadlines or the pressure to publish findings may mean that data are misrepresented, or that exhaustive experiments to attempt to falsify a hypothesis are not carried out. The availability of existing data on a topic, the practicality of and resources available for collecting data, and whether the subject matter is open to the use of certain methods or not will all influence what is researched.

All such influences on scientific research, summarized in figure 5.5, raise important questions about whether natural science, or indeed any research, lives up to its own supposedly objective scientific procedures. Science is itself a social product, produced within a set of agreed, taken-for-granted assumptions and methods (a paradigm). Evidence that doesn't fit the dominant paradigm may be dismissed or downgraded. This suggests that natural science, far from being the detached,

Figure 5.5 Social influences on scientific research

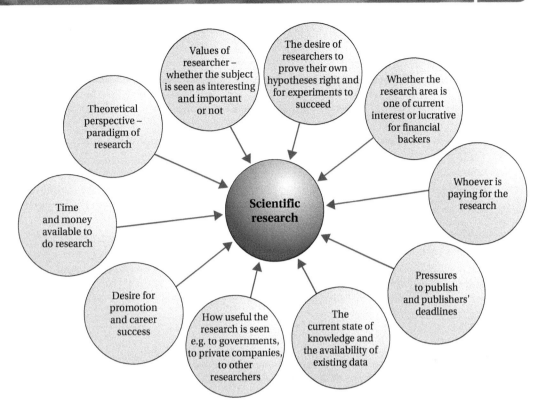

objective and rigorous process we are led to believe, is very much a social product created by the interpretations and values of the scientists themselves.

The discussion above suggests the positivists are perhaps exaggerating how objective and value-free the natural science model really is. The answer to those critics who accuse sociologists of sloppiness and question whether sociology is scientific, might well be 'Does natural science live up to its own criteria of objectivity and lack of bias?' In short, people in glasshouses shouldn't throw stones, as natural science and social research are equally vulnerable to the influences and biases summarized in figure 5.5.

Activity

Drawing on the material in the previous sections and figure 5.5:
1 Go through each of the points in figure 5.5 and explain briefly in each case how the factors identified might distort the objectivity and value freedom that is meant to be a feature of science, drawing on examples from both sociology and the natural sciences.
2 Identify and explain three reasons why scientific knowledge might be regarded as socially constructed.

Postmodernism, sociology and science

The debate in sociology between positivism and interpretivism over whether sociology can or should adopt the scientific method is largely dismissed by postmodernists as a pointless waste of time. Postmodernists take the view that:

1   Science is simply a metanarrative, another big theory claiming a monopoly of the truth, along-side similar social theories like Marxism and functionalism that seek to explain everything, with other ways of seeing the world regarded as inadequate and inferior.

2 There is a loss of faith in the modernist view that rational thinking and the application of scientific methods can control and improve the world. Science has failed, and has created problems like genetically modified foods, climate change, environmental pollution and antibiotic-resistant superbugs, leaving uncertainty and risk instead of solutions. Sociology has nothing to learn from copying from the natural sciences.

3 No sociological research of any kind provides a factual description of social life, and such research is a social construction created by sociological researchers. Concepts such as social structure, social class, gender and ethnicity are simply frameworks imposed on the world by sociologists, and have no meaning or existence separate from the interpretations of those sociologists.

4 It is pointless trying to find the social causes of behaviour. Social structures like class, ethnicity and gender have diminished in importance, and society has become fragmented into so many different groups, interests and lifestyles, all of which are constantly changing, that society is essentially chaotic. There is no longer anything called 'society' or 'a social structure', and there is only a mass of individuals making separate choices about their lifestyles. It is pointless to try to find the wider causes of their behaviour or even the construction of their meanings, as these will be specific to each individual.

5 Claims of objectivity and value freedom by scientists, which some sociologists seek to copy, are simply a pretence aimed at presenting their views as somehow superior to others, when all are equally valid, because all are just social constructions.

Is sociology a science? Some conclusions

The debate over whether sociology is or isn't, or can be or should be, a science raises a range of issues, which have been seen as important in sociology, even if postmodernists are rather dismissive of them. The question is whether sociology can be regarded as a science, to the extent that its findings should be taken at least as seriously as those in the natural sciences. There are at least four positions in this debate which have been discussed in this topic:

1 *Positivists* argue sociology should be a science, and can be if it searches for explanations by the study of social facts following as closely as possible the detached, objective, empirical and quantitative methods making up the scientific method found in the natural sciences;

2 *Interpretivists* argue sociology cannot be a science, because of the different nature of the social world, the unpredictability of human behaviour, and the need to explore people's subjective states of mind and the meanings they give to their actions;

3 *Realists* argue that both positivists and interpretivists have an incorrect understanding of what science is, and that science deals with both observable empirical data and hidden underlying structures. This suggests both positivism and interpretivism can be regarded as using scientific methods.

4 *Social constructionists, and postmodernists,* suggest that what counts as science is a product of a wide range of social influences, that scientists frequently don't live up to their own criteria of good science, and that there is no objective science or scientific method 'out there' which is somehow independent of the beliefs and activities of scientists themselves or the society of which they are a part.

It is most unlikely that sociological theory will ever be as accurate as a theory in physics, and those formed in the closed systems of laboratory experiments. We are not dealing with emotionless electrons but with people with consciousness, emotions, free will and values. Ultimately, whether sociology is or can be a science depends on what people define as a science in the first place. There are no clear-cut answers. In both the natural and social worlds, reputable researchers want to make sure they are testing hypotheses and producing statements or theories which are based on the best possible evidence available, whatever form that may take, and that the evidence they collect is valid, and not so manipulated, distorted or simply made up by researchers as to be completely worthless.

As long as sociologists *strive* to achieve objectivity and keep their personal values out of the research process, then sociologists of any perspective can justly claim that their work is no less objective or scientific than research which is carried out in the natural sciences. Sociology may then be regarded as scientific, regardless of the perspective used, as long as it strives to achieve the following five objectives.

1 *Value freedom*: the personal beliefs and prejudices of the researcher, while obviously affecting the topic chosen for study, are kept out of the research process itself, and not allowed to distort or manipulate data collection.
2 *Objectivity*: the sociologist approaches topics with an open mind, considering all the evidence in a detached and fair-minded way.
3 *The use of systematic research methods to collect evidence*, whatever perspective is used. For example, the use of careful sampling techniques and skilfully designed questionnaires in positivist survey research, or the careful recording of observations and interpretations in unstructured interviews or participant observation in interpretivist research.
4 *The careful analysis and evaluation of data and hypotheses in the light of evidence and logical argument*, and the use of evidence to support research and the conclusions drawn from it, rather than personal opinion or hearsay.
5 *Findings should be open to inspection, criticism, debate and testing by other researchers*, if necessary by replicating the research (carrying out the same or similar research again to check the findings of earlier research). This may be difficult with interpretivist research, such as participant observation, but even here the published findings and research notes should be open for other researchers to assess.

You should be aware that the 'rules' for rigorous scientific sociology discussed above, and particularly the issue of values, are themselves the subject of debate in sociology, and are considered in Topic 5.

Practice questions

1 Outline and explain **two** reasons why positivist sociologists suggest the methods and procedures of the natural sciences should be applied to the study of society. **(10 marks)**
2 Outline and explain **two** arguments for the view that sociology is a science. **(10 marks)**
3 Read **Item A** below and answer the question that follows.

Item A

Sociologists disagree about whether or not sociology can study society using similar scientific methods to those used by natural scientists, because of significant differences between the social and natural worlds. Some argue that whether or not sociology is a science depends on how science is defined, and point to the way the natural sciences are subject to similar social influences to those affecting sociology.

Applying material from **Item A** and your knowledge, evaluate the view that sociology is not, and cannot be, a science. **(20 marks)**

Topic 4

SPECIFICATION AREA

The relationship between theory and methods

> This topic links back to the various sociological methods and the influences on researchers' choice of topic and method which were considered during the first year of your A level course and Topic 1 on structuralist and social action theories, and Topic 3 on the debates over whether or not sociology can be a science in this chapter. You should refer back to these areas if necessary during this topic.

This topic is concerned with the way in which the theories sociologists hold influence the ways they go about researching society, and the different methods they use to collect data either to test their theories or to help in forming them. Tables 5.3 and 5.4 on pages 417 and 419 show the broad links which exist between the two different approaches of positivism and interpretivism, other wider theories of society identified with them, and the research methods most likely to be used, and you should use them for reference throughout this topic, and as a revision tool.

Positivism, interpretivism and research methods

As seen in the last topic, positivists and interpretivists have differing conceptions of the nature of society. For positivists, society has a reality external to individuals – there are social structures and social facts independent of the individual which exercise constraint over her or him and mould their behaviour. For interpretivists, society is a socially created set of meanings shared by a social group. As a result there are conflicting views and a basic disagreement about what counts as proper sociological research evidence, and different explanations and understandings of human behaviour.

Since they begin with different assumptions about the nature of society, positivist and interpretivist perspectives employ different research methods to gain knowledge about society.

Positivism and quantitative data

As seen in Topic 3, positivism holds to the position that social behaviour can be measured and explained objectively and can be and should be researched according to the same or similar principles and methods used in the natural sciences. This involves using the hypothetico-deductive model, whereby hypotheses or possible explanations for some social phenomena are formed, and then these are tested against observable (empirical), measurable data. Positivist research is therefore more likely to involve large-scale or macro research on large numbers of people, and is generally associated with structural theories of society, like those of Marxism and functionalism (discussed in Topic 1). This means they tend to record social facts, using *quantitative*, statistical techniques, including:

- The use of official statistics, like those on suicide, crime, or social class
- The experiment
- The comparative method
- Social surveys
- Structured questionnaires
- Formal/structured interviews
- Non-participant observation.

Table 5.3 A summary of the links between positivism, sociological theories and research methods

Key features	Explanation/comment
View of society	
Society is an objective reality, made up of social structures/social facts that exist independently of the individuals living in society.	Individuals are constrained/moulded by and react to external social forces and social structures that exist outside of them and cause their behaviour. The job of sociologists is to examine and measure these social-structural constraints, involving a macro or large-scale approach.
Theoretical perspective	
Structural theories, like functionalism and Marxism: how society moulds and controls individual behaviour.	Structural theories adopt a macro approach, studying the role of social institutions/social structures like the family, education, the law, religion, the media and the economy in shaping and moulding behaviour.
Methodological approach	
Positivist or scientific approaches.	Sociology can and should study society using similar methods and procedures to those used in the natural sciences. This may enable discovery of the causes of human behaviour, and predictions of future trends. Such methods include using the hypothetico-deductive model to test theories, and quantitative methods to collect empirical (observable) data to measure social facts.
Research methods used to collect data	
More *quantitative* (statistical) methods, applied with objectivity and detachment, to collect statistics on empirical (observable) data.	The use of standardized research methods and careful sampling techniques enables the collection of statistical data that is reliable (can be checked and replicated), and representative. This enables positivists to apply their findings to the whole of society and make generalized statements about the causes and effects of social activities.
Use of statistics, either collected by sociologists using surveys or existing official statistics, such as those on crime, suicide, health, unemployment or poverty.	The use of representative samples and quantitative methods, or large-scale official statistics collected nationally by government agencies, provide reliable quantitative data. *Interpretivists* reject the use of official statistics because they see them as socially and politically constructed and therefore as lacking validity. They are simply a record of official decision-making, labelling and interpretations, and political decisions about what statistics to collect and what not to collect, rather than objective social facts. For example, official suicide statistics are simply a record of decision-making and labelling by coroners.
Experimental method – controlled laboratory experiments, field experiments or the comparative method as an alternative.	Comparative method most likely to be used, as closest alternative to natural science laboratory method. This avoids problems of using the experimental method to study society, such as artificial conditions, ethical risks of harm to participants, practical difficulties of controlling variables in open systems, and small scale creating issues of representativeness and generalizability.
Large-scale sample surveys, using structured questionnaires and structured interviews.	These produce representative quantitative data on large numbers of people that is reliable – it can be checked and replicated (repeated). They involve personal detachment on the part of the researcher, and reduce risks of interviewer bias and promote objectivity. *Interpretivists* see detachment as not getting at what people really think, and structured questions risk the imposition problem, where the researcher imposes their framework and assumptions on those being researched.
Non-participant observation.	Retains detachment, and possible to collect quantitative data by categorizing observations. *Interpretivists* say data lack validity as researchers don't know what meanings and interpretations those being observed give to their behaviour.

Positivists regard such methods as valuable, as they provide quantitative empirical data, which, by using representative samples and survey techniques, can be generalized to the whole of society. They regard such data as *reliable*, as the findings can be checked and replicated (repeated) by other researchers using the same or similar methods. Such methods also involve objectivity and the personal detachment of researchers from those they study, and avoid the risk of personal values and prejudices influencing research. This is similar to what they claim is achieved by natural scientists using the scientific method. Positivists see such methods as producing the kind of data that enables the creation of cause-and-effect explanations of human behaviour, and of predictions of what might happen in similar circumstances in the future.

Criticisms of positivist approaches

The main criticisms of the positivist approach come from the interpretivist view discussed in table 5.4 and in the following section. Interpretivists suggest that the methods adopted by positivists do not produce a valid or true account of society, as they simply impose the researcher's own framework and assumptions on those being studied. For example, they decide what questions to ask (or not to ask), and give little opportunity for people to explain and elaborate about what they think and feel. The detachment of the researcher means they do not develop the empathy and closeness necessary to really understand the meanings and interpretations that people hold. They argue the statistics positivists produce through surveys are simply social constructions created by the categories and questions positivists themselves create. Official statistics, which positivists regard as factual information, are also seen by interpretivists as social constructions – simply a record of decision-making by officials, over what statistics to collect and not to collect, and how they categorize events. The classic example is suicide statistics, which interpretivists suggest are nothing more than a record of coroners' decision-making in classifying sudden unexplained deaths.

Interpretivism and qualitative data

Interpretivists are more concerned with understanding the meanings that individuals give to situations – how they see things and how these perceptions direct social action. They regard using the methods and procedures of the natural sciences as wholly inappropriate for the study of society, as society is fundamentally different from the natural world, and people's meanings and motivations cannot be measured or discovered by quantitative methods.

Interpretivists generally adopt an **inductive approach** to form theories, rather than the hypothetico-deductive method used by the positivists. This approach, instead of first forming a hypothesis and then testing it against the evidence as positivists do, is much more of an open-ended process. Theories emerge from the accumulation of insights, issues and evidence gained through research into the meanings and interpretations that people hold, providing the possibility of discovering ideas that those using the hypothetico-deductive method may not even have thought of. Glaser and Strauss (1999 [1967]) refer to theory arising from an inductive approach as **grounded theory**, as it is grounded in an analysis of data that have been collected.

Interpretivists generally adopt the *Verstehen* approach suggested by Weber – developing closeness and empathy with people to understand the world through their eyes, rather than the detachment preferred by the positivists. They therefore see a need to get personally involved with people, through deep conversations with them in unstructured interviews, by close observation, and participation in their activities, in order to understand how they see the world and the motives and meanings behind their actions. For example, interpretivist research on crime is less likely to use the positivist approach of looking for the *causes* of crime, but is more likely to study, as Becker did, how and why some behaviour becomes labelled as deviant while other similar behaviour does not, and how people respond to being labelled as deviant or criminal. Interpretivists are therefore more likely to use *qualitative* research methods, giving in-depth description of and insight into the attitudes, values, meanings, interpretations and feelings of individuals and groups. Interpretivists see close involvement with those they are studying as the only means of producing a valid (or truthful) understanding of society. Such methods involve small-scale or *micro* research on small numbers of people, associated with social action theories such as symbolic interactionism and ethnomethodology.

An **inductive approach** is one which develops theories on the basis of evidence that has been collected.

Grounded theory is theory that arises from (is grounded in) analysis of data that have been collected.

Table 5.4 A summary of the links between interpretivism, sociological theories and research methods

Key features	Explanation/comment
View of society	
Society is a social construction of meaning, that has no objective reality or existence independent of the meanings and interpretations people hold.	Individuals have free will and choice. They actively construct society through their social action, driven by the meanings and interpretations they give to their own behaviour and that of others. The job of sociologists is to understand these meanings and interpretations, involving a micro or small-scale approach.
Theoretical perspective	
Social action or interpretivist theories, like symbolic interactionism and ethnomethodology: how the action of individuals is based on the meanings they hold, and how they make sense of the world.	Social action theories adopt a micro approach, studying interaction between individuals in small groups to discover the meanings and motivations behind their actions and how these are created in the process of interaction.
Methodological approach	
Interpretivist approaches.	Society is fundamentally different from the natural world. Sociologists have to adopt *Verstehen* approaches that enable them to gain insight into people's motivations and meanings by seeing the world as they do, and building grounded theories using an inductive approach and qualitative data.
Research methods used to collect data	
More *qualitative* methods, aimed at achieving validity through involvement and empathy, to gain insight and understand meanings.	Qualitative methods enable greater understanding of people's meanings, interpretations and motives, and how these influence their behaviour. *Verstehen* sociology, with researchers putting themselves in the position of the person or group being studied, is the key to understanding social life.
Newspapers, autobiographies, personal diaries, letters and other personal documents, personal oral histories (people telling their own stories about the past).	The study of these can provide insights into people's personal views and opinions as told by the people themselves. So-called 'social facts' preferred by positivists, like official statistics, are social constructions. For example, official suicide statistics are simply a social construction, and interpretivists prefer to study coroners' decision-making to understand the rules they use to interpret sudden deaths and label them as suicides, and thereby create the official statistics.
Uncontrolled experiments, like some field experiments, and small-scale case studies of group interaction.	Field experiments, like those of Garfinkel (see page 385), enable the discovery of the meanings and assumptions people attach to everyday interaction; case studies can provide an in-depth account of social life from the point of view of those being researched.
Unstructured/semi-structured open-ended questionnaires and interviews, and group interviews and focus groups.	Involvement and closeness of the researcher with the researched help to provide valid, in-depth information. Building trust and empathy (*Verstehen*) and group interaction through focus groups and group interviews can draw out people's real thoughts and feelings and gain insights into what they really think, as they can express and develop answers in their own words. This helps to avoid the imposition problem in the structured questionnaires and interviews used by positivists. *Positivists* argue such small-scale research tends not to be representative. It is hard to replicate to check findings, and the closeness and involvement of the researcher with the researched can produce distorted, invalid findings generated by factors like interviewer bias.
Participant observation.	This enables *Verstehen* by fully immersing the researcher in the world of the researched. This produces highly valid, in-depth and detailed accounts of the world as seen by those being researched. *Positivists* see this closeness and involvement producing data that are not reliable, as it is hard to check findings, which depend on the researcher's interpretations of what they observe.

Interpretivist methods include

- The use of personal accounts and personal documents like diaries and letters
- Unstructured/semi-structured open-ended questionnaires
- Informal (unstructured/in-depth) interviews, focus groups and group interviews
- Small-scale case studies of group interaction
- Participant and (sometimes) non-participant observation.

Criticisms of interpretivist approaches

It is worth noting (particularly for exam questions) that just as the main criticisms of positivist methods come from the interpretivists, so the main criticisms of the interpretivists come from the positivists. The strengths of each approach are the weaknesses of the other.

Positivists generally criticize interpretivist research methods for their lack of reliability and the subjective nature of their findings. They suggest interpretivist research depends on the researcher's own interpretations of the meanings people hold, or of the answers they give. The close involvement of the researcher means that findings may be invalid (untruthful) because of interviewer bias, or the Hawthorne effect changing the behaviour of those being researched. It is often difficult for other sociologists to check the findings of interpretivist research or to repeat the research as it depends so much on the personal characteristics and skills of the researcher. The small scale of the research means it is not generalizable to the whole population, or even to other groups, and so is of limited use.

Feminist methodology

Feminist theories were considered in Topic 1, and you will recall that the main focus of these theories was the unequal position of women in societies, combined with a commitment to improve the lives of women. Feminist methods flow from these theories, and are concerned with the best methods for capturing the experiences of women.

Positivism: male bias and malestream methods

Feminist researchers have generally been critical of much quantitative positivist research in the past for several reasons.

1 *It ignored and excluded women and issues of concern to women.* Mies (1983) argues much positivist research has a masculine bias, and produces a male view of social life that ignores the experiences of women. For example, the examination of 'work' all too often refers to paid employment, and ignores the unpaid work that women do in the home. Oakley (1974) found this in her pioneering study of housework, which encountered opposition at first for not being regarded by some (male) sociologists as a serious topic worthy of sociological study.
2 *It simply treated women as appendages or insignificant extensions of men.* For example, Stanley and Wise (1993) suggest the findings from research on men are generalized to women, despite the different experiences and inequalities women face.
3 *It uses 'malestream methods' to research the experiences of women.* Westmarland (2001) cites the conduct of positivist structured interviews as an example of a 'malestream method'. These are conducted with distance and detachment between the interviewer and interviewee, and researchers do not reveal their feelings or views, and do not share their knowledge with the respondents. Oakley (1981a) regards such positivist methods as an aspect of the power relationships which she sees as a feature of malestream sociology. This is because such methods involve the researcher taking control of the research situation, in the sense of deciding what the important issues are, what questions to ask, what is worth (or not worth) talking about, and limiting the responses that can be given. Oakley argued that such approaches contradicted the aims of feminist research, which are concerned with encouraging women to open up and describe and share their experiences.

Feminists regard many positivist approaches as like smash-and-grab raids, where researchers burst upon the scene, grab the information they want as quickly as possible from their victims (respondents), offer nothing in exchange, and then move on to their next victim. The researcher has as little involvement as possible with those being researched, who probably have little or no idea of what the research is about, and have little opportunity to discuss or explain their answers, and are given little encouragement to open up and describe their experiences and discuss their lives.

Feminism and interpretivism

Because of the criticisms of positivist methods already described, feminist researchers have generally been more sympathetic to the use of interpretivist methods to research the lives of women, though they are more likely to develop more equal and intimate relationships with the women they are researching than is perhaps associated with the work of male interpretivists. Feminists emphasize the importance of warmth, co-operation, information sharing and empathy – *Verstehen* – to explore women's lives. This means using the more informal, open-ended methods associated with interpretivism, such as informal unstructured interviews, case studies of women's lives, group interviews/discussions, and oral histories in which women tell the story of their lives in their own words. Feminists argue these provide valid, in-depth accounts of women's lives, and may encourage women to open up about aspects of their lives they may otherwise be reluctant to talk about to dominating and detached sociology experts. Such areas might include domestic violence, sexual harassment at work, relationships with their partners or the experience of motherhood. Feminists argue such methods enable feminist theory to emerge from the research itself, rather than being imposed by the theoretical framework of the researcher, and feminist theory is therefore frequently a form of the grounded theory discussed earlier (see page 418).

An example of such an approach was adopted by Oakley (1981b) in her studies of first-time motherhood and the experience of becoming a mother in British society. She used informal, unstructured conversational interviews, involving two-way interaction, with a close and equal relationship with the mothers concerned. Oakley shared her own experiences of motherhood and offered advice to first-time mothers to help them overcome anxieties. By sharing her own experiences and feelings, Oakley was able to establish more equal relations with the mothers, and draw out their feelings, opinions and confidences, and produce valid and detailed information about the lives of women, which could be shared to improve their lives.

The feminist perspective and value commitment

It would be misleading to suggest that all feminists regard positivist research methods as inappropriate, and that only interpretivist methods can and should be used in feminist research. Westmarland suggests that positivist large-scale surveys and official statistics may be useful to discover the scale of problems. She points out, for example, that it is useful to know, via surveys and official statistics, that women are more likely to be raped by acquaintances and partners (88 per cent of rapes) than by strangers (12 per cent of rapes), and that only 6 per cent of rapes reported to the police result in a prosecution and conviction. However, she suggests statistical information like this is in itself inadequate, as feminists want to know how this affects the lives of women. She argues unstructured interviews are needed to fully understand what lies beneath quantitative statistical data, such as how women experience events and how these affect their lives, and to provide information that can promote social change and improve women's lives.

Westmarland argues that different feminist issues need different research methods, and that both positivist quantitative methods and interpretivist qualitative methods can be used as long as they are applied from a feminist perspective, and that there is no need for an 'us against them', quantitative versus qualitative divide. Westmarland suggests that many research methods can be adapted for feminist use, and supports the view of Kelly et al. that 'what makes feminist research feminist is less the method used, and more how it is used and what it is used for' (Kelly et al. (1992: 150), cited in Westmarland (2001)).

What really makes feminist approaches different from positivist and much interpretivist research is that there is nearly always a clear value commitment behind the research, and that is to improve the lives of women. For example, many of the interpretivist participant observation studies carried out by men do not seem to be associated with any desire to improve the lives of those they have been participating with. This issue of value commitment is discussed further in the next topic.

Is theory all that affects methods?

It is easy to get the impression that sociological research is divided into opposing camps, with positivists pursuing methods generating quantitative data, and interpretivists and feminists using methods generating qualitative data. The real world of practical research is somewhat more confused than this. While positivists might prefer more scientific, quantitative techniques, and interpretivists and feminists might prefer more qualitative methods, most sociologists will use a range of methods to collect different kinds of data, regardless of whether they are quantitative or qualitative. They will use whatever methods seem best suited and most practical for producing the fullest possible data to understand the subject being studied.

This use of a variety of methods is known as *methodological pluralism*, and is very useful for increasing sociological understanding of social life. Sociologists will also often use a variety of methods, and different types of data, to check that the results obtained by a particular method are valid and reliable. For example, positivists might conceivably use participant observation to check the accuracy or validity of statistical (quantitative) evidence collected by questionnaires in a survey, or to check whether people act as they said they did in an interview. Interpretivists might well use structured questionnaires to collect background data or to check whether their observations are valid. This approach of using a range of methods (usually two or three) to check findings is called *triangulation*.

The theoretical/methodological issues related to positivism, interpretivism and feminism considered in this topic will have important effects on:

- *How* something is investigated – the research *methods* sociologists choose to investigate and collect information about society
- *What* is studied – the choice of research *topic*.

The sociological perspective held by a researcher will influence not only how she or he investigates a topic, but also the research topic that she or he sees as important and interesting to study. Functionalists, for example, are likely to focus on those aspects which show how social institutions contribute to the maintenance of society as a whole, and their role in contributing to social stability. Marxists are more likely to emphasize inequality, conflict and division, and to investigate research topics which highlight these areas, and to emphasize class inequality, rather than, for example, ethnicity and gender. Feminists are concerned with issues of gender inequality and to discover women's experiences and to improve their lives, and this will guide their choice of research topic.

While such theoretical and methodological issues are major influences on the choice of research topic and research method(s), there are also practical and ethical considerations.

- *Practical issues* include things like funding, ease of access to the place or group being studied, time available, and whether the researcher has the personal skills and characteristics to carry out the research.
- *Ethical issues* include considerations like whether the research will have any harmful consequences, whether participants have given their *informed consent*, and whether research is reported accurately and honestly.

You should already be familiar with these issues from your first-year studies, but figure 5.6 provides a summary of some of the theoretical, practical and ethical influences on the choice of research topic and the methods used.

Figure 5.6
Influences on choices of research topic and method

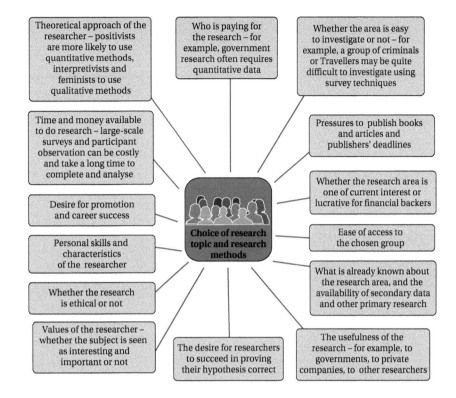

Theoretical approach of the researcher – positivists are more likely to use quantitative methods, interpretivists and feminists to use qualitative methods

Who is paying for the research – for example, government research often requires quantitative data

Whether the area is easy to investigate or not – for example, a group of criminals or Travellers may be quite difficult to investigate using survey techniques

Time and money available to do research – large-scale surveys and participant observation can be costly and take a long time to complete and analyse

Pressures to publish books and articles and publishers' deadlines

Desire for promotion and career success

Whether the research area is one of current interest or lucrative for financial backers

Personal skills and characteristics of the researcher

Ease of access to the chosen group

Whether the research is ethical or not

What is already known about the research area, and the availability of secondary data and other primary research

Values of the researcher – whether the subject is seen as interesting and important or not

The desire for researchers to succeed in proving their hypothesis correct

The usefulness of the research – for example, to governments, to private companies, to other researchers

Choice of research topic and research methods

Activity

Consider the following topic area:

Women's experiences of working both inside the home (housework and childcare (domestic labour)) and in paid employment

1 Outline:
   a) A hypothesis that positivists might wish to test, and what method(s) they might use.
   b) A question that interpretivists might wish to explore and what method(s) they might use.
   c) How feminists researchers might explore this issue, and the methods they might use. Give reasons for your answers in each case.
2 In each case, explain how *valid* and *reliable* the research by these different methods might be, giving your reasons.

   Refer to figure 5.6, and the research topic considered in question 1.
3 Outline two ways in which sources of funding for research might influence the research.
4 Outline two ways in which the personal skills and characteristics of the researcher may influence the research.
5 List three practical considerations that might influence whether or not a researcher chose to investigate this topic.
6 Outline two ethical issues that might influence the researcher's choice of research method in this area.

Practice questions

1   Outline and explain **two** advantages of using quantitative (statistical) data in sociological research. **(10 marks)**

2   Outline and explain **two** reasons why positivist research methods may not provide a valid (or true) understanding of society. **(10 marks)**

3   Read **Item A** below and answer the question that follows.

Item A

The theoretical and methodological perspectives held by sociologists, such as whether they are functionalists, Marxists or feminists, or positivists or interpretivists, will have important influences on their choice of topics for research and the research methods they use to investigate them. However, their research is also influenced by a series of important practical and ethical considerations.

Applying material from **Item A** and your knowledge, evaluate the view that sociologists' choice of research topics and the methods they use to investigate them are primarily based on practical considerations. **(20 marks)**

Topic 5

SPECIFICATION AREA

Debates about subjectivity, objectivity and value freedom

Subjectivity, objectivity and values in sociology

Subjectivity

Subjectivity is the idea that sociologists are part of the society they are studying, and therefore involved in what they are researching and that their own values and beliefs will affect the research in some way; it is therefore impossible for them to be completely objective and detached. Sociologists are routinely involved in making choices about the things they are researching, and there are always some elements of personal judgement and interpretation in any research. Subjectivity is most commonly associated with interpretivists and feminists, who believe that it is necessary to have interaction, personal involvement and closeness to those being studied in order to fully understand the meanings and interpretations they hold, and the collection of qualitative data inevitably involves a subjective dimension of selection and interpretation.

Objectivity

Objectivity is generally taken to mean that researchers approach topics with a totally open mind and with complete detachment, separation and distance from those being researched. The research process and findings remain completely independent of, and uninfluenced by, subjective influences such as the personal feelings, prejudices, opinions, beliefs, values or interpretations of researchers. Research should provide completely unbiased knowledge about the world, and the researcher simply collects data which are totally external to their own views. Objectivity has generally been associated with positivism and the use of quantitative scientific methods in sociological research, and was considered in Topics 3 and 4 on sociology and science, and the links between theory and methods.

Objectivity and subjectivity are often seen as two extremes, but the following sections will suggest that all research, including natural science research, is influenced by subjective elements and values to a greater or lesser extent. Subjectivity and objectivity should therefore be seen not as an either/or situation, but as a continuum: a line with two very different extremes at either end, but with each in-between stage having only small differences between them. Much sociology falls in a mid-position between the two extremes, as shown in figure 5.7.

Values in sociology

There has been a long-running debate in sociology about whether it is possible or desirable for sociologists to study society in a completely value-free, objective way, or whether there is inevitably subjectivity involved, with the researcher's values influencing research. There are three main competing positions adopted by sociologists in the 'values debate':

1 That sociology should be and can be value-free
2 That sociology cannot be value-free
3 That sociology should not be value-free, even if it were possible.

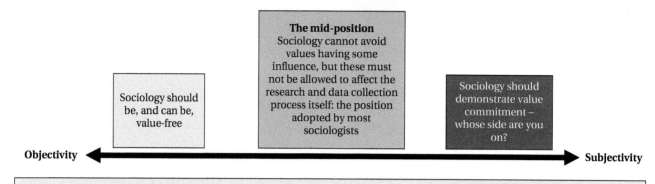

Figure 5.7 Subjectivity, objectivity and the values debate

There is a further position in this discussion taken by postmodernists, who basically dismiss the whole subjectivity/objectivity and values debate as pointless and meaningless, as they see all knowledge as relative and value-laden anyway.

This continuum between subjectivity and objectivity, and the various positions in the 'values debate' are illustrated in figure 5.7.

A value-free sociology is desirable and possible

Sociology should be value-free

When sociology was being established as a subject, positivists like Comte and Durkheim were concerned to show that it was possible to study society objectively in the same way as scientists studied the natural world, untainted by personal values, and thereby to establish sociology as a science in the same way as the natural sciences. They thought sociology *should* be value-free in order to give the subject the status and authority that would enable it to be regarded as a source of impartial, objective information, in the same way as the natural sciences were. Such an objective, value-free sociology could then provide the facts that might be used to influence social policy and improve the world.

Sociology can be value-free

Positivists like Comte and Durkheim believed that not only *should* sociology be value-free, but that it *could* be objective and value-free so long as it used similar methods to those used in the natural sciences, as discussed in Topic 3. They believed society was made up of social structures and social facts that existed independently of researchers and these facts could be clearly separated from the values of the researcher, and studied in the same detached and objective way as natural scientists studied the natural world, in subjects like physics and chemistry. Through the study of social facts and the collection of empirical quantitative data using the hypothetico-deductive scientific method (see pages 404–5), it was possible to test theories using reliable and valid data, which could be checked/replicated by other researchers, establish the causes of social behaviour, uncover the laws of human society, and make predictions. This is what Durkheim sought to do in his study of suicide using official suicide statistics, and that Marx did in his studies of capitalism, which led him to believe in the inevitability of communism. Since the collection of facts could be wholly separated from the subjective views and values of researchers (assuming they didn't cheat or distort or fiddle with the data), sociology could become an unbiased, objective, value-free science of society.

A value-free sociology is not possible: the myth of value-freedom

It is impossible for any natural or social scientist to avoid the influence of values completely. For example, their academic training, the paradigm or perspective they have learnt for interpreting and evaluating evidence, their assumptions about society, and their beliefs about what are important or unimportant areas to study are all sources of values. Sociological research – like research in the natural sciences – does not consist of facts that 'speak for themselves'. 'Facts', whether they take quantitative or qualitative forms, are not meaningful in themselves. For example, untrained observers looking at an X-ray picture will see only meaningless blotches and shadows, and will have difficulty in making sense of what they see because they lack the theoretical background and training. Radiologists, however, can make sense of the X-ray as they have the theoretical training to do so. In sociology, participant observers must have some framework for identifying what they should look at and for interpreting the significance of what they see. Without a theoretical framework, it is impossible to know what to observe, or what research methods to use, or to make sense of what is observed. These depend on the theoretical assumptions and interpretations of the researcher.

The assumptions of positivists and interpretivists as a source of values

Sociological investigation is ultimately based on researchers' assumptions – their subjective assumptions – about the nature of people in society. Positivists, for example, believe society exists as an objective reality, with social structures moulding and constraining individual behaviour. This leads positivists to search for the causes of social behaviour by the collection of quantitative data which they regard as reliable because it is untainted by the values of the researcher and can be replicated and checked by other researchers. In contrast, interpretivists believe society is socially constructed by the actions of individuals, who act in the ways they do because of the meanings and interpretations they give to their behaviour. The only way of discovering these meanings and producing valid data is to collect qualitative data through close involvement with those being researched, and by a process of subjective interpretation of what those meanings and interpretations are.

The facts never speak for themselves, and only become meaningful because people apply their understandings and interpretations to them, and make judgements about what they see. Everyone will see the same X-ray picture, but only some people will be able to understand and interpret what they see.

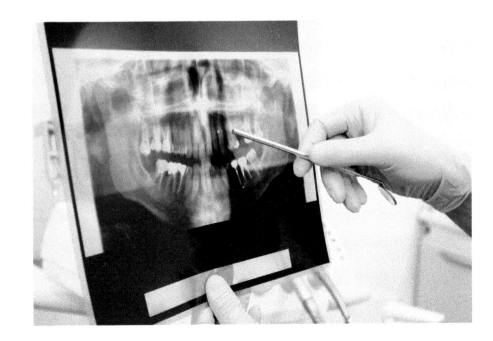

Is the wine bottle half-full or half-empty? Such difficulties in interpretation affect both natural and social science.

Consider, for example, the differing assumptions underlying the analysis of suicide. Positivists look at the social facts which constrain individuals and make some more vulnerable to suicide than others, while interpretivists are more likely to examine the process by which some sudden, unnatural deaths come to be labelled as suicide while others do not.

The different assumptions of sociologists – subjective value judgements – guide the selection of what is regarded as a worthwhile topic or problem for investigation, the questions to be asked or explored, the research methods employed, what types of data (quantitative or qualitative) are collected, and what information is interpreted and selected as 'significant' and 'important' (and what isn't).

Other sources of values

The personal prejudices and political views of the researcher may influence the selection of the subjects studied. For example, feminist sociologists, who are concerned with the male dominance of sociology ('malestream' sociology) and the unequal position of women in a patriarchal society, are likely to study subjects that highlight these inequalities. Marxist sociologists will begin with a conception that society is fundamentally class-divided and in social conflict, and investigate issues with a view to highlighting evidence of exploitation and the need for social change. Functionalists, such as Durkheim and Parsons, begin with an assumption that society is fundamentally based on harmony and consensus, and investigate issues which highlight this consensus and threats to it. Durkheim and Comte, from the very beginnings of sociology, and most contemporary functionalists, Marxists and feminists take the view that sociological research is worth doing because it provides a means for what they see as improving society in some way and resolving social problems. All these involve values to some extent, and they are unavoidable.

In both the natural and social sciences, there are a wide range of other factors that introduce subjectivity and values into *all* research, as seen in Topics 3 (see pages 409–15) and 4 (see pages 422–3), so it is simply not possible for sociology to be value-free, even if that was desirable, and value-freedom is therefore a myth.

A value-free sociology is not desirable: the need for value-commitment

The preceding section suggested that sociological research cannot avoid some influence from values. However, other sociologists have posed the question differently – even if a value-free sociology were possible, would it actually be desirable?

IF YOU ARE NEUTRAL IN SITUATIONS OF INJUSTICE, YOU HAVE CHOSEN THE SIDE OF THE OPPRESSOR. ARCHBISHOP DESMOND TUTU

OCCUPY   OCCUPYWALLST.ORG   TWITTER: #OWS   OCCUPYSTUDENTDEBT.COM

OCCUPYDESIGN.ORG

Should sociologists wash their hands of all moral responsibility for their work? Is there such a thing as being neutral and value-free in an unequal society? Should sociologists take sides when they do their research?

Value freedom as ideology

Gouldner (1962, 1971) argues that it is not possible to be free from value judgements in sociology, for the kinds of reasons discussed in the previous section. But he goes further and suggests that value-freedom is itself a value-laden concept. It is, he argues, little more than a convenient ideology that serves the career interests of sociologists who will take funding from anyone and sell their research to the highest bidders, and avoid taking any moral responsibility for the uses or consequences of their research. Those clinging to the ideology of value-freedom have sold out to the establishment to protect their careers by refusing to take a stand and criticize society as it is and those with power within it. For example, if you were observing a fight between a large bully and a small victim, would you really be neutral and value-free if you stood aside and let the victim get beaten up? Or would your supposed neutrality really be supporting the bully and more concerned with self-preservation than neutrality?

Gouldner argues that pretending to be value-free and not taking sides supports the powerful in an unequal society. Can you and should you be neutral when you are studying the poorest and most disadvantaged people in society? Or should you be applying your research skills to help them to escape their poverty and to tackle social exclusion? Can you avoid taking moral responsibility for your work?

Gouldner's argument is that sociologists should not even try to be value-free, but that there should be a clear value-commitment in sociology, with a public responsibility for – and value-commitment to – improving the lives of the downtrodden, the exploited and the oppressed in an unequal society, and taking their sides against the powerful groups in society who are the sources of their oppression.

Whose side are you on?

Becker (1967) echoed Gouldner's argument when he challenged sociologists to ask themselves the question 'Whose side are we on?' Becker argues no knowledge is value-free, and all knowledge must favour somebody, and therefore we have to choose whom to favour. Sociologists should be committed to social change for human improvement and take responsibility for the moral implications and uses of their work. In other words, they should abandon any idea of value-freedom. This does not mean that such sociological work is any less 'scientific' than any other research, but that the choice of research area is committed to a particular value position. Becker's own research reflected this, as it was clearly aimed at understanding how some people became labelled as 'outsiders' (such as criminals, misfits, the mentally ill and the poor) by those with power (see pages 384 and 459–63 for a discussion of labelling theory). Such a view of sociology involves siding with the underdogs in society, seeing what life is like from their points of view, and giving society's deprived and other outsiders a voice through such research, and thereby hopefully leading to social change.

From this perspective, research should not be neutral, but ought to be driven by a desire to change and improve the world for the most disadvantaged. This value-committed position is the one that has been taken by many feminists and Marxists. Many feminists, for example, see their research as driven by a desire to challenge patriarchy, to fight against male oppression and to improve the position and lives of women and achieve equality with men. It is this value-commitment that has enabled feminist research to increase awareness of gender inequalities, to expose and challenge social institutions, social policies and practices that discriminate against women, to promote more positive images of women, and to raise the status and perception of women in society.

Marxist sociologists have taken similar positions, with a clear value-commitment to exposing the structures of social class inequality, exploitation and conflict in capitalist society, and the power and privilege of the dominant class, with a view to destroying them. Marx himself demonstrated such clear value-commitment when he wrote, as long ago as 1845, that 'The philosophers have only interpreted the world in various ways; the point is to change it.'

Postmodernism and the values debate

Postmodernists like Lyotard (1984) and Baudrillard (2001) suggest the subjectivity/objectivity and value-freedom debate simply reflects the values and assumptions of competing sociologists. Postmodernists say there is no objective truth, and all forms of knowledge are social constructions, all involve values, none are more objective or valuable than others, and all are equally valid. The assertion of the importance of value-free knowledge is simply an attempt by some groups who may have more power than others to establish their interpretation as the only true or valid approach to studying society. Sociology, whether or not it claims to be value-free, is just another metanarrative claiming its knowledge and understanding of the world is better than other forms of knowledge.

Conclusion: dealing with values in social research

As discussed above, sociology can't be completely value-free, and most sociologists will have political views about society, such as about the extent of inequality, and the need for social change and how it should be achieved. Nonetheless, all sociologists, whatever their theoretical or methodological perspective, would agree that they should *strive* to produce research evidence that provides the fullest, most reliable and most valid explanations of social life. No reputable sociologist would wish to produce research that is so manipulated and distorted by their own political beliefs and personal values – for example by concealing data that they disagree with – that it is little better than poorly researched, value-laden and politically loaded tabloid journalism. Research data that were selectively collected and manipulated to justify and promote the political beliefs of the researcher are unlikely to be taken seriously either by fellow sociologists, or by policy makers whom sociologists might be trying to influence.

The fact that sociology can't escape the influence of values, just as natural science can't, does not mean that it is completely value-laden and worthless. The key issue is the extent to which these values are allowed to influence the actual research and data collection process. There are three ways that we can accept the existence of values in sociology, and still produce valid and/or reliable data.

1   *Values can't (and some would say shouldn't) be avoided when choosing the topic to research, but values and personal prejudices should never be allowed to enter the research process itself or allowed to distort or manipulate data collection.* Weber argued the topic chosen for research is bound to reflect what the sociologist thinks important and relevant, and also the values of those funding the research. But once these value judgements have been made, sociologists should tackle research with an open mind and consider all the evidence in a detached and fair-minded way. Evidence should be collected using systematic research methods, whatever perspective is used – for example, the use of careful sampling techniques and skilfully designed questionnaires in positivist survey research, or the careful recording of observations

and interpretations in unstructured interviews or participant observation in interpretivist research. Any conclusions reached should be based on this evidence, not on personal values.

2 *Values and personal prejudices should be considered when examining the ethics of research.* For example, what should researchers do if they come across serious crime like murder or armed robbery in their research, or offences like child abuse or paedophilia? Should they shop the respondents to whom they have promised confidentiality? Should they publish data likely to harm those researched? These ethical considerations ultimately rest on the moral values of researchers, but they should properly be considered as part of sociological research. Sociologists have to take some responsibility for avoiding harm caused by their research.

3 *Findings should be open to inspection, criticism, debate and testing by other researchers.* Weber emphasized researchers should be open and clear about their own values, so any personal biases, or distortion and manipulation of results as a result of these values, even if unintended, can be checked by others who scrutinize their work. This may be achieved, for example, by scrutinizing the methodology used, replicating the research (carrying out the same or similar research again to check the findings of earlier research) in positivist research, or examining interview transcripts or research notes in interpretivist research.

Activity

Imagine you were an advisor to a researcher about to start a study of child poverty. You know this researcher holds very strong beliefs that child poverty is due to inadequate parents and parenting. What advice would you give the researcher to ensure that the research findings are not simply seen as a reflection of her or his values?

Practice questions

1 Outline and explain **two** ways in which a sociologist's subjective beliefs and values may influence sociological research. **(10 marks)**

2 Outline and explain **two** arguments for the view that sociological research should *not* be value-free. **(10 marks)**

3 Read **Item A** below and answer the question that follows.

> **Item A**
> Some argue that it is possible and desirable for sociologists to study society in a completely value-free, objective way. Others suggest that sociologists cannot avoid the influence of values completely, and it is therefore impossible for them to conduct value-free research. A third position is that sociology should not be value-free, even if it were possible, and research should involve a value commitment to improve the lives of the disadvantaged.

Applying material from **Item A** and your knowledge, evaluate the view that value-freedom is an ideal to strive for in sociology, but is impossible to achieve. **(20 marks)**

Topic 6

SPECIFICATION AREA

The relationship between sociology and social policy

Sociology, social policy and social problems

Social policy refers to the packages of plans and actions adopted by national and local government or various voluntary agencies to solve social problems or achieve other goals that are seen as important. A **social problem** is something that is seen as being harmful to society in some way, causing, as Worsley (1978) put it, public friction and/or private misery, that needs some collective action to solve it. This 'collective action' to reduce social problems involves that raft of social policies implemented through the services governments provide and the measures they take to achieve goals which have an impact on the life chances and welfare of citizens, such as those concerned with health, housing, employment, social care, education, crime and transport.

Social problems and sociological problems

Sometimes social problems are confused with sociological problems, but they are not the same things. A **sociological problem** is any social or theoretical issue that needs explaining, whether it is a social problem or not. For example, the huge improvement in the achievement of girls in education might need explaining, but it is not a social problem. However, all social problems are sociological problems.

Research by sociologists has shown that many social problems, like ill-health, obesity, crime, poverty and educational failure, have social explanations and are created by wider social factors rather than simply the behaviour of individuals, and they need social policy solutions to tackle them. Such research has enabled sociology to make major contributions to the formation of social policies adopted by national and local government or various voluntary agencies.

The contribution of sociology to social policy

Governments are more likely to produce social policies that are effective and work as intended if they base them on proper evidence gained through research. The work of sociologists in areas such as education, health, poverty and crime has had quite important effects on the social policies of governments, and often government will commission research from academics in universities to assist policy-making. There are also a number of bodies which are specifically concerned with social policy research within which sociologists work. For example, the Institute of Public Policy Research (www.ippr.org) and the Joseph Rowntree Foundation (www.jrf.org.uk) are both concerned with research to feed into the formation of social policy.

Social policy refers to the packages of plans and actions adopted by national and local government or various voluntary agencies to solve social problems or achieve other goals that are seen as important.

A **social problem** is something that is seen as being harmful to society in some way, and needs something doing to sort it out.

A **sociological problem** is any social or theoretical issue that needs explaining.

Activity

Go to www.jrf.org.uk and:
1 Identify three pieces of social policy research the Joseph Rowntree Foundation is currently involved with.
2 Explore one of these pieces of research. Identify the aims, the sociological research methods used, the conclusions reached and how you think the research might influence government policy.

Nine ways sociology contributes to social policy

Giddens (2006) suggests a number of ways that 'sociology can help us in our lives', and his ideas are incorporated into the following discussion of nine ways that sociology can contribute to the formulation of social policy.

1 Providing an awareness of cultural differences

Seeing society from different perspectives, and developing an 'informed awareness' of and sensitivity to the ways of life, needs and problems of others helps policy makers to tailor policies more effectively – such insight is provided by, for example, research on ethnicity or disability.

2 Providing self-awareness and understanding

Sociology develops a knowledge and understanding of ourselves, why we behave as we do, and our position within society. There is a growing reflexivity in late modernity, which was discussed in terms of Giddens and Beck earlier in this chapter (see pages 401–2); sociological research can enable individuals and groups to develop self-awareness and understanding of their positions in society by reflecting on it. Reflecting on experiences like racism, domestic violence, sex discrimination, and prejudice and discrimination arising from disability can have the effect of empowering people to change their lives. This can encourage people to form support and pressure groups with those facing similar experiences. Such groups are often concerned with criticizing the inadequacies of existing social policies, forming new ones to address their needs with evidence to support them, and exerting pressure on government to implement them. Late modernity has seen the development of a wide range of new social movements and self-help groups which demand new policies from governments to meet their needs, such as disability and gay rights, environmental changes, and equal opportunity, anti-racist, anti-ageist, and anti-sexist policies.

3 Changing assumptions

McNeill (1986) suggests social research can indirectly influence social policy by being absorbed into the taken-for-granted common-sense assumptions involved in society's dominant culture. This can make government social policies seem either reasonable and acceptable, or subjects of ridicule. For example, social policies aimed at tackling the problem of crime by locking up everyone with a specific body type, on the grounds they were more prone to criminality, would face ridicule, while one based on the provision of social facilities for young people to divert them from crime might be seen as more reasonable and sensible.

4 Providing a theoretical framework

Sociology can often provide a theoretical framework for social policies adopted by governments. Between 1979 and 1992, the Conservative governments were strongly influenced by the New Right ideas of Charles Murray (1984), whose views about poverty and the undeserving workshy welfare-dependent underclass provided a basis for savage cuts in welfare benefits and welfare state funding and attacks on the poor throughout the 1980s. This was combined with a prime minister, Margaret Thatcher, who had a contempt for most sociology and sociological research, reflecting her almost postmodern view that 'there is no such thing as society. There are individual men and women, and there are families' (Margaret Thatcher, in an interview with *Woman's Own* magazine, 31 October 1987). Such a New Right-inspired policy framework resurfaced in the Conservative-led coalition government after 2010, which again reinstated attacks on welfare benefits based on the idea of the workshy underclass.

By contrast, the New Labour government of 1997–2010 was led for ten years by a prime minister who was a fan of sociologist Anthony Giddens. In his book *The Third Way* (1998), Giddens provided the theoretical basis for new social policies based around building social cohesion and social solidarity, and reducing social problems posing threats to social order. These were implemented by the Labour Government in the late 1990s and the early years of the twenty-first century, and included welfare, health and education policies which were more supportive of the most disadvantaged in society, and policies to tackle social exclusion, including the national minimum wage to reduce poverty. Similar theoretical frameworks have been provided by Townsend's work on poverty, which helped to establish the concept of relative poverty, and Left and Right Realism, which both had important influences on crime policy (see pages 464–9 and 532–7 in chapter 6).

5 Providing practical professional knowledge

Sociologists are not just academics working in universities or sociology teachers. They work in a wide range of other occupations, such as town planning, social work, journalism, human resource management, and in the civil service. All of these can provide professional inputs as social policy is formed in a range of areas. Journalism, for example, has an important role in setting the agenda for publicly acceptable social policies. Sociologists are also employed as civil servants in government departments like the Departments for Work and Pensions and the Home Office, where they play a direct role in shaping and evaluating policy. For example, it was researchers in the Home Office who helped to improve the validity of crime statistics by the development of the British Crime Survey (now called the Crime Survey for England and Wales). Such researchers are constantly involved in both commissioning and carrying out research, and briefing the media, MPs and government ministers about the effectiveness of social policies.

6 Identifying social problems

Sociologists, particularly academics who are not locked into applied research for very specific already-identified policy purposes, can do some 'blue sky' thinking, peering into the future, and can ask questions and identify social problems that arise from more open sociological thinking. Sociological ideas can also help shape policy by showing that social problems have wider structural causes beyond the behaviour of individuals, as shown by sociological research on poverty and crime.

Many social problems have been identified by the work of sociologists. Feminist sociologists have carried out a great deal of theoretical and practical research revealing the nature and extent of inequalities and discrimination against women in areas such as pay and employment, and suggesting solutions to them. This has fed into legal changes such as the Sex Discrimination, Equal Pay and Equality Acts. In the UK, poverty research by Townsend (1979), as well as that carried out by the Joseph Rowntree Foundation, has exposed the extent of poverty, and the *Black Report* of 1980 revealed the huge inequalities in health. Similar examples are research highlighting the continuing problems of racism, and studies of attacks on and harassment of gays.

7 Providing the evidence

This is the most obvious form of input, as sociologists are frequently those who do the surveys, collect the statistics, analyse the problems, suggest explanations and so on, which policy makers can then draw on to form evidence-based policies. The use of research evidence can guide practice and decision-making, and often provide some assurance that policies will work as intended.

8 Identifying the unintended consequences of policies

Sociological research can evaluate existing policies, to see if they have any unintended consequences, such as the latent functions or dysfunctions discussed by Merton on page 373. For example, have policies aimed at reducing crime in a community simply displaced it to other areas or onto more vulnerable targets?

9 Assessing the results

Sociological research can help to establish whether policies have worked, whether they achieved what they set out to, and whether they need changing or scrapping.

Influences on social policy-making

The previous section suggests a range of ways sociology might influence social policies. However, it would be naive to think that social policies were formed purely on the basis of evidence, with sociologists producing clear research reports, documenting the evidence of social problems, identifying explanations for them, and making policy recommendations to governments which were then accepted and implemented. This rarely happens. Part of the explanation for this lies in the nature of sociology and the multidimensional, changing and slippery causes of social phenomena which have been discussed throughout this chapter. Sociological research therefore rarely produces clear-cut explanations and solutions, such as those that natural scientists generally can when they identify the causes of disease and means of preventing it. Crime, for example, has been a social problem from time immemorial, and has probably been the subject of more social research than any other social area. Every new government rehearses old arguments, commissions more research, and draws up new or recycled policies to defeat crime, but still it continues. It is this complex nature of social explanation that makes it relatively easy for governments to choose to ignore research, or elements of it that do not conform to their preconceptions.

The politics of social policy-making

The process of social policy formation involves something much more complex than simply looking at the evidence produced by sociologists and acting on it. Governments may not be able to afford to implement social policies, or may have to make financial savings which can actually generate social problems rather than solve them, such as cutting welfare benefits which produces social problems like hardship, family breakdown and homelessness as a consequence. Government policy-making has to take into account wider global issues, such as membership of the European Union, which means governments can't adopt just any policy they like if it is in breach of European Union law or other commitments.

Governments can, and frequently do, choose to ignore evidence when they form policy, or only use research selectively to justify social policies which are driven by their political ideologies rather than by hard research evidence. Policy advice to political parties and governments is often provided by research institutes ('think tanks') which are broadly politically aligned, such as Demos and the Institute for Public Policy Research which are generally more sympathetic to Labour Party approaches to social policy, and the Centre for Social Justice and Policy Exchange which are closer to Conservative Party policies. Such think tanks will often provide evidence that supports the ideological and political preferences of governments and political parties.

Whether policy advice is accepted by governments or political parties will also be influenced by their desire to win elections, and if a policy – no matter how sound the evidence might be – is unlikely to be popular with the public, then it stands less chance of being adopted. Toynbee (2012) cites the example of crime – she argues that there is little evidence that putting more criminals in prison lowers crime rates, and the Ministry of Justice's own research suggests that prison cuts crime so little that it hardly justifies the money it costs to lock up prisoners. Toynbee points out that cries by politicians for more police on the beat to cut crime ignores the fact that each police officer on the beat will only come within 100 metres of a crime once every eight years – and then probably won't see it. Yet politicians ignore such evidence, and call for tougher measures on crime, more police and more imprisonment, even when crime rates are falling. They ignore more effective policies for reducing crime, like policies to stop people offending in the first place, because calls for more police and more imprisonment are what works with the voters.

McNeill (1986) suggests that what becomes defined as a social problem will depend on individuals or groups being able to whip up enough support among those with power to make their concerns or interests an issue for public debate and public action.

Davies (2008) points out that debates about social policy do not take place in a vacuum, but have an ideological basis to them, and depend on current public and other perceptions of the problem or issue. For example, if governments or others with power consider something to be morally offensive in some way, like prostitution, or politically sensitive and unlikely to be popular with the electorate, like the decriminalization of cannabis use, they may, when formulating policy, ignore evidence that doesn't fit their preconceptions.

Davies cites the findings of the Parliamentary Science and Technology Select Committee (*Guardian*, 8 November 2006), showing that the government often misused or distorted scientific

research to justify policy decisions that were really based on ideological or social grounds. The findings suggested that the government hid behind a fig-leaf of scientific respectability to make controversial policies more acceptable to voters. The investigation highlighted several examples of misuse of research, including evidence from a criminologist at Keele University, who told the committee that his work on crime statistics had been given a different interpretation by the Home Office for political reasons. Two examples illustrating this are policies on prostitution and cannabis.

Social policies on prostitution and cannabis are both examples of where expert advice based on research evidence has been ignored by government.

Prostitution

Davies found the government's Coordinated Prostitution Strategy of 2006 was highly selective in its use of social research in order to bolster support for its own hostile view of prostitution. Davies argued that, while the government didn't ignore social research in formulating its prostitution policy, it did ignore, dismiss or misrepresent research that might undermine its policy. In particular, the government ignored:

- Research on prostitutes' clients, which showed they were fairly typical men, and not the violent and abusive stereotypes assumed in the strategy
- Evidence from Sweden that undermined their own strategy
- The effectiveness of alternative approaches adopted in other countries.

Cannabis

The government decided in May 2008 to reclassify the legal status of cannabis from a Class C (less harmful) to a Class B (more harmful) drug, reversing its own policy of downgrading the drug from Class B to Class C in January 2004. It did this despite advice from its own scientific advisors, the Advisory Council on the Misuse of Drugs, that such a reclassification was not necessary and would not have the desired effect in curbing cannabis use (this advice was repeated in a further report by the independent UK Drug Policy Commission (2012), based on a six-year study of Britain's drug laws, which said that no serious rise in consumption was likely if possession of small amounts of controlled drugs were allowed). The reasons given for the reclassification were that the government had to take into consideration public perceptions, the health of children, and the pressures on policing. This was despite evidence that cannabis use among young people had fallen from 13.4 per cent to 9.4 per cent since downgrading to category C, so there were declining risks to health and less demands on policing. This policy of reclassification, then, was based not on any kind of research evidence, but was about giving a message to young people that this was not a safe drug to take.

McNeill points out much sociological work is ignored by governments and others with power because sociology often concerns itself with politically sensitive issues like social inequalities and

Figure 5.8
Influences on the formation of social policy

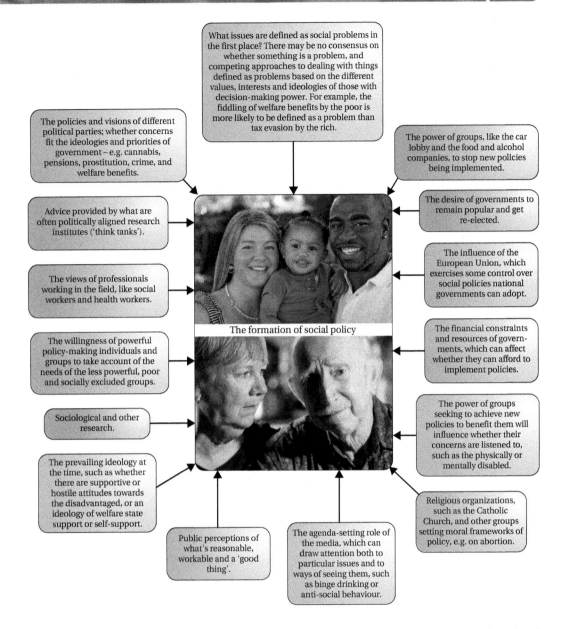

What issues are defined as social problems in the first place? There may be no consensus on whether something is a problem, and competing approaches to dealing with things defined as problems based on the different values, interests and ideologies of those with decision-making power. For example, the fiddling of welfare benefits by the poor is more likely to be defined as a problem than tax evasion by the rich.

The policies and visions of different political parties; whether concerns fit the ideologies and priorities of government – e.g. cannabis, pensions, prostitution, crime, and welfare benefits.

The power of groups, like the car lobby and the food and alcohol companies, to stop new policies being implemented.

Advice provided by what are often politically aligned research institutes ('think tanks').

The desire of governments to remain popular and get re-elected.

The influence of the European Union, which exercises some control over social policies national governments can adopt.

The views of professionals working in the field, like social workers and health workers.

The formation of social policy

The financial constraints and resources of governments, which can affect whether they can afford to implement policies.

The willingness of powerful policy-making individuals and groups to take account of the needs of the less powerful, poor and socially excluded groups.

Sociological and other research.

The power of groups seeking to achieve new policies to benefit them will influence whether their concerns are listened to, such as the physically or mentally disabled.

The prevailing ideology at the time, such as whether there are supportive or hostile attitudes towards the disadvantaged, or an ideology of welfare state support or self-support.

Public perceptions of what's reasonable, workable and a 'good thing'.

The agenda-setting role of the media, which can draw attention both to particular issues and to ways of seeing them, such as binge drinking or anti-social behaviour.

Religious organizations, such as the Catholic Church, and other groups setting moral frameworks of policy, e.g. on abortion.

related social problems, such as those to do with income and wealth inequalities, educational underachievement, poverty and ill-health. In addition, sociologists have not been slow in questioning the effects of government policies and highlighting uncomfortable truths about society – for example, the 1980 *Black Report* and the *Marmot Review* (Marmot 2010), which exposed deep social class inequalities in health rooted in wide cultural and structural factors. Those with power, therefore, often prefer to see sociology as a biased and value-laden subject, rather than confront the uncomfortable information it places before them.

The final decisions on what constitute social problems and what measures should be taken are ultimately political decisions, and in an unequal society, it is those who have the most power who will ultimately decide which policies are adopted and implemented, no matter how good sociological research may be. For example, the *Black Report* in 1980 was buried by the Conservative government of the time, yet in the 1990s similar research, like the *Acheson Report* (1998), had a direct influence on health policy under a Labour government more sympathetic to reducing health inequalities. This is the real world of politics, and not the sheltered world of the sociology classroom.

Figure 5.8 shows a range of social, political and economic factors that influence the formation of social policy, and, in this context, the work of sociologists would appear to be a relatively small one.

Activity

Refer to figure 5.8.
1 Outline and explain one example of a social policy to illustrate each of the points in the boxes.
2 Outline three ways that the unequal distribution of power in society influences:
   a) Whether or not something is defined as a social problem, illustrating your answer with examples.
   b) Whether or not social policies are formed to solve the problems.
3 Outline three reasons why governments may choose not to support social policies even when sociological research suggests such policies could be effective in reducing or solving social problems.

Sociological theories/perspectives and social policy

There are few direct links between sociological theories and perspectives and social policy. Quantitative positivist research is generally more favoured by governments, and positivists themselves often take the view that their research provides objective data on which governments can form policies. Sociologists working from a functionalist or New Right perspective, or from a feminist perspective, often see their research as a means of changing society through social policies, though often with completely different outcomes. For example, the New Right, such as found in the work of Charles Murray, sees the aim of social policy as reducing the involvement of the state in people's lives and encouraging self-help, such as by cutting back on what they regard as an over-generous welfare state, eliminating the dependency culture and strengthening the traditional family and marriage as alternative sources of support. Many feminists see their research as a means of providing evidence to implement social policies that undermine patriarchy and remove discrimination against women. Conflict theorists of all kinds are likely to emphasize research that promotes social policies that reduce social inequality and poverty, and the social conflict that arises from them. Nonetheless, there is a disagreement among sociologists of all kinds about the extent to which they should involve themselves in research simply geared towards forming social policy.

Should sociologists be involved in social policy research?

Throughout this chapter, and particularly in Topic 5, there have been discussions about objectivity, value-freedom and detachment in sociological research, and such discussions are often particularly heated when it comes to the link between sociology and social policy. So far, an emphasis has been placed on the factors influencing whether policy makers choose to use sociological research, but there is another issue of how sociologists themselves see the role of sociology in relation to social policy. There are two broad positions in this discussion – those who argue sociologists should get involved in applied research for policy ends, and those who believe they shouldn't.

The view that sociology should be involved in applied social policy research

The founders of sociology, such as Comte, Durkheim and Marx, all saw the study of the social world as a means of improving society, reflecting the modernist concern with scientific study and a belief in progress. Since that time, many sociologists have taken the view that their work in identifying and explaining social problems should lead them to make specific social policy recommendations for the implementation of practical measures to solve the problems they've identified. Not to do so is simply refusing to take any responsibility for the findings of their work.

Many feminist sociologists, particularly liberal feminists, take such a view. They regard many existing social policies as supporting patriarchy and discrimination against women, and therefore

The Economic and Social Research Council (ESRC) is an important source of funding for social research.

they seek to change them through their research evidence. They have undertaken research on a wide range of issues, such as the changing nature of families; lone parenthood; unequal opportunities for, and discrimination against, women in employment; domestic violence, and the continuing underachievement of girls in education, with a view to changing laws and policies to improve the position of women. Other sociologists, like Townsend (1979) and those supported by the Joseph Rowntree Foundation, have studied issues like poverty and health with a view to making recommendations to government for social policies to reduce poverty and improve health in the community.

Another very practical reason to get involved in applied research is the issue of funding. In order to carry out research, grants are needed, and the largest funding agency for research is the government and other public bodies. For example, the Departments of Health, Work and Pensions and Education, and the Home Office, all have large research budgets, and commission research from universities to develop their policies.

The Economic and Social Research Council (ESRC) is an independent government-funded body for the promotion of social science research, with research spending of around £139 million in 2012–13, providing substantial grants to social science researchers, often linked to social policy issues. Other funding bodies are charitable trusts like the Joseph Rowntree Foundation, which is specifically concerned with applied research on poverty and related issues, and provides over £5 million a year for these purposes, much of it to university researchers. These research funds are so substantial that those who choose not to get involved in applied social research are likely to find themselves short of funds for any research.

Marsland (1994), generally identified with the New Right, argues for a 'fully engaged' sociology that is committed to social policy, and that 'systematic empirical sociological research has a necessary, important, and constructive role to play in relation to policy formulation, implementation and evaluation'. He suggests that much policy work doesn't take proper account of sociological research, but that most sociologists themselves lack commitment to applied policy research, and would rather 'shout or hiss from the sidelines' than risk getting their hands dirty by becoming involved in policy-making. Marsland argues that sociologists should be fully and actively involved in the policy process, and this would produce positive benefits for the community through evidence-based policy-making, and assessment of policy objectives and achievements. He argues that, if sociologists don't involve themselves in applied research, this won't stop the research being carried out, but sociology will become marginalized, and policy areas will be less well informed. He also suggests that either 'social policies will take account of relevant sociological knowledge or they are bound to fail'.

As seen earlier, social policy-making is a complex process with a diversity of influences, but if sociologists do not involve themselves in social policy research, then social policy will be even more vulnerable to manipulation by powerful groups with particular interests of their own to promote.

The view that sociology should not be involved in applied social policy research

The arguments for sociologists not involving themselves in applied social policy research relate to the issues of detachment, objectivity and non-involvement which were discussed in Topic 5, and how funding issues can constrain the nature of research.

Funding for research comes from government and other agencies, which, understandably enough, will only fund research which meets with their approval. Sometimes, as with ESRC funding, these approval criteria regarding the value of research may be quite broad, but for government and some charitable foundations, like the Joseph Rowntree Foundation, only research for particular purposes is funded. Such funding sources can have theoretical and methodological implications for the way research is conducted. For example, government agencies generally prefer what they regard as more reliable positivist research methods, producing easily digestible quantitative data, rather than in-depth qualitative research. Funding sources can also limit the parameters of research. The Department for Work and Pensions research strategy specifically states that 'all the research which is carried out flows directly from the policy agenda, and there is no "blue skies" research'. In other words, there is no scope for open-ended free thinking outside of the policy framework.

There are also potential ethical difficulties. As seen earlier, sociological research is only one of many influences on the formation of social policy. Radical sociologists, like radical feminists and Marxists, may well regard detachment and non-involvement in policy research as preferable to inadvertently contributing to social policies that might be used to reinforce patriarchy, or that might eventually be used against the interests of the poorest and least powerful groups in society on which they carried out research and for bolstering and legitimizing the power of the dominant social class.

Sociological research may well produce findings that are opposed to the interests of the government or actively challenge existing policies by throwing up dysfunctional aspects which create, rather than solve, social problems, as was the case with the Black Report's highlighting the serious consequences for health of social inequality. There is a risk that too close an involvement in applied research can mean that policy-making – a political process – becomes the driving force of sociology, with sociology being reduced to an extension of the political arm of government and serving its needs. What happens then to objectivity in research? Governments may be able to pick and choose which research evidence they accept or ignore, but sociologists who wish to retain some professional integrity and scientific objectivity cannot do the same thing.

Sociologists may have different conceptions of what social problems are, and what measures are necessary to solve them, from those with power. In such circumstances, applied social research in which sociologists have no control over the use to which their research is put may involve them in unreasonable compromises and unwittingly contribute to policies dealing with the symptoms of a problem rather than the problem itself. For example, the view of many Marxist and radical feminist sociologists is that most social problems are rooted in social inequality and/or patriarchy, which only radical change, rather than a few new policy initiatives, will resolve.

The postmodernist view

Postmodernists adopt a position that sociology should not be involved in social policy research, because sociology has no contribution to make to social policy-making, and the discussion between sociologists about whether or not they should involve themselves in such research is irrelevant. This is because they argue sociology provides only interpretations of the world, rather than universal truths or firm evidence on which social policy should be based. Bauman and May (2001) suggest all sociology does is to provide a commentary on social life, but it does not possess a monopoly of wisdom in understanding society, nor is its interpretation the only one. All sociologists do is provide their own interpretations, which are no better than any others. Bauman and May argue any successful use of sociological evidence in influencing social policy would simply be imposing their view of reality on others, displacing alternative views and values, contributing to the management of society, and enhancing the control of those who are already in control of society by providing questionable evidence to bolster their positions. They suggest that sociology's role is to contribute, not to the formation of social policy, but to social understanding and tolerance by enabling people to understand more about themselves and others and the social context of their personal lives and those of others.

There is no simple or obvious answer to the two contrasting points of view considered above, but perhaps improvement of human lives is more likely to be achieved, as Marsland put it above, by sociologists risking getting their hands dirty by becoming involved in policy-making than by shouting or hissing from the sidelines. Certainly, as long as sociological research, whether applied to social policy or not, aspires to the five principles identified on page 415 (avoiding personal values influencing the data collection process; keeping an open mind; using systematic research methods to collect evidence; carefully analysing and evaluating data and hypotheses in the light of evidence; and opening up findings to inspection, criticism and testing by other researchers), then it should retain high research value of potential use to social policy makers, whether or not they choose to use it.

Ultimately, perhaps, the issue is a political one, and sociologists may decide how to proceed once they answer the question posed by Becker: Whose side are we on?

Activity

1 Suggest two areas where sociological research has influenced social policy.
2 Suggest, with examples, two possible dysfunctions or unintended consequences of government social policies.
3 Identify and explain two reasons why postmodernists might see sociology as having no useful contribution to make to social policy formation.
4 Outline two reasons in each case why (a) Marxists (b) radical feminists might think that sociological research should not be applied to the development of social policy.

Practice questions

1 Outline and explain **two** ways in which sociologists may contribute to the understanding of a society's social problems. **(10 marks)**

2 Outline and explain **two** reasons why some sociologists suggest researchers should not involve themselves in applied research to assist governments in forming their social policies. **(10 marks)**

3 Read **Item A** below and answer the question that follows.

Item A

Sociological research can make important contributions to the formulation of government social policies. Sociological evidence can help, for example: to identify and explain social problems; to assess how well existing policies are working (or why they are not); to identify the unintended consequences of existing policies; and to develop new social policies to help solve social problems. However, social policy formation is often influenced by factors other than sociological research evidence.

Applying material from **Item A** and your knowledge, evaluate the extent to which sociological research may have an influence on the formation of government social policies. **(20 marks)**

CHAPTER SUMMARY AND REVISION CHECKLIST

After reading this chapter, and having revised the research methods studied in the first year, you should be able to:

- Distinguish between quantitative and qualitative data, and the advantages and limitations of each

- Identify the difference between primary and secondary sources, and the strengths and limitations of the data obtained from each

- Identify the differences between, and the uses, advantages and limitations of, public and private documents

- Explain the usefulness and problems of using content analysis

- Explain the uses, advantages and limitations of official statistics, with examples

- Explain the issues of reliability and validity of research evidence

- Identify the ethical considerations sociologists must consider when carrying out social research

- Explain the uses and problems of the experimental method in sociology

- Explain how the comparative method might be used as an alternative to the experimental one

- Explain the main features and stages of the social survey, and the various sampling methods sociologists use to gain representative samples, and their strengths and weaknesses

- Explain the uses, strengths and weaknesses of different types of questionnaires and interviews, including the problems of imposition and the validity and reliability of these methods

- Explain fully the problem of interviewer bias

- Explain the uses, strengths and weaknesses of participant and non-participant observation as research methods, including theoretical and practical problems, and the issues of validity and reliability

- Discuss the strengths and weaknesses of longitudinal studies, case studies and life histories

- Explain what is meant by methodological pluralism and triangulation, and why sociologists might want to use a range of methods in sociological research

- Briefly outline how sociology as a subject and many sociological theories are linked to modernity

- Describe and explain consensus and conflict theories in sociology

- Outline what is meant by the problem of determinism and choice in sociology

- Describe the main features and aims of structural and action (interpretivist) theories in sociology, and evaluate them, including functionalism, classical Marxism and neo-Marxism, symbolic interactionism and ethnomethodology

- Describe and evaluate integrated approaches, including Weberian sociology and Giddens's theory of structuration

- Describe, explain and evaluate a range of feminist theories, and the contribution of feminist theory and research to sociology and the understanding of contemporary societies

- Describe the features of modernity and postmodernity, the differences between them, and evaluate the contribution of postmodernism to sociological theory and to an understanding of society

- Explain what is meant by late modernity, reflexivity, and risk society

- Explain what is meant by the scientific method, and assess the extent to which it can be used in the study of society

- Describe and evaluate the features of, and difference between, positivism and interpretivism

- Explain the realist view of science

- Explain how scientific knowledge is socially constructed and the social influences on scientific research

- Discuss the arguments for and against the view that sociology can be or should be a science, including the views of postmodernists

- Examine the ways in which sociological theories, including positivism, interpretivism and feminism, influence the research methods used and the different types of data collected

- Examine a range of practical, ethical and theoretical factors that influence sociologists' choice of research topic, choice of method(s) and the conduct of research

- Explain what is meant by subjectivity and objectivity in sociology, and examine the range of arguments for and against whether sociology can be or should be value-free, including the contribution of postmodernists to this debate

- Explain what is meant by social policy, and the difference between social problems and sociological problems

- Explain the links between sociology and social policy, including the various ways sociology can contribute to social policy, the range of other factors apart from sociological evidence that influence social policy-making, and the arguments adopted by different sociologists over whether or not they should involve themselves in applied research for social policy purposes.

KEY TERMS

Definitions can be found in the glossary at the end of this book, as well as these terms being defined in the margin where they first appear in the chapter.

bourgeoisie	hegemony	modernity	social integration
capitalists	hyperreality	moral regulation	social order
class consciousness	ideological state	New Right	social policy
collective conscience	apparatuses	objectivity	social problem
communism	impression management	paradigm	sociological problem
dependency culture	inductive approach	positivism	structural differentiation
determinism	interpretivism	proletariat	structuralism
disembedding	labour power	realism	structuration
dominant ideology	latent function	reflexivity	surplus value
dysfunction	macro approach	relations of production	symbol
empirical evidence	malestream	relative autonomy	value freedom
false consciousness	manifest function	repressive state apparatus	*Verstehen*
functional prerequisites	means of production	simulacra	
grounded theory	micro approach	social facts	

There are a variety of free tests and other activities that can be used to assess your learning at

www.politybooks.com/browne
You can also find new contemporary resources by following @BrowneKen on Twitter.

See also the revision guide to accompany this book:
Sociology for AQA Revision Guide 2: 2nd-Year A level

Please note that the above resources have not been endorsed by AQA.

Answer to question 1 of the activity on page 385
Ethnomethodology is a sociological discipline which studies the ways in which people make sense of their world, display this understanding to others, and produce the mutually shared social order in which they live. The term was initially coined by Harold Garfinkel in 1954.

Crime and Deviance

KEN BROWNE

SPECIFICATION TOPICS

- **Topic 1:** Crime, deviance, social order and social control
- **Topic 2:** The social distribution of crime and deviance by ethnicity, gender and social class, including recent patterns and trends in crime
- **Topic 3:** Globalisation and crime in contemporary society; the media and crime; green crime; human rights and state crimes
- **Topic 4:** Crime control, surveillance, prevention and punishment, victims, and the role of the criminal justice system and other agencies

Contents

CHAPTER 6

Crime and Deviance

Topic 1

SPECIFICATION AREA

Crime, deviance, social order and social control

Social control, deviance and crime

Social control and socialization are the main processes involved in encouraging people to conform to the dominant social norms and values of a society or group, and in preventing **deviance**. These processes therefore aim to avoid society collapsing into chaos and disorder and to maintain *social order* – a relatively stable society in which people generally comply with social norms and values.

Social control is achieved by a range of positive and negative sanctions which are applied by both formal agencies of social control – those which are specifically set up to ensure that people conform to a particular set of norms, particularly the law – such as the police, courts and prisons, and informally through family, community and peer group pressures, and other institutions like the education system, religion, the workplace, and the media.

> **Social control** refers to the various methods used to persuade or force individuals to conform to the dominant social norms and values of a society or group.

> **Deviance** refers to rule-breaking behaviour of some kind, which fails to conform to the norms and expectations of a particular society or social group.

The family is an important agency of informal social control.

446

The social construction of crime and deviance

The social construction of crime

Crime is the term used to describe behaviour which is against the criminal law – law-breaking.

Newburn (2007) suggests that **crime** is basically a label that is attached to certain forms of behaviour which are prohibited by the state, and have some legal penalty against them. While crime therefore seems to be easy to define, as the law states what a criminal act is, there is no act that is in itself criminal. An act only becomes a crime when a particular label of 'crime' has been applied to it, and even very similar acts can be treated very differently depending on the interpretations of the law enforcement agencies, and the context in which the act takes place. For example, killing someone is not in itself a criminal act: if it happens during a knife fight outside a pub in Britain, it is likely to be defined as criminal, but not if that knife fight is with an enemy soldier in wartime. Changing social attitudes can also mean acts once seen as criminal are no longer regarded as such, and laws are consequently changed over time. The most recent example of this is the altered and more flexible legal position on the level of 'reasonable force' people can use to defend themselves when faced with an intruder in their homes. As Newburn points out, even if crime is defined as whatever the criminal law says it is, the fact that the criminal law varies from country to country, and changes over time, reinforces the idea that there is nothing that is in itself criminal. Even with an act that appears to be against the law, the police and other criminal justice agencies have to interpret – or make a judgement – about whether it was prohibited. If the police do decide to define the act as a criminal one, that does not necessarily mean they will do anything about it, in terms of recording the offence or prosecuting the offender. Crime is therefore socially constructed because there is no act that is, in itself, criminal or deviant – it largely depends on how other members of society see and define it.

Crime also covers a very wide range of behaviour, from relatively trivial acts like pilfering from work to very serious acts like rape and murder. It is extremely difficult to develop explanations that account for the vast diversity of acts that are labelled as criminal, since it is not difficult to see that the reasons for shoplifting are likely to be different from those for premeditated murder.

The social construction of deviance

The wider concept of deviance is even more difficult to define than crime. Deviance includes both criminal and non-criminal acts, but it is quite difficult to pin down what members of any society or group actually regard as deviant behaviour. Downes and Rock (2007) suggest that *ambiguity* is a key feature of rule-breaking, as people are frequently unsure whether a particular episode is truly deviant or what deviance is. Their judgement will depend on the context in which the act occurs, who the person is, what they know about them, and what their motives might be. What is defined as deviance will depend on the social expectations about what constitutes 'normal' behaviour, and therefore whether something is defined as deviant or not will depend on how others react to it. For example, swearing at your mates in your peer group is unlikely to be defined as deviant, but swearing at your teacher in a school is likely to be viewed quite differently.

Societal and situational deviance

Plummer (1979) discusses two aspects of defining deviance, using the concepts of societal deviance and situational deviance.

Societal deviance refers to forms of deviance that most members of a society regard as deviant because they share similar ideas about approved and unapproved behaviour – murder, rape, child abuse and driving over the alcohol limit in the UK are likely to fall into this category. Situational deviance refers to the way in which an act being seen as deviant or not depends on the context or location in which it takes place. These two conceptions of deviance suggest that, while there may be some acts that many people agree are deviant in a particular society, those same acts may not be regarded as deviant across a range of different societies. Similarly, those acts defined as deviant may vary between groups within the same society, and they change over time. Whether or not an act is defined as deviant will therefore depend on the time, the place, the society and the attitudes of those who view the act. The following examples illustrate how definitions of deviance can vary according to a range of circumstances, and therefore show quite clearly that deviance, like crime, is very much a social construction, rather than something that is a characteristic of the act itself.

> **Societal deviance** refers to acts which are seen by most members of a society as deviant.

> **Situational deviance** refers to acts which are only defined as deviant in particular contexts.

1 *Non-deviant crime?* Most people commit deviant and even illegal acts at some stage in their lives, and there are many illegal acts which most people don't regard as particularly deviant. For example, parking and speeding offences, under-age drinking, use of soft drugs like cannabis, pinching office stationery, and littering are all extremely common, so it is difficult to see them as being deviant.
2 *The time.* Definitions of deviance change over time in the same society, as standards of normal behaviour change. For example, cigarette smoking used to be a very popular and socially acceptable activity, but is increasingly becoming branded as deviant. Since July 2007 it has been illegal in the UK to smoke indoors in workplaces, pubs, nightclubs, restaurants and buildings open to the public. Attitudes to homosexuality have also changed dramatically. Homosexuality was illegal in the UK before 1967, but is now legal and widely accepted, and in 2013 gay men and lesbians were legally enabled to marry on the same basis as heterosexual couples.
3 *The society or culture.* Deviance is culturally relative – what is regarded as deviance in one society or group is not necessarily so in another. For example, consumption of alcohol is seen as deviant and illegal in most Islamic countries, but is seen as normal in Britain.
4 *The social group.* What may be acceptable in a particular group may be regarded as deviant in the wider society. For example, smoking cannabis is perfectly acceptable behaviour among many young people, although it is regarded as deviant by many adults, and it is illegal.
5 *The place or context.* It is seen as deviant if people have sex in public, but not if it takes place between couples in private. Killing someone may be interpreted as heroic, as an accident, manslaughter, self-defence, murder, a 'crime of passion', justifiable homicide or euthanasia (mercy killing).

Activity

Apart from the examples given above:
1 Outline and explain **two** examples of acts which are against the law but are not usually regarded as deviant by most people.
2 Give **three** examples of deviant acts which are not against the law.
3 Outline and explain **two** examples of acts which are generally accepted by the majority of people in Britain, but which might be regarded as deviant in some social groups, for example minority ethnic or religious groups.
4 Devise a small survey to explore among your friends and family their attitudes regarding which acts they regard as deviant in contemporary society. You might do this by drawing up a list of both criminal and non-criminal acts, and asking them whether they regard them as deviant or not. Bring your conclusions together as a class, and see whether there appears to be any widespread consensus on what constitutes deviance, or whether there are variations according to age, gender, ethnicity, context and so on. Try to reach some conclusions around the concepts of societal and situational deviance.

In 1948, over half (53 per cent) of the UK adult population smoked cigarettes, but today cigarette smoking is a minority activity, restricted to around 19 per cent (in 2013) of the population, and falling. What was once seen as a common, normal practice, is now increasingly viewed as a deviant one and, in many circumstances, also an illegal one, due to health education and government legislation.

Sociological and non-sociological theories of crime and deviance

Crime and deviance have always existed in some form, and have been regarded as social problems to be tackled. There have consequently been a huge number of attempts to explain the causes of deviance, and particularly crime, and why some people commit crime while the majority appear not to. Many explanations have come from biology and psychology, but sociologists generally regard such explanations as, at best, inadequate, and in many cases as simply wrong.

Biological and psychological theories suggest that deviant/criminal behaviour is determined by conditions arising from nature (biology and physiology) or nurture (psychology) which prevent some individuals conforming to conventional norms and legal rules. Crime is put down to there being 'something wrong' with criminals, rather than with society.

Biological theories suggest that there is something in the genetic make-up of criminals that make them more disposed to turn to crime – the idea of the 'born criminal'. For example, Cesare Lombroso in the nineteenth century suggested that criminals had abnormal physical features that distinguished them from the rest of the population, such as having large jaws and cheekbones, and other features more associated with humans from an earlier stage of evolution. Phrenology, which was very popular in Victorian times, claimed that people's personality could be explained by the shape of their skulls, and criminals could be identified in this way.

Psychologists have linked criminal behaviour to genetically based personality characteristics, such as the presence of an extra Y-chromosome creating neurotic extroverts, who are less rational, less cautious and more risk-taking, more aggressive, and more impulsive and excitement-seeking than normal people. Current technology, such as PET scans, have shown that known psychopaths often have brain abnormalities which suggest organic reasons for their deviant behaviour. Modern studies have suggested that childhood experiences can have long-term psychological effects which may lead to maladjusted personalities and potential criminality in later life.

Sociologists generally reject these explanations, as they fail to recognize that the very meanings attached to crime and deviance are created by social and cultural factors, and there is no act that in itself is ever always regarded as criminal or deviant. It is very difficult to see how some people can have a biological or psychological predisposition to crime and deviance when such behaviour involves breaking socially defined rules which are subject to change over time and vary between cultures and sub-groups in the same society. To suggest that criminals are different from normal

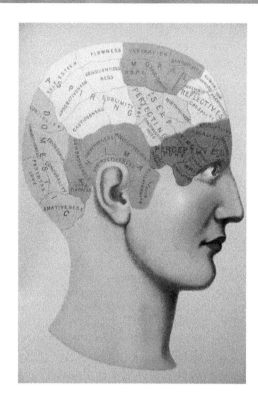

Early attempts to explain crime were derived from the physical features of criminals, such as their facial features and the shapes of their skulls.

people fails to recognize that many people will commit acts of deviance and crime, albeit trivial offences, at some time in their lives, and many criminals are never detected. Many biological and psychological theories are based on an unrepresentative sample of criminals who have been caught, and publicly labelled as criminals. Finally, crime is not randomly distributed by genes or personality, but follows a social pattern, linked to features such as age, class, gender and ethnicity. For example, many young people engage in deviant or criminal acts, but most eventually give it up – something they could not easily do if they were driven by their biological or psychological make-up.

The following sections consider the main sociological theories of crime and deviance.

Functionalist and subcultural theories of crime and deviance

Functionalism is a consensus structuralist theory, which sees the source of crime and deviance located in the structure of society. Social order and cohesion are based on a value consensus, and the agencies of social control seek to protect this by controlling the threat posed by crime and deviance. Despite this, Durkheim saw some benefits of deviance.

The benefits or functions of crime and deviance

Durkheim (1982 [1895]) argued that crime is an inevitable feature of social life, because individuals are exposed to different influences and circumstances, and so not everyone can be equally committed to the shared values and moral beliefs of society. Despite the potential threats to social order, he saw some deviance and crime as necessary and beneficial, as it could perform positive functions in contributing to the well-being of society in the following ways.

1 *By strengthening collective values.* Values can 'atrophy' (waste away) unless people are reminded of the boundaries between right and wrong behaviour. For example, sensationalized reporting in the media of incidents of child abuse has the effect of reinforcing social control against

child abusers and improving the protection of vulnerable children. The media frequently carry dramatic stories of crime and deviance, which spark a sense of public outrage against the acts or groups concerned. This often unites the public in displays of disapproval, and provides the opportunity for society to condemn deviant behaviour and, by punishing criminals, to reassert the boundaries of acceptable behaviour, and strengthen collective values.

2   *By enabling social change.* Some deviance is necessary to allow new ideas to develop, and enable society to change and progress.

3   *By acting as a 'safety valve'.* Deviance can act as a 'safety valve' releasing stresses in society. For example, mass violent protest demonstrations might be seen as an outlet for expressions of discontent avoiding wider and more serious challenges to social order.

4   *By acting as a warning device* that society is not working properly. For example, high rates of suicide, truancy from school, drug addiction, divorce and crime point to underlying social problems that need solving before serious threats to social order develop.

Strain theory and anomie

Merton (1968 [1957]) develops functionalist theory by attempting to explain why deviance arises in the first place. He suggests that social order is based on a consensus around social goals and approved means of achieving them. Most people share goals – for example, financial success, having their own home and possessing consumer goods – and most conform to the approved means of achieving them, like working in paid employment. However, in an unequal society, Merton argues not all individuals have the same opportunity of realizing these goals by approved means because of things such as, for example, unemployment, low pay, racism or lack of educational success. This means they face a sense of strain and anomie (normlessness), as the dominant rules about how to achieve success don't meet their needs. He argues there are different 'modes of adaptation' or responses to this situation, ranging from the conformity most people display, to one of four forms of deviance, which he calls innovation, ritualism, retreatism and rebellion. These are illustrated in table 6.1.

Evaluation of Merton's strain theory

While Merton's strength is that he clearly explains deviance as arising from the structure of society, there are some criticisms.

Table 6.1 Merton's strain theory

Mode of adaptation	Accept means?	Accept goals?	Example
Conformity	✓	✓	The non-deviant, non-criminal conformist citizen
Innovation	✗	✓	Factors like poor educational qualifications or unemployment mean some can't achieve goals by approved means so turn to crime as an alternative
Ritualism	✓	✗	Give up on achieving goals, but stick to means, e.g. teachers who have given up caring about student success, or office workers who have abandoned hopes of promotion and are just marking time until they retire
Retreatism	✗	✗	Drop-outs like drug addicts or tramps who give up altogether
Rebellion	✗ (✓)	✗ (✓)	Reject existing social goals and means, but substitute new ones to create a new society, like revolutionaries or members of some religious sects

✓ = accept ✗ = reject

Activity

1 Explain, with examples, how deviance and crime might be important as a source of social change.
2 Classify each of the following as one of Merton's five modes of adaptation, and explain your reasons:
   - A successful banker
   - A drug-dealer
   - A monk living in a monastery
   - A person cheating in exams
   - A shoplifter
   - An alcoholic
   - An indifferent Jobcentre clerk

1 He takes a consensus around means and goals for granted, assuming most people accept them. But some people do not accept goals like financial success, and, for example, may value job satisfaction and helping others more than a high income.
2 He focuses on individual responses, and doesn't recognize there is a social pattern of crime and deviance affecting whole groups of people, linked to social class, age, gender and ethnicity.
3 He doesn't explain why most people who face strain do not turn to crime or other deviance.
4 He doesn't recognize that there may be many outwardly respectable, apparently conforming successful people who are 'innovators' engaged in illegal activities, as in white-collar crime and corporate crime (see pages 494–9).

Subcultural theories

The subcultural theories of Cohen (1971) and Cloward and Ohlin (1960) build on Merton's work, but their theories focus on the position of groups in the social structure rather than just on individuals, and how these groups adapt in different ways to the strain facing them in achieving social goals. They deal with working-class juvenile delinquency, as these young people constitute the largest group of criminals and deviants.

Cohen: status frustration and the reactive delinquent subculture

Cohen argues that working-class youth believe in the success goals of mainstream culture, but their experiences of failure in education, living in deprived areas and having the worst chances in the job market mean they have little opportunity to attain them by approved means. They feel they are denied status in mainstream society, and experience status frustration. They react to this situation by developing an alternative distinctive set of values – a *delinquent subculture*. This subculture is based on a reaction to, and deliberate reversal of, accepted forms of behaviour. For example, stealing replaces hard work, vandalism replaces respect for property, and intimidation and threats replace respect for others. This gives working-class youth an opportunity to achieve some status in their peer group which they are denied in the wider society. Cohen identifies elements of revenge in this subculture, to get back at the society that has denied them status. This element of revenge helps to explain why a lot of juvenile offences, such as vandalism, joy-riding, fighting and general anti-social behaviour, are not motivated by a desire for financial gain, but rather by a desire for peer-group status by being malicious, intimidating, having a laugh at the expense of others, and generally causing trouble.

Evaluation of Cohen

A strength of Cohen's theory is that it helps to explain working-class delinquency as a group response rather than being a focus on individuals, as is the case with Merton's theory. However, Cohen makes an assumption that young working-class delinquents accept the mainstream values as superior

White-collar crime refers to offences committed by middle-class individuals who abuse their work positions for personal gain at the expense of the organization or its clients.

Corporate crime refers to offences committed by groups or individuals on behalf of large companies, which directly profit the company rather than individuals.

Delinquency is crime committed by those under age 18, though the term 'delinquency' is often used to describe any anti-social or deviant activity by young people, even if it isn't criminal.

Status frustration is a sense of frustration arising in individuals or groups because they feel they are denied status in society.

and desirable, and develop delinquent values only as a reaction to what they can't achieve. Miller (1962) cast doubt on this. He argues that it is false to suggest lower-working-class delinquents reject mainstream values, as the lower working class has always had its own independent subculture. This means that young people couldn't generate delinquent subcultures seeking revenge and rejecting and reacting against mainstream goals, as they never held them. Matza's (1964) studies of delinquency found most young delinquents were not committed to delinquent values. Many showed a commitment to mainstream values and merely drifted in and out of occasional delinquency rather than showing any serious commitment to it. Miller's and Matza's theories are outlined in the following sections.

Cloward and Ohlin: three working-class delinquent subcultures

Cloward and Ohlin (1960) argue that Cohen's theory doesn't allow for the diversity of responses found among working-class youth who find the approved means for achieving society's goals blocked. They suggest the varied social circumstances in which working-class youth live give rise to three types of delinquent subculture.

1 *Criminal subcultures* are characterized by utilitarian (useful) crimes, such as theft. They develop in more stable working-class areas where there is an established pattern of adult crime. This provides a learning opportunity and career structure for aspiring young criminals, and an alternative to the legitimate job market as a means of achieving financial rewards. Adult criminals exercise social control over the young to stop them carrying out non-utilitarian delinquent acts – such as vandalism – which might attract the attention of the police.
2 *Conflict subcultures* emerge in socially disorganized areas where there is a high rate of population turnover and a consequent lack of social cohesion. These prevent the formation of a stable adult criminal subculture. Conflict subcultures are characterized by violence, gang warfare, 'mugging' (street robbery with violence) and other street crime. Both approved and illegal means of achieving mainstream goals are blocked or limited, and young people express their frustration at this situation through violence or street crime, and at least obtain status through success in subcultural peer-group values. This is a possible explanation for the gang culture which is increasingly appearing in the run-down estates and inner-city areas of Britain's largest cities, and which has been a common feature of American cities for a long time.
3 *Retreatist subcultures* emerge among those lower-class youth who are 'double failures' – they have failed to succeed both in mainstream society and in the crime and gang cultures of the criminal and conflict subcultures. The response is a retreat into drug addiction and alcoholism, paid for by petty theft, drug-dealing, shoplifting and prostitution.

Evaluation of Cloward and Ohlin

Cloward and Ohlin's research is helpful, as it gives insights into why working-class delinquency may take different forms in different social circumstances. However, they exaggerate the differences between the three types of subculture, as there is overlap between them. For example, utilitarian crime features in all three subcultures, and criminal subcultures may involve drug-dealing inside the retreatist subculture, and many drug addicts in the retreatist subculture are also money-making drug-dealers. Goods stolen in the retreatist subculture areas to pay for drugs may be disposed of in the more stable criminal areas where there is more of a market for stolen goods.

Miller: the independent subculture and the focal concerns of working-class life

Miller explains deviance and crime in terms of a distinctive working-class subculture which he suggests has existed for centuries. This subculture, which mainly relates to males, revolves around central characteristics that Miller calls *focal concerns*. These focal concerns include an emphasis on toughness and masculinity; smartness (being shrewd, quick-witted, clever and amusing); autonomy and freedom (a resentment of authority and being pushed around); trouble (an acceptance that life involves violence and fights); and a search for excitement and thrills. Such values carry with them the risk of law-breaking. These values become exaggerated in the lives of young people, as the search for peer-group status – for example, through being the toughest – leads them into delinquency. It is therefore over-conformity to lower-working-class subculture, rather than the rejection of dominant values, that explains working-class delinquency.

Criticisms of functionalist-based explanations of crime and deviance

1   They generally assume there is some initial value consensus, from which people deviate in some way. Taylor et al. (1973) say it is wrong to assume this, pointing out that not everyone is committed to mainstream goals. For example, some religious sects reject the struggle for material success in favour of alternative spiritual goals, and job satisfaction may be more important to some workers than career progression, financial success and lots of consumer goods.
2   Subcultural explanations only explain working-class delinquency, and do not explain white-collar (middle-class) and corporate crimes. These are discussed in Topic 2.
3   They rely on the pattern of crime shown in official crime statistics. However, a lot of crime is never reported, and a lot of offenders are never caught. This makes it difficult to know who the real offenders are, so subcultural explanations are inadequate as they are based on an unrepresentative sample of offenders.
4   The idea of a delinquent subculture implies that working-class youth are socialized into and committed to central values of delinquency. If true, this should lead to delinquent behaviour being widespread and persistent, but, as Matza found, most working-class youth don't engage regularly in illegal acts, and those who do give it up in early adulthood.
5   Matza criticizes subcultural theories for making the delinquent out to be different from other people. Matza stresses the similarity between the values held by delinquents and those of mainstream society, and shows how ordinary delinquents actually are. He points out, for example, that they show feelings of outrage about crime in general similar to those of most people. When they are caught offending, most delinquents express feelings of remorse, guilt and shame, and use what Matza calls techniques of neutralization rooted in mainstream values to explain away their actions as justifiable or excusable temporary lapses in otherwise conformist behaviour – as exceptions to the rule. For example, they were only shoplifting because they wanted to get their mum a birthday present and didn't have any money, or the person they were fighting with was a bully who deserved it. This shows a commitment to mainstream values, not a rejection of them. Matza also suggests that many young people commit only occasional delinquent activities as a means of achieving identity, excitement and peer-group status for a short period of 'drift' in their lives before reaching full independent adult status. They have little serious commitment to delinquent values or a delinquent way of life, and many give it up as they grow older.

Techniques of neutralization are justifications used to excuse acts of crime and deviance, such as by denying responsibility; denying that there was a victim or any injury to a victim; claiming that those casting blame had no right to do so, or the deviance was justified by the circumstances.

Control theory: Hirschi's social bonds theory of crime and deviance

Hirschi (1969) is the figure most associated with control theory, and he shares a similar view to Durkheim: that social order is based on shared values and socialization through institutions integrating individuals into society. However, control theory takes the opposite approach from other theories in criminology. Instead of asking what drives people to commit crime, Hirschi asks why most people do *not* commit crime. Control theorists argue that all human beings suffer from weaknesses which make them unable to resist temptation and turn to crime, but that there are social bonds with other people that encourage them to exercise self-control, tie them to conformity and restrain them from committing crime. If these social bonds with other people are weakened or broken, their self-control is weakened, and they will turn to crime.

Four social bonds

Hirschi identifies four social bonds which pull people away from crime and towards conformity: commitment, attachment, belief, and involvement. These are illustrated in figure 6.1. Gottfredson

Figure 6.1 Hirschi's control theory

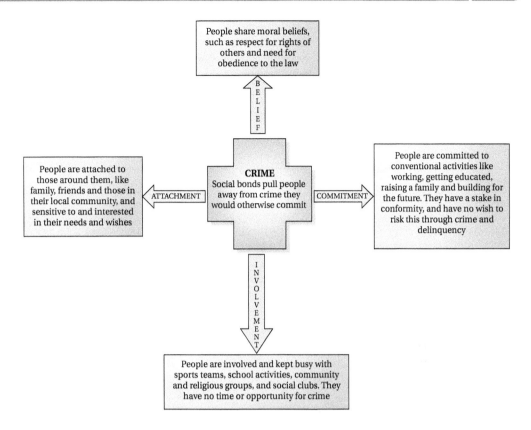

and Hirschi (1990) later added that inadequate self-control arising from weakened social bonds is not in itself enough to explain crime; opportunities for offending must also be present for a crime to be committed. This opportunity theory is explored later in Right Realism, and the crime prevention sections of Topic 4.

Activity

Refer to figure 6.1 on Hirschi's control theory.
1 Identify all the social bonds that you think prevent you from committing crime, or how those bonds were weakened if you have committed crime, been involved in anti-social behaviour or other forms of deviance.
2 Suggest how Hirschi's theory might explain juvenile delinquency.

Evaluation of control theory

1 It recognizes the importance of socialization and social control in maintaining a cohesive society, and the idea of social integration through social bonds is well-established in functionalist theory.
2 It assumes that those who commit crime and deviance have broken away from the bonds tying them into mainstream values, but Merton's theory and Matza's work suggest that criminals are committed to those values.
3 It doesn't explain why some have weaker bonds than others, or for that matter why all those with weaker bonds don't turn to crime.
4 It doesn't explain the variety of forms of deviance and crime.
5 It doesn't recognize that it is possible to be deviant *and* have tight social bonds, as for example among well-integrated middle-class drug users or white-collar criminals with successful careers.

6   It suggests that everyone is a potential criminal, and therefore our behaviour should be closely controlled and monitored. Those who conform may well resent the constant surveillance this implies, and some groups may be stereotyped and subjected to unwarranted harassment, as labelling theory (discussed on pages 459–63) suggests. This may in itself undermine respect for belief in the law and justice, and weaken social bonds.

Radical criminology: traditional Marxist and neo-Marxist theories of crime

Traditional Marxist theories

Marxist theories of crime are conflict approaches, as opposed to the consensus approaches of the functionalist-based theories of Merton and the subcultural theorists. Marxists – like functionalists – see people's behaviour moulded by the social structure, but Marxists regard this structure as based on conflict between social classes, with social inequality as the driving force behind crime. Traditional Marxist theories have the following features.

1   *Capitalist society is criminogenic.* 'Criminogenic' means that crime is an in-built and 'natural' outgrowth of a capitalist society which emphasizes economic self-interest, greed and personal gain. Crime is a rational response to the competitiveness and inequality of life in capitalist societies, in which profit, individual gain and looking after number 1 are seen as more important than concern for the well-being of others. Relative poverty means some struggle to survive or are excluded from participation in the consumer society, encouraging crimes like theft, or vandalism and violence arising from hostility to and frustration at social exclusion. Gordon (1971) suggests that what is surprising in these circumstances is not that the working class commit crime, but that they don't commit more of it.

2   *The law reflects ruling-class interests and ideology.* Laws are *not* an expression of value consensus, as functionalists contend, but, as writers like Chambliss (1975) argue, instruments of the ruling class, and they reflect the values and beliefs found in ruling-class ideology. At the heart of the capitalist system is the protection of private property and other ruling-class interests, and the state defines acts as criminal in line with these basic concerns. Box (1983) argues that what is defined as serious crime is ideologically constructed. Serious crime is identified as offences such as property crime and violence committed by members of the working class, rather than as the major harm caused by corporations – such as environmental damage caused by oil spills or the production of dangerous and faulty products – or by governments – such as human rights violations, illegal wars and genocide. The agencies of social control protect ruling-class interests and power, criminalize those who oppose them, and are used to control the workforce.

    Snider (1991) argues capitalist states will pass health and safety laws, or laws against pollution and other laws that regulate private business, only when forced to do so by public crises or union agitation. They will strengthen them reluctantly, weaken them whenever possible, rarely enforce them or enforce them only in a manner calculated to do as little as possible to seriously impede profitability or frighten off potential investors.

    Laws that appear to benefit everyone, or the occasional prosecution of members of the ruling class, have an ideological, manipulative function of providing a smokescreen suggesting that the law is impartial and even-handed, and that even ruling-class offenders are properly handled, when the opposite is more often the case.

3   *Selective law enforcement.* The impression in official statistics that crime is mainly a working-class phenomenon is largely due to the selective enforcement of the law. Chambliss suggests there's one law for the rich and another for the poor, with crime control focused on the working class, who are those most likely to be prosecuted for crime. Those of higher social classes are less likely to be prosecuted for offences, and, if they are, generally get treated more leniently. The biggest crimes of all are those committed by the ruling class – what Pearce (1976) called 'the crimes of the powerful' – in the form of white-collar and corporate crime (see pages 494–9),

Social exclusion is where people are excluded from full participation in education, work, community life, access to services and other aspects of life seen as part of being a full and participating member of mainstream society.

like fraud, tax evasion, corporate manslaughter and breaches of health and safety regulations. Such crimes are rarely prosecuted, even if they are discovered. Selective law enforcement gives the false impression most crime is committed by disturbed working-class individuals, and this diverts the working class's attention away from the exploitation they experience and the crimes of the capitalist class, and directs it toward other members of their own class. Individuals, not the system of inequality, are blamed for crime.

Neo-Marxist theories

Neo-Marxists are more recent Marxist theorists who attempt to develop a more sophisticated approach to crime than the rather crude traditional Marxist view that the law and law enforcement are simply aspects of ruling-class power and control of the working class. Neo-Marxists argue that traditional Marxist theories are too deterministic in suggesting people are driven into crime by forces beyond their control. They suggest no one is forced to commit crime, and many facing the same circumstances do not commit crime, and so choosing crime is a voluntary act.

Neo-Marxist theories couple this choice to commit crime with a view that working-class crimes like theft, burglary and vandalism are meaningful and symbolic political acts of resistance to ruling-class oppression. Working-class criminals are seen almost as Robin Hood figures, taking forms of political action against inequalities in power and wealth, misdirected into criminal activities rather than more traditional forms of political protest. This was the approach adopted by Gilroy (1982) in his discussion of black crime in the 1970s, in which black crime was seen as a form of resistance to ruling-class oppression in the form of police racism and harassment.

The New Criminology

Hegemony describes the dominance in society of the ruling class's set of ideas over others, and acceptance of and consent to them by the rest of society.

The neo-Marxist approach is generally associated with the (now-not-so-) New Criminology developed by Taylor et al. (1973) in the 1970s. Taylor et al., while accepting many of the features of traditional Marxist theories, suggested that, to fully understand crime and deviance, how it was socially constructed and the motivations of offenders and the meanings they gave to their crimes, it was necessary to draw on both structural and interactionist approaches. They sought therefore to develop what they called 'a fully social theory of deviance' blending labelling theory and Marxism, involving an exploration of the six dimensions shown in table 6.2.

A **moral panic** is a wave of public concern about some exaggerated or imaginary threat to society, stirred up by overblown and sensationalized reporting in the media.

The New Criminology was applied by Hall et al. (1978) in their study of black crime, particularly the street crime of mugging in the 1970s. Hall et al. suggested crime was used to reassert the dominance of ruling-class **hegemony** at a time when it was under threat due to an economic and political crisis. This was achieved by diverting people's attention away from the wider structural causes of the crisis onto the problem of mugging by scapegoating young black people. To reassert hegemony, the ruling-class-owned media stirred up the public by exaggerating the problem of black crime and created demands for something to be done to stamp it out. Hall et al. suggested societal reaction to crime, fuelled by media exaggeration, created a **moral panic** (see glossary box), shown by mounting public concerns about an alleged black crime wave, which helped to justify more repressive and aggressive policing. This became a means of re-establishing ruling-class hegemony in society generally, and cracking down on all opposition to the ruling class.

Criticisms of Marxist and neo-Marxist theories of crime

1 *They over-emphasize property crime*, and don't have much to say about non-property offences like rape, domestic violence, the physical and sexual abuse of children and murder. It is difficult to conceive how the vast majority of such offences could ever have any political motivation or meaning.
2 *They over-emphasize class inequality in relation to crime*, and neglect other inequalities like those relating to ethnicity and gender.

Table 6.2 The New Criminology and a 'fully social theory of deviance'

Dimension to be explored	Explanation
The wider social origins of the deviant act	The wider context of crime, like capitalism and its unequal distribution of wealth and power, or a period of economic and political crisis.
The immediate origins of the deviant act	The specific situation leading criminals to choose to commit a deviant act, such as police racism or unemployment.
The actual act and what it means to the deviant	Is it seen as a political act against the ruling class or resistance to police racism? Is it a Robin Hood act, robbing the rich to help the poor? Is it just an alternative to a job in paid employment? Is it to support a drug habit?
The immediate origins of societal reaction	How do other people react to the discovery of the act, like the police, or family and neighbours of the deviant or victim.
The wider origins of societal reaction	How does the wider social system or society react to the act, such as those with the power to define acts as deviant and label offenders, like the mass media or the police? Why are some acts treated more harshly than others?
The outcomes of the societal reaction on the deviants' further action	What happens to deviants once they've been labelled as a deviant? Does it stop them re-offending, or does it just lead to bitterness and resentment and acceptance of the label, and the development of a deviant career and further deviance?

3   *Feminists regard many Marxist theories of crime as malestream,* for focusing primarily on male criminality, and making assumptions that their theories can automatically be applied to women.

4   *Traditional Marxist theories are too deterministic,* in the sense that they see people as forced into crime by circumstances beyond their control. They ignore the point made by neo-Marxists that people might choose crime for various reasons, and certainly most working-class people, even the poorest, do not commit crime.

5   *It is difficult to interpret* all *laws as reflecting ruling-class interests;* there are many that are in everyone's interests, such as traffic and consumer protection laws, those against household and vehicle theft and personal violence of all kinds. The police do try to protect the public from victimization, and are not simply ruling-class agents solely in the business of repressing and criminalizing the working class.

6   *They pay little attention to the victims of crime.* Neo-Marxists, in particular, tend to romanticize working-class crimes as symbolic political acts. Left Realists point out (see pages 465–8) that the crimes that matter most to people in their everyday lives, such as burglary, vehicle crime, street violence and anti-social behaviour, are mainly committed by working-class criminals against other working-class people. It is therefore difficult to see them as Robin Hood figures who rob the rich to feed the poor.

Later theories came to condemn traditional Marxism and some neo-Marxist theories of crime for trivializing and romanticizing the problem of crime; for not taking seriously the reality of crime in working-class communities; and for not producing realistic policies to prevent crime and protect the victims, who were overwhelmingly working-class. It was disillusionment with these approaches among some conflict theorists that led Lea and Young (1984) to develop a more realistic theory of crime called Left Realism, which is considered later in this topic.

Interactionist theories of crime and deviance: labelling theory

Interactionist theories of crime and deviance are most commonly referred to as labelling theory. This suggests many people involve themselves in some deviant or illegal behaviour, so it is hard to sustain a distinction between deviants and non-deviants; attempts to find the *causes* of crime (as in many of the theories examined so far) are therefore pointless. Official crime statistics are regarded as *social constructions*, showing only an unrepresentative group of offenders who have been caught and publicly labelled as 'criminal', because of the stereotypes and explanations that the police and other social control agencies themselves believe give rise to crime.

Labelling theory seeks to explain why only *some* people and *some* acts are defined as deviant or criminal, while others carrying out similar acts are not.

Labelling theory therefore takes as its focus:

1 *The interaction between deviants and those who define them as deviant*, and why particular individuals and groups are defined as deviant, and the circumstances in which this occurs.
2 *The process whereby rules are selectively enforced*, and why the response to rule-breaking is not always the same. What assumptions are used by the police when they choose whether or not to take action? For example, why might the police respond differently to groups of black male youths compared to white youths engaged in similar activities?
3 *The consequences of being labelled 'deviant'*. How do others react – societal reaction – to those labelled as deviant, and what effect does the attachment of the label 'deviant' have on the self-concept – or the way they see themselves – of those labelled? For example, does it prevent further deviance? Is it a self-fulfilling prophecy? Does it make deviance worse (this is called deviancy amplification, and is discussed in relation to the media in Topic 3 – see pages 518–22)
4 *The circumstances in which a person becomes set apart and defined as deviant.*
5 *An analysis of who has the power to attach deviant labels and make them 'stick'.*
   Becker (1997 [1963]) (www.home.earthlink.net/~hsbecker/index.html) is the key figure in labelling theory. He suggests that an act only becomes deviant when others perceive and define it as such, and whether or not the deviant label is applied will depend on *societal reaction* (how an act is interpreted by those whose attention is drawn to it).

The following quotation from Becker's *Outsiders* is a classic, and sums up well the problematic nature of deviance:

> Social groups create deviance by making the rules whose infraction constitutes deviance, and by applying those rules to particular people and labelling them as outsiders. From this point of view, deviance is not a quality of the act the person commits, but rather a consequence of the application by others of the rules and sanctions to an 'offender'. The deviant is one to whom the label has successfully been applied. Deviant behaviour is behaviour that people so label.

Becker calls agencies, such as the media and the police, who have the power and resources to create or enforce rules and impose their definitions of deviance, moral entrepreneurs.

A **moral entrepreneur** is a person, group or organization with the power to create or enforce rules and impose their definitions of deviance.

Selective law-enforcement

Agencies of social control use considerable discretion and selective judgement in deciding whether and how to deal with illegal or deviant behaviour. The police, for example, can't prosecute all crime: it would require very heavy policing, which would not enjoy much public support, and would be a massive drain on resources. So 'criminal' labels are not attached to every breach of the law, even if discovered, and the same courses of action are not always taken in response to the same offence. Labelling theorists therefore suggest it is necessary to study how, and to whom, deviant labels are attached.

Becker suggests that the police operate with pre-existing conceptions and stereotypical categories of what constitutes 'trouble', criminal types and criminal areas and so on, and these influence their responses to behaviour they come across. What action is taken will depend not so much on actual offences or behaviour, but on the stereotypes of groups and offences they hold.

The police force is made up of people from all social classes and, in theory, the police work for everyone in society. However, the institution can work in favour of the ruling class by treating different groups unequally. For example, drug use in a deprived area is much more likely to be investigated and punished than drug use among rich city bankers or celebrities.

The work of Cicourel

Cicourel (1976) uses a phenomenological approach to understand how law-enforcers make sense of and interpret what they see. He suggests their subjective perceptions and stereotypes can affect whether criminal labels are attached, and how these lead to the social construction of crime statistics. In his study of juvenile delinquency in two US cities, he found juvenile crime rates to be consistently higher in working-class areas than in middle-class areas. He found this was because the police viewed the behaviour of middle-class and working-class juveniles differently even when they were engaged in the same behaviour. Cicourel argued that this was because the police had a perception that middle-class youth came from 'good backgrounds' with lots of family support, and so their behaviour was interpreted as temporary lapses, and charges weren't brought. They held the opposite perception of working-class youth, and so more formal police action was taken against them. Cicourel's research suggests we need to look at the choices made by police over where they patrol, who they regard with suspicion, and therefore who they choose to stop and search, arrest and charge.

The labelling process – primary and secondary deviance

Lemert (1972) distinguishes between **primary deviance** and **secondary deviance**.

Primary deviance is deviance that has not been publicly labelled as such. For example, people might break traffic laws, use illegal drugs, pinch stationery from work, or even download child pornography to their computers. This has few consequences for the person, so long as no one knows about it. However, once an offender is discovered and publicly exposed and the label of 'deviant' is attached, then secondary deviance may occur. The stigma attached to people caught downloading child pornography is a good example.

Becker points out that the attachment of the label may have major consequences for the individual's view of themselves – their self-concept – and their future actions. This is because the deviant label can become a **master status** – a status that overrides all other characteristics which the individual may possess. For example, if caught downloading child porn, other identities like manager, worker, husband, father, sportsman or vicar become displaced by labels like 'paedophile', 'child pornographer' and 'sex offender', which become seen by others as that person's defining status.

Primary deviance is deviance that has not been publicly labelled as such.

Secondary deviance is deviance that follows once a person has been publicly labelled as deviant.

A **master status** is one which displaces all other features of a person's social standing, and a person is judged solely in terms of that one defining characteristic.

Others see and respond to the individual in light of this master status, and assume that he or she has all the negative attributes of the label. This is where secondary deviance begins, arising from the attachment of the label, and societal reaction to the deviant. Sustaining an alternative image in the deviant's own eyes and in those of others becomes difficult once the master status is applied.

Deviant careers and the self-fulfilling prophecy

> A **deviant career** is what arises when people who have been labelled as deviant find conventional opportunities blocked to them, and so are pushed into committing further deviant acts.

Becker suggests that the labelling process and societal reaction can lead to a self-fulfilling prophecy and a deviant career similar to an occupational career, as those labelled face rejection from many social groups, are placed outside conventional society and become 'outsiders', and continue to act even more in the way they have been labelled. Institutions like prisons for the punishment of offenders help to make the label stick, and, even after leaving prison, labels like 'ex-con' are still applied. Such labelling may lead to further deviance due to the closing off of alternative legitimate opportunities and a lack of means by which to live their lives and shake off the label. A deviant career begins when the individual eventually joins or identifies with a deviant group facing similar problems, which provides support and understanding for the deviant identity. This may generate further deviance. Becker therefore suggests societal reaction and the application of the deviant label produce more deviance than they prevent. Cohen's (2002 [1972]) work on deviancy amplification and moral panics, discussed later in Topic 3 (see pages 518–22) illustrated this process, with labelling by the media generating more of the deviance it apparently condemned. Young's (1971) participant observation study of hippie marijuana-users in Notting Hill carried out between 1967 and 1969 also demonstrated this process. The two examples shown in figure 6.2, one fictional and one based on Young's research, illustrate the labelling process and its possible consequences.

Evaluation of labelling theory

Plummer (2011) argues that, although few contemporary sociologists now describe themselves as labelling theorists, labelling theory has been enormously influential and is embedded in a vast range of contemporary sociology, such as in the theory of moral panics and the dramatization of crime in the media; crime and popular culture; public attitudes to, and perceptions of crime; stereotyping; social control through police, courts and prisons in the context of reactions to crime; and in postmodernist theories. This influence is demonstrated in the various strengths of the theory, and is also shown in the extensive debates arising from criticisms and weaknesses of the theory.

Strengths of labelling theory

1   It provides insights into the nature of deviance not provided by structural theories.
2   It challenges the idea that deviants are different from 'normal' people.
3   It shows the importance of the reactions of others in defining and creating deviance.
4   It reveals the importance of stereotyping in understanding deviance.
5   It reveals the way official crime statistics are a product of bias in law-enforcement.
6   It reveals the importance of those with power in defining acts and people as deviant.
7   It highlights the role of moral entrepreneurs, like the media, in defining and creating deviance and generating moral panics.
8   It shows how labelling can lead to a self-fulfilling prophecy and to deviant careers.
9   It shows how the deviant label can affect the self-concept of the deviant.

Weaknesses of labelling theory

1   It tends to remove the blame for deviance away from the deviant and onto those who define him or her as deviant: the deviant becomes a victim too.
2   It assumes an act isn't deviant until it is labelled as such, yet many know perfectly well that what they are doing is deviant.
3   It doesn't explain the causes of deviant behaviour which precede the labelling process (primary deviance), nor the different kinds of acts that people commit – for example, taking drugs is a different act from murder.

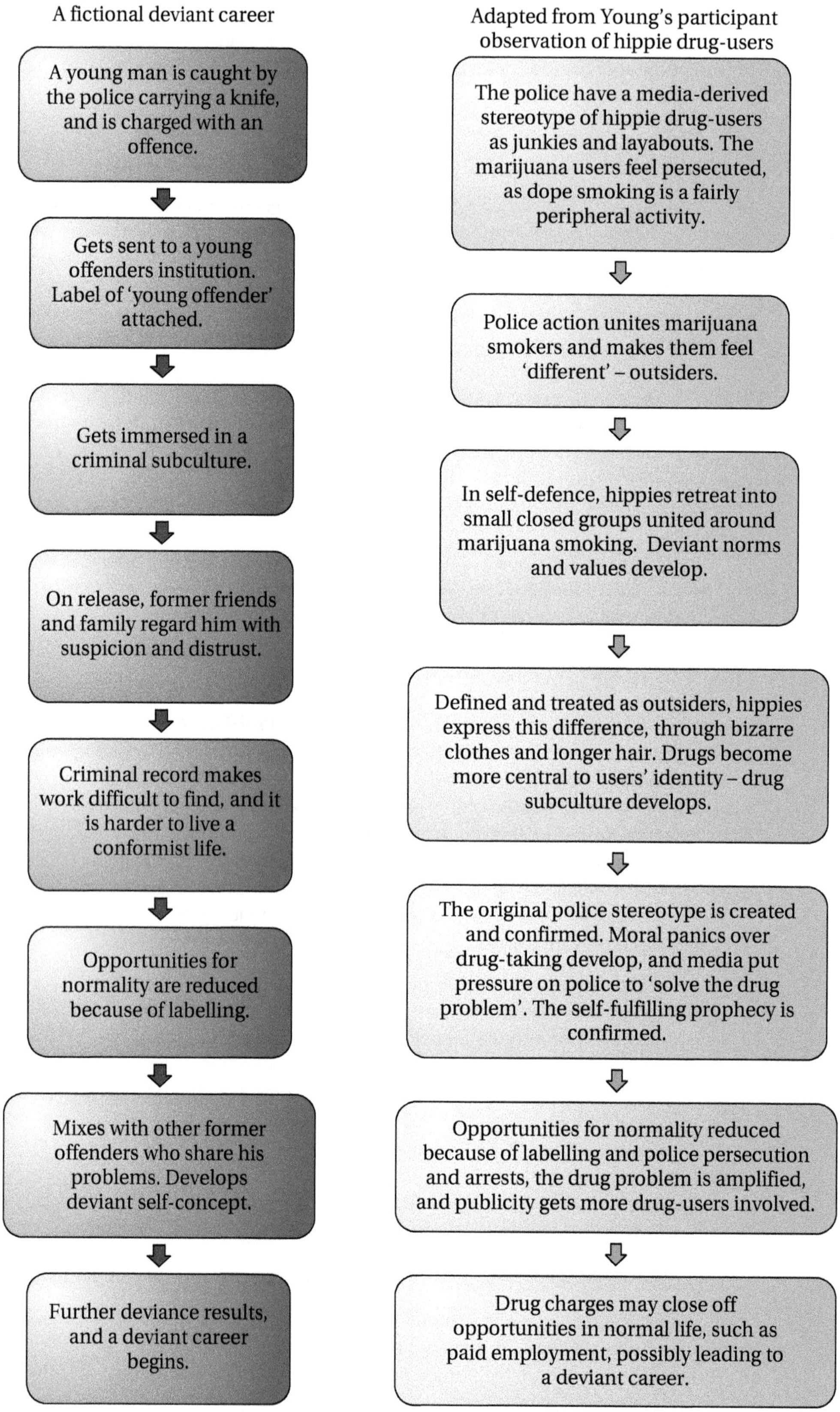

A fictional deviant career

A young man is caught by the police carrying a knife, and is charged with an offence.

Gets sent to a young offenders institution. Label of 'young offender' attached.

Gets immersed in a criminal subculture.

On release, former friends and family regard him with suspicion and distrust.

Criminal record makes work difficult to find, and it is harder to live a conformist life.

Opportunities for normality are reduced because of labelling.

Mixes with other former offenders who share his problems. Develops deviant self-concept.

Further deviance results, and a deviant career begins.

Adapted from Young's participant observation of hippie drug-users

The police have a media-derived stereotype of hippie drug-users as junkies and layabouts. The marijuana users feel persecuted, as dope smoking is a fairly peripheral activity.

Police action unites marijuana smokers and makes them feel 'different' – outsiders.

In self-defence, hippies retreat into small closed groups united around marijuana smoking. Deviant norms and values develop.

Defined and treated as outsiders, hippies express this difference, through bizarre clothes and longer hair. Drugs become more central to users' identity – drug subculture develops.

The original police stereotype is created and confirmed. Moral panics over drug-taking develop, and media put pressure on police to 'solve the drug problem'. The self-fulfilling prophecy is confirmed.

Opportunities for normality reduced because of labelling and police persecution and arrests, the drug problem is amplified, and publicity gets more drug-users involved.

Drug charges may close off opportunities in normal life, such as paid employment, possibly leading to a deviant career.

Figure 6.2 Deviant self-concepts, deviant careers and the self-fulfilling prophecy

4 It is too deterministic:
- It doesn't allow that some people *choose* deviance and the attachment of a deviant label or of a deviant identity, like those who, in the past, adopted a gay identity; it is not simply or always imposed on them by societal reaction.
- Labelling doesn't always lead to a self-fulfilling prophecy and more deviance: the attachment of a deviant label and the stigma attached by societal reaction may reduce deviance rather than increase it, for example a shoplifter may be so mortified by being caught they never want to do it again; Becker himself recognizes that individuals can choose to avoid a deviant career by seeking to rehabilitate themselves.

5 It doesn't explain why there are different reactions to deviance, nor where stereotypes come from in the first place.

6 It ignores the importance of wider structural factors in creating deviance, and assumes it is all down to societal reaction.

7 It has little to say about the victims of crime.

8 It has no real policy solutions to crime, beyond making fewer rules and not 'naming and shaming' offenders. This isn't much consolation for the victims of crime.

9 It does not explain why some individuals are labelled rather than others, and why some activities are against the law while others aren't. It points to the issue of power in the labelling process, but not, as the Marxists have done, at the structures of power in society which create the wider framework for the labelling process.

Activity

1 Explain, with examples, how the definition of deviance does not depend on the act itself but on societal reaction to it.
2 List some deviant labels you know of. Explain how and why these labels are applied, and what groups and circumstances are important in making the labels stick.
3 Outline and explain two ways that the mass media can act as moral entrepreneurs and how this might affect official crime statistics.
4 Outline, with examples, what assumptions you think the police operate with when they go about their work, such as their stereotypes of typical criminals and criminal areas.
5 Outline and explain ways how, in the process of interaction, a delinquent may avoid being labelled as such.
6 Drawing on Cicourel's research, explain how phenomenologists might explain the pattern in official crime statistics that most criminals are young, male and working-class, with an over-representation of black youth.

Feminist theories of crime and deviance

Feminist theories and research are applied in the gender and crime section in the next topic (see pages 487–93). This section will therefore focus on the main features underlying feminist contributions.

'Malestream' sociology and the invisibility of women

Feminism views society as patriarchal, and early feminist critiques of the sociology of crime and deviance focused on the way the subject was male-dominated and characterized by what Heidensohn and Silvestri (2012) called the two themes of 'amnesia' and 'neglect and distortion'. Gender issues and female offending were forgotten or ignored, until fairly recently, in most sociological theories of crime; most studies were about male offenders and deviants. There was therefore little attempt to explain female offending, the gender gap between male and female offending, and other forms of female deviance. For example, studies of working-class crime paid little attention to the fact that working-class women in the same social class position as men committed far less crime. Feminists also point out that female victimization was ignored, and particularly female victimization by men in the form of domestic and sexual violence. Feminists therefore saw male dominance in society reflected in a male dominance of the sociology of crime, which was seen as 'malestream' sociology.

Heidensohn (1996) suggests various reasons for this invisibility of females:

- Academics and researchers in the sociology of crime and deviance were predominantly men
- 'Malestream' middle-class sociologists had a kind of romanticized male preoccupation with macho working-class deviance – by studying rogue males, male academics might attach to themselves some of the alleged glamour, and increase their 'street cred'
- There is actually less to study, due to the relatively low level of female crime, and the often invisible nature of the offences committed by women, which are more likely to be *less detectable offences*, like prostitution and shoplifting.

The growth of feminist criminology

Like other areas in sociology, since the women's movement of the 1960s and 1970s, there has been a growing interest in female crime and deviance, led by feminist researchers, and this is now one of the key areas of sociological research. Much feminist criminology focuses on female offending, women's treatment by the criminal justice system, the study of female victimization, and the gender gap in offending. This involves both applying existing theories of male deviance to explain female deviance, and criticizing their shortcomings and developing new theories to explain female offending. Feminists bring the issue of gender and male power into the sociological study of crime and deviance. A major theme has been the importance of gender identity in understanding crime and deviance, rather than simply focusing on offending and structural features like strain, subcultures, social class or power. Smart (1976), for example, pointed out that women offenders are often seen as double deviants, as they not only break the law but breach traditional gender roles too, which means that their offences are more highly stigmatized than those committed by men, even if they are less serious.

This focus on gender and identity is also developed to explore how conceptions of femininity and female gender roles might lead women to be less deviant than men, but also why men are more deviant than women. For example, Messerschmidt's (1993) research into how crime and violence, including domestic violence, can be a means of 'accomplishing masculinity' (achieving a masculine image) for men who have failed to achieve this in other areas of their lives owes much to the impact of feminist ideas in sociology (this is discussed on page 492).

The feminist perspective has made a number of contributions to the study of crime and deviance, including the following:

- A new focus on female offending and the experiences of women in the criminal justice system
- The application of existing theories, criticisms of them, and the development of new theories, to explain female deviance
- A new focus on the various types of victimization suffered by women, particularly from male physical and sexual violence, including rape and domestic violence
- A challenge to the popular misconception that women enjoy 'chivalry' from the criminal justice system, and are treated more leniently than men
- An important new focus on gender and gender identity issues in explaining deviance, and the adaptation of existing theories to refocus them on gender rather than simply offending – feminists have raised questions in control theory, for example, concerning how men and women experience different levels of control, and in labelling theory concerning why female offending carries higher levels of stigmatization than male offending.

Realist theories of crime

Realist theories differ from other rather abstract theories of crime in that they focus on the reality of crime: what's actually happening, the impact of crime on victims and local communities, and the development of practical policies to reduce crime. There are two versions of realist theory: Left Realism and Right Realism, which are linked to different political perspectives. Left Realism tends to take an approach of 'tough on crime, and tough on the causes of crime', generally linked to Labour Party policies, while Right Realism puts greater emphasis on being tougher on the criminals than on the causes, and is associated more with Conservative Party and New Right policies. The following sections focus on the main features of Left and Right Realist theories, with the practical policy solutions arising from them discussed in Topic 4 (see pages 532–7).

Left Realism

Left Realism developed in the 1980s and is particularly identified with Lea and Young (1984). It developed as a response to traditional Marxist and neo-Marxist approaches, which it accused of:

- Not taking working-class crime seriously, and romanticizing working-class criminals as 'Robin Hood' characters fighting against social inequality and injustice, or reducing working-class crime to simple moral panics induced by the capitalist state, or regarding it as socially constructed through selective law enforcement and the labelling process
- Failing to take victimization seriously, and the fact that most victims were the poor and deprived
- Having no practical policies to reduce crime.

Through victim surveys (see pages 476–7) like the Islington crime surveys, Left Realists found crime was a serious problem, particularly in more deprived inner-city areas, and needed policies to tackle it. The sort of crime that worries people most is primarily street crime like mugging, violence, car crime and burglary, which is mainly carried out by young working-class males. Those at the greatest risk of becoming victims of these offences, and who have the highest fears about crime, are not the rich but the poor – the deprived white and minority ethnic residents living in inner-city areas. Left Realists accept that most people don't care much about white-collar and corporate crime, as they do not regard it as having any impact on their lives.

Explaining crime

Like Marxists, Left Realists accept that structural inequalities, social conditions and perceptions of injustice are the major causes of crime. Lea and Young attempt to explain why people turn to crime using three key concepts.

- *Relative deprivation.* It is not deprivation as such which causes people to commit crime, as most deprived people do not turn to crime, but whether they see themselves as deprived relative to others they compare themselves with. This can generate discontent and resentment as their expectations are not met.

Marginality is where some people are pushed to the margins or edges of society by poverty, lack of education, disability, racism and so on, and face social exclusion.

- *Marginalization.* Some groups experience marginality, as they find themselves politically and economically 'on the edge' of mainstream society, and face social exclusion through factors like poor educational achievement, unemployment and lack of involvement in community organizations. Such marginality, combined with relative deprivation, can lead to anti-social behaviour, crime, violence and rioting as there are few other means of expressing their frustrations and resentments at their exclusion.
- *Subculture.* Working-class deviant subcultures emerge as group solutions to the problems of relative deprivation and marginality arising from social inequality, though they take different forms over time and in different contexts, such as street gangs or various youth subcultures. These can act as motivators for crime, as some working-class subcultures see offending as acceptable behaviour.

Late modernity and the bulimic society

Young (1999, 2003) has more recently developed Left Realism and linked the explanations for crime to changes in society emerging in late modernity. Young argues that late modern societies are media saturated, and everyone, even the poorest, is included in consumer culture through constant exposure to advertising of consumer goods and media-generated lifestyles, which raise everyone's expectations of what the good life is like. However, this cultural inclusion is accompanied for those at the bottom of the class structure by social and economic exclusion, which means they cannot afford to actively participate in consumer society, as they can't afford to buy the goods necessary to forge new identities and lifestyles. Young argued this process whereby cultural inclusion was combined with social and economic exclusion was creating a 'bulimic society', in which people gorge themselves on media images of expensive consumer lifestyles, but are then forced by economic circumstances to vomit out their raised expectations. This intensifies the sense of frustration, resentment and anger among young people at their relative deprivation. Lewis et al. (2011) found the desire to consume by looting what was otherwise denied them in a bulimic society was a significant factor motivating some of the 13,000 to 15,000 people involved in riots and looting in English cities in August 2011.

Young argues the intensified sense of relative deprivation is made worse by three further features of late modernity.

1 *Growing individualism.* There is a growing emphasis on self-seeking, individual freedom and self-centredness, and less community spirit and concern for the welfare of others.
2 *The weakening of informal controls.* Traditional social structures like the family and close-knit communities have been breaking up, and are no longer able to provide support and informal controls on the behaviour of those living in the community.
3 *Growing economic inequality and economic change.* Globalization has meant the gap between the wealthiest and the poorest has grown massively, with staggering rewards for those at the top gained through participation in a global economy – such as footballers and music stars who are global media stars – while at the same time there has been a decline in traditional manufacturing industries, loss of unskilled work and more unemployment or part-time or short-term temporary work, which affected young working-class males the most.

The toxic mix that generates crime

The factors of late modernity considered above combine in a toxic mix that generates crime among young people in the most deprived communities. In such communities, the life of young people is marked by greater risk, more uncertainty and less informal control over their behaviour than ever before. With no other outlets for their anger and frustration at being excluded from the lifestyles they aspire to, they are more likely to involve themselves in various forms of what Lyng (1990, 2005) called 'edgework'. This involves all manner of thrill-seeking and risk-taking behaviour, not necessarily criminal or deviant, but the pursuit of peril may include exploring the boundaries between legal and criminal behaviour. This can lead to crime and violence, anti-social behaviour, rioting and self-destructive confrontations with the law.

Understanding and tackling crime: the square of crime

To understand and tackle crime, Lea and Young suggest it is necessary to examine the inter-relationships between four elements of what has been called 'the square of crime' – illustrated in figure 6.3 – and how they influence or interact with one another in influencing crime levels in any community.

- *Social structural factors and formal social control by the state.* These influence the context of crime, such as how crime is defined and its social causes, how law enforcement is carried out and decisions whether an act is labelled as criminal or not, styles of policing and the ability of the police to influence crime levels by deterring and catching offenders.
- *The public and the extent of informal social control.* How do people react to crime in their communities? Are offenders condemned by family, peer groups and neighbours? Do the public report offences? Do they trust the police? Do they buy stolen goods? Is the offence just seen as part of normal life in their community?
- *The role of victims.* Why do people become victims and what do they do about it? Victims are often of the same ethnic group, class and community as the offenders, or partners in a relationship with them. How do victims view offenders? Will they report them? Could or would the police do anything?
- *The offenders.* What meaning does the act have to the offender? Why do they choose to offend? Is it because they feel marginalized? Because they belong to a deviant subculture? Because they

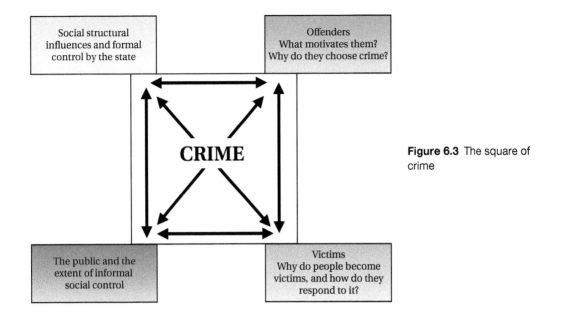

Figure 6.3 The square of crime

feel relatively deprived? Offenders choose to commit crimes – to what extent are they driven to it by outside forces, and how is this choice influenced by the other three factors?

Activity

Look at the four elements in figure 6.3 making up the square of crime, and suggest and explain how:
1 a) The attitudes of the public might affect whether or not an act is defined as a crime;
   b) The attitudes of the public towards the police might affect the police's ability to reduce crime levels in a community;
   c) The attitudes of a community towards offenders might influence whether or not they commit offences in the future;
   d) The attitudes of victims and their relationship with offenders might affect crime reporting in a community;
   e) The attitudes of the police towards offending and their clear-up rates might influence crime levels in a community.
2 On the basis of this activity and your understanding of Left Realism, suggest four practical policies that Left Realists might adopt for reducing crime in a deprived community.

Evaluation of Left Realism

Strengths

Left Realism draws on a range of theories, such as Marxist ideas of the importance of social inequality, Merton's concept of strain and anomie, Cohen's ideas of status frustration, subcultural theories, labelling, and the growth of individualism and consumerism in late modernity to produce a fuller explanation for crime than that offered by any one single theory. It does not glamorize crime as Marxist writers do, and takes the importance of tackling crime and the fear of crime seriously – it recognizes that crime can have devastating consequences for the most deprived communities, and that most offenders *and* victims are poor and working-class. It also sees the importance of community solutions to crime – these are discussed in Topic 4 (see pages 532–4).

Limitations

1   It neglects other responses to relative deprivation and marginality apart from crime, such as Merton's *retreatism* and *ritualism*, though it does recognize Merton's *rebellion*.

2   It neglects gender as a significant issue, and particularly those crimes of which females are the more likely victims, such as domestic violence and rape. Left Realism tends to be part of that 'malestream criminology' which feminists are critical of.

3   It doesn't pay much attention to white-collar and corporate crime, even though crimes such as fraud, neglect of health and safety and pollution controls, and sale of unsafe products often have the greatest impact on the most deprived communities.

4   It doesn't really explain why most deprived working-class youth *don't* turn to crime. If the 'toxic mix' is as toxic as it appears to be, why isn't there more crime, and why have crime rates been generally falling rather than increasing in recent years, despite a growing emphasis on consumerism combined with prolonged economic recession, unemployment and austerity?

Right Realism and rational choice and opportunity theories

Right Realism is associated with the New Right, and is now, arguably, the greatest influence on current Home Office policy of all theories of crime, because of the practical policies for crime prevention which derive from it (see Topic 4 pages 534–7).

Right Realism has the following key features:

1   *Value consensus and shared morality underpin society.* This is reflected in the law, and criminals are immoral because they breach this consensus. Social order is crucial, and individuals should be able to live their lives without fear of crime.

2   *People are naturally selfish.* Like control theory, it suggests people are essentially self-seeking, and need to have their natural tendency to take shortcuts by committing crime regulated by the agencies of socialization and social control, including the law. This links to the next point on community control.

3   *Community control.* It is poor socialization and lack of community controls that lie behind crime and anti-social behaviour. The most effective form of crime control is through strengthening the bonds of community – the types of bond suggested by Hirschi's control theory. Stricter socialization through the family and education and community pressure, and re-establishing social cohesion and a sense of individual responsibility, are all likely to be more effective in preventing crime than police action. These views are reflected in the work of New Right theorists like Murray (1989, 1990), who link crime to an unemployed workshy underclass, who live in broken communities with high rates of social disorder and crime. Murray suggests this underclass is characterized by welfare dependency, lack of individual responsibility and respect for authority, dysfunctional family life, high rates of family breakdown and lone parenthood, which mean parents fail to properly socialize and control their children, and to teach them proper moral standards, and there is a lack of community pressure to control deviance.

4   *Rational choice and opportunity.* People are rational, and weigh up the costs and benefits before choosing what action to take. Cornish and Clarke (1986) applied this rational choice and opportunity theory to crime, and suggested that people choose to commit crime because they decide that the benefits to be gained are greater than the potential costs, the opportunities are available, and the risks are therefore worth it. The solution is, then, to increase the costs, such as heavier policing to increase the risks of being caught, and to reduce the opportunities for crime (this is discussed further on pages 534–7).

5   *Crime will always exist.* There will always be some people whose natural selfishness and greed will slip through other controls. It's a waste of time trying to find out what the social causes of crime are as the Left Realists and Marxists seek to do, because, for example, most deprived people don't commit crime. The most that can be achieved is to reduce the impact of crime on victims, particularly crimes like violence and burglary, which are of major concern to the public. White-collar and corporate crimes have relatively little impact on individuals in their daily lives, so they shouldn't be a major focus for policing.

Rational choice theory suggests people weigh up the costs and benefits before choosing whether to commit a crime.

Evaluation of Right Realism

Strengths

1 It addresses the immediate causes of crime, and provides policies for reducing the opportunities for crime (see Topic 4).
2 It recognizes, like Left Realism, the importance of community control and community responses to crime in affecting crime levels.

Limitations

1 It doesn't address the wider structural causes of crime that other theories do.
2 It doesn't pay any attention to white-collar and corporate crime, and other 'hidden crimes' like domestic violence and child abuse.
3 It suggests that offenders act rationally, weighing up costs and benefits, but some crimes are impulsive or irrational, and do not bring any obvious gain, like vandalism or violence; Lyng's (1990, 2005) conception of 'edgework' or Katz's (1988) work on the seductions of crime (see pages 470–1), which suggest people might offend for the seductiveness, attractiveness and fun derived from the risk-taking, thrill and buzz involved in committing crime, are not explained by rational choice theory.

Postmodernist theories of crime

Postmodernists argue that society is changing so rapidly and constantly that it is marked by uncertainty and risk, and society is diverse and fragmented, with a huge variety of groups with different interests and lifestyles. Postmodernists view the category 'crime' as simply a social construction, based on a narrow legal definition, reflecting an outdated metanarrative of the law which does not reflect the diversity of postmodern society. In postmodern society, people are increasingly freed from the constraints arising from social norms and social bonds to others, yet crime as presently defined is simply an expression of a particular view among those with power of how people should conduct themselves, and denies people's freedom, self-identity and difference. It is necessary to develop a transgressive approach, which goes beyond the usual boundaries of defining crime as simply law-breaking, and to develop a conception of crime based on respect for people's chosen identities and lifestyles.

A transgressive approach: crime as social harm

Henry and Milovanovic (1996) adopt such a transgressive approach to crime. They suggest that crime should be reconceptualized as people using power to show disrespect for, and causing harm of some sort to, others, whether or not it is illegal, embracing all threats and risks to people pursuing increasingly diverse lifestyles and identities. They identify two forms of harm:

1 *Harms of reduction.* Power is used to cause a victim to experience some *immediate* loss or injury.
2 *Harms of repression.* Power is used to restrict *future* human development. This conception of harm brings a wider range of actions into the criminal net, which are either not illegal or not traditionally taken very seriously or perceived as part of the current crime 'problem'. These include harms threatening human dignity and respect, such as sexual harassment, and hate crimes, in which people are attacked or abused because of some characteristics which mark them out as different, such as their ethnicity, religion, gender, sexual orientation, disability or nationality.

> **Hate crimes** are those which are perceived by the victim or any other person to be motivated by hostility or prejudice based on a person's ethnicity, religion, sexual orientation or disability.

The causes of crime

Most sociological theories explain crime and deviance in relation to a social structure and core values or a dominant ideology which the criminal deviates from or rejects for some reason, such as through:

- Marginalization
- Relative deprivation
- Anomie and strain
- Inadequate socialization
- Being part of a workshy welfare-dependent underclass
- Subcultural values
- Weakened social bonds.

Postmodern society is characterized by a fragmentation of this social structure, and a growing diversity of values. The metanarratives of social class, work and family, which formed people's identity and gave them their social roles and values, and integrated them into society, have been replaced by uncertainty and individual choice of identity. Individuals increasingly focus on themselves, often with little sense of obligation to others, or regard and respect for them, which reduces constraints over committing crime.

The individualism of identity in postmodern society means that the social causes of crime are undiscoverable. Each crime becomes a one-off event, expressing whatever identity an individual chooses – a lifestyle choice – and is motivated by an infinite number of individual causes, including intangible emotional reasons. For example, low individual self-esteem may be overcome by criminal activities designed to earn respect from others by harming them, perhaps by humiliating, bullying or intimidating victims as in anti-social behaviour or bullying at school – or hate crimes directed at others simply because of such characteristics as ethnicity, religion, gender, sexual orientation, disability, or nationality. Levin and McDevitt (2008) suggest perpetrators of some hate crimes derive thrills, joys, excitement and pleasure and an escape from everyday routines by inflicting suffering on those they perceive to be different from themselves. The earlier section on feminist theories mentioned Messerschmidt's work on crime as an expression of masculinity for some men (see page 492 for more on this).

Edgework and the seductions of crime

Katz (1988) explores the pleasures and seductions of crime for individuals, and Lyng (1990, 2005) studied crime as 'edgework', with individuals committing crime for the excitement and thrills they get from the risk-taking involved and from living 'on the edge' as they explore the boundaries between legal and criminal behaviour.

Crime and anti-social behaviour may be just one more way in which people set about constructing their identities, alongside or as alternatives (for poorer people) to other high-risk (and often high-cost) adrenaline-inducing activities like motor racing, paragliding, skydiving, base jumping, deep sea diving and high-altitude mountaineering. Committing crime may be a gratifying, seductive adventure, generating a 'buzz' of emotion from the risk-taking, excitement and thrills involved in acts like shoplifting, joyriding, vandalism, fighting, being drunk, taking drugs and winding up or intimidating the public, and more important than any worry about the risk of being caught or the need for items stolen. The 'thrills and spills' of edgework as a motivation for crime may appeal to all people at various times, but are likely to appeal particularly to young people. This applies especially to young working-class men who lack the means of winning peer group respect and status and the accolades others might achieve by non-criminal leisure-based activities, and for whom it may be a way of expressing the masculinity that Miller suggested was a focal concern in lower-working-class subculture. For postmodernists, there are a diverse range of motivations for crime other than simply material gain, and the causes of crime lie in the individual, not in society. Crime may be committed simply for the kicks derived from doing so.

The implications of postmodernist approaches for the control of crime are considered in Topic 4 (see pages 538–40).

Evaluation of the postmodernist approach

Strengths

1 It recognizes that there are other dimensions to the causes of crime beyond the more structural theories which have dominated in the sociology of crime and deviance.
2 It offers explanations for non-utilitarian crime, with no material benefit, like hate crimes and anti-social behaviour.
3 It provides a fuller picture of the pattern of crime than that traditionally provided, as the transgressive conception of crime as 'harm' encompasses a range of behaviour that has been largely neglected in the law and in sociological theories.

Limitations

1 It doesn't explain why most people don't use their power to harm others, and why particular individuals or groups find it necessary to actively engage in acts of harm as a means of asserting their identity. Lea (1998) suggests traditional theories like marginality, relative deprivation and subculture still provide a useful starting point for explaining why certain groups have been denied access to less harm-causing sources of identity.
2 It fails to recognize that the consumer society, in which personal identity and fulfilment are tied up with the purchase of consumer goods, can lead to resentment among those who can't afford to participate.
3 It fails to recognize that many people still have strong conceptions of right and wrong behaviour, which underpin the law and much sociological theory of crime.
4 Lea points out that postmodernist theories are not much more than a re-discovery of labelling theory or radical criminology, which concluded long ago that crime was simply a social construction, and that power was a crucial element in that construction.

The implications of a number of the theories discussed in this Topic for policies for crime control and prevention are explored in Topic 4 (pages 532–40).

Practice questions

1 Outline **two** ways in which crime and deviance are socially constructed. **(4 marks)**

2 Outline **three** reasons why some crime may be necessary and beneficial for the well-being of society. **(6 marks)**

3 Read **Item A** below and answer the question that follows.

Item A

Labelling theorists suggest that many people commit acts of crime and deviance, but it is the stereotypes and assumptions held by the police and other agencies of social control that influence who gets caught and defined as criminal. Officially classified criminals are an unrepresentative group of offenders who have had their behaviour publicly labelled as 'criminal'.

Applying material from **Item A**, analyse **two** reasons why labelling theory may not provide an adequate explanation for the causes of crime. **(10 marks)**

4 Read **Item B** below and answer the question that follows.

Item B

Some Marxist sociologists argue that capitalist society is criminogenic, that is, crime is an in-built and natural outgrowth of a capitalist society. Crime is a rational response to the competitiveness and inequality of life in capitalist society, and the law reflects ruling-class interests and ideology.

Applying material from **Item B** and your knowledge, evaluate the usefulness of Marxist approaches to an understanding of the causes of crime. **(30 marks)**

Topic 2

SPECIFICATION AREA

The social distribution of crime and deviance by ethnicity, gender and social class, including recent patterns and trends in crime

Crime statistics

The picture of crime that is generally presented to the public, and used by sociologists, is the one derived from official statistics. These statistics are used for a variety of purposes:

- For comparison with previous years to discover trends in crime
- To look at the police clear-up rate to measure police efficiency
- To show where the police should concentrate resources to reduce crime
- To provide the public (often via the media) with information on crime patterns
- To provide a basis for sociologists to explain crime, including what is and what is not shown in the statistics
- To reveal police assumptions and stereotyping, as the statistics are in part generated by the activities of the police themselves and the offenders they choose to pursue and the offences they choose to record.

The source of crime statistics

Crime statistics are compiled from several main sources.

1 *Police recorded crime (PRC)*. These are offences either detected by or reported to the police, and recorded by them.
2 *Victim surveys*. These survey the victims of crime and include unreported and unrecorded crime. They give a more accurate picture than police recorded crime, and are not affected by the recording/counting rules that police statistics are bound by. They include, for example, the *Crime Survey for England and Wales* (CSEW). This is a face-to-face survey in which people resident in households in England and Wales are asked about their experiences of crime in the twelve months prior to the interview.
3 *Self-report studies*. These are anonymous questionnaires in which people are asked to own up to committing crimes, whether or not they have been discovered. An example of this was the Home Office's *Offending, Crime and Justice Survey*, which was carried out annually between 2003 and 2006.
4 *Court and prison records, and records on police cautions*. These reveal some of the characteristics of offenders who have been caught.

Police recorded crime (PRC) and the *Crime Survey for England and Wales* (CSEW)

Police recorded crime (PRC) and the *Crime Survey for England and Wales* (CSEW) form the main basis for official crime statistics, and together they provide a more comprehensive picture of crime than either source alone can provide. This is particularly the case for offences committed against the public involving physical harm, loss or damage to property.

PRC covers a wider range of offences than the CSEW – it includes crimes against businesses and non-residents, such as visitors and tourists – but it does not include crimes that are not reported to, discovered by or recorded by the police, and excludes some less serious offences. The CSEW covers crimes even if they are not reported to or recorded by the police, but excludes crimes against businesses and those not resident in households, and excludes some more serious crimes. In 2014/15, despite covering a narrower range of offences, the CSEW recorded around 50 per cent more crimes than were recorded by the police.

The social construction of crime statistics

Many sociologists approach official crime statistics with caution. They question the extent to which they are *reliable*, in so far as there may be inconsistencies in the way crimes might be classified – for example, several offences committed at the same time might be rolled up into a single (most serious) offence, and individual police forces and officers have some discretion in how they classify offences.

There are also questions raised over their *validity* in providing a true and complete picture of the amount of crime, and the characteristics of offenders. This is because many offences are not discovered, many of those that are discovered are not reported to the police, and many of those that are reported are not recorded. For example, in 2014 HM Inspectorate of Constabulary calculated that almost one in five (19 percent) of crimes reported to the police were not recorded, following an investigation into claims that PRC statistics are routinely fiddled. These 'hidden' crimes are commonly referred to as the 'dark figure' of undiscovered, unrecorded and unreported crime. In addition, only about 27 per cent of recorded crimes were detected or 'cleared up' in 2014/15, with an offender identified and action taken against them. Maguire (2002) estimates only about 3 per cent of all crime in England and Wales ends with a conviction.

Unreported crime

A large number of people who are victims of crime don't bother to report it to the police. For example, as shown in figure 6.4, the CSEW suggests around 60 per cent of the crimes it covers are never reported to the police.

Like an iceberg, where most of the ice is hidden beneath the surface, so it is with crime, with a hidden 'dark figure' of undiscovered, unreported or unrecorded crime. Only about 3 per cent of all crimes are estimated to result in an offender being convicted.

Figure 6.4
Percentage of *Crime Survey for England and Wales* (CSEW) incidents reported to the police 2014–15

Source: Crime in England and Wales, Annual Trend & Demographic Tables, Office for National Statistics, July 2015

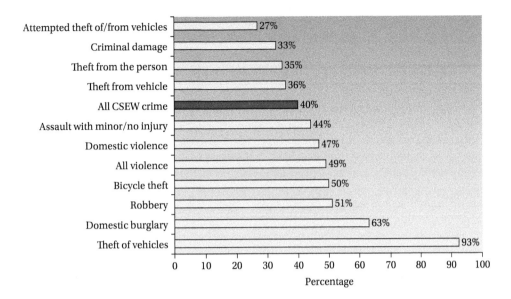

Attempted theft of/from vehicles 27%
Criminal damage 33%
Theft from the person 35%
Theft from vehicle 36%
All CSEW crime 40%
Assault with minor/no injury 44%
Domestic violence 47%
All violence 49%
Bicycle theft 50%
Robbery 51%
Domestic burglary 63%
Theft of vehicles 93%

Percentage

Activity

Study figure 6.4 and answer the following questions:
1 What percentage of crimes of criminal damage were *not* reported to the police in 2014/15?
2 What percentage of thefts from vehicles were reported in 2014/15?
3 Which offence was most likely to be reported in 2014/15?
4 With reference to figure 6.4, suggest three reasons, with examples, why some offences are reported to the police much more than others.

The CSEW found the three main reasons people don't report a crime to the police are because:

1 It was too trivial, involved no loss, or the police would not have been interested or could not do anything.
2 It was a private matter which they dealt with themselves.
3 It was inconvenient to report.

Other reasons included: the offence was a common occurrence; it was the victim's own fault; the offender was not responsible for their actions; fear of reprisals, and dislike or fear of the police or previous bad experiences with the police and courts. In some circumstances, a crime may not be reported as doing so may harm the reputation of the institution in which the offence occurs, such as white-collar crime, for example fraud by a bank employee, or theft or drug abuse in schools.

Reported but unrecorded crime

The police may decide not to record an offence that has been reported to or observed by them because:

- They may regard the matter as too trivial to waste their time on, such as anti-social behaviour or the theft of a very small sum of money.
- It has already been satisfactorily resolved, or because the victim does not wish to proceed with the complaint.
- They may regard the person complaining as too unreliable to take his or her account of the incident seriously, as in the case of complaints made by a tramp, a drug addict, or someone who is drunk.
- They may interpret the law in such a way that what is reported is not regarded as an offence.

Changes in reporting, and counting and recording of crime

Official statistics can also give a distorted picture of crime because of a range of other factors, which may give the impression of an increase in crime, when the rise is really due to the public reporting more crimes or changes in the way police record crime, rather than a real increase in the number of crimes. These factors include:

1   *The media.* The bulk of recorded crimes – around 85 per cent – are first brought to the attention of the police by reports from the public. Whether the public choose to report crime is influenced partly by their awareness or feelings about crime, which are in turn influenced by the preoccupations of the media. Media reports may exaggerate and distort events, generate moral panics, and make problems seem worse than they are (these media effects are discussed on pages 515–23). This sensitizes people and groups to particular offences or groups of people, and may consequently lead to more reporting of incidents by a more intolerant public demanding police action.

2   *Changing police attitudes, priorities and policies.* A stronger desire by the police to prosecute certain offenders due to changing police attitudes and policies towards some offences (possibly provoked by the media), such as a crack-down on prostitution, drug-dealing, knife crime or drink-driving. This may give the impression of an increase in crimes of that type, when it is simply that the police are making extra efforts and allocating more officers to tackle such crimes, and therefore recording more offences.

3   *People may be bringing to the attention of the police less serious incidents which they may not have reported in the past.* For example, they may have become less tolerant of vandalism and anti-social behaviour, and expect the police to stop it. This could be another effect of media reporting. Maguire (2007) suggests that growing privatization and the break-up of close-knit community life means that people may now be reporting to the police incidents that they may once have dealt with by taking action themselves.

4   *Changing social norms and public attitudes.* For example, changing attitudes to offences like rape, domestic violence and child abuse among the police and the public may have resulted in more offences being reported, even though no more have been committed.

5   *Community policing and higher policing levels.* This means more crimes may be recorded and detected/offenders caught. Neighbourhood policing teams, which involve engagement by the police with local communities, and Neighbourhood Watch schemes may also lead to more crimes being detected and reported.

6   *Changing counting rules.* Changing rules for the way police count or record crimes can lead to higher numbers of offences being recorded, but not necessarily more crime.

7   *More sophisticated police training, communications and equipment.* For example, the use of computers, CCTV, forensic science, and DNA testing can lead to increasing detection of crime.

8   *Changes in the law.* These can lead to more things becoming illegal – for example, in the year ending May 2014, 280 new criminal offences were created, while 213 were abolished.

9   *Easier communications.* Mobile phones, SMS, email and police community websites, for example, all make reporting of crime easier.

10 *People have more to lose today.* People tend to have more consumer goods, and more people have household contents insurance cover. Insurance claims for crimes such as theft or criminal damage need a police crime number, so more crime is reported. For example, nearly all thefts of cars and burglaries with loss are reported today so people can claim the insurance money.

Attempts to overcome the limitations of official statistics: victim surveys and self-report studies

Victim surveys

Victim surveys, like the CSEW, ask the public whether they have been victims of crime, whether or not they reported it to the police. They help to overcome the problem of offences not reported to or recorded by the police, and they provide insights into the victims of crime. They do have a number of limitations:

1 *People may exaggerate*, or lie, perhaps because of a desire to impress researchers or be dramatic.

2 *People may forget they were victimized*, particularly the more trivial incidents, or forget *when* they were victimized. They may have repressed and totally forgotten what they regard as traumatic incidents, or they may construct false memories of victimization they haven't actually experienced (psychology students may recognize these as selective and constructed memories). In an annual survey like the CSEW, errors may arise if victims think incidents occurred outside the time period (the previous 12 months) covered by the survey, even if they were in it, or report incidents outside the time period.

3 *People may not realize they have been the victims of a crime*, nor that what happened to them was actually a criminal act. For example, in the case of white-collar and corporate crimes, they may not realize that they have been duped, 'conned' or sold dangerous products.

4 *They often don't include all crimes.* The CSEW, for example, surveys households, and excludes commercial premises and, therefore, business crime, shops and fraud.

5 *As with all surveys, there is the issue of whether the survey is representative*, and therefore whether the findings can be generalized to the whole population.

6 *Victims may feel embarrassment or guilt at admitting to being a victim*, such as in the case of sexual offences or domestic violence, or of those who get conned by internet scams.

7 *Consensual or victimless crimes*, where both parties agree to commit an offence and both have something to lose, such as white-collar crimes like bribery and corruption, or taking someone else's penalty points for speeding offences, or buying and selling illegal drugs, are not likely to be reported.

Self-report studies

Self-report studies are surveys that ask people to 'own up' to their offending and tell researchers what offences they have committed, whether or not they were caught. They are useful as they provide information on the characteristics of offenders not reported to or caught by the police, and offences not recorded by them; they also help to find out about victimless crimes like fraud, bribery and corruption or illegal drug use, and may help to discover some of the factors associated with risks of offending, such as difficult childhoods or being taken into care, or unemployment. Despite their usefulness, they do have some limitations.

1 *The validity of findings.* The validity or truthfulness and accuracy of responses is a major issue in any self-report survey – perhaps not surprisingly, given that many offences involve dishonesty. Offenders may exaggerate, understate or lie about the number of crimes they've committed, perhaps because of a desire to impress researchers or be dramatic. Young male offenders, for example, may make up or exaggerate their offences to assert their masculinity. Offenders may not be willing to admit to more serious offences, and especially those with a strong social stigma, like domestic violence, child abuse or paedophilia. This means such surveys tend to over-emphasize more minor or trivial offences, like vandalism/criminal damage.

2 *They may ignore respondents' own definitions of crime.* For example, in some communities or subcultures some crimes may be such a common and accepted occurrence – such as handling stolen goods – that offenders may not see them as criminal and therefore don't report them.

3 *They rely on memory.* Individuals may not remember all the offences they have committed over a period of time, perhaps because they have repressed and totally forgotten what they regard as embarrassing or traumatic incidents, or they may construct false memories of offences they haven't actually committed (in psychology, these refer to selective and constructed memory).

4 *Lack of representativeness.* Those who live more chaotic lifestyles, probably like many young offenders, and those who are persistent, prolific and serious offenders are the least likely to participate in such surveys, so they may therefore be unrepresentative.

The use of crime statistics by sociologists

The social construction of the crime statistics described above means we cannot be certain we have very valid evidence about the nature and extent of crime, who is committing the majority of offences, and the social characteristics of criminals. Those who appear in official statistics may be an unrepresentative sample of a minority of officially classified criminals who happen to have been caught (or voluntarily admitted to offending in self-report surveys), leaving open the possibility that much crime may be committed by very different types of people from those who come before the courts. Interpretivists argue that the crime statistics are such a socially constructed manufactured product that they tell us more about the process of reporting by the public, the way the media report crime, and the stereotypes and activities of the police and other agencies of social control than they do about the real number of crimes and the characteristics of criminals.

Sociologists from different theoretical perspectives have responded to the ambiguity and uncertainty in the official statistics in various ways, which are outlined in table 6.3. The rest of this topic discusses sociological explanations for the pattern of crime shown in official statistics, but those statistics may give a misleading impression of the criminal population as a whole.

Table 6.3 Theoretical approaches to the use of official crime statistics

Functionalism, New Right, Right Realism	Broadly accept statistics as accurate and representative of most crime, and useful for establishing patterns and trends in crime, and as a base for forming hypotheses and building theories.
Interactionism/labelling theory	Statistics are social constructions, and useful only to reveal the stereotypes, labelling and assumptions of the public, and the institutional sexism and racism of the criminal justice system. The pattern shown in statistics further fuels these stereotypes, which generates a self-fulfilling prophecy, as they provide a guide for the police on the 'typical offender' as they go about their work.
Marxism/neo-Marxism	Statistics provide a biased view of crime, as they under-represent crimes of the powerful – white-collar and corporate crime – and give the impression that the main criminals are working-class.
Feminism	Statistics under-represent the extent of female crime, and crimes by men against women, such as domestic violence and rape.
Left Realism	Statistics are broadly correct, though they under-represent white-collar and corporate crime, and exaggerate the extent of working-class crime, particularly by some minority ethnic groups.

Trends in crime

Official statistics show the following trends in recorded crime:

- From the 1930s to the early 1950s, there was a gradual rise
- From the 1950s and the early 1980s, there was a steeper rise
- From the 1980s to the mid-1990s, there was a rapid increase
- From the mid-1990s to 2015, there was a gradual annual decline.

Figure 6.5 shows that both PRC and CSEW crime in England and Wales peaked in the mid-1990s. CSEW crime has more than halved since its peak in 1995, and in 2015 was the lowest estimate since the survey began in 1981. PRC crime has dropped by about 25 per cent in the last ten years. The apparent increase in PRC crime after 1999/2000 is due to changes in the methods the Home Office used to record and count crimes in 1998 and 2002, and the introduction of the National Crime Recording Standard (NCRS) in 2002/3, rather than representing a real increase in the number of crimes committed. Although crime today is at a much higher level than it was before the 1960s, the overall crime level seems to have stabilized or to be dropping each year, though this is not the case for all offences, some of which are increasing, such as police-recorded violence with injury, sexual offences, fraud and cybercrime.

Figure 6.6 shows a breakdown of the main types of offence recorded by the police in 2014/15, and those revealed by the CSEW.

Figure 6.5 Trends in police recorded crime (PRC) and CSEW crime, 1981 to year ending June 2015

Source: Crime in England and Wales, Office for National Statistics, 2015

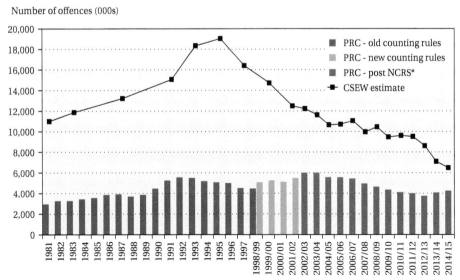

*the new National Crime Recording Standard (counting rules) adopted in 2002/3

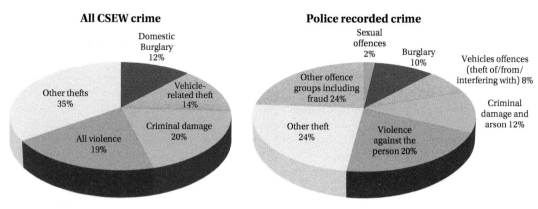

Total number of CSEW crimes = 6.5 million

Total number of PRC crimes = 4.3 million

Figure 6.6 The pattern of crime in official statistics: *Crime Survey for England and Wales* (CSEW) crime and police recorded crime (PRC), England and Wales, year ending June 2015

Source: Crime in England and Wales, Office for National Statistics, 2015

The pattern of offending

The pattern of offences and the characteristics of offenders revealed by the various statistical sources mentioned above show that most crime is committed:

- By working-class males
- In urban areas
- By young people (a third of all those convicted in any year are aged 10–21, with the peak age for crime being 18 for males, and 14 for females)
- Against property (about 70–80 per cent of all crime).

For some offences, such as street crime and some drug offences, there is – according to official statistics – an over-representation of some minority ethnic groups, particularly black minority ethnic groups.

Despite the various limitations arising from the social construction of crime statistics, sociologists need to work with the best evidence available to them, and the rest of this topic examines explanations for some aspects of the pattern of offending shown in official statistics.

An important note on the rest of this topic

Many of the explanations for the patterns of crime which are referred to in the rest of this topic from this point on have been considered in Topic 1, and some will be in Topic 3. It is important that you refer to any page references indicated to ensure you have a full understanding of the points being made, as these will not be reproduced here in full.

Ethnicity and crime

Contemporary official statistics suggest what *appear* to be higher levels of criminality among some minority ethnic groups, particularly the black (African-Caribbean) population. For example, the Ministry of Justice, in 2013, reported that, compared to white people, black people were:

- Over twice as likely to be cautioned by the police
- Around three times more likely to be arrested

Table 6.4 Proportion of individuals at different stages of the Criminal Justice System (CJS) process by ethnic group compared to general population, England and Wales

	White	Black	Asian	Mixed	Chinese or Other	Unknown	TOTAL
Population aged 10 or over 2011	87%	3%	6%	2%	2%	–	49,443,451
Stop and searches (s1) 2011–12	67%	14%	10%	3%	1%	4.2%	1,120,084
Arrests 2011–12	79%	8%	6%	3%	1%	2%	1,235,028
Cautions 2012	84%	7%	5%	–	1%	3%	188,610
Court proceedings (indictable*) 2012	71%	8%	5%	2%	1%	13%	375,874
Convictions (indictable*) 2012	73%	7%	4%	2%	1%	12%	308,124
Sentenced to immediate custody (indictable*) 2012	71%	9%	5%	2%	2%	11%	81,082
Prison population (aged 15+) 2013	74%	13%	8%	4%	1%	–	86,067

Figures are rounded to nearest whole percentage

* Indictable offences are more serious criminal offences that can be tried at the Crown Court (indictable only) or at the magistrates' court (either-way offences)

Source: Statistics on Race and the Criminal Justice System; Offender Management Statistics, Ministry of Justice, 2013

Indictable offences are more serious criminal offences that can be tried at the Crown Court (indictable only) or at the magistrates' court (either-way offences). These contrast with less serious Summary Offences, such as motoring offences, common assault and small-scale criminal damage up to £5,000, which are usually tried only by a magistrates' court.

- If arrested, more likely to be charged, remanded in custody, and face court proceedings than to receive a caution
- More likely, if found guilty, to receive a custodial (prison) sentence and for a longer term
- Five times more likely to be in prison.

Asians compared to white people were:

- More likely to be charged and face court proceedings than to receive a caution;
- More likely to receive a custodial sentence if found guilty and for a longer term.

Table 6.4 shows the proportions of different ethnic groups involved at various stages of the criminal justice system process.

Activity

Referring to table 6.4, analyse the data and describe what conclusions you might draw about the links between ethnicity and crime. Give figures to back up your conclusions.

Sociologists have developed a number of explanations for the higher levels of offending in some ethnic minorities shown in official statistics.

Sociological explanations of the links between ethnicity and offending

Neo-Marxist approaches

Black crime as resistance
Gilroy (1982) argued that crime by black people, particularly in the 1970s, was a form of political action, representing a culture of resistance to inequality and oppressors in the form of police racism

Figure 6.7 Ethnicity and crime

Black crime is exaggerated to justify aggressive styles of policing and, in the 1970s, to reassert the power of the state, which was facing a crisis of hegemony

Offers a form of political resistance against oppressive white society and culture

Relative deprivation means young black people have a sense of injustice, intensified by racism, at lacking things others in society have

Labelling, stereotyping and racism in the criminal justice system, e.g. racist canteen culture in police forces, stop and search, and institutional racism

Poverty and social exclusion encourage the search for a powerful identity otherwise denied in a predominantly white culture

Marginality creates powerlessness and resentment

Subcultures combined with marginality and relative deprivation provide support for crime as an alternative means of achieving mainstream goals that are otherwise blocked

and harassment. He denied there was greater criminality among black people than whites, suggesting this was a myth created by negative stereotyping by the police and the media, who saw minority ethnic groups as untrustworthy, with African-Caribbean youth labelled as potential 'muggers' and Asians as potential illegal immigrants.

Black crime and scapegoating – the crisis of hegemony and the creation of the 'black mugger'

As discussed in Topic 1 (see page 457) Hall et al. (1978) argue that in the 1970s Britain was facing an economic and political crisis which threatened the dominance of ruling-class ideology in society – a crisis of hegemony. At the same time, there was growing conflict between the police and the African-Caribbean community. This was fuelled by selective publication of crime statistics showing black youth involvement in particular offences, including street robbery (theft with actual or threatened use of force, now commonly called 'mugging'). The media picked up on this, as making good headlines, and promoted the idea that black people were more prone to criminality than whites, and the media image of the 'black mugger' was born. A moral panic developed – a media-fuelled exaggeration of the problem of black crime – with growing demands by the public that something should be done to stamp out the problem. The 'black mugger' came to be a folk devil and a scapegoat for all of society's problems. (Moral panics are discussed further on pages 518–22).

Hall et al. argued that there had not been a real increase in street robbery (mugging) but the moral panic was used to justify more repressive and aggressive policing against the black community, like repeated stop and search. All black youth were seen as a threat, even when they weren't doing anything wrong, and this generated growing distrust, and hostility and resistance to the police in the black community, which in many ways continues today. The media-exaggerated extent of black crime therefore became a means of reasserting the dominance of ruling-class ideas, and re-establishing their hegemony in society generally, as the public shared their concerns over black criminality, and this diverted people's attention from the wider crisis in British society.

In the 1970s, the 'black mugger' emerged during a crisis of hegemony of the British state, and came to symbolize all of society's problems, and also helped to justify more repressive and aggressive policing in some inner-city areas. Britain's police riot squads, using paramilitary equipment such as shields and riot sticks, first emerged in 1970s Britain.

Evaluation of neo-Marxist explanations

While neo-Marxist theories offer an explanation for black crime, as a form of resistance and as a response to aggressive policing arising from an unjustified moral panic, there are three main criticisms.

1 The conflicts between minority ethnic groups, the police and criminal justice agencies and negative media stereotypes still exist, but the 'crisis of hegemony' of the 1970s does not, suggesting that the explanation is inadequate.
2 Gilroy seems to be imposing his own interpretation of the meaning of black crime when he describes it as a political act against oppressors. Black crime, including mugging, is often committed against other black or poor people, so it is hard to see it as resistance to oppression.
3 Lea and Young (1984) point out that most crimes are reported by the public, not uncovered by the police, so it is hard to explain black crime in terms of police racism.

Left Realism

Lea and Young's Left Realist approach (see pages 465–8) accepts that black crime, for some offences, is higher than for the white population. They suggest three factors contribute to this.

1 *Marginality.* Some minority ethnic groups are pushed to the edges of mainstream society by underachievement in education, lack of employment or low pay, and lack of legitimate opportunities to influence events. These create resentments and a sense of powerlessness, further fuelled by the experience of racism.
2 *Relative deprivation.* This is most likely to be felt by those facing more deprived social situations, as many of those in minority ethnic groups do.
3 *Subculture.* Marginality and relative deprivation can combine in contributing to the formation of subcultures in deprived communities, which provide a form of peer-group support for young black males, and may involve gang culture, violence, and street crime as a response to the resentments and status frustration they feel.

Poverty, social exclusion and the search for identity

Bowling and Phillips (2002) suggest higher levels of robbery by black people could be linked to poverty and social exclusion, which black communities are more likely to suffer from, and such activities can generate both peer-group status and a sense of a powerful black identity otherwise denied. Poverty and social exclusion clearly affect Asians as well, particularly Pakistanis and Bangladeshis, who are among the poorest groups in British society. However, their lower crime rate may be because Asian cultures offer a much clearer cultural identity, and there are generally stronger controls within Asian families and communities, limiting the opportunities and perhaps the desire to commit crime.

Labelling, stereotyping and racism in policing and the criminal justice system

As considered earlier, many sociologists have argued that official crime statistics are socially constructed. Labelling theorists (see pages 459–63) and Marxists (see pages 456–7) argue that statistics suggesting black and Asian people are more likely to be offenders than whites are misleading, and are evidence of selective law enforcement rather than higher rates of criminality. Racism and racist stereotypes in police culture and practice mean the behaviour of black and Asian people is more likely to be labelled as criminal, and the law selectively enforced to target them, accounting for their higher arrest rates compared to whites. In support of this view, Reiner (2000) points to a racist 'canteen culture' among the police, which includes suspicion, macho values and racism, and this encourages racist stereotypes and a mistrust of those from non-white backgrounds. From this point of view, the link between crime and ethnic minorities is a socially constructed fabrication – a product of racial prejudice and discrimination against black people and Asians by the police and other criminal justice agencies. Phillips and Bowling (2012) suggest evidence of racial discrimination is shown in the following ways.

Indirect racial discrimination

1 *Mistrust of the police.* This means minority ethnic suspects are less likely than white offenders to cooperate with police officers or prosecutors, and less likely to admit offences during interview or before trial. Refusing to admit to offences means they are ineligible for a caution or reduced sentences.
2 *Social position.* Minority ethnic groups are more likely than white offenders to display the social characteristics which make a remand in custody more likely than release on bail, because they are thought to be more likely to abscond. This includes factors like poor housing and a lack of community.

Direct racial discrimination

1 *Stop and search.* Black and Asian people, and especially youth, fit police stereotypes of 'troublemakers' and they are therefore targeted for heavier policing. Fitzgerald (1993) found police discrimination against ethnic minorities was greatest in situations where police officers had scope to exploit their own intuition, stereotypes and racial prejudices, such as stopping and searching people. The Ministry of Justice in 2013 reported that, compared to white people, Asians were twice as likely, and black people (African Caribbeans) were six times more likely (though this rises to thirty times under some police stop and search powers) to be stopped and searched by the police, as shown in figure 6.8; that this seems to be based on unjustified assumptions and racial stereotypes, rather than reasonable suspicion, is shown by the fact that only about one in ten stop and searches results in an arrest, so at least 90 per cent of 'suspects' are in fact not guilty of anything. Phillips and Bowling (2012) note that stop and search contributes to the unfair criminalization of ethnic minorities, and undermines public support for the police in their communities. The resentments created by over-policing and stop and search were one of the sparks behind the UK riots in British cities in 2011. Bowling and Phillips (2002) suggest regular stop and searches by the police can lead to a self-fulfilling prophecy, with higher levels of robbery among black youth arising as a response to labelling, as they act in accordance with the stereotypes the police have of them.

Black and Asian people are between twice and thirty times more likely than white people to be stopped and searched by the police.

Figure 6.8 Stop and search rates by ethnicity in England and Wales

Source: Home Office

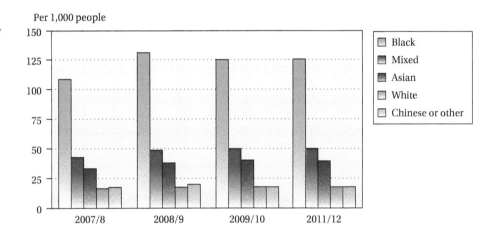

Per 1,000 people

Legend: Black, Mixed, Asian, White, Chinese or other

2 *Institutional racism.* The investigation into the police handling of the murder of 18-year-old Stephen Lawrence by five white youths in 1993 led to the Macpherson Report in 1999. This was highly critical of the Metropolitan Police, pointing to a series of mistakes, professional incompetence, and a 'lack of urgency' and mishandling of the police investigation, including their assumption that Stephen Lawrence was involved in a street brawl rather than being the victim of an unprovoked racist attack. It pointed to the existence of institutional racism in the police force. The persistence of this racism in the Metropolitan Police led the Metropolitan Black Police Association, in 2008, to warn people from minority ethnic groups not to join the force, because of 'a hostile atmosphere where racism is allowed to spread'.

Institutional racism refers to patterns of discrimination based on ethnicity that have become structured into social institutions.

3 *Arrests, charges and court proceedings.* Police officers appear to arrest and charge some black and Asian suspects without sufficient evidence. The Crown Prosecution Service (CPS) are more likely to drop cases against ethnic minorities before they reach court, and those cases the CPS brings to court have a lower conviction rate than those involving white offenders. This suggests there wasn't enough evidence for the police to charge them in the first place, nor for the CPS to secure convictions as they were bringing such weak cases to court.

4 *Discrimination in sentencing.* Black people, compared to white offenders in the same position, face a greater likelihood both of being given a prison sentence and of receiving longer sentences.

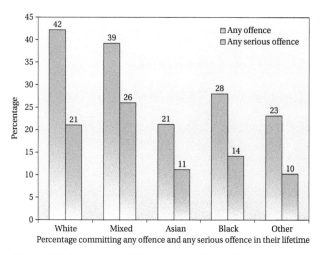

Figure 6.9 Self-reported lifetime offending (%)

Source: Sharp and Budd (2005)

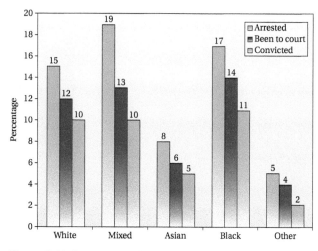

Figure 6.10 Percentage of respondents aged 10–65 who have ever been arrested, been to court, or been convicted (2003 *OCJS*)

Source: Sharp and Budd (2005)

5   *Over-representation in prison.* The cumulative effects of social exclusion, and direct and indirect discrimination, are shown in the disproportionate rates of imprisonment for people from minority ethnic groups. In 2013, they made up over twice the proportion of prisoners (26 per cent) compared to their proportion in the general population (12 per cent), and black people were over-represented by four times (13 per cent) compared to their 3 per cent proportion of the general population. Phillips and Bowling (2012) cite evidence showing that, in prison, black and Asian prisoners face a more brutal regime than white prisoners, including abuse, violence and intimidation, denial of earned privileges and disproportionate disciplinary action. Asian prisoners face stereotyping as 'Islamic terrorists' and as 'security risks' in prison.

Further evidence of discrimination in policing and the criminal justice system is suggested by self-report studies. Sharp and Budd (2005), based on findings from the Home Office's *2003 Offending, Crime and Justice Survey* (*OCJS*), found that white people had the highest rate of lifetime offending, as shown in figure 6.9, and black and Asian people were significantly less likely to offend than white respondents. For offences committed in the previous twelve months, white males aged from 10 to 25 were far more likely to have committed an offence than 10- to 25-year-old males in other ethnic groups, and were more likely to be classed as serious or frequent offenders compared to Asian or black males in this age group. Despite this generally lower level of offending, figure 6.10 shows that people of Mixed or Black ethnicity are more likely to have been arrested, been to court or been convicted in their lifetimes.

In the light of such evidence, it is perhaps then not surprising that many of those from minority ethnic groups see the criminal justice system as discriminatory, causing them to lack confidence and trust in the police, and creating the sense of grievance that Gilroy and Hall et al. first identified in the 1970s but which continues in contemporary Britain.

Evaluation of ethnicity and crime

The links between ethnicity and offending are complex, and it is quite difficult to discover whether differences between ethnic groups are a result of their ethnic identity, or because of differences in age, social class and the areas in which they live. For example, compared to white people, minority ethnic groups tend to have higher proportions of young people, those suffering social and economic deprivation, and those living in deprived urban communities; higher crime rates may be related to these factors rather than ethnicity itself.

On the other hand, there is substantial evidence, confirmed in self-report studies, that the higher rate of offending by some minority ethnic groups shown in official statistics may be an exaggerated distortion created by racist stereotyping, unjustified assumptions and labelling by the police, and by racial discrimination in the criminal justice system.

Activity

1 Referring back to Topic 1 if necessary, explain how each of the following concepts or theories might be applied to explain apparently higher levels of criminality among some minority ethnic groups:
   ● strain theory and anomie (see pages 451–2)
   ● marginality and social exclusion (see pages 465–6)
   ● control and rational choice and opportunity theories (see pages 454–6 and 468–9).
2 Identify four pieces of evidence in each case that outline that minority ethnic groups are: (a) more involved, and (b) no more, or less, involved, in crime than the white ethnic majority.

Gender and crime

Official statistics show that, in most countries of the world, males commit far more crime than females, in what is sometimes called the 'crime–gender gap' or the 'crime–sex ratio'. In England and Wales in 2014, men accounted for three-quarters of all persons convicted and 85 per cent of those convicted for more serious (indictable) criminal offences, and 95 per cent of prisoners. Men are convicted for about six *known* indictable offences for every one committed by women, they are more likely to be repeat offenders and in general they commit more serious offences. The proportion of men found guilty of or cautioned for indictable offences peaks at ages 17 to 20 when it is around ten times higher than the rate for women. Men are many times more likely to be found guilty of offending than women (as shown in figure 6.11) – for example:

● About sixty times more likely for sex offences
● About fourteen times more likely for robberies
● About thirteen times more likely for possession of weapons
● About ten times more likely for public order offences
● About eight times more likely for violence against the person (though it is much greater for violence which results in serious injury)
● About seven times more likely for criminal damage
● About six times more likely for all indictable offences overall
● About four times more likely for theft.

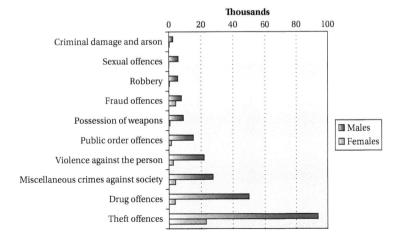

Figure 6.11 Offenders found guilty in all courts by sex and type of offence, England and Wales 2013–14

Source: Statistics on Women and the Criminal Justice System, Ministry of Justice, November 2014

Why do females appear to commit less crime than men?

Less detectable offences

Women, compared to men, tend to commit more of those offences which are less likely to be detected or reported, like shoplifting. Theft from shops is the most common offence among women, and around one-third of women in prison are there for theft and handling stolen goods. Although men do most shoplifting, women tend to steal smaller, less detectable items such as clothing, groceries, health products and perfumes, while males go for larger, more detectable and higher-value items like electrical equipment and power tools.

Sex-role theory and gender socialization

Sex-role theory, generally associated with functionalism and the New Right, is concerned with gender socialization and the different roles of men and women in society. Women's traditional 'expressive' roles involve caring for partners, children and dependent elderly relatives, and these are combined with responsibilities for housework and family management, and often paid employment. Gender socialization encourages women to adopt feminine characteristics such as being more emotional, less competitive, less tough and aggressive, and more averse to taking risks than men. These combine to make many women avoid the risk-taking involved in crime, as well as giving them fewer opportunities than men to commit crime.

Control theory and rational choice and opportunity in a patriarchal society

Carlen (1988) and Heidensohn (1996) combine a feminist approach with control and rational choice and opportunity theories (see pages 454–6 and 468–9) to explain women's lower level of offending. Heidensohn suggests that the differences between male and female crime arise from their different social circumstances, opportunities, the socialization process and the different impacts of informal and formal social control in a patriarchal society.

The gender deal and the class deal

Following a study of a small number of working-class women who had a criminal conviction, Carlen suggested that women are encouraged to conform by what she calls the *class deal* and the *gender deal*.

- The *class deal* refers to the material rewards that arise from working in paid employment, enabling women to purchase things like consumer goods and enjoy a respectable life and home.
- The *gender deal* refers to the rewards that arise from fulfilling their roles in the family and home, with material and emotional support from a male breadwinner.

Most women accept and achieve these deals and the rewards and security arising from them, and therefore conform. However, the rewards arising from the class or gender deals are not available to some women, because of things like poverty, unemployment, lack of a family through being brought up in care, or abusive partners. Such women may then make a rational decision to choose crime: such a choice has few costs, as they have little to lose (like loss of a job, family or status) but at least crime, like shoplifting or fraud, offers potential benefits like money, food and consumer goods which are not otherwise available through the approved or legitimate class and gender deals.

The constraints of socialization

Heidensohn suggests that women, in a patriarchal society, have more to lose than men if they get involved in crime and deviance, because they face a greater risk of stigma or shame. Carlen suggests women are socialized into performing a central role as 'guardians of domestic morality', and they risk social disapproval when they fail to do so. Women who take the risk of involving themselves in crime therefore face the double jeopardy of being condemned for both committing a crime and behaving in an unfeminine way – unlike a 'proper woman'.

Social control and different spheres

Agencies of social control work to discourage people from choosing crime over conformity. Heidensohn suggests that there is a patriarchal ideology of different spheres, with men dominating the public sphere – in which most crime is committed – including locations such as workplaces, pubs and clubs, and the streets at night, and women the private sphere of the home. Social control deters women from crime in the following ways:

1   In the *private domestic sphere* of the home, patriarchal control through the allocation to women of responsibilities for domestic labour and childcare provides less time and opportunity for crime, and women face more serious consequences if they do become involved. Teenage girls are likely to be more closely supervised by their parents than boys, reducing their chances of getting into trouble.

2   In the *public sphere* outside the home, women are faced with patriarchal controls arising from fear of physical or sexual violence if they go out alone at night, and at work they are often subject to sexual harassment and supervision by male bosses, which restricts their opportunities to deviate. Women are also likely to face a 'glass ceiling' at work. This is an invisible barrier of discrimination which makes it difficult for women to reach the same top levels in their chosen careers as similarly qualified men, and this restricts their opportunities to engage in white-collar crime like fraud.

3   Women face the threat of losing their reputation for being 'respectable' if they engage in deviance, for example through gossip, the application of labels like 'slag' or 'slapper' by men, and the threat to their reputation that comes from being caught, as men will condemn them for a lack of femininity.

All these put greater pressure to conform on women than on men, because of their greater risks of losing more than they might gain by law breaking, and also reducing their opportunities to do so.

Figure 6.12 Gender and crime

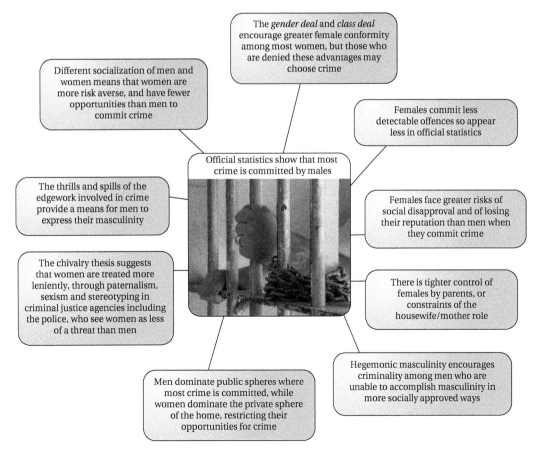

Different socialization of men and women means that women are more risk averse, and have fewer opportunities than men to commit crime

The *gender deal* and *class deal* encourage greater female conformity among most women, but those who are denied these advantages may choose crime

Females commit less detectable offences so appear less in official statistics

Official statistics show that most crime is committed by males

The thrills and spills of the edgework involved in crime provide a means for men to express their masculinity

Females face greater risks of social disapproval and of losing their reputation than men when they commit crime

The chivalry thesis suggests that women are treated more leniently, through paternalism, sexism and stereotyping in criminal justice agencies including the police, who see women as less of a threat than men

There is tighter control of females by parents, or constraints of the housewife/mother role

Men dominate public spheres where most crime is committed, while women dominate the private sphere of the home, restricting their opportunities for crime

Hegemonic masculinity encourages criminality among men who are unable to accomplish masculinity in more socially approved ways

The chivalry thesis

Pollak (1950) first proposed the chivalry thesis, which suggests that the male-dominated criminal justice system (CJS), such as the police and the courts, takes a more benevolent, protective and patriarchal view of female offending. This means that women offenders are seen as 'less guilty' as they are more vulnerable and in need of protection, and they are therefore treated more leniently than men.

Evidence for the chivalry thesis

According to the Home Office, supported by statistics provided by the Ministry of Justice, women are consistently treated more leniently by the law, with first offenders about half as likely to be given a sentence of immediate imprisonment as their male counterparts. Women are also less likely to be remanded in custody, more likely to receive suspended or community sentences rather than imprisonment, and, when they are imprisoned, to receive, on average, shorter prison sentences. Female offenders are also generally regarded by the police as a less serious threat than men, and therefore benefit from more informal approaches to their offences, particularly for minor offences – such as cautions or warnings rather than being charged.

Evidence against the chivalry thesis: double deviance and double jeopardy

It does not appear that there is much evidence of a leniency towards female defendants, and women's less severe treatment by the CJS is mainly due to the fact that they commit less serious offences than men. They also have more 'mitigating factors' which reduce the length of sentences, such as showing remorse, having caring responsibilities and a lack of previous relevant convictions. Men generally have more 'aggravating factors' leading to their longer sentences.

Walklate (2004) argues that, in general, the crimes that result in imprisonment for women are of a less serious nature than those that lead to imprisonment for men. On the other hand, Heidensohn (1996) suggests that, although women are far less likely to commit serious offences than men, those who violate socially acceptable patterns of feminine behaviour risk harsher punishment than men. She criticizes the chivalry thesis on the grounds that female offenders are subjected to double jeopardy, in that they are on trial both for the crime they commit and for the extent to which they conform to, or deviate from, stereotypes of femininity. Women are often defined in terms of their relationships with others, in which they are expected to act with warmth, emotion and caring – for example as mothers, daughters or partners. Feminist writers regard the CJS as patriarchal – run by men, for men. Carlen (1988) suggests that women's sentences reflect this double jeopardy, as judges, magistrates and juries are partly influenced by their assessment of women's characters and performance in relation to their traditional wife/partner and mother roles, rather than simply by the severity of the offence. Many feminist writers have referred to this as the 'evil woman' theory. This suggests that women who are seen as sexually promiscuous, as neglectful mothers or as violent women – and particularly violent against children – are perceived by the CJS in far worse terms than men in similar situations. They are seen as 'really bad', doubly deviant evil women, as they both commit crimes and violate the norms of traditional gender stereotypes of feminine behaviour. Men are in general far more violent than women, but are given comparatively lighter sentences for similar levels of violence as they are perceived as just overstepping the mark of what men are expected to be like anyway. There is also some evidence that, although women offenders are less likely than men to be remanded in custody (imprisoned) rather than given bail while awaiting trial, a higher proportion of those women who are remanded, compared to men, eventually receive a suspended or community sentence, or are acquitted or not tried, even though they've already spent time in prison.

Conclusion on the chivalry thesis

For most offences, there is not much evidence to support either the chivalry thesis or the 'evil woman' theory. In most cases, women seem to receive less harsh treatment from the criminal justice system because they commit less serious offences than men, rather than because of a chivalrous, protective and patriarchal CJS. The 'evil woman' is most likely to be found in the most serious offences where women violate norms relating to gender roles, motherhood and childcare – such as serious violence, child neglect and abuse, child cruelty or child murder, where they suffer markedly more severe consequences than men who commit similar offences. This may well be because, in a patriarchal society, women are expected to be 'good' – feminine and conformist – and punished when they're not, while men are expected to be a bit tough and aggressive and periodically go off the rails, and so are punished less severely when they do so.

Police assumptions and stereotyping

Labelling theorists suggest that police assumptions and stereotypes mean women who commit crimes may benefit from the police stereotype (reflecting the pattern shown in official statistics) that they are less likely than men to be criminals, and so are less likely to have their behaviour watched, to get caught, to be labelled as criminal, and therefore less likely to become a criminal statistic.

Growing female criminality

Although men still commit a lot more crime than women, that pattern is slowly changing in the UK and internationally, and there is a growing increase in the proportion of crime committed by females, most noticeably by young women. In 1957, for example, men were responsible for eleven times as many offences as women, but by 2014 that ratio had narrowed to about three-to-one. There was a decrease in the male crime rate between 2002 and 2014, but the female crime rate increased in the same period, and although this started decreasing after 2010, it was at a much slower rate than that of men. The number of crimes committed by girls (aged 10–17) in England and Wales went up by around 25 per cent between 2004 and 2010, with significant increases in minor assaults, robberies, public order offences and criminal damage.

Changing gender roles: the liberation thesis and ladette culture

Adler (1975), in what is sometimes called the 'liberation thesis', suggested growing female crime may be due to changing gender roles. Women in contemporary Britain have more independence than in the past, and they are becoming more successful than men in both education and the labour market. At the same time, some of the traditional forms of control on women discussed above are weakening, particularly among younger women. Younger women are spending more leisure time outside 'on the streets' away from the home, so they are more visible and accessible to formal and informal surveillance and control by agencies of social control like the police. As Denscombe (2001) found, there is much more of a masculinized 'ladette' culture, in which young women are adopting behaviour traditionally associated with young men, as they assert their identity through binge drinking, gang culture, risk-taking, being hard and in control, and peer-related violence. Heidensohn and Silvestri (2012), however, cite a range of evidence that suggests that the reported increase in girls' violence is due more to changes in the labelling and criminalization of girls' bad behaviour than to real changes in their behaviour or that they are becoming more criminal. There is some evidence that the police and the CJS are now reacting in a more serious way – arresting, prosecuting and imprisoning girls and women involved in violence and other offences – rather than dealing with it informally by other means, which increases the statistics for such offences. It is also worth emphasizing that the main offences women commit – drug offences, criminal damage, shop-lifting and violence – still tend to be much less serious than those committed by men, and women's violence consists of fairly low-level minor assaults and rarely involves the serious injury or use of weapons which are more associated with male violence.

Why do males commit more crime than women?

Sex-role theory and gender socialization

Men's traditional role has been as family provider/breadwinner – what the functionalist Parsons refers to as the 'instrumental role'. Men's traditional roles in employment, their lack of responsibility for housework and childcare, and the lack of the various constraints encouraging women's conformity that were identified above, all give men more independence than women, and more opportunities to commit crime. A development of this kind of explanation centres on the features of masculinity and male gender identity, rather than simply the different roles performed by men and women in the family and society.

The assertion of masculinity

Connell (1987, 2005) suggests there is what she calls a hegemonic masculinity associated with the traditional masculine image in the world. This is a male gender identity that defines what it means to be a 'real man'; men who don't want to be regarded as 'wimps', abnormal or odd are meant to accomplish this masculinity. It features such things as independence, self-confidence, toughness, aggression, competitiveness, risk-taking, control, success and power over – and subordination of – women. It is the masculinity that was identified earlier by Miller as a focal concern of lower-working-class subculture (see pages 453–4). The male peer group reinforces these tendencies, particularly among younger men, and this can lead to higher risks of crime and delinquency.

> A **hegemonic masculinity** is a male gender identity that defines what is involved in being a 'real man', and is so dominant that those who don't conform to it are seen as odd or abnormal in some way.

Messerschmidt (1993) suggests that men sometimes turn to crime and violence as a means of asserting their masculinity when legitimate and traditional means of demonstrating masculinity and being 'real men' are blocked. Legitimate means include things like success at school, having a steady, reliable well-paid job, a stable family life and secure status as a family breadwinner. When these are missing, Messerschmidt suggests, men seek out alternative, 'masculine-validating resources', such as the threatened or actual use of violence, through fights and defending themselves, violence against women as an assertion of power, and crime. Those lacking legitimate masculine-validating resources are most likely to be those from more deprived backgrounds (the most common offenders).

The 'thrills and spills' involved in what Lyng called 'edgework' (see pages 470–1) may also be a motivating factor for some men to get involved in crime as a means of expressing their masculinity. This is more likely to occur among those for whom legitimate means of asserting masculinity are blocked or missing, but the nature of hegemonic masculinity might also explain why middle-class men try to assert masculinity through ruthlessness, ambition and thrill-seeking in business, leading to white-collar and corporate crimes (discussed later), such as computer hacking, embezzlement, fraud, and illegal stock market or money market trading. The nature of hegemonic masculinity might also explain why men from all social classes commit domestic violence and rape.

Evaluation of the masculinity thesis

The difficulty with Messerschmidt's analysis is that, while it provides a plausible explanation for why men might commit more crime than women, it doesn't have explanations for why all men who don't have access to legitimate means of asserting masculinity don't turn to crime – and most don't – or for the different types of crime that are committed. Not all male crime can be interpreted as an expression of masculinity.

Police assumptions and stereotyping

Labelling theorists suggest that police assumptions and stereotypes are the opposite of those discussed above in relation to women. Because of the pattern shown by official statistics, the police are more likely to see men than women as potential offenders, to label their behaviour as criminal, to press charges against them, and they are therefore more likely to appear in the crime statistics.

Control theory and rational choice and opportunity

The discussion above on control theory and rational choice and opportunity in relation to why women commit less crime than men can be reversed to explain why men commit more crime. Men dominate the public sphere where most crime is committed, and they face fewer constraints than women, such as responsibility for housework and childcare; also, they have less to lose in terms of reputation. Indeed, crime and deviance may actually enhance their reputation, particularly among young men for whom it might provide peer-group status. The demands of hegemonic masculinity may mean that some men who lack legitimate means of accomplishing masculinity may have more to gain than lose by choosing to commit crime or other forms of deviance, and they have more independence and opportunities to do so than women.

Activity

Read the previous section on gender and crime, then answer the following questions.

1 Outline the ways that the crime–gender ratio might be explained by sex role theory and gender socialization, linking them to examples of offences that men and women are most likely and least likely to commit.
2 Explain, with examples, the ways hegemonic masculinity is linked to male criminality, and why most men don't turn to crime.
3 Suggest ways that the changing role of women might explain the fact that females are committing an increasing proportion of all crimes.
4 Explain what is meant by each of the following concepts and theories, and suggest how they might be used to explain why, among offenders who have been caught, it is mainly working-class men and women who seem to turn to crime:
   - Sex role theory
   - Masculinity and femininity
   - Rational choice and opportunity
   - Control theory
   - Personal reputation
   - Police stereotyping.
5 Given that women commit far less crime than men, identify and explain *three* reasons why those women who do turn to crime might choose to do so.

Social class and crime

Newburn (2007) has noted that the sociology of crime and deviance has tended to focus on the crimes of the powerless rather than those of the powerful. This is largely because official statistics show that working-class people, particularly those with the least power from the lower working class, are the main offenders. It was Sutherland (1983 [1949]) who first sought to show crime was not simply a working-class phenomenon, but was widespread throughout all sections of society. He introduced the ideas of white-collar and corporate crime to describe those offences committed by the more affluent in society, and suggested many of these remain undetected, unreported and unrecorded in official statistics, or even manage to escape altogether being labelled as criminal acts. The crime statistics may therefore give a misleading, invalid picture of the reality of crime.

The working class and crime: crimes in the streets

It is predominantly *working-class* young males, both black and white, living in the *working-class* neighbourhoods of towns and cities, who appear, according to official statistics, to be the main offenders. Topic 1, and parts of this topic, cover a range of theories which provide explanations for this pattern of working-class crime; figure 6.13 and table 6.5 provide a summary of these explanations, and page references to which you can refer.

Evaluation of explanations for working-class crime

Many evaluative points concerning the explanations for working-class crime have been made throughout Topic 1 and this topic, but there are two major criticisms which you should bear in mind.

1 The explanations don't give any reason why all those in the same circumstances in the poorest sections of the working class do not turn to crime (and most don't).

2 There is widespread evidence of crime committed by members of other social classes which may be undetected and unrecorded, or dealt with outside of the criminal law even though criminal offences have been committed. The suggestion that most criminals are working-class may therefore be exaggerated.

Activity

1 Refer to table 6.5, and the relevant page references, and briefly outline three explanations for working-class crime suggested by each theory.
2 Link each of the following ideas or concepts to the explanation of working-class crime: criminogenic capitalism; selective law enforcement; social deprivation; relative deprivation; marginalization; subculture; bulimic society; anomie; social exclusion; rational choice; status frustration; focal concerns; edgework; underclass; labelling; stereotyping.
3 Outline three reasons why agencies of socialization and social control might be less effective in integrating people into society in deprived communities than in more affluent ones.
4 Identify and briefly explain all the reasons you can for why those living in deprived communities might decide that choosing crime is a rational way to behave. Be sure to consider both the costs and the benefits.
5 Suggest reasons why middle-class offenders might be treated less harshly by the criminal justice system than working-class offenders.

White-collar and corporate crime: crimes in the suites

Timmer and Eitzen (1989) described white-collar and corporate crimes committed in the suites of offices and boardrooms of the businesses of the middle classes as 'crimes in the suites', in contrast to the more familiar and visible everyday 'crimes in the streets', such as the violent crime and property crimes more associated with working-class offending. Many of the crimes in this section are what Pearce (1976) called 'the crimes of the powerful', and often the amounts of money involved in these crimes are so colossal, and the human misery arising as a consequence so serious, that they dwarf the everyday crimes committed by working-class offenders.

What is white-collar and corporate crime?

The terms 'white-collar crime' and 'corporate crime' are often, and confusingly, used interchangeably, and sometimes they are described simply as 'economic crime'; it is therefore sometimes difficult to know quite what is being discussed. Croall (2007) suggests the following distinction is widely accepted, and it is the one that is used here.

- *White-collar crime*, sometimes called *occupational crime*, is that committed by middle-class individuals who abuse their work positions for *personal gain*, at the expense of employers, the government or clients.
- *Corporate crime*, sometimes called *organizational crime*, is defined by Slapper and Tombs (1999) as offences committed by large companies, or individuals acting on behalf of those companies, which directly benefit the company rather than individuals, and involve increased profits or the survival of the organization.

Examples of white-collar crime

White-collar crime includes offences such as bribery and corruption in government and business; fiddling expenses; professional misconduct; fraud; and embezzlement. Croall (2001) cites examples of crimes against the NHS committed by doctors, pharmacists and dentists, who falsify prescriptions and patient records to claim millions of pounds more than that to which they are entitled – including one GP who made £700,000 over five years writing fake prescriptions. The millionaire press baron Lord Conrad Black, former owner of the *Daily* and *Sunday Telegraph*, was in 2007 convicted and jailed for six and a half years in the United States for misusing his position as

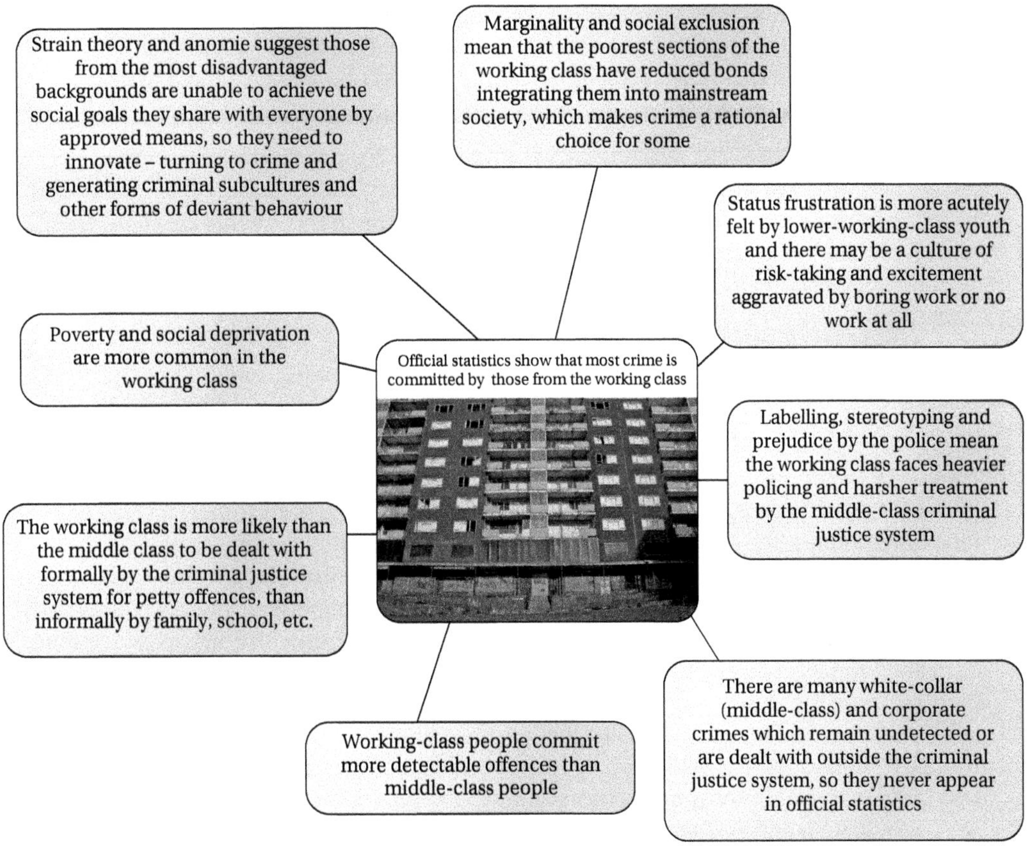

Figure 6.13 Social class and crime

Strain theory and anomie suggest those from the most disadvantaged backgrounds are unable to achieve the social goals they share with everyone by approved means, so they need to innovate – turning to crime and generating criminal subcultures and other forms of deviant behaviour

Marginality and social exclusion mean that the poorest sections of the working class have reduced bonds integrating them into mainstream society, which makes crime a rational choice for some

Status frustration is more acutely felt by lower-working-class youth and there may be a culture of risk-taking and excitement aggravated by boring work or no work at all

Poverty and social deprivation are more common in the working class

Official statistics show that most crime is committed by those from the working class

Labelling, stereotyping and prejudice by the police mean the working class faces heavier policing and harsher treatment by the middle-class criminal justice system

The working class is more likely than the middle class to be dealt with formally by the criminal justice system for petty offences, than informally by family, school, etc.

There are many white-collar (middle-class) and corporate crimes which remain undetected or are dealt with outside the criminal justice system, so they never appear in official statistics

Working-class people commit more detectable offences than middle-class people

Table 6.5 Theoretical explanations for working-class crime

Theories	Main causes of crime	Page references
Strain and anomie (Merton)	Blocked opportunities lead to innovation to achieve success.	Pages 451–2
Subcultural theories (Cohen; Cloward and Ohlin; Miller)	Status frustration, focal concerns of lower-working-class culture and search for peer group status generate delinquent subcultures.	Pages 452–4
Control theory (Hirschi)	Lack of integrating and controlling social bonds.	Pages 454–6
Marxist/neo-Marxist theories (Gordon; Chambliss; Box; Snider; Pearce; Gilroy; Taylor, Watson and Young; Hall)	Criminogenic capitalism; crime as rational response to social inequality and social deprivation/poverty; selective law enforcement; crime as resistance to capitalism; distraction from white-collar and corporate crimes of the powerful.	Pages 456–8
Labelling theory (Becker; Cicourel; Lemert)	Working-class offenders are more likely to be labelled as criminal and to have the law selectively enforced against them.	Pages 459–63
Left Realism (Lea and Young; Young)	Relative deprivation, marginalization and subcultures combine to generate crime in a media-saturated bulimic consumer society from which the lower working class are socially excluded and in which they lack legitimate opportunities to access the consumer lifestyles they crave.	Pages 465–8
Right Realism/rational choice and opportunity/New Right (Murray; Cornish and Clarke)	Inadequate/poor socialization by a welfare-dependent workshy underclass combines with lack of community controls to make crime a rational choice in deprived communities.	Pages 468–9
Postmodernism (Lea; Henry and Milovanovic; Katz; Lyng)	Crime (harm to others) is committed for the sheer hell of it – the pleasure, excitement and thrills derived from edgework in otherwise boring lives arising from social exclusion.	Pages 469–71

Chair of Hollinger International to defraud shareholders of millions of dollars for private gain. In November 2012, a rogue financial City trader in London was jailed for seven years for committing what police described as the UK's biggest ever fraud – 'fraud by abuse of position' – after recklessly gambling huge sums in unauthorized off-the-book rogue deals which ended up costing the Swiss banking giant UBS more than £1.5bn.

> 'Bank robbers are masked and they use guns. Burglars wear dark clothes and use crowbars. These men dressed in ties and wore suits. They did it with memos and documents and a few lies.'
> From the opening statement of the US prosecutor in the trial of Conrad Black, the millionaire fraudster and racketeer.

Examples of corporate crime

Slapper and Tombs identify six types of corporate offence.

1 *Paperwork and non-compliance.* These are offences such as where correct permits or licences are not obtained, or companies fail to comply with health and safety and other legal regulations. An example is the *Herald of Free Enterprise* disaster in 1987, when this cross-Channel ferry capsized in a calm sea just outside Zeebrugge harbour. Because the rules governing the closing of the bow doors of the ship had not been complied with, 193 people died. In 2015, Volkswagen illegally evaded environmental regulations by fitting 11 million cars with a defeat device aimed at cheating emissions tests. This is also an example of an environmental corporate crime.

2 *Environmental (or 'green') crimes.* These involve damage to the environment caused either deliberately or through negligence, and include the pollution of land, water supplies and air through the discharge, emission and dumping of dangerous or toxic substances and waste from industry, farming and transport. Environmental crime is covered extensively in Topic 3 (see pages 506–11) and you may wish to refer to this now.

3 *Manufacturing offences.* These involve offences such as the incorrect labelling or misrepresentation of products and false advertising, producing unsafe or dangerous articles, and producing counterfeit goods. These are mainly offences against consumers, such as ignoring or failing to correct or recall unsafe or dangerous products. For example, inadequate testing and government regulation of the morning-sickness drug thalidomide in the late 1950s and early 1960s led to birth defects in thousands of babies.

4 *Labour law violations.* These include offences such as neglect of health and safety regulations, failing to pay legally required minimum wages, and causing or concealing industrial diseases. Such offences hit the lowest-paid workers the hardest, and kill or injure thousands worldwide each year.

5 *Unfair trade practices.* These include things like false advertising and anti-competitive practices, such as price fixing and illegally obtaining information on rival businesses. For example, in 2011, UK supermarkets and dairy companies were fined £50 million for fixing the price of milk and cheese, costing consumers £270m more than they would have paid without price fixing.

6 *Financial offences.* These are offences like tax evasion and concealment of losses and debts. In the USA in 2001, Enron concealed large debts of around $50 billion, eventually causing the company to collapse, many people to lose large amounts of their investments, and thousands of employees to lose their jobs. In 2012, global companies like Amazon and Starbucks came under attack in the UK for failing to pay their fair share of taxes, through using various legal offshore financial centres where taxes were lower than in the UK. Pensions, mortgage endowment policies and payment protection policies have all been the subject of proceedings, fines and compensation in the UK over misselling – i.e. being sold with misleading indications about their benefits.

You should be aware that some corporate crimes have global and transnational dimensions to them – for example, large Western corporations may try to avoid laws and regulations in the West by moving production to poorer, less developed countries, which have less stringent laws and law enforcement. They may also involve various forms of cybercrime, and may sometimes be carried out in collusion with governments and organized crime. These wider issues are considered in Topic 3.

The under-representation of white-collar and corporate crime

There are several reasons why white-collar and corporate crimes are under-represented in official statistics.

1 *They are hidden from view and hard to detect.* Clarke (1990) and Croall (2001) point out that these offences are relatively invisible, as they take place in the workplace and offenders simply appear to be doing their normal jobs and are quite justified in being present at the scene. Corporate cover-ups and networks of influence by powerful businesses mean some corporate offences may never actually be discovered, or discovered only much later when the damage might already have been done, as in the example of the thalidomide drug mentioned earlier.

2 *They are often without personal or individual victims.* Croall (2007) points out that there is less obvious, personal harm – or 'blood on the streets' – and victims appear impersonal, like a company, the government, the NHS, the taxpayer or the public at large, rather than individuals. Clarke points out that these are often 'complainantless' crimes, as there is no individual victim to report an offence.

3 *They may benefit both the parties concerned.* For example, in cases of bribery and corruption, whether for business or personal reasons, both parties stand to gain something, and therefore both parties will be in trouble if discovered and seek to conceal the offence, making it hard to detect.

4 *They are hard to investigate.* Even if offences like business or computer fraud are suspected, they often involve some form of technical or insider knowledge, making many offences complex. Their investigation requires a lot of skill and expert knowledge, which local – and even national – police forces may lack, and this makes the extent and duration of offending, and the offenders themselves, hard to discover and investigate.

5 *There is often a lack of awareness that a crime has been committed* and therefore it is not reported. Croall (2007) suggests victims may lack the expertise to know whether they are, for example, being misled or defrauded, and may be unaware of any harm to them. She suggests this happens with offences such as pollution, food adulteration (such as the scandal in 2013 of horsemeat found in burgers in UK supermarkets), false descriptions of consumer goods, internet scams and financial frauds, or offences where individual losses are very small or barely perceptible – as in cases in which a bank employee steals one penny from thousands of customer accounts. Victims may also blame themselves, for example for making 'risky' investments, or being otherwise gullible.

6 *Even if these crimes are detected, they are often not prosecuted and dealt with as criminal acts.* Many of the harmful corporate crimes of businesses, like violations of health and safety legislation, price fixing and environmental offences often lead only to a reprimand, a fine or enforcement notices from regulatory bodies and government agencies like the Health and Safety Executive, the Financial Services Authority, the Office of Fair Trading or the Environment Agency, rather than to police action and prosecution through the criminal justice system. White-collar crimes are often concealed by *institutional protection* – for example, employee crimes such as embezzlement from customer accounts in a bank – and are rarely reported, to protect the interests or reputation of the profession or institution, and avoid the loss of public confidence which the surrounding scandal might cause. Suspected offenders may consequently be dealt with by internal administrative systems of control, such as being sacked or forced to retire rather than being prosecuted.

7 *Even if reported and prosecuted, offenders have a better chance of being found not guilty.* Most juries, like the public at large, hold the stereotype that crime is a mainly working-class phenomenon, rather than committed by affluent, well-educated, outwardly respectable middle-class people. Defendants are often of the same background as judges and magistrates, and may appear more plausible, honest and respectable to juries, and so may be less likely to be found guilty, and are more likely to have their offences seen as temporary lapses in otherwise good behaviour, and receive more lenient sentences than working-class offenders.

In general, the higher up you are in the social class hierarchy:
- The less likely are your crimes to be detected
- The less likely are your crimes, if detected, to result in your arrest
- The less likely you are, if arrested, to be prosecuted
- The less likely you are, if prosecuted, to be found guilty
- The less likely you are, if found guilty, to be given a prison sentence.

Explanations for white-collar and corporate crime

Strain theory and relative deprivation

It is hard to see successful middle-class people as having legitimate means of achieving social goals blocked, as Merton's strain theory (see pages 451–2) might suggest, as many are already successful in terms of these goals. Nonetheless, they may still have a sense of relative deprivation – of lacking things they see others having – and want even more than they can achieve by legitimate, approved means, so they innovate, and turn to crime. This may be further fuelled, quite simply, by greed and power – they have a lot, but want more. Corporate crimes can also be seen as forms of innovation, whereby businesses seek to by-pass laws and regulations to maintain profits in difficult circumstances of competitive markets.

Control theory

Control theory (see pages 454–6) suggests that the individuals who carry out corporate crimes to benefit companies are driven by socialization into, and conformity to, self-seeking, aggressive management cultures, which encourage ruthless business practices when competing with other companies. This might well involve taking illegal shortcuts which are not regarded as really doing wrong, but simply as extensions of acceptable business practice, and so there are reduced moral controls about doing wrong. This may be extended to bring some personal rewards to employees as well, through white-collar offences such as giving or accepting bribes when negotiating orders.

Nelken (2012) suggests strain and control theories converge in explaining some white-collar offenders. He suggests some are successful people who have the material goods associated with success, but may have got into financial difficulties in trying to maintain their lifestyles. They are so strongly tied to the social expectations of and obligations to those in the same social group that they innovate by using illegitimate means to resolve their financial difficulties, and to maintain the lifestyles expected by those around them, through using the opportunities provided by their jobs to commit embezzlement, fraud and similar offences. This helps to explain offences that are committed by people who are often quite affluent, and even very rich, and are very successful in terms of society's values and goals.

Differential association

Sutherland's (1983 [1949]) theory of differential association suggests that if people associate with others who commonly support illegal activities, then they are more likely to commit crime themselves – either for personal gain (white-collar crime) or to benefit the business (corporate crime). The aggressive management cultures in business circles referred to above may generate a favourable climate for corporate crime, driven by loyalty to the firm, the need to take illegal shortcuts to compete to sell goods in the marketplace, and a dislike of government regulation.

Marxist explanations

Marxists like Box (1983) and Slapper and Tombs (1999) argue that the push to corporate crime is driven by criminogenic capitalism (see page 456). The need to maintain profits in an increasingly global market means that, if this cannot be achieved legally, then illegal means will be used. This leads to crimes such as industrial espionage; price fixing; lying about losses to avoid hitting share prices and upsetting investors (as in Enron); concealment of profits to avoid taxation; deceiving consumers by fraud, misleading advertising, and the sale of dangerous or unsafe products – or the export to developing countries of products that fail safety tests in their own countries, such as happens with drug companies who continue to sell drugs in developing countries which are either banned at home or out-of-date.

Labelling theory

Labelling theory (see pages 459–63) has not had much to say about white-collar and corporate crime, but Nelken suggests these offences are more likely to escape labelling as 'criminal' because they are often similar to normal business practices. Croall (2007) notes corporate crime is often not accompanied by a direct intent to cause harm – for example, breaches of health and safety or the dumping of toxic waste are not deliberately intended to kill or injure people, even if this is the effect, and so they appear to be 'less criminal' than offences like burglary. Nelken points out powerful individuals or corporations employ accountants and lawyers to develop techniques of neutralization (see pages 454 and 514–15) in order to redefine their crimes as non-criminal oversights, mistakes or errors, rather than as deliberate attempts to break the law. This avoidance of the attachment of the label of 'criminal' to white-collar and corporate offences can encourage further crimes by reducing the risks associated with offending.

The seduction of crime and edgework

As postmodernists like Katz (1988) and Lyng (1990, 2005) suggest, crime can be a seductive, pleasurable experience, and thrill-seeking and risk-taking may be motivations for crime rather than simply material gain. Nelken (2012) cites evidence from the world of high finance which shows a subculture in which the excitement for young men of living life in the fast lane and making hard choices in high-risk situations is as important as the money benefits themselves. This is a plausible explanation for some white-collar crime, especially among those who are already rich.

Evaluation of white-collar and corporate crime

The study of white-collar and corporate crime is important as it contributes to an understanding of the social construction of crime statistics, and the relative over-representation of working-class crime.

However, as with working-class crime, the explanations fail to give reasons why not all individuals or corporations turn to crime to resolve their problems, or are prepared to take the risks in doing so. As Nelken suggests, while the best way to rob a bank may be to own one, most of those in this position do not take advantage of it. Marxist explanations, which see corporate crime as an inevitable part of the search for profits in competitive criminogenic capitalist societies, do not explain why, in countries where there was no pressure for profitability, as in the former communist countries of Russia and Eastern Europe, or in public organizations like the army, police or government, corporate crimes and corruption are still found.

Activity

1 Outline and explain, with examples of offences, two differences between corporate and white-collar crime.
2 Outline and explain three reasons why white-collar and corporate offences may not result in a criminal conviction.
3 Outline and explain three ways in which the study of corporate and white-collar crimes contributes to the view that official crime statistics are misleading social constructions.
4 Outline and explain three sociological reasons for why successful, affluent and outwardly conformist individuals might choose to commit crime.

Practice questions

1   Outline **two** ways in which the criminal justice system may discriminate against some minority ethnic groups.   **(4 marks)**

2   Outline **three** reasons why official crime statistics may not provide a valid picture of the patterns of crime in society.   **(6 marks)**

3   Read **Item A** below and answer the question that follows.

> **Item A**
>
> White-collar crime is that committed by middle-class individuals who abuse their work positions for personal gain, at the expense of employers, the government or clients. Many white-collar crimes remain undetected, unreported and unrecorded in criminal statistics, or even manage to escape altogether from being labelled as criminal acts.

Applying material from **Item A**, analyse **two** reasons why white-collar crime may be less likely to be reported to the police than crimes committed by working-class people.   **(10 marks)**

4   Read **Item B** below and answer the question that follows.

> **Item B**
>
> Statistics show that women commit less crime than men. Some suggest this may be because women are treated more leniently by the criminal justice system, and so are less likely to have their offences recorded. Others suggest it is because of different gender roles, which leads more men into crime, and women to commit fewer and less serious offences.

Applying material from **Item B** and your knowledge, evaluate sociological explanations for gender differences in the patterns of crime.   **(30 marks)**

Topic 3

Globalization and crime in contemporary society

Held and McGrew (2007) define globalization as 'the widening, deepening, and speeding up of worldwide interconnectedness'. Globalization involves a process of *deterritorialization*. This means that an increasing number of social, political and economic activities are no longer attached to specific countries, but are transnational and stretched across the globe. Instant communication technologies like the internet and fast international travel mean we now live in a shrinking world in which national borders become less relevant. The local and the global are increasingly interconnected, and activities and decisions in one place can have significant consequences for people in a totally different part of the world. With globalization, the world has become a single territory for both legal and illegal business.

The nature and extent of global crime

Karofi and Mwanza (2006) and Castells (2010) argue globalization has led to a global criminal economy, in which new opportunities for crime and new types of crime have emerged, such as the illegal trade in weapons, nuclear materials, body parts and drugs; human-trafficking of women and children for prostitution, and/or of illegal migrant workers; child sex tourism (for illegal sex with children); cybercrimes, including identity theft, fraud and theft of intellectual property rights; green crimes (discussed later in this topic); international terrorism; and money-laundering. Some of these are examined below.

The international illegal drug trade

Estimates of the value of the global illegal drug trade are very difficult to calculate and vary widely, and are often little more than educated guesses – unsurprisingly, given it is an illegal and hidden activity – but the UNODC (United Nations Office on Drugs and Crime) *World Drug Report 2007* suggested this trade was worth $322 billion each year (no new breakdown has been established

The international trade in illegal drugs begins with the growth of crops, like poppies in Afghanistan (shown here) or coca in Colombia, which eventually appear on the streets of Western cities as heroin and crack cocaine, where they become the generators of more crime, as people turn to theft to support their addiction.

since). This was higher than the Gross Domestic Product (GDP) in 88 per cent of the countries in the world.

The international drugs trade provides the drugs that are available in local communities in the UK. The Home Office estimates that up to half of acquisitive crime, such as theft and burglary, is drug-related as people steal to support their drug habits.

Gross Domestic Product (GDP) refers to the total value of goods and services produced by a country in a particular year.

Human-trafficking

Human-trafficking is the illegal movement and smuggling of people, for a variety of purposes ranging from the illegal removal of organs for transplants, the exploitation of women and children for prostitution and other forms of sexual exploitation, to forced labour and practices similar to slavery. The National Crime Agency in 2014 estimated there were as many as 13,000 people in Britain who were victims of slavery, including women forced into prostitution, domestic staff, and workers in fields, factories and fishing (for more information, see www.modernslavery.co.uk). There is also a related global criminal network dealing with the trade in illegal immigrants: smuggling people at high costs into countries which they are unable to enter legally.

Money-laundering

Money-laundering is concerned with making money obtained illegally look like it came from legal sources. Castells calls this the 'matrix of global crime', because criminals, like drug-dealers and human-traffickers, deal with large amounts of cash, which they need to 'launder' to avoid their criminal activities from coming to the attention of law-enforcement agencies. The deregulation of global financial markets, banking secrecy and modern communications technology, like the internet, make it possible to launder 'dirty money' through complex financial transactions involving almost instantaneous repeated electronic movement of vast sums around the world. This makes it very difficult for law-enforcement agencies to track the sources of money, and hard to identify which country is responsible for law-enforcement.

Cybercrime

Cybercrime refers to a wide range of criminal acts committed with the help of communication and information technology, predominantly the internet. Cybercrime is one of the fastest-growing criminal activities in the world. Cybercrimes are 'glocal' (discussed below), in the sense that many offenders and offences in the UK often have links outside the country. Detica (2011) estimates financial cybercrimes such as identity theft, online scams, fraud relating to tax, pensions and benefits, local and central government and the NHS, and intellectual property theft (stealing copyright, ideas, designs and trade secrets) cost the UK £27 billion each year. Examples of cybercrimes include:

- Internet-based fraud, such as various financial scams (like the infamous 'Nigerian letters'), credit card fraud and the money-laundering discussed above
- Child pornography and paedophilia
- Terrorist websites and networking, involving recruitment, illegal acquisition of weaponry and planning of attacks. For example, in 2015, there were major concerns about the way the terrorist group ISIS (Islamic State), which had seized large areas of land in Syria and Iraq, was using social media like YouTube, Twitter, Instagram and Tumblr to conduct a high-tech media jihad (holy war) to advertise and spread its message globally, to create a network of militants recruited from all over the world (including the UK), and to plan terrorist attacks in Western countries.
- Cyber-attacks, such as virus attacks and hacking – gaining illegal or unauthorized access to computers to steal data or other forms of disruptive activity. An example of this was the cyber-attack on the telecoms company TalkTalk in October 2015, in which cybercriminals targeted its website in an attempt to steal details of customer identities and financial information.
- Identity theft, in which criminals trawl the web or other public databases, as well as discarded documents, for people's personal details, which they then use to take on another person's identity to apply for credit cards and loans, running up large bills that are then sent to the person whose identity they have stolen.

Transnational organized crime

Castells argues that globalization has created transnational networks of organized crime, which operate in many countries. These employ millions of people, and often work in collusion with corrupt state officials and legitimate businesses. Farr (2005) suggests there are two main forms of global criminal networks.

1 *Established mafias*, like the Italian-American mafia, the Japanese Yakusa, and the Chinese Triads, which are very long-established groups, often organized around family and ethnic characteristics. These have adapted their activities and organization to take advantage of the various new opportunities opened up by globalization.
2 *Newer organized crime groups*, which have emerged since the advent of globalization, and the collapse of the communist regimes of Russia and Eastern Europe in the 1980s and 1990s. These newer groups include Russian, East European and Albanian criminal groups, and the Colombian drug cartels, which connect with both one another and the established mafias to form part of the network of transnational organized crime.

Between them, these organizations control much of the world's human-trafficking for sex/prostitution and/or illegal immigration, money-laundering, pornography, weapon and drug smuggling, as well as operating a range of legal businesses funded by the money-laundered profits of their criminal activities.

Castells emphasizes the increasing international linkages between criminal groups, with once regional and local criminal groupings in individual countries becoming deterritorialized (less tied to specific countries) and globalized. Glenny (2009), uses the term 'McMafia' to describe the way transnational organized crime mirrors the activities of legal transnational corporations like McDonald's, who seek to provide and sell the same products across the world. In a sense, they, like McDonald's, are operating as purely self-interested economic organizations which, instead of fast food, provide drugs, sex, guns, body organs, pornography and opportunities for illegal immigration.

From global to local – glocalism

Hobbs and Dunnighan (1998) suggest that global criminal networks work within local contexts as interdependent local units. For example, the international drugs trade and human-trafficking require local networks of drug dealers, pimps and sex clubs to organize supply at a local level, and existing local criminals need to connect to the global networks to continue their activities, such as accessing drugs, counterfeit goods and illegal immigrants for cheap labour or prostitution. Hobbs (1998) coined the term 'glocal' to describe this interconnectivity between the local and the global, with transnational crime really rooted in glocalities – local contexts with global links. This glocalism means the precise forms of criminal organization and actual crimes will be shaped by the cultural, political and economic circumstances of the local and global contexts – glocalities – in which they occur.

How globalization has affected crime

Globalization has affected crime in the following ways (these are summarized in figure 6.14):

1 Disorganized capitalism

Lash and Urry (1987) argue globalization has been accompanied by less regulation and fewer state controls over business and finance – they refer to this as 'disorganized capitalism'. Corporations now operate transnationally in global markets, moving money, manufacturing, staff and waste around the globe to countries where profits are higher and labour costs are lower, and where health and safety and environmental pollution regulations are less demanding and less likely to be enforced than in Western countries.

Taylor (1997, 1999) argues this process has led to fewer job opportunities and more job insecurity, an increase in unemployment and more part-time and temporary jobs, in developed

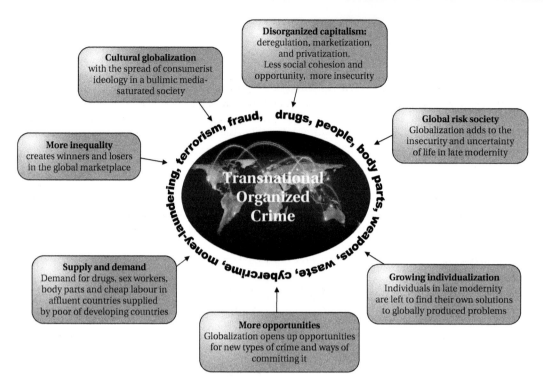

Figure 6.14 How globalization influences crime

countries, and intensified exploitation of the labour force in developing countries. This has been accompanied by a reduction in state provision in areas like health and welfare. These factors undermine social cohesion, and combine with the lack of opportunity to fuel crime as people search for alternative opportunities of obtaining the consumerist lifestyles which are promoted by a global media (see point 5).

2 Growing inequality

Globalization produces new patterns of inequalities, and Taylor (1997) suggests that the winners from globalization are the rich financial investors and transnational corporations based in the developed Western countries, and the losers are the workers in both the developed and developing countries. The most disadvantaged in both developed and developing countries are exposed to ever more risks and insecurity in their lives, and experience growing relative deprivation. This feeds crime.

3 Supply and demand in a globalized world

Growing global inequality, and particularly poverty in the developing world, coupled with rising expectations generated by a global media, has led to factors that push people to emigrate to the developed Western countries where they think they will be better-off. At the same time, most of those countries have made immigration more difficult. This has created a market in illegal human-trafficking. Many illegal immigrants are in debt to the smuggling gangs, leading them into virtual slavery to repay their debts, or women are forced into prostitution.

In the affluent developed countries, demand for illegal drugs like heroin and cocaine provides a means of making money by drug-dealing for those deprived of other opportunities, and supply is met by poverty-stricken farmers in countries like Colombia, Bolivia and Afghanistan who gain the highest income by growing opium poppies and coca for heroin and cocaine. Demands by the affluent for body parts for transplants, and women as sex workers, have been met by people from poor countries selling their organs, or by women who are forced into prostitution. This highly profitable illegal trade is managed by transnational organized criminal networks.

4 More opportunities for crime

Growing globalization and global communications offer:

- *Opportunities for new types of crime*, as discussed above.
- *New means of carrying out crimes*, such as through the speed, convenience and anonymity of the internet, especially the hidden so-called 'dark web', invisible to normal web browsers, which enables criminals to commit almost any illegal activity anywhere in the world with little risk of detection. For example, credit cards 'skimmed' (copied) in the UK can be used a few minutes later in Australia, and millions of pounds can be moved around the world in seconds to conceal their origins in crime (money-laundering). Crime committed in one country may have its perpetrators located in another country, and without the cooperation of other states, it may be impossible for a police investigation in any one country to track down and convict the offenders, or even to decide which country is responsible for prosecuting the perpetrators of crime. This substantially reduces the risks involved in committing crimes.

Activity

Go to the websites of Interpol (www.interpol.int) and Europol (www.europol.europa.eu).
1 Identify three types of transnational crime (which spans more than one country) which these agencies are currently tackling.
2 Identify two ways that cooperation between different countries is being used to combat the crimes you identify.
3 Suggest reasons why the crimes you have identified might be difficult for the criminal justice agencies of a single country to tackle.

---

5 Cultural globalization and the ideology of consumerism

Globalization through mass tourism, migration and the influence of the media has spread a similar culture and ideology of consumerism across the globe. In media-saturated contemporary societies, everyone in both developed and developing countries is constantly exposed to the ideology that the 'good life' lies in obtaining the consumer goods associated with affluent Western lifestyles. Young, from a Left Realist perspective (see pages 465–6) points out many people have little chance of achieving this, and a bulimic society encourages a turn to crime in many countries, including crimes like the international illegal drug trade, and human-trafficking for illegal migration and prostitution organized by transnational criminal networks.

6 Growing individualization

Bauman (2000) argues that, in late modernity, there is growing individualization. Any improvement to the living conditions and happiness of individuals now depends on their own efforts, and they can no longer count on the safety nets provided by the welfare state to protect them from unemployment or poverty. Taylor suggests individuals are left alone to weigh the costs and benefits of their decisions, and to choose the course that brings them the best chances of gaining the highest rewards. These rewards are increasingly seen in terms of the ideology of consumerism promoted by a Western-based global media. This individualism and global consumer ideology put personal gain above community benefit. Crimes like drug-dealing and trafficking, and enabling illegal migration through human-trafficking, provide individuals with a means of achieving rewards which are otherwise unobtainable, and offer individuals from poor nations the hope (nearly always unfulfilled) of achieving individual salvation through (illegal) migration to the West.

7 Global risk society

Globalization adds to the insecurity and uncertainty of life in late modernity, and generates what Beck (1992) calls a 'global risk society'. People become more 'risk conscious', and fearful of things like losing their jobs, of having their computers hit by viruses, of having their identities stolen, of having their food supplies contaminated, of threats from asylum seekers and illegal immigrants, of terrorism, of drug-dealers threatening their children, of nuclear accidents, of climate change and so on. The causes of these risks are often located globally, and it is not always easy to identify who is responsible. The media play on these fears, with scare stories and moral panics induced by over-blown, sensationalized reporting of events like terrorist threats, gun crime, and threats to people's ways of life and of growing social disorder allegedly posed by 'scroungers', such as migrant workers, illegal immigrants and asylum seekers, arising from global population movements. These can fuel hate crimes, where people are attacked or abused because of their ethnicity or religion or other features which mark them out as different.

Evaluation of crime and globalization

The study of this area is valuable as it focuses on some of the newest, most dramatic and serious forms of crime, and links them to the local and global contexts. However, its secretive and complex nature means it is a difficult area for sociologists to investigate – for example, the investigation of global financial crime requires specialist skills. For many crimes there is a dependence on secondary sources, and reliable statistics may not be available. This raises questions over the valid-ity of some of the research. Research may also be dangerous, as global crime involves powerful and dangerous individuals. While some might see research into global crime as important, others may regard it as a distraction from research into the more routine crimes which concern people and have a more significant impact on their daily lives.

It is easy to exaggerate the significance of the impact of globalization. The crime rate for most offences has been dropping in the UK, and it is likely that globalization has affected crime more significantly in some parts of the world than in others, particularly in countries where law enforce-ment is limited or less efficient, or where corruption is rife. Much crime tends to consist of fairly routine, low-level offences which are committed in local communities by local offenders, rather than being influenced by wider forces of globalization. It is worth noting that globalization has also meant more interconnectedness in global law enforcement, with more agencies working across national borders to tackle crimes that have global dimensions, and make the lives of offenders more difficult.

Green or environmental crime

Environmental issues are of increasing importance, particularly in the context of globalization and the growing inter-connectedness of the world, as harm to the environment in one part of the world has implications for the rest of the world. Issues like climate change, waste disposal, nuclear power, genetically modified crops and the extinction of non-human animal species have given rise to new global environmental social movements, organizing through new media like the internet. These have pushed green issues onto political agendas, and this has been reflected in sociology in the emergence of green or environmental criminology.

What is green or environmental crime?

Wolf (2011) points out that the term 'green crime' (also called 'environmental crime' and 'eco-crime') was first used in traditional criminology to describe actions that break laws protect-ing the environment. The problem with this approach is that the same harmful environmental action may be defined as illegal in some countries but not in others. Laws also change over time, and a wide range of actions that harm the environment may be regarded as breaches of health and safety regulations rather than as criminal offences – and even such regulations vary over time and between countries.

A transgressive approach to green crime: crime as environmental harm

To overcome this problem of legal/illegal, Lynch and Stretsky (2003) suggest environmental or green criminology should adopt a more transgressive or wider approach which goes beyond defining environmental crime simply as law-breaking. White (2008) adopts such an approach, and considers environmental crime to be any human action that causes *environmental harm*, whether or not it is illegal. He regards as crimes all actions that harm the physical environment, including all people, animals and plants that live within it. This is sometimes referred to as an *environmental justice* approach.

Examples of green crime

Green crimes may involve various violations of national and international laws and regulations, or they may not be against the law at all. They include the pollution and contamination of land, water supplies and air through the discharge and emission of dangerous or toxic substances from manufacturing processes, farming and transport; pollution through the burning of fossil fuels; and species decline caused by the destruction of natural habitats. Some are caused either by the deliberate breaking or avoidance of rules that seek to regulate and prevent environmental damage or disasters, or through negligence. Such crimes include the deliberate or negligent release of controlled toxic emissions; the illegal disposal and dumping of toxic/hazardous waste; the illegal trafficking of endangered animals and plants; unregulated fishing, like illegal whaling – which threatens the survival of species of fish – in contravention of controls imposed by various regional fisheries management organizations; and deforestation, such as the destruction of the Amazon rainforest by logging companies – increasing CO_2 emissions and contributing to global warming and climate change.

The 1984 disaster in Bhopal in India is an example of an environmental crime that illustrates both the traditional criminological and environmental justice approaches. The Union Carbide chemical company plant leaked poisonous gas, which affected half a million people; by 2012, there had been approximately 25,000 deaths, with at least 120,000 people still suffering severe symptoms – like blindness and birth defects in children – from ailments caused by the accident and the subsequent pollution at the plant site (see www.bhopal.org for more information on the Bhopal disaster). The traditional criminological approach suggests the disaster arose because Union Carbide broke local health and safety laws, while the more transgressive environmental justice approach suggests Union Carbide deliberately located plants in countries where health

Do you regard destroying the Amazon rainforest as an environmental crime, even if the companies involved aren't technically breaking the law? Do you think environmental damage and destruction of the environment for business interests and profit should be outlawed and officially classified as crimes?

and safety laws were weak and there was less concern for the environment. The explosion at BP's Deepwater Horizon oil rig in the Gulf of Mexico in 2010 led to the largest accidental marine oil spill in the history of the oil industry, which, as well as causing the deaths of eleven people working on the platform, caused extensive damage to marine and wildlife habitats and to the Gulf's fishing and tourism industries.

The Volkswagen emissions scandal of 2015, in which 11 million vehicles were illegally fitted with a defeat device aimed at cheating emissions tests, breaching environmental regulations, meant the company was possibly responsible for nearly 1m tonnes of extra air pollution every year – roughly the same as the UK's combined emissions from all power stations, vehicles, industry and agriculture (see http://www.theguardian.com/business/2015/sep/22/vw-scandal-caused-nearly-1m-tonnes-of-extra-pollution-analysis-shows).

Green crime, globalization and global risk society

Beck (1992) has shown that many environmental disasters in the past, such as droughts, famine and flooding, were of natural origin and largely outside human control. In late modern societies, he suggests there are new kinds of risk that are created by the actions of human beings through the application of science and technology. Beck emphasizes that these are global risks in what he refers to as 'global risk society', which include potentially disastrous consequences for the global environment.

Environmental harm cannot be limited to one locality, and events in one country can have consequences in many. For example, actions like the deforestation of the Amazon rainforest by hi-tech logging companies, and carbon emissions arising from the use of fossil fuels, are creating major climate changes which have potentially catastrophic consequences for the planet. The use of nuclear energy creates a growing problem of nuclear waste disposal, as well as increasing risks of nuclear accidents, like the explosion at the Chernobyl nuclear power plant in the Ukraine in 1986, and the meltdown at the Fukushima Daiichi nuclear plant in Japan in 2011, which released (and in 2013 was continuing to release) large quantities of radioactive contamination. The explosion at BP's Deepwater Horizon oil rig referred to above caused extensive damage to marine and wildlife habitats; floating plastic and other human debris has created the Great Pacific Garbage Patch, a vast area of thousands of square kilometres of polluted sea. The increasing use of genetically modified crops poses any number of potential unforeseen risks (see http://en.wikipedia.org/wiki/Genetically_modified_food_controversies).

White (2008) illustrates the globalized character of environmental harms by the way transnational corporations move manufacturing operations to the Global South to avoid pollution laws in more developed countries, and either illegally dump European waste or send it for processing to developing countries where disposal costs and health and safety standards are lower, and enforcement action is less effective.

Activity

Go to one of the following websites, or use Wikipedia, and familiarize yourself with some of the disasters mentioned above.

The Chernobyl nuclear accident 1986: http://news.bbc.co.uk/1/shared/spl/hi/guides/456900/456957/html/nn1page1.stm (or do a search of the BBC on Chernobyl)

The Deepwater Horizon oil spill 2010: www.guardian.co.uk/environment/bp-oil-spill

The Fukushima nuclear plant meltdown 2011: www.newscientist.com/special/fukushima-crisis

1 Explain how they illustrate Beck's idea of the 'global risk society'.
2 Explain how they show that environmental harm is a global issue.
3 Explain what the main underlying causes of the disasters appeared to be, such as a breach of health and safety regulations, state or corporate corruption and so on.
4 Explain in what ways these might be regarded as examples of green crimes.

Who commits green crimes?

Wolf identifies four groups who commit environmental crimes.

1   *Individuals* can have a powerful cumulative impact on the environment, through things such as individual littering, the illegal disposal of household waste ('fly tipping'), collecting eggs of protected birds, and dealing in endangered animals.
2   *Private business organizations* cause the most devastating environmental harms. Environmental crime is a typical example of corporate crime, and it is large corporations that are responsible for the bulk of land, air and water pollution, through emissions of toxic materials, the dumping of waste, and breaches of health and safety regulations.
3   *States and governments* cause environmental harm, often in collusion with private businesses. Santana (2002) points out that the military is the largest institutional polluter. Warfare plays a major role in generating risk and environmental destruction, but environmental harms can last well beyond the conflicts themselves, such as through unexploded bombs and landmines and the lasting effects of toxic chemicals. The nuclear arms race of the twentieth century, as well as the nuclear power industry, has generated millions of tons of nuclear waste and other radioactive material.
4   *Organized crime.* Wolf points out that organized crime has had a long-standing involvement in green crime, often in collusion with governments and industry. According to Interpol, a significant proportion of environmental crime is carried out by organized global criminal networks, attracted by the low-risk and high-profit nature of these types of crime. For example, research by Massari and Monzini (2004) revealed collusion between mafia-type organizations, legal businesses and local authorities in illegal hazardous waste disposal in Italy. This was driven by the demand for cheap means of disposal, and was made possible by the unscrupulous and unethical behaviour of government and business leaders, combined with a low public awareness of the threat posed by eco-crimes.

The victims of green crimes

Wolf points out that there are wide inequalities in the distribution of harm and risks to victims caused by environmental destruction, and in how laws are made, applied and enforced. Potter (2010) points out that current social divisions are reinforced by environmental harms, with the least powerful – the working class, the poor and minority ethnic groups – being the most likely victims of green crimes, in both developed and developing countries. He also suggests there is 'environmental racism' whereby those suffering the worst effects of environmental damage are of different ethnicity from those causing the damage, with the latter, most often, being white. White (2003) shows that people living in the developing world, which increasingly provides legal and illegal dump sites for the developed world's unwanted waste, face far greater risks of exposure to environmental air, water and land pollution than those in the developed world. In the developed world, it is working-class areas, rather than middle-class areas, that face the greatest risks from environmental pollution and the consequences of industrial accidents.

Enforcement action against green crimes

Governments are mainly responsible for creating and enforcing laws and regulations that control green crime, but they often form these policies in collaboration with the businesses who are most likely to be the principal offenders. Snider (1991), from a Marxist perspective, argues states are often reluctant to pass laws and regulations against pollution and other environmental harm by private business, and generally do so only when pressured by public opposition or environmental crises. They will strengthen them reluctantly, weaken them whenever possible, and often enforce them only weakly in a manner calculated to avoid threatening profits and employment, or frightening off potential investors.

Sutherland (1983 [1949]) pointed out that, like other types of white-collar and corporate crimes, environmental crimes often do not carry the same stigma as conventional crimes, like street crime, and rich multinational corporations which commit environmental offences often have the power and legal resources to avoid having them even being labelled as criminal. This means that, even where laws and regulations exist, they may not be enforced, or may be enforced only through the imposition of fines rather than by criminal prosecution and punishment through the criminal justice system. For example, the UK's Environment Agency (2012) says waste crime is often organized, large-scale and profitable, yet in England and Wales in 2011–12, the highest fine for waste crime was £170,000; there were just sixteen prison sentences handed out, and the longest was twenty-seven months. In the face of such relatively minor sanctions, offenders may find it more profitable to take the risk of paying a fine or serving a short prison sentence rather than fixing the problem or ceasing illegal and harmful activities. Wolf points out that poor countries may not have the resources, political will or power to enforce restrictions on things like the dumping of toxic materials, illegal logging, or trading in or poaching of endangered species.

Explaining green crimes

White (2008) argues green crime arises because transnational corporations and nation-states tend to hold a broadly *anthropocentric* view of the world. This suggests that the most important consideration for nations is the well-being of their citizens achieved through economic development and growth, and the environment is only a secondary consideration when forming economic policies, exploiting raw materials, manufacturing goods or disposing of waste by-products.

Wolf suggests that green crime is motivated by many of the same factors as ordinary crime, such as those considered by the rational choice, strain, control and Marxist theories discussed earlier in this chapter. These suggest that individuals and companies are motivated to break environmental laws or commit harm because crime pays, for example in terms of reducing financial costs, or the personal hassle and costs involved in socially responsible disposal of household waste, and perpetrators face less stigma and weaker sanctions than other criminals, as their offences are not taken as seriously or regarded as so 'wrong' as more conventional crimes.

Marxists suggest that the most serious green crimes are examples of what Pearce (1976) called 'the crimes of the powerful' – corporate crimes arising from criminogenic capitalism: corporations seek to minimize costs and maximize profits, through, for example, the dumping or recycling of toxic waste in developing countries where health and safety and environmental regulations are less demanding and less likely to be enforced, so waste disposal costs are much lower.

Problems of researching green crimes

Sociologists face a number of difficulties in researching green crimes.

- *Different laws*. Countries have different laws about green crime, which means that official statistics may not always be comparable between different countries.
- *Different definitions*. As discussed above, there is some dispute over what counts as a green crime, and this will vary between different researchers as well as between nations. Some define green crime as activities that break the law, others as any harm to the environment. Wolf points out this generates problems in the measurement, monitoring and reporting of green crimes, and there are few reliable and standardized sources of data.
- *Difficulties in measurement*. Green crime is often carried out by individuals, organized crime syndicates, powerful states and multinational corporations, who all have the capacity to conceal their crimes, and the most powerful can often avoid prosecution even if their crimes are discovered. This means it can be difficult to discover and measure the extent of green crime.
- *The use of case studies*. Much research has taken the form of case studies of individual cases of green crime, such as the Bhopal disaster of 1984, or the BP oil spill of 2010, but Wolf suggests

these have limited use in explaining and making generalizations about the causes of green crime.

Evaluation of green criminology

Green criminology is useful in addressing the growing threats of environmental harm, and locates this within the context of globalization, in what White (2011) has referred to as *eco-global criminology*. It also locates green crime within a wider framework of sociological theories of crime, state and corporate crime, and other theories such as the manufactured nature of risks in a global risk society, and rising risk consciousness, discussed by Beck. However, White points out that there is a lack of clarity and agreement about what environmental crime actually is, and that 'much depends upon who is defining the harm, and what criteria are used in assessing the nature of the activities'. This can mean that green criminology is accompanied by even greater risks of influence by the value-judgements and subjective interpretations of researchers than are normally found in most areas of sociological or scientific research.

Human rights and state crimes

It is ironic that the state that is responsible for making and enforcing the law also sometimes breaks the law itself. These crimes carried out by the agents of the state are known as state crimes.

What are state crimes?

Green and Ward (2004) describe state crimes as illegal or deviant activities perpetrated by, or with the complicity of, state agencies to further state policies. State crimes are generally taken to include offences like torture; the illegal treatment, imprisonment or punishment of citizens; corrupt or criminal policing; corruption; war crimes; assassination; genocide; state-sponsored terrorism; and other violations of human rights (which are discussed below).

Problems with defining state crimes

There is considerable controversy in defining what a state crime is. This is because the state is the source of law within nations, and itself defines what a crime is. It therefore has the power to avoid defining its own acts as criminal – for example, the persecution of Jews in 1930s and 1940s Nazi Germany was permitted under German law at the time.

Even when states commit acts that are clearly illegal under international law, such as violations of human rights conventions like the United Nations' Universal Declaration of Human Rights, the Geneva Conventions, and the Conventions against Torture and Genocide, states have the power to disguise, decriminalize and justify these offences by defining them as something other than crimes (see 'techniques of neutralization' below).

A transgressive approach: state crime as the violation of human rights

Because of the problems of defining state crime, sociologists have adopted a more *transgressive* approach, which involves going outside the usual boundaries of defining crime as simply law-breaking. Schwendinger and Schwendinger (1975) and Green and Ward (2012) suggest that state crimes should be considered as violations of human rights. Green and Ward (2012: 717) therefore adopt the following definition of state crime:

> *State organizational deviance* involving the *violation of human rights*.

Green and Ward's definition involves two aspects (shown in italics) and includes acts which may not be defined in law as criminal. It is worth emphasizing the aspect of *state organizational deviance*, to distinguish state crimes from the acts of rogue individuals who might work for the state, such as soldiers or police officers who abuse or injure prisoners without authority to do so, and may face disciplinary or criminal action if discovered. State crimes are committed on behalf of, or with the complicity of, state agencies, and are implementing official or unofficial state policy.

What are human rights?

Human rights are those that suggest that everyone, because of their common humanity, is entitled to the same fair and just treatment wherever they might be in the world. The United Nations Universal Declaration of Human Rights of 1948 has established a legal framework for defining and enforcing universal human rights, which Green and Ward suggest have now become global social norms, and nearly all countries in the world now have to pay at least lip-service to human rights. In the contemporary world, O'Byrne (2012) argues states are increasingly assessed by the extent to which they preserve human rights, and by the extent to which they fail to do so through injustice, discrimination, torture, violence, slavery or genocide.

Schwendinger and Schwendinger and Green and Ward see human rights as involving a wider package of basic social and economic rights, such as security, subsistence and well-being, as well as civil and political rights, like rights to life, liberty, free speech, voting, equal treatment before the law, and no imprisonment without a fair trial. This human rights dimension puts the study of state crime within a wider context of social harm rather than as simply law-breaking, so things like state-induced famine, the denial of basic welfare services as a result of state corruption and other deliberate denials of basic human rights are state crimes.

Activity

1 Go to www.un.org/en/rights or watch the videos at www.humanrights.com and identify ten human rights you have.
Go to www.yourrights.org.uk or www.liberty-human-rights.org.uk.
2 Identify four human rights which are contained in the UK Human Rights Act.
3 Identify three breaches of the Human Rights Act which the British government has recently been found guilty of.

Examples of state crimes

States have the power and resources to commit crimes on such a vast scale that it dwarfs the scale and harm caused by conventional crime. All of the following examples include extensive violations of human rights, but there are also huge numbers of less serious state crimes involving human rights abuses.

- *The torture and illegal treatment or punishment of citizens.* Examples include the systematic torture, disappearances and mass murder of thousands of political opponents of the Gaddafi regime in Libya, which was overthrown in 2011; the Pol Pot-led Khmer Rouge regime in Cambodia in 1975–9, when an estimated 1.5–3 million people (one-fifth to a quarter of the country's total population) died through the combined effects of forced labour, malnutrition, poor medical care, and executions of those regarded as 'enemies' and 'traitors'; the UK was found guilty in the 1970s of using 'white noise' to torture IRA suspects, and by 2012 the UK Ministry of Defence had paid out £14 million in compensation and costs to hundreds of Iraqis who complained that they were illegally detained and tortured by British forces following the invasion of Iraq in 2003. The United States still holds prisoners (at the time of writing) at the US Guantánamo Bay naval base in Cuba who have been subjected to torture, and have not been charged with any offence or given a trial. In 2014, a US Senate report found the CIA frequently (and illegally) used torture as an interrogation technique in secret prisons run by the CIA across the world in the years after the 11 September 2001 terror attack on New York's World Trade Center.

One of the worst state crimes of the twentieth century was the systematic attempted genocide of European Jews by Hitler's Nazi regime between 1933 and 1945. In Auschwitz concentration camp, shown here, an estimated 1 million Jews were murdered in gas chambers, out of a total of about 6 million murdered across Europe.

- *Corruption.* This involves the organized plunder of national resources by a ruling elite, such as the former Egyptian dictator Mubarak, overthrown in 2011, who was allegedly worth around $70 billion, embezzled from Egyptian state coffers.
- *Assassination or 'targeted killing',* which have been used as instruments of state power. For example, Mahmoud al-Mabhouh, the Palestinian Hamas commander, at the top of an Israeli hit list, was killed in a hotel in Dubai in 2010; the Russian state is widely believed to be behind the 2006 murder by radiation poisoning of Alexander Litvinenko in London.
- *War crimes.* These involve illegal acts committed during wars, like the murder, ill-treatment, torture or deliberate targeting or enslavement of civilian populations or prisoners of war, and the plundering/looting of property. Israel has repeatedly been condemned for the deliberate targeting of civilian populations in the Israel–Palestine conflict. Former Yugoslav president Slobodan Milošević was brought to trial for war crimes, including the forced deportation and murder of thousands of ethnic Albanians from Kosovo, and of non-Serbs in Croatia and Bosnia in 1998–9.
- *Genocide.* This involves the attempted elimination by mass murder of people belonging to a particular ethnic, national or religious group, and is normally carried out by state action or with its support. Hitler's Nazi regime murdered 6 million Jews between 1933 and 1945; in Sudan's Darfur region, an estimated 300,000 died between 2003 and 2009, with millions forced into refugee camps; in the Rwanda genocide of 1994, an estimated 500,000–1,000,000 people from the Tutsi minority were killed by the majority Hutu people in a period of around 100 days.
- *State-sponsored terrorism.* This involves the state itself carrying out terrorist acts or supporting others that do. For example, Iran has been accused of backing Shia militias in Iraq, and the United States has a long history of supporting illegal rebel groups against elected regimes it regards as unfriendly, particularly in Central and South America. The De Silva report in 2012 into the murder of a Belfast lawyer in 1989 concluded that agents of the British state were involved in carrying out serious violations of human rights up to and including murder, in what

British prime minister David Cameron described as 'shocking levels of state collusion' between the army, police and terrorists.

Explaining state crimes

Integrated theory and the crimes of obedience model

Green and Ward (2012) identify two main explanations for state crime.

Integrated theory

This suggests state crime arises from similar circumstances to those of other crimes, like street crimes, and involves integrating the three elements of the motivations of offenders, opportunities to commit crimes, and failures of control (whether or not intentional) and how these interact to break rules and generate state crimes. This approach draws on many of the theories of crime discussed in this chapter, but applies them to state crime.

The crimes of obedience model

This was developed by Kelman and Hamilton (1989) and emphasizes not rule-breaking, but conformity to rules. They suggest violent states encourage obedience by those who actually carry out state-backed systematic human rights abuses, like torture, murder, genocide or other atrocities, even when they may personally regard them as deviant and immoral acts, in three ways.

1 *Authorization:* making it clear to individuals they are acting in accordance with official policy, and with explicit state authority and support.
2 *Dehumanization.* This involves the state's promotion of a monolithic (single and inflexible) cultural identity, which is based on the marginalization and social exclusion of minorities, who are portrayed as a sub-human species to whom normal rules of behaviour do not apply, which enables state discrimination, atrocities, torture and genocide to become acceptable to ordinary people. This is what happened to the Jews in Nazi Germany, who were systematically stripped of all human rights and who became defined as a sub-human species, to whom the normal rules of civilized behaviour therefore did not apply. Much the same might be said to apply to terrorists today, who are regarded as monsters to whom the normal rules of human rights do not apply.
3 *Routinization.* This involves organizing the actions in such a way that they become part of a regular routine, and can be performed in a detached way that denies perpetrators the need or opportunity to raise moral questions or make moral decisions about the acts they are committing. Violent states reinforce and manage this by creating what de Swann (2001) called 'enclaves of barbarism' – places or situations where state violence is encouraged and rewarded, and which the perpetrators of violence can then afterwards leave, returning to an everyday life where ordinary social norms prevail.

Bauman (1989) suggests the Holocaust – the Nazi genocide of the Jews – was made possible by these three processes. He points to the way it was, for those who actually carried out the crimes in the 'enclaves of barbarism' of the death camps, turned into a state-approved routine administrative task. This involved the detached application of modern science and technology to the mass destruction of an ethnic group defined as sub-human. Those carrying out the genocide went about their work in much the same routine and detached way as a contemporary pest-control worker might apply scientific techniques to eliminate an infestation of rats. This type of approach can be applied to many types of human rights abuses committed by states, particularly to the use of torture, and not just to the horrors of genocide.

Techniques of neutralization

Cohen (2001) applies Sykes and Matza's (1957) concept of techniques of neutralization to explain how states can deny they have committed serious breaches of human rights. They do this by trying to neutralize their crimes by re-labelling them as something else, or excusing them as regrettable but justifiable – for example, illegal torture and detention of terrorists is justified by denying they are victims of abuse as they themselves show no regard for human life or human rights, or by appeals to higher loyalties such as the need to stop ruthless terrorists from massacring innocent people, or as necessary steps to protect national security in the war on terror. By such techniques of neutralization, states provide the necessary excuses and justifications to explain their human rights breaches to themselves, to those who actually carry out the acts, and to other countries in the rest of the world who might seek to condemn them for it.

Problems of researching state crimes

Traditional sociological research on crime has been fairly straightforward, with the use of official crime statistics, victim surveys and a range of other sociological methods to discover acts of law-breaking, who commits them and why. Researching state crime is rather different.

Cohen shows it is difficult to find the true extent of state crime because governments adopt strategies of denial to either deny or justify their actions, or reclassify them as something else. State crimes are carried out by powerful people, who have a huge armoury of state agencies at their disposal to control information, and to cover up any of the state's criminal activity. This state secrecy means there are no official statistics or victim surveys to show the extent of such crime, and the 'dark figure' of hidden state crime is probably much greater than that of unreported and unrecorded conventional crime. Researchers are often reliant on secondary data like media reports, but even these tend to focus on state crimes in developing countries, and largely ignore state crimes committed by Western democracies, such as those of the United Kingdom or the United States.

Tombs and Whyte (2003) point out that researchers are likely to face strong official resistance, and states can use their power to prevent or hinder sociologists doing research – by threats, by refusals to provide funding, and by denying access to state officials and to official documents. In dictatorships, researchers additionally risk imprisonment, torture and death as enemies of the state. Greene and Ward (2012) point out research can therefore be difficult, harrowing (because of the nature of the offences) and dangerous, and the state can use the law and criminal justice system to control and persecute researchers whom it perceives to be its enemies, even in democracies. All these factors make it difficult to access information on state crime.

The media and the social construction of crime and deviance

Crime as consumer spectacle

Crime and deviance have long been major themes in popular culture. Fictional and non-fictional crime stories have provided significant sources of spectacle and mass entertainment, and are staple parts of the media diet. In fiction, comic books, thrillers and films often have acts of crime and violence, particularly murder and theft, and the detection of offenders, as central features. Media news is full of stories of crime and deviance, which have become an integral part of contemporary media *infotainment*, in which information about crime is packaged to entertain. For example, programmes like *Crimewatch* present crime in the form of dramatized reconstructions giving quite frightening insights into the crimes committed, and TV reality shows like *Police, Camera, Action!* use footage shot from police cars as entertainment. Hayward and Young (2012) argue advertisers have turned images of crime and deviance into tools for selling products in the consumer market, such as the way, for the youth market, things like gangsta rap, urban hip hop, and videogames like *Grand Theft Auto* combine images of criminality, street gang culture and designer chic that represent crime as a style and fashion choice that is romantic, exciting and cool. Some designer gear, like hoodies, has itself become a symbol of deviance.

Agenda-setting

Many of the issues that people think about and discuss are based on the list of subjects (agenda) that media reports tell them about. This influence of the media is known as agenda-setting. The media provide knowledge or impressions about crime and deviance for most people in society, including politicians, the police, social workers and the public at large. The media clearly can't report every single criminal or deviant act that occurs, and media personnel are necessarily very selective in the incidents they choose to report. People are only able to discuss and form opinions about the crime and deviance they have been informed about, and for most people this information is provided by the traditional mainstream mass media rather than by personal experience or through social media networking sites, like Facebook, YouTube or Twitter, which are more likely to provide alternative views of events. This means that people's perceptions of crime and deviance in society are influenced by what media personnel choose to include in or leave out of their newspapers, television programmes, films or websites. Media representations may therefore influence what people believe about crime and deviance, regardless of whether or not these are accurate.

> **Agenda-setting** involves the power to manage which issues are to be presented for public discussion and debate and which issues are to be kept in the background.

News values

Greer and Reiner (2012) point out that in news, documentaries and fiction, stories of sexual and violent crimes are the stuff that titillates, excites and captures the popular imagination. The media are always seeking out newsworthy stories of crime and deviance, and they exploit the possibilities for a 'good story' by dramatizing, exaggerating, over-reporting and sensationalizing some crimes out of all proportion to their actual extent in society, in order to generate audience interest and encourage audiences to consume or buy their media products.

Reiner (2007) suggests that media coverage of crime and deviance is filtered through the values and assumptions of crime-thriller and film-script writers, and of journalists, about what makes a story worth telling or 'newsworthy' – exciting, interesting, and that media audiences want to know about. These values and assumptions are known as news values. Jewkes (2011) suggests that the news values that influence the reporting of crime and deviance include those shown in table 6.6. These guide the choices writers, editors and journalists make when they decide what stories are sufficiently newsworthy to report, and what to leave out; which elements of a story to include and play up; and how what they choose to report should be presented. The stories that are most likely to be reported are those which include many newsworthy aspects. Greer (2005) suggests it is these news values that explain why all mainstream media, both fact and fiction, tend to exaggerate the extent of violent crime, and why practically any form of deviance by celebrities, no matter how trivial, receives massive coverage.

> **News values** are the values and assumptions held by editors and journalists which guide them in choosing what is 'newsworthy' – what to report and what to leave out, and how what they choose to report should be presented.

The backwards law: public perceptions and the distortion and exaggeration of crime

Surveys such as the CSEW (see, for example, the Office for National Statistics report, *Public Perceptions of Crime*, 26 March 2015), show that the majority of people base their knowledge of crime and the criminal justice system (CJS) on the media, including crime fiction, rather than on their own direct experience. However, Surette (2010) suggests that there is what he calls a 'backwards law', with the media constructing images of crime and justice which are an opposite or backwards version of reality. Greer (2003) and Greer and Reiner (2012) suggest this backwards law is shown by media news and fiction misrepresenting the reality of crime in the following ways:

- By hugely over-representing and exaggerating sex, drug and (particularly) serious violence-related crimes, such as sexual assault, murder or armed robbery, and by under-representing the risks of the most common offence of property crime
- By portraying property crime as far more serious and violent than most recorded offences, which are fairly routine, trivial and non-dramatic, and typically involve little or no loss or damage, and no violence or threat to victims

- By over-exaggerating police effectiveness in clearing-up (solving) crimes
- By exaggerating the risks of becoming victims faced by higher-status white people, older people, women and children
- By emphasizing individual incidents of crime, rather than providing any understanding or analysis of crime patterns or the causes of crime.

Left Realists suggest media reporting of crime disguises the reality that both offenders and victims are mainly from the working class and the poor, and Marxists point to the concealment of the significance of white-collar and corporate crimes, such as widespread tax and other frauds, environmental pollution, and the manufacture of harmful drugs, which rarely get reported.

Table 6.6 News values and crime and deviance

News value	Meaning
Threshold	Events have to be considered significant or dramatic enough to be in the news – a single rape might make it into a local paper, but a serial rapist might become a national story.
Proximity	Items which will have some cultural meaning or geographical closeness (proximity) to media audiences. For example, in the British media, British criminals or victims are more newsworthy than foreigners (except for foreign criminals who prey on the British in Britain), significant national crimes are generally considered more important than local ones, and the murder of a 'respectable' woman is more likely to be reported than that of a prostitute.
Predictability	Stories that are predictable (known in advance) are more likely to be covered, like the publication of the latest crime statistics, as media can plan ahead.
Individualism	Focus on the actions of, or conflict between, individuals, avoiding complex explanations.
Simplification	Events that are easily understood and not too complicated, without the need for lots of background explanation and detail.
Risk	Crime becomes newsworthy when it can be presented (or misrepresented) as sufficiently serious, random and unpredictable for us all to be at risk of becoming victims, and to have something to fear.
Spectacle and graphic images	Events, particularly violent ones, accompanied by film, video, CCTV, or mobile phone footage are more newsworthy as they enable the media to provide a visual and dramatic portrayal for audiences.
Celebrity or high-status people	Crime and deviance, even if quite trivial, involving celebrities or important or powerful people, whether they are victims or offenders, is seen as more newsworthy than that involving ordinary people.
Children	Children as offenders or victims of crime have the potential to be newsworthy (see, for example, the Madeleine McCann story on page 209 of chapter 3).
Sex	Sex crimes, crimes with a sexual dimension, women as victims, and non-criminal sexual deviance like BDSM (bondage domination sado-masochism) – especially involving celebrities or other famous people – are more newsworthy.
Violence	Violent events enable media to report using the drama, excitement and action which appeal to audiences.
Conservatism	Events are made newsworthy by calls for more punishment and deterrence, e.g. more police, higher fines, jailing young people, more prisons, and longer sentences.

Source: devised from Jewkes (2011)

> **Activity**
>
> With reference to table 6.6, choose any two current big media news stories, fiction or non-fiction TV dramas or films about crime and deviance, and try to identify those news values that have made them newsworthy or have given them 'audience appeal'.

The hyperreality of crime

The backwards law, combined with the agenda-setting and news values discussed above, means the media socially construct a distorted view of crime and the CJS, exaggerate the risks of becoming a victim of crime, and unnecessarily increase the public's fear of crime. This illustrates Baudrillard's (2001) postmodernist idea of *hyperreality* (see pages 198–9 and 399–400), which suggests that the media do not reflect reality but actively create it, as most people's only knowledge of crime is through media-created images which have little connection with the real world. The effects of this backwards hyperreality are illustrated by Flatley et al. (2010), who show that although all crime in England and Wales had been falling or steady between 1995 and 2010, between three-quarters and two-thirds of the population wrongly thought it was rising.

Activity

1 Study some media reports (such as national newspapers, TV news, websites and social media) for a few days, and think about TV dramas and films you've seen. What impressions do they give about the levels and seriousness of crime in society?
2 On the basis of what you found above, draw up a profile of the media stereotype of a 'typical criminal', explaining where you got your ideas from.
3 To what extent do you think media reporting tends to exaggerate the risks of individuals becoming victims of crime? Give reasons for your answer.
4 Outline three contemporary examples of media accounts of the criminal justice system (criminals, victims, police, courts, prisons etc.) which you think might illustrate the backwards law, i.e. show the opposite of reality.

The media as moral entrepreneurs

Moral entrepreneurs are people, groups or organizations with the power to create or enforce rules which define deviance. The media act as moral entrepreneurs and establish themselves as the self-appointed guardians of national morality by labelling and stereotyping certain groups and activities as deviant and as social problems, by presenting them as acting outside the boundaries of normal, rational behaviour, and by suggesting they are a threat to society which should be condemned. Even if much of what is reported is exaggerated or even untrue, media stories can demonize as folk devils those involved in some activities, and sensitize the public to such an extent that it is encouraged to support action taken against them. Some examples of issues and groups that have been defined in such ways are shown in figure 6.16 on page 521. One of the ways the media carry out their roles as moral entrepreneurs is through the creation of a moral panic, which is discussed below.

Folk devils are individuals or groups posing an imagined or exaggerated threat to society.

Deviancy amplification, folk devils and moral panics

Hall et al. (1978), in their study about the crime of mugging in 1973 (see pages 222, 457 and 482), and Cohen (2002 [1972]) (see below) show how the media, through their exaggerated and sensationalized reporting of crime and deviance, can whip up a moral panic – a wave of public concern about some exaggerated or imaginary threat to society – generating growing public anxiety and concern about the alleged deviance. The deviants themselves are labelled as folk devils and troublemakers who present a threat to society, and provide visible reminders of what we should *not* be. Hall et al. and Cohen suggest these media-generated moral panics tend to appear during periods of uncertainty, such as during periods of rapid social change or political and economic crisis. In this context, those defined as deviants play much the same role as witches in the past, as easy scapegoats to blame for a range of social problems, and this is seen by some sociologists as part of the process of strengthening the status quo and marginalizing those who challenge or threaten it.

The creation of a moral panic can sensitize the police, courts and other agencies of social control to the group or problem, and lead to demands by the media and the media-fuelled public for action to stamp down on the alleged deviance. Often these agencies, such as newspaper editors, the churches, politicians, schools, social services, the police and magistrates, will respond to the exaggerated threat presented in the media by pulling together to take harsher measures against the demonized folk devils of alleged troublemakers. These measures might include heavier policing levels, more arrests, stiffer fines, more imprisonment of offenders, and sometimes changes in the law to criminalize deviant activities. Such action, particularly by the police, can often amplify (or make worse) what was originally minor or isolated deviant behaviour, for example by causing more arrests. It's possible that such action, combined with media coverage and pre-publicity over the possible trouble looming, might even create deviance where there was none before, as people get swept away by the excitement of events. The presence and attention of reporters and TV cameras might encourage people to act up for the cameras and misbehave when they might not otherwise have done so. The way the media may actually create or make worse the very problems they condemn is known as deviancy amplification.

Figure 6.15 illustrates the way the media can amplify deviance and generate a moral panic, and figure 6.16 shows a range of moral panics which have arisen in Britain since the 1950s.

> **Deviancy amplification** is the way the media may actually make worse or create the very deviance they condemn by their exaggerated, sensationalized and distorted reporting of events and their presence at them.

An example of deviancy amplification: Stanley Cohen's *Folk Devils and Moral Panics*

In *Folk Devils and Moral Panics* (2002 [1972]), Stanley Cohen showed how the media helped to create two opposing youth groups in the 1960s – the Mods (who drove scooters and wore parkas) and the Rockers (who drove motorbikes and wore leather gear).

On an Easter bank holiday weekend in 1964, at Clacton and other seaside resorts, there were some minor acts of vandalism and a few scuffles between some Mods and Rockers, though the level of violence was little different from that occurring anywhere else in the country. However, the media carried hugely exaggerated reports of what happened, and front-page headlines gave the misleading impression that Clacton had been terrorized and torn apart by pitched battles between rival gangs.

This generated a moral panic, with widespread public fear of, and hostility towards, the Mods and Rockers, who came to be seen in the period after this as folk devils posing major threats to public order. The police were forced to stamp down hard on these groups in response to the alleged deviant behaviour, which had been so exaggerated by the media. This resulted in a growing number of arrests.

1960s Rockers hanging out, and some 'born-again' present-day Mods out for a spin. Are there any similar rivalries among competing youth groups today which the media suggest might be folk devils?

Before these events, the Mods and Rockers had not seen themselves as rival groups, and most young people did not identify with either of them. However, the publicity created by the media's exaggerated, distorted and sensationalized reporting encouraged more young people to identify with the two groups, and to adopt their styles as fashionable and exciting lifestyle choices. This raised public fears to even greater heights. The example of the Mods and Rockers shows how the media's reporting of deviance can actually create the very problems they are allegedly concerned about, and generate public concerns about a problem that only existed because the media created it.

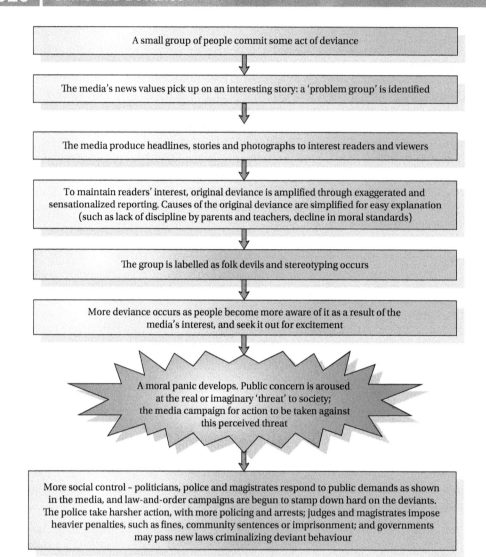

A small group of people commit some act of deviance

↓

The media's news values pick up on an interesting story: a 'problem group' is identified

↓

The media produce headlines, stories and photographs to interest readers and viewers

↓

To maintain readers' interest, original deviance is amplified through exaggerated and sensationalized reporting. Causes of the original deviance are simplified for easy explanation (such as lack of discipline by parents and teachers, decline in moral standards)

↓

The group is labelled as folk devils and stereotyping occurs

↓

More deviance occurs as people become more aware of it as a result of the media's interest, and seek it out for excitement

↓

A moral panic develops. Public concern is aroused at the real or imaginary 'threat' to society; the media campaign for action to be taken against this perceived threat

↓

More social control – politicians, police and magistrates respond to public demands as shown in the media, and law-and-order campaigns are begun to stamp down hard on the deviants. The police take harsher action, with more policing and arrests; judges and magistrates impose heavier penalties, such as fines, community sentences or imprisonment; and governments may pass new laws criminalizing deviant behaviour

Figure 6.15
Deviancy amplification, moral panics and the media

How relevant is the concept of moral panic today?

McRobbie and Thornton (1995) suggest that the concept of moral panic is no longer useful for understanding crime, and is outdated in the age of the new media. This is because new media technology, the growing sophistication of media audiences in a media-saturated society, constant 24/7 rolling news reporting, and intense competition both between media organizations and between different types of media – such as web-based news, blogs, social networking through Twitter, YouTube and Facebook, and cable, print, broadcast and satellite news – have changed the reporting of, and reaction to, events that might once have caused a moral panic. Pluralists and postmodernists argue there is now such a huge diversity of media reports and interpretations of events, and of opinions on and reactions to these events by the public through citizen journalism and social media, that people today are much more sceptical of mainstream media reports and less likely to believe them. This means it has become more difficult for the media to define issues or events in such a way that they can develop into a moral panic. This is also made more difficult by the way news is reported and updated by both social media and mainstream news organizations on an ongoing, almost minute-by-minute basis, 24 hours a day. As a result, most deviant or criminal events now have such short shelf-lives in sustaining audience interest that they are unlikely to be newsworthy for long enough to become a moral panic.

Hunt (2003, cited in Hall (2012)) suggests that the boundaries separating moral and immoral behaviour have become blurred, and late modernists like Beck (1992) argue that in contemporary

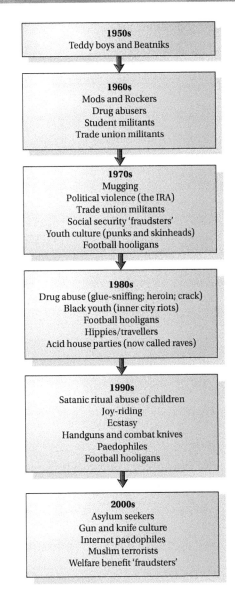

Figure 6.16 Folk devils and moral panics: Great Britain, 1950s–2010s

'risk society' there are now so many risks and uncertainties that many of the things that used to generate moral panics have become a normal part of daily life, and no longer seem to have the exceptional and anxiety-inducing qualities required to whip up moral panics. He suggests that the concept of moral panic is now too vague to explain a situation in which daily life is routinely marked by new crises of some kind, and where 'crime consciousness' is a part of normal, everyday life. It is therefore now less easy to define what a moral panic might be.

Steve Hall (2012), a critical theorist, dismisses the whole concept of moral panics. He suggests that newspaper headlines about 'the grinding selfishness and anti-social behaviour of numerous groups ranging from troublesome youths on sink estates to spoilt and unruly sportspeople, over-paid celebrities, faceless bureaucrats and corporate executives, corrupt politicians, irresponsible bankers and financial traders and organized criminal traffickers' reflect a real sense of exasperation felt by many, but these headlines have not produced moral panics. He suggests the concept of moral panics is wholly unfounded. He argues that the media do sensationalize specific crimes, and this sensationalism does cause concern amongst the public, but the media also overstate the criminal justice system's ability to solve these crimes and bring criminals to justice. Therefore, public concern is generated only to be soothed by the media in a way that increases the public's faith in the existing political and administrative system and creates complacency – the opposite of panic.

Hall also argues that there are rational concerns (not artificial fears manufactured by media headlines) about real crimes, particularly in disadvantaged communities where crime and disorder are high and policing lax, and where family structures and communities are unable to provide informal controls as they are breaking down under economic pressures, such as those of unemployment, temporary and part-time work, and low pay. Hall argues that criminality is not a figment of the imagination that a fearful and stupid population are duped into believing by the media, but that crime produces real and distressing harms to all sorts of victims. Sociologists who dismiss such events as myths – moral panics – generated by a conservative media are denying the justified anxieties that people have. Hall argues the concept of moral panics is simply an ideological construction by liberal sociologists who dismiss people's anxieties as a product of overblown and sensationalized media reporting to avoid stampeding people into supporting greater repression by the state. At the same time, liberal sociologists don't concern themselves enough with the rational fears that people have as they face the risks and uncertainties of an unstable contemporary capitalism. Hall sees 'moral panic' as a zombie concept, and regards the importance attached to moral panics in contemporary sociology as comparable to living with the undead.

Activity

1 Outline and explain three reasons why the mass media might distort, exaggerate and sensationalize the extent of deviance and crime in society. Try to illustrate your answer with examples drawn from current media reports.
2 Refer to figures 6.15 and 6.16 and try to fill in each of the stages of any current moral panic in society.
3 To what extent do you agree with the view that the nature of the media in the contemporary world has made the concept of moral panic largely redundant? Give reasons for your answer.
4 Outline reasons why the lifestyles and activities of young people are often the focus of media amplification of deviance, and why they are most often portrayed as folk devils.

Do the media cause crime?

Greer and Reiner (2012) point out there has been a very long history of what Pearson (1983) called 'respectable fears' (concerns of 'respectable' people) about the media causing crime and deviance. They identify several ways that the media might do this, and a number of these are discussed in more depth elsewhere in this book, and you may wish to refer to the pages shown.

1 *Labelling, moral entrepreneurship and deviancy amplification* suggest that media reporting can create and/or make crime and deviance worse (see above, and pages 222, 457 and 482 on mugging, and pages 459 and 479–82 on labelling theory).
2 Motives for crime. The media's promotion of consumerist culture through images of affluent lifestyles creates crime by intensifying relative deprivation in what Young called a bulimic society (see Left Realism, pages 465–6), or generating the strain Merton identified (see pages 451–2), or through images of crime and violence encouraging people to commit crime by imitating (copycatting) what they pick up from the media, or by desensitizing them to violence (see pages 249–51).
3 *Knowledge and learning of criminal techniques,* such as the way the video *Child's Play 3* is alleged to have influenced the murderers of toddler James Bulger (see pages 249–51), and videogames like *Grand Theft Auto* in which players act out the roles of criminals.
4 *New means of committing crimes.* The new media and media technology, like the internet, provide new opportunities for cybercrimes and the organization of transnational crime and terrorism (see pages 502–3, 505).
5 *The reduction of social controls over crime.* Drawing on control theory (see pages 454–6) and rational choice theory (see page 468), Greer and Reiner suggest that, even if people are motivated to commit crime, they may not do so if there are effective *internal* controls, through

self-control and conscience, and *external* controls, through the risk of police action and arrest, that prevent them. The media may undermine these controls in two ways.

- By stories mocking the police and criminal justice system, and/or suggesting they are corrupt, ineffective and inefficient. This undermines external controls by reducing both public cooperation in controlling crime and the perception by potential offenders of the risks they face of getting caught.
- By stories and images which undermine internal controls by presenting crime sympathetically, or as glamorous, exciting and seductive, or which desensitize people to the use and effects of violence.

6 *Providing targets for crime.* Media hardware and software provide new targets for property crime, such as smartphones, laptop and tablet computers, TVs, DVD recorders, and DVDs and CDs.

There are many difficulties and controversies surrounding research into the effects of the media (see, for example, pages 240 and 249–52) and many of the suggestions about how the media may encourage people who might otherwise not have done so to commit acts of crime or violence have little conclusive evidence to support them.

Practice questions

1 Outline **two** ways in which green or environmental crimes may reinforce existing social inequalities. **(4 marks)**

2 Outline **three** reasons why the media may exaggerate the extent of crime in society. **(6 marks)**

3 Read **Item A** below and answer the question that follows.

> **Item A**
> State crimes are those carried out by the state in pursuit of its policies, and involve violations of human rights as defined by international law. It can be difficult to investigate the extent of state crimes, because governments have the power to adopt strategies to either deny or justify human rights abuses, or reclassify them as something else that is not criminal.

Applying material from **Item A**, analyse **two** reasons why it may be difficult for sociologists to investigate the extent of state crimes. **(10 marks)**

4 Read **Item B** below and answer the question that follows.

> **Item B**
> Globalization has created a global criminal economy and transnational networks of organized crime. New opportunities for crime and new types of crime have emerged. Less financial regulation and fewer state controls over business and finance have contributed to the globalization of crime, along with other factors such as growing inequality, cultural globalization and the ideology of consumerism.

Applying material from **Item B** and your knowledge, evaluate sociological views of the effects of globalization on crime. **(30 marks)**

Topic 4

SPECIFICATION AREA

Crime control, surveillance, prevention and punishment, victims, and the role of the criminal justice system and other agencies

The criminal justice system (CJS)

The criminal justice system (CJS) refers to all the different agencies and organizations that are involved in law, order, crime and punishment, and how they work together. It consists of agencies such as the police, Crown Prosecution Service (CPS), courts, prisons and the probation service. These are overseen by the government departments of the Home Office and the Ministry of Justice. The Youth Justice Board oversees youth justice, and advises the Ministry of Justice on youth offending. (These agencies relate to England and Wales, and arrangements differ to some extent in Scotland and N. Ireland.) These agencies are the main means of identifying, controlling and punishing known offenders.

The CJS establishment is massively dominated by older, middle-class people, and, in crown courts, senior judges are predominantly white and male, and drawn from very privileged social backgrounds, including education at top private schools and at the elite Oxford and Cambridge universities. Those dispensing justice to the most disadvantaged are therefore among the most advantaged in our society.

The role of the criminal justice system in crime control and prevention

The CJS is concerned with four inter-related aims.

1 *Deterrence.* Deterring people from committing crime is a key aim of the CJS, and in an ideal world it would be so effective that people who were tempted to commit crime would be so afraid of being caught and the consequences that followed that they would be deterred from committing crime at all.
2 *Public protection.* It is the primary role of the police to maintain public order, prevent crime and catch offenders, and the courts, through a wide range of penalties, aim to stop criminals causing further harm to people or property.
3 *Retribution.* Retribution or retributive justice is concerned with punishing criminals to make sure they get their 'just deserts' for wrongdoing, and is perhaps the most popular conception of what the CJS is about.
4 *Rehabilitation.* Rehabilitative justice is the idea that, often alongside, or instead of, being punished, criminals should be rehabilitated – turned into reformed characters, so that they never offend again.

Changing approaches to criminal justice

Garland (2001) suggests that, in most of the twentieth century, the focus of the CJS was on the rehabilitation (reform) of offenders, but that since the 1970s there has been a growing emphasis on retributive justice, with more punitive – harsher – penalties, giving criminals what Newburn (2007) calls their 'just deserts'. This was shown by a huge increase in imprisonment, with the number of prisoners in the UK more than doubling between 1970 and 2014. This has been accompanied by more rhetoric from politicians about protecting the public – 'cracking down hard on crime' – by controlling and supervising offenders by imposing penalties such as imprisonment, parole, probation, and being placed on sex offender registers.

Even though there are much higher levels of imprisonment, primarily aimed at retribution ('just deserts'), this has also been accompanied by growing uncertainty over the extent to which the deterrent effects of expensive punishments, including imprisonment, and ideas of reforming/rehabilitating offenders are working. Victim surveys like the Crime Survey for England and Wales (CSEW) show that most crime never gets reported, and Crawford and Evans (2012) note that the emphasis on crime reduction has since the 1980s been changing to give higher priority to prevention of crime in the future, rather than to simply the prosecution and retributive punishment of offenders after the event. There has been a growing recognition that criminal justice should also be concerned with protecting the rights and needs of victims of crime, as well as punishing the criminals ever more heavily.

The culture of control: from Left Realism to Right Realism

Garland sees these changes in criminal justice also reflected in sociological theory, in which there was a shift from Left Realist-style theories which focused on the causes of crime rooted in social injustice and inequality, towards more Right Realist-style approaches. Right Realist approaches have more focus on the consequences of crime and emphasize the need for more social control, stricter socialization, harsher punishment, measures to reduce the opportunities for criminal acts to be committed, and reducing the harm and fears that crime produces in the public. These policies are discussed shortly. Garland argues there is now a 'culture of control', concerned with controlling, preventing and reducing the risks of people becoming victims of crime, rather than with rehabilitating criminals. This new approach is accompanied by the growing use of private security, alongside official criminal justice agencies like the police, to protect the public and prevent crime.

Restorative justice – naming, shaming and facing the victims

> **Restorative justice** is a process which brings together victims of crime and the offenders responsible, usually in face-to-face meetings, to help repair the harm done, restore the dignity and self-respect of victims, reduce their fear of crime, and make offenders take responsibility for the consequences of their actions.

Recently, in view of rising uncertainty about the impact of imprisonment on reducing crime, there are more attempts being made, particularly in the field of youth justice, to divert people involved in low-level minor offending away from formal sanctions in the CJS. This aims to avoid the unnecessary criminalization of those on the fringes of criminal activity, and to avoid them entering the 'universities of crime' – prisons and youth justice institutions. There is more use of restorative justice processes (see glossary box), and of community sentences for less serious offences, whereby offenders involve themselves in unpaid community work, such as cleaning up litter or removing graffiti, rather than being imprisoned.

Braithwaite (1999) claims restorative justice is most effective when it involves what he calls 'reintegrative shaming' – where offenders not only face their victims, but are also publicly 'named and shamed' so offenders come to realize the extent to which society disapproves of their offending, to shame them into future conformity and to make them take responsibility for the consequences of their actions.

Postmodernists draw attention to the growing detachment of the criminal justice system from centralized control to more informal localized arrangements, as it starts to take account of people's different lifestyles and needs. For example, policing policies become more localized and community-based, reflecting the fragmentation of society into a diverse range of smaller groupings of localized identities, such as those around ethnic and gender identities. The voluntary use of Sharia courts, based on Islamic rather than British law, among some sections of the Muslim community to deal with disputes might be seen as an example of the growing informality and localism of criminal justice, as it becomes more responsive to local identities. A further element of this is the growing use of private security by people and businesses who seek to customize the control of crime and disorder to their own needs, rather than relying simply on the formal agencies of the CJS.

The role of punishment in crime control and prevention

Newburn (2007) suggests there are five main reasons for punishing criminals:

1 To discourage them from reoffending (rehabilitation) or to deter other people from offending in the future (deterrence)
2 To force them to make amends to victims for the harm they have done to them (restorative justice)
3 To protect society from those who are dangerous (incapacitation – prevention through imprisonment or, in some countries, execution)
4 To reinforce social values and bonds (the functionalist view discussed below)
5 To punish them simply because they deserve to be punished for their crimes (retribution – making sure offenders get their just deserts).

Types of punishment

The punishment of offenders is part of the state regulation of the behaviour of its citizens. There have been many different forms of punishment of criminals over time, with some taking the form of public spectacles for which crowds would gather to watch and cheer. Some have involved highly brutal, sadistic punishments, focusing on retribution through the infliction of pain and suffering on criminals – such as public hanging, drawing and quartering (where people were hanged, cut down while still alive, disembowelled and then cut into four pieces); burning alive at the stake; beheadings; mutilation through removal of hands, feet, etc.; and branding, torture, whipping and being put in the stocks. Such punishments are most associated in Britain with the Middle Ages (twelfth to fifteenth centuries) and up to the eighteenth century, but they are still found in some societies today. For example, amputations of the hands of thieves, floggings, and public executions by beheading are still found in some Muslim countries like Saudi Arabia. The death penalty is still a legal form of punishment in around 58 countries in the world, and in 2013, 778 executions were carried out according to Amnesty International, with the highest number in China, Iran, Iraq, North Korea, Saudi Arabia, the USA and Somalia. In contemporary Britain, punishment of offenders involves less brutal and more private forms of punishment, such as life imprisonment as an alternative to execution, imprisonment, parole, probation, community service sentences, fines, Criminal Behaviour Orders (CBOs), curfew orders, restorative justice, and monitoring devices like electronic tagging.

The changing form of punishments

Why have the forms of punishment changed over time, from the public spectacles of cruel brutality and the infliction of bodily pain to the more 'civilized' forms of punishment we see in most contemporary societies today? Two types of explanation are offered below, from the broadly postmodernist Foucault (1991), and from the Marxists Rusche and Kirchheimer (2003 [1939]).

Foucault: from sovereign power to disciplinary power

Foucault relates the decline in public forms of physical punishment and the infliction of pain to the changing structures of power in society. He saw public brutal punishments as concerned not with deterring people from crime, but as public demonstrations of the supreme power of the sovereign – the monarch – over criminals, including their bodies. He referred to this form of state power and control as sovereign power.

As the supreme power of sovereigns declined, there developed a new form of state power and control over criminals which Foucault referred to as disciplinary power. Criminals were to be controlled and disciplined by surveillance – constantly having their behaviour monitored, managed, controlled and regulated.

Foucault saw this change from sovereign power to disciplinary power reflected in the way punishments changed from the infliction of pain to the development of the prison, and other forms

Inside one of the prison buildings at Presidio Modelo, Isla de la Juventud, Cuba. An example of a panopticon-style design

of the less brutal punishment with which we associate justice in contemporary Britain. As Newburn (2007) puts it, 'occasional bursts of bodily punishment of offenders were replaced by a system of control and regulation at all times'.

Foucault illustrated this change from sovereign power to disciplinary power through surveillance using the idea of the disciplinary mechanism of the panopticon. This was a prison design in which prisoners in their cells were permanently visible to the guards in a central tower (an example is shown in the photo above) but the prisoners could not see the guards, nor other prisoners. Foucault suggested that, because the prisoners could never be sure whether the guards were watching them or not, the uncertainty of surveillance would encourage criminals to exercise self-surveillance and control their behaviour through self-discipline or self-control. In short, Foucault's theory is that the disciplinary power of constant external monitoring through surveillance would be internalized – transformed into self-surveillance – and change people's behaviour because they would know they were being monitored constantly.

Foucault saw this disciplinary power of the state over offenders through surveillance as extending beyond prisons and the wider CJS into wide areas of life in contemporary society. This has been variously referred to, as Newburn points out, as 'disciplinary society', the 'age of panopticism' and 'surveillance society'. This is discussed below.

Rusche and Kirchheimer: punishment, class domination and control

From a Marxist perspective, Rusche and Kirchheimer (2007 [1939]) see punishments as part of the system of social control and class domination in unequal societies. They see the changing forms of punishment over time, ranging from the barbarous public spectacles of physical cruelty, to transportation/exile with hard labour, to the contemporary use of criminals as cheap labour in prisons, arising from the changing economic interests of the dominant class. The scale of brutality generally rose while labour was plentiful, and declined when there was a labour shortage. In other words, forms of punishment reflect whatever was in the economic interests of the dominant class at any particular time.

Sociological approaches to punishment

The precise form of punishment adopted in the CJS will depend on the intended effects of punishment on the offender and society – such as whether the punishment is intended to deter others, to rehabilitate offenders, to satisfy victims – or wider considerations of what the role or functions of punishment are in society. These wider considerations are outlined below.

Functionalist approaches: bolstering the collective conscience

Functionalist writers like Durkheim argue societies can only exist if they have a system of shared beliefs and values (a value consensus) that form moral ties binding communities together – what he called the collective conscience – and this regulates the behaviour of individuals living within them. Laws are an expression of this collective conscience, and those who break them are violating the collective conscience. Retribution (punishment):

- Provides an outlet for public anger and outrage at violation of the collective conscience, and an opportunity to express its disapproval of criminal behaviour
- Reasserts the boundaries between right and wrong behaviour and re-establishes social order
- Reaffirms and strengthens collective values and the laws which are an expression of them
- Reinforces social regulation and social control
- Contributes to building social solidarity and social cohesion for the benefit of all.

Durkheim's approach to punishment has been criticized for assuming that the law reflects a value consensus, and for ignoring the inequalities in wealth and power that Marxists consider (see below). Punishments like imprisonment may also not assist in re-establishing social order, but actually threaten it and make things worse, as prisons often prove to be institutions for the manufacture of crime rather than for deterrence or the rehabilitation of offenders and their eventual reintegration into society. This is considered shortly.

Marxist approaches: maintaining the position of the powerful

In contrast to the functionalist view, Marxists argue that laws are not an expression of so-called collective values, but of ruling-class ideology. Punishment is part of what Althusser (1971) called the repressive state apparatus – those parts of the state which are concerned with mainly repressive, physical means of keeping a population in line, through police, courts and prisons. Rusche and Kirchheimer regard the law and punishment as mechanisms of social control of the working class and as means of reinforcing ruling-class power in unequal class societies. The unequal distribution of power in society is reflected in the unequal distribution of punishment, and the way some acts are criminalized. The criminal law and the punishments handed down by the CJS are directed overwhelmingly and systematically against the most disadvantaged in society, such as the unemployed, the poor, the homeless, those who are mentally ill and people from minority ethnic groups, and particularly black men. It is these people who are most severely punished. As Newburn (2007, p. 531) notes, 'it is rare for the wealthy, the powerful and the influential to find themselves the focus of prosecution and punishment'. The way the CJS and the media focus on working-class crime diverts attention from the crimes of the powerful, and socially advantaged white-collar and corporate criminals either escape punishment altogether or are treated leniently.

Criticisms of this Marxist approach have been considered earlier (see pages 457–8) but it is difficult to see all punishments as linked simply to the interests of the dominant class, and much depends on what the purposes of those punishments are intended to be. Some would argue that the working class fill the prisons because they commit some of the most harmful offences, and, as Left Realists point out, their victims are most commonly other disadvantaged people like themselves.

Weberian approaches: the rationalization of punishment

For Weber, modern societies have undergone a process of rationalization, based around laws, rules and regulations. Only the state now has the power to punish offenders (not, for example, landowners or factory owners as in the past). There has been a rationalization of the punishment of offenders, based on what Weber called legal-rational authority. This means punishment is based on impersonal rules and regulations, and administered by complex bureaucracies of officials, rather than by the arbitrary (and often brutal) treatment handed out by the sovereign power of the kings and queens of the past. In democratic societies, rules and regulations governing punishment are based on legislation decided by elected and accountable governments, which gives them some claim to being legitimate (justifiable) in the eyes of the public, and with which it is reasonable for offenders to comply (albeit reluctantly).

The entire CJS is now a huge and complex hierarchical bureaucratic organization, with a range of professional groups (the police, prison service, the Crown Prosecution Service, social workers, probation officers, psychiatrists, etc.) dealing with offenders in a tightly managed impersonal process governing the forms of punishment that can be applied – such as the type and length of sentences for particular offences – and where those punishments are carried out – such as in prison, the home (curfews) or the community (community service sentences). Some insight into the rationalization and bureaucratization of crime and punishment can be gained by visiting the website of the Crown Prosecution Service (www.cps.gov.uk).

The main criticisms of the Weberian view arise from the issues surrounding the extent to which the rules and regulations are really fair, and the extent to which officials actually follow those rules. There are many cases of miscarriages of justice, in which judges seem to discriminate unfairly against some groups, and individual law enforcement officers have considerable discretion in interpreting the rules, as the Marxists and labelling theorists suggest.

Does imprisonment prevent crime?

Prison – or Young Offender Institutions, Secure Training Centres or Secure Children's Homes for those aged between 10 and 21 – is the most serious sanction available to the CJS. Right Realists see prison as a key way of deterring people from offending by increasing the costs of crime, and politicians are always 'talking tough' on crime and calling for ever more people to be imprisoned. In the past 100 years, the number of offenders in prison in England and Wales has quadrupled (see figure 6.17), and in the period 2001–11, it rose by about 30 per cent.

However, prison doesn't actually seem to work very well as a crime prevention measure. Research by the Downing Street Strategy Unit in 2003 showed that a 22 per cent increase in the prison population since 1997 was estimated to have reduced crime by only around 5 per cent, at a time when overall crime had fallen by 30 per cent, and suggested that there was no convincing evidence that putting more people in prison would significantly reduce crime. Nonetheless, the prison population continued to grow; in 2012 it reached a record all-time high, and England and Wales has the highest imprisonment rate in the European Union. Ministry of Justice research shows that nearly half (47.5 per cent) of prisoners released in 2010 were proven to have reoffended within a year of being released, and for juveniles it was around 70 per cent, with each former prisoner committing an average of four offences. And this was just for those who had their further offending discovered. Boorman and Hopkins (2012), in findings based on the *Surveying Prisoner Crime Reduction* (SPCR) survey, found around half (54 per cent) of the SPCR sample had committed *at least* one proven offence within one year, and 68 per cent within two years, after release from prison. This means imprisonment isn't stopping re-offending, nor are high levels of imprisonment making much impact on reducing crime.

There is a range of possible reasons for this, other than an assumption that criminals are 'born bad'. One may be that crime has a range of complex social causes. Boorman and Hopkins, for

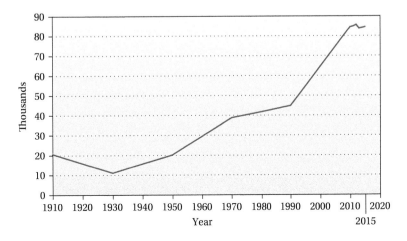

Figure 6.17 Average prison population, England and Wales 1910–2015

Source: Offender Management Caseload Statistics; Prison Population Figures, Ministry of Justice

example, cite evidence that re-offending former prisoners had chaotic childhoods, during which many had experienced abuse, witnessed violence in the home, and had been taken into care. Many had been unemployed, had problems with accommodation and many had histories of mental illness. Prison may also make pre-existing problems worse, such as by destabilizing family ties, and disrupting employment opportunities by stigmatizing offenders. Interactionist sociologists like Goffman (1991 [1961]) suggest prisons have their own subcultures, which provide training grounds for criminals, and confirm the 'criminal' label. This becomes what Becker (1997 [1963]) calls a master status, over-riding all other characteristics; the stigmatized master status of 'ex-con' makes it difficult for released prisoners to re-enter conforming mainstream society successfully, and increases the likelihood of re-offending as legitimate opportunities in society are blocked. Prisons therefore become institutions for the manufacture of crime rather than the rehabilitation of criminals.

Surveillance and crime control and prevention

Foucault (1991), as discussed earlier in relation to punishment (see pages 526–7), suggested surveillance was a key means of monitoring, controlling and changing the behaviour of criminals. He saw surveillance as a form of disciplinary power, as the fear and uncertainty of whether or not they were being watched would encourage people to internalize surveillance and exercise self-surveillance, and control their behaviour through self-discipline or self-control.

Foucault sees such surveillance extending across many institutions in contemporary society, and penetrating ever more into every sphere of life, including the private aspects of our lives. He argued contemporary society has been transformed into a surveillance or disciplinary society, in what he called the 'age of panopticism' in which everyone is subject to the disciplinary gaze of the panopticon (see p. 527).

The use of surveillance technology – what Foucault calls 'technologies of power' and 'disciplinary technologies' – has become a means for the state and other institutions to exercise disciplinary power and control by casting the net of surveillance over the entire population. Lyon (2009), argues that surveillance – which he defines as 'focused attention to personal details for the purposes of influence, management or control' – in technologically advanced societies has been enhanced and amplified by information and communication technologies (ICTs). He emphasizes that 'in addition to those who may be "suspects" (because of committing alleged offences) ordinary persons in everyday life – workers, consumers, citizens, travellers – find that their personal data are of interest to others', and that everyday life has become less 'private' and that ordinary people have become more vulnerable to monitoring and intrusion. He suggests that surveillance has become so pervasive and such a routine and inescapable part of everyday life in technologically advanced contemporary societies that it now makes sense to talk of 'surveillance societies' in which ICTs enable total social control.

Round-the-clock surveillance technologies like CCTV, face-recognition software and automatic number plate recognition (ANPR) systems now monitor the movements of all people, and such technology has become a key means of controlling crime and disorder, by avoiding the risk of them occurring in the first place, and of tracking potential offenders. Foucault used the concept of a *carceral archipelago* (meaning a prison consisting of a series of islands) to describe contemporary societies, with every public location like a small panopticon in which everyone is subject to surveillance.

Government agencies have consequently gathered huge amounts of data on every individual, and surveillance is now used not just to track criminals, but also to prevent potential crime and monitor any non-conformist behaviour. Foucault summed up this disciplinary power of surveillance in controlling criminal and deviant behaviour in the following way:

> If the inmates are convicts, there is no danger of a plot, an attempt at collective escape, the planning of new crimes for the future, bad reciprocal influences; if they are patients, there is no danger of contagion; if they are madmen [sic] there is no risk of their committing violence upon one another; if they are schoolchildren, there is no copying, no noise, no chatter, no waste of time; if they are workers, there are no disorders, no theft, no coalitions, none of those distractions that slow down the rate of work, make it less perfect or cause accidents.

Widespread surveillance through CCTV is endemic throughout the UK, which had, in 2013, according to the British Security Industry Association, an estimated 5 million cameras across Britain, most of them indoors and privately operated, which is about 1 camera for every 13 UK citizens. This makes Britain one of the most heavily surveilled countries in Europe, and the police routinely draw on video footage to identify criminals. This surveillance also takes the form of consumer tracking, in which huge amounts of data are collected on individuals. Google, for example, collects vast amounts of information about people through data collection of their website searches, and the Tesco Clubcard collects information about every product a customer purchases in their stores, providing a profile of the lifestyle of that person. New digital technologies, such as data-mining systems and the use of sophisticated algorithmns, are now used to track people's emails, websites visited and social media messaging. Internet Service Providers (ISP) are now legally required to hang on to their users' communications, and often an individual's digital footprint provides more information than direct, physical observation. In surveillance society, everything people do is visible to the state or the large corporations like Apple, Google, Facebook, Amazon and Microsoft that collect data about the lives and choices of individuals, and control who gets to see it. Whatever people do, wherever they go and whoever they are, the chances are they might be under surveillance. Car drivers, people at their places of work, school children, hospital users, call centre users and workers, shoppers, those going to clubs, and anyone using a public space, like a street, shop or a shopping mall, or using a computer, a mobile phone, an ATM or a credit card, is providing information that can be used to monitor the time, location and likely purpose of their activities and movements. Such surveillance allows the state to track individuals' activities throughout their lives.

Foucault suggests we are now living in a carceral (prison-like) culture, in which the panoptic model of surveillance has been spread throughout society. Society itself has become a gigantic panopticon, in which everyone is being watched by those with power – whom Foucault calls 'the judges of normality' – in order to impose conformist behaviour through self-discipline, and to prevent and undermine any threat to social order through crime and disorder, and indeed any deviant behaviour.

Evaluation of the surveillance society

The strength of Foucault's analysis is that he shows how the power of surveillance can increase the power of the state. He regards this as a fundamentally oppressive form of social control, inducing

Surveillance is now widespread in every area of society, and is a key means of preventing, controlling, and detecting crime and disorder.

conformity and limiting opposition to a society that has profound inequalities in wealth and power. However, such surveillance is now so pervasive (found everywhere) that it is likely that people have ceased to be aware of it, and this particularly applies to their use of the internet and social media. Even when they are aware of surveillance, they may then take steps to avoid that surveillance (see for example the criticisms of situational crime prevention on pages 535–6). and it is therefore questionable how far surveillance alters people's behaviour through self-surveillance. At the same time, some surveillance can be useful, for example for monitoring hospital patients, or for reducing crime and social disorder in communities where it is a real problem. Evidence suggests those living in the most deprived communities that suffer the greatest harm from crime and disorder welcome surveillance cameras as improving their sense of safety, as well as reducing crime in their neighbourhoods. Surveillance also appears to be of growing assistance in the fight against terrorism and the threats it might pose to public safety, though some regard this as a convenient excuse by the state to undermine civil liberties and justify ever-increasing levels of surveillance over everyone.

Theoretical approaches and social policies for crime control and prevention

Realist theories and crime prevention

Realist theories, which were considered on pages 464–9, regard themselves as 'real' as they primarily concern themselves with practical policies to prevent the crimes that matter most to people and impact on their daily lives. Although there is some overlap in their policies, Left and Right Realism have different emphases. Left Realism tends to emphasize the social causes of crime, which might be characterized as *tough on the causes of crime*, while Right Realism lays more emphasis on situational crime prevention (discussed below) and being *tough on the criminals*.

Left Realism: social crime prevention and being tough on the causes of crime

Left Realist approaches to crime prevention recognize that both the offenders and the victims of the crimes that worry people most are found in the more disadvantaged communities – those with the highest levels of marginality and social exclusion. They therefore emphasize the need to tackle the material and cultural deprivation – such as poverty, unemployment, poor housing and education, poor parental supervision, and broken families and family conflict – that generate anger and frustration, and are the risk factors for crime, particularly among young people.

Kinsey et al. (1986) suggest police need to improve clear-up rates (crimes solved and offenders caught), and to spend more time investigating crime to deter offenders and restore confidence among the public that it is actually worth their while to report crimes. The lack of confidence in the police in deprived communities means the police often have to resort to military styles of policing, such as the use of surveillance technology, stopping and searching people, and flooding an area with police in order to find suspects. This is often completely counter-productive, as it results in increased antagonism with the community, particularly among young black people, who regard the police as acting like an occupying army. Lewis et al. (2011) found it was resentment of a perceived lack of respect from the police, and of the experience of innocent people being repeatedly stopped and searched, that was one of the major factors behind the 2011 English riots.

Preventing crime involves addressing these social issues through policies such as:

- Building community cohesion and strong communities, enabling them to develop more informal controls over behaviour, and to work out local solutions to local crime problems
- Multi-agency working, such as Community Safety Partnerships, where a variety of agencies – such as the police, the local council, and the health and probation services – work together with local people to tackle crime, rather than just relying on the police and the criminal justice system

How might a deprived neighbourhood contribute to crime? How might responses to this differ between Left and Right Realists?

- More democratic and community control of policing, so it becomes more responsive to local needs, concerns and priorities, with more time spent by the police on investigating local crimes. The police need to be more tolerant of, rather than harassing or discriminating against, those with different lifestyles or from non-white ethnic groups. Only by building more public confidence will victims and the wider community be encouraged to report crime and provide leads on offenders, and, without this flow of information from the public, the police are unable to protect the main victims of crime – working-class people. Safer Neighbourhood teams, Community Forums and the election of local Police and Crime Commissioners (see https://www.gov.uk/police-and-crime-commissioners) for the first time in 2012 might all be seen as part of this process
- Tackling social deprivation and the other risk factors for crime by improving community facilities – for example, youth leisure activities – to divert potential offenders from choosing crime, and reducing unemployment and improving housing
- Intensive parenting support, getting parents and young offenders together to work out solutions, and early intervention through strategies like Sure Start Children's Centres to help get children in the poorest communities, where the risk factors for crime are greatest, off to a better start in life by bringing together early-years education, childcare, health and family support (go to www.gov.uk and search 'family support' for more information on what's available in your area).

Criticisms of Left Realist crime prevention approaches

1. They are 'soft' on crime, as they focus too much on the social causes of crime, and downplay the role of the offender in choosing to commit crime. The offender almost becomes a victim him- or herself.
2. The explanations are inadequate, as the majority of those living in deprived communities and sharing similar risk factors do not turn to crime.
3. They deflect attention away from more practical crime prevention measures, like the tighter social control and situational crime prevention advocated by Right Realists.
4. They (like Right Realists) ignore white-collar and corporate crimes, which can have serious consequences for victims (see page 496).

5   Neighbourhood policing, in which police try to integrate themselves into communities as part of community approaches to tackling crime, might be seen as an extension of control and surveillance by the state over the whole population, whether or not they are involved in offending.

Right Realism: situational crime prevention and being tough on the criminals

Right Realist approaches to crime prevention tend to have a focus on individuals and the specific location of crime rather than on wider social issues. They reject broad social and structural theories of crime as unproven and impractical, and they argue policies should focus on what is practical and achievable, and what works. They emphasize individuals *choose* crime and must be persuaded not to do so, by reducing the opportunities for crime and increasing the chances of being caught and punished. These approaches are underpinned by four interlinked theories: the 'broken windows' thesis, routine activity theory and rational choice and opportunity theories.

Environmental crime prevention and the 'broken windows' thesis

The origins of Right Realist policies for crime prevention are found in the work of Wilson (1985 [1975]), and Wilson and Kelling (1982), who developed what has become known as the 'broken windows' thesis. This is the idea that if a broken window – a symbol for social disorder of all kinds and a lack of community concern – is not repaired, then others are likely to be broken and further neglect will follow (see broken windows picture below). Wilson suggests that, unless 'incivilities' – for example, anti-social behaviour of all kinds – are kept to the minimum, then there will be a gradual deterioration of neighbourhoods, as a sense that no one cares and of 'anything goes' develops. There will be growing anti-social behaviour like noise, litter, graffiti and vandalism, and petty crimes will eventually grow into bigger, more serious crimes. Wilson suggested that to prevent such a deterioration of social cohesion and the sense of community, and to keep neighbourhoods safe, it was necessary to keep environments in good physical condition, and that the police should have a policy of zero tolerance – cracking down on all anti-social and criminal behaviour which threatened social order, even if it wasn't strictly illegal.

Wilson's broken windows thesis suggests that, if a few broken windows are left unrepaired, further damage and anti-social behaviour will occur, more serious crime will follow, and whole neighbourhoods will deteriorate into high crime areas. The solution? Zero tolerance of all anti-social and criminal behaviour, no matter how trivial. What problems might be created if a zero tolerance policy is introduced into a neighbourhood?

Routine activity theory

This is associated with the work of Felson and Clarke (1998), and suggests that a crime occurs as part of everyday routines, when there are three conditions present.

1 There is a suitable target for the potential offender, which could be a person, a place or an object.
2 There is no 'capable guardian', like a neighbour, police or CCTV surveillance, to protect the target.
3 There is a potential offender present, who thinks the first two conditions are met (suitable target and no guardian), and then makes a rational choice whether or not to commit the crime.

Rational choice and opportunity theories

These related theories are associated with the work of Cornish and Clarke (1986), and focus on the decision-making process of the potential offender. They argue that offenders, when they see an opportunity for crime, act rationally, and weigh up the benefits and costs/risks before choosing whether or not to commit an offence. To deter potential offenders, it is necessary to reduce the opportunities for crime and increase the costs/risks of offending, so conformity offers greater benefits.

The 'broken windows' thesis, routine activity theory and rational choice and opportunity theories have led Right Realists to adopt two main approaches to crime prevention: situational crime prevention, and increased social control.

Situational crime prevention (SCP): reducing opportunities for crime

Clarke (1992) emphasizes that situational crime prevention (SCP) is concerned with preventing crime in particular locations rather than catching offenders, and merely aims to make crime a less attractive choice for offenders, rather than eliminating criminal behaviour through the improvement of society or the threat of punishment. This is achieved by 'designing out crime' and 'target hardening' measures – what Pease (2002) called 'bars, bolts and barriers' – such as post-coding goods, use of anti-climb paint, Smartwater, CCTV, locks, alarms in premises and car alarms, alcohol-free zones and targeted policing. Other examples include what has been called 'hostile architecture', such as public benches with graffiti-resistant sloping surfaces to deter both sleeping and skateboarding, 'anti-homeless' spikes outside buildings to deter rough sleepers, and ground markings by ATMs to increase the privacy and security of cash machine users. Such measures aim to reduce opportunities for crime and disorder in particular locations by making possible targets more difficult and risky for potential offenders. Cornish and Clarke (2003) suggested this could be further reinforced by putting up notices warning people of surveillance and of the rules operating in the area, which would remove excuses and encourage people to regulate their behaviour – or face consequences such as arrests, fines or Dispersal Orders (these enable the police to move on groups from areas where there is persistent anti-social behaviour).

Criticisms of situational crime prevention

1 It removes the focus from other forms of crime prevention, such as looking at wider economic and social policies which cause crime.
2 It doesn't pay sufficient attention to catching criminals or punishments to deter offenders.
3 Crawford and Evans (2012) point out that SCP in an unequal society can increase inequality with, at the extremes, the more affluent living in the target-hardened fortresses of gated communities, and poorer people unable to afford the security paraphernalia required for target hardening. This may mean the affluent become even more immune to crime, and the poor ever more vulnerable. Many of the 'hostile architecture' measures mentioned above have been criticized for particularly targeting the poor, and limiting their ability to use public spaces.
4 *Displacement theory* is perhaps the major criticism. This suggests SCP does not prevent crime overall, but only in particular locations, and simply *displaces* it to other areas, as potential offenders are diverted to committing crime somewhere else, at some other time, or against

Right Realists focus on reducing the opportunities for crime through situational crime prevention, like the use of surveillance cameras and alcohol-free zones to deter potential offenders.

other more vulnerable targets (such as poorer people in less protected areas, as Crawford and Evans suggest) where the risks are lower. Against this view, Felson and Clarke (1998) argue that SCP can still have positive effects beyond the immediate location, as potential offenders may believe that measures, like CCTV, that are in place in one location may also be in place in others, even if they aren't. Bowers et al. (2011) confirmed this; their review of forty-four international studies of targeted policing in high-crime areas found SCP led to a 'diffusion of benefits', with neighbouring districts also seeing reductions in crime. They found potential offenders prefer familiar environments, and if SCP blocks opportunities there, then they do not simply 'move round the corner', but find legitimate activities more appealing, particularly as they are uncertain of the scope of police operations.

Increased social control

This second major Right Realist policy for crime prevention is linked to Hirschi's control theory (see pages 454–6), which suggests that individuals are encouraged to choose conformity over deviance and crime when there are strong social bonds integrating them into communities. The focus is then on tighter family and community control and socialization, to promote conformity and isolate deviant individuals through community pressure. This approach also suggests that it is possible to predict crime, and therefore prevent it, by identifying those from 'at risk' backgrounds, such as young people in deprived communities facing family breakdowns, drug use or social exclusion.

Policies flowing from this include:

1 Making parents take more responsibility for supervision of their children, and socializing them more effectively into conformist behaviour. Those who don't may be issued with Parenting Orders – court orders issued to parents of persistent young offenders who fail to properly supervise their children. These compel a parent to attend parenting classes or counselling, or to meet other requirements to improve their child's behaviour.

2 Schemes like Neighbourhood Watch, which help to build community controls over crime through informal surveillance and 'good neighbourliness' – for example, by keeping an eye on each other's homes.

3 Cracking down on anti-social behaviour like graffiti, hoax calls, verbal abuse, noisy neighbours, drug and alcohol abuse in public places, and intimidating behaviour by groups of youths through measures like Criminal Behaviour Orders (CBOs – nicknamed 'crimbos') or Dispersal Orders.

4 Supervision of offenders – for example, electronic tagging and curfew orders to restrict and monitor their movements.

5 Adopting zero tolerance policing (in keeping with the 'broken windows' thesis), which involves taking steps against all crimes, even low-level offences like graffiti, vandalism and anti-social behaviour, to prevent community breakdown and nip problems in the bud before they destroy a sense of community and individuals come to believe they can get away with offending, and crime subsequently escalates.

6 Heavier policing and more arrests, particularly targeted on high-crime areas, to deter potential offending.

7 Fast-track punishment of offenders, with more imprisonment and harsher sentences.

Criticism of Right Realist crime prevention policies

As well as the criticisms of SCP, others are:

1   Zero tolerance policing and a strong police presence in neighbourhoods with high levels of crime and social disorder may involve a wasteful over-emphasis on minor and trivial offences, which may divert police resources away from more serious offences which cause greater harm to people and property. Labelling theorists suggest that zero tolerance policing can result in giving people who have committed only very minor offences criminal records, and such labelling may have long-term negative consequences for their lives and careers. Labelling theorists also argue that some groups of people may be targeted and victimized unfairly by police, for example through stereotyping and racism, generating resentment and a self-fulfilling prophecy creating more disorder rather than less. This is precisely the situation Lewis et al. (2011) found was one of the causes behind the 2011 riots in English cities.
2   They ignore white-collar and corporate crimes, which can have serious consequences for victims.
3   They don't address the wider social causes of crime that the Left Realists do.
4   They assume offenders act rationally in choosing crime and derive some benefits from it, but some crimes like vandalism, joy-riding, drug-taking, hate crime or violence are impulsive or irrational, and do not bring any obvious gain. Edgework and the seductiveness of the risk-taking, thrill and buzz of crime, as discussed by Lyng and Katz (see pages 470–1 and 499) are not addressed by rational choice and opportunity theories.

Feminism and the control and prevention of crime

Feminist theories of crime have been discussed on pages 463–4 and 488–93, and the issue of gender and victimization is discussed later in this topic.

Feminist approaches to crime control and prevention mainly focus on the issues that directly impact on women. These largely relate to the fear of crime among women, and particularly their fears of going out at night or being forced to avoid certain areas for fear of patriarchally based violence. They also draw attention to the ongoing problems of domestic and sexual violence, of which women are the main victims. They regard patriarchy as the key factor contributing to both crimes *against* women, and women themselves turning to crime.

Newburn (2007) suggests feminist solutions to the problem of crime involve:

1   Making visible forms of victimization that hitherto had been largely ignored, such as the extent of domestic violence, sexual harassment and sexual violence
2   Exposing the extent to which violence against women is primarily an issue of men's violence against women, and particularly in the home, rather than 'stranger danger'
3   Recognizing that sexual violence by men against women is primarily an issue of male power, and in some cases of misogyny (hatred or dislike of women or girls), not of sex
4   Showing how a male-dominated and patriarchal CJS holds stereotyped views of women and fails to respond appropriately to crimes against them
5   Identifying those features of the CJS that lead to the further victimization of women. For example, Walklate (2004) points out that the CJS may contribute to the further victimization of women in rape trials, where it is often the female victims rather than the male suspects who seem to be on trial, with women's reputation and respectability scrutinized through embarrassing and intensive questioning, and quite often their evidence is not taken seriously or regarded as believable.

Crimes committed against women

Feminist solutions to crimes against women include the points made above. Liberal feminists particularly emphasize improving the circumstances that might encourage more women to report crimes against them – such as sexual assaults and rape, sexual harassment, and domestic violence – and for the police to record them. The under-reporting of such offences is partly due to the generally unsympathetic approach of the police and other criminal justice agencies. Newburn has suggested that the police need more specialist training of officers to deal with offences such as rape and domestic violence. Feminists suggest these issues need to be tackled in order that more of these crimes are reported and prosecuted, so that men begin to realize they can no longer get away with such offences. Other policies include things such as better street lighting, self-defence classes and rape alarms to boost the confidence of women and reduce their fears of crime.

Crimes committed by women

To reduce crimes committed by women, most of which are related to poverty, debt and drug abuse, there need to be more supportive welfare policies and better-paid jobs to avoid women getting trapped in debt-crime-drugs spirals. These policies would involve similar approaches to Left Realist solutions to crime, but with a clear focus on the particular circumstances of women.

Marxist feminist solutions to crime focus on how inequality in capitalist society has its hardest impact on women, and particularly working-class women, which drives women to commit 'female' crimes such as prostitution and shoplifting through economic necessity, as well as making them the main victims of crime. Tackling female crime therefore means tackling social inequality. Radical feminists are more likely to focus on the crimes committed against women by men in a patriarchal society, but they also emphasize the way women sometimes turn to crime as a result of the responsibilities placed on them by a patriarchal society, such as for housework and childcare, and managing limited household budgets. Radical feminists emphasize policies like opening more rape crisis centres, and highlighting the sexual exploitation and abuse of women through things like 'slut walks' and 'reclaim the night' marches. Men need to undergo re-socialization so they no longer treat women as sexual objects or as objects over which they can exert their power through violence, harassment and intimidation.

Evaluation of feminism and crime control

The Marxist and radical feminist solutions to crime ultimately point to huge social change, with revolutionary action against patriarchy and capitalism, but they would also support the various more practical short-term measures, as outlined above by Newburn, such as exposing the extent of crimes against women, encouraging women to report them, and exposing and tackling patriarchy and stereotyping in the CJS. By exposing the extent of male crimes against women, and taking steps to prevent men from committing them, by re-socialization, tighter controls and tougher sanctions, then men might be persuaded, as Right Realist rational choice theories suggest, that committing crimes against women might become an increasingly dangerous path for men to follow.

Postmodernism and the control and prevention of crime

Postmodernists (see pages 469–71) regard crime as a social construction, based on a narrow legal definition. The law is an outdated metanarrative that is simply an expression of a particular view, among those with power, of how people should conduct themselves, and does not reflect the growing diversity and choice of identities in contemporary societies. Lea (1998) suggests the postmodernist approach to crime reduction involves a need for the CJS to recognize the diversity of social groups and to respect their particular social identities and lifestyle choices, for example by the police becoming more sensitive to and tolerant of, for example, ethnic and gender identities, and the diversity of sexual relations. Lea points out that the postmodernists' stress on the fragmentation of social structures and the growing choice and diversity of identities leads them to emphasize more informal localized arrangements for preventing and controlling harms caused by crime and disorder. This involves the replacement of centrally managed formal CJS processes by, for example, localized customized community policing, the use of private security firms, and informal controls through the family, community, school and work. The increasing use of private control agencies, like security firms, and the use of surveillance technology enable crime control and the reduction of harm to be customized to the demands and needs of particular communities and groups, rather than being reliant on the formal agencies of criminal justice like the police. This is accompanied by growing control of entry to certain areas, such as shopping malls, streets and housing complexes in gated communities, for which entry is only permitted to particular social groups, such as shoppers or residents, rather than skateboarders or the homeless.

Postmodernists emphasize that crime is caused by complex individual motives. To reduce offending and the infliction of harm, justice needs to be more individualized, reflecting the particular needs of the individual offender and the wider public interest. This involves exploring whether alternatives other than prosecution are more suited to the needs of those causing harm, and to reducing the risks of them creating further harm in the future. Any sentencing, rather than following national formulas that apply to all, should be customized to each individual, and recognize the particular circumstances – such as economic conditions, inadequate welfare support, homelessness or mental illness – which make individuals vulnerable to causing harm.

Evaluation of the postmodernist approach

Strengths

- It draws attention to the diversity of identities and lifestyle choices in postmodern societies, and to the idea that a centralized criminal justice system may not meet all needs, and that the law, policing and criminal justice need to be flexible if they are to be effective in controlling crime.
- It provides insights into the way contemporary developments like extensive surveillance – for example by CCTV – the growing use of private security, more localized policing, and control of entry to some private 'public' areas like shopping malls can reduce the harms, including fear, caused by crime and disorder.

Weaknesses

- It doesn't recognize the importance or impact of social inequality. It pays little attention to the poorest social groups who can't afford to establish identities by consuming goods in the consumer society, and who are not significant consumers and customers. Such groups face increasing exclusion from public places like shopping malls, more surveillance and stricter control, for example through heavier and more repressive policing.
- It doesn't recognize that decentralized and more informal arrangements for crime control to respond to more local identities – like the use of private security firms and localized policing – are likely to benefit the most well-organized, articulate and affluent middle-class groups, who have the power and resources to get their needs attended to. The needs of the poorest in society are likely to be neglected.

Activity

1 Go to www.popcenter.org/25techniques and study *Twenty-five techniques of situational prevention* developed by Cornish and Clarke. Write a brief paragraph on each of the following five groups of techniques, explaining how each puts into practice routine activity and rational choice and opportunity theories, and illustrating it with explanations of the examples given. If you are in a group, you could divide these up between you.
   - Increase the effort
   - Increase the risks
   - Reduce the rewards
   - Reduce provocations
   - Remove excuses
2 Go to the Home Office website (www.gov.uk/government/organisations/home-office) and search for two current social policies for preventing crime which might be associated with (a) Left Realism and (b) Right Realism.
3 What do you think are the major causes of crime and deviance in society, and what social policies do you think are most likely to reduce crime? Explain your reasons, linked to sociological theories of crime.

- It doesn't really consider the implications of the growing use of customized private 'policing' and surveillance for people's civil liberties and human rights. Private security firms are not subject to the same controls as the police.
- It fails to recognize that there may be a fairer, more equal distribution of justice for all through a centrally managed, publicly run and accountable CJS, so everyone has – at least in theory – an equal opportunity for protection from harm, and for the same rules to be applied equally to all.

The victims of crime

Victimology

Since the 1980s, **victimology** has been a growing concern in both academic research and the criminal justice process. This has been accompanied by a rapid growth in victim surveys – like the *Crime Survey for England and Wales* (CSEW) – to uncover the 'dark figure' of hidden victims of crime who never come to the attention of the police or the criminal justice system (CJS).

Victims of crime are increasingly viewed as consumers or customers of the CJS, and its success is now judged by the extent to which it meets the needs of victims, not just on how effectively it deals with offenders. For example, a new National Crime Recording Standard (NCRS) for recording crimes was adopted in 2002 by all police forces in England and Wales which gave priority to victims' account of a crime occurring, rather than to the police view of the evidence; Victim Support schemes (see www.victimsupport.org.uk) are now an integral part of the CJS; there is a growing emphasis on restorative justice, which gives victims an opportunity to confront offenders with the consequences of their actions and encourage them to make amends; and the Home Office announced in 2013 that victims of anti-social behaviour and low-level crime will be able to have their say on out-of-court punishments of offenders, selected from a list of options. In 2014, there was a proposal from the government for a new 'victims' law' which would give crime victims the legal right to be kept informed about their case and to confront offenders in court.

This greater importance attached to victims is part of a growing recognition that, if the victims of crime do not have confidence in the CJS to support them and catch and punish offenders, then most crime will remain unreported, victims will be unwilling to give evidence and offenders will go unpunished.

> **Victimology** is the term used for the study of the impact of crime on victims, victims' interests, and patterns of victimization.

The social construction of victimization

Who counts as a victim in the CJS is, like crime and official crime statistics, socially constructed – it depends on the attachment of the label of 'victim'. There are many unreported and unrecorded victims who never come to the attention of the CJS, such as victims of domestic violence, sexual assaults and of all kinds of white-collar frauds and corporate crimes like environmental harm, the sale of dangerous products, and industrial accidents and diseases. In some cases, like fraud, victims may not even realize they have been victimized. Victims may refuse to accept they have been victimized – for example, some victims of domestic violence blame themselves for provoking their victimization, whilst others may reject the label of 'victim' as it may show them to be weak or foolish, such as victims of internet scams. Some are denied the status of victim because others regard them as responsible for their own victimization, as sometimes occurs with women who are victims of sexual assault, or gay men or transgender people suffering homophobic or transphobic attacks, who are seen as bringing it on themselves by their dress or behaviour; a further example of the denial of victim status is provided by Tombs and Whyte (2007) who suggest accident victims of corporate crimes arising from employer neglect of health and safety regulations are themselves blamed for being accident-prone or negligent.

The effects of victimization

Hoyle (2012) points to a range of possible effects of victimization, apart from physical harm or financial/material loss or damage; these include anger, anxiety, depression, withdrawal, panic attacks, shock, post-traumatic stress disorder, disrupted sleep, poor physical health, feelings of powerlessness and fear of further victimization, though these effects will depend on the nature of the offence and the characteristics of the victims. The CSEW shows that high levels of worry about crime rise among those who have been victimized, and there is a whole security industry that has developed around the fear of crime. Other consequences may include restrictions over movement, for example feminists have drawn attention to women victims fearing to go out at night or forced to avoid certain areas for fear of patriarchally based violence. There may be an ongoing sense of fear, such as in cases of vandalism, domestic violence or racial harassment where there are high levels of repeat victimization – around three-quarters of incidents of domestic violence, half of vandalism and violence, and one-third of burglaries are experienced by those who have been victimized before, often several times. Victimization can also have wider effects beyond the victims themselves – for example, whole neighbourhoods or groups of people can be put in fear as a result of hate crimes against minority ethnic groups or gays.

In some cases, further victimization – *secondary* (or double) *victimization* – occurs as a result of the original or *primary victimization*. For example, Walklate (2004) points out that the CJS may contribute to secondary victimization in rape trials, where it is often the female victims rather than the male suspects who seem to be on trial, with their reputation and respectability scrutinized through embarrassing and intensive questioning before their evidence is taken seriously or regarded as believable. This form of secondary double victimization is also found in cases of 'honour crime', where some ethnic minority women who have been sexually assaulted or raped can face further victimization by threats, attacks, beatings, mutilation and murder ('honour killings') by family members for the 'dishonour' and shame that their victimization has wrought on the family's reputation.

> ### Activity
>
> Devise a small survey among your friends, family and neighbours to see how many have been victims of crime, and try to discover the effects this had on their lives, and how it affected their attitudes towards policing and the criminal justice system. Bring your conclusions together as a class, and see if you reach any general conclusions about the impact of crime on victims.

The pattern of victimization

Gender and victimization

The CSEW shows that women are more likely than men to have high levels of worry about being victims of burglary and violent crime. Young men (aged 16–24) have about twice the risk of young women of being the victim of most violent crime, but this declines with age, and older men and women are the least likely to be victims of violent crime.

There are certain types of crime of which women are far more likely than men to be the victims. Apart from honour crimes in minority ethnic groups, these are 'intimate crimes', like sexual assault and rape, and non-sexual physical violence committed in the home: domestic violence. These crimes are also the least likely to be reported to the police, to be recorded in official statistics, or to result in offenders being convicted.

Domestic violence

There is widespread evidence of violence by men and women against their partners. It is estimated that one in four women, and one in six men, will suffer some form of domestic violence at some point in their relationships. Most of the assaults and physically most violent incidents resulting

Every week 2 women die due to domestic violence. Don't let your friend be 1 of them.

ENOUGH If you know your friend's being hit, it's time to put a stop to her abuse, before the abuser puts a stop to her. Help her take the first step: call the National Domestic Violence Helpline for support: 0808 2000 247

Free helpline run by Refuge and Women's Aid. Open 24 hours.

in injury – 89 per cent – are committed by men against their female partners, and those men who experience domestic violence suffer less serious attacks and do so less frequently than women. Each year about 150 people are killed by a current or former partner, and 80 per cent of them are women. An estimated two-thirds of victims of domestic violence do not report it or seek help from any source, because they are afraid the violence will get worse, are ashamed or see it as a private matter. Many female victims of domestic violence suffer repeat victimization – meaning they suffer the same offence many times – yet many do not leave their partners, because of lack of resources for economic independence, they have nowhere else to go, they blame themselves, or they are afraid of further violence, or of losing their children.

In the past, domestic violence was not taken very seriously by the police or courts, as it was seen as a private family or personal matter rather than their responsibility. Walklate (2004) points out, though, that the police are now beginning to take domestic violence more seriously, with domestic violence units and rape suites in police stations. Nevertheless, only about 40 per cent of all incidents are reported to the police and, as Hester and Westmarland (2006) found, only around 5 per cent of those that are reported result in a conviction.

Rape

About 90 per cent of rape victims are women, and the CSEW estimates only about one in ten rape victims report the offence to the police. They may be deterred from doing so partly because, as Walklate suggests (see above), in rape trials it often seems to be the female victims rather than the male suspects who are put on trial; another reason may be that the rapes that are reported have a very low conviction rate: only about 6 per cent of all reported rapes lead to a prosecution and conviction.

A common conception is that rapists are strangers unknown to the victim and that they suffer from social or psychological problems which make them different from normal men. The reality is that a high proportion of rape victims are likely to be attacked by men they know in some way, with a considerable proportion experiencing repeated attacks by the same man. As figure 6.18 shows,

Figure 6.18
Relationship to perpetrator for incidents of any serious sexual assault experienced by women since the age of 16, Crime Survey for England and Wales, 2013/14

Source: Crime Statistics, Focus on Violent Crime and Sexual Offences, 2013/14, Office for National Statistics, 2015

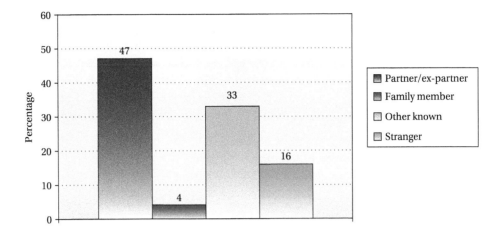

around 84 per cent of female victims of serious sexual assaults (which largely means rapes) knew the perpetrator, with only 16 per cent victimized by strangers. Only about 30 per cent of rapes, according to the CSEW, take place in public or other places – 70 per cent occur in the homes of the victim or offender.

The misleading stereotype of the rapist as an abnormal stranger means that when the police and courts are faced with a person accused of rape, the fact that he is often acquainted with the victim and appears to be no different from other men, leads to doubts about whether what occurred was really rape at all, and that the victim may in some ways have been partly to blame for what occurred. This may contribute towards explaining the low conviction rates.

Activity

1 Women are more likely to be victims of some crimes than men. Suggest, with reasons, examples of some of these crimes.
2 Describe the types of male criminality which occur within the family unit, and suggest three explanations for it.
3 Suggest reasons why male victims of rape (by other males) – an estimated 10 per cent of all rapes – might be even less likely to report it to the police than female victims of rape by men.

Age and victimization

The lifestyles of the young, as well as giving them greater opportunity to commit crime, also expose them to greater risk of being victims of crime. The 2013/14 CSEW found the likelihood of being a victim of crime decreases with age, with a much higher proportion of adults aged 16–24 reporting they had been victims of personal crimes (that is, crimes against the individual, for example assault and theft) than other age groups, and people in this age group were around nine times more likely to be victims than those aged 75 and over.

While young people are more likely to be the perpetrators of violent crime, they are also most likely to be the victims of it. The 2013/14 CSEW found 16- to 24-year-olds faced about three times the risk of violent crime, compared to all adults. The survey also found that 6 per cent of children aged 10–15 had experienced violent crime and theft in that year.

Ethnicity and victimization

The 2013/14 CSEW showed that the risk of being a victim of personal crime was higher for minority ethnic groups than for the white group. With the exception of racial incidents, these differences in victimization may in part be explained by the younger age profile of minority ethnic groups, their social class and living in areas of social deprivation. Nonetheless, even allowing for age, social class and locality differences, all minority ethnic groups report higher levels of worry about crime than do the white population.

Victims from minority ethnic groups made up 23 per cent of homicides in 2007–10 – more than twice the risk facing the white population, and this risk rises to four times higher for black people (African Caribbeans). The Home Office (Corcoran et al. 2015), based on data from the CSEW for 2012/13 to 2014/15, estimates that there were an average of 106,000 incidents of racially motivated hate crime per year, including harassment, personal theft, abuse, threats, intimidation and violence – the equivalent of nearly 300 incidents every day of the year. Those from Black, Asian or Mixed Ethnic backgrounds were up to fourteen times more likely to be victims of racially motivated incidents than white people.

Honour crimes and forced marriages – where pressure or abuse is used to compel a marriage without the consent of both people, which became a criminal offence in 2012 – are exclusively linked to ethnic minority groups, and women are overwhelmingly the victims.

Social class and victimization

The poorest sections of the working class are the most likely victims of crime. The highest rates of victimization are found:

- *Among the 'hard pressed'* – the unemployed, the long-term sick, low-income families and those living in rented accommodation
- *In areas of high physical disorder*, with widespread vandalism, graffiti and deliberate damage to property, rubbish and litter, and homes in poor condition
- *In areas with high levels of deprivation.*

The 2014/15 CSEW showed that, compared to the 20 per cent most affluent areas, those in the 20 per cent of poorest areas faced much higher risks of being victims of household crime and of all CSEW crimes, and faced higher risks than the other four-fifths of the population (see figure 6.19).

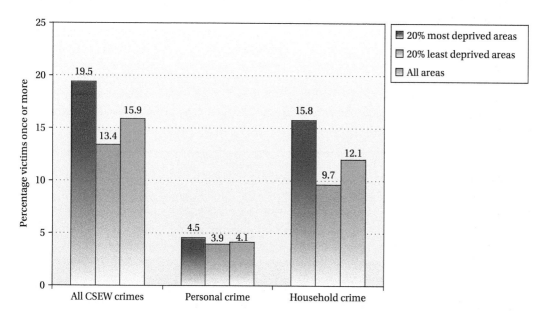

Figure 6.19 Risk of CSEW crime by level of deprivation, England and Wales, 2014/15

Source: Crime in England and Wales, Annual Trend & Demographic Tables, 2014/15, Office for National Statistics, July 2015

The double whammy and the inverse victimization law

A great irony of crime and victimization is what we might call the 'inverse victimization law'. This is that those who have the least power, who are the most deprived, and have the fewest and least valuable material possessions are those most likely to be the victims of all forms of crime, and to have their few possessions stolen or vandalized; by contrast, the affluent with the most power, and the most valuable material possessions, are the least likely to be victims of crime, and to have their possessions stolen or vandalized. The second irony is that those who steal from the poor are mainly other poor people.

Explaining victimization

The section above suggests that much crime is not random, and that some social groups are more likely to be the victims of crime than others. The two major approaches to explaining this are positivist victimology and radical victimology.

Positivist victimology

Tierney (1996) suggests the positivist approach to victimology involves identifying something in the characteristics or circumstances of victims which makes them different from non-victims: *victim proneness* and *victim precipitation*.

- *Victim proneness* identifies the characteristics of individuals or groups that make them more vulnerable to victimization.
- *Victim precipitation* suggests that victims are actively involved in, or to blame for, their victimization – for example, women making themselves vulnerable by dressing 'provocatively' or 'leading men on' in rape offences, or victims failing to lock doors or conceal valuables in cars, or carrying large amounts of cash around.

Positivist victimology has been criticized in a number of ways:

1 *It tends to blame the victims rather than the offenders*, in effect making the victims more responsible than the criminals themselves. Feminist writers, for example, have been particularly critical of suggestions arising from positivist victimology that victims of rape and other sexual offences or domestic violence are somehow to blame for making themselves vulnerable.
2 *It downplays the role of the law*, the police and other criminal justice agencies in not tackling crime effectively and thereby contributing to victimization.
3 *It focuses too much on the characteristics of individual victims*, and does not pay enough attention to the wider structural factors, like powerlessness, poverty, unemployment, and corporate neglect, that often make some groups and communities more vulnerable to crime than others.
4 *It does not recognize that there are situations where people may wholly unwittingly become victims* or are not aware of their victimization, such as in white-collar, corporate or environmental crimes.

Radical (or critical) victimology

Radical victimology is associated with conflict theories such as Marxism and feminism. This focuses on how wider social issues and circumstances – including the CJS – produce victimization. For example, social deprivation means it is the weakest and most deprived members of society who are most likely to be victims; feminist writers suggest 'intimate crimes' like rape and other sexual assaults, and domestic violence, of which women are the main victims, are an aspect of male power in a patriarchal society, in which men are socialized into a sense of superiority over women, and sexual and physical violence are aspects of the network of male control of women. The higher rates of victimization among ethnic minorities have been explained by under-protection by a racist police force that over-polices minority ethnic communities, which it regards as perpetrators rather than as victims of crime.

The main criticism of radical victimology is that it ignores the issues of victim precipitation and proneness that positivist victimology identifies. For example, many people would regard burglars injured by householders trying to protect their property, or drug users who get ripped off by a drug-dealer, as responsible for their victimization.

Activity

1 Outline one explanation from the perspective of positivist victimology, and one from the perspective of radical victimology, for each of the patterns of victimization by gender, age, ethnicity and social class.

2 Enter the following address into your browser – www.homeoffice.gov.uk/crime-victims/victims. Click on the UK Government Web Archive link, and then follow the crime link. Explore the site, and identify three government policies that have been used for reducing the number of victims of crime, which might suggest:

  a) Positivist approaches, focusing on the characteristics that make individuals vulnerable to and/or responsible for their own victimization;

  b) Radical victimology approaches, focusing on offenders and issues and circumstances in wider society rather than the individual victims, such as community safety or youth crime strategies. Explain also how these policies remove the focus away from victim-blaming.

Practice questions

1 Outline **two** ways in which situational crime prevention may reduce the incidence of crime in an area. **(4 marks)**

2 Outline **three** reasons why increasing surveillance in society may not be effective in reducing crime and disorder. **(6 marks)**

3 Read **Item A** below and answer the question that follows.

Item A

Who is counted as a victim of crime is socially constructed, as it depends on the attachment of the label of 'victim'. Some may deny their victimization, and there are many unreported and unrecorded victims who never come to the attention of the criminal justice system, such as victims of domestic and sexual violence, and of white-collar and corporate crime.

Applying material from **Item A**, analyse **two** reasons why victimization in crime is considered to be socially constructed. **(10 marks)**

4 Read **Item B** below and answer the question that follows.

Item B

Punishment of criminals may act in various ways: as retribution or revenge; as rehabilitation to prevent reoffending; as deterrence to others; as restoration of the harm caused to victims; as social protection from those who are dangerous; as reinforcement of social values; or as an assertion of the power and authority of a sovereign or of a dominant social class.

Applying material from **Item B** and your knowledge, evaluate sociological explanations of the role of punishment in the prevention and reduction of crime. **(30 marks)**

CHAPTER SUMMARY AND REVISION CHECKLIST

After studying this chapter you should be able to:

- Identify a range of agencies of social control, and how they seek to ensure social conformity

- Identify and explain how crime and deviance are socially constructed

- Outline and criticize non-sociological theories of crime and deviance, and explain how sociological approaches differ from them

- Explain and evaluate the following theories of crime and deviance: functionalist; strain; subcultural; control; Marxist and neo-Marxist, including the New Criminology; interactionist (labelling); feminist; Left Realism; Right Realism and rational choice and opportunity; and postmodernist

- Identify the sources of crime statistics, explain the limitations of their use and how they are socially constructed

- Explain the strengths and limitations of victim surveys and self-report studies, and how they might contribute to the validity of crime statistics

- Describe how different sociological theories regard and use crime statistics

- Describe the pattern and trends in crime shown in official statistics, and provide and evaluate a range of explanations for patterns of offending in relation to ethnicity, gender and social class

- Describe and explain the nature of white-collar and corporate crime, why they are under-represented in crime statistics, and explanations for them

- Examine, with examples, how globalization affects crime

- Describe and explain what is meant by green or environmental crime, and its victims, causes and the problems of researching it

- Describe and explain, with examples, what are meant by state crimes, including human rights offences, their causes and the problems of researching them

- Explain the role of the media in constructing and distorting perceptions of crime and deviance, acting as moral entrepreneurs, generating moral panics and amplifying deviance, and discuss whether the media causes crime

- Examine the role of the criminal justice system in controlling and preventing crime, including the role and effectiveness of punishment, the changing forms of punishment and changing approaches to criminal justice

- Examine the role of surveillance in the control and prevention of crime

- Identify and evaluate strategies for controlling and preventing crime, including the theories behind them: Left and Right Realism, the broken windows thesis, routine activity and rational choice and opportunity theories, situational crime prevention, displacement theory, feminist approaches and postmodernism

- Explain how victimization is socially constructed, the effects of victimization, and identify and explain patterns of victimization by gender, age, ethnicity and social class, and the different approaches of positivist and radical victimology

KEY TERMS

Definitions can be found in the glossary at the end of this book, as well as these terms being defined in the margin where they first appear in the chapter.

agenda-setting	Gross Domestic Product	moral entrepreneur	social exclusion
corporate crime	hate crimes	moral panic	societal deviance
crime	hegemonic masculinity	news values	techniques of neutralization
delinquency	hegemony	primary deviance	victimology
deviance	indictable offences	restorative justice	white-collar crime
deviancy amplification	institutional racism	secondary deviance	
deviant career	marginality	situational deviance	
folk devils	master status	social control	

There are a variety of free tests and other activities that can be used to assess your learning at

www.politybooks.com/browne
You can also find new contemporary resources by following @BrowneKen on Twitter.

See also the revision guide to accompany this book:
Sociology for AQA Revision Guide 2: 2nd-Year A level

Please note that the above resources have not been endorsed by AQA.

PRACTICE QUESTION

Crime and Deviance with Theory and Methods

Answer **all** questions   **Time allowed: 2 hours**

Crime and Deviance

0 1   Outline **two** ways in which globalization has affected crime.   **[4 marks]**

0 2   Outline **three** reasons why white-collar crimes may be less likely than typical working-class offences to be reported to the police.   **[6 marks]**

0 3   Read **Item A** below and answer the question that follows.

Item A

Imprisonment appears to have relatively little impact on reducing or preventing crime, and around half of all prisoners reoffend after they leave prison. Some suggest prisons act more as training grounds for crime rather than as a means of rehabilitating or deterring offenders, and make the pre-existing problems of offenders worse.

Applying material from **Item A**, analyse **two** reasons why imprisonment may not be effective in reducing crime.   **[10 marks]**

0 4   Read **Item B** below and answer the question that follows.

Item B

Marxist theories regard crime as an inbuilt feature of an unequal class-divided capitalist society that emphasizes self-interest, greed and personal gain. Laws reflect ruling-class interests, and are selectively enforced against the working class. It is rare for the wealthy, the powerful and the influential to find themselves the focus of prosecution and punishment.

Applying material from **Item B** and your knowledge, evaluate the usefulness of Marxist approaches to the understanding of crime.   **[30 marks]**

Turn over >

Theory and Methods

0 5 Outline and explain **two** advantages of using unstructured interviews in sociological research.

[10 marks]

0 6 Read **Item C** below and answer the question that follows.

Item C

Feminists have argued that women were once marginalized in 'malestream' sociological research. Areas of interest to women, such as the household division of labour, domestic violence, women's health, female criminality and the significance of gender differences and inequality were largely ignored. Feminist theory and research have now put women and gender at the heart of sociological thinking and research.

Applying material from **Item C** and your knowledge, evaluate the contribution of feminist theories and research to our understanding of society. **[20 marks]**

Glossary

Words in blue within entries refer to terms found elsewhere in the glossary

absolute rate of mobility   Total number of movements within a class structure within a given period of time.

agenda-setting   The power to manage which issues are to be presented for public discussion and debate and which issues are to be kept in the background.

aid   Economic, military, technical and financial assistance given (or loaned) to developing countries.

alienation   The lack of power, control, fulfilment and satisfaction experienced by workers in a capitalist society, where the means of producing goods are privately owned and controlled.

anomie   A sense of normlessness, confusion and uncertainty over social norms, often found in periods of rapid social change and other disruptions of the routines and traditions of everyday social life.

anti-globalization movement   A loose network of groups and organizations globally opposing neoliberal economic globalization (but using globalized communications).

apartheid   A system whereby society is divided on the basis of ethnic grouping – more especially, skin colour. Found in South Africa until the mid-1990s.

appropriate technology   Technology which is people-centred, small-scale, energy-efficient and environmentally sound, and uses local resources.

authority   Legitimate or accepted power – for example, parents are said to have authority over children and governments over their citizens.

beliefs   Ideas about things we hold to be true.

bias   Presenting a subject in a one-sided way, favouring one point of view over others, or ignoring, distorting or misrepresenting issues.

bilateral aid   Aid involving only the donor and the recipient, usually government to government.

biodiversity   Refers to the number and variety of species in ecosystems, threatened by human activity.

bio-piracy   Refers to the appropriation, generally by means of patents, of legal rights over indigenous knowledge – particularly biomedical knowledge – developed by indigenous groups, without permission from and without compensation to the indigenous groups themselves.

black economy   Running parallel to the official economy, the black economy is informal and most people in it work for cash-in-hand which thus avoids payment of various taxes. It is illegal.

blogosphere   A collective term to describe all the online diaries or reports known as blogs.

bottom billion   Collier's term for the poorest billion of the world's population; also 'Africa plus'.

bourgeoisie   (or capitalists) The class of owners of the means of production in industrial societies, whose primary purpose is to make profits.

Bretton Woods   The place where an agreement in 1944 set up the International Monetary Fund, the World Bank and what became the World Trade Organization (WTO).

bureaucracy   A term derived from the works of Weber. A system of organization in which there is a hierarchy of officials, each with a different level of authority. All officials must stick to the rules, and detailed records are kept of every action.

capitalism   An economic system in which investment in and ownership of the means of production, distribution and exchange of wealth are made and maintained chiefly by private individuals or corporations, whose primary aim is to make profits.

capitalists   The class of owners of the means of production in industrial societies whose primary purpose is to make profits.

cash crops   Crops that are grown for sale in the market, and especially for export; colonialism imposed cash crop cultivation as the main form of agriculture in many colonies.

caste   A system of closed social hierarchy based on the Hindu belief in reincarnation which determines one's social position during this lifetime.

child labour   Where children, usually under the age of 10, are employed, often for very low wages.

churnalism   A form of journalism in which journalists produce news articles based on pre-packaged material in press releases provided by sources such as government spin doctors, public relations consultants and news agencies, without doing further research or checking facts.

citizen journalism   Where members of the public, rather than professional journalists and media companies, collect, report and spread news stories and information.

class   For Weber, this relates to an individual's market position, and how scarce and needed their skills are. More generally, it refers to a broad group of people who share a similar economic situation and interests.

class consciousness   An awareness in members of a social class of their real interests.

closed belief system   One that cannot be disproved, because it relies on faith or beliefs rather than empirical evidence, and rejects or explains away any evidence that challenges that belief system.

closed system/society   A society in which there is very little social mobility. Usually members of this society are likely to spend their whole lives in the class/group into which they were born. Status is therefore ascribed rather than achieved.

collective conscience   The shared beliefs and values which form moral ties binding communities together, and regulate individual behaviour.

collective intelligence   The way users of new media collaborate and share knowledge, resources and skills to build a shared or group intelligence that is greater than that of any one individual.

colonialism   A system in which European powers had direct political control over most of today's developing countries.

communism   An equal society, without social classes or class conflict, in which the means of production are the common property of all.

conditionality   The setting of conditions on aid, so that it will be withheld if those conditions are not met.

conservative force   One that maintains, or seeks to restore, traditional beliefs and customs and maintains the status quo (the way things are currently organized in society). This may sometimes involve supporting social change in order to return to traditional values and ways of life that are at risk of disappearing, or have already disappeared.

consumption patterns   Ways in which people spend their money. Some sociologists, such as Giddens, suggest these are as important as class in demonstrating identity.

corporate crime   Offences committed by large companies, or by individuals on behalf of large companies, which directly profit the company rather than individuals.

crime   Behaviour which is against the criminal law – law-breaking.

cultural capital   The knowledge, education, attitudes and values usually associated with the upper social classes.

cultural convergence   The way new media users engage with a range of media content delivered in a variety of ways, and the ways they seek out, share and make connections between this content, and make sense of it.

cultural defence   Where culture, such as religion, acts as a focal point for the defence of community identity which is seen as under threat in some way from an external force.

cultural homogenization   The process whereby the separate characteristics of two or more cultures are erased, and become blended into one uniform culture. Often linked to the ideas of globalization and cultural imperialism, with world cultures becoming increasingly the same global culture.

cultural imperialism   The imposition of Western, and especially American, cultural values on non-Western cultures, and the consequent undermining of local cultures and cultural independence. Often linked to cultural homogenization, media imperialism and global culture.

cultural transition   Where groups make the transition to a new culture, for example through migration, with their own culture, as shown through such facets as religion, providing a source of identity and support during the period of transition and adaptation to the new culture.

debt boomerang   George's term to describe the ways in which the debt crisis has negative effects in the developed world.

debt crisis   Caused by the inability (and sometimes refusal) of indebted countries to pay interest on loans or to repay the original loan; debt repayments hold back development by diverting money and resources.

delinquency   Crime committed by those under age 18, though the term 'delinquency' is often used to describe any anti-social or deviant activity by young people, even if it isn't criminal.

demographic transition   In demography, the change from high birth and death rates to low birth and death rates.

deforestation   The fall in the amount of land covered by forest as a result of human activity.

dependency culture   A set of values and beliefs, and a way of life, centred on dependence on others. It is normally used by New Right writers in the context of those who depend on welfare state benefits.

dependency theory   Alternative Marxist-influenced theory to modernization, focused on external factors which impede development, including relationships with developed countries.

desacralization   The loss of the capacity to experience a sense of sacredness and mystery in life.

desertification   The spread of deserts, as land on the edges of deserts loses its vegetation and top soil.

deskilling   A situation in which the skills and knowledge previously needed to do a job are no longer required. A good example would be in printing photographs which used to need four specialized workers, but can now be done by a computer operated by a relatively unskilled person.

determinism   The idea that people's behaviour is moulded by their social surroundings, and that they have little free will, control or choice over how they behave.

deterritorialization   The blurring or severance of social, political or cultural practices, like religion, from their original places and populations.

development   The process by which societies change; a controversial term, with different writers having different conceptions of what processes are involved and what the outcome should be.

development state   A state which sees its main purpose as development and leads the country's development programme.

deviance   Rule-breaking behaviour of some kind, which fails to conform to the norms and expectations of a particular society or social group.

deviancy amplification   The way the media may actually make worse or create the very deviance they condemn by their exaggerated, sensationalized and distorted reporting of events, and their presence at them.

deviant career   What arises when people who have been labelled as deviant find conventional opportunities blocked to them, and so are pushed into committing further deviant acts.

digital divide   The gap between those people with effective access to the digital and information technology making up the new media and those who lack such access.

digital underclass   A group of people, mainly those from the lowest social classes, the least educated and the unemployed, who are increasingly disadvantaged in comparison to those who have full access to and use of the internet and other digital media.

disability A physical or mental impairment which has a substantial and long-term adverse effect on a person's ability to carry out normal day-to-day activities.

disembedding The way social relations are lifted out of local contexts, and are no longer confined by time and space.

disenchantment The process whereby the magical and mystical elements of life are eroded, as understandings of the world based on religion, faith, intuition, tradition, magic and superstition are displaced by rational argument, science and scientific explanation.

Disneyization (or Disneyfication) The process whereby something is transformed into a diluted or simplified, trivialized and sanitized version of its original form, to create an inoffensive neutral product resembling the Disneyland theme parks.

dominant ideology A set of ideas which justifies the social advantages of wealthy, powerful and influential groups in society, and the disadvantages of those who lack wealth, power and influence.

dual labour market A theory that says there are two types of employment – the primary labour market with secure, permanent jobs, and the secondary one with insecure, often temporary, part-time work.

dysfunction When a part of the social structure does not contribute to the maintenance and well-being of society, but creates tensions and other problems.

ecofeminism Feminist theory based on the idea that women's relationship with nature and the environment is different from that of men.

ecological footprint A measure of the environmental impact of an individual's or country's lifestyle, taking into account what resources are consumed.

economic capital People's wealth, earnings, assets and savings.

economic growth The growth of national income, usually measured by Gross National Product.

elite A small group holding great power and privilege in society.

embourgeoisement The notion that working-class manual workers were adopting more middle-class norms and values.

empirical evidence Observable evidence collected in the physical or social world.

epidemiologic transition In health, the change from the main problem in a society being infectious diseases to it being 'diseases of affluence' such as cancer and heart disease.

establishment An elite group of people with a belief in the free-market economy whose shared beliefs and financial interests bind them together.

ethnic identity One in which individuals assert their identity primarily in terms of the ethnic group and culture to which they belong.

ethnicity The shared culture of a social group which gives its members a common identity in some ways different from that of other social groups.

ethnocentrism The belief that one's own culture is the most important one.

exhaustible resources Those that can be renewed, but that can also be exhausted and destroyed if overused – for example, fish stocks and forests.

existential security The feeling that survival is sufficiently secure for it to be taken for granted. Religious participation is highest in societies or groups with low levels of existential security, and lowest in societies or groups with high levels of existential security.

export-oriented industrialization An industrialization strategy based on production for export.

Export Processing Zones Areas in developing countries where the normal workplace regulations are relaxed to encourage transnational corporations (TNCs) to invest.

expressive role The nurturing, caring and emotional role, often linked by functionalists to women's biology and seen as women's 'natural' role in the family.

Fair Trade A movement to try to alter the terms of trade so that producers in developing countries receive a higher proportion of the profit.

false consciousness   A lack of awareness among people about what their real interests are, and the false belief that everyone benefits from the present organization of society, which is presented as fair and just.

fatalism   A state of mind in which someone believes there is nothing they can do to alter their situation or circumstances.

feudal/estate system   A system of society in which the hierarchy of power and prestige is closely tied to the ownership of land.

folk devils   Individuals or groups posing an imagined or exaggerated threat to society.

forced labour   Where individuals work for another person with no control over any aspect of their lives, but do get paid, usually a very small amount.

forced marriage   A marriage in which at least one party, usually the woman, has no chance to refuse. Often involves the exchange of money.

functional prerequisites   The basic needs that must be met if society is to survive.

fundamentalism   A return to the literal meaning of religious texts and associated behaviour.

future generations   The concept of sustainable development requires consideration of the future of today's children, and also of people not yet born, even though there is no established way of representing their interests.

gatekeeping   The power of some people, groups or organizations to limit access to something valuable or useful. For example, the mass media have the power to refuse to cover some issues and therefore not allow the public access to some information.

gender   The culturally created differences between men and women which are learnt through socialization.

Gini coefficient   A method of measuring one person's income against those of all other individuals in that society. A coefficient of 0 means all incomes are equal and there is no inequality; a coefficient of 1 means all income goes to one individual. Thus the nearer to 1, the more unequal the society.

glass ceiling   An invisible barrier of discrimination which makes it difficult for women to reach the same top levels in their chosen careers as similarly qualified men.

glass floor   The opposite of a glass ceiling – an invisible baseline below which more advantaged groups prevent their children from falling.

global civil society (GCS)   A loose collection of non-governmental organizations (NGOs), activist groups and others, overlapping with the anti-globalization movement; there is a debate as to whether there is a coherent GCS or whether the organizations are too different and lack any common focus.

global culture   The way cultures in different countries of the world have become more alike, sharing increasingly similar consumer products and ways of life. This has arisen as globalization has undermined national and local cultures.

global decision-making   Refers to states acting together and taking decisions at a global level through international governmental organizations (IGOs) to resolve issues that states acting alone are unable to do.

global village   The way that the media and electronic communications now operate on a global scale and so shrink barriers of space and time that the world has become like one village or community.

global warming   The rise in global temperatures now acknowledged to be caused mainly by human activity, likely to lead to severe consequences such as rising sea levels and increased desertification.

globalists   In the globalization debates, those who argue that globalization is a positive and irreversible force from which all will eventually benefit, and are associated with neoliberalism.

globalization   The growing interconnectedness of societies across the world, with the spread of the same culture, consumer goods and economic interests across the globe.

glocalization   The processes leading to the permanent intertwining of the global with the local, and the way, for example, global products might be adapted to fit local cultural needs.

green revolution   Scientific and technological developments that improved agricultural yields, enabling more food to be produced in developing countries but creating some environmental problems because of heavy use of pesticides and insecticides.

Gross Domestic Product (GDP)   One of the ways, along with Gross National Income (GNI), used by economists to measure the total wealth (value of goods and services) produced by a country in a particular year.

Gross National Income (GNI)   One of the ways, along with Gross Domestic Product (GDP), used by economists to measure the total wealth (value of goods and services) produced by a country in a particular year. It differs from GDP in that it also includes income obtained from other nations.

grounded theory   Theory that arises from (is grounded in) analysis of data that have been collected.

hate crimes   Criminal offences which are perceived by the victim or any other person to be motivated by hostility or prejudice based on a person's ethnicity, religion, sexual orientation or disability.

Hawthorne effect   When the presence of the researcher, or the group's (or individual's) knowledge that it has been specially selected for research, changes the behaviour of the group or individual, raising problems with the validity of the research.

hegemonic masculinity   A male gender identity that defines what is involved in being a 'real man', and is so dominant that those who don't conform to it are seen as odd or abnormal in some way.

hegemony   The dominance in society of the ruling class's set of ideas over others, and acceptance of and consent to them by the rest of society.

heterosexuality   A sexual orientation towards people of the opposite sex.

hierarchy of credibility   The greatest importance being attached by journalists to the views and opinions of those in positions of power, like government ministers, political leaders, senior police officers or wealthy and influential individuals.

high culture   Specialist cultural products, seen as of lasting artistic or literary value, which are particularly admired and approved of by intellectual elites and predominantly the upper and middle classes.

Highly Indebted Poor Countries (HIPC) initiative   A system by which heavily indebted countries can apply to have debt written off, provided they keep to conditions.

homosexuality   A sexual orientation towards people of the same sex as oneself.

host immigrant/assimilation model   A view of race relations which sees the host community as homogenous and expects the immigrant groups to be absorbed into this community by adapting their culture to that of the original population.

human capital   The theory that a country's people are a potential source of wealth; by educating its people, a country can increase its human capital.

Human Development Index   A composite measure of social and economic indicators, giving a statistical value to the level of development.

hybrid culture   A new culture formed from a mix of two or more other cultures.

hybrid identities   Identities created by a mixing of different cultural identities – for example British Asian.

hybridization   The creation of a new hybrid culture when aspects of two or more different cultures combine.

hydraulic society   A society in which power is related to the control of access to water.

hyperreality   A view of the world which is created and defined by the media, with the image of an event more real than the event it is meant to be depicting.

ideal type   A model of a phenomenon, like a religious organization, built up by identifying the essential characteristics of many factual examples of it. The purpose of an ideal type is not to produce a perfect category, but to provide a measuring rod that enables the researcher to compare particular examples and identify the extent to which they are similar to or different from the ideal type.

ideological state apparatuses   Agencies that spread the dominant ideology and justify the power of the dominant social class.

ideology   A set of ideas, values and beliefs that provides a means of interpreting the world, and represents the outlook, and justifies the interests, of a social group.

immediate gratification   A desire to have rewards now rather than waiting to acquire them in the future, which is known as deferred gratification.

impairment   Some loss, limitation or difference of functioning of the body or mind, either that one is born with or arising from injury or disease.

imperialism   The process of empire-building associated with the colonial system.

import substitution industrialization   An industrialization strategy based on domestic production of consumer goods to replace imported ones.

impression management   The way individuals try to convince others of the identity they wish to assert by giving particular impressions of themselves to other people.

income   An inward flow of money over time. For most people this consists of wages or salary, but other sources are benefits, pensions, interest on savings and dividends from shares.

indictable offences   More serious criminal offences that can be tried at the Crown Court (indictable only) or at the magistrates' court (either-way offences). These contrast with less serious summary offences, such as motoring offences, common assault and small-scale criminal damage up to £5,000, which are usually heard only by a magistrates' court.

inductive approach   One which develops theories on the basis of evidence that has been collected.

Industrial Revolution   A phrase coined by Tawney in the 1880s to describe the process by which Britain had developed from an agricultural society into a society based on manufacturing.

industrialized   Countries are industrialized if their economies are based on industry rather than agriculture or extraction.

informal sector   An employment sector, characterized by lack of regular work and wages, including petty trading, self-employment, casual work and so on; the dominant sector in cities in developing countries.

institutional racism   Patterns of discrimination based on ethnicity that have become structured into existing social institutions.

instrumental role   The provider/breadwinner role in the family, often associated by functionalists with men's role in family life.

instrumental orientation   An attitude in which wages/money are the most important aspect of work.

intergenerational social mobility   When the class of the child is different from the class of the parent. The move can be either upwards or downwards.

international governmental organizations (IGOs)   These are established by states; examples include the International Monetary Fund (IMF), the World Bank and World Trade Organization (WTO).

International Monetary Fund (IMF)   A key international governmental organization (IGO), which gives loans to members and which has helped to spread neoliberal economic globalization.

international non-governmental organizations (INGOs)   Non-profit groups which are independent of the state; they are largely funded by private contributions and work internationally on a range of global humanitarian, development and environmental issues.

interpretivism   An approach emphasizing that people have consciousness involving personal beliefs, values and interpretations, and these influence the way they act. People have choices and do not simply respond to forces outside themselves. To understand society, it is therefore necessary to understand the meanings people give to their behaviour, and how these are influenced by the behaviour and interpretations of others.

intragenerational social mobility   When an individual moves from one class to another during their own working life. It can be either upwards or downwards.

inverse care law   Those whose need is least get the most resources, while those in greatest need get the fewest resources.

Islamophobia   An irrational fear and/or hatred of or aversion to Islam, Muslims or Islamic culture.

labour power   People's capacity to work. In capitalist societies, people sell their labour power to employers in return for a wage, and employers buy only their labour power, but not the whole person as they did, for example, under slavery.

latent function   The unrecognized or unintended outcome of the action of an individual or institution.

life chances   The chances of obtaining those things defined as desirable and of avoiding those things defined as undesirable in a society.

looking-glass self   The suggestion that our image of ourselves as a social being is built up by reflecting on the opinions of others, seeing ourselves as we think others see us.

low culture   A derogatory (critical and insulting) term used to suggest popular culture or mass culture is of inferior quality compared to the high culture of the elite.

lumpenproletariat   A term used by Marx to describe the group of unorganized working-class people. Now seen as synonymous with the underclass by many commentators.

macro approach   One that focuses on the large-scale structure of society as a whole, rather than on individuals.

male gaze   Where men look (gaze) at women as sexual objects.

malestream   A word coined by feminists to describe the type of sociology that concentrates on men, is mostly carried out by men and then assumes that its findings can be applied to women as well.

manifest function   The recognized and intended outcome of the action of an individual or institution.

marginality   Where some people are pushed to the margins or edges of society by poverty, lack of education, disability, racism and so on, and face social exclusion.

marginalization   The process whereby some people are pushed to the margins or edges of society or organizations (marginality), often by poverty, lack of education, disability, discrimination and so on.

mass culture   Commercially produced culture, involving cultural products manufactured as entertainment for sale to the mass of ordinary people. These involve mass-produced, standardized, short-lived products, which many see as of little lasting value and which demand little critical thought, analysis or discussion.

master status   A status which overrides all other features of a person's social standing, with a person being judged solely in terms of that one defining characteristic.

matrilocal   Describes family systems in which the husband is expected to live near the wife's parents.

McDonaldization   Ritzer's term for the ways in which the organizing principles of a fast-food restaurant chain are coming to dominate and standardize many aspects of economic and cultural life globally.

media gaze   The way the media view society and represent it in media content.

media imperialism   The suggestion that the media, particularly satellite television and global advertising, have led to the Westernization of other cultures, with Western, and especially American, cultural values being forced on non-Western cultures, and the undermining of local cultures and cultural independence. Often linked to cultural imperialism.

media representations   The categories and images that are used to present groups and activities to media audiences, which may influence the way we think about these activities and groups.

media text   Any media product which describes, defines or represents something, such as a movie or video clip, TV or radio programme, a newspaper or magazine article, a book, a poster, a photo, a popular song, an advertisement, a CD or DVD, or a webpage.

means of production   The key resources necessary for producing society's goods, such as land, factories and machinery.

meritocracy   A social system in which rewards are allocated on the basis of merit or ability.

meta-analysis   A statistical technique of collating many different research findings and testing the reliability of the results by controlling the variables within each individual study.

metanarrative   A broad, all-embracing big theory or story providing an explanation for how the world and societies operate.

metropolis   In dependency theory, the centre of economic activity, profiting from an exploitative relationship with satellites.

micro approach   One that focuses on small groups or individuals, rather than on the structure of society as a whole.

micro-credit   Schemes to allow poor people to borrow small sums of money.

millenarianism   The beliefs (millenarian beliefs) that existing society is evil, sinful or otherwise corrupt, and that supernatural or other extra-worldly forces will intervene to completely destroy existing society and create a new and perfect world order.

Millennium Development Goals (MDGs)   A set of eight development goals adopted by the United Nations in 2000, to be achieved by 2015.

minority ethnic group   A social group that shares a cultural identity which is different from that of the majority population of a society, such as African-Caribbean, Indian Asian and Chinese ethnic groups in Britain.

modern world system   In world systems theory, the global capitalist system.

modernity   Refers to the period of the application of rational principles and logic to the understanding, development and organization of human societies.

modernization theory   Dominant development theory of the 1960s, based on factors internal to Third World countries inhibiting their development.

monopoly   When one person or company is the only possible provider of goods or services.

moral entrepreneur   A person, group or organization with the power to create or enforce rules and impose their definitions of deviance.

moral panic   A wave of public concern about some exaggerated or imaginary threat to society, stirred up by exaggerated and sensationalized reporting in the mass media.

moral regulation   The control or regulation by social values of the actions and desires of individuals.

multilateral aid   Donors contribute to a shared fund, from which aid is then given to recipients.

multinational corporations (MNCs)   Sometimes used interchangeably with transnational corporations (TNCs), but more usefully used to mean corporations that have some global aspects but are still clearly based in one nation.

need for achievement   In modernization theory, the desire to be entrepreneurial and to make money, essential for modernization.

NEETs   People between the ages of 16 and 25 who are not in education, employment or training.

negotiated reading   A reading or interpretation of a media text by media audiences which amends the preferred (or dominant) reading of media content to suit their own values and beliefs. *See also* oppositional reading; preferred (or dominant) readings.

neo-colonialism   Refers to the continuation of past economic domination by former colonial powers over ex-colonies.

neoliberal economic theory   The dominant theory influencing development policies in the 1980s and 1990s, based on a minimal role for states and liberalization of trade to allow the free market (capitalism) to work without restrictions.

neo-Malthusian   Modern followers of Malthus's main argument: that population growth will overtake food supply.

neophiliacs   People who dislike and get bored with tradition and routine, and welcome, rapidly embrace and adapt to new technology and other changes.

new barbarism   Kaplan's theory, a variant of Malthusian theory, that overpopulation and exhaustion of resources were leading to civil wars in developing countries.

new international division of labour (NIDL)   The new global economic order said to be produced by factory production moving from the developed world to some developing countries.

New Right   A political ideology and an approach to social and political policies that stresses individual freedom; self-help and self-reliance; reduction of the power and spending of the state; the free market and free competition between private companies, schools and other institutions; and the importance of traditional institutions and values.

newly industrializing countries (NICs)   Those countries that seemed to make rapid progress in the late twentieth century, notably the 'Asian tigers'.

news values   The values and assumptions held by editors and journalists which guide them in choosing what is 'newsworthy' – what to report and what to leave out – and how what they choose to report should be presented.

non-governmental organizations (NGOs)   Non-profit groups which are independent of the state; they are largely funded by private contributions and are mostly involved in humanitarian activities.

non-renewable resources   Natural resources which are finite, and cannot be replenished, such as coal and oil. They can be distinguished from renewable resources such as wind, solar power and (if used sustainably) timber.

norm-setting   The way the media emphasize and reinforce conformity to social norms, and seek to isolate those who do not conform by making them the victims of unfavourable media reports.

North   The world's richer countries – developed nations; sometimes known as the 'Global North' or the 'First World'.

objectivity   Approaching topics with an open mind, avoiding bias, and being prepared to submit research evidence to scrutiny by other researchers.

open belief system   One that is open to questioning, testing and falsifying by others, and may subsequently change as a result of these processes.

open system   A social system in which it is possible for an individual to move from the social group in which he or she was born into a different social group.

opportunity hoarding   The ability of more socially privileged groups to manipulate situations, organizations and opportunities to prevent their own children from losing advantages over other children from more disadvantaged backgrounds.

oppositional reading   A reading or interpretation of a media text by media audiences which opposes or rejects the preferred (dominant) reading (or interpretation) of media content. *See also* preferred (or dominant) reading; negotiated reading.

paradigm   A framework of scientific laws, concepts, theories, methods and assumptions within which scientists operate, and which provides guidelines for the conduct of research and what counts as proper evidence. These are rarely called into question until the evidence against them is overwhelming.

parastatals   State-run organizations such as marketing boards, which played a leading role in the development policies of many states before neoliberal policies were enforced.

participatory culture   A media culture in which the public do not act only as consumers, but also as contributors or producers of media content. This new culture, as it relates to the internet, has been termed 'Web 2.0'.

party   A term used by Weber to describe the way in which political organization will appear in any group of individuals who work together because they have common backgrounds, aims or interests.

paternity leave   Time off from work, with pay, given to men so they can be with their partner and child during a short time in the first six months of the child's life.

patriarchal ideology   A set of ideas that supports and justifies the power of men.

patriarchy   Power and authority held by males.

patrilocal Describes family systems in which the wife is expected to live near the husband's parents.

people-trafficking   Where individuals are traded across national boundaries and often sold into prostitution, frequently becoming slaves.

perfect social mobility   Where every position in society is filled on merit and individuals move easily between the class of birth and the class of achievement based on their ability and nothing else.

pluralism   A view that sees power in society spread among a wide range of interest groups and individuals, with no group or individual having a monopoly of power.

pluralist ideology   A set of ideas that reflects the pluralist view of the distribution of power, with no one particular ideology able to dominate others, and with the prevailing ideas in society reflecting the interests of a wide range of competing social groups and interests.

polysemic   This means that a sign (such as a media message, picture or headline) can be interpreted in different ways by different people.

popular culture   Cultural products liked and enjoyed by the mass of ordinary people. Often associated with mass culture.

positivism   The view that the logic, methods and procedures of the natural sciences, as used in subjects like physics, chemistry and biology, can be applied to the study of society with little modification.

power   The capacity of individuals or groups to get their own way in any given situation.

predatory state   A state that preys upon its own people, through appropriation and corruption, preventing development.

preferred (or dominant) reading   The interpretation of messages that those producing media content would prefer their audiences to accept. *See also* negotiated reading; oppositional reading.

present-time orientation   Concentrating on today without much consideration for the future or the past.

pressure groups   Organizations that try to put pressure on those with power in society to implement policies they favour.

primary definers   Powerful individuals or groups whose positions of power give them greater access to the media than others, and therefore put them in a more privileged position to influence what journalists define as news and how they present it.

primary deviance   Deviance that has not been publicly labelled as such.

professions   Types of occupation which are self-governing and usually of relatively high status.

proletarianization   The process whereby other groups take on the attributes and characteristics of the proletariat.

proletariat   The social class of workers who have to work for wages as they do not own the means of production.

pull factors   The advantages of city life which attract people to move there from rural areas.

push factors   The disadvantages of rural life which push people into moving to cities.

race hate crimes   Criminal offences which are perceived by the victim or any other person to be motivated by hostility or prejudice based on a person's ethnicity or religion.

racism   Treating people differently on the basis of their ethnic origin.

radicals   In globalization debates, those who argue that globalization is a powerful negative force; associated with dependency theory and neo-Marxists.

realism   The view that events in both the social and natural worlds are produced (caused) by underlying structures and processes, which may be unobservable.

reflexivity   The way the knowledge people gain about society can affect the way they behave in it, as people (and institutions) reflect on what they do and how they do it.

relations of production   The forms of relationship between those people involved in production, such as cooperation or private ownership and control.

relative autonomy   The idea in neo-Marxist theory that social institutions in the superstructure of society can have some independence from the economy and the interests of the dominant class, rather than being directly determined by them.

relative deprivation   The sense of lacking something compared to the group with which people identify and compare themselves.

relative rate of mobility   Actual number of movements within a class structure within a given period of time, adjusted to take account of changes in the occupational structure of a society.

religiosity   The extent of importance of religion, religious beliefs and feelings in people's lives.

religious market theory   Also known as rational choice or market supply theory. Suggests that religious organizations are like businesses that compete in the spiritual marketplace for customers. Diversity, choice and competition between religious organizations leads to a greater variety of religion and improved quality of religious products tailored to the needs of consumers, which leads to more religious participation.

religious pluralism　A situation where there are a variety of different religions, different groups within a religious faith, and a range of beliefs of all kinds, with no one religious belief or organization reasonably able to claim to hold a monopoly of truth or to have the support of most members of society.

remittances　The transfer of money by a migrant worker back to family and friends in their country of origin.

repressive state apparatus　The parts of the state concerned with mainly repressive, physical means of keeping a population in line, such as the army, police, courts and prisons.

resacralization　The renewal and continuing vitality of religious beliefs.

reserve army of labour　Refers to a group of people not normally in the paid workforce who can be called on in time of need. Marx saw them as members of the lumpenproletariat; feminists see them as married women and mothers.

restorative justice　A process which brings together victims of crime and the offenders responsible, usually in face-to-face meetings, to help repair the harm done, restore the dignity and self-respect of victims, reduce their fear of crime, and make offenders take responsibility for the consequences of their actions.

role allocation　Ensuring that the most suitable individuals fill the roles needed for society to function properly and maintain social consensus.

satellite　In dependency theory, the deformed and dependent economies of the under-developed countries.

scapegoating　Blaming an individual or group for problems which are not necessarily their fault.

scientism　A belief system or ideology that claims science and the scientific method alone can provide true knowledge and understanding of the world, and rejects any alleged truths that cannot be explained by the scientific method.

secondary deviance　Deviance that follows once a person has been publicly labelled as deviant.

secularization　The process whereby religious thinking, practice and institutions lose social significance.

selective biomedical intervention　In healthcare, interventions such as immunization campaigns to try to prevent the spread of disease.

sexual orientation　The type of people that individuals are either physically or romantically attracted to, such as those of the same or opposite sex.

sexuality　People's sexual characteristics and their sexual behaviour.

shared resources　Those resources that are not privately owned and whose use is freely shared – for example air, water (unless you choose to buy bottled water) and parts of the countryside. They are also sometimes referred to as 'public goods'.

simulacra　Images or reproductions and copies which appear to reflect things in the real world but have no basis in reality.

situational deviance　Acts which are only defined as deviant in particular contexts.

slavery　A situation in which people are sold like objects, forced to work for no pay and have their whole lives controlled by their owners.

social capital　The social networks of influence and support that people have.

social closure　A system whereby members of a group can act to prevent others from joining the group.

social construction　The way something is created through the individual, social and cultural interpretations, perceptions and actions of people. Official statistics, notions of health and illness, deviance and suicide are all examples of social phenomena that only exist because people have constructed them and given these phenomena particular labels.

social control　The various methods used to persuade or force individuals to conform to the dominant social norms and values of a society or group.

social exclusion　Being excluded from full participation in education, work, community life, access to services and other aspects of life seen as part of being a full and participating member of mainstream society.

social facts   Phenomena which exist outside individuals and independently of their minds, but which act upon them in ways that constrain or mould their behaviour.

social integration   The integration of individuals into social groups, binding them into society and building social cohesion.

social media   Websites and other online means of communication that are used for social interaction among large groups of people, in which they create, share and exchange information and develop social networks.

social mobility   The movement of individuals or groups from one social class to another, both upward and downward.

social order   A relatively stable state of society, with some shared norms and values which establish orderly patterns that enable people to live together and relate to one another in everyday life.

social policy   The packages of plans and actions adopted by national and local government or various voluntary agencies to solve social problems or achieve other goals that are seen as important.

social problem   Something that is seen as being harmful to society in some way, and needs something doing to sort it out.

social solidarity   The integration of people into society through shared values, a common culture, shared understandings and social ties that bind them together.

societal deviance   Acts that are seen by most members of a society as deviant.

sociological problem   Any social or theoretical issue that needs explaining.

South   The world's poorer countries, those that are developing; sometimes known as the 'Global South'.

stages of economic growth   In Rostow's version of modernization, the five stages through which societies pass as they move from being traditional to fully developed.

standardized mortality ratio   A measure of actual deaths against expected deaths. Figures below 100 suggest fewer than expected, and those above 100 indicate a higher-than-expected death rate.

status   The amount of prestige or social importance a person has in the eyes of other members of a group or society.

status frustration   A sense of frustration arising in individuals or groups because they are denied status in society.

stigmatized identity   An identity that is in some way undesirable or demeaning, and stops an individual or group being fully accepted by society.

Structural Adjustment Programme   A programme of actions imposing neoliberal policies on governments used by international governmental organizations (IGOs), especially the International Monetary Fund (IMF).

structural differentiation   The way new, more specialized social institutions emerge to take over functions that were once performed by a single institution.

structural violence   The term used by Galtung (1969) to describe the way in which, even in an apparently peaceful society, a group can be exploited.

structuralism   A perspective that is concerned with the overall structure of society, and sees individual behaviour moulded by social institutions like the family, the education system, the media and work.

structuration   The two-way process by which people are constrained or shaped by society and social institutions, but they can at the same time take action to support, shape and change them.

subsistence farming   Farming to produce crops and livestock for consumption by the family rather than for sale in the market.

surplus value   The extra value added by workers to the products they produce, after allowing for the payment of their wages, and which goes to the employer in the form of profit.

sustainability   When something can continue at the same level indefinitely; for example, using trees from a forest for fuel is sustainable only if the wood is taken at the rate that the trees grow, so that the number of trees in the forest remains constant.

sustainable development   Development that sustains the natural environment, thereby ensuring that future generations can have the same level of development.

Sustainable Development Goals (SDGs)   A set of seventeen development goals adopted by the United Nations in 2015, to be achieved by 2030 and replacing the earlier Millennium Development Goals (MDGs).

symbol   Something, like an object, word, expression or gesture, that stands for something else and to which individuals have attached some meaning.

symbolic annihilation   The lack of visibility, under-representation and limited roles of women or other groups in media representations, as they are omitted, condemned or in many roles.

synergy   Where a product is produced in different forms which are promoted together, either through different arms of the same company or through collaboration of different companies, to enable greater sales than would be possible through the sale of a single form of that product or by the efforts of one company.

tabloidization   The process whereby there is a decline of serious news reporting, coverage of current affairs and documentaries, and their replacement by a more dumbed-down, entertaining, sensationalized or gossipy style of journalism – focusing on human interest stories, celebrity culture and scandal – entertainment, crime drama, soap opera and reality TV shows.

take-off   In Rostow's five stages of economic growth, the third stage at which societies achieve a momentum that ensures development.

techniques of neutralization   Justifications used to excuse acts of crime and deviance.

technological convergence   Where several media technologies, once contained in separate devices, are combined in a single device.

technological leapfrogging   The use of a new technology when the previous version of that technology has not been used.

teenagers   Young people at a time of life between childhood and adulthood – in their 'teen' years. The teenager's status is often ambiguous and changes from one situation to another, which reflects the confusion felt by teenagers themselves as to their exact status.

terrorism   In war and conflict, the use of tactics intended to persuade the opponents, or civilians, not to resist.

theodicy   An explanation for the contradiction in the existence of a God who is assumed to be all-powerful and benevolent, and, at the same time, the prevalence of widespread suffering and evil in the world.

theodicy of disprivilege   A religious explanation and justification for social inequality and social deprivation, explaining the marginalization (or disprivilege) of believers, often used as a test of faith, with the promises of compensating rewards in a future after death.

Third World   A term used to describe the world's poorer countries, distinct from the First World (developed capitalist countries) and Second World (developed communist, or, today, ex-communist countries).

totem   A sacred object representing, and having symbolic significance and importance for, a group.

trade liberalization   Removal of barriers to free trade, such as tariffs and subsidies.

trade union   An organization of workers whose aim is to protect the interests of its members and improve their life chances.

transformationalists   In the globalization debates, those who see globalization as a force whose outcomes are uncertain, but which can be controlled and used to promote development.

transnational capitalist class   A global power elite or ruling class made up of the owners and controllers of transnational corporations and the globalized media, top officials, professionals and politicians who operate globally, and top business people who trade in global markets.

transnational corporations (TNCs)   Large business enterprises which produce and sell globally and have global supply chains.

triangular trade   The slave trade linking West Africa, Europe and the Americas.

typology   A generalization used to classify things into groups or types according to their characteristics, which do not necessarily apply in every real-world example.

underclass   A concept developed by Murray to describe a group considered to be outside the mainstream of society, below the working class. See also lumpenproletariat.

underdevelopment   Used by dependency theorists, the process of exploitation by which the North became and stayed rich at the expense of the South.

universe of meaning   A set of beliefs and values which enable people to give life some focus, order and meaning.

urbanization   The process by which a growing proportion of people live in towns and cities, and the social and other changes which accompany this process.

value consensus   A widespread agreement around the main values of a society.

value freedom   The idea that the beliefs and prejudices of a researcher should not influence the way research is carried out and evidence interpreted.

Verstehen   The idea of understanding human behaviour by putting yourself in the position of those being studied, and trying to see things from their point of view.

victimology   The study of the impact of crime on victims, victims' interests, and patterns of victimization.

Washington Consensus   A set of neoliberal policies which were argued to be essential for reforming economies and promoting development.

wealth   The total value of the possessions held by an individual or society.

white-collar crime   Offences committed by middle-class individuals who abuse their work positions within organizations for personal gain at the expense of the organization or its clients.

World Bank   A key international governmental organization (IGO) which gives aid and loans to members to fight poverty; often accused of spreading neoliberal economic globalization.

World Economic Forum   An annual gathering of the world's business and political leaders.

World Social Forum   An annual gathering of the anti-globalization movement.

Bibliography

Abercrombie, N. (1996) *Television and Society*. Cambridge: Polity.

Acheson Report (1998) *Independent Inquiry into Inequalities in Health*. London: Stationery Office.

Adamson, P. (1980) 'The Rich, the Poor and the Pregnant', *New Internationalist* 088.

Adler, F. (1975) *Sisters in Crime: The Rise of the New Female Criminal*. New York: McGraw-Hill.

Adonis, A. and Pollard, S. (1997) *A Class Act: Myth of Britain's Classless Society*. London: Hamish Hamilton.

African Economic Outlook (2012) 'Burundi', www.africaneconomicoutlook.org/en/countries/east–africa/burundi.

Ahmed, L. (1992) *Women and Gender in Islam*. New Haven: Yale University Press.

Aldridge, A. (2007) *Religion in the Contemporary World*. Cambridge: Polity.

Aldridge, A., Parekh, A., MacInnes, T. and Kenway, P. (2011) *Monitoring Poverty and Social Exclusion 2011*. York: Joseph Rowntree Foundation.

Allen, K. (2014) 'Poor Nations Pushed into New Debt Crisis', *Guardian*, 20 October.

Allen, R. (2015) *Missing Talent*. London: Sutton Trust.

Althusser, L. (1969) *For Marx*. Harmondsworth: Penguin.

Althusser, L. (1971) *Lenin and Philosophy and Other Essays*. London: New Left Books.

Alvarado, M., Gutch, G. and Wollen, T. (1987) *Learning the Media: Introduction to Media Teaching*. London: Palgrave Macmillan.

Amin, S. (1976) *Unequal Development*. New York: Monthly Review Press.

Anderson, C. A., Berkowitz, L., Donnerstein, E., et al. (2003) 'The Influence of Media Violence on Youth', *Psychological Science in the Public Interest* 4/3.

Anderson, M. (2015) 'Africa Losing Billions from Fraud and Tax Avoidance', *Guardian*, 2 February.

Arber, S., Dale, A. and Gilbert, G. Nigel. (1986) 'The Limitations of Existing Social Class Classifications for Women', in A. Jacoby (ed.), *The Measurement of Social Class*. London: Social Research Association.

Ariès, P. (1973) *Centuries of Childhood*. Harmondsworth: Penguin.

Ashuri, T. (2012) 'Activist Journalism: Using Digital Technologies and Undermining Structures', *Communication, Culture & Critique* 5/1.

Ashworth, J. and Farthing, I. (2007) *Churchgoing in the UK: A Research Report from Tearfund on Church Attendance in the UK*. Teddington: Tearfund (www.tearfund.org).

Atkinson, J. Maxwell (1971) 'Societal Reactions to Suicide: The Role of Coroners' Definitions', in S. Cohen (ed.), *Images of Deviance*. Harmondsworth: Penguin.

Atkinson, J. Maxwell (1983) *Discovering Suicide: Studies in the Social Organization of Sudden Death*. Basingstoke: Palgrave MacMillan.

Aune, K., Sharma, S. and Vincett, G. (eds.) (2008) *Women and Religion in the West: Challenging Secularization*. Aldershot: Ashgate Publishing.

Ayoob, M. (2001) 'State Making, State Breaking and State Failure', in C. Crocker, F. E. Hampson and P. R. Aall (eds.), *Turbulent Peace*. Washington, DC: US Institute of Peace.

Bagdikian, B. H. (1989) 'Conquering Hearts and Minds: The Lords of the Global Village', *The Nation*, 12 June.

Bagdikian, B. H. (2004) *The New Media Monopoly*. Boston: Beacon Press.

Bales, K. (2002) 'Because She Looks Like A Child', in B. Ehrenreich and A. Hochschild (eds.), *Global Woman: Nannies, Maids and Sex Workers in the New Economy*. London: Granta.

Bandura, A., Ross, D. and Ross, S. A. (1961) 'Transmission of Aggression Through Imitation of Aggressive Models', *Journal of Abnormal and Social Psychology* 63: 575–82.

Barber, B. (1963) 'Some Problems in the Sociology of Professions', *Daedalus* 92/4.

Barker, E. (1984) *The Making of a Moonie*. Oxford: Blackwell.

Barker, E. (1989) *New Religious Movements: A Practical Introduction*. London: Stationery Office Books.

Barnes, C. (1992) *Disabling Imagery and the Media*. Halifax: Ryburn Publishing.

Barnett, S. (2002) 'Will a Crisis in Journalism Provoke a Crisis in Democracy?' *Political Quarterly* 73(4).

Barnett, S. and Gaber, I. (2001) *Westminster Tales: The Twenty-first Century Crisis in British Political Journalism*. London: Continuum.

Barnett, S. and Seymour, E. (1999) *A Shrinking Iceberg Travelling South. Changing Trends in British Television: A Case Study of Drama and Current Affairs.* London: Campaign for Quality Television.

Barrett, L. (1977) *The Rastafarians: The Dreadlocks of Jamaica.* Kingston, Jamaica: Sangster Books.

Barrett, M. and McIntosh, M. (1982) *The Anti-social Family.* London: Verso.

Baudrillard, J. (1988) *The Ecstasy of Communication*, trans. Bernard and Caroline Schutze. New York: Semiotext.

Baudrillard, J. (2001) *Selected Writings*, ed. M. Poster. Cambridge: Polity.

Bauer, P. (1995) 'Foreign Aid: Central Component of World Development?' in S. Corbridge (ed.), *Development Studies: A Reader.* London: Arnold.

Bauman, Z. (1989) *Modernity and the Holocaust.* Cambridge: Polity.

Bauman, Z. (1992) *Intimations of Postmodernity.* London: Routledge & Kegan Paul.

Bauman, Z. (1996) 'From Pilgrim to Tourist – or, A Short History of Identity', in S. Hall and P. du Gay (eds.), *Questions of Cultural Identity.* London: Sage.

Bauman, Z. (2000) *Liquid Modernity.* Cambridge: Polity.

Bauman, Z. (2007) *Consuming Life.* Cambridge: Polity.

Bauman, Z. and May, T. (2001) *Thinking Sociologically.* Oxford: Blackwell.

Beall, J. (2000) 'Life in the Cities', in T. Allen and A. Thomas (eds.), *Poverty and Development into the Twenty-first Century.* Oxford: Oxford University Press.

Beattie, L., Khan, F. and Philo, G. (1999) 'Race and the Public Face of Television' in G. Philo (ed.), *Message Received.* Harlow: Longman.

Beck, U. (1992) *Risk Society: Towards a New Modernity.* London: Sage.

Becker, H. (1950) *Through Values to Social Interpretation.* Durham, NC: Duke University Press.

Becker, H. S. (1967) 'Whose Side Are We On?' *Social Problems* 14/3.

Becker, H. S. (1997 [1963]) *Outsiders: Studies in the Sociology of Deviance.* New York: Free Press.

Beishon, S., Modood, T. and Virdee, S. (1998) *Ethnic Minority Families.* York: Joseph Rowntree Foundation.

Bellah, R. N. (1976) 'New Religious Consciousness and the Crisis in Modernity', in C. Y. Glock and R. N. Bellah (eds.), *The New Religious Consciousness.* Berkeley and Los Angeles: University of California Press.

Bellah, R. N., Madsen, R., Sullivan, W. M., Swidler, A. and Tipton, S. M. (1996) *Habits of the Heart: Individualism and Commitment in American Life.* London: University of California Press.

Ben-Nun Bloom, P., Arikan, G. and Sommer, U. (2014) 'Globalization, Threat and Religious Freedom', *Political Studies* 62/2.

Berger, P. L. (1990) *The Sacred Canopy: Elements of a Sociological Theory of Religion.* New York: Anchor Books.

Berger, P. L. (2001) 'Reflections on the Sociology of Religion Today', *Sociology of Religion* 62: 443–54.

Bernard, J. *The Future of Marriage.* New Haven, CT: Yale University Press.

Berthoud, R. (2006) *The Employment Rates of Disabled People*, DWP Research Report 298. London: Department for Work and Pensions.

Bhaskar, R. (1998) *The Possibility of Naturalism: A Philosophical Critique of the Contemporary Human Sciences.* London: Routledge & Kegan Paul.

Bhatti, G. (1999) *Asian Children at Home and at School.* London: Routledge.

Biggs, S. (1993) *Understanding Ageing: Images, Attitudes and Professional Practice.* Milton Keynes: Open University Press.

Bivens, R. K. (2008) 'The Internet, Mobile Phones and Blogging: How New Media are Transforming Traditional Journalism', *Journalism Practice* 2/1.

Black, D., Morris, J. N., Smith, C. and Townsend, P. (1980) *Inequalities in Health: Report of a Working Party.* London: Department of Health and Social Security.

Blanden, J. and Machin, S. (2007) *Recent Changes in Intergenerational Mobility*, Report for the Sutton Trust. London: Sutton Trust.

Blumer, H. (1969) *Symbolic Interactionism: Perspective and Method.* Englewood Hills, NJ: Prentice-Hall.

Bond, M. (2012) 'The Bases of Elite Social Behaviour: Patterns of Club Affiliation among Members of the House of Lords', *Sociology.* 46/4.

Boorman, R. and Hopkins, K. (2012) *Prisoners' Criminal Backgrounds and Proven Re-offending after Release: Results from the Surveying Prisoner Crime Reduction (SPCR) Survey*, Research Summary 8/12. London: Ministry of Justice.

Booth, D. (1985) 'Marxist Sociology: Interpreting the Impasse', *World Development* 13: 761–87; repr. in S. Corbridge (ed.), *Development Studies: A Reader.* London: Edward Arnold, 1995.

Bottero, W. (2005) *Stratification: Social Division and Inequality.* London: Routledge.

Bowers, K. J., Johnson, S. D., Guerette, R., Summers, L. and Poynton, S. (2011) 'Do Geographically Focussed Police Initiatives Displace Crime or Diffuse Benefits? A Systematic Review', *Journal of Experimental Criminology* 7/4.

Bowling, B. and Phillips, C. (2002) *Racism, Crime and Justice.* Harlow: Pearson Education.

Box, S. (1983) *Power, Crime and Mystification.* London: Routledge & Kegan Paul.

Boyle, R. (2007) 'The "Now" Media Generation', *Sociology Review* 17/1 (September).

Bradley, H. (1996) *Fractured Identities: Changing Patterns of Inequality*. Cambridge: Polity.

Bradley, H. (2014) 'Class Descriptors or Class Relations? Thoughts Towards a Critique of Savage et al.', *Sociology* 48/3.

Brah, A. (1992) 'Women of South Asian Origin in Britain: Issues and Concerns', in P. Braham, A. Rattiansi and R. Skellington (eds.), *Racism and Antiracism: Inequalities, Opportunities and Policies*. London: Sage.

Braithwaite, J. (1999) *Crime, Shame and Reintegration*. Cambridge: Cambridge University Press.

Brandt, W. (1980) *North, South: A Programme for Survival*, Report of the Independent Commission on International Development (The Brandt Report). London: Pan.

Brantingham, P. and Brantingham, P. (1995) 'Criminality of Place: Crime Generators and Crime Attractors', *European Journal of Criminal Policy and Research* 3/3.

Braverman, H. (1974) *Labor and Monopoly Capital: The Degradation of Work in the Twentieth Century*. New York: Monthly Review Press.

Briant, E., Philo, G. and Watson, N. (2011) *Bad News for Disabled People: How the Newspapers Are Reporting Disability*. Glasgow: University of Glasgow (Glasgow Media Group, Strathclyde Centre for Disability Research and Inclusion London).

Broadcasting Standards Commission (2003) *Ethnicity and Disability on Television, 1997 to 2002*. Briefing update. London: Broadcasting Standards Commission.

Browne, K. (2011) *An Introduction to Sociology*, 4th edn. Cambridge: Polity.

Browne, K. (2015) *Sociology for AQA Volume 1: AS and 1st-Year A Level*, 5th edn. Cambridge: Polity.

Bruce, S. (1995) *Religion in Modern Britain*. Oxford: Oxford University Press.

Bruce, S. (1996) *Religion in the Modern World: From Cathedrals to Cults*. Oxford: Oxford University Press.

Bruce, S. (2001) 'Christianity in Britain, RIP', *Sociology of Religion* 62/2.

Bruce, S. (2002a) 'God and Shopping', *Sociology Review* (November).

Bruce, S. (2002b) *God Is Dead: Secularization in the West*. Oxford: Blackwell.

Bruce, S. (2008) *Fundamentalism*, 2nd edn. Cambridge: Polity.

Bryman, A. (2004) *The Disneyization of Society*. London: Sage.

Bryson, V. (1999) *Feminist Debates*. Basingstoke: Palgrave.

Bunting, M. (2010) 'The Great Cotton Stitch-Up – Fairtrade Foundation Lifts Lid on Mali's Entrenched Poverty', *Guardian*, 15 November.

Butler, C. (1995) 'Religion and Gender: Young Muslim Women in Britain', *Sociology Review* 4/2.

Butsch, R. (2003) 'Ralph, Fred, Archie and Homer: Why Television Keeps Re-creating the White Male Working Class Buffoon', in G. Dines and J. M. Humez (eds.), *Gender, Race, and Class in Media: A Text Reader*. London: Sage.

Cameron, D. (2007) *The Myth of Mars and Venus*. Oxford: Oxford University Press.

Cannadine, D. (1998) *Class in Britain*. London: Yale University Press.

Carlen, P. (1988) *Women, Crime and Poverty*. Milton Keynes: Open University Press.

Carroll, R. (2002) 'The Eton of Africa', *Guardian*, 25 November.

Castells, M. (2010) *End of Millennium*, 2nd edn. Oxford: Wiley-Blackwell.

Catto, R. (2014) 'What Can We Say about Today's British Religious Young Person? Findings from the AHRC/ ESRC Religion and Society Programme', *Religion* 44/1.

Chambliss, W. J. (1975) 'Toward a Political Economy of Crime', *Theory and Society* 2/2.

Chang, Ha Joon (2003) 'Kicking Away the Ladder: Infant Industry Promotion in Historical Perspective', *Oxford Development Studies* 31/1: 21–32.

Chapman, S. (2008) 'Any Dream Will Do: Equality of Opportunity in 2008', *Social Science Teacher* 37/3.

Children Now (1999) *Boys to Men: Media Messages About Masculinity*. Children Now. Three related reports are available at: www.childrennow.org/issues/media/.

Children Now (2001) *Fair Play? Violence, Gender and Race in Video Games*. www.childrennow.org.

Cicourel, A. (1976) *The Social Organisation of Juvenile Justice*. London: Heinemann.

Clarke, R. V. (1992) 'Introduction', in R. V. Clarke (ed.), *Situational Crime Prevention: Successful Case Studies*. Guilderland, NY: Harrow and Heston.

Clarke, R. V. (2005) 'Seven Misconceptions of Situational Crime Prevention', in N. Tilley (ed.), *Handbook of Crime Prevention and Community Safety*. Cullompton: Willan.

Clarke, M. (1990) *Business Crime: Its Nature and Control*. Cambridge: Polity.

Cloward, R. and Ohlin, L. (1960) *Delinquency and Opportunity: A Theory of Delinquent Gangs*. New York: Free Press.

Coates, K. and Silburn, R. (1970) *Poverty, The Forgotten Englishmen*. Harmondsworth: Penguin.

Cochrane, A. and Pain, K. (2004) 'A Globalizing Society?' in D. Held (ed.), *A Globalizing World: Culture, Economics, Politics*, 2nd edn. London: Routledge & Kegan Paul.

Coghlan, B., Ngoy, P., Mulumba, F., et al. (2008) *Mortality in the Democratic Republic of Congo: An Ongoing Crisis*. International Rescue Committee. Available at http://news.bbc.co.uk/2/shared/bsp/hi/ pdfs/22_1_08congomortality.pdf.

Cohen, A. K. (1971) *Delinquent Boys: The Culture of the Gang*. New York: Free Press.

Cohen, B. C. (1963) *The Press and Foreign Policy.* Princeton, NJ: Princeton University Press.

Cohen, P. (2002 [1972]) 'Subcultural Conflict and Working Class Community', in *Working Papers in Cultural Studies 2*, 3rd edn. Birmingham: University of Birmingham.

Cohen, R. and Kennedy, P. (2012) *Global Sociology*, 3rd edn. Basingstoke: Palgrave.

Cohen, S. (2001) *States of Denial: Knowing About Atrocities and Suffering.* Cambridge: Polity.

Cohen, S. (2002 [1972]) *Folk Devils and Moral Panics.* London: Routledge & Kegan Paul.

Collier, P. (2007) *The Bottom Billion: Why the Poorest Countries Are Falling Apart and What Can Be Done About It.* Oxford: Oxford University Press.

Compaine, B. M. (2005) *The Media Monopoly Myth: How New Competition is Expanding Our Sources of Information and Entertainment.* Washington, DC: New Millennium Research Council.

Connell, R. W. (1987) *Gender and Power: Society, the Person and Sexual Politics.* Cambridge: Polity.

Connell, R. W. (2005) *Masculinities*, 2nd edn. Cambridge: Polity.

Cooley, C. H. (1998 [1902]) *On Self and Social Organization*, ed. H.–J. Schubert. London: University of Chicago Press.

Coontz, S. and Henderson, P. (eds.) (1986) *Women's Work, Men's Property.* London: Verso.

Corcoran, H., Lader, D. and Smith, K. (2015) *Hate Crime, England and Wales 2014/15*, Statistical Bulletin 05/15. London: Home Office.

Cornish, D. B. and Clarke, R. V. (1986) *The Reasoning Criminal.* New York: Springer-Verlag.

Cornish, D. B. and Clarke, R.V. (2003) 'Opportunities, Precipitators and Criminal Decision'. *Crime Prevention Studies* 16.

Cottle, S. (2000) *Ethnic Minorities and the Media: Changing Cultural Boundaries.* Buckingham: Open University Press.

Cowan, K. (2007) *Living Together: British Attitudes to Lesbian and Gay People.* London: Stonewall. (Available at www.stonewall.org.uk.)

Cowan, K. and Valentine, G. (2005) *Tuned Out: The BBC's Portrayal of Lesbian and Gay People.* London: Stonewall. (Available at www.stonewall.org.uk.)

Coyle, D. (2001) 'Trade: The Great Debate', *Developments* 15.

Crawford, A. and Evans, K. (2012) 'Crime Prevention and Community Safety', in M. Maguire, R. Morgan and R. Reiner (eds.), *The Oxford Handbook of Criminology*, 5th edn. Oxford: Oxford University Press.

Croall, H. (2001) *Understanding White Collar Crime.* Buckingham: Open University Press.

Croall, H. (2007) 'Victims of White Collar and Corporate Crime', in P. Davies, P. Francis and C. Greer (eds.), *Victims, Crime and Society.* London: Sage.

Crompton, R. and Jones, G. (1984) *White-collar Proletariat: Deskilling and Gender in Clerical Work.* London: Macmillan.

Crow, B. (2000) 'Understanding Famine and Hunger', in T. Allen and A. Thomas (eds.), *Poverty and Development into the Twenty-first Century.* Oxford: Oxford University Press.

Cuddy, A. J. C. and Fiske, T. S. (2004) 'Doddering but Dear: Process, Content, and Function in Stereotyping of Older Persons', in T. D. Nelson (ed.), *Ageism: Stereotyping and Prejudice Against Older Persons.* Cambridge, MA: Bradford Books/MIT Press.

Cudworth, E. (2003) *Environment and Society.* London: Routledge & Kegan Paul.

Cumberbatch, G. (1994) 'Legislating Mythology: Video Violence and Children', *Journal of Mental Health* 3/4.

Cumberbatch, G. (2004) *Video Violence: Villain or Victim?* Borehamwood: Video Standards Council (www.videostandards.org.uk).

Cumberbatch, G. and Negrine, R. M. (1992) *Images of Disability on Television.* London: Routledge & Kegan Paul.

Cumberbatch, G., Maguire, A., Lyne, A. and Gauntlett, S. (2014) *Diversity Monitoring: The Top TV Programmes.* Birmingham: CRG / Creative Diversity Network.

Curran, J. and Seaton, J. (2010) *Power without Responsibility: Press, Broadcasting and the Internet in Britain*, 7th edn. Abingdon: Routledge.

Curran, J., Iyengar, S., Brink Lund, A. and Salovaara-Moring, I. (2009) 'Media System, Public Knowledge and Democracy: A Comparative Study', *European Journal of Communication* 24/1.

Cusack, C. M. (2011) 'Some Recent Trends in the Study of Religion and Youth', *Journal of Religious History* 35/3.

Dahrendorf, R. (1959) *Class and Class Conflict in an Industrial Society.* London: Routledge & Kegan Paul.

Davie, G. (1994) *Religion in Britain Since 1945: Believing Without Belonging.* Oxford: Blackwell.

Davie, G. (2002) *Europe: The Exceptional Case.* London: Darton, Longman and Todd Ltd.

Davies, N. (2008) *Flat Earth News: An Award-winning Reporter Exposes Falsehood, Distortion and Propaganda in the Global Media.* London: Chatto and Windus.

Davies, T. (2008) 'Sociology and Social Policy', *Sociology Review* 17/3: February.

Davis, K. and Moore, W. E. (1967 [1945]) 'Some Principles of Stratification', in R. Bendix and S. M. Lipset (eds.), *Class, Status and Power*. London: Routledge & Kegan Paul.

De Beauvoir, S. (1953) *The Second Sex*. London: Jonathan Cape.

De Swann, A. (2001) 'Dyscivilization, Mass Extermination and the State', *Theory, Culture and Society* 18/2–3.

Dench, G., Gavron, K. and Young, M. (2006) *The New East End: Kinship, Race and Conflict*. London: Profile Books.

Denscombe, M. (2001) 'Uncertain Identities and Health-risking Behaviour: The Case of Young People and Smoking in Late Modernity', *British Journal of Sociology* 52/1.

Detica (2011) *The Cost of Cyber Crime: A Detica Report in Partnership with the Office of Cyber Security and Information Assurance in the Cabinet Office*. Guildford: Detica Limited.

Devine, F. (1992) *Affluent Workers Revisited*. Edinburgh: Edinburgh University Press.

Dorling, D. (2011) *So You Think You Know about Britain*. London: Constable & Robinson.

Dorling, D. et al. (2007) *Poverty, Wealth and Place in Britain 1968–2005*. London: Joseph Rowntree Foundation.

Dowden, R. (2006) 'In Africa It's Good to Talk – Even Better to Sell', *Society Matters* 9: 10.

Dowling, T. (2007) 'They come over here . . .', *Guardian*, 22 November.

Downes, D. and Rock, P. (2007) *Understanding Deviance*. Oxford: Oxford University Press.

Duffield, M. R. (2001) *Global Governance and the New Wars*. London: Zed Books.

Durkheim, E. (1982 [1895]) *The Rules of Sociological Method*. London: Palgrave Macmillan.

Durkheim, E. (2001 [1912]) *The Elementary Forms of the Religious Life*. Oxford: Oxford University Press.

Durkheim, E. (2002 [1897]) *Suicide: A Study in Sociology*. London: Routledge & Kegan Paul.

Dutton, W. H. and Blank, G., with Groselj, D. (2013) *Cultures of the Internet: The Internet in Britain. Oxford Internet Survey 2013*. Oxford: Oxford Internet Institute, University of Oxford.

Dworkin, A. (1981) *Pornography – Men Possessing Women*. London: The Women's Press.

Easterley, W. (2006) *The White Man's Burden*. Oxford: Oxford University Press.

Edgell, S. (1980) *Middle-Class Couples*. London: Allen & Unwin.

Edgell, S. (1993) *Class*. London: Routledge & Kegan Paul.

Edwards, D. and Cromwell, D. (2009) *Newspeak in the 21st Century*. London: Pluto Press.

Ehrenreich, B. and Hochschild, A. (eds.) (2002) *Global Woman: Nannies, Maids and Sex Workers in the New Economy*. London: Granta.

El Saadawi, N. (1980) *The Hidden Face of Eve: Women in the Arab World*. London: Zed Books.

Elson, D. and Pearson, R. (1981) '"Nimble Fingers Make Cheap Workers": An Analysis of Women's Employment in Third World Export Manufacturing', *Feminist Review* 7/1 (Spring).

Engels, F. (1972 [1891]) *The Origins of the Family, Private Property and the State*. London: Lawrence & Wishart.

Environment Agency (2012) *Cracking Down on Waste Crime: Waste Crime Report 2011–2012*. Bristol: The Environment Agency.

Escobar, A. (2011) *Encountering Development: The Making and Unmaking of the Third World*. Princeton: Princeton University Press.

Eurobarometer and European Commission (2010) *Special Eurobarometer 341 Wave 73.1 Biotechnology Report*. Brussels: European Commission. Available at http://ec.europa.eu/public_opinion/archives/ebs/ebs_341_en.pdf.

Evans, H. (2011 [1983]) *Good Times, Bad Times*. London: Bedford Square Books.

Evans, H. (2012) 'Myth, memory and Murdoch's imagination', *Guardian*, 26 April.

Evans, P. B. (1989) 'Predatory, Developmental and Other Apparatuses: A Comparative Political Economy Perspective on the Third World State', *Sociological Forum* 4/4: 561–87.

Fanon, F. (1963) *The Wretched of the Earth*. Harmondsworth: Penguin.

Farr, K. (2005) *Sex Trafficking: The Global Market in Women and Children*. New York: Worth Publishers.

Felson, M. and Clarke, R. V. (1998) *Opportunity Makes the Thief: Practical Theory for Crime Prevention*. Home Office Police Research Series Paper 98. London: Home Office. Available at: www.homeoffice.gov.uk/rds/prgpdfs/fprs98.pdf.

Fenton, N. (1999) 'Mass Media', in S. Taylor (ed.), *Sociology: Issues and Debates*. Basingstoke: Macmillan.

Ferguson, C. J. (2014) 'Does Media Violence Predict Societal Violence? It Depends on What You Look at and When', *Journal of Communication* 65/1.

Ferguson, M. (1983) *Forever Feminine: Women's Magazines and the Cult of Femininity*. London: Heinemann.

Finkelstein, V. (1980) *Attitudes and Disabled People: Issues for Discussion*. New York: World Rehabilitation Fund.

Firestone, S. (1972) *The Dialectic of Sex*. London: Paladin.

Fitzgerald, M. (1993) *Ethnic Minorities and the Criminal Justice System*. Royal Commission on Criminal Justice, Research Study 20. London: HMSO.

Flatley, J., Kershaw, C., Smith, K., Chaplin, R. and Moon, D. (2010) *Crime in England and Wales 2009/10*. London: Home Office.

Flew, T. (2002) *New Media: An Introduction*. Oxford: Oxford University Press.

Forero, J. and Goodman, P. S. (2007) 'Continental Drift Towards Venezuela's Economic Alternatives', *Guardian Weekly*, 30 March–5 April.

Foucault, M. (1991) *Discipline and Punish: The Birth of the Prison*. Harmondsworth: Penguin.

Fox, K. (2005) *Watching the English*. London: Hodder & Stoughton.

Frank, A. G. (1966) 'The Development of Underdevelopment', *Monthly Review* (September 1966).

Frank, A. G. (1969) *Capitalism and Underdevelopment in Latin America*. Harmondsworth: Penguin.

Frank, R. H. (2007) *Falling Behind: How Rising Inequality Harms the Middle Class*. Berkeley: University of California Press.

Fröbel, F., Heinrichs, J. and Kreye, O. (1980) *The New International Division of Labour*. Cambridge: Cambridge University Press.

Fulcher, J. and Scott, J. (2007) *Sociology*. Oxford: Oxford University Press.

Gallie, D. (1988) *Employment in Britain*. Oxford: Blackwell.

Gallie, D. (1994) 'Are the Unemployed an Underclass?' *Sociology* 28/3.

Galtung, J. (1969) 'Violence, Peace and Peace Research', *Journal of Peace Research* 6/3.

Galtung, J. and Ruge, M. H. (1970) 'The Structure of Foreign News: The Presentation of the Congo, Cuba and Cyprus Crises in Four Foreign Newspapers', in J. Tunstall (ed.), *Media Sociology: A Reader*. London: Constable.

Garfinkel, H. (1984 [1967]) *Studies in Ethnomethodology*. Cambridge: Polity.

Garland, D. (2001) *The Culture of Control: Crime and Social Order in Contemporary Society*. Oxford: Oxford University Press.

Garrod, J. (2004) 'What is Reality TV and Why Do We Like It?' *Sociology Review* (February).

Gauntlett, D. (1998) 'Ten Things Wrong with the "Effects Model"', in R. Dickinson, R. Harindranath and O. Linné (eds.), *Approaches to Audiences – A Reader*. London: Arnold; also available at www.theory.org.uk/david/effects.htm.

Gauntlett, D. (2008) *Media, Gender and Identity: An Introduction*. Abingdon: Routledge.

George, S. (1991) *The Debt Boomerang: How Third World Debt Harms Us All*. London: Pluto.

Gerbner, G. (1988) *Violence and Terror in the Mass Media*. Reports and Papers on Mass Communication No. 102. Paris, France: UNESCO.

Gerbner, G. and Gross, L. (1976) 'Living with Television: The Violence Profile', *Journal of Communication* 26/2.

Giddens, A. (1973) *The Class Structure of the Advanced Societies*. London: Hutchinson.

Giddens, A. (1986) *The Constitution of Society: Outline of the Theory of Structuration*. Cambridge: Polity.

Giddens, A. (1990) *The Consequences of Modernity*. Cambridge: Polity.

Giddens, A. (1991) *Modernity and Self-identity: Self and Society in the Late Modern Age*. Cambridge: Polity.

Giddens, A. (1998) *The Third Way: The Renewal of Social Democracy*. Cambridge: Polity.

Giddens, A. (2006) *Sociology*, 5th edn. Cambridge: Polity.

Giddens, A. and Sutton, P.W. (2013) *Sociology*, 7th edn. Cambridge: Polity.

Giddings, A. (2010) 'Cultural Differences: High, Low and Mass Culture' *Journoblog*, www.journoblog.com/2010/05/cultural-differences.

Gill, R. (2007) *Gender and the Media*. Cambridge: Polity.

Gilmore, D. (1991) *Manhood in the Making: Cultural Concepts of Masculinity*. London: Yale University Press.

Gilroy, P. (1982) 'Police and Thieves', in Centre for Contemporary Cultural Studies, *The Empire Strikes Back: Race and Racism in '70s Britain*. London: Hutchinson.

Glaser, B. G. and Strauss, A. L. (1999 [1967]) *The Discovery of Grounded Theory: Strategies for Qualitative Research*. Piscataway, NJ: Aldine Transaction.

Glasgow Media Group (2000) 'Content Study' and 'Audience Study', in *Viewing the World: A Study of British Television Coverage of Developing Countries*. London: Department for International Development.

Glasgow University Media Group (1976) *Bad News*. London: Routledge & Kegan Paul.

Glasgow University Media Group (1980) *More Bad News*. London: Routledge & Kegan Paul.

Glasgow University Media Group (1982) *Really Bad News*. London: Writers and Readers Cooperative.

Glass, D. (1954) *Social Mobility in Britain*. London: Routledge & Kegan Paul.

Glendinning, T. and Bruce, S. (2006) 'New Ways of Believing or Belonging: Is Religion Giving Way to Spirituality?' *The British Journal of Sociology* 57/3.

Glennie, A., Straw, W. and Wild, L. (2012) *Understanding Public Attitudes to Aid and Development*. London: ODI/IPPR.

Glenny, M. (2009) *McMafia: Seriously Organised Crime*. London: Vintage Books.

Global Media Monitoring Project (2010) *Who Makes the News?* World Association for Christian Communication (WACC). Available at www.whomakesthenews.org.

Glock, C. Y. and Stark, R. (1965) *Religion and Society in Tension.* Chicago: Rand McNally.

Goffman, E. (1990a [1959]) *The Presentation of Self in Everyday Life.* Harmondsworth: Penguin.

Goffman, E. (1990b [1963]) *Stigma: Notes on the Management of Spoiled Identity.* Harmondsworth: Penguin.

Goffman, E. (1991 [1961]) *Asylums: Essays on the Social Situations of Mental Patients and Other Inmates.* London: Penguin.

Goldberg, D. T. (1993) *Racist Culture: Philosophy and the Politics of Meaning.* Oxford: Blackwell.

Goldthorpe, J. (1980) *Social Mobility and Class Structure in Modern Britain.* Oxford: Clarendon Press.

Goldthorpe, J. (1987) *Social Mobility and Class Structure in Modern Britain,* 2nd edn. Oxford: Clarendon Press.

Goldthorpe, J. (1995) 'The Service Class Revisited', in T. Butler and M. Savage (eds.), *Social Change and the Middle Classes.* London: UCL Press.

Goldthorpe, J. and Jackson, M. (2007) 'Intergenerational Class Mobility in Contemporary Britain: Political Concerns and Empirical Findings', *British Journal of Sociology* 58/4.

Goldthorpe, J. and Payne, C. (1986) 'On the Class Mobility of Women', *Sociology* 20/4.

Goldthorpe, J. H., Lockwood, D., Bechhofer, F. and Platt, J. (1969) *The Affluent Worker in the Class Structure.* Cambridge: Cambridge University Press.

Gordon, D. M. (1971) 'Class and the Economics of Crime', *Review of Radical Political Economics* 3/3.

Gottfredson, M. R. and Hirschi, T. (1990) *A General Theory of Crime.* Stanford: Stanford University Press.

Gouldner, A. W. (1962) 'Anti-Minotaur: The Myth of a Value-free Sociology', *Social Problems* 9/3.

Gouldner, A. W. (1971) *The Coming Crisis of Western Sociology.* London: Heinemann.

Gramsci, A. (1971) *Selections from the Prison Notebooks.* London: Lawrence & Wishart.

Greeley, A. M. (1995) *Sociology and Religion: A Collection of Readings.* New York: HarperCollins College Publishers.

Green, P. and Ward, T. (2004) *State Crime: Governments, Violence and Corruption.* London: Pluto Press.

Green, P. and Ward, T. (2012) 'State Crime: A Dialectical View', in M. Maguire, R. Morgan and R. Reiner (eds.), *The Oxford Handbook of Criminology,* 5th edn. Oxford: Oxford University Press.

Greer, C. (2003) *Sex Crime and the Media: Sex Offending and the Press in a Divided Society.* Cullompton: Willan.

Greer, C. (2005) 'Crime and Media: Understanding the Connections', in C. Hale, K. Hayward, A. Wahidin and E. Wincup (eds.), *Criminology.* Oxford: Oxford University Press.

Greer, C. and Reiner, R. (2012) 'Mediated Mayhem: Media, Crime, Criminal Justice', in M. Maguire, R. Morgan and R. Reiner (eds.), *The Oxford Handbook of Criminology,* 5th edn. Oxford: Oxford University Press.

Gross, L. (1991) 'Out of the Mainstream: Sexual Minorities and the Mass Media', *Journal of Homosexuality* 21:19–46.

Grusky, D. (1996) 'Theories of Stratification and Inequality', in D. B. Grusky, J. N. Barron and D. J. Treiman (eds.), *Social Differentiation and Inequality.* Boulder, CO: Westview Press.

Hakim, C. (2000) *Work–Lifestyle Choices in the 21st Century: Preference Theory.* Oxford: Oxford University Press.

Hall, S. (1999) 'Encoding/decoding', in S. Hall, D. Hobson, A. Lowe and P. Willis (eds.), *Culture, Media, Language.* London: Hutchinson/CCCS.

Hall, S. (2003) 'The Whites of Their Eyes: Racist Ideologies and the Media', in G. Dines and J. M. Humez (eds.), *Gender, Race, and Class in Media: A Text-reader,* 2nd edn. London: Sage.

Hall, S. (2012) *Theorizing Crime and Deviance: A New Perspective.* London: Sage.

Hall, S., Critcher, C., Jefferson, T., Clarke, J. and Robert, B. (1978) *Policing the Crisis: Mugging, the State and Law and Order.* London: Macmillan.

Halloran, J. D. (1970) *The Effects of Television.* London: Panther.

Halman, L. and Draulans, V. (2006) 'How Secular is Europe?' *The British Journal of Sociology* 57/2.

Halsey, A. H., Heath, A. and Ridge, J. M. (1980) *Origins and Destinations.* Oxford: Clarendon Press.

Hanlon, J. (2006) 'External Roots of Internal War', in H. Yanacopulos and J. Hanlon (eds.), *Civil War, Civil Peace.* Oxford: James Currey.

Hardt, A. and Negri, M. (2004) *Multitude.* New York: Penguin.

Hargrave, A. M. (ed.) (2002) *Multicultural Broadcasting: Concept and Reality.* London: Broadcasting Standards Commission.

Harris, N. (1995) *The New Untouchables: Immigration and the New World Worker.* London: Penguin.

Harvey, D. (1990) *The Condition of Postmodernity.* Oxford: Blackwell.

Hayter, T. (1971) *Aid as Imperialism.* Harmondsworth: Penguin.

Hayward, K. and Young, J. (2012) 'Cultural Criminology', in M. Maguire, R. Morgan, and R. Reiner (eds.), *The Oxford Handbook of Criminology,* 5th edn. Oxford: Oxford University Press.

Heath, A. (1981) *Social Mobility.* Glasgow: Fontana.

Heath, A. and Britten, N. (1984) 'Women's Jobs Do Make a Difference', *Sociology* 18/4.

Heelas, P. (1996) *The New Age Movement: The Celebration of the Self and the Sacralization of Modernity*. Oxford: Blackwell.

Heelas, P. (1998) 'Introduction', in P. Heelas (ed.), *Religion, Modernity and Postmodernity*. Oxford: Blackwell.

Heelas, P., Woodhead, L., Seel, B., Szerszynski, B. and Tusting, K. (2004) *The Spiritual Revolution: Why Religion is Giving Way to Spirituality*. Oxford: Blackwell.

Heidensohn, F. (1996) *Women and Crime*. Basingstoke: Macmillan.

Heidensohn, F. and Silvestri, M. (2012) 'Gender and Crime', in M. Maguire, R. Morgan and R. Reiner (eds.), *The Oxford Handbook of Criminology*, 5th edn. Oxford: Oxford University Press.

Held, D. and McGrew, A. (2007) *Globalization/Anti-globalization: Beyond the Great Divide*, 2nd edn. Cambridge: Polity.

Helsper, E. J. (2011) *The Emergence of a Digital Underclass: Digital Policies in the UK and Evidence for Inclusion*, Media policy brief 3. London: LSE Media Policy Project, http://blogs.lse.ac.uk/mediapolicyproject.

Henry, S. and Milovanovic, D. (1996) *Constitutive Criminology: Beyond Postmodernism*. London: Sage.

Herberg, W. (1960) *Protestant–Catholic–Jew: An Essay in American Religious Sociology*. New York: Anchor Books.

Herman, E. S. and Chomsky, N. (2002) *Manufacturing Consent: The Political Economy of the Mass Media*. New York: Pantheon Books.

Hester, M. and Westmarland, N. (2006) *Service Provision for Perpetrators of Domestic Violence*. Bristol: University of Bristol.

Hewitt, T. (2000) 'Half a Century of Development', in T. Allen and A. Thomas (eds.), *Poverty and Development into the Twenty-first Century*. Oxford: Oxford University Press.

Hewitt, T. and Smyth, I. (2000) 'Is the World Overpopulated?' in T. Allen and A. Thomas (eds.), *Poverty and Development into the Twenty-first Century*. Oxford: Oxford University Press.

Hill, S. (1976) *The Dockers*. London: Heinemann.

Hills, J., Brewer, M., Jenkins, S., et al. (2010) *An Anatomy of Economic Inequality in the UK: Report of the National Equality Panel*. London: Government Inequalities Office.

Himmelweit, H. T., Oppenheim, A. N. and Vince, P. (1958) *Television and the Child*. Oxford: Oxford University Press.

Hirschi, T. (1969) *Causes of Delinquency*. Berkeley: University of California Press.

Hirst, P. and Thompson, G. (1999) *Globalization in Question*, 2nd edn. Cambridge: Polity.

Hobbs, D. (1998) 'Going Down the Glocal: The Local Context of Organised Crime', *The Howard Journal of Criminal Justice* 37/4.

Hobbs, D. and Dunnighan, C. (1998) 'Glocal Organised Crime: Context and Pretext', in V. Ruggiero, N. South and I. Taylor (eds.), *The New European Criminology: Crime and Social Order in Europe*. London: Routledge.

Hobbs, D., Hadfield, P., Lister, S. and Winlow, S. (2003) *Bouncers: Violence and Governance in the Night-time Economy*. Oxford: Oxford University Press.

Holm, J. (1994) 'Introduction: Raising the Issues', in J. Holm and T. Bowker, *Women in Religion*. London: Pinter Publishers.

Holm, J. and Bowker, T. (1994) *Women in Religion*. London: Pinter Publishers.

Hoogvelt, A. (2005) 'Intervention as Management of Exclusion', in *OU Course Readings: War, Intervention and Development*, TU875. Milton Keynes: The Open University.

Hoselitz, B. F. (1995 [1952]) 'Non-economic Barriers to Economic Development', in S. Corbridge (ed.), *Development Studies: A Reader*. London: Edward Arnold.

Hoyle, C. (2012) 'Victims, the Criminal Justice Process, and Restorative Justice', in M. Maguire, R. Morgan and R. Reiner (eds.), *The Oxford Handbook of Criminology*, 5th edn. Oxford: Oxford University Press.

Huish, R. and Kirk, J. M. (2007) 'Cuban Medical Internationalism and the Development of the Latin American School of Medicine', *Latin American Perspectives* 34.

Hulme, D. and Edwards, M. (eds.) (2013) *NGOs, States and Donors: Too Close for Comfort?* London: Palgrave Macmillan.

Hunt, A. (2003) 'Risk and Moralization in Everyday Life', in R. Ericson and A. Doyle (eds.), *Risk and Morality*. Toronto: University of Toronto Press.

Hunt, P. (1966) *Stigma: The Experience of Disability*. London: Geoffrey Chapman.

Huntington, S. P. (2002) *The Clash of Civilizations and the Remaking of World Order*. London: Free Press.

ILO (2013) *Marking Progress Against Child Labour: Global Estimates and Trends 2000–2012*. Geneva: International Labour Office.

Inness, S. A. (1999) *Tough Girls: Women Warriors and Wonder Women in Popular Culture*. Philadelphia: University of Pennsylvania Press.

IWMF (2010) *Global Report on the Status of Women in the News Media*. Washington, DC: International Women's Media Foundation.

Jacobson, J. (1998) *Islam in Transition: Religion and Identity Among British Pakistani Youth.* London: Routledge & Kegan Paul.

Jenkins, H. (2008) *Convergence Culture: Where Old and New Media Collide.* New York: New York University Press.

Jerven, M. (2012) 'Lies, damn lies and GDP', *Guardian,* 20 November.

Jewell, J. (2014) 'Branded Content: How Online Advertorials are Changing the Shape of Modern Journalism', *The Conversation,* 14 October.

Jewkes, Y. (2011) *Media and Crime,* 2nd edn. London: SAGE.

Johal, S. (1998) 'Brimful of Brasia', *Sociology Review* (November).

Jones, A. (2006) *Dictionary of Globalization.* Cambridge: Polity.

Jones, O. (2011) *Chavs: The Demonization of the Working Class.* London: Verso.

Jones, O. (2014) *The Establishment: And How They Get Away With It.* London: Allen Lane.

Jones, P. (2010) *EHRC Triennial Review: Education (Lifelong Learning). Internet Access and Use.* University of Southampton. Available from the Equality and Human Rights Commission, Triennial Review web pages.

Jones, S. (1994) *The Language of the Genes.* London: Flamingo.

Kaldor, M. (1999) *New and Old Wars.* Cambridge: Polity.

Kaplan, A. (1973) *The Conduct of Inquiry: Methodology for Behavioral Science.* New York: Chandler Publishing.

Kaplan, R. (1994) 'The Coming Anarchy: How Scarcity, Crime, Overpopulation and Disease Are Rapidly Destroying the Social Fabric of our Planet', *Atlantic Monthly* (February): 44–76.

Karofi, U. A. and Mwanza, J. (2006) 'Globalisation and Crime', *Bangladesh e-Journal of Sociology* 3/1 (January).

Katz, E. and Lazarsfeld, P. F. (1955) *Personal Influence: The Part Played by People in the Flow of Mass Communication.* New York: Free Press.

Katz, J. (1988) *Seductions of Crime.* New York: Basic Books.

Keat, R. N. and Urry, J. R. (2010 [1975]) *Social Theory as Science.* Abingdon: Routledge Revivals/Taylor and Francis e-Library.

Kellner, D. (1995) *Media Culture: Cultural Studies, Identity and Politics between the Modern and the Postmodern.* London: Routledge.

Kellner, P. and Wilby, P. (1980) 'The 1:2:4 Rule of Class in Britain', *Sunday Times,* 13 January.

Kelly, L., Regan, L. and Burton, S. (1992) 'Defending the Indefensible? Quantitative Methods and Feminist Research', in H. Hinds, A. Phoenix and J. Stacey (eds.), *Working Out: New Directions for Women's Studies.* London: RoutledgeFalmer.

Kelman, H. C. and Hamilton, V. L. (1989) *Crimes of Obedience: Toward a Social Psychology of Authority and Responsibility.* New Haven and London: Yale University Press.

Kinsey, R., Lea, J. and Young, J. (1986) *Losing the Fight Against Crime.* Oxford: Blackwell.

Klapper, J. T. (1960) *The Effects of Mass Communication.* New York: Free Press.

Klug, F. (2001) 'The Human Rights Act: A "Third Way" or "Third Wave" Bill of Rights', *European Human Rights Law Review* 4: 361–72.

Knight, G. L. (2010) *Female Action Heroes: A Guide to Women in Comics, Video Games, Film, and Television.* Santa Barbara, CA: Greenwood/ABC-CLIO.

Kuhn, T. S. (2012 [1962]) *The Structure of Scientific Revolutions,* 4th edn. Chicago: University of Chicago Press.

Kunstler, J. H. (2005) 'Globalization is an Anomaly and its Time is Running Out', *Guardian,* 24 August.

Kurtz, L. R. (2012) *Gods in the Global Village: The World's Religions in Sociological Perspective,* 3rd edn. London: Sage.

Lankester, T. (2012) *The Politics and Economics of Britain's Foreign Aid: The Pergau Dam Affair.* London: Routledge.

Lash, S. and Urry, J. (1987) *The End of Organized Capitalism.* Cambridge: Polity.

Lawler, S. (2005) 'Disgusted Subjects: The Making of Middle-class Identities', *The Sociological Review* 53/3.

Lea, J. (1998) 'Criminology and Postmodernity', in P. Walton and J. Young (eds.), *The New Criminology Revisited.* Basingstoke: Palgrave Macmillan.

Lea, J. and Young, J. (1984) *What is to be Done About Law and Order?* London: Penguin.

Lee, N. (2005) *Childhood and Human Value.* London: Open University Press.

Leftwich, A. (1995) 'Bringing Politics Back In: Towards a Model of the Development State', *Journal of Development Studies* 31/3: 400–27.

Lemert, E. M. (1972) *Human Deviance, Social Problems and Social Control.* Englewood Cliffs, NJ: Prentice Hall.

Leonard, M. (2003) 'Women and Development: Examining Gender Issues in Developing Countries', in G. McCann and S. McCloskey (eds.), *From the Global to the Local.* London: Pluto.

Leveson, The Right Honourable Lord Justice (2012) *An Inquiry into the Culture, Practices and Ethics of the Press: Report.* London: The Stationery Office.

Levin, J. and McDevitt, J. (2008) 'Hate Crimes', in L. Kurtz (ed.) *Encyclopedia of Violence, Peace, & Conflict*, 2nd edn. Oxford: Academic Press.

Lewis, P., Newburn, T., and Roberts, D. (2011) *Reading the Riots*. London: Guardian Books.

Li, N. and Kirkup, G. (2007) 'Gender and Cultural Differences in Internet Use: A Study of China and the UK', *Computers and Education* 48/2 (February).

Lister, M., Dovey, J., Giddings, S., Grant, I. and Kelly, K. (2003) *New Media: A Critical Introduction*. London: Routledge & Kegan Paul.

Livingstone, S. (1996) 'On the Continuing Problems of Media Effects Research', in J. Curran and M. Gurevitch (eds.), *Mass Media and Society*. London: Edward Arnold.

Livingstone, S. and Bovill, M. (1999) *Young People, New Media: Research Report*. London: Department of Media and Communications, London School of Economics and Political Science. Available at http://eprints.lse.ac.uk/21177.

Livingstone, S. and Wang, Y. (2011) *Media Literacy and the Communications Act: What Has Been Achieved and What Should Be Done?* Media Policy Brief 2. London: LSE Media Policy Project. Available at http://blogs.lse.ac.uk/mediapolicyproject.

Livingstone, S. M. (1988) 'Why People Watch Soap Operas: An Analysis of the Explanations of British Viewers', *European Journal of Communication* 3/1.

Lloyd, P. (1979) *Slums of Hope? Shanty Towns of the Third World*. Harmondsworth: Penguin.

Lockwood, D. (1958) *The Black-coated Worker*. London: Allen & Unwin.

Lockwood, D. (1966) 'Sources of Variation in Working Class Images of Society', *The Sociological Review* 14/3.

Longhi, S. and Platt, L. (2008) *Pay Gaps across Equalities Areas*. Manchester: Equalities and Human Rights Commission.

Longhi, S., Nicoletti, C. and Platt, L. (2009) *Decomposing Wage Gaps across the Pay Distribution: Investigating Inequalities of Ethno-Religious Groups and Disabled People*, ISER Working Paper 2009–31. Colchester: Institute for Social and Economic Research.

Longhi, S., Nicoletti, C. and Platt, L. (2012) 'Interpreting Wage Gaps of Disabled Men: The Roles of Productivity and of Discrimination', *Southern Economic Journal* 78/3.

Lull, J. (1990) *Inside Family Viewing: Ethnographic Research on Television's Audiences*, London: Routledge & Kegan Paul.

Lull, J. (1995) *Media, Communication, Culture*. Cambridge: Polity.

Luttwak, E. (1999) 'Give War A Chance', *Foreign Affairs* 78/4: 36–44.

Lynch, G. (2008) 'Understanding the Sacred', *Sociology Review* 17/2 (November).

Lynch, M. J. and Stretsky, P. B. (2003) 'The Meaning of Green: Contrasting Criminological Perspectives', *Theoretical Criminology* 7/2.

Lyng, S. (1990) 'Edgework: A Social Psychological Analysis of Voluntary Risk-taking', *American Journal of Sociology* 95/4.

Lyng, S. (2005) 'Edgework and the Risk-taking Experience', in S. Lyng (ed.), *Edgework: The Sociology of Risk-taking*. Abingdon: Routledge.

Lyon, D. (2000) *Jesus in Disneyland: Religion in Postmodern Times*. Cambridge: Polity.

Lyon, D. (2009) 'Surveillance, Power and Everyday Life', in R. Mansell, C. Avgerou, D. Quah and R. Silverstone (eds.), *The Oxford Handbook of Information and Communication Technologies*. Oxford: Oxford University Press.

Lyotard, J.–F. (1984) *The Postmodern Condition: A Report on Knowledge*. Manchester: Manchester University Press.

MacDonald, T. (2005) *Third World Health: Hostage to First World Wealth*. London: Radcliffe Publishing.

MacKenzie, R., Stuart, M., Forde, C., Greenwood, I., Gardiner, J. and Perrett, R. (2006) '"All That is Solid?": Class, Identity and the Maintenance of a Collective Orientation amongst Redundant Steelworkers', *Sociology* 40/5.

MacKinnon, R. (2012) *Consent of the Networked: The Worldwide Struggle for Internet Freedom*. New York: Basic Books.

Maduro, O. (1982) *Religion and Social Conflicts*. New York: Orbis.

Maguire, M. (2002) 'Crime Statistics: The "Data Explosion" and its Implications', in M. Maguire, R. Morgan and R. Reiner (eds.), *The Oxford Handbook of Criminology*, 3rd edn. Oxford: Oxford University Press.

Maguire, M. (2007) 'Crime Data and Statistics', in M. Maguire, R. Morgan and R. Reiner (eds.), *The Oxford Handbook of Criminology*, 4th edn. Oxford: Oxford University Press.

Malik, K. (1996) *The Meaning of Race*. Basingstoke: Macmillan.

Malik, S. (2002) *Representing Black Britain: Black and Asian Images on Television*. London: Sage.

Malinowski, B. (2004 [1926]) *Magic, Science and Religion and Other Essays*, ed. Robert Redfield. Whitefish, MT: Kessinger Publishing.

Mannheim, K. (1985 [1936]) *Ideology and Utopia: An Introduction to the Sociology of Knowledge*, trans. L. Wirth and E. Shils. San Diego, CA: Harcourt Brace.

Manning, P. (1999) 'Who Makes the News?' *Sociology Review* (September).

Marcuse, H. (2002 [1964]) *One-dimensional Man*. London: Routledge.

Marmot, M. (chair) (2010) *Fair Society, Healthy Lives: The Marmot Review, Strategic Review of Health Inequalities in England post-2010*. Available at www.marmotreview.org.

Marshall, B. and Johnson, S. (2005) *Crime in Rural Areas: A Review of the Literature for the Rural Evidence Research Centre*. London: Jill Dando Institute of Crime Science.

Marshall, G., Swift, A. and Roberts, S. (1997) *Against the Odds? Social Class and Social Justice in Industrial Societies*. Oxford: Clarendon Press.

Marshall, G., Rose, D., Newby, H. and Vogler, C. (1988) *Social Class in Modern Britain*. London: Hutchinson.

Marsland, D. (1989) 'Universal Welfare Provision Creates a Dependent Population: The Case For', *Social Studies Review* 5/2.

Marsland, D. (1994) 'Sociologists and Social Policy: The Need for Intelligent Involvement', *Sociological Notes* No. 21. London: Libertarian Alliance.

Martin, D. (1969) *The Religious and the Secular*. London: Routledge & Kegan Paul.

Martinson, J. (2014) 'Journalist Olenka Frenkiel says BBC Sexism and Ageism Still an Issue', *Guardian*, 7 November.

Martin, J. and Roberts, C. (1984) *Women and Employment: A Lifetime Perspective*, Department of Employment and Office of Population Censuses and Surveys. London: HMSO.

Marx, K. and Engels, F. (1848) *The Manifesto of the Communist Party* (also known as the *Communist Manifesto*). Available as a free download at www.marxists.org/archive/marx/works/1848/communist-manifesto.

Massari, M. and Monzini, P. (2004) 'Dirty Businesses in Italy: A Case-study of Illegal Trafficking in Hazardous Waste', *Global Crime* 6/3–4.

Matza, D. (1964) *Delinquency and Drift*. New York: Wiley.

Mayhew, H. (1985 [1851]) *London Labour and the London Poor*. Harmondsworth: Penguin.

McClelland, D. (1961) *The Achieving Society*. Princeton: Princeton University Press.

McCombs, M. (2004) *Setting the Agenda: The Mass Media and Public Opinion*. Cambridge: Polity.

McGiffen, P. (2002) *Globalisation*. Harpenden: Pocket Essentials.

McGrew, A. (2000) 'Sustainable Globalization?' in T. Allen and A. Thomas (eds.), *Poverty and Development into the Twenty-first Century*. Oxford: Oxford University Press.

McGrew, A. (2004) 'Power Shift: From National Government to Global Governance?' in D. Held (ed.), *A Globalizing World: Culture, Economics, Politics*, 2nd edn. London: Routledge & Kegan Paul.

McGuire, M. B. (2001) *Religion: The Social Context*, 5th edn. London: Wadsworth.

McKendrick, J. H., Sinclair, S., Irwin, A., O'Donnell, H., Scott, G. and Dobbie, L. (2008) *The Media, Poverty and Public Opinion in the UK*. York: Joseph Rowntree Foundation. Available at www.jrf.org.uk/sites/files/jrf/2224-poverty-media-opinion.pdf.

McKnight, A. (2015) *Downward Mobility, Opportunity Hoarding and the 'Glass Floor'*. London: Social Mobility and Child Poverty Commission.

McLuhan, H. M. (1962) *The Gutenberg Galaxy: The Making of Typographic Man*. Toronto: University of Toronto Press.

McNair, B. (2006) *Cultural Chaos: Journalism, News and Power in a Globalised World*. London: Routledge.

McNeill, P. (1986) 'Social Research', in P. McNeill and C. Townley (eds.), *Fundamentals of Sociology*. London: Hutchinson.

McQuail, D. (1972) *The Sociology of Mass Communications*. Harmondsworth: Penguin.

McRobbie, A. (1994) *Postmodernism and Popular Culture*. London: Routledge & Kegan Paul.

McRobbie, A. (1999) *In the Culture Society: Art, Fashion and Popular Music*. Abingdon: Routledge.

McRobbie, A. and Thornton, S. (1995) 'Rethinking "Moral Panic" for Multi-mediated Social Worlds', *British Journal of Sociology* 46/4.

Mead, M. (1935) *Sex and Temperament in Three Primitive Societies*. New York: HarperCollins.

Merton, R. K. (1968 [1957]) *Social Theory and Social Structure*. New York: Free Press.

Messerschmidt, J. M. (1993) *Masculinities and Crime: Critique and Reconceptualization of Theory*. Lanham, MD: Rowman & Littlefield.

Meyer, K., Barker, E., Ebaugh, H. R. and Juergensmeyer, M. (2011) 'Religion in Global Perspective: SSSR Presidential Panel', *Journal for the Scientific Study of Religion* 50/2.

Mies, M. (1983) 'Towards a Methodology for Feminist Research', in G. Bowles and R. D. Klein (eds.), *Theories of Women's Studies*. London: Routledge.

Milanovic, B. (2011) *The Haves and the Have-nots: A Brief and Idiosyncratic History of Global Inequality*. New York: Basic Books.

Miliband, R. (1973) *The State in Capitalist Society*. London: Quartet Books.

Miller, A. S. and Hoffmann, J. P. (1995) 'Risk and Religion', *International Journal of the Addictions* 30/10: 1207–41.

Miller, T. (2011) 'Falling Back into Gender? Men's Narratives and Practices around First-time Fatherhood', *Sociology* 45/6.

Miller, W. B. (1962) 'Lower-class Culture as a Generating Milieu of Gang Delinquency', in M. E. Wolfgang, L. Savitz and N. Johnson (eds.), *The Sociology of Crime and Delinquency*. New York: Wiley.

Millett, K. (1970) *Sexual Politics*. New York: Doubleday.

Mills, C. (2014) 'The Great British Class Fiasco: A Comment on Savage et al.', *Sociology* 48/3.

Mirza, H. (1992) *Young, Female and Black*. London: Routledge & Kegan Paul.

Mirza, M. (2008) 'Religious Extremism and British Muslims', *Sociology Review* 17/4 (April).

Mirza, M., Senthilkumaran, A. and Ja'far, Z. (2007) *Living Apart Together: British Muslims and the Paradox of Multiculturalism*. London: Policy Exchange.

Modood, T., Beishon, S. and Virdee, S. (1994) *Changing Ethnic Identities*. London: Policy Studies Institute.

Monbiot, G. (2008) 'The Great Green Land Grab', *Guardian*, 13 February.

Moore, B. (1967) *Social Origins of Dictatorship and Democracy: Lord and Peasant in the Making of the Modern World*. Harmondsworth: Penguin.

Morley, D. (1999 [1980]) 'The Nationwide Audience: Structure and Decoding', in D. Morley and C. Brunsdon, *The Nationwide Television Studies*. London: Routledge.

Moyo, D. (2010) *Dead Aid: Why Aid is Not Working and How There is a Better Way for Africa*. Harmondsworth: Penguin.

Mulvey, L. (2009 [1975]) 'Visual Pleasure and Narrative Cinema', *Screen* 16/3; included in L. Mulvey, *Visual and Other Pleasures (Language, Discourse, Society)*. Basingstoke: Palgrave Macmillan.

Murray, C. (1984) *Losing Ground*. New York: Basic Books.

Murray, C. (1989) 'Underclass', *Sunday Times Magazine*, 26 November.

Murray, C. (1990) *The Emerging British Underclass*. London: Institute of Economic Affairs.

Naidoo, K. (2008) 'Let's Change the Climate', *Developments* 40: 14.

Nanda, M. (2008) 'Rush Hour of the Gods', *New Humanist* 123/2 (March/April).

Nandi, A. and Platt, L. (2010) *Ethnic Minority Women's Poverty and Economic Wellbeing*. Colchester: Institute for Social and Economic Research.

Nelken, D. (2012) 'White-collar and Corporate Crime', in M. Maguire, R. Morgan and R. Reiner (eds.), *The Oxford Handbook of Criminology*, 5th edn. Oxford: Oxford University Press.

Neumayer, E. (2003) 'What Factors Determine the Allocation of Aid by Arab Countries and Multilateral Agencies?', *The Journal of Development Studies* 39/4.

Newburn, T. (2007) *Criminology*. Cullompton: Willan.

Newburn, T. and Hagell, A. (1995) 'Violence on Screen: Just Child's Play?', *Sociology Review* 4/3.

Newson, E. (1994) 'Video Violence and the Protection of Children', *Journal of Mental Health* 3: 221–6.

Niebuhr, H. R. (1957 [1929]) *The Social Sources of Denominationalism*. New York: Meridian Books.

Norris, P. and Inglehart, R. (2010) *Are High Levels of Existential Security Conducive to Secularization?* Paper for Mid-west Political Science Association annual meeting, Chicago, 22 April 2010.

Norris, P. and Inglehart, R. (2011) *Sacred and Secular: Religion and Politics Worldwide*. Cambridge: Cambridge University Press.

O'Byrne, D. (2012) 'On the Sociology of Human Rights: Theorising the Language-structure of Rights', *Sociology* 46/5.

Oakley, A. (1972) *Sex, Gender and Society*. London: Temple Smith.

Oakley, A. (1974a) *Housewife*. London: Allen Lane.

Oakley, A. (1974b) *The Sociology of Housework*. Oxford: Martin Robertson.

Oakley, A. (1981a) 'Interviewing Women: A Contradiction in Terms', in H. Roberts (ed.), *Doing Feminist Research*. London: Routledge & Kegan Paul.

Oakley, A. (1981b) *From Here to Maternity*. Harmondsworth: Penguin.

Oakley, A. (2002) *Gender on Planet Earth*. Cambridge: Polity.

OECD (2012) 'Development: Aid to Developing Countries Falls because of Global Recession', OECD.org Newsroom.

Ofcom (2005) *The Representation and Portrayal of People with Disabilities on Analogue Terrestrial Television*. London: Office for Communications.

Ofcom (2011) *The Communications Market Report*. London: Ofcom.

Ofcom (2012) *The Communications Market Report*. London: Ofcom.

Ofcom (2014) *The Communications Market Report*. London: Ofcom.

Oliver, M. (1990) *The Politics of Disablement*. London: Macmillan.

Ortner, S. (1974) 'Is Female to Male as Nature is to Culture?', in M. Z. Rosaldo (ed.), *Women, Culture and Society*. Stanford: Stanford University Press.

Oxfam (2014) *Even It Up: Time to End Extreme Inequality*. Oxford: Oxfam GB.

Pahl, R. (1993) 'Money, Marriage and Ideology: Holding the Purse Strings', *Sociology Review* (September).

Pakulski, J. and Waters, M. (1996) *The Death of Class*. London: Sage.

Park, N., Kee, K. F. and Valenzuela, S. (2009) 'Being Immersed in Social Networking Environment: Facebook Groups, Uses and Gratifications, and Social Outcomes'. *CyberPsychology & Behavior* 12/6.

Parry, N. and Parry, J. (1976) *The Rise of the Medical Profession*. London: Croom Helm.

Parsons, T. (1951) *The Social System*. New York: Free Press.

Parsons, T. (1964) *Social Structure and Personality*. London: Collier-Macmillan.

Parsons, T. (1967) *Sociological Theory and Modern Society*. New York: Free Press.

Patterson, S. (1965) *Dark Strangers*. London: Penguin.

Payne, G. and Abbott, P. (1990) *The Social Mobility of Women*. Basingstoke: Falmer Press.

Pearce, F. (1976) *Crimes of the Powerful*. London: Pluto Press.

Pearson, G. (1983) *Hooligan: A History of Respectable Fears*. London: Macmillan.

Pearson, R. (2000) 'Rethinking Gender Matters in Development', in T. Allen and A. Thomas (eds.), *Poverty and Development into the Twenty-first Century*. Oxford: Oxford University Press.

Pease, K. (2002) 'Crime Reduction', in M. Maguire, R. Morgan and R. Reiner (eds.), *The Oxford Handbook of Criminology*, 3rd edn. Oxford: Oxford University Press.

Phillips, C. and Bowling, B. (2012) 'Ethnicities, Racism, Crime, and Criminal Justice', in M. Maguire, R. Morgan, and R. Reiner (eds.) *The Oxford Handbook of Criminology*, 5th edn. Oxford: Oxford University Press.

Phillips, T. (2007) Interview with Chris Arnot, 'Doyen of Diversity', *Guardian*, 31 January.

Philo, G. (1990) *Seeing and Believing*. London: Routledge.

Philo, G. (2008) *Debates on the Active Audience: A Comparison of the Birmingham and Glasgow Approaches*. Glasgow University Media Group. Available at www.glasgowmediagroup.org/images/stories/pdf/actaud.pdf.

Philo, G. (2012) 'The Media and the Global Banking Crisis', *Sociology Review* 21/3 (February).

Philo, G. and Berry, M. (2004) *Bad News from Israel*. London: Pluto Press.

Philo, G. and Berry, M. (2011) *More Bad News From Israel*. London: Pluto Press.

Philo, G., Henderson, L. and McCracken, K. (2010) *Shifting Attitudes to Mental Illness – Making a Drama out of a Crisis: Authentic Portrayals of Mental Illness in TV Drama?* Glasgow Media Group and Shift. Available at www.glasgowmediagroup.org.

Piketty, T. (2014) *Capital in the Twenty-First Century*. Cambridge, MA: Belknap Press of Harvard University Press.

Platt, L. (2005) 'Intergenerational Social Mobility of Minority Ethnic Groups', *Sociology* 39/3.

Platt, L. (2007) *Poverty and Ethnicity in the UK*. London: Joseph Rowntree Foundation.

Platt, L. (2011) *Understanding Inequalities: Stratification & Difference*. Cambridge: Polity.

Plummer, K. (1979) 'Misunderstanding Labelling Perspectives', in D. Downes and P. Rock (eds.), *Deviant Interpretations: Problems in Criminological Theory*. Oxford: Martin Robertson.

Plummer, K. (2011) 'The Labelling Perspective Forty Years On', in H. Peters and M. Dellwing (eds.), *Langweiliges Verbrechen: Warum Kriminologinnen den Umgang mit Kriminalität interessanter finden als Kriminalität*. Wiesbaden: VS Verlag für Sozialwissenschaften.

Pollak, O. (1950) *The Criminality of Women*. Philadelphia: University of Pennsylvania Press.

Pollert, A. (1996) 'Gender and Class Revisited; or, the Poverty of "Patriarchy"', *Sociology* 30/4.

Popper, K. (2002 [1935]) *The Logic of Scientific Discovery*. London: Routledge.

Postman, N. (1994) *The Disappearance of Childhood*. New York: Vintage Books.

Potter, G. (2010) 'What is Green Criminology?', *Sociology Review* 20/2.

Preston, P. (2012) 'If You Choose Your Own News, You'll Be Less Well Read', *Observer*, 1 January.

Pryce, K. (1979) *Endless Pressure: A Study of West Indian Lifestyles in Bristol*. Harmondsworth: Penguin.

Putnam, R. (2000) *Bowling Alone*. New York: Simon and Schuster.

Raghuram, P. (2009) 'Migration: Changing, Connecting and Making Places', in S. Bromley, J. Clarke, S. Hinchliffe and S. Taylor (eds.), *Exploring Social Lives*. Milton Keynes: The Open University.

Ransom, D. (2006) *The No-nonsense Guide to Fair Trade*. Oxford: New Internationalist.

REACH (2007) *An Independent Report to Government on Raising the Aspirations and Attainment of Black Boys and Young Black Men*. London: Department for Communities and Local Government.

Reay, D. (2007) 'Education and Social Class', *Sociology Review* 17/2.

Reiner, R. (2000) *Politics of the Police*. Oxford: Oxford University Press.

Reiner, R. (2007) 'Media Made Criminality: The Representation of Crime in the Mass Media', in M. Maguire, R. Morgan and R. Reiner (eds.), *The Oxford Handbook of Criminology*, 4th edn. Oxford: Oxford University Press.

Reuters Institute for the Study of Journalism (2014) *Reuters Institute Digital News Report 2014: Tracking the Future of News*. Edited by N. Newman and D. A. L. Levy. Oxford: Reuters Institute for the Study of Journalism. Available online at www.digitalnewsreport.org.

Reuters Institute for the Study of Journalism (2015) *Reuters Institute Digital News Report 2015: Tracking the Future of News*. Edited by N. Newman, D. A. L. Levy and R. K. Nielsen. Oxford: Reuters Institute for the Study of Journalism. Available online at www.digitalnewsreport.org.

Reynolds, T. (2001) 'Black Mothering, Paid Work and Identity', *Ethnic and Racial Studies* 24.

Richards, P. (1996) *Fighting for the Rain Forest: War, Youth and Resources in Sierra Leone*. Oxford: James Currey.

Ritzer, G. (2008) *The McDonaldization of Society*, 5th edn. London: Pine Forge Press.

Robinson, L. (2001) 'When Will Revolutionary Movements Use Religion?' in S. Monahan, W. A. Mirola and M. O. Emerson (eds.), *Sociology of Religion: A Reader*. Englewood Cliffs, NJ: Prentice Hall.

Rodney, W. (1972) *How Europe Underdeveloped Africa*. London: Bogle-L'Ouverture Publications.

Rollock, N., Gillborn, D., Vincent, C. and Ball, S. (2012) 'The Public Identities of the Black Middle Classes: Managing Race in Public Spaces', *Sociology* 45/6.

Roof, W. C. (2001) *Spiritual Marketplace: Baby Boomers and the Remaking of American Religion*. Princeton, NJ: Princeton University Press.

Rosaldo, M. Z. (1974) *Women, Culture and Society*. Stanford, CA: Stanford University Press.

Rostow, W. W. (1960) *The Stages of Economic Growth: A Non-Communist Manifesto*. Cambridge: Cambridge University Press.

Runciman, W.G. (1990) 'How Many Classes Are There in Contemporary British Society?' *Sociology* 24/3.

Rusche, G. and Kirchheimer, O. (2003 [1939]) *Punishment and Social Structure*. Piscataway, NJ: Transaction Publishers.

Ryan, L. (2004) 'Family Matters: (E)migration, Familial Networks and Irish Women in Britain', *Sociological Review* 5/3.

Sachs, J. (2005) *The End of Poverty*. London: Penguin.

Salway, S. et al. (2007) *Long-term Ill Health, Poverty and Ethnicity*. York: Joseph Rowntree Foundation.

Sancho, J. (2003) *Disabling Prejudice: Attitudes Towards Disability and Its Portrayal on Television*. London: The British Broadcasting Corporation, the Broadcasting Standards Commission and the Independent Television Commission.

Santana, D. B. (2002) 'Resisting Toxic Militarism: Vieques Versus the U.S. Navy', *Social Justice* 29/1–2.

Saul, J. R. (2004) 'The Collapse of Globalism and the Rebirth of Nationalism', *Harper's Magazine* (March).

Saunders, P. (1990) *Social Class and Stratification*. London: Routledge & Kegan Paul.

Saunders, P. (1999) 'Capitalism and the Environment,' in M. J. Smith (ed.), *Thinking Through the Environment*. London: Routledge & Kegan Paul.

Savage, M. (2014) 'Focus: Social Change in the 21st Century: The New Sociology of "Wealth Elites"', *Discover Society 15*, Social Research Publications. Available online at http://discoversociety.org/2014/12/01/focus-social-change-in-the-21st-century-the-new-sociology-of-wealth-elites.

Savage, M., Bagnall, G. and Longhurst, B. (2001) 'Ordinary, Ambivalent and Defensive Class Identities in the North West of England', *Sociology* 35/4.

Savage, M., Barlow, J., Dickens, P. and Fielding, T. (1992) *Property, Bureaucracy and Culture: Middle Class Formation in Contemporary Britain*. London: Routledge & Kegan Paul.

Sayer, A. (1992) *Method in Social Science: A Realist Approach*. London: Routledge & Kegan Paul.

Sayer, A. (2000) *Realism and Social Science*. London: Sage.

Sayer, A. (2014) 'The Rich: The Elephant in the Sociology Room', *Discover Society 15*, Social Research Publications. Available online at http://discoversociety.org/2014/12/01/viewpoint-the-rich-the-elephant-in-the-sociology-room.

Scambler, G. (2013) 'Resistance in Unjust Times; Archer, Structured Agency and the Sociology of Health Inequalities', *Sociology* 47/1.

Schuurman, F. J. (2002) 'The Impasse in Development Studies', in V. Desai and R. B. Potter (eds.), *The Companion to Development Studies*. London: Arnold.

Schwendinger, H. and Schwendinger, J. (1975) 'Defenders of Order or Guardians of Human Rights?' in I. Taylor, P. Walton and J. Young (eds.), *Critical Criminology*. London: Routledge and Kegan Paul.

Seagar, A. and Lewis, J. (2007) 'How Top London Law Firms Help Vulture Funds Devour Their Prey', *Guardian*, 17 October.

Sen, A. (1999) *Development as Freedom*. Oxford: Oxford University Press.

Sen, A. (1999) *Development as Freedom*. Oxford: Oxford University Press.

Shah, A. (2010) 'Women's Rights'. Available at www.globalissues.org/article/166/womens-rights.

Shakespeare, T. (1994) 'Cultural Representations of Disabled People', *Disability and Society* 9/3.

Shakespeare, T. (1998) *The Disability Reader: Social Science Perspectives*. London: Cassell.

Shakespeare, T. (1999) 'Art and Lies? Representations of Disability on Film', in M. Corker and S. French (eds.), *Disability Discourse*. Buckingham: Open University Press.

Sharot, S. (2002) 'Beyond Christianity: A Critique of the Rational Choice Theory of Religion from a Weberian and Comparative Religions Perspective', *Sociology of Religion* 63/4.

Sharp, C. and Budd, T. (2005) *Minority Ethnic Groups and Crime: Findings from the Offending, Crime and Justice Survey 2003*. Online report. London: Home Office.

Sharpe, S. (1994) *Just Like a Girl*, 2nd edn. Harmondsworth: Penguin.

Shildrick, T., MacDonald, R. and Webster, C. (2007) 'Class, Consumption and Prejudice: Contemporary Representations of "the Social Scum"'. Paper presented at ESRC research seminar '"Money's Too Tight to Mention": Consumption on the Margins'. University of Teeside, 23 April.

Sidwell, M. (2008) *Unfair Trade*. London: Adam Smith Institute.

Singleton, A. (2014) *Religion, Culture and Society: A Global Approach*. London: Sage.

Sklair, L. (1995) *Sociology of the Global System*, 2nd edn. Hemel Hempstead: Prentice Hall.

Sklair, L. (2000) 'The Transnational Capitalist Class and the Discourse of Globalization', *Cambridge Review of International Affairs* 14/1.

Sklair, L. (2012) 'Sociology of the Global System', in F. J. Lechner and J. Boli (eds.), *The Globalization Reader*, 4th edn. Oxford: Wiley-Blackwell.

Slapper, G. and Tombs, S. (1999) *Corporate Crime*. Harlow: Longman.

Slatterthwaite, D. (2007) 'Humanity Crosses Urban Milestone', *Society Matters* 10.

Smart, C. (1976) *Women, Crime and Criminology: A Feminist Critique*. London: Routledge & Kegan Paul.

Snider, L. (1991) 'The Regulatory Dance: Understanding Reform Processes in Corporate Crime', *International Journal of Sociology of Law* 19.

Social Mobility & Child Poverty Commission (2014) *State of the Nation 2014: Social Mobility and Child Poverty in Great Britain*. London: HMSO.

Southerton, D. (2002) 'Class, Mobility and Identification in a New Town', *Sociology* 36/1.

Spencer, H. (1996 [1885]) *The Study of Sociology*. London: Routledge & Kegan Paul.

Stanley, L. and Wise, S. (1993) *Breaking Out Again: Feminist Ontology and Epistemology*. Abingdon: Routledge.

Stanworth, M. (1984) 'Women and Class Analysis', *Sociology* 18/2.

Stark, R. and Bainbridge, W. S. (1985) *The Future of Religion: Secularization, Revival and Cult Formation*. Berkeley: University of California Press.

Stark, R. and Bainbridge, W. S. (1996) *A Theory of Religion*. New Brunswick, NJ: Rutgers University Press.

Stark, R. and Finke, R. (2000) *Acts of Faith: Explaining the Human Side of Religion*. London: University of California Press.

Stewart, A., Prandy, K. and Blackburn, R. M. (1980) *Social Stratification and Occupations*. London: Macmillan.

Stiglitz, J. (2002) *Globalization and its Discontents*. London: Penguin.

Stonewall (2010) *Unseen on Screen: Gay People on Youth TV*. London: Stonewall.

Storey, A. (2003) 'Measuring Development', in G. McCann and S. McCloskey (eds.), *From the Global to the Local*. London: Pluto.

Strinati, D. (1995) *An Introduction to Theories of Popular Culture*. London: Routledge & Kegan Paul.

Surette, R. (2010) *Media, Crime and Criminal Justice: Images, Realities and Policies*, 4th edn. Belmont, CA: Wadsworth.

Sutcliffe, B. (2001) *100 Ways of Seeing An Unequal World*. London: Zed Books.

Sutcliffe, S. J. (2003) *Children of the New Age: A History of Spiritual Practices*. London: Routledge & Kegan Paul.

Sutherland, E. H. (1947) *Principles of Criminology*. Philadelphia: J. B. Lippincott.

Sutherland, E. H. (1983 [1949]) *White Collar Crime: The Uncut Version*. New Haven CT: Yale University Press.

Swain, J. (2007) 'Performing masculinities', *Sociology Review* 17/2.

Swift, R. (1998) 'The Cocoa Chain', *New Internationalist* 304 (August).

Sykes, G. and Matza, D. (1957) 'Techniques of Neutralization: A Theory of Delinquency', *American Sociological Review* 22/6.

Szmigin, I. and Carrigan, M. (2000) 'Does Advertising in the UK Need Older Models?' *Journal of Product and Brand Management* 9/2.

Taylor, I. (1997) 'The Political Economy of Crime', in M. Maguire, R. Morgan and R. Reiner (eds.) *The Oxford Handbook of Criminology*, 2nd edn. Oxford: Oxford University Press.

Taylor, I. (1999) *Crime in Context: A Critical Criminology of Market Societies*. Cambridge: Polity.

Taylor, I., Walton, P. and Young, J. (1973) *The New Criminology: For a Social Theory of Deviance*. London: Routledge & Kegan Paul.

Tebbel, C. (2000) *The Body Snatchers: How the Media Shapes Women*. Sydney: Finch Publishing.

Thekaekara, M. M. (2005) 'Tsunami Business', *New Internationalist* 383 (October).

Thiel, D. (2008) *Policing Terrorism: A Review of the Evidence*. London: Policing Foundation.

Thomas, A. (2000) 'Meanings and Views of Development', in T. Allen and A. Thomas (eds.), *Poverty and Development into the Twenty-first Century*. Oxford: Oxford University Press.

Thomas, W. I. and Thomas, D. S. (1928) *The Child in America: Behavior Problems and Programs*. New York: Knopf.

Thussu, D. K. (2007) *News as Entertainment: The Rise of Global Infotainment.* London: Sage.

Tierney, J. (1996) *Criminology: Theory and Context.* London: Harvester Wheatsheaf.

Tiger, L. and Fox, R. (1972) *The Imperial Animal.* London: Secker & Warburg.

Time to Change (2014) *Making a Drama out of a Crisis.* London: Time to Change.

Timmer, D. A. and Eitzen, S. (1989) *Crime in the Streets and in the Suites: Perspectives on Crime and Criminal Justice.* Boston, MA: Allyn and Bacon.

Tombs, S. and Whyte, D. (2003) 'Scrutinizing the Powerful: Crime, Contemporary Political Economy, and Critical Social Research', in S. Tombs and D. Whyte (eds.), *Unmasking the Crimes of the Powerful: Scrutinizing States and Corporations.* New York: Peter Lang.

Tombs, S. and Whyte, D. (2007) *Safety Crimes.* Uffculme: Willan Publishing.

Tomlinson, J. (1999) *Globalization and Culture.* Cambridge: Polity.

Townsend, P. (1979) *Poverty in the United Kingdom.* Harmondsworth: Penguin.

Toynbee, P. (2012) 'Why Politicians Won't Tell You the Truth about Crime', *Guardian,* 22 October.

Troeltsch, E. (1992 [1931]) *The Social Teaching of the Christian Churches.* Louisville, KY: Westminster John Knox Press.

Tuchman, G., Daniels, A. K. and Benet, J. W. (eds.) (1978) *Hearth and Home: Images of Women in the Mass Media.* Oxford: Oxford University Press.

Tudor-Hart, J. (1971) 'The Inverse Care Law', *Lancet* 1.

Tumin, M. (1967 [1953]) 'Some Principles of Stratification: A Critical Analysis', in R. Bendix and S. M. Lipset (eds.), *Class, Status and Power.* London: Routledge & Kegan Paul.

Tyler, I. (2008) 'Chav Mum, Chav Scum: Class Disgust in Contemporary Britain', *Feminist Media Studies* 8/1.

UK Drug Policy Commission (2012) *A Fresh Approach to Drugs.* London: UK Drug Policy Commission.

UN (2005) *Millennium Development Goals.* Available at: www.un.org/millenniumgoals/pdf/mdg2007.pdf.

UNESCO (2015) *Education for All Global Monitoring Report: Achievements and Challenges.* Available online at http://unesdoc.unesco.org/images/0023/002322/232205e.pdf.

UNIFEM (2006) *Progress of the World's Women 2005: Women, Work and Poverty.* Available at www.un.org.

United Nations (2014) *World Urbanization Prospects: The 2014 Revision, Highlights.* New York: Department of Economic and Social Affairs, United Nations.

United Nations Office on Drugs and Crime (2007) *World Drug Report 2007.* New York: United Nations.

Uvin, P. (1998) *Aiding Violence: The Development Enterprise in Rwanda.* West Hartford: Kumarian Press.

van der Gaag, N. (2008) *The No Nonsense Guide to Women's Rights.* Oxford: New Internationalist Publications.

van Dijk, T. (1991) *Racism and the Press.* London: Routledge & Kegan Paul.

Voas, D. (2009) 'The Rise and Fall of Fuzzy Fidelity in Europe', *European Sociological Review* 25/2.

Voas, D. (2010) 'Explaining Change over Time in Religious Involvement', in S. Collins-Mayo and P. Dandelion (eds.), *Religion and Youth.* Farnham: Ashgate.

Voas, D. (2015) *The Mysteries of Religion and the Lifecourse.* London: Centre for Longitudinal Studies.

Voas, D. and Crockett, A. (2005) 'Religion in Britain: Neither Believing Nor Belonging', *Sociology* 39/1.

Walby, S. (1990) *Theorizing Patriarchy.* Oxford: Blackwell.

Walklate, S. (2004) *Gender, Crime and Criminal Justice,* 2nd edn. Cullompton: Willan.

Wallerstein, I. (2004) 'The Rise and Future Demise of the World Capitalist System', in F. Lechner and J. Boli (eds.), *The Globalization Reader,* 2nd edn. Oxford: Blackwell.

Wallis, R. (1974) 'Ideology, Authority and the Development of Cultic Movements', *Social Research* 41.

Wallis, R. (1984) *The Elementary Forms of the New Religious Life.* London: Routledge & Kegan Paul.

Walter, T. and Davie, G. (1998) 'The Religiosity of Women in the Modern West', *British Journal of Sociology* 49/4.

Warren, B. (1980) *Imperialism: Pioneer of Capitalism.* London: New Left Books.

Watson, H. (1994) 'Women and the Veil: Personal Responses to Global Process', in A. S. Ahmed and H. Donnan, *Islam, Globalization and Postmodernity.* London: Routledge & Kegan Paul.

Webber, R. (2008) 'Postcodes and Social Class: Which Tells Us More?' *Social Science Teacher* 37/2.

Weber, M. (1947) *The Theory of Social and Economic Organization,* trans. A. R. Henderson and T. Parsons. London: William Hodge.

Weber, M. (1993 [1920]) *The Sociology of Religion.* Boston: Beacon Press.

Weber, M. (2001 [1904]) *The Protestant Ethic and the Spirit of Capitalism.* Chicago: Fitzroy Dearborn.

Weisbrot, M., Baker, D., Kraev, E. and Chen, J. (2001) *The Scorecard on Globalization 1980–2000: Twenty Years of Diminished Progress.* Available at: www.cepr.net/documents/publications/globalization_2001_07_11.pdf.

Weltman, D. (2008) *Popular Representations of the Working Class: Contested Identities and Social Change.* Beyond Current Horizons: www.beyondcurrenthorizons.org.uk/.

Westergaard, J. and Resler, H. (1975) *Class in a Capitalist Society.* London: Heinemann.

Westmarland, N. (2001) 'The Quantitative/Qualitative Debate and Feminist Research: A Subjective View of Objectivity', *Forum Qualitative Sozialforschung / Forum: Qualitative Social Research*, 2(1), Art. 13, http://nbn–resolving.de/urn:nbn:de:0114–fqs0101135.

White, C., Morrell, G., Luke, C., Young, P. and Bunker, D. (2012) *Serving All Ages: The Views of the Audience and Experts*. London: BBC, NatCen and Creative Diversity Network.

White, R. (2003) 'Environmental Issues and the Criminological Imagination', *Theoretical Criminology* 7(4).

White, R. (2008) *Crimes Against Nature: Environmental Criminology and Ecological Justice*. Uffculme: Willan Publishing.

White, R. (2011) *Transnational Environmental Crime: Toward an Eco-global Criminology*. Abingdon: Routledge.

Wield, D. and Chataway, J. (2000) 'Unemployment and Making a Living', in T. Allen and A. Thomas (eds.), *Poverty and Development into the Twenty-first Century*. Oxford: Oxford University Press.

Wilkinson, R. and Pickett, K. (2009) *The Spirit Level: Why Equality is Better for Everyone*. London: Penguin.

Wilson, B. R. (1959) 'An Analysis of Sect Development', *American Sociological Review* 24/1.

Wilson, B. R. (1966) *Religion in Secular Society: A Sociological Comment*. London: Watts.

Wilson, B. R. (1970) *Religious Sects: A Sociological Study*. London: Weidenfeld & Nicolson.

Wilson, B. R. (1982) *Religion in Sociological Perspective*. Oxford: Oxford University Press.

Wilson, J. Q. (1985) *Thinking about Crime*, rev. edn. New York: Vintage.

Wilson, J. Q. and Kelling, G. L. (1982) *The Police and Neighborhood Safety: Broken Windows*. Available at: www.manhattan-institute.org/pdf/_atlantic_monthly-broken_windows.pdf.

Winlow, S. (2001) *Badfellas: Crime, Tradition and New Masculinities*. Oxford: Berg.

Wittfogel, K. (1957) *Oriental Despotism: A Comparative Study of Total Power*. New York: Vintage Books.

Wolf, B. (2011) '"Green-Collar Crime": Environmental Crime and Justice in the Sociological Perspective', *Sociology Compass* 5/7.

Wolf, N. (1991) *The Beauty Myth*. London: Vintage Books.

Woodhead, L. (2002) 'Christianity' and 'Women and Religion', in L. Woodhead, P. Fletcher, H. Kawanami and D. Smith (eds.), *Religions in the Modern World*. London: Routledge.

Woodhouse, P. (2000) 'Environmental Degradation and Sustainability', in T. Allen and A. Thomas (eds.), *Poverty and Development into the Twenty-first Century*. Oxford: Oxford University Press.

World Bank, Migration and Remittances Team, Development Prospects Group (2015) *Migration and Development Brief 24*. Washington, DC: World Bank.

World Commission on Environment and Development (1987) *Our Common Future*. Oxford: Oxford University Press.

World Health Organization, Global Health Observatory (GHO) data. Available online at www.who.int/gho/malaria/en.

Worsley, P. (1978) *Introducing Sociology*. Harmondsworth: Penguin.

Wright, E. O. (1978) *Class, Crisis and the State*. London: New Left Books.

Young, J. (1971) 'The Role of the Police as Amplifiers of Deviancy, Negotiators of Reality and Translators of Fantasy', in S. Cohen (ed.), *Images of Deviance*. Harmondsworth: Penguin.

Young, J. (1999) *The Exclusive Society*. London: Sage.

Young, J. (2003) 'Merton with Energy, Katz with Structure: The Sociology of Vindictiveness and the Criminology of Transgression', *Theoretical Criminology* 7/3.

Young, M. and Willmott, P. (1962) *Family and Kinship in East London*. London: Pelican.

Illustration credits

Index